BOARD OF EDUCATION
FOR THE CITY OF HAMILTON

You are given the use of this book on the understand... ... ... with care. Do not
ma... ... ... student will use
... ... books.
it next ...

Name Nicole Lewis
Form   Year 98   Room 208

Name
Form   Year   Room

Name
Form   Year   Room

Name
Form   Year   Room

Name
Form   Year   Room

Name
Form   Year   Room

FOUNDATIONS
OF MATHEMATICS

9

SECOND EDITION

THE McGRAW-HILL RYERSON MATHEMATICS PROGRAM

MATH 1 SOURCE BOOK
MATH 2 SOURCE BOOK
MATH 3
MATH 4
MATH 5
MATH 6

TEACHER'S EDITIONS FOR:
MATH 3
MATH 4
MATH 5
MATH 6

BLACKLINE MASTERS FOR:
MATH 3
MATH 4
MATH 5
MATH 6

LIFE MATH 1
LIFE MATH 2
LIFE MATH 3

INTERMEDIATE MATHEMATICS 1
INTERMEDIATE MATHEMATICS 2
INTERMEDIATE MATHEMATICS 3

TEACHER'S EDITIONS FOR:
INTERMEDIATE MATHEMATICS 1
INTERMEDIATE MATHEMATICS 2
INTERMEDIATE MATHEMATICS 3

BLACKLINE MASTERS FOR:
INTERMEDIATE MATHEMATICS 1
INTERMEDIATE MATHEMATICS 2

APPLIED MATHEMATICS 9
APPLIED MATHEMATICS 10
APPLIED MATHEMATICS 11
APPLIED MATHEMATICS 12

TEACHER'S EDITION FOR:
APPLIED MATHEMATICS 9

TEACHER'S GUIDES FOR:
AM 10
AM 11
AM 12

FOUNDATIONS OF MATHEMATICS 9
FOUNDATIONS OF MATHEMATICS 10
FOUNDATIONS OF MATHEMATICS 11
FOUNDATIONS OF MATHEMATICS 12

TEACHER'S EDITION FOR:
FOUNDATIONS OF MATHEMATICS 9

TEACHER'S GUIDES FOR:
FM 10
FM 11
FM 12

FOUNDATIONS
OF MATHEMATICS

SECOND EDITION

Dino Dottori, B.Sc., M.S.Ed.
George Knill, B.Sc., M.S.Ed.
Robert McVean, B.A., B.Sc.
Patricia Leuty, B.A., M.A.

McGRAW-HILL RYERSON LIMITED

TORONTO MONTREAL NEW YORK AUCKLAND BOGOTÁ CAIRO CARACAS HAMBURG
LISBON LONDON MADRID MEXICO MILAN NEW DELHI PANAMA PARIS SAN JUAN
SÃO PAULO SINGAPORE SYDNEY TOKYO

FOUNDATIONS OF MATHEMATICS 9
SECOND EDITION

ISBN 0-07-548726-8

7890 JD 65432

Cover Art Direction/Display Headings by Dan Kewley
Cover Design by Marc Mireault
Cover Photography by Imtek Imagineering
Technical Illustrations by Frank Zsigo

Printed and bound in Canada

Canadian Cataloguing in Publication Data
Dottori, Dino, date —
Foundations of mathematics 9

(The McGraw-Hill Ryerson mathematics program)
2nd ed.
ISBN 0-07-548726-8

1. Mathematics — 1961 — . I. Knill, George, date — .
II. McVean, Robert, date — .
III. Title. IV. Series.

QA39.2.D689 1987   512'.14   C87-093947-5

Communications Branch, Consumer and Corporate Affairs Canada, has granted permission for the use of the National Symbol for Metric Conversion.

TABLE OF CONTENTS

APPLICATIONS OF WHOLE NUMBERS AND DECIMALS

CHAPTER

1

The science of pure mathematics, in its modern developments, may claim to be the most original creation of the human spirit.

Alfred North Whitehead

REVIEW AND PREVIEW TO CHAPTER 1

SETS

A well-defined collection of objects is called a set.

The set of natural numbers is
N = {1, 2, 3, ...}

A prime number is a natural number with no divisor except itself and 1.

EXERCISE

List the following sets in brace brackets, { }.

1. The set of natural numbers less than 6.

2. The set of natural numbers between 11 and 16.

3. The set of even natural numbers less than 9.

4. The set of odd natural numbers between 30 and 36.

5. The set of prime numbers less than 10.

6. The set of vowels in the alphabet.

7. The set of multiples of 7 between 19 and 43.

8. The set comprised of the Great Lakes.

9. The set comprised of the provincial capitals of Canada.

10. The set comprised of the Confederate States.

SUBSETS

If every element of A is an element of B, then A is a subset of B.

(A ⊆ B)

EXERCISE

1. Write all the subsets of {a, b, c}.

2. Is { } a subset of {a, b, c}?

3. Is {a, b, c} a subset of {a, b, c}?

4. Complete the table in your notebook.

Sets	Number of Elements	List of Subsets	Number of Subsets
{1}			
{1, 2}			
{1, 2, 3}			
{1, 2, 3, 4}			

INTERSECTION AND UNION

If A = {2, 3} and B = {3, 4}, then
(i) the intersection of A and B is {3}.

A ∩ B = {3}
      = A and B

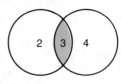

(ii) the union of A and B is {2, 3, 4}.

A ∪ B = {2, 3, 4}
      = A or B

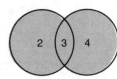

EXERCISE

1. If A = {5, 6, 7, 8} and B = {7, 8, 9}, list

(a) A ∩ B   (b) A ∪ B
(c) B and A   (d) B or A

2. If P = {1, 2, 3}, Q = {3, 4, 5}, and R = {4, 5, 6, 7}, list

(a) P ∩ Q
(b) Q or R
(c) P ∩ R
(d) R ∪ P
(e) Q and R
(f) P ∩ (Q ∪ R)

3. If N = {1, 2, 3, ...} and W = {0, 1, 2, 3, ...} list the following sets and graph them on a number line.

(a) {x | x < 7, x ∈ N}
(b) {x | x ≤ 5, x ∈ W}
(c) {x | 2 < x < 9, x ∈ N}
(d) {x | x ≠ 5, x ∈ W}
(e) {x | x > 3, x ∈ W}
(f) {x | x ≥ 10, x ∈ N}
(g) {x | x ≤ 5, x ∈ W} ∩ {x | x ≥ 2, x ∈ W}
(h) {x | x > 4, x ∈ N} ∪ {x | x ≤ 5, x ∈ N}
(i) {x | x ≤ 3, x ∈ W} ∩ {x | x > 6, x ∈ W}

PROPERTIES OF WHOLE NUMBERS

W = {0, 1, 2, 3, ...} and the W-line is

If a, b, c ∈ W		
Property	Addition	Multiplication
Closure	(a + b) ∈ W	(a × b) ∈ W
Commutative	a + b = b + a	a × b = b × a
Associative	(a + b) + c = a + (b + c)	(a × b) × c = a × (b × c)
Distributive	a(b + c) = ab + ac	
Identity Element	a + 0 = a	a × 1 = a

EXERCISE

1. Name the property illustrated in each case.

(a) 7 + 4 = 4 + 7
(b) 5 × 3 = 3 × 5
(c) 3 × (5 × 2) = (3 × 5) × 2
(d) (5 + 4) + 2 = 5 + (4 + 2)
(e) 5 + 0 = 5
(f) 8 × 1 = 8
(g) 8 + 7 is a whole number
(h) 9 × 3 is a whole number
(i) 3(5 + 2) = 3 × 5 + 3 × 2

2. Use the distributive property to remove brackets in each of the following.

(a) 2(x + y)   (b) 3(x + 4)
(c) 4(2 + t)   (d) 5(m + 8)
(e) 7(x + 9)   (f) 8(n + 11)
(g) (x + 1)3   (h) (y + 3)5
(i) (t + 3)7   (j) (5 + x)9
(k) 10(x + 4)   (l) 2(x + 13)
(m) 3(x + y + 6)   (n) 4(m + 7 + n)
(o) 5(r + s + 8)   (p) (x − y − 3)2

1.1 APPLICATIONS OF WHOLE NUMBERS

Whole numbers can be ordered by placing them on a place value chart. The number 3 425 000 000 is read "three billion, four hundred twenty-five million." The number 3 081 000 000 is read "three billion, eighty-one million."

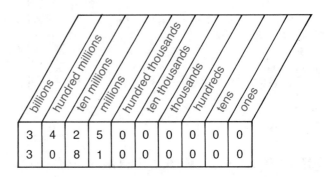

The number 3 425 000 000 is larger than 3 081 000 000 because the 3 in the billions place means 3 000 000 000, three billion, while 425 and 081 in the millions place mean 425 000 000 and 81 000 000 respectively.

EXERCISE 1.1

A 1. Read the following numbers.
(a) 524 000
(b) 13 500
(c) 6215
(d) 21 624 316 528
(e) 508 000 000

2. What number does the 2 represent in the following numbers?
(a) 14 286 536
(b) 265 304
(c) 12 345 816
(d) 624 145
(e) 72 345 915 308

B 3. Write the following numbers.
(a) thirteen million, two hundred thousand
(b) four hundred twenty-five thousand
(c) thirty-seven million
(d) five thousand, four hundred eighteen
(e) one billion, two hundred thousand

4. Add.

(a)	(b)	(c)
576	175	97 406
493	3814	38 505
+318	+767	+64 767

(d) 678, 2156, 38, 9005
(e) 5183, 803, 9265, 56 834
(f) 7663, 59 205, 491, 7849

5. Subtract.

(a)	(b)	(c)
593	491	9438
−461	−384	−7659

(d) 82 867 from 93 474
(e) 756 from 8009
(f) 5004 from 8000

6. Multiply.

(a)	(b)	(c)
733	586	7156
×9	×21	×37

(d)	(e)	(f)
597	6853	525
×300	×7002	×683

7. Divide.

(a) 1216 ÷ 8
(b) 944 ÷ 2
(c) 2016 ÷ 126
(d) 116 736 ÷ 256
(e) $\dfrac{5586}{57}$
(f) $\dfrac{29\ 456}{526}$
(g) $\dfrac{30\ 375}{243}$
(h) $\dfrac{75\ 339}{99}$
(i) $291\overline{)35\ 502}$
(j) $56\overline{)2688}$
(k) $801\overline{)34\ 443}$
(l) $96\overline{)96\ 384}$

8. Perform the indicated operation.

(a) $\begin{array}{r} 527 \\ \times 27 \end{array}$
(b) $\begin{array}{r} 64\ 258 \\ -27\ 724 \end{array}$
(c) $\dfrac{1512}{24}$
(d) $\begin{array}{r} 509 \\ \times 78 \end{array}$
(e) $\begin{array}{r} 12\ 837 \\ -7\ 485 \end{array}$
(f) $\dfrac{5418}{63}$
(g) $\begin{array}{r} 345\ 278 \\ +782\ 300 \end{array}$
(h) 1161 ÷ 27

9. Simplify.

(a) 6124 + 5236 + 2112 + 4567
(b) 65 254 − 37 612
(c) 35 253 − 12 458 − 14 625
(d) 625 × 23 × 18
(e) 38 880 ÷ 864 × 36
(f) 463 926 + 728 497
(g) 1012 ÷ 11 ÷ 14

10. Simplify.

(a) 52 376 − 21 837 + 9602
(b) 364 × 28 ÷ 56
(c) 966 ÷ 46 × 25
(d) 31 274 + 18 555 − 45 707
(e) 3476 + 32 640 − 27 531
(f) 26 × 16 800 ÷ 32
(g) 650 ÷ 25 + 7

11. The results of an election are as follows.

Cloutier, J.	32 635
Howe, A.	27 538
Marsini, G.	41 207
Skinner, W.	18 356

(a) Arrange the four candidates in order with the winner first.
(b) By how many votes did the winner defeat the second place candidate?
(c) How many people voted if there were no spoiled ballots?

12. A person uses about 240 L of water a day. About how much water would a person use in one week?

13. The distance around the earth at the Equator is about 40 000 km. How long will it take to fly around the earth non-stop, in an aircraft that flies at a speed of 800 km/h?

14.

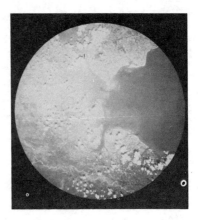

The total area of the earth is about 510 000 000 km². The water area of the earth is about 362 000 000 km². What is the land area of the earth?

15. The approximate areas of the five largest countries in Europe are as follows.

Finland	337 009 km²
France	547 026 km²
Norway	324 219 km²
Spain	504 782 km²
Sweden	449 964 km²

(a) Arrange these five countries from largest to smallest.
(b) What is the total area of these five countries?
(c) The largest country is how much larger than the smallest country?

Find three whole numbers whose sum is equal to their product.
$$a + b + c = a \times b \times c$$

1.2 APPLICATIONS OF DECIMALS

The number 524.525 is read "five hundred twenty-four and five hundred twenty-five thousandths." The position of each digit in the number determines the place value of the digit. This can be shown by putting the number on a place value chart.

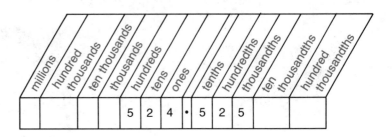

Numbers can be written in expanded form as follows.

32.645 = 30 + 2 + 0.6 + 0.04 + 0.005
= 3 × 10 + 2 × 1 + 6 × 0.1 + 4 × 0.01 + 5 × 0.001

A number in expanded form can be written in standard form.

5 × 10 + 2 × 1 + 3 × 0.1 + 8 × 0.01 + 7 × 0.001
= 50 + 2 + 0.3 + 0.08 + 0.007
= 52.387

In the number 124.637, the 3 has a place value of 0.01 while the face value is 3. Since 0.03 = 3 × 0.01, we can make the following statement.

Total value = face value × place value

EXERCISE 1.2

A 1. Read the following numbers.
(a) 16.25   (b) 0.325
(c) 1.625   (d) 20.095
(e) 0.0025   (f) 0.000 25
(g) 0.0125   (h) 0.25
(i) 5.6   (j) 3.04

2. State the place value of the indicated digit.
(a) 12.6**8**7   (b) 1.034 7**6**
(c) 0.0**2**5 46   (d) 123.7**5**6 38
(e) 4.2**1**5 04   (f) 50.002 35**6**

3. State the total value of the 4.
(a) 2.405   (b) 3.042
(c) 0.425 68   (d) 10.264 85
(e) 0.325 46   (f) 43.2653

B 4. Write the following numbers in standard form.
(a) five and four tenths
(b) twelve and one hundred twenty-five thousandths
(c) one hundred five and three tenths
(d) fifty-two thousandths
(e) eleven and thirteen thousandths
(f) four and five thousandths

5. Write in expanded form.
(a) 2.625   (b) 15.23
(c) 8.35   (d) 0.835
(e) 24.300 14   (f) 6.205 07
(g) three and fifteen hundredths
(h) one hundred twenty-five thousandths

(i) ten and twenty-five hundredths

(j) one hundred and five tenths

6. Add.

(a) 32.45
      15.64
    + 54.76

(b) 12.654
     243.28
    + 3.647

(c) 0.65, 34.307, 7.8904, 22.006 06

(d) 23.809, 2.75, 243.6577, 0.275 35

(e) 0.265, 1.25, 0.04, 365.24, 0.25

7. Subtract.

(a) 345.658
   − 204.735

(b) 34.85
    − 6.245

(c) 12.65 from 32.5

(d) 1.325 from 3.5008

8. Multiply.

(a) 6.25
    × 7

(b) 0.375
    × 8

(c) 325
    × 0.7

(d) 42.65
    × 0.25

(e) 0.25 × 0.65

(f) 3.25 × 2.625

9. Divide.

(a) 81.6 ÷ 12

(b) 812.5 ÷ 25

(c) 13.5 ÷ 0.25

(d) 4.32 ÷ 0.12

(e) $\dfrac{98.64}{3.6}$

(f) $\dfrac{2.55}{0.75}$

(g) 2.6)‾36.92

(h) 0.36)‾5.148

10. Perform the indicated operation.

(a) 35.657
    − 9.623

(b)   12.5
      534.835
        0.425 36
       54.064
    +   4.206 65

(c) 42.65
    × 0.53

(d) $\dfrac{120}{25}$

(e) 52.45
    × 0.75

(f) 0.75)‾6.3

(g) 5.35 × 1.25

11. Simplify.

(a) 56.25 + 1.7 + 3.565 + 14.8

(b) 456.5 − 267.48

(c) 653.6 × 21.4

(d) 3432 ÷ 6.5

(e) 35.625 + 51.7 − 66.65

12. The area of a soccer field is 7300 m². The area of an American football field is 5358.2 m². How much larger is the soccer field?

13. Noah's Ark was about 137 m long. Nelson's ship, Victory, was about half that length. About how long was Nelson's Victory?

14. The height of the Statue of Liberty from the sandals to the top of the torch is 46.02 m. The total height with the pedestal is 92.96 m. What is the height of the pedestal?

15. Twenty-four theatre tickets cost $408.00. What is the cost of one ticket?

16. A wire 8.00 m long is to be cut into five equal pieces. What is the length of each piece?

17. Louise bought the following computer equipment.

computer	$456.75
colour monitor	359.95
keyboard	249.95
printer	479.50
modem	389.50

What is the total cost before the sales tax?

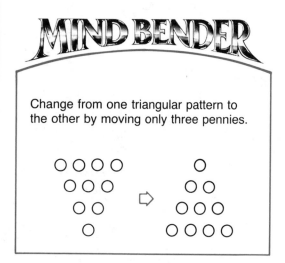

MIND BENDER

Change from one triangular pattern to the other by moving only three pennies.

1.3 ROUNDING AND ESTIMATING

Statements such as "There are seven trees in the yard" are considered exact because the trees can be counted. In a statement like "The circumference of the earth is 40 000 km" an exact number is not required and a rounded number is used. The following chart shows the method used to round to a given place value. The first digit to be discarded is called the key digit.

Rule	Number	Required Place	Key Digit	Rounded Number
If the key digit is less than 5, round down.	5.262 438 3475	0.001 1000	5.262 438 3475	5.262 3000
If the key digit is greater than 5, or if it is a five followed by digits other than zero, round up.	5.414 83 5.267 509 42 583	0.001 0.001 100	5.414 83 5.267 509 42 583	5.415 5.268 42 600
If the key digit is 5, followed only by zeros, round to the nearest even digit.	6500 5500 85 000 4.75 1.265	1000 1000 10 000 0.1 0.01	6500 5500 85 000 4.75 1.265	6000 6000 80 000 4.8 1.26

Estimates are found using rounded numbers. For example if compact discs cost $17.95 each, then an estimate for 12 compact discs is

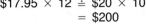
$$\$17.95 \times 12 \doteq \$20 \times 10$$
$$= \$200$$

≐ means approximately equal

Estimation is used to determine whether a solution is reasonable, and to check computations mentally. In some problems, an estimate is all that is required.

> To find an estimate, round the numbers first, then calculate using the rounded numbers.

EXAMPLE. Estimate the answer.
(a) 42.6×68.7
(b) $\dfrac{9.2 \times 52.1}{88}$

SOLUTION:
(a) $42.6 \times 68.7 \doteq 40 \times 70$
$$= 2800$$
(b) $\dfrac{9.2 \times 52.1}{88} \doteq \dfrac{9 \times 50}{90}$
$$= 5$$

EXERCISE 1.3

A 1. Round off to the nearest hundred.
(a) 752
(b) 761
(c) 2735
(d) 47 265
(e) 34 915
(f) 26 407
(g) 850
(h) 55 500
(i) 645 650

2. Round off to the nearest hundredth.
(a) 3.525
(b) 0.235 85
(c) 25.850
(d) 234.875
(e) 37.535
(f) 0.375 165
(g) 0.065
(h) 7.025

3. Round off to the nearest tenth.
(a) 56.25
(b) 5.875
(c) 4.625
(d) 32.85
(e) 0.465
(f) 4.65
(g) 0.0853
(h) 0.001 25

4. Round off to the nearest thousandth.
(a) 5.125 125
(b) 0.525 821
(c) 1.045 456
(d) 23.2655
(e) 23.2645
(f) 5.006 035
(g) 425.425 425
(h) 1.124 52

5. Estimate to insert the decimal point.
(a) 24.8 × 57.2 = 141856
(b) 6374 × 32.6 = 2077924
(c) 46.3 × 21.8 = 100934
(d) 0.854 × 28.8 = 245952
(e) 46.655 ÷ 2.15 = 217
(f) 159.84 ÷ 4.8 = 333
(g) 15.9375 ÷ 3.75 = 425
(h) 0.050 625 ÷ 0.125 = 405

B 6. Estimate to insert the decimal point.

(a) $\dfrac{345 \times 278}{125} = 76728$

(b) $\dfrac{1240}{52 \times 18} = 13247862$

(c) $\dfrac{74\,560.28}{53.6 \times 21.5} = 647$

(d) $\dfrac{34.2 \times 58.5}{61.6} = 32478896$

(e) $\dfrac{(6.25)^2}{4.25 \times 65.75} = 1397897$

7. Estimate the answer.
(a) 475 × 256
(b) 639 × 28.4
(c) 1422.4 ÷ 63.5
(d) 3.8931 ÷ 0.683
(e) 843.6 ÷ 88.8

(f) $\dfrac{487 \times 315}{625}$

(g) $\dfrac{6425}{38 \times 325}$

(h) $\dfrac{53.6 \times 21.4}{0.485}$

8. Estimate the cost of the following.
(a) 12 pens at $1.95 each
(b) 18 dictionaries at $8.95 each
(c) 1 protractor if 12 cost $14.28
(d) 1 floppy disk if 48 cost $102.00
(e) 12 sweaters if 78 cost $2336.10

9. Estimate the following sums.
(a) 8 + 27 + 15 + 32
(b) 5.8 + 3.2 + 6.4 + 9.3
(c) 2.95 + 1.19 + 6.75 + 5.29
(d) 32.6 + 45.8 + 56.2 + 12.9

10. Use estimation to determine which is larger.
(a) 32.8 + 21.7 or 21.6 × 2.12
(b) 456 ÷ 23 or 4.25 × 6.75
(c) 65.72 − 38.6 or 56.5 ÷ 4.14

1.4 NUMERICAL EXPRESSIONS

All of the following expressions have the value 12.

$$10 + 2 \qquad 4 \times 3 \qquad 24 \div 2 \qquad 15 - 3$$
$$6 \times 2 \qquad 10.5 + 1.5 \qquad 6 + 4 + 2 \qquad 18 - 4 - 2$$

A numerical expression is a name for a number. The number is the value of the expression. A numerical expression is simplified when it is replaced by the simplest name of its value.

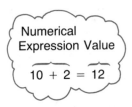

Numerical Expression Value

$$\overbrace{10 + 2} = \overbrace{12}$$

EXAMPLE 1. Simplify. $(40 - 4) \times 2$

SOLUTION:

The parentheses ( ) show how the numbers are to be grouped.

$$(40 - 4) \times 2 = 36 \times 2$$
$$= 72$$

Brackets [ ], and brace brackets { } are also used as grouping symbols along with the division bar.

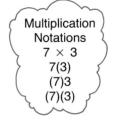

Multiplication Notations

7×3
$7(3)$
$(7)3$
$(7)(3)$

EXAMPLE 2. Simplify. $\dfrac{13 + 5}{6}$

SOLUTION:

The fraction bar in $\dfrac{13 + 5}{6}$ is a division symbol and a grouping symbol.

$$\frac{13 + 5}{6} = \frac{(13 + 5)}{6}$$
$$= \frac{18}{6}$$
$$= 3$$

Sometimes numerical expressions are written without grouping symbols. For example

$$12 \div 2 + 4 = \begin{cases} (12 \div 2) + 4 = 10 \\ 12 \div (2 + 4) = 2 \end{cases}$$

To obtain the correct answer in any given problem, it is necessary to agree on an order for performing calculations. The order that has been agreed upon is:

(i)   if there are grouping symbols, perform the operations within the grouping symbols
(ii) then perform all multiplications and divisions, in order from left to right
(iii) then perform all the additions and subtractions, in order from left to right.

EXAMPLE 3. Simplify. $4(15 - 8) + 6 \div 3$

SOLUTION:
$$4(15 - 8) + 6 \div 3 = 4(7) + 6 \div 3$$
$$= 28 + 2$$
$$= 30$$

EXAMPLE 4. Simplify. $[7 - (4 - 2)] \times 6 - 3$

SOLUTION:
First perform the operation within the inner grouping symbol.

$$[7 - (4 - 2)] \times 6 - 3 = [7 - 2] \times 6 - 3$$
$$= 5 \times 6 - 3$$
$$= 30 - 3$$
$$= 27$$

EXERCISE 1.4

A 1. Simplify.

(a) $5 \times 2 - 3$ (b) $7 + 4 - 5$
(c) $8 + 8 + 4$ (d) $10 \div 2 + 1$
(e) $9 - 1 + 3$ (f) $(7 - 3) + 2$
(g) $3 \times (5 - 4)$ (h) $16 \div (3 + 5)$
(i) $(4 + 3)5$ (j) $4(12 - 5)$
(k) $\dfrac{7 + 3}{5} + 4$ (l) $\dfrac{16 - 2}{7} - 1$
(m) $\dfrac{10}{7 - 2} + 3$ (n) $\dfrac{12}{8 \div 2} \div 3$

B 2. Simplify.

(a) $33 + (5 \times 4)$
(b) $59 - 28 \div 2$
(c) $3(5 - 2) + 16$
(d) $34 - 16 + 25 - 18$
(e) $42 \times 5 - 17$
(f) $36 \div 4 \times 14$
(g) $(21 + 4) - (13 + 5)$
(h) $(8 - 5)(11 + 6)$
(i) $(21 - 6) \div (30 - 25)$
(j) $(18 - 4) \times (54 \div 3)$
(k) $[53 - (8 + 9)] \times 4$
(l) $(20 - 15 \div 3) + 42$
(m) $(3.7 + 4.3) \times 8$
(n) $6.5(2.8 - 1.2)$
(o) $\dfrac{3.6 + 4.4}{5.2 - 1.2}$
(p) $\dfrac{3.6(4.8 - 2.7)}{3 \times 1.2}$

3. Simplify.

(a) $[7(5 - 2)] \div 7$ (b) $\dfrac{56 \div 8}{7} + 46$
(c) $\dfrac{13 + 21}{20 - 3}$ (d) $\dfrac{24 + 3 \times 6}{12 \div 6}$
(e) $29 + \dfrac{32}{16 \div 8}$
(f) $[7 \times 12 - (4 + 6)] \times 8$
(g) $(36 + 5)(27 - 9)$
(h) $24(16 - 3) \div (10 - 2)$
(i) $\dfrac{93 - 55}{38 \div 2} + 74$
(j) $5.2 [4.7 - (3.6 - 2.1)]$
(k) $[7.5 - (3.4 + 1.6)] + 4.2$
(l) $[7.3(12.8 - 4.6) + 3] + 2.1$

4. Make each of the following a true statement by replacing each ■ with $=$ or $\neq$.

(a) $\dfrac{14 + 8}{2}$ ■ $\dfrac{4(31 - 9)}{8}$
(b) $\dfrac{41 + 22}{9 \times 7}$ ■ $21 - 4(7 - 2)$
(c) $\dfrac{8 \times 6 - 12}{36 \div 9 + 2}$ ■ $1 + \dfrac{20 - 5}{35 \div 7}$
(d) $3[24 \div (5 + 1)]$ ■ $[(4 + 1) \times (6 \div 3)]$
(e) $\dfrac{20 - 5}{4 + 1} + 4$ ■ $7(6 - 3) - 28 \div 2$
(f) $\dfrac{67 - [5(7 + 2)]}{23 - 12}$ ■ $\dfrac{74 - [16 \times 4 \div 2]}{72 \div (4 \times 3)}$

1.5 USING YOUR CALCULATOR

When using a calculator, it is important to press the keys in the proper sequence. Different models of calculators have special features that require investigation in order to use these machines efficiently in problem solving. For special features that are not covered in this book, it is necessary to check the user's manual.

Calculator keys can be classified into three groups.

Number Keys	Operation Keys	Special Function Keys
7 8 9 4 5 6 1 2 3 0	× ÷ + − √	M+ M− MR MC % c/ce +/− ·

Most calculators will perform the following operations as shown.

Problem	Press	Display
345 + 624 − 588	C 3 4 5 + 6 2 4 − 5 8 8 =	381
806 ÷ 24.8	C 8 0 6 ÷ 2 4 · 8 =	32.5
486.3 × 21.7	C 4 8 6 · 3 × 2 1 · 7 =	10552.71

Many calculators have a constant feature that operates automatically with the equal key = . The following exercise investigates how constants for addition, subtraction, multiplication, and division operate.

EXERCISE 1.5

B 1. Constant for addition:

Press   C 5 + 2 = = = =

If the display reads:

7 — there is no repeating function

13 — there is a repeating function

(a) What will your calculator display after you press the following?

(i)   C 3 + 1 0 = = = =

(ii)   C 5 + = = = = =

(iii)   C 3 + 4 = = = = =

(b) Start with 5 and make your calculator count by 10.

2. Constant for subtraction:

Press   C 2 0 − 2 = = =

If the display reads:

18 — there is no repeating function

14 — there is a repeating function

(a) What will your calculator display after you press the following?

(i)   C 3 2 − 4 = = = =

(ii)   C 2 5 − 5 = = = = =

(iii)   C 3 3 − 5 = = = =

(b) Start with 125 and make your calculator count backwards by 10.

3. Constant for multiplication:

Press [C] [4] [×] [5] [=] [=] [=] [=] [=]

If the display reads:

`5120` — the 4 is the constant multiplier

`12500` — the 5 is the constant multiplier

(a) What will your calculator display after you press the following?

(i) [C] [3] [×] [4] [=] [=] [=] [=]

(ii) [C] [2] [×] [5] [=] [=] [=] [=]

(iii) [C] [3] [×] [5] [=] [=] [=] [=]

(iv) [C] [3] [×] [2] [=] [=] [=] [=]

(v) [C] [1] [×] [5] [=] [=] [=] [=]

(b) Start with 8 and multiply by 4 five times.
(c) Start with 3 and multiply by 7 four times.
(d) Explain how the constant for multiplication operates.

4. Constant for division:

Press [C] [5] [1] [2] [÷] [2] [=] [=] [=] [=]

If the display reads:

`256` — there is no repeating function

`16` — the constant divisor is 2

(a) What will your calculator display after you press the following?

(i) [C] [1] [2] [5] [÷] [5] [=] [=] [=]

(ii) [C] [2] [1] [8] [7] [÷] [7] [=] [=] [=] [=]

(iii) [C] [3] [1] [2] [5] [÷] [5] [=] [=] [=] [=]

(iv) [C] [4] [0] [9] [6] [÷] [2] [=] [=] [=] [=]

(v) [C] [4] [0] [9] [6] [÷] [4] [=] [=] [=] [=]

(b) Divide 65 536 by 4 six times.
(c) Divide 531 441 by 9 seven times.
(d) Explain how the constant for division operates.

5. Investigate the following on a calculator. Explain the results.

(a) [C] [+] [1] [0] [=] [=] [=] [=] [=]

(b) [C] [−] [1] [0] [=] [=] [=] [=] [=]

(c) [C] [×] [1] [0] [=] [=] [=] [=] [=]

(d) [C] [÷] [1] [0] [=] [=] [=] [=] [=]

6. Use the information from questions 1 to 5 to answer the following.
Write the answer for each.
Check with a calculator.

(a) [C] [4] [+] [5] [=] [=] [=] [=] [=]

(b) [C] [2] [4] [−] [2] [=] [=] [=] [=] [=]

(c) [C] [1] [0] [2] [4] [÷] [2] [=] [=] [=] [=]

(d) [C] [6] [5] [6] [1] [÷] [9] [=] [=] [=] [=]

CALCULATOR MATH

CLEAR ENTRY

The clear entry key is used to correct the last number that has been entered. This key is labelled [CE] or [CL] depending on the calculator. The clear entry key must not be confused with the general clear key [C] or [ON/C] . The clear key will clear all calculations except the memory.

An incorrect number can be replaced as long as it has not been followed by a function key. By pressing the clear entry key, the latest entry is cleared while all previous entries are retained.

Suppose you have entered

[5] [·] [3] [×] [2] [·] [4]

and the 2.4 should be 3.4.
Make this correction by pressing

[CE] [3] [·] [4] [=]

and the displayed answer will be `18.02`

Perform the following corrections if possible, and complete the calculation.

1. Enter [C] [4] [×] [8]

Change the 8 to 7.

2. Enter [C] [6] [·] [3] [−] [2] [·] [7]

Change 2.7 to 2.5.

3. Enter [C] [2] [·] [4] [+] [3] [·] [8]

Change 3.8 to 5.8.

1.6 VARIABLES IN ALGEBRAIC EXPRESSIONS

In algebra we work with algebraic expressions such as

$$7n \qquad y + 5 \qquad 2x - 3$$

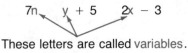

These letters are called variables.

A variable is a symbol used to represent one or more numbers. When we write a product that contains a variable, such as 7n, the multiplication symbol is understood.

The value of an expression depends on the number used to replace the variable.

When n = 3, the value of 7n is 7 × 3 or 21.
When n = 8, the value of 7n is 7 × 8 or 56.

The set of numbers that the variable represents is called the domain of the variable.

EXAMPLE 1. Evaluate. $2x + 3$ when $x \in \{2, 3, 4\}$

SOLUTION:
$\{2, 3, 4\}$ is the domain of x.

When x = 2, $\quad 2x + 3 = 2(2) + 3 = 4 + 3 = 7$
When x = 3, $\quad 2x + 3 = 2(3) + 3 = 6 + 3 = 9$
When x = 4, $\quad 2x + 3 = 2(4) + 3 = 8 + 3 = 11$

The calculations in Example 1 can also be written as follows, where E(x) is read "the expression in x."

$$E(x) = 2x + 3$$
$$E(2) = 2(2) + 3 = 7$$
$$E(3) = 2(3) + 3 = 9$$
$$E(4) = 2(4) + 3 = 11$$

EXAMPLE 2. If $E(x) = 3x - 5$, evaluate
(a) E(4) $\qquad$ (b) E(7) $\qquad$ (c) E(6.2) $\qquad$ (d) E(4.45)

SOLUTION:
$\quad E(x) = 3x - 5$
(a) $E(4) = 3(4) - 5 = 12 - 5 = 7$
(b) $E(7) = 3(7) - 5 = 21 - 5 = 16$
(c) $E(6.2) = 3(6.2) - 5 = 18.6 - 5 = 13.6$
(d) $E(4.45) = 3(4.45) - 5 = 13.35 - 5 = 8.35$

Algebraic expressions may contain more than one variable. For example, $w + 2x + y$ is an algebraic expression with three variables.

EXAMPLE 3. If $x = 5$, $y = 3$, and $z = 2$, evaluate $7x + 4y - 5z$.

SOLUTION:
$$7x + 4y - 5z = 7(5) + 4(3) - 5(2)$$
$$= 35 + 12 - 10$$
$$= 37$$

Whenever a variable appears in the denominator of a fraction we shall understand that the domain of the variable excludes those elements which makes the denominator zero, since division by zero is not defined.

EXAMPLE 4. If $x = 4$ and $y = 2$, find the value of $\dfrac{5x + 4y}{3x - 4y}$.

SOLUTION:

$$\frac{5x + 4y}{3x - 4y} = \frac{5(4) + 4(2)}{3(4) - 4(2)}$$
$$= \frac{20 + 8}{12 - 8}$$
$$= \frac{28}{4}$$
$$= 7$$

EXERCISE 1.6

A 1. If $E(x) = 3x$, find

(a) E(1)   (b) E(4)   (c) E(0)
(d) E(2.3) (e) E(50)   (f) E(a)

2. If $E(x) = 2x - 1$, find

(a) E(4)   (b) E(10)   (c) E(40)
(d) E(1.5) (e) E(100) (f) E(m)

3. If $E(x) = 7 + 3x$, find

(a) E(1)   (b) E(2)   (c) E(10)
(d) E(2.5) (e) E(200) (f) E(y)

B 4. If $x = 2$, $y = 3$, and $z = 4$, evaluate the following algebraic expressions.

(a) x + y (b) y + z   (c) 5x   (d) 3z
(e) xy   (f) 2yz   (g) 3x + 2 (h) 5z − 1

5. If $r = 1.2$, $s = 2.5$, and $t = 4$, find the value of each of the following.

(a) 5r + s   (b) 7st
(c) r + s + t   (d) s − r
(e) 4rs   (f) 5s + r
(g) 3r + 2t   (h) 2r + 4

6. Evaluate $9x - 4$ when $x \in \{8, 9, 10, 11, 12\}$.

7. Evaluate $33x + 5$ when $x \in \{21, 22, 23, 24\}$.

8. If $E(x) = 17x + 34$, find

(a) E(4)   (b) E(7)   (c) E(10)
(d) E(1.2) (e) E(0)   (f) E(0.5)

9. If $E(x) = 9x - 8$, find

(a) E(9)   (b) E(13)   (c) E(20)
(d) E(2.1) (e) E(m)   (f) E(1)

10. If $x = 3$, $y = 2$, and $z = 5$, find the value of each of the following.

(a) 12xy   (b) 7x + 5y + 13
(c) 11x + 7y + 8z   (d) 10z − 3x + 4y
(e) 13x − 2y − 3z   (f) 43 − 7x − z
(g) 3xyz − 4   (h) 7(y + z)
(i) 10z − xy   (j) z(2x − y)
(k) xy(x + z) + 9   (l) 4xz − 3yz

C 11. If $r = 5$, $s = 4$, and $t = 3$, find the value of each of the following.

(a) (r + s)(s + t)   (b) 2t(3r − 5)

(c) (5s − 2t)(4r + t)   (d) $\dfrac{t + s}{r - s}$

(e) $\dfrac{4r + 7s}{s}$ (f) $s(r - t) + \dfrac{rs}{2}$

(g) $\dfrac{6t + 2s}{4r + 6}$ (h) $\dfrac{9t + 3r}{4s - 2r}$

(i) $\dfrac{4t - 2s + 6}{r} + 7$ (j) (s + r)(t + r)(t + s)

1.7 FACTORS AND EXPONENTS

When two or more numbers are multiplied, each of the numbers is called a factor of the product.

Since $5 \times 3 = 15$, 5 and 3 are called factors of 15.
The numbers 2, 3, and 5 are factors of 30 since $2 \times 3 \times 5 = 30$.

Exponents are used when a number can be expressed as the product of equal factors.

$$16 = 2 \times 2 \times 2 \times 2 \qquad \text{This tells us there are four}$$
$$= 2^4 \qquad \qquad \text{equal factors.}$$

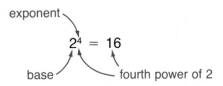

When a number can be expressed as the product of equal factors, except 1, the number is called a power of the repeated factor. The following illustrates the first four powers of 3.

First Power: $3 = 3^1$
Second Power: $9 = 3^2$
Third Power: $27 = 3^3$
Fourth Power: $81 = 3^4$

In general, if $n \in \{1, 2, 3, 4, ...\}$, then x^n means $x \times x \times x \times x \times x \times x \, ...$ to n factors.

Factored Form

$$x^4 = x \times x \times x \times x \times x \times x$$

Exponential Form

EXAMPLE 1. If $x = 3$, find the value of
(a) x^4 (b) $4x^2$ (c) $(4x)^2$

SOLUTION:

(a) $x^4 = 3^4$
$= 3 \times 3 \times 3 \times 3$
$= 81$

(b) $4x^2 = 4(3)^2$
$= 4 \times 3 \times 3$
$= 36$

(c) $(4x)^2 = (4 \times 3)^2$
$= 12^2$
$= 12 \times 12$
$= 144$

EXAMPLE 2. If $E(x) = 3x^2 + 2$, evaluate
(a) $E(2)$ (b) $E(5)$ (c) $E(1.5)$ (d) $E(m)$

SOLUTION:

$E(x) = 3x^2 + 2$
(a) $E(2) = 3(2)^2 + 2 = 3(4) + 2 = 12 + 2 = 14$
(b) $E(5) = 3(5)^2 + 2 = 3(25) + 2 = 75 + 2 = 77$
(c) $E(1.5) = 3(1.5)^2 + 2 = 3(2.25) + 2 = 6.75 + 2 = 8.75$
(d) $E(m) = 3(m)^2 + 2 = 3m^2 + 2$

EXAMPLE 3. If $x = 2$, $y = 3$, and $z = 4$, evaluate $\dfrac{5x^2 + 3yz}{x^2}$.

SOLUTION:

$$\frac{5x^2 + 3yz}{x^2} = \frac{5(2)^2 + 3(3)(4)}{2^2}$$

$$= \frac{5(4) + 3(3)(4)}{4}$$

$$= \frac{20 + 36}{4}$$

$$= \frac{56}{4}$$

$$= 14$$

EXERCISE 1.7

A 1. State the expression in factored form.

(a) $3x^4$ (b) $4y^2$ (c) $(2x)^2$ (d) t^3
(e) $(xy)^3$ (f) $3(rs)^2$ (g) $4a^2b^3$ (h) $(x + y)^3$

2. State the expression in exponential form.

(a) $x \times x \times x \times x$
(b) $y \times y \times y \times y \times y$
(c) $4 \times x \times x \times x \times y$
(d) $3 \times m \times n \times n \times n$
(e) $3x \times 3x \times 3x$
(f) $5 \times (x + y)(x + y)$
(g) $(x - y)(x - y)(r + s)(r + s)(r + s)$

3. State the value of

(a) the fourth power of 2
(b) the second power of 5
(c) the third power of 3
(d) the second power of 4
(e) the fifth power of 2
(f) the third power of 10

B 4. If $x = 2$, state the value of

(a) x^2 (b) $3x^2$ (c) $x^2 - 1$
(d) $x^3 + 2$ (e) $(x + 1)^2$ (f) $5x - 1$

5. If $y = 1.5$, state the value of

(a) $2y^2$ (b) $(2y)^2$ (c) $(y - 1)^2$
(d) y^3 (e) $(y + 1)^2$ (f) $y^3 - 1$

6. If $w = 1$, state the value of

(a) w^5 (b) $4w^9$ (c) $(3w)^2$
(d) $(w + 2)^2$ (e) $4w^5 - 1$ (f) $(w + 1)^3$

7. If $E(x) = x^2 + 2$, find

(a) $E(1)$ (b) $E(3)$ (c) $E(4)$
(d) $E(0)$ (e) $E(1.2)$ (f) $E(a)$

8. If $E(x) = x^3 - 1$, find

(a) $E(3)$ (b) $E(2)$ (c) $E(1)$
(d) $E(1.5)$ (e) $E(2.8)$ (f) $E(y)$

9. Given the value of the variable, evaluate each of the following expressions.

(a) y^4; 5   (b) x^3; 6
(c) t^4; 4   (d) $3x^2$; 8
(e) $7z^5$; 2   (f) $(3y)^2$; 4
(g) $(7x)^3$; 2   (h) 2^3x^2; 5

10. If $x = 2$ and $y = 3$, find the value of

(a) $x^2 + y^2$ (b) $(x + y)^2$
(c) $2(3x + 2y)$ (d) $(3x - y)^2$
(e) $x^3 + y^3$ (f) $2(x^2 + y)$
(g) $3x^3 - y^2$ (h) $(3x)^2 - y$

11. If $r = 3$, $s = 4$, and $t = 5$, find the value of

(a) $\dfrac{r^2 + s^2}{t}$ (b) $\dfrac{t^2 - r^2}{2s}$

(c) $\dfrac{3st - s^2}{2t + 1}$ (d) $\dfrac{s^3 - 2rt - 4}{2t}$

(e) $\dfrac{2(3s^2 - st) - 2s^2}{rs}$

(f) $\dfrac{(2r + 1)^2 + 2r^2t - 19}{2rst}$

1.8 THE EXPONENT RULES

2^3 means $2 \times 2 \times 2$ and $2^3 = 8$.

2^n means $2 \times 2 \times 2 \times \dots$ to n factors.

On a calculator, press

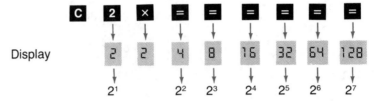

Display

2^1 2^2 2^3 2^4 2^5 2^6 2^7

This result can be described using exponents as shown above.
We can multiply 128 and 16 using exponents. First, express 128 and 16 as powers with the same base.

$$128 \times 16 = 2^7 \times 2^4$$

$$\overbrace{}^{128} \qquad \overbrace{}^{16}$$

$$= 2 \times 2 \times 2 \times 2 \times 2 \times 2 \times 2 \times 2 \times 2 \times 2 \times 2$$
$$= 2^{11}$$
$$= 2048$$

or
$$2^7 \times 2^4 = 2^{7+4}$$
$$= 2^{11}$$
$$= 2048$$

Multiplying with Powers

> To find the product of powers with the same base, we add the exponents.
>
> $$x^m \times x^n = x^{m+n}$$

We can also divide 128 by 16 using exponents.

$$128 \div 16 = \frac{2^7}{2^4}$$

$$= \frac{2 \times 2 \times 2 \times 2 \times 2 \times 2 \times 2}{2 \times 2 \times 2 \times 2}$$

$$= 2 \times 2 \times 2$$
$$= 2^3$$
$$= 8$$

or
$$2^7 \div 2^4 = 2^{7-4}$$
$$= 2^3$$
$$= 8$$

Dividing with Powers

> To find the quotient of powers with the same base, we subtract the exponents.
>
> $$x^m \div x^n = x^{m-n}$$

The following example illustrates the procedure for raising a power to a power.

$$16^3 = 16 \times 16 \times 16 \qquad \text{or} \qquad 16^3 = (2^4)^3 \qquad\qquad \text{or} \qquad 16^3 = (2^4)^3$$
$$= 4096 \qquad\qquad\qquad\qquad = 2^4 \times 2^4 \times 2^4 \qquad\qquad\qquad = 2^{4 \times 3}$$
$$= 2^{4+4+4} \qquad\qquad\qquad\qquad = 2^{12}$$
$$= 2^{12} \qquad\qquad\qquad\qquad = 4096$$
$$= 4096$$

Power of a Power

To find the power of a power, we multiply the exponents.

$$(x^m)^n = x^{m \times n}$$

EXAMPLE. Simplify.

(a) $(x^5)(x^3)$ 　　　　　　(b) $\dfrac{x^9}{x^6}$ 　　　　　　(c) $(x^4)^2$

SOLUTION:

(a) $(x^5)(x^3) = x^{5+3}$ 　|　(b) $\dfrac{x^9}{x^6} = x^{9-6}$ 　|　(c) $(x^4)^2 = x^{4 \times 2}$
$\qquad\qquad\quad = x^8$ 　　　|　$\qquad\quad = x^3$ 　　|　$\qquad\qquad = x^8$

EXERCISE 1.8

A 1. Find the value of ■ in each of the following.
  (a) $3^5 \times 3^7 = 3^■$ 　　　(b) $4^6 \times 4 = 4^■$
  (c) $7^3 \times 7^7 = 7^■$ 　　　(d) $10^8 \times 10^8 = 10^■$
  (e) $2^3 \times 2^5 \times 2^2 = 2^■$ (f) $5 \times 5^6 \times 5^2 = 5^■$
  (g) $x^3 \times x^7 \times x^4 = x^■$ (h) $y \times y^2 \times y^3 = y^■$

2. Find the value of ■ in each of the following.
  (a) $6^5 \div 6^2 = 6^■$ 　　　(b) $2^8 \div 2^3 = 2^■$
  (c) $5^6 \div 5 = 5^■$ 　　　(d) $10^{12} \div 10^8 = 10^■$
  (e) $x^7 \div x^3 = x^■$ 　　　(f) $y^3 \div y^2 = y^■$

3. Find the value of ■.
  (a) $(2^3)^2 = 2^■$ 　　　(b) $(3^2)^4 = 3^■$
  (c) $(5^3)^3 = 5^■$ 　　　(d) $(7^4)^2 = 7^■$
  (e) $(x^2)^5 = x^■$ 　　　(f) $(y^3)^5 = y^■$

B 4. Find the value of ■.
  (a) $2^2 \times 2^■ = 2^7$ 　　　(b) $3^4 \div 3^■ = 3^2$
  (c) $4^■ \times 4^3 = 4^9$ 　　　(d) $5^■ \div 5 = 5$
  (e) $(2^4)^■ = 2^{12}$ 　　　(f) $(3^■)^2 = 3^{14}$

5. Simplify.
  (a) $5^4 \times 5^3 \times 5^2$ 　　　(b) $2^3 \times 2 \times 2^7$
  (c) $7^3 \times 7^4 \times 7^3$ 　　　(d) $5 \times 5^4 \times 5^4$
  (e) $2^8 \times 2^3 \times 2^5$ 　　　(f) $x^7 \times x^4 \times x^{10}$

6. Simplify.
  (a) $x^2 \times x^4 \div x^3$ 　　　(b) $y^3 \times y^5 \times y^8$
  (c) $m^4 \div m^2 \times m$ 　　　(d) $t^8 \times t^2 \div t$
  (e) $x^{10} \div x^3 \times x^4$ 　　　(f) $w^7 \times w^7 \times w^3$
  (g) $(x^2)^4$ 　　　　　　(h) $(y^3)^7$
  (i) $(m^2)^3 \div m^2$ 　　　(j) $(x^4)^4 \times x^2$
  (k) $(t^3)^2 \div t^5$ 　　　(l) $m^7 \div m^7 \times m^2$

CALCULATOR MATH

Some calculators have an exponential key **yˣ** to find the power of a number. To use the "y to the exponent x" key, first enter y, press **yˣ** and then enter x.

Use the "y to the exponent x" key to evaluate the following.
  1. 57^3 　　　　　2. 36^2
  3. 55^4 　　　　　4. 25^5
  5. 2.5^5 　　　　　6. 3.7^4
  7. 4.8^4 　　　　　8. 2.65^3
  9. 92.6^3 　　　　10. 55.5^4

1.9 ORDER OF OPERATIONS

In earlier work, the order of operations was established as a rule of mathematics. If the order is not followed, it is quite likely that answers will be different.

What does your calculator display as the answer to $4 + 3 \times 2$, when you enter

$$\boxed{C}\ \boxed{4}\ \boxed{+}\ \boxed{3}\ \boxed{\times}\ \boxed{2}\ \boxed{=}$$

If your calculator displayed the answer 10, then it performs $\times$ and $\div$ before $+$ and $-$.

If your calculator displayed the answer 14, then the order in which the operations are performed is determined by the person using the calculator. To calculate $4 + 3 \times 2$ with this type of calculator, enter

$$\boxed{C}\ \boxed{3}\ \boxed{\times}\ \boxed{2}\ \boxed{+}\ \boxed{4}\ \boxed{=}$$

The order of operations is summarized in the acronym BEDMAS as described in the following chart.

BEDMAS is an acronym. The following words are also acronyms. What do they mean?
SCUBA
NATO
RADAR
LASER

B	E	D M	A S
Do the computations in brackets first.	Simplify numbers with exponents and "of."	Divide or multiply in the order in which $\div$ and $\times$ appear from left to right.	Add or subtract in the order in which $+$ and $-$ appear from left to right.

With a calculator, it is often necessary to use the memory key $\boxed{M}$ to perform some of the more complicated calculations.

EXAMPLE 1. Simplify. $(4 + 5) \times (9 - 4)$

SOLUTION:
$(4 + 5) \times (9 - 4) = 9 \times 5$ B
$ = 45$ M

This key puts the display into memory.

Press $\boxed{C}\ \boxed{4}\ \boxed{+}\ \boxed{5}\ \boxed{=}\ \boxed{M}\ \boxed{C}\ \boxed{9}\ \boxed{-}\ \boxed{4}\ \boxed{=}$
$\boxed{\times}\ \boxed{MR}$

The display is 45

This key recalls the display from memory.

EXAMPLE 2. Simplify. $6^2 \div (5 - 1^2) - 4$

SOLUTION:
$6^2 \div (5 - 1^2) - 4 = 6^2 \div (4) - 4$ B
$ = 36 \div 4 - 4$ D
$ = 9 - 4$ S
$ = 5$

Press $\boxed{C}\ \boxed{5}\ \boxed{-}\ \boxed{1}\ \boxed{=}\ \boxed{M}\ \boxed{C}\ \boxed{6}\ \boxed{\times}\ \boxed{6}\ \boxed{=}$
$\boxed{\div}\ \boxed{MR}\ \boxed{=}\ \boxed{-}\ \boxed{4}\ \boxed{=}$

The display is 5

EXAMPLE 3. Simplify. $39.06 \div (12.8 - 3.5) \times 2.4^3$

SOLUTION:

$ 39.06 \div \overbrace{(12.8 - 3.5)} \times 2.4^3 \qquad$ B,E
$= 39.06 \div 9.3 \times 13.824 \qquad$ D
$\doteq 4.2 \times 13.824 \qquad$ M
$= 58.0608$

Press [C][1][2][·][8][−][3][·][5][=][M]
[C][3][9][·][0][6][÷][MR][×]
[2][·][4][yˣ][3][=]

The display is   `58.0608`

EXERCISE 1.9

A 1. Simplify.

(a) $5^2 - 1$ (b) $16 - 5 + 3$

(c) $27 \div 3 + 4$ (d) $12 - 6 \times 0$

(e) $10 + 1 + 3^2$ (f) $(5^2 + 1) - 3$

(g) $10 \times 5 \div 25$ (h) $0 \div 4^2 + 7$

(i) $18 \div 9 + 4$ (j) $15 - 2^2 + 5 \times 4$

(k) $7 \times 5 + 6 - 4$ (l) $5(9 - 7) + 6$

(m) $\dfrac{8 + 2}{2}$ (n) $\dfrac{30 \div 5}{3}$

(o) $\dfrac{4^2 - 1}{5}$ (p) $\dfrac{19 - 5 + 7}{7}$

B 2. Simplify the following.

(a) $5 + 7 - 6 \div 2 + 11$

(b) $6 \times 4 - (13 - 5) \div 2$

(c) $2 \times 3^2 - (5 \times 2) + 15$

(d) $(3^2 - 1) \div 4 + 5 - 2$

(e) $6 \times 4 \div 2 + 15 \div 3$

(f) $6 \times (4 \div 2) + 15 \div 3$

(g) $12^2 - 8^2 + 3^2 - 5$

(h) $6^2 \div (5 + 2^2) - 1$

(i) $3(2^4 - 11) + 3 \times 2^2 - 4$

(j) $5[10 - (4 \times 1)] \div 3$

3. Simplify.

(a) $\dfrac{8^2 - 4 \times 3}{2^4 - 3}$ (b) $\dfrac{17 \times 4 - 2^3}{3^2 + 1}$

(c) $\dfrac{2^4 - 3 + 12 \div 4}{64 \div 2^3}$ (d) $\dfrac{8^2 - 14}{(3 + 2) \times 10}$

(e) $5 \times 3^3 - 6(11 + 2^2)$

(f) $13 \times 6 \div 3 \times 2 \div 13$

(g) $55 - 3[(4 + 3) - (18 \div 3)]$

(h) $(7^2 - 4)(5^2 - 2)$

(i) $3(7 - 3)^3 + 130 \div (14 - 1)$

(j) $\dfrac{22[14 - (12 \div 6)]}{3^3 - 5}$

4. Evaluate each expression if $x = 2, y = 3,$ and $z = 1.$

(a) $(x + y)^2$ (b) $x^2 + 2xy + y^2$

(c) $xyz - x^2$ (d) $4x^2 + 3y^2 - 7z^2$

(e) $y^4 - x^3 + z^2$ (f) $3x^2y^2 + 2x^3z$

(g) $(x + y + z)(y - x + z)$

(h) $(x + z)^2(y - z)^3$

(i) $\dfrac{x^3y^2 - 10(y^2 - x)}{2z}$

(j) $y^x - x^y$

5. Simplify using a calculator.

(a) $2.4^3 \div 3.75 + 7.4 \times 2.6$

(b) $5.7(7.2 - 2.8) \div 1.9 + 4.3 - 2.5$

(c) $(3.5^3 - 5.2 \times 2.6) \div 5 - 2.371$

(d) $3.5^2 - (1.5 \div 0.5) + 1.3$

(e) $1.5^2 - (2.75 + 6.13) \div 7.4$

6. Simplify using a calculator.

(a) $2.4(2.7 \times 9.1 - 3.5 \times 2.6) + 4.2^3$

(b) $2.5^5 \div 2.5^3 \div 2.5^2$

(c) $\dfrac{3.4^2 - 2.3 \times 2.3 - 1.9}{1.6^2 - 1.5}$

(d) $\dfrac{(10^2 + 4.6^3) \div 2}{4} + 16.7$

7. Evaluate each expression if $x = 2.1,$ $y = 3.2,$ and $z = 1.5.$

(a) $\dfrac{3x + 2y + 4z}{2.5}$

(b) $x^2yz - 4$

(c) $9x^4 \div 2y^2 - 7.85$

(d) $\dfrac{5x^2 - 2y}{6z + 1}$

(e) $\dfrac{2y - x - z}{3x^5y^2z}$

1.10 ADDING AND SUBTRACTING MONOMIALS

A term is a mathematical expression using numerals or variables or both to indicate a product or quotient. The following are examples of terms

$$5x \qquad 8xy \qquad m \qquad 7 \qquad 4x^2 \qquad \frac{x}{7}$$

In expressions such as $3x + 4y - 2z$, the parts separated by $+$ and $-$ signs are terms.

Expressions such as $4x^2$, consisting of only one term, are called monomials. Expressions with two terms are called binomials, and those with three terms are called trinomials.

Name	Number of terms	Examples
Monomial	1	$7x, 13, y, 8x^3$
Binomial	2	$3x + 4, 4m - n$
Trinomial	3	$x^2 + x + 4, m + 3n + 7$

Polynomial is the general name for such mathematical expressions. It is sometimes used to refer to expressions with more than three terms.

In the expression $7xy$, the 7, x, and y are factors of the term. Each factor is the coefficient of the product of the other factors. For example

7 is the coefficient of xy

$7x$ is the coefficient of y

xy is the coefficient of 7

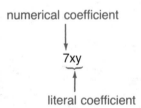

Usually when the word coefficient is used, it refers to the numerical coefficient.

Terms with the same literal coefficient are called like terms. For example $3xy$ and $5xy$ are like terms while $3x^2$ and $5x^3$ are not like terms.

Expressions with more than one term can be simplified if they contain like terms.

EXAMPLE 1.   Simplify.   3x + 5x

SOLUTION:
$$3x + 5x = x(3) + x(5)$$
$$= x(3 + 5)$$
$$= x(8)$$
$$= 8x$$
$$3x + 5x = 8x$$

An expression is simplified when it is replaced with an equivalent expression with as few terms as possible.

EXAMPLE 2.   Simplify.
(a) 7x + 9x   (b) 3y + 4y + 8y

SOLUTION:
(a) 7x + 9x = (7 + 9)x | (b) 3y + 4y + 8y = (3 + 4 + 8)y
$\qquad\quad = 16x$ | $\qquad\qquad\qquad\quad = 15y$

EXAMPLE 3.   Simplify.
(a) 17x − 6x   (b) 6y − 2y + 5y

SOLUTION:
(a) 17x − 6x = (17 − 6)x | (b) 6y − 2y + 5y = (6 − 2 + 5)y
$\qquad\qquad = 11x$ | $\qquad\qquad\qquad = 9y$

EXAMPLE 4.   Simplify.   5x + 4y + 3x − y

$$-y = -1y$$

SOLUTION:
$$5x + 4y + 3x - y = 5x + 3x + 4y - y$$
$$= 8x + 3y$$

Note that 8x + 3y cannot be expressed as a monomial because 8x and 3y are not like terms.

Addition and subtraction may also be done vertically as in the following examples.

EXAMPLE 5.   Add.

(a)   9x   (b)   6w   (c)   5x
     + 7x   + 13w   + 3y

SOLUTION:

(a)   9x | (b)   6w | (c)   5x
     + 7x | + 13w | + 3y
    ────── | ─────── | ───────
      16x | 19w | 5x + 3y

EXAMPLE 6.   Subtract.

(a)   10x   (b)   15w   (c)   9x
     − 3x   − 7w   − 5y

SOLUTION:

(a) $10x$
$-3x$
$7x$

(b) $15w$
$-7w$
$8w$

(c) $9x$
$-5y$
$9x - 5y$

EXERCISE 1.10

A 1. Identify the following as a monomial, binomial, or trinomial.

(a) $x + y$
(b) $7xy$
(c) $x^2 + 7x + 12$
(d) $3x^4y^3$
(e) $5x^2 + 3$
(f) 8
(g) $3x^3 - 4x$
(h) $1 + 7y + 3y^2$

2. Name the

(a) numerical coefficients and
(b) literal coefficients of each of the following monomials.

(i) $4x$ (ii) $7x^2y$ (iii) x (iv) $3x^4y$ (v) xyz

3. Simplify.

(a) $3x + 7x$
(b) $4y + 5y$
(c) $8w + 9w$
(d) $10x + 13x$
(e) $9x - 4x$
(f) $10w - 3w$
(g) $6w - w$
(h) $5x + x$
(i) $6s + 3s + 2s$
(j) $8x + 2x + 5x$
(k) $7x + 3x - 2x$
(l) $9w + w - 5w$

4. Add.

(a) $5x$
$+3x$

(b) $9w$
$+4w$

(c) $10s$
$+12s$

(d) $8t$
$+11t$

(e) $15x$
$+6x$

(f) $9w$
$+w$

(g) x
$+x$

(h) $4t$
$+13t$

(i) $21s$
$+5s$

(j) $4x$
$+3y$

5. Subtract.

(a) $7x$
$-4x$

(b) $9w$
$-3w$

(c) $12x$
$-x$

(d) $13s$
$-7s$

(e) $80t$
$-60t$

(f) $12t$
$-7t$

(g) $8x$
$-3y$

(h) $3r$
$-r$

(i) $16x$
$-5x$

(j) $21y$
$-11y$

B 6. Simplify.

(a) $6x + 7x - 4x$
(b) $8x + 7x - 3x + 5x$
(c) $15w + 11w - 3w + 4w$
(d) $13x - 3x + 4x - 2x$
(e) $15w + 21w - 13w + w$
(f) $24x + 19x - 11x + 51x$
(g) $19t + 49t + 33t$
(h) $87x - 24x + 68x$
(i) $97w - 14w + 83w + 9w$
(j) $47x + 54x - 9x + 28x$
(k) $49w + w + 51w - 3w$
(l) $89t - 13t + 42t + 6t$

7. Simplify.

(a) $5x + 13x + 6y - 2y$
(b) $15t + 5x + 3t + 15x$
(c) $33s + 5y - 13s + 51y$
(d) $15x^2 + 14x - 3x^2 - 9x$
(e) $41t + 13 + 64t + 33$
(f) $43x + 15y - 21x - 3y$
(g) $14x + 9xy + 13xy + 42x$
(h) $12x^3 + 17x^2 - 3x^2 + 14x^3$
(i) $21 + 53x - 9 - 14x + 8$
(j) $13xy + 15x + 17y - 9xy + 14x - 2y$
(k) $15x^2 + 14x + 7 - x^2 - x - 1$
(l) $15x^2y + 14xy^2 + 13xy^2 - 2x^2y$
(m) $24r + s + 43r + 16s + 9$
(n) $17x^2 + 14x + 9 - 6x^2 + 8 - 2x + 15$
(o) $18x^3 + 41x + 5x^2 - x^3 - 2x^3 + 61x + x^2$

8. Simplify, then evaluate for $x = 2$.

(a) $5x + 7x - 2x$
(b) $13x + 9x - 2x + 6x$
(c) $13x + 9 + 24x - 2$
(d) $x^2 + 5x + 3x^2 - x$
(e) $14x + 9 - 2 + 13x - 1$
(f) $5x^2 + 8x - 3x - x^2$
(g) $7x^2 + 9x - 3x + 7$
(h) $5x + 6x^2 - x^2 + 7x$
(i) $x^2 + 4x^2 + 9x + 4$

9. Simplify, then evaluate for $x = 2$ and $y = 3$.

(a) $5x + 11y + 9y - 2y$
(b) $15x + 11y - 4x - y$
(c) $5xy + 9xy - 2xy$
(d) $x^2 + y^2 + x^2 - y^2$
(e) $7x + 6xy + 9xy - x$
(f) $7y + 8xy - xy + y$

10. Evaluate.

(a) $3x + 2y - x + 3y$ for $x = 1$, $y = 2$
(b) $5x + 7y - x - y$ for $x = 3$, $y = 5$
(c) $2xy + 3xy - xy$ for $x = 5$, $y = 3$
(d) $3x^2 - 2x$ for $x = 5$
(e) $7x + 2y + 5xy$ for $x = y = 3$
(f) $5xy - 2x - 3y$ for $x = 4$, $y = 5$

11. Evaluate for $x = 2.5$.

(a) $x^2 + x + 6.25$
(b) $3x + 7.3 - 2x + 6.4$
(c) $2.5x + 8.75 - 1.1x + 1.25$
(d) $6.2x - 2.5x + 3.8x - x$
(e) $4x^2 - 2x + 4.5x - 6.25$
(f) $25 - 4.1x + 3.6x$

12. Evaluate for $x = 3.1$ and $y = 2.4$

(a) $2x + 3y + 4x - y$
(b) $x^2 + y^2$
(c) $x^2 - y^2$
(d) $(x + y)^2$
(e) $x^2 + 2xy + y^2$
(f) $3xy + 2yx - 8.75$

13. Use $x = 3.5$ and $y = 2.8$ to determine which is greater.

(a) $(x + y)^2$ or $x^2 + 2xy + 2y$
(b) $(x + y)^2$ or $x^2 + y^2$
(c) $(x - y)^2$ or $2x^2 - y^2$
(d) $(x - y)^2$ or $5x^2 - 2y$
(e) $x + 2.6$ or $y + 3.3$

1.11 MULTIPLYING AND DIVIDING MONOMIALS

Monomials are multiplied in the following manner.

$$2x \times 3y = 2 \times x \times 3 \times y$$
$$= 2 \times 3 \times x \times y$$
$$= 6xy$$

6 is the result of multiplying the numerical coefficients. xy is the result of multiplying the literal coefficients.

EXAMPLE 1. Simplify.
(a) $5x \times 11y$

(b) $(4x^2)(3y)(2z)$

SOLUTION:
(a) $5x \times 11y = (5 \times 11)(x \times y)$
$$= 55xy$$

(b) $(4x^2)(3y)(2z) = (4 \times 3 \times 2)(x^2 \times y \times z)$
$$= 24x^2yz$$

Division is the inverse operation of multiplication.

$$5 \times 3 = 15 \text{ and } \begin{cases} 15 \div 3 = 5 \\ 15 \div 5 = 3 \end{cases}$$

Since $(5x)(2y) = 10xy$,
then $10xy \div 5x = 2y$

EXAMPLE 2. Simplify.
(a) $24wxy \div 8wx$

(b) $\dfrac{39x^2y}{13x^2}$

SOLUTION:
(a) $24wxy \div 8wx = \dfrac{24wxy}{8wx}$
$$= \left(\dfrac{24}{8}\right)\left(\dfrac{wxy}{wx}\right)$$
$$= 3y$$

(b) $\dfrac{39x^2y}{13x^2} = \dfrac{\cancel{(13x^2)}(3y)}{\cancel{(13x^2)}}$
$$= 3y$$

EXAMPLE 3. Evaluate. $18xyz \div 3xy$, for $x = 2.5$, $y = 3.6$, $z = 4.5$

SOLUTION:
METHOD I

$$18xyz \div 3xy = \dfrac{18xyz}{3xy}$$
$$= 6z$$

for $z = 4.5$, $\quad 6z = 6(4.5)$
$$= 27$$

Simplify or substitute first?

METHOD II

$$18xyz \div 3xy = 18(2.5)(3.6)(4.5) \div 3(2.5)(3.6)$$
$$= 729 \div 27$$
$$= 27$$

EXERCISE 1.11

1. Simplify.

(a) $(7x)(4y)$

(b) $4w \times 8t$

(c) $11y \times 5x$

(d) $(6xy)(7w)$

(e) $(8r)(7st)$

(f) $15x \times 3y^2$

(g) $8xy \times 3$

(h) $(5pq)(7r)$

2. Multiply.

(a) $\begin{array}{r} 3xy \\ \times\, 5z \\ \hline \end{array}$

(b) $\begin{array}{r} 3x^2 \\ \times\, 4wt \\ \hline \end{array}$

(c) $\begin{array}{r} 8xy \\ \times\, z \\ \hline \end{array}$

(d) $\begin{array}{r} 7m^2 \\ \times\, 5n \\ \hline \end{array}$

3. Simplify.

(a) $\dfrac{24xy}{3x}$

(b) $(35rs) \div (5r)$

(c) $\dfrac{30xyz}{6xyz}$

(d) $(18pqr) \div (3pq)$

(e) $\dfrac{30xy}{10xy}$

(f) $(20rst) \div (10rt)$

(g) $\dfrac{21x^2y}{7x^2}$

(h) $\dfrac{45x^3y}{9y}$

B 4. Simplify.

(a) $(9xy)(17w)$

(b) $(8x)(9y)(3w)$

(c) $27x^2y \times 15t$

(d) $(33t)(17rs)$

(e) $(11x)(27wy)$

(f) $43x^2y \times 19w^3$

(g) $(19pqr)(29st)$

(h) $25x^3y^2 \times 43w^5$

(i) $(17x)(21y)(52z)$

(j) $51p^2q^2 \times 24s^2$

5. Simplify.

(a) $\dfrac{144xyz}{24xy}$

(b) $\dfrac{300xy}{15xy}$

(c) $(240x^2y) \div (16x^2)$

(d) $\dfrac{615xyz}{5xz}$

(e) $\dfrac{2745st^2}{61t^2}$

(f) $(273xyz) \div (13xy)$

(g) $(532x^2y^2) \div (28x^2y^2)$

(h) $\dfrac{168rst}{12r}$

(i) $(1850t) \div (74)$

C 6. Simplify.

(a) $\dfrac{(3x)(4y)}{6x}$

(b) $\dfrac{(5x^2)(12y)}{10y}$

(c) $\dfrac{(6x^2)(9y)}{27x^2}$

(d) $(9x)(5y) \div (15y)$

(e) $(16x)(2y) \div 32$

(f) $(21x)(8y) \div (14xy)$

(g) $\dfrac{(36s)(15t)}{45st}$

(h) $\dfrac{(25w^2)(18x)}{30x}$

(i) $\dfrac{(34x)(6y)}{51xy}$

(j) $\dfrac{(10x)(20y)}{(5x)(4y)}$

7. Simplify, then evaluate for $w = 2$, $x = 3$, $y = 4$.

(a) $(3w)(2x)(4y)$

(b) $(7w)(16x)(0)$

(c) $(2w^2)(x)(2y)$

(d) $(5w)(2x)(5y)$

(e) $(3w^2)(x^2)(4y)$

(f) $(2w)(3x)(4y)$

8. Evaluate for $w = 3.7$, $x = 2.8$, $y = 4.4$, $z = 2.2$, and round off to the nearest tenth.

(a) $(5w)(2x)(3y)$

(b) $(4x)(5y)(4z)$

(c) $\dfrac{(5x)(2y)}{3z}$

(d) $\dfrac{8y}{(5x)(5z)}$

(e) $(3x)(2y) \div (z)$

(f) $11y \div xz$

(g) $(24xyz) \div (8yz)$

(h) $(32wxyz) \div (4xy)$

(i) $(3wx)(2yz)$

(j) $12wxy \div 3xy$

1.12 FORMULAS FOR PERIMETER, AREA, AND VOLUME

Many formulas for physical measurements contain variables. The most common formulas deal with perimeter, area, and volume. When applying formulas, the formula must be stated and then used correctly.

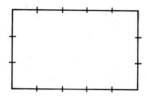

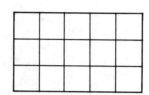

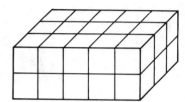

The perimeter, P, of a geometric figure is the number of linear units around it.

The area, A, of a surface is the number of square units the surface contains.

The volume, V, of a solid is the number of cubic units the solid contains.

EXERCISE 1.12

B 1. The perimeter of a rectangle is twice the length plus twice the width. We use the formula

$$P = 2\ell + 2w \text{ or } P = 2(\ell + w)$$

Rectangle

$P = 2(\ell + w)$

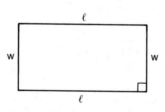

(a) Find P if w = 6 cm and ℓ = 15 cm.
(b) Find P if w = 147 m and ℓ = 206 m.

2. To determine the perimeter of a square we use the formula $P = 4s$.

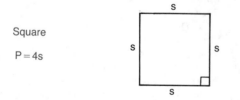

Square

$P = 4s$

(a) Find P if s = 32 cm.
(b) Find P if s = 143 m.

3. To determine the perimeter of a triangle the lengths of the three sides are added.

Triangle

$P = a + b + c$

(a) Find P if a = 9 cm, b = 11 cm, and c = 16 cm.
(b) Find P if a = 136 m, b = 181 m, and c = 157 m.

4. The opposite sides of a parallelogram are equal. We use the formula $P = 2a + 2b$ or $P = 2(a + b)$.

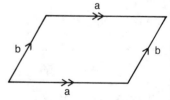

Parallelogram

$P = 2(a + b)$

(a) Find P if a = 63 cm and b = 86 cm.
(b) Find P if a = 277 m and b = 246 m.

5. To determine the perimeter of any quadrilateral the lengths of the four sides are added.

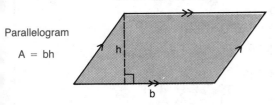

Quadrilateral

$P = a + b + c + d$

(a) Find P if a = 17 cm, b = 22 cm, c = 19 cm, and d = 18 cm.
(b) Find P if a = 107 m, b = 118 m, c = 137 m, and d = 99 m.

6. To determine the area of a rectangle we use the formula $A = \ell w$.
(a) Find A if w = 31 cm and ℓ = 64 cm.
(b) Find A if w = 101 m and ℓ = 147 m.

7. The formula for the area of a square is $A = s^2$.
(a) Find A if s = 39 cm.
(b) Find A if s = 62 m.

8. The formula for the area of a triangle is $A = \frac{1}{2}bh$.

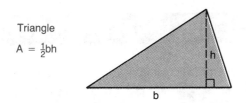

Triangle

$A = \frac{1}{2}bh$

(a) Find A if b = 28 cm and h = 12 cm.
(b) Find A if b = 62 m and h = 131 m.

9. The area of a parallelogram can be determined using the formula $A = bh$.

Parallelogram

$A = bh$

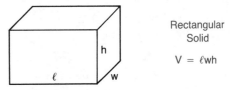

(a) Find A if b = 38 cm and h = 14 cm.
(b) Find A if b = 101 m and h = 33 m.

10. The area of a trapezoid can be found using the formula $A = \frac{1}{2}h(a + b)$.

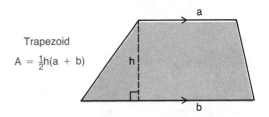

Trapezoid

$A = \frac{1}{2}h(a + b)$

(a) Find A if a = 10 cm, b = 13 cm, and h = 8 cm.
(b) Find A if a = 24 m, b = 17 m, and h = 36 m.

11. The area of a quadrilateral can be determined using the formula $A = \frac{1}{2}d(h_1 + h_2)$.

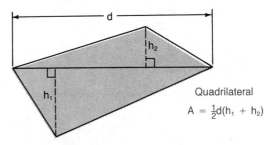

Quadrilateral

$A = \frac{1}{2}d(h_1 + h_2)$

(a) Find A if d = 16 cm, h_1 = 5 cm, and h_2 = 7 cm.
(b) Find A if d = 22 m, h_1 = 17 m, and h_2 = 21 m.

12. To determine the volume of a rectangular solid we use the formula $V = \ell wh$.

Rectangular Solid

$V = \ell wh$

(a) Find V if ℓ = 5 cm, w = 3 cm, and h = 2 cm.
(b) Find V if ℓ = 13 m, w = 7 m, and h = 11 m.

13. The volume of a cube is given by the formula $V = s^3$.
(a) Find V if s = 7 cm.
(b) Find V if s = 13 m.

1.13 FORMULAS ASSOCIATED WITH CIRCLES

In this section the formulas for the circumference and area of a circle are reviewed.

EXERCISE 1.13

B 1. The perimeter of a circle is given a special name, circumference. We use the formulas $C = \pi d$ or $C = 2\pi r$.

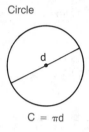

Circle

$C = \pi d$

Circle

$C = 2\pi r$

(a) Find C if d = 30 cm (use π = 3.14).
(b) Find C if r = 140 m.

2. The formula for the area of a circle is $A = \pi r^2$.

Circle

$A = \pi r^2$

(a) Find A if r = 10 cm (use π = 3.14).
(b) Find A if r = 24 m.

3. The volume of a cylinder is determined using the formula $V = \pi r^2 h$.

Cylinder

$V = \pi r^2 h$

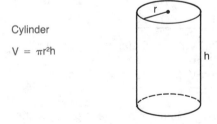

(a) Find V if r = 10 cm and h = 15 cm (use π = 3.14).
(b) Find V if r = 8 m and h = 20 m.

4. The volume of a sphere is determined using the formula $V = \frac{4}{3}\pi r^3$.

Sphere

$V = \frac{4}{3}\pi r^3$

(a) Find V if r = 5.6 cm (use π = 3.14).
(b) Find V if r = 2.5 cm.

CALCULATOR MATH

Some calculators have parentheses keys, **(** and **)**, and follow order of operations according to the BEDMAS acronym.

For $(7 - 4)^3 + 2 \times 8$

Press

The display is `43`

Perform the calculations.

1. $4^2 - (3 + 5) \div 2$
2. $(5 + 3)^2 - (5^2 + 3^2)$
3. $\dfrac{2^5 - 5 \times 2}{11}$

1.14 APPLICATIONS OF FORMULAS FROM GEOMETRY

EXERCISE 1.14

1. Find the perimeter of a rectangle if the length is 67 m and the width is 44 m.

2. Find the circumference of a circle if the diameter measures 86 m (use $\pi = 3.14$).

3. Find the perimeter of a triangle with sides measuring 981 cm, 873 cm, and 766 cm.

4. Determine the area of a rectangle with length 891 m and width 764 m.

5. Find the area of a square if each side measures 643 cm.

6. Determine the area of a circle with a diameter 286 cm.

7. Find the volume of a rectangular solid that is 1.9 m long, 1.3 m wide, and 0.7 m high.

8. Find the volume of a cylinder where $r = 12$ cm and $h = 33$ cm (use $\pi = 3.14$).

9. Find the volume of a sphere which has a radius of 12 cm (use $\pi = 3.14$).

10. Find the volume of a sphere whose diameter is 10 cm.

11. Find the area of the shaded figures.

(a)

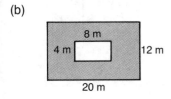

(b)

12. Find the perimeter and area of each of the following.

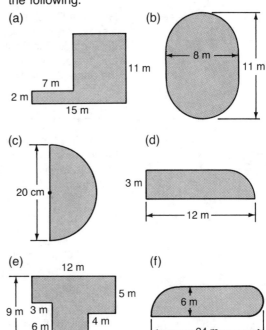

(a) 11 m, 7 m, 2 m, 15 m
(b) 8 m, 11 m

(c) 20 cm
(d) 3 m, 12 m

(e) 12 m, 9 m, 3 m, 6 m, 5 m, 4 m
(f) 6 m, 24 m

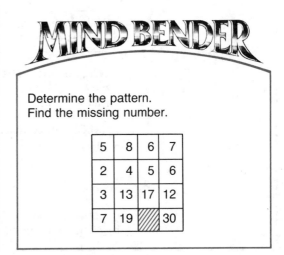

1.15 INDUCTIVE REASONING

Heron, a Greek mathematician, discovered that when a ball hits a flat surface, the angle at which the ball strikes the surface is equal to the angle at which it rebounds.

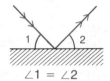

$\angle 1 = \angle 2$

EXERCISE 1.15

1. (a) The three diagrams below show the path of a ball hit from the lower-left corner of a game table so that it travels at 45° angles with the sides of the table. (We will assume that the ball stops when it hits a corner.)

(b) Construct a table with dimensions 12 by 4. Draw the path of a ball hit from the lower-left corner at an angle of 45°. (From now on, assume that all balls are hit from the lower-left corner at an angle of 45°.)

(c) The four tables do not have the same dimensions; yet there is something similar about their dimensions. What is it?

(d) What do the paths of the balls on the four tables have in common?

(e) Where will a ball hit on a 15 by 5 table stop?

> The process of drawing a conclusion based on several specific cases is called inductive reasoning.

2. What do the paths of balls hit on square tables have in common? (Assume that balls are always hit from the lower-left corner at an angle of 45°.)

3. (a) Construct tables with dimensions

(i) 3 by 2   (ii) 6 by 4   (iii) 9 by 6

and draw the paths of the balls.

(b) What do the paths of the balls have in common?

(c) What do the dimensions of the tables have in common?
(d) Where would a ball hit on a 12 by 8 table stop?

4. On the tables below the ball crosses every square.

(a) Draw a table with dimensions 5 by 4 and show the path of
the ball.

(b) Draw a table with dimensions 6 by 5 and show the path of
the ball.

(c) Where will a ball stop on a table with dimensions 7 by 6?
(d) Where will a ball stop on a table with dimensions 54 by 53?

5. The table below has dimensions 4 by 5. The ball stops in the
top-left corner.

(a) Draw a table with dimensions 4 by 6 and show the path of
the ball.

(b) Where will a ball stop on a 4 by 7 table? Use a diagram to
verify your guess.
(c) Using inductive reasoning we might conclude that a ball will
stop in the upper-right corner of a 4 by 8 table. Does it?

The results of this exercise illustrate an important aspect of
inductive reasoning: some conclusions that appear reasonable
do not apply to all cases. However, inductive reasoning is still a
very important process in mathematics and science.

1.16 REVIEW EXERCISE

1. Perform the indicated operation.

(a) 52 426
× 625

(b) 378 475
− 156 847

(c) 347 674
258 125
+847 888

(d) 87)22 272

(e) 36.265 − 12.87
(f) 534.26 + 45.926
(g) 36.5 × 11.7
(h) 57.436 ÷ 9.92

2. Round off the following numbers as indicated.

(a) 32 205 to the nearest hundred
(b) 525 876 to the nearest thousand
(c) 16 450 to the nearest hundred
(d) 0.625 to the nearest tenth
(e) 12.8356 to the nearest hundredth
(f) 5.75 to the nearest tenth
(g) 34.845 to the nearest hundredth

3. Estimate the following.

(a) 36.25 × 17.895
(b) 628.35 ÷ 28.8
(c) $\dfrac{28.7 \times 53.9}{41.6}$
(d) $\dfrac{475}{63.25 \times 18.65}$

4. Estimate the cost of the following.

(a) 12 photo albums at $6.95 each
(b) 18 purses at $18.95 each
(c) 48 cookies at $0.12 each
(d) 96 ride tickets at $4.75 each
(e) 8 radios at $49.95 each

5. Simplify.

(a) 8 × 3 − 10
(b) 8 + 6 − 5
(c) 21 ÷ 7 − 1
(d) 7 + 6 ÷ 2
(e) (8 − 4) + 5
(f) 8(5 − 3)
(g) 5 + 3 × 2
(h) 10 − 12 ÷ 6

6. If E(x) = 5x, find

(a) E(1)   (b) E(4)   (c) E(12)   (d) E(20)

7. If x = 3, y = 4, and z = 2 evaluate the following algebraic expressions.

(a) x + y
(b) 7z
(c) 3x − 4
(d) 5xy
(e) 10z + 5
(f) 2x + 3z − 2y

8. If y = 2, state the value of each of the following.

(a) y^2
(b) $3y^3$
(c) $y^2 − 1$
(d) $(y + 3)^2$
(e) $y^4 − 1$
(f) $5y^2$
(g) $(5y)^2$
(h) $(7 − y)^3$

9. Simplify.

(a) 6x + 4x
(b) 3y + y + 7y
(c) 12x − 7x
(d) 7x + 3x − 2x
(e) 10x − x − 4x
(f) 11y − 3y − 4y
(g) 9z + 3z − 4z
(h) 20y + 5y − 11y

10. Simplify.

(a) 56 + (7 × 13)
(b) 77 − (48 ÷ 2)
(c) 56 ÷ 4 × 13
(d) (41 + 5)(63 − 4)
(e) (51 − 11) ÷ (16 ÷ 2)
(f) [5 × 3 − (6 + 1)] × 9

11. Simplify the following.

(a) $3.6^2 ÷ 1.2 + 2.5 × 5.58$
(b) $4.8(16.2 − 12.3) ÷ 1.8 + 5.7 − 4.6$
(c) $(4.5^2 − 2.6 × 3.2) × 2.1 − 4.65$
(d) $8.5^2 − (3.75 + 2.13) × 4.5$
(e) $3.5(4.6 + 2.7) − 3.2^2 + 2.25$

12. If x = 4, y = 5, and z = 3, find the value of each of the following.

(a) (x + y)(y + z)
(b) 2x(3y + 5)
(c) (2x − 3)(3z + 4)
(d) 7xy − 3yz
(e) $\dfrac{9x + 2y + 2}{z}$
(f) (7x − 2y)(8z + x)

13. If r = 4, s = 3, and t = 2, find the value of each of the following.

(a) $5r^2 − 7s$
(b) $r^2 + s^2 + t^2$
(c) $3r^2s − 6t$
(d) $(5s^2) − 4st$
(e) $\dfrac{2r^2 − 3s + 1}{t}$
(f) $\dfrac{2s^3 − 6rt}{2s}$
(g) $\dfrac{5t − 6}{r + s}$
(h) $\dfrac{3r^2 + (3r)^2}{6t}$
(i) $\dfrac{7s^2t^3}{3s} + 5$
(j) $5r^2 − 3s^2 + 4t^2$
(k) (r + s + t)(r − s + t)
(l) $r^3 − s^2 + t^4$

14. Simplify.
(a) $97x + 13y - 14x + 15y$
(b) $15x^2 + 43x^2 + 7x + 3x$
(c) $5x + 6y + 4 + 11x + 9y$
(d) $73x^2 + 15x^2 + 8x^3 - x^3$
(e) $24xy + 4yz + 17xy$
(f) $9r + 7s + 12s + 15r$

15. Evaluate for $x = 2$, $y = 3$.
(a) $15x + 5y - 11x + 3y$
(b) $14x + 9y + 8y - y$
(c) $9xy + 8x + 9x - 6xy$
(d) $3x^2 + 5x + 2x + 7x^2$
(e) $9x + 8xy - 7x + 5xy$
(f) $7x^2 + 3y^2 - y^2 + 4x^2$

16. Substitute and find the value of the indicated variable.
(a) If $A = \ell \times w$, find A when $\ell = 27$ cm and $w = 22$ cm.
(b) If $P = 2(\ell + w)$, find P when $\ell = 53$ cm and $w = 47$ cm.
(c) If $A = \frac{1}{2}bh$, find A when $b = 406$ cm and $h = 168$ cm.
(d) If $A = \frac{1}{2}(a + b)h$, find A when $h = 194$ cm, $a = 64$ cm, and $b = 78$ cm.
(e) If $V = \ell wh$, find V when $\ell = 34$ cm, $w = 16$ cm, and $h = 9$ cm.
(f) If $P = 2(\ell + w)$, find P when $\ell = 3.7$ cm and $w = 2.8$ cm.
(g) If $A = \frac{1}{2}(a + b)h$, find A when $a = 3.8$ cm, $b = 4.7$ cm, and $h = 4.5$ cm.

17. For $C = \pi d$, and $A = \pi r^2$, find the circumference and area for each of the following circles.
(a) $r = 76$ cm   (b) $d = 84$ cm
(c) $r = 2.5$ m   (d) $d = 3.7$ m

18. Find the area of the shaded figure.

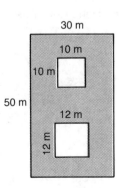

30 m
10 m
10 m
50 m
12 m
12 m

19. An Air Canada jet takes off every two minutes for eighteen hours every day, seven days per week. How many take offs are there for Air Canada in one year?

20. Boris earns \$5.50/h and Debbie earns \$6.25/h. Together in one weekend, they earned \$88.50 for 15 h of work. How many hours did they each work?

21. The length of a rectangle is 3.2 cm longer than the width. The perimeter of the rectangle is 25 cm. What is the length of the rectangle?

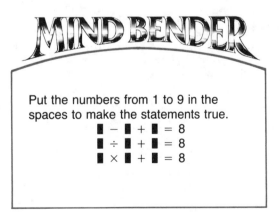

MIND BENDER

Put the numbers from 1 to 9 in the spaces to make the statements true.

■ − ■ + ■ = 8
■ ÷ ■ + ■ = 8
■ × ■ + ■ = 8

1.17 CHAPTER 1 TEST

1. Simplify.
(a) 32 526 + 6358
(b) 435.28 − 174.489
(c) 356.6 × 21.5
(d) 934.8 ÷ 28.5

2. Round off the following.
(a) 2.658 24 to the nearest thousandth
(b) 34.45 to the nearest tenth
(c) 63 457.726 45 to the nearest hundred

3. Find an estimate for $\dfrac{32.6 \times 78.5}{48.6}$.

4. Simplify.
(a) 4(24 − 13) + 5 × 3.6
(b) (2.8 − 1.5)(4.3 + 2.7) ÷ (5 − 2.6)(3.7 + 4.2)
(c) 5[3.4 − (7.8 − 7.2)] + 7.1

5. Given $E(x) = x^2 - 2$, evaluate.
(a) E(4)
(b) E(10)
(c) E(2)

6. Evaluate for x = 2, y = 3.
(a) $(x + y)^2$
(b) $x^2 + y^2 - 2xy$

7. Evaluate for x = 2.6, y = 3.5.
(a) $x^2 + y$
(b) 2xy + 2(y − x)

8. Simplify.
(a) (3x)(2yz)
(b) 2x + 3y − x + 4y + 5xy
(c) $x^2 + 3x + 2x^2 + 5x$
(d) 3(2x − y) + 4(x + 2y)

9. The area of a trapezoid is found using the formula
$$A = \tfrac{1}{2}(a + b)h$$
Find the area of a trapezoid with a = 6.5 cm, b = 4.3 cm, and h = 2.1 cm.

10. Find the volume of the given cylinder using the formula
$$V = \pi r^2 h, \ (\pi = 3.14).$$

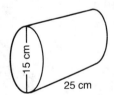

15 cm

25 cm

PROBLEM SOLVING

CHAPTER

Every age and generation has its special mysteries.
Stephen Leacock

REVIEW AND PREVIEW TO CHAPTER 2

PERCENT

EXERCISE

1. Write the percents as decimals.

(a) 50%   (b) 25%
(c) 75%   (d) 10%
(e) 15%   (f) 20%
(g) 21%   (h) 37%
(i) 42%   (j) 81%
(k) 93%   (l) 62%
(m) 8%   (n) 5%
(o) 24.2%   (p) 15.7%
(q) 60.4%   (r) 82.3%
(s) 91.5%   (t) 36.6%

2. Calculate.

(a) 30% of 80   (b) 24% of 600
(c) 60% of 92   (d) 52% of 150
(e) 72% of 66   (f) 4% of 40
(g) 7% of 77   (h) 31% of 8000

3. Calculate.

(a) 42.5% of 700   (b) 63.8% of 9000
(c) 70.2% of 550   (d) 6.6% of 100
(e) 120% of 84   (f) 200% of 65
(g) 150% of 70   (h) 125% of 80

4. Copy and complete the sales tax table.

Article	Price	Rate of Sales Tax	Sales Tax	Total Cost
Lamp	$80.00	7%		
Boat	$96 000	6%		
Disks	$21.50	5%		
Tickets	$90.00	7%		
Lunch	$18.80	5%		
Pens	$36.40	7%		

PROBLEMS

EXERCISE

1. Find the cost of 75 m of fencing at $15/m.

2. If Tony averaged 75 km/h for 7 h, how far did he travel?

3. A telethon raised $183 365 towards a goal of $250 000. How much more money needs to be raised?

4. A football stadium holds 45 000 people. Tickets cost $15 each and there were 3125 tickets not sold. What is the value of the tickets that were sold?

5. At 85 km/h, how long will it take Sandra to drive 935 km?

6. How many 40 cm sections can be cut from a 50 m coil of wire?

7. The average mass of an adult is 68 kg. If a commuter train system carries 55 500 adults per day, what is the total mass carried by the system in five days?

8. In a row of 10 houses the distance between each house is 13 m. What is the total distance between the houses?

9. A loaded truck has a mass of 5155 kg. If the unloaded truck has a mass of 2197 kg, what is the mass of the load?

10. Assuming exactly 52 weeks in a year and exactly 28 d in a complete cycle of the moon, how many cycles are completed in a year?

PERIMETER, AREA, AND VOLUME

EXERCISE

Perimeter

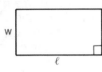

Rectangle
$P = 2(\ell + w)$

Square
$P = 4s$

1. Calculate the perimeter.

(a)

6 m

9 m

(b)

133 cm

133 cm

(c)

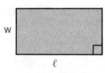

8.4 m

15.1 m

(d)

109 m

213 m

Area

Rectangle
$A = \ell w$

Square
$A = s^2$

2. Calculate the area.

(a)

21 cm

46 cm

(b)

15 m

15 m

(c)

8.7 m

5.2 m

(d)

63 cm

121 cm

Volume

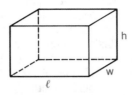

Rectangular Solid
$V = \ell wh$

Cube
$V = s^3$

3. Calculate the volume.

(a)

6 m

11 m   3 m

(b)

9 cm

9 cm
9 cm

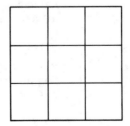

MIND BENDER

Place the numbers 1, 2, 3, 4, 5, 6, 7, 8 in the circles so that the sum of each line equals 13.

Place the numbers from 1 to 9 in the squares so that the sum of any vertical, horizontal, or diagonal line is 15.

2.1 A PLAN FOR PROBLEM SOLVING

An important goal in the study of mathematics is to develop the ability to solve problems. There are no set rules or formulas for solving problems. Sometimes it is done in a systematic manner, but often in flashes of creativity and intuition. In some problems drawing a picture is helpful. In others, the given information can be sorted out using a list or table. Reading, understanding, paraphrasing, and summarizing are also helpful in recognizing relevant and irrelevant information.

Problem solving is not exclusive to the domain of mathematics; it is an integral part of all subjects and everyday life. We can solve problems in a systematic manner by using the

READ — PLAN — SOLVE — ANSWER

model.

In this section the model will be introduced. Each of the problem solving strategies found in the PLAN step will be dealt with in the sections that follow.

READ

Read the problem carefully to understand it. Identify relevant and irrelevant information. Look at the picture if there is one. Identify what information you are given. Determine what you are asked to find. Paraphrase and summarize.

PLAN

Think of a plan. Find a connection between the given information and the unknown which will enable you to calculate the unknown.

1. Classify information. Study the information carefully to determine what is needed to solve the problem. Identify the important information. Some information may be unnecessary or extra. You may find it helpful to summarize the information or make lists.

2. Search for a pattern. Try to recognize patterns. Some problems are solved by recognizing that some kind of pattern is occurring. The pattern could be geometric, numerical, or algebraic. If you can see that there is some sort of regularity or repetition in a problem, then you might be able to guess what the continuing pattern is, and then solve the problem.

3. Draw a diagram or flow chart. For many problems it is useful to draw a diagram and identify the given and required quantities on the diagram. A flow chart can be used to organize a series of steps that must be performed in a definite order.

4. Estimate, guess, and check. This is a valid method to solve a problem where a direct method is not apparent. You may find it necessary to improve your guess and "zero in" on the correct answer.

5. Sequence operations. To solve many problems, several operations performed in a definite order are needed.

6. Work backwards. Sometimes it is useful to imagine that your problem is solved and work backwards step by step until you arrive at the given data. Then, you may be able to reverse your steps to solve the original problem.

7. Use a formula or an equation. In some problems, after analyzing the data, the problem can be written as an equation, or the data can be substituted into a formula.

8. Solve a simpler problem. A problem can sometimes be broken into smaller problems that can be solved more easily.

9. Make a table. In some problems, it is helpful to organize the data in a table, chart, or grid.

10. Conclude from assumptions. In some problems, it will be necessary to make assumptions. The conclusions that you draw from these assumptions should be those that you have made in the past, from the same types of information.

SOLVE

Carry out the strategy. Perform the calculation, working with care. Present your ideas clearly. Persist.

ANSWER

Make a statement. Check your answer in the original problem and use estimation to decide if your answer is reasonable. Search for a better solution.

READ

EXAMPLE 1. During a performance test a ball was dropped from a height of 27 m. The ball bounced to a height two thirds that of the previous height. If the ball was allowed to keep bouncing, how far would it travel when it hit the floor the fourth time?

SOLUTION:

PLAN

Make a diagram and calculate the distance travelled.

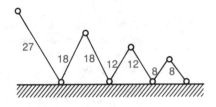

SOLVE

$$27 + 18 + 18 + 12 + 12 + 8 + 8 = 103$$

ANSWER

The ball travelled 103 m.

READ

EXAMPLE 2. A bus can carry 48 passengers. How many buses will be needed to take 312 people to the Shakespearian festival, which is 350 km away?

SOLUTION:

PLAN

Divide the number of people by the number of passengers per bus.

The 350 km is extra information.

SOLVE

```
        6.5
48)312.0
    288
    240
    240
      0
```

ANSWER

7 buses will be needed.

Estimate.
$312 \div 48 \doteq 300 \div 50$
$= 6$

EXERCISE 2.1

B 1. The Conrad's orchard has 63 rows of apple trees and each row has 47 trees. If each tree produces an average of 17 baskets of apples, how many baskets can the Conrads expect to harvest?

2. It is just before 10:00 and you are waiting in line to get on the Blue Line Ferry to Sangster Island. Your car is eighty-third in line. The ferry can take twenty cars at a time. The round trip to Sangster Island, including loading and unloading, takes forty-five minutes. The ferry is just arriving and it will leave promptly at 10:00. About what time can you expect to arrive on Sangster Island?

3. Robert has a sheet of cardboard that measures 30 cm by 21 cm. He cuts the cardboard into six rectangles exactly the same size. What are the dimensions of each rectangle?

4. Susan bought a pair of jeans for $41.90 and a shirt for $23.75. Assuming both prices included the sales tax, how much change did Susan get from $70?

5. The following are the first four of eight triangular numbers.

How many dots are there in the eighth triangular number?

6. The ship has four different coloured flags: a red, a black, a white, and a green. How many different ways can the four flags be raised up the flagstaff?

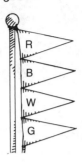

7. An electrician wants to cut a piece of wire 350 cm long into two pieces so that one piece is 63 cm longer than the other. How long will each piece be?

8. Two shirts cost $46.80. One of the shirts costs $6.50 more than the other. How much does each shirt cost?

9. Three consecutive whole numbers have a sum of 246. What are the numbers?

10. Passenger pigeons are now extinct, although at one time they existed in great numbers. Someone once described a flock as follows.

> The column was 500 m wide and flew overhead at 500 m/min. It took 3 h to fly by. Each square metre was occupied by ten pigeons.

About how many pigeons were in the flock?

11. Peter earns $21.50/h, with time and a half for overtime. Overtime is any time worked over forty hours in one week. One week his time card indicated the following number of hours worked each day.

Monday	8
Tuesday	9
Wednesday	8.5
Thursday	8
Friday	9

What were his earnings for the week?

12. Maria's bowling average for three games was 184. She bowled 181 and 195 for the first two games. What did she bowl in the third game?

13. What is the sum of the five smallest whole numbers that are multiples of 8?

14. If the Governor General delivered the Speech from the Throne in Ottawa at 14:00, at what time would people be hearing the speech in:
(a) Halifax?
(b) Vancouver?

15. There are fourteen teams in the American Baseball League. In one season, each team plays 162 games. How many games are played in one season?

16. If 9285 posters came off a printing press at a rate of 5 posters per second, for how many minutes and seconds did the press run?

17. Suppose you were given a billion dollars and you spent it at the rate of one dollar per second. How long would it take you to spend it all? Give your answer in days, hours, minutes, and seconds.

18. How many different routes are there from A to B?

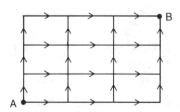

19. Place the numbers from 1 to 9 in the circles so that the sum of each row is 25.

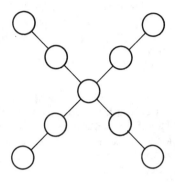

20. Two days ago Peggy was fifteen years old. Next year Peggy will be eighteen years old. What is today's date and when is Peggy's birthday?

21. Tom agreed to work for one year for $15 400 and a car. He left the job after seven months and received $6275 and the car. What was the value of the car?

22. Find the next three numbers.

2, 4, 9, 16, 28, ■, ■, ■

23. The gift shop sells small, medium, and large bags of seashells. Small bags cost $1.50. Medium bags cost $2.25. Large bags cost $3.75. On one weekend 74 small bags and 57 medium bags were sold. The total revenue from all three sizes of bags was $389.25. How many large bags were sold?

24. A cashier gave Margaret change for a dollar bill in dimes and quarters. How many coins did Margaret receive?

25. At the beginning of September, Derek had $123.47 in his chequing account. During the month he made deposits of $45.60, $82.00, and $56.80, and wrote cheques for $13.80, $110.00, and $22.20. How much did he have in his account at the end of the month?

26. A car rental agency charges $120 a week plus $0.22/km. How far can you travel, to the nearest kilometre, on a budget of $400.00?

27. If snow is falling at a rate of 6 cm/h, how much snow will fall in fifteen minutes?

28. Ten fence posts are spaced 2.8 m apart in a row. What is the distance from the first post to the last post?

29. Carol bowled games of 231 and 206. What will she have to bowl in her third game to have a three-game average of 218?

30. A dinner bill was to be divided equally among 8 people. When one person could not pay because he had forgotten his money, each of the others had to pay $6.10 more. What was the total value of the bill?

31. How old will you be, in seconds, on your next birthday?

32. What number times itself is 56 169?

33. What is the maximum number of times that four straight lines can intersect?

34. You speak an average of 125 words in a minute. How many words could you speak in 1.5 h?

35. Light travels at a speed of 300 000 km/s. How far does light travel in one billionth of a second?

36. If you start at zero and write each of the whole numbers out in words, as in:

zero, one, two, three, four, ...

what is the first number that contains the letter a?

37. How many math textbooks placed end to end will it take to go from Moncton, N.B. to Windsor, Ont. by road?

In 1514 the famous painter and printmaker Albrecht Dürer created an engraving called *Melancholia*. The engraving contained a magic square. The magic square was made up of the numbers from 1 to 16. Part of the magic square is shown below.

	3	2	13
5	10	11	8
	15		1

EXERCISE

1. (a) Copy and complete the magic square.
(b) What is the sum of the four centre squares?
(c) What is the sum of the four corner squares?
(d) What is the sum of the squares of the numbers in the first and third rows?
(e) What is the sum of the squares of the numbers in the second and fourth rows?

Each letter represents a different digit in this division question. Find the values of A, B, C, D, and E.

$$
\begin{array}{r}
1B \\
A\overline{)C7} \\
A \\
\hline
3B \\
D5 \\
\hline
E
\end{array}
$$

2.2 CLASSIFYING INFORMATION

In many problems it is necessary to sort out the information that is given. Some useful questions to ask are:

— Am I given enough information to solve the problem?
— Is there conflicting information?
— Is there extra information?
— How are the important facts related?

READ

EXAMPLE. Tickets for the concert cost $55 each. 17 946 people attended the concert. 18 234 tickets were sold. The expenses for the concert totalled $900 000. How much money was collected on the ticket sales?

SOLUTION:

PLAN

17 946 people attending is extra information.
$900 000 in concert expenses is extra information.
The important information is that 18 234 tickets were sold at $55 each.

Multiply 18 234 by $55.

SOLVE

$$
\begin{array}{r}
18\ 234 \\
\times\ 55 \\
\hline
1\ 002\ 870
\end{array}
$$

ANSWER

$1 002 870 was collected on the ticket sales.

EXERCISE 2.2

In some questions you will need to supply missing information.

B 1. Sandra bought two pairs of jeans and three shirts. She paid $45.20 for each pair of jeans and $23.15 for each shirt. How much did she pay for the shirts?

2. A human being has a body temperature of 37.0°C. A python can have a body temperature of 28.6°C. A blue jay has a body temperature of 43.0°C. What is the difference in body temperatures between the python and the blue jay?

3. The mass of a diamond is measured in carats. What is the mass, in grams, of a 4.5 carat diamond?

4. During one season a professional baseball player earned $5200 for every game he played. Assuming he played all the games, how much did he earn?

5. The planet Mercury has a maximum distance from the sun of about 70 000 000 km. How much closer is Mercury to the sun than the planet Pluto?

6. The longest river in the world is the Nile. It is 6648 km long. How much longer is the Nile than the Fraser River in British Columbia?

7. Tickets bought in advance of a play cost $18.50. Tickets bought at the door on the night of the play cost $20. Denise bought 35 tickets in advance. What did she pay?

8. What is the total number of gifts given in the "Twelve Days of Christmas" song?

9. How long does it take a ray of light to travel from the sun to the earth?

10. Ponderosa pines grow about 0.45 m each year. The Sax family has two pines in their back yard. One is 22.2 m tall and the other is 19.5 m tall. How tall will the shortest pine be in five years?

11. The Blue Sox hockey team won 34 games, tied 6 games, and lost 14 games. If they received two points for a win and one point for a tie, how many points did they earn?

12. The price tag on a T-shirt is $11. What would you pay for the shirt, including sales tax?

13. A new car depreciates by about one fifth of its value each year. Shelly bought a new car. What will it be worth after four years?

14. When is the next year that July 1 will fall on Sunday?

15. Frank bought a TV set. He paid $100 down and made 11 monthly payments of $85 each. How much did he pay in total in monthly payments?

16. The Market Garden received 2 truckloads of tomatoes. Each truck delivered 76 crates of tomatoes. There were about 150 tomatoes in each crate. Each crate cost $24. How much was paid for the tomatoes?

17. At rest, a human heart beats about 8 times in 6 s. A canary's heart beats 130 times in 12 s. How many times does a canary's heart beat in a day?

18. The Student Council organized a dance. A local record store donated prizes worth $80.00. The disc jockey charged $300.00. The dance tickets cost $2.75 each. Enough tickets were sold to just cover the cost of the disc jockey. How many tickets were sold?

19. A long distance telephone call from Blue Ridge to Trentville costs $1.45 for the first minute and $1.10 for each additional minute. It is 720 km from Blue Ridge to Trentville. How much will a seven minute phone call cost?

CALCULATOR MATH

Multiply some 2-digit numbers by 99. Record your results. What do you observe about the product of 99 and 2-digit numbers?

2.3 SEARCHING FOR A PATTERN

Searching for a pattern is another problem solving strategy.

READ

EXAMPLE. Determine the number of diagonals that can be drawn for polygons with 3 sides to 12 sides.

SOLUTION:

PLAN

Start with 3 sides and continue drawing diagonals until you see a pattern.

SOLVE

Number of Sides	3	4	5	6	7	8	9	10	11	12
Number of Diagonals	0	2	5	9	14	20	27	35	44	54

$+2 \quad +3 \quad +4 \quad +5 \quad +6 \quad +7 \quad +8 \quad +9 \quad +10$

ANSWER

Sides	3	4	5	6	7	8	9	10	11	12
Diagonals	0	2	5	9	14	20	27	35	44	54

EXERCISE 2.3

B 1. Use the method from the example to determine the number of squares on an 8 by 8 checkerboard.

1   5   14

2. The triangular set of numbers shown below is the first five rows of Pascal's triangle.

1 · · · · · · · · · · · · · · Row 1

1   1 · · · · · · · · · · · · Row 2

1   2   1 · · · · · · · · · Row 3

1   3   3   1 · · · · · · · Row 4

1   4   6   4   1 · · · · · Row 5

(a) Determine the pattern and write the numbers for the next four rows.
(b) Use a pattern to determine the sum of the numbers in the twelfth row.

3. The numbers 345 and 346 are called consecutive numbers. There is a pattern that will let you evaluate $346^2 - 345^2$ mentally. This pattern applies to this operation for all consecutive numbers. What is it?

4. The numbers 1, 8, 27, 64, ... are called cubes. Use patterns to determine the sum of the first seven cubes.

CALCULATOR MATH

Find some products of 2-digit numbers AB × AC where B + C = 10.

63 × 67 is an example

Record your results. What can you infer from your answer?

2.4 SOLVING BY GUESS AND CHECK

Guessing at an answer and checking your guess is a reasonable problem solving method. If your guess is incorrect, the check helps you improve the next guess.

READ

EXAMPLE. A rectangular shed has edges measured in whole numbers. The areas of the faces are 20 m², 30 m², and 24 m². Find the dimensions of the shed.

SOLUTION:

PLAN

Set up a table. Try different factors of 20 and see what the other two area numbers become.

SOLVE

20 m²		30 m²		24 m²		
w	h	w	ℓ	h	ℓ	
1	20	1	30	20	30	No
2	10	2	15	10	15	No
4	5	4	7.5	5	7.5	No
5	4	5	6	4	6	Yes

ANSWER

The dimensions of the shed are 4 m by 5 m by 6 m.

EXERCISE 2.4

1. Use the digits 1, 2, 3, 4, 5, and 6 to write two whole numbers whose product is as large as possible.

2. If you multiply a number by 4, then subtract 6, and then add 10 you get 33. What is the number?

3. The cube of a whole number is close to 6000. What is the number?

4. Allan has $4 in dimes and nickels. He has twice as many dimes as nickels. How many dimes does he have?

5. Find five consecutive numbers whose sum is 125.

6. The perimeter of a rectangle is 150 cm. The length is 5 cm longer than the width. Find the dimensions of the rectangle.

7. A 71 m piece of cable is cut into two pieces. One piece is 14 m longer than the other. How long is each piece?

8. The sum of the angles of a triangle is 180°. Two angles of a triangle are equal. The third angle is 11° less than each of the other two. How large is each angle?

CALCULATOR MATH

Use each of the digits from 1 to 9 once to make three 3-digit numbers. Each number must be a perfect square.

2.5 DRAWING A DIAGRAM OR FLOW CHART

The solution to many problems can be simplified by using a diagram or flow chart. A flow chart provides a way of checking the overall process involved in solving a problem. It also provides a way of describing the process to someone. The following flow chart is used by a library to explain how to find library materials.

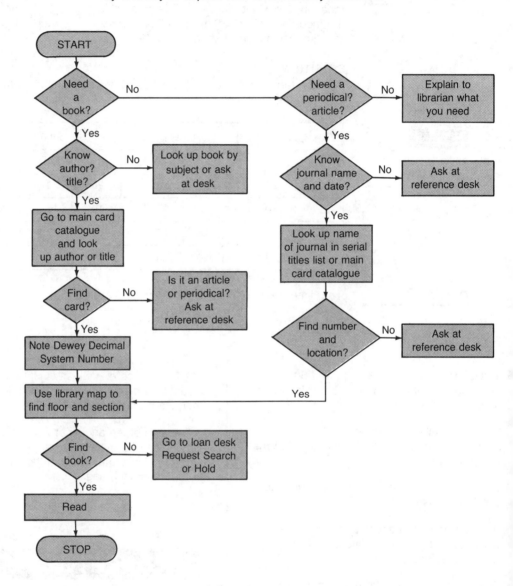

READ

EXAMPLE. Dawn can swim the width of the pool in 15 s. It takes Terry 20 s. They started swimming widths at the same time from opposite sides of the pool. How many times will they pass each other in 2 min?

PLAN

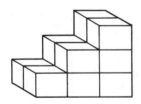

SOLVE

SOLUTION:
Draw a diagram.

Dawn _____
Terry _____

| Time | 0 | 5 | 10 | 15 | 20 | 25 | 30 | 35 | 40 | | 50 | | 60 | | 70 | | 80 | | 90 | | 100 | | 110 | | 120 |

| Time | | | 15 | 20 | | | 45 | | 60 | | 75 | | | 100 | 105 |

ANSWER

They pass each other 6 times.

EXERCISE 2.5

1. Draw a flow chart to show the steps involved in making a telephone call to a friend.

2. Draw a flow chart to explain the steps to be followed in organizing a concert at school.

3. A staircase was built with twelve cement blocks. There are three steps.

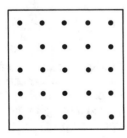

How many cement blocks are needed to build a staircase with seven steps?

4. How many different-sized squares can you make on a 5 by 5 geoboard?

5. You can cut a pizza into 7 pieces using three straight cuts. What is the maximum number of pieces you can get with five straight cuts?

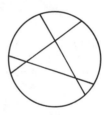

6. In a scalene triangle, all the sides have a different length. How many scalene triangles can you draw with a perimeter less than 13 cm and have the lengths of the sides be whole numbers?

7. A farmer has to take a wolf, a goat, and some cabbages across a river. The boat has enough room for the farmer plus either the wolf, or the goat, or the cabbages. If he takes the cabbages, the wolf will eat the goat. If he takes the wolf, the goat will eat the cabbages. The goat and the cabbages are only safe when the farmer is present. How does the farmer get the wolf, goat, and cabbages across the river?

2.6 CHOOSING AND SEQUENCING THE OPERATIONS

Some problems require the use of more than one arithmetic operation. In this section we will solve problems where two or more arithmetic operations must be performed in a specific order.

READ

EXAMPLE. In one week, Justine worked 23 h as a lifeguard for $13.75/h and 14 h at the museum for $15.50/h. How much did she earn in that week?

SOLUTION:

PLAN

Calculate her earnings for each job and then add to get her total earnings.

SOLVE

Lifeguard: $13.75 × 23 = $316.25
Museum: $15.50 × 14 = $217.00
Total: $316.25 + $217.00 = $533.25

ANSWER

Justine earned $533.25.

EXERCISE 2.6

B 1. Sal and Corine started their rally cars from the same spot on the highway and drove in opposite directions. Sal drove at 65 km/h and Corine drove at 75 km/h. How far apart will they be after 2.5 h?

2. Peter is reading a 510-page book. He has read 118 pages. If he reads 25 pages each day, how many more days will it take him to finish the book?

3. The framing material for a painting is 5 cm wide. What length of the material is required to frame the painting?

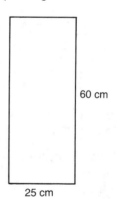

60 cm

25 cm

4. The distance between Fredricton and Vancouver is 4200 km. A plane averaged 750 km/h from Fredricton to Vancouver. On the return trip the plane averaged 800 km/h. How much longer did the flight from Fredricton to Vancouver take?

5. At one time the record for consecutive sit-ups was 1750. How many minutes and seconds would it take to break the record if you could do 40 sit-ups per minute?

6. What is the smallest number that 2, 4, 6, and 8 all divide evenly?

7. Jean and Paula went on a vacation together. Paula paid $934.76 for the hotel room and $56.88 for gas. Jean paid $344.90 for food. They decided to share the expenses equally. How much does Jean owe Paula?

8. The sum of two whole numbers is 25. Their difference is 7. What is their product?

9. Brent had a balance of $432.89 in his bank account. He wrote cheques for $23.89, $67.09, and $101.90. What is his new balance?

10. Susan was born on June 12, 1979. Shelly was born on October 29, 1981. How much older is Susan?

11. A baseball team won 24 games. It lost 11 more games than it won. How many games did it play?

12. Fifty-two more girls than boys are attending Pinegrove school. There are 1468 students at Pinegrove. How many of them are boys?

13. A 5.5 m by 7.5 m rug was bought for a 8.5 m by 7 m room. How much of the floor will not be covered by the rug?

14. A car costs $19 600. You can either pay cash for the car or buy it on the instalment plan. On the instalment plan you pay $4000 as a down payment and $500 a month for 36 months. How much more does the car cost using the instalment plan?

15. David bought the food and drinks for a beach party. He spent $54.78 for food and $23.34 for drinks. Before he went to the store he collected $70.00. How much more money does he need to collect to cover the total spent?

16. Frank left the highway service station at 09:00 and drove at 80 km/h. Margaret left the same station one-half hour later and drove in the same direction at 90 km/h. How far apart will they be at 12:00?

17. A theatre has 850 seats. For a benefit performance, orchestra seats sold for $65 each and balcony seats sold for $45 each. The total receipts were $39 125. If 400 balcony seats were sold, how many orchestra seats were sold?

CALCULATOR MATH

Multiply some 2-digit numbers by 9999. Record your results. Draw a conclusion.

2.7 WORKING BACKWARDS

Many problems can be solved by working backwards. The following example illustrates this problem solving technique.

READ

EXAMPLE. Nicla's plane leaves at 16:15. She must be at the airport one hour before flight time. She lives 75 km from the airport and she can drive at 50 km/h. On the way she must make a twenty minute stop at her lawyer's office. Nicla decides to allow fifteen minutes for possible traffic problems and parking. When should she leave for the airport?

Passengers with tickets

SOLUTION:

PLAN

Start at the flight time and work backwards.

3·2·1

SOLVE

Flight time: 16:15
Airport arrival (1 h early): 15:15
Driving time $\left(\frac{75}{50} = 1\ h\ 30\ min\right)$: 13:45
Lawyer stop (20 min): 13:25
Traffic and parking time (15 min): 13:10

ANSWER

Nicla should leave for the airport at 13:10.

EXERCISE 2.7

B 1. If you multiply a number by 11 and add 36 you get 300. What is the original number?

2. Kim received his pay on Friday. He gave $20 to his sister and then spent one-half of what he had left on clothes. Then he put $30 in the bank. He had $27 left. How much pay did Kim receive?

3. The number of people at an outdoor concert doubles every hour. At 20:00 there are 64 000 people. How many people were there four hours before, at 16:00?

4. The Orient Express was scheduled to leave for Paris at 16:45. Dr. Tremell planned to arrive at the station at 16:35. His hotel was a 24 min cab ride from the station. On the way, he needed to stop for ten minutes to meet with the ambassador. It would take him fifteen minutes to pack. Before packing he had to make four phone calls which would take a total of twenty minutes. In order to be on time for the train, what is the latest time Dr. Tremell could start making the phone calls?

5. Sandra paid a total of $1284, including 7% sales tax, for a stereo system. What was the cost of the system before the sales tax?

6. Frank's power boat was assessed at $36 000. He bought it a year ago. Power boats depreciate 10% in value each year. What did Frank pay for the boat a year ago?

7. Sylvia owns a painting worth $14 400. She bought the painting two years ago. During the two years, the painting increased in value by 20% of its previous year's worth.

(a) What did Sylvia pay for the painting?
(b) What will the painting be worth in two years?

8. Tanya carves chess sets. When she completes a set, she calculates her costs, adds 50%, and sells the set to a distributor. The distributor adds 20% to the price and sells the set to a wholesaler. The wholesaler adds 10% and sells the set to a retailer. The retailer adds 20% to the price and sells the set to a customer. If a customer pays $2376 for the set, what does it cost Tanya to make it?

POLYOMINOES

Polyominoes are shapes made by joining the same sized squares along one or more edges.

One square —Monomino

Two squares —Domino

Three squares —Tromino

Four squares —Tetromino

Five squares —Pentomino

There are eleven other different pentominoes. Draw them.

2.8 SOLVING PROBLEMS USING FORMULAS

Many problems can be solved using formulas. You have used formulas to calculate perimeter, area, and volume. In this section we will use other types of formulas.

READ

EXAMPLE. The SONAR equipment on a boat measures the time it takes sound waves to reach an object and return. To find the distance from the boat to the object we use the formula

$$d = 800t$$

where d is the distance from the boat to the object, in metres, and t is the time, in seconds, for the sound waves to leave the SONAR equipment, hit the object, and return. If t = 4.7 s, how far is the object from the boat?

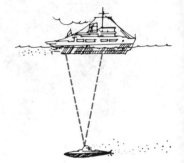

SOLUTION:

PLAN

Substitute for t in the formula.

$$d = 800t$$
$$d = 800(4.7)$$
$$= 3760$$

SOLVE

ANSWER

The object is 3760 m from the boat.

EXERCISE 2.8

B 1. As you increase altitude the air temperature drops at the rate of 1°C for every 150 m. The temperature changes according to the formula

$$T = t - \frac{h}{150}$$

where T is the air temperature at altitude h, and t is the ground temperature. Find the temperature at a height of 7500 m when the air temperature at ground level is 28°C?

2. The following formula relates the time, t, in seconds it takes for an object to fall from a height, h, in metres.

$$h = 4.9t^2$$

It takes 10.6 s for an object to fall from the top of the CN Tower. How high is the CN Tower?

3. A baseball pitcher's earned run average is the average number of runs an opposing team will score against the pitcher in 9 innings. To calculate an earned run average we use the formula

$$\text{ERA} = \frac{9 \times r}{i}$$

runs $\nearrow$

innings pitched

Calculate the earned run average of a pitcher who gave up 15 runs in 27 innings.

4.

The volume of a pyramid is given by the formula

$$V = \frac{\ell \times w \times h}{3}$$

Calculate the volume of a pyramid where $\ell = 28$ m, w = 28 m, and h = 30 m.

5. The following formula determines an amount of sleep needed for people 19 a old or younger.

$$h = \frac{35 - n}{2}$$

where h is the hours of sleep and n is the age in years. How much sleep does a thirteen year-old need?

6. The following formula determines the day of the week for any date based on our current calendar. This calendar was introduced in 1592. In the formula,

d = the day of the month of the given date
m = the number of the month of the given year

> January is regarded as the thirteenth month and February as the fourteenth month of the previous year. For example, January 17, 1992, which is normally 1992–01–17 becomes 1991–13–17.
> The other months are numbered 3 through 12 as usual.

y = the year

$$W = d + 2m + \left[\frac{3(m + 1)}{5}\right] + y + \left[\frac{y}{4}\right] - \left[\frac{y}{100}\right] + \left[\frac{y}{400}\right] + 2$$

The brackets [ ] mean the integer part of the quotient. For example

$$\left[\frac{23}{5}\right] = 4$$

Once you calculate W, you divide it by 7. The remainder is the day of the week.

          0 = Saturday
          1 = Sunday
          2 = Monday
          3 = Tuesday
          4 = Wednesday
          5 = Thursday
          6 = Friday

(a) On what day of the week were you born?
(b) On what day of the week will January 1, 2000 fall?

2.9 SOLVING A SIMPLER PROBLEM

Many complicated problems can be solved by first solving a similar but simpler problem.

READ

EXAMPLE. A rectangular piece of property measures 468 m by 104 m. It is located on the bank of a river. A fence is to be built along three of the sides. The posts are to be 2 m apart. How many posts are required?

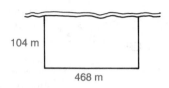

104 m

468 m

SOLUTION:

PLAN

Determine the number of posts needed for smaller areas and look for a pattern.

SOLVE

Start with smaller fields.
$\ell = 4$ m
$w = 2$ m

2 4 2

8 m of fence require 5 posts or (4 + 1) posts

$\ell = 6$ m
$w = 4$ m

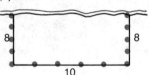

4 4

6

14 m of fence require 8 posts or (7 + 1) posts

$\ell = 10$ m
$w = 8$ m

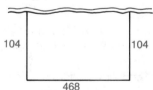

8 8

10

26 m of fence require 14 posts or (13 + 1) posts

The pattern indicates that you need one post for every 2 m of fence plus another end post.

$\ell = 468$ m
$w = 104$ m

104 104

468

There are 676 m of fence.
$\frac{676}{2} = 338$ posts plus 1 end post
$\qquad = 339$

ANSWER

339 posts are required.

EXERCISE 2.9

B 1. About how many times does your heart beat in one year?

2. Find the sum of

    $1 + 2 + 3 + 4 + ... + 1000$

3. How many strides would it take to run 10 km?

4. A rectangular field measures 243 m by 93 m.

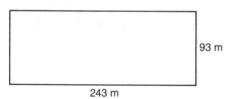

A fence is to be constructed around the field. Fence posts are to be 3 m apart. How many fence posts are required?

5. How thick is a page in a telephone book?

6. Two hundred people entered a handball tournament. If players are eliminated after 1 lost game, how many games will be required to determine a winner?

7. Students, representing each of the ten provinces, met in Ottawa to discuss a student exchange program. When they gathered for their first meeting each student shook hands with every other student. How many handshakes were exchanged?

8. Cans are stacked for display in layers that increase in size as shown.

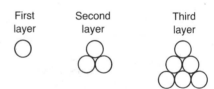

| First layer | Second layer | Third layer |

The layers are arranged on top of one another to form a display.

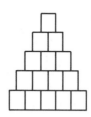

How many cans are in a display that has 12 layers?

9. How long would it take you to walk to the sun and back?

MIND BENDER

At McWings you can order chicken wings in boxes of 6, 9, or 20. By ordering two boxes of 6 you can get 12 wings. But you cannot order 13 wings, since no combination of 6, 9, and 20 adds to 13. What is the greatest number of wings you cannot order (Hint: it is a number less than 100.)

2.10 CONSTRUCTING A TABLE

Organizing information in a table is another useful problem solving strategy.

READ

EXAMPLE. Peter has twenty metres of fence. He wants to enclose a rectangular field. What should the dimensions of the enclosed field be to give Peter maximum area?

SOLUTION:

PLAN

Construct a width, length, area table.

SOLVE

w (m)	ℓ (m)	A (m²)
1	9	9
2	8	16
3	7	21
4	6	24
5	5	25	← maximum area
6	4	24

ANSWER

The maximum area is reached when the length is 5 m and the width is 5 m.

EXERCISE 2.10

B 1. There are twenty-five students in the class. Sandra is arranging them into three groups with an odd number of students in each group. How many possible arrangements are there?

2. The sum of two whole numbers is 90 and their product is less than 300. What are the possible combinations of whole numbers that fit these two conditions?

3. A rectangle has an area of 240 m². Its length and width are whole numbers.
(a) What are the possible dimensions for the length and width?
(b) What length and width in (a) give the smallest perimeter?

4. The number 4 has three different factors, namely 4, 2, and 1. Find all the positive integers less than 50 that have an odd number of different factors.

5. Make a table to show the number of different ways to make change for fifty cents.

25¢	10¢	5¢	1¢
2	0	0	0

6. During the summer, Don makes and sells boomerangs. If he charges $40 for a boomerang, he will sell 300. For every dollar drop in price, he will sell 10 more boomerangs. Complete the table to find what price Don should charge for the greatest receipts.

Price	Number	Receipts
$40	300	$12 000
$39		
$38		
$37		
$36		
$35		
$34		
$33		
$32		

7. You have been given a 3 L container, a 5 L container, and an unlimited supply of water. Your task is to obtain four litres of water. Record your solution in a table as shown.

3 L container	5 L container

8. Sandra earns $60 a day as a tour guide. Jennifer earns $40 a day as a lifeguard. Jennifer works five more days than Sandra, but they each earn the same amount of money. How many days does each one work?

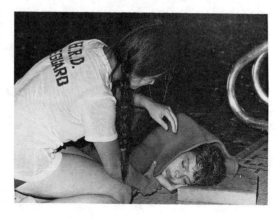

9. Socks cost $9.95 a pair. T-shirts cost $17.42 each. The track coach spent $92.06 for socks and T-shirts. How many of each did he buy?

10. Using the powers of 2 in a table to multiply is shown below. To multiply 19×51, we proceed as follows.

1×51	51
2×51	102
4×51	204
8×51	408
16×51	816

Since $16 + 2 + 1 = 19$

$$\begin{array}{rl} 16 \to & 816 \\ 2 \to & 102 \\ \underline{1 \to} & \underline{51} \\ 19 & 969 \end{array}$$

$\therefore 19 \times 51 = 969$

Use this method to multiply the following.
(a) 23×47
(b) 31×66
(c) 48×24

2.11 CONCLUDING FROM ASSUMPTIONS

To solve many problems we must sometimes make assumptions about the information given.

READ

EXAMPLE. Jan surveyed 24 students in her school and found that 12 of them would buy school scarves. If there are 980 students in the school, how many scarves can she expect to sell?

SOLUTION:

PLAN

Since one half of the 24 students surveyed will buy scarves, assume that one half of all the students will buy them.

SOLVE

One half of 980 is

$$\frac{980}{2} = 490$$

ANSWER

Jan can expect to sell 490 scarves.

EXERCISE 2.11

In the following, state the assumptions made to solve the problem.

B 1. The Blue Flame rocket car can travel at 1046 km/h. How far can the car travel in 4.5 h?

2. In one week 53 students were absent from school. About how many will be absent in three months?

3. Justine scored 23 points in the first basketball game. How many points could she score in the 24-game season?

4. It takes Phil 2.5 h to cut his neighbour's lawn. How long will it take him to cut all 14 of the lawns on his street?

5. The school band sells cases of grapefruits to raise money. Last year each band member sold 18 cases. How many cases can the band expect to sell this year if there are 64 band members?

6. For each of the following make an assumption to identify the pattern and list the next three numbers.
(a) 4, 6, 9, 13, 18, 24, ...
(b) 63, 48, 35, 24, ...
(c) 64, 32, 16, 8, 4, ...
(d) 1, 1, 2, 3, 5, 8, 13, ...
(e) 5, 8, 7, 10, 9, 12, 11, 14, ...
(f) 3, 4, 6, 7, 9, 11, 12, ...

7. You have three apples. You eat one every half hour. How long will the apples last?

2.12 A MODEL FOR DECISION MAKING

One reason to study mathematics is to develop the ability to make decisions. When making decisions, it is helpful to have an organized plan. The following example illustrates the PACED plan for decision making.

EXAMPLE.

PROBLEM

IDENTIFY THE PROBLEM.

Laura is an avid tennis fan. She has saved $700 to go to a professional tennis tournament for two days. Courtside tickets cost $150 for the two days. Bleacher seats cost $50. An airline flight to the tournament would take two hours and cost $300. The bus trip takes seven hours and costs $100. Laura does not like long bus trips. If she goes by plane she will need to spend two nights in a hotel. If she goes by bus she will need to spend three nights. The hotel rates are:

Royal Hotel .... $200 per night
Sunrise Hotel .... $150 per night
Paradise Hotel .... $120 per night

What should Laura do to stay within her budget, and yet enjoy her trip?

ALTERNATIVES

STATE THE ALTERNATIVES OR CHOICES.

1. $150 seats or $50 seats
2. $300 by plane or $100 by bus
3. Two or three nights in a hotel
4. Royal, Sunrise, or Paradise Hotels

CRITERIA

STATE THE RESTRICTIONS ON THE ALTERNATIVES.

1. Laura is a tennis fan
2. She has $700
3. She doesn't like long bus trips

EVALUATE THE ALTERNATIVES BASED ON THE CRITERIA.

In this problem, a tree diagram helps to organize the information.

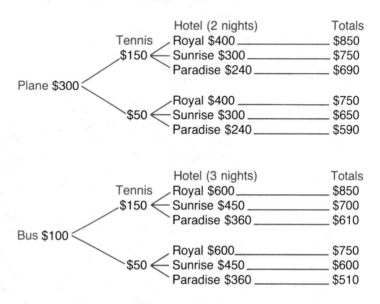

		Hotel (2 nights)	Totals
Tennis		Royal $400	$850
$150		Sunrise $300	$750
		Paradise $240	$690
		Royal $400	$750
$50		Sunrise $300	$650
		Paradise $240	$590

Plane $300

		Hotel (3 nights)	Totals
Tennis		Royal $600	$850
$150		Sunrise $450	$700
		Paradise $360	$610
		Royal $600	$750
$50		Sunrise $450	$600
		Paradise $360	$510

Bus $100

DECISION

DECIDE ON THE BEST ALTERNATIVE.

Laura should fly, pay $150 for the seats, and stay at the Paradise Hotel. The total cost is $690.

EXERCISE 2.12

B 1. Fifty-six boys and sixty-four girls from Central School plan to stay one night at a hotel while on a white water rafting trip. The trip organizers must decide which hotel would provide the least expensive accommodation. The following prices for the local hotels were provided by the provincial tourist bureau.

Hotel	Single	Double	Extra Person	Maximum in a room
Regency	$148	$180	$20	5
Fife	$128	$160	$20	4
Waterfront	$140	$172	$16	4
Star	$152	$176	$20	5

Room maximums cannot be exceeded. Boys and girls cannot share rooms.

(a) Which hotel will provide the least expensive accommodation for the group?

(b) If costs are distributed among the students evenly, how much would each pay?

(c) What other considerations other than cost might go into selecting a hotel?

2. For his vacation, Paul has decided to spend seven days and nights at the ocean. The train fare is $200 return. The airfare is $800 return. The hotel rates per night are as follows.

Sands	$200
Driftwood	$120
Seabreeze	$90

The Sands is described as an "ocean front" hotel. The Driftwood is an "ocean view" hotel. The Seabreeze is described as "near ocean." Paul has estimated that it will cost $350 for food for the week. He has saved $2000 for the trip. What he does not spend on travel, accommodation, and food, he will spend on surfing, sailing, and deep sea fishing. Plan Paul's trip so that he will get the most enjoyment for his money.

3. The manager of the recreation centre has $1000 to spend on volleyballs, baseballs, basketballs, and footballs. The price list for regular balls and professional balls is as follows.

Volleyballs:	regular	$20
	pro	$25
Baseballs:	regular	$8
	pro	$10
Basketballs:	regular	$35
	pro	$50
Footballs:	regular	$40
	pro	$60

The centre needs a minimum of 10 volleyballs, 30 baseballs, 5 basketballs, and 6 footballs. How should the manager use the money to get the best quality balls for $1000?

LEONHARD EULER (1707-1783)

Leonhard Euler was a Swiss mathematician who became famous for his incredible capacity for mental calculations. He was able to perform calculations in his head that required answers of up to fifty digits.

Euler became especially well-known in the old city of Königsberg, Germany. The centre of the city was located on two islands in the Pregel River. The islands and the river banks were joined by seven bridges. It was a long-standing puzzle for the people to try to travel through the city, crossing each of the bridges once and only once. Euler took a special interest in the puzzle, eventually proving mathematically that it could not be done.

Although Euler was completely blind during the last seventeen years of his life, his tremendous memory enabled him to continue his work. He produced over 800 books and papers in his lifetime.

2.13 DYNAMIC PROGRAMMING — WORKING BACKWARDS

A driver for a courier service can use many routes to deliver parcels. If the driver determines the route that takes the least amount of time, the driver has solved an optimization problem.

Problems of this type occur often. Bus companies need to know the best routes to take. Fire stations and emergency vehicles must be located near as many potential victims as possible. Subways must serve as many people as possible.

Many of these problems can be expressed mathematically. When this is done, each solution is given a score. The object in solving an optimization problem is to find the solution that gives the best score; that is, shortest time, best route, and lowest expense.

There are many methods that can be used to solve optimization problems. In this section we will use Dynamic Programming. We will apply Dynamic Programming to traffic route problems.

The map at the right is drawn on a 2 by 2 block. It shows the possible routes between A and B with the distances between each point marked in kilometres. (In all problems we will restrict travel to two directions: vertical and to the right.)

The brute force method of determining the shortest route between A and B is to list all of the possible routes and calculate the distances.

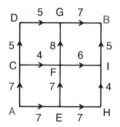

Route	Distances	Total Distance
A–C–D–G–B	7 + 5 + 5 + 7	24
A–C–F–G–B	7 + 4 + 8 + 7	26
A–C–F–I–B	7 + 4 + 6 + 5	22
A–E–H–I–B	7 + 7 + 4 + 5	23
A–E–F–I–B	7 + 7 + 6 + 5	25
A–E–F–G–B	7 + 7 + 8 + 7	29

The shortest route is A–C–F–I–B, which is 22 km. Each route required 3 additions to find the distance. There are 6 different routes, so a total of 18 additions are needed to solve the problem.

Consider another similar problem, drawn on a 3 by 3 block at the right. There are 20 different routes to get from A to B.

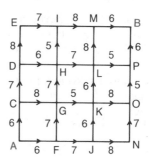

(a) Complete the following table in your notebook (one route is done for you).

Route	Distances	Total Distance
A–C–D–E–I–M–B	6 + 7 + 8 + 7 + 8 + 6	42

Route	Distances	Total Distance

(b) What is the shortest route from A to B?
(c) How many additions are required for each route?
(d) How many additions are required for the 20 routes?

As the number of blocks increases, the number of routes and additions increases rapidly. A computer can be programmed to solve large route problems using the brute force method, however, there is a time restriction. For example, a 30 by 30 block problem would have approximately 120 000 000 000 000 000 different routes and require 7 100 000 000 000 000 000 additions. It would take a computer one hundred years to solve such a problem.

Using Dynamic Programming, a 30 by 30 block problem can be solved on a computer in less than one second.

Dynamic Programming solves problems by working backwards. We will use the 2 by 2 block problem to illustrate the technique.

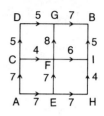

We work backwards from B and find the shortest distance to B from every intersection. We will write the shortest distance to B in red and indicate the direction to go by an arrow.

From I there is one way to get to B: 5 km vertically.

From G there is one way to get to B: 7 km right.

From F there are two choices:
    (i) going vertically 8 + ⑦ = 15
    (ii) going to the right 6 + ⑤ = 11

Going to the right is the shortest distance at 11 km, so we mark it on the diagram.

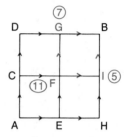

From D you must go right.
The distance is 5 + ⑦ = 12

From H you must go vertically.
The distance is 4 + ⑤ = 9

There are two options at C:
    (i) going vertically 5 + ⑫ = 17
    (ii) going to the right 4 + ⑪ = 15

Going to the right is shorter, so we mark the direction and distance at C.

There are two options at E:
    (i) going vertically 7 + ⑪ = 18
    (ii) going to the right 7 + ⑨ = 16

Going to the right is shorter, so we mark the direction and distance at E.

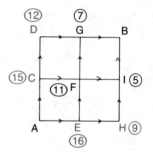

There are two options at A:
    (i) going vertically 7 + ⑮ = 22
    (ii) going to the right 7 + ⑯ = 23

Going vertically is shorter, so we mark the direction and distance.

The arrows indicate the direction to leave each intersection. The shortest path is A–C–F–I–B and the distance is 22 km.

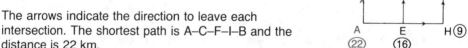

When this problem was solved using brute force, 18 additions were needed. Using Dynamic Programming, only 10 additions were needed.

The following steps illustrate the solution to the 3 by 3 block problem. In practice you will use one diagram.

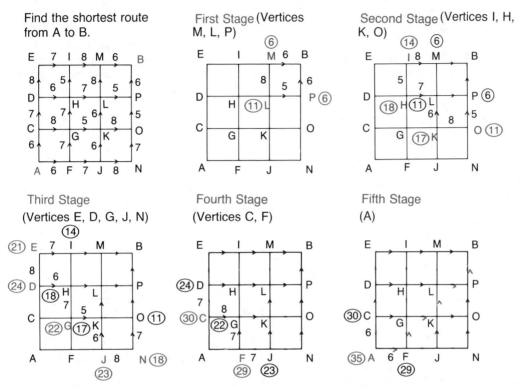

Find the shortest route from A to B.

First Stage (Vertices M, L, P)

Second Stage (Vertices I, H, K, O)

Third Stage
(Vertices E, D, G, J, N)

Fourth Stage
(Vertices C, F)

Fifth Stage
(A)

The shortest path is A–F–G–K–L–P–B and the distance is 35 km.

The brute force method required 100 additions to do this problem. Using Dynamic Programming only 22 additions were needed and we saved time by not having to list all of the possible routes.

Dynamic Programming reduces the 30 by 30 block problem from
7 100 000 000 000 000 000 additions to 1858 additions. A computer can solve this problem in less than one second.

EXERCISE 2.13

1. Find the shortest route from A to B in each of the following.

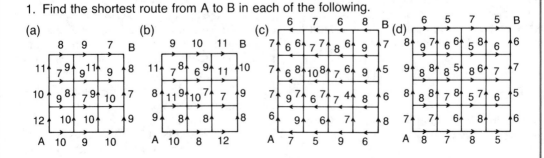

(a)

(b)

(c)

(d)

2.14 REVIEW EXERCISE

1. One tent can sleep 6 people. How many tents will be needed if 29 boys and 23 girls go on an overnight camping trip with boys and girls in separate tents?

2. Three consecutive numbers have a sum of 195. What are the numbers?

3. Tom and Marcia made a total of $126.90 on their weekend jobs. Tom made $7.90 more than Marcia. How much did each make?

4. Place the numbers from 1 to 9 in the circles so that the sum of each side of the triangle is 20.

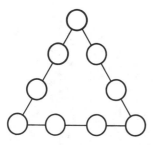

5. Canada has an area of approximately 9 976 000 km². Which country is larger, Canada or the United States, and by how much?

6. Black and white television sets cost $101.75. Colour television sets cost $566.90. A hotel bought 46 colour sets. What was the cost, not including the sales tax?

7. A table tennis ball is the lightest officially approved ball for sporting activities. It has a mass of 2.4 g. A 10-pin bowling ball is the heaviest. It has a mass of 7.3 kg. How many table tennis balls would it take to equal the mass of one 10-pin bowling ball?

8. What is the sum of the first fifty odd numbers?

9. Find the pattern and determine the three missing numbers.

1, 3, 6, 10, 15, ■, ■, ■

10. The area of a rectangle is 91 m². The length is 6 m longer than the width. Find the dimensions of the rectangle.

11. A 30 cm by 40 cm rectangular piece of cardboard has a 5 cm by 5 cm square cut out of each corner. The sides are then folded up to make an open box. Find the volume of the box.

12. Four squares are arranged so that each square touches at least one other square along a side.

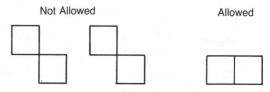

Draw as many possible arrangements as possible and find the perimeter of each arrangement.

13. Make a table to show the number of different ways you can make change for a quarter.

10¢	5¢	1¢

14. Frank found three brass house numbers, a 6, a 7, and a 2. How many possible 3-digit numbers can he make?

15. Jackie and Pamela decided to have a party. Jackie spent $45.60 for food and $21.35 for drinks. Pamela spent $12.65 for prizes. If they want to share the expenses equally, how much does Pamela owe Jackie?

16. The sponsor of a soccer team had the following expenses.

> 15 jerseys at $12.50 each
> 15 shorts at $9.75 each
> 4 soccer balls at $32.50 each

What were the total expenses?

17. When Saroj started on a 1280 km auto trip the odometer on her car read 56 789.9 km. After eight hours the odometer read 57 343.8 km. How many more kilometres did she have to drive?

18. How many minutes are there in the month of September?

19. The train left Arndale station. Fourteen passengers got on at the Beacon stop and five got off. Twenty-one passengers got on at Chester and twenty-three got off. Eleven passengers got on at Dundurn and six got off. Seven passengers got on at Elmvale. When the train left Elmvale there were ninety-eight passengers on board. How many passengers were on the train when it left Arndale?

20. How many pencils laid end to end would it take to make one kilometre?

21. How many of the first 300 page numbers in a book contain at least one 5?

22. Four hundred seventy students attended the first school dance. How many can you expect to attend the next three dances? What assumption did you make to solve this problem?

23. There are three ways to add four odd numbers to get 10.
$$1 + 1 + 3 + 5 = 10$$
$$1 + 1 + 1 + 7 = 10$$
$$1 + 3 + 3 + 3 = 10$$
There are eleven ways to add eight odd numbers to get 20. Changing the order of the numbers does not count as a new solution. Find the eleven ways.

24. Each of the three letters stands for a different digit. Find the digit for each letter that makes the addition true.

$$OK + OK + OK + OK = GO$$

25. A train travelling at 100 km/h takes three seconds to completely enter a tunnel. It takes the train another thirty seconds to completely pass through the tunnel.
(a) How long is the train?
(b) What is the length of the tunnel?

26. Each number in the large squares is found by adding the numbers in the small squares next to it.

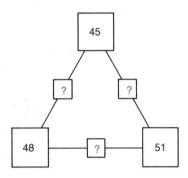

Find the numbers in the small squares.

2.15 CHAPTER 2 TEST

1. A major league baseball costs $12.75. There are exactly 216 stitches in each ball. How much do 24 baseballs cost, excluding the sales tax?

2. A train is 2 km long. It is travelling at 60 km/h. How long will it take to pass through a tunnel that is 1 km long?

3. Determine the pattern and find the three missing numbers.
    30, 29, 27, 24, 20, ■, ■, ■

4. A piece of rope is 67 m long. It is to be cut into two pieces. One piece is to be 9 m longer than the other. How long is each piece?

5. Karen has to put a fence along 32 m of field. The fence posts are to be 4 m apart. How many posts does she need?

6. There are twenty children at the playground. Frank wants to arrange them in 3 groups with an even number of children in each group. How many ways can he do it?

7. Brent's pay was $345.64. He bought some computer software for $125.70 and spent $135.45 on clothes. How much did he have left?

8. The cost of renting a car is given by the formula
    $$C = 21n + 0.2k$$
where C is the cost, n is the number of days, and k is the number of kilometres driven. How much would you pay if you rented a car for 3 d and drove 1200 km?

APPLICATIONS OF INTEGERS AND MICROCOMPUTERS

CHAPTER

Number rules the universe.
The Pythagoreans

REVIEW AND PREVIEW TO CHAPTER 3

WORDS AND NUMBERS

In many applications and problems, certain words or phrases are used to represent arithmetic operations.

EXERCISE

1. Write the expression, then calculate the value of each. The answers must belong to the set of whole numbers $W = \{0, 1, 2, 3, ...\}$.

(a) The sum of 1056 and 927.
(b) The product of 125 and 73.
(c) The difference between 93 and 68.
(d) 563 subtracted from 958.
(e) Twice 2385.
(f) The sum of 85 and 132, subtracted from 500.
(g) The square of 89.
(h) 95 multiplied by itself.
(i) The average of 186 and 254.
(j) The quotient of 658 and 14.
(k) The difference between the square of 18 and twice 18.
(l) The cube of 6.
(m) The sum of the product of 25 and 6, and the difference between 207 and 981.
(n) The average of 56, 48, 79, 46, and 96.
(o) The difference between 127 and 1027.
(p) The product of 56 and 9, decreased by 207.
(q) The sum of 435 and 863, divided by 22.
(r) The amount by which 537 exceeds 189.
(s) The sum of 43 and 97, subtracted from the product of 102 and 50.
(t) The value of 15^2.
(u) The product of 56 and 81, divided by 14.
(v) 1853 diminished by 475.

NUMBER LINES

EXERCISE

Graph the following sets on a whole number line.

1. $\{x \mid x < 6\}$

2. $\{x \mid 3 < x \leqslant 8\}$

3. $\{x \mid x > 4\}$

4. $\{x \mid x \leqslant 4\}$

5. $\{x \mid 2 \leqslant x \leqslant 7\}$

6. $\{x \mid 1 \leqslant x \leqslant 5\}$

7. $\{x \mid 4 \leqslant x < 9\}$

8. $\{x \mid 0 < x \leqslant 5\}$

9. $\{x \mid 3 < x \leqslant 10\}$

10. $\{x \mid x \neq 6\}$

Write descriptions for the following sets using set notation.

11.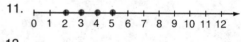

12.

13.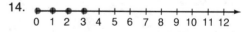

14.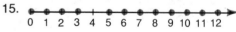

15.

16.

SUBSTITUTION

EXERCISE

1. Evaluate each of the following for
x = 3, y = 4, z = 7.
(a) 2x + y
(b) 3x − 2y
(c) xyx − (x + y + z)
(d) (x + y)² − z²
(e) (x + y)² − (x² + y²)

2. Given E(x) = 3x² − 2x + 5,
evaluate
(a) E(2)   (b) E(5)   (c) E(3)   (d) E(0)

3. Given E(x) = 8x − 7.5, evaluate
(a) E(2.5)   (b) E(1.25)
(c) E(5.6)   (d) E(2.75)

4. Given E(x) = 0.5x + 2.8, evaluate
(a) E(1.24)   (b) E(0.8)
(c) E(4.46)   (d) E(3.5)

5. Evaluate each of the following for
x = 2.5, y = 3.6, z = 4.5.
(a) x + y − z
(b) x(y + z)
(c) x(z − y)
(d) x + z − y
(e) 2x + 3y − 4z

6. Evaluate x² + 3xy + y², for
(a) x = 4, y = 7
(b) x = 3, y = 8
(c) x = 0, y = 1
(d) x = 1, y = 0
(e) x = y = 5
(f) x = 4, y = x + 2
(g) x = y − 2, y = 5

7. Evaluate 1.5x + 3.2y − 1.7xy for
(a) x = 2.5, y = 3.6
(b) x = 4.6, y = 2.7
(c) x = 8.2, y = 3.7
(d) x = 0.8, y = 0.4
(e) x = 2.9, y = 3.2

8. When an object is dropped from a hot air balloon, the amount of distance it has fallen depends on the time it is in the air. The formula

$$d = 4.9t^2$$

where d is in metres and t is in seconds gives the distance the object has fallen.
(a) Complete the following table.

t	d
0.25	
0.5	
0.75	
1.0	
1.25	
1.5	
1.75	
2.0	
2.25	
2.5	
2.75	
3.0	

(b) How far does the object fall in the first second?
(c) How far does the object fall during the second second?
(d) How high is the balloon if the object reached the ground in exactly 3 s?

9. The perimeter of a rectangle is given by the formula

$$P = 2(\ell + w)$$

Complete the following table.

ℓ	w	P
35	24	
63		200
	32	360

3.1 INTEGER NOTATION

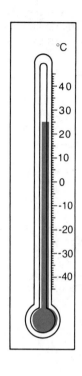

Starting with 0, we can make a calculator count.

Press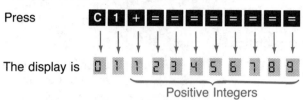

The display is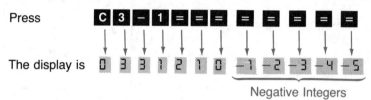

Positive Integers

Similarly, starting with 3, we can make a calculator count backwards.

Press

The display is

Negative Integers

The positive and negative integers, including zero (0), which is neither positive nor negative, form the set of integers This set of integers can be represented graphically as a number line.

$$I = \{..., -3, -2, -1, 0, 1, 2, 3, ...\}$$

zero is neither
positive nor negative

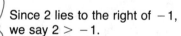

Negative Integers   Positive Integers

Integers are used in many problems to illustrate ideas that are opposite in direction or meaning:

1542 m above sea level	$+1542$
13°C below zero	-13
a profit of $156	$+156$
6 under par	-6
a deposit of $78 followed by a withdrawal of $27	$(+78)+(-27)$

The order of integers may be determined by their position on the number line. An integer to the right of another integer on the number line is greater than the preceding integer.

Since 2 lies to the right of -1, we say $2 > -1$.

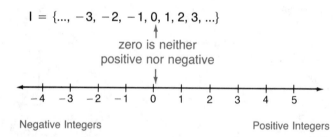

Since -3 lies to the left of -1, we say $-3 < -1$.

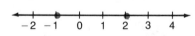

It is possible to express integer problems in simpler notation.

The brackets are used here to eliminate confusion between the sign of operation and the sign of the integer.

$+1542$	becomes	1542
$(+78)+(-27)$	becomes	$78+(-27)$
$(+7)+(+3)$	becomes	$7 + 3$
$(-2)-(+7)$	becomes	$-2 - 7$
$(+6)-(-7)$	becomes	$6 - (-7)$

EXAMPLE 1. Describe $\{-2, -1, 0, 1, 2, 3, ...\}$ using:
(a) words
(b) a number line
(c) set notation

SOLUTION:

(a) The set of integers greater than negative three; or the set of integers greater than or equal to negative two.

(b)

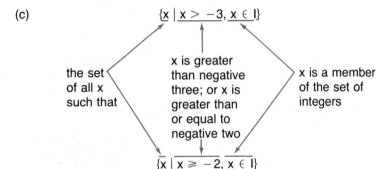

(c)

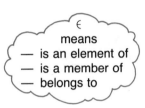

$\{x \mid x > -3, x \in I\}$

the set of all x such that

x is greater than negative three; or x is greater than or equal to negative two

x is a member of the set of integers

$\{x \mid x \geq -2, x \in I\}$

ϵ means
— is an element of
— is a member of
— belongs to

EXAMPLE 2. Describe the set of integers defined by the graph using:
(a) words
(b) a list of the elements
(c) set notation

SOLUTION:

(a) The set of integers greater than negative four and less than positive three.
(b) $\{-3, -2, -1, 0, 1, 2\}$
(c) $\{x \mid x > -4 \text{ and } x < 3, x \in I\}$

This may also be written in one of the following ways.
    (i) $-4 < x < 3$
    (ii) $-3 \leq x < 3$
    (iii) $-4 < x \leq 2$
    (iv) $-3 \leq x \leq 2$

EXERCISE 3.1

A 1. Describe each of the following by a suitable integer.

(a) a fall of 6 m
(b) 4°C below zero
(c) a decrease of $3
(d) 7 kg more
(e) 1560 m above sea level
(f) a profit of $560
(g) 5 cm shorter
(h) a debt of $20

2. Describe each of the following sets in words.

(a) $\{-2, -1, 0, 1, 2, ...\}$
(b) $\{..., -1, 0, 1, 2, 3, 4\}$
(c) $\{9, 10, 11, ...\}$
(d) $\{..., -9, -8, -7\}$
(e) $\{-1, 0, 1, 2, 3, 4\}$
(f) $\{0, 1, 2, 3, 4\}$

(g)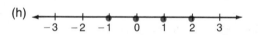

(h)

(i)

(j)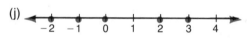

B 3. Using a number line as a guide, replace ■ with $<$ or $>$ to form a true statement.

(a) $+5$ ■ $+3$ (b) 7 ■ 0 (c) -5 ■ 1
(d) 2 ■ -2 (e) -1 ■ -3 (f) 2 ■ -9
(g) -5 ■ 0 (h) 0 ■ -1 (i) -7 ■ -12
(j) -19 ■ 19 (k) -4 ■ 4 (l) -8 ■ -7

4. Write each of the following sets using set notation.
$$\{x \mid \qquad \}$$
(a) $\{-2, -1, 0, 1, ...\}$
(b) $\{-3, -2, -1, 0, 1, 2, 3\}$
(c) $\{0, 1, 2, 3, ...\}$
(d) $\{..., -3, -2, -1, 0\}$
(e) $\{-1, 0, 1, 2, 3, ...\}$
(f) $\{..., -6, -5, -4\}$
(g) $\{-1, 0, 1\}$

5. For each set below,
(a) list the elements
(b) graph the set on a number line.
(i) $\{x \mid x > -2, x \in I\}$
(ii) $\{x \mid x \leqslant 4, x \in I\}$
(iii) $\{x \mid x < -4, x \in I\}$
(iv) $\{y \mid y \neq -1, y \in I\}$
(v) $\{y \mid y \geqslant -2, y \in I\}$
(vi) $\{x \mid -2 < x < 3, x \in I\}$
(vii) $\{x \mid 0 \leqslant x < 5, x \in I\}$
(viii) $\{x \mid x < 0 \text{ or } x > 2, x \in I\}$
(ix) $\{x \mid -3 \leqslant x < 1, x \in I\}$
(x) $\{x \mid -1 < x < 1, x \in I\}$

6. For the domain $\{-3, -2, -1, 0, 1, 2, 3\}$, list the elements in each set below.

(a) $\{x \mid x > 1\}$ (b) $\{x \mid x \leqslant 2\}$
(c) $\{x \mid -1 < x < 6\}$ (d) $\{x \mid x < -3\}$

C 7. For each set,
(a) list the elements
(b) graph the set on a number line.
(i) $\{y \mid y > -3, y \in I\} \cap \{y \mid y \leqslant 2, y \in I\}$
(ii) $\{x \mid x < 1, x \in I\} \cup \{x \mid x \geqslant 3, x \in I\}$
(iii) $\{x \mid x \leqslant 0, x \in I\} \cap \{x \mid x > -5, x \in I\}$

MIND BENDER

Can you walk through this maze? Start at the top. Walk through each path exactly once and come out at B. Then try to walk through each path just once and come out at A or C.

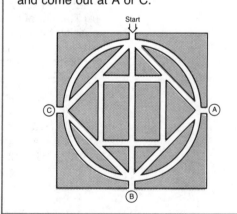

3.2 ADDITION OF INTEGERS

In many problems, integers may be used in constructing a mathematical model to aid in solving the problem.

EXAMPLE 1. To test an elevator, John went up 4 floors, down 2 floors, up 3 floors, and finally, down 8 floors. Represent each of these trips by an integer, and determine if John stopped above or below where he started.

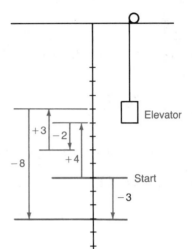

SOLUTION:

up 4 floors	$+4$
down 2 floors	-2
up 3 floors	$+3$
down 8 floors	-8

The results may be illustrated on a vertical number line. Since the result is -3, John stopped 3 floors below where he started.

Mathematically, we write
$$4 + (-2) + 3 + (-8) = -3$$

Addition in I:
If $x, y \in I$, (i) $(+x) + (+y) = +(x + y)$
(ii) $(-x) + (-y) = -(x + y)$
(iii) $(+x) + (-y) = +(x - y)$ if $x > y$
$= -(y - x)$ if $y > x$

EXAMPLE 2. Represent each of the following calculations on a number line, and determine the net result.
(a) $5 + (-3)$
(b) $-3 + (-2)$
(c) $-8 + 6$

SOLUTION:

(a)

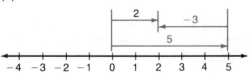

$\therefore 5 + (-3) = 2$

(b)

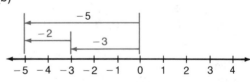

$\therefore -3 + (-2) = -5$

(c)

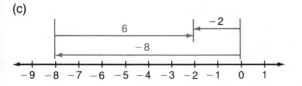

$\therefore -8 + 6 = -2$

EXERCISE 3.2

A number line may be used if necessary for the problems in this exercise.

A 1. Add.

(a) $+12$
$\underline{+3}$

(b) -5
$\underline{+7}$

(c) $+8$
$\underline{-10}$

(d) -2
$\underline{-5}$

(e) -12
$\underline{+12}$

(f) -5
$\underline{-17}$

(g) -8
$\underline{-4}$

(h) $+7$
$\underline{-17}$

(i) $+32$
$\underline{-15}$

(j) $+22$
$\underline{-13}$

(k) -15
$\underline{-7}$

(l) $+27$
$\underline{-44}$

2. Find the sum in each of the following.

(a) $8 + (-5)$
(b) $-12 + 14$
(c) $9 + (-3)$
(d) $-2 + 3$
(e) $-5 + 1$
(f) $-8 + 8$
(g) $-4 + (-6)$
(h) $-9 + (-8)$
(i) $0 + (-3)$
(j) $(-7) + (-3)$

3. Simplify.

(a) $-6 + 9$
(b) $12 + (-3)$
(c) $2 + (-7)$
(d) $-15 + 2$
(e) $-3 + (-8)$
(f) $-5 + 5$
(g) $23 + (-23)$
(h) $18 + (-19)$
(i) $-21 + 0$
(j) $-11 + (-3)$
(k) $-14 + (-1)$
(l) $1 + (-17)$

B 4. Complete the statements.

(a) ■ $+ 3 = 7$
(b) $-3 +$ ■ $= 9$
(c) ■ $+ (-2) = 7$
(d) $3 +$ ■ $= -5$
(e) ■ $+ (-5) = 0$
(f) ■ $+ (-1) = -6$
(g) $-12 +$ ■ $= -11$
(h) ■ $+ 6 = -4$
(i) $-12 +$ ■ $= 5$
(j) ■ $+ (-7) = -4$

5. Simplify.

(a) $19 + 7 + (-12)$
(b) $-7 + 4 + 8$
(c) $12 + 6 + (-10)$
(d) $-11 + (-2) + 8$
(e) $0 + (-5) + 8$
(f) $7 + 12 + (-7)$
(g) $-7 + (-4) + 11$
(h) $-2 + (-7) + (-9)$
(i) $-1 + (-1) + (-1)$
(j) $15 + (-8) + (-8)$
(k) $-2 + 5 + (-8)$

(l) $5 + 0 + (-9)$
(m) $-12 + 5 + (-3) + 10$
(n) $-2 + (-7) + 6 + (-3)$
(o) $8 + (-9) + (-11) + 11$
(p) $7 + (-3) + (-5) + 5$

6. Complete the tables in your notebook.

(a)

x	x + 2
2	
1	
0	
-1	
-2	
-3	

(b)

x	x + (-5)
2	
1	
0	
-1	
-2	
-3	

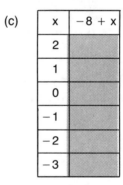

(c)

x	-8 + x
2	
1	
0	
-1	
-2	
-3	

(d)

x	-x + 3
2	
1	
0	
-1	
-2	
-3	

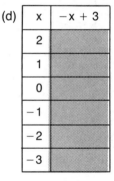

In the problems that follow, represent the values by suitable integers before attempting the calculations.

7. The temperature in Moose Factory was recorded as 3°C. In a 24 h period, the temperature dropped 5°C.

(a) Represent the temperature change as an integer.
(b) Find the new temperature.
(c) What temperature change will cause the temperature to drop from 2°C to -7°C?

8. The temperature in Edmonton at midnight was −1°C. The temperature changes were recorded hourly as shown in the table.

Time	Temp. Change	New Temperature
01:00	−2°C	
02:00	−3°C	
03:00	−2°C	
04:00	−1°C	
05:00	+1°C	
06:00	+2°C	

(a) Complete the table for the new temperatures in your notebook.
(b) Find the net temperature change over a 6 h period.

9. The average mass of the five member heavyweight wrestling team is 92 kg. Their individual mass is

87 kg, 93 kg, 90 kg, 92 kg, 98 kg

(a) Express each mass above or below the average as an integer.
(b) Find the sum of these integers.

10. The terms often used by golfers and sports broadcasters are:

double bogey : 2 over par
bogey : 1 over par
par
birdie : 1 under par
eagle : 2 under par

Represent each term by a suitable integer.

11. On the first nine holes of golf, Judy kept score as follows:

par, bogey, par, par, eagle,
birdie, par, double bogey, par.

Par is a rating used for each hole and represents the number of strokes a good player would take to complete the hole.

(a) Is Judy over or under par for the first nine holes?
(b) If par for the nine holes was 35, what was Judy's score?

12. The height above sea level of the Dead Sea in Asia is −400 m.
(a) What is the height above sea level of Mount Everest if it is 9248 m above the Dead Sea?
(b) What is the height of Kilimanjaro if it is 6295 m above the Dead Sea?
(c) What is the height of Mount McKinley if it is 6594 m above the Dead Sea?

13. The height above sea level of Death Valley, the lowest point in North America, is −86 m. The highest point in North America is Mount McKinley, which is 6280 m above Death Valley. What is the height above sea level of Mount McKinley?

14. During the first year of operation of Ben's Diner, the restaurant had a loss of $27 465. In the next two years, the restaurant operated with profits of $17 835 and $43 724. Express the net profit, or loss, for the three year period as an integer.

CALCULATOR MATH

ENTERING NEGATIVE NUMBERS

To enter a negative number, press the +/− key after the numeral. For example, to calculate

50 + (−20) + (−34)

Press C 5 0 + 2 0
+/− + 3 4 +/− =

and the display is −4

Calculate the following.

1. −3 + 5 + (−4)

2. 25 + (−3) − (−15)

3. −16 + (−10) + 25

3.3 SUBTRACTION OF INTEGERS

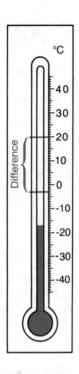

°C

40

30

20

10

0

-10

-20

-30

-40

Difference

In winter there is usually a difference between indoor and outdoor temperatures. On a typical day the outdoor temperature may be $-3°C$ and the indoor, 20°C.

Integers may be used to set up a model of this situation to determine the temperature difference.

EXAMPLE 1. Represent the temperatures 20°C and $-3°C$ by suitable integers and determine the temperature difference.

SOLUTION:

20°C becomes 20

$-3°C$ becomes -3

From the thermometer, we see that the difference is 23. Mathematically, we write

$$20 - (-3) = 23$$

In general, subtraction is the inverse operation of addition. That is, if $10 + (-3) = 7$, then $7 - (-3) = 10$. This idea provides one method for subtracting integers:

if $12 - (-7) = x$, then $x + (-7) = 12$
$$\therefore x = 19$$

To subtract an integer, we add its opposite.

EXAMPLE 2. Simplify.

(a) $9 - (-7)$ (b) $-3 - 12$ (c) $15 + (-8) - 3$

SOLUTION:

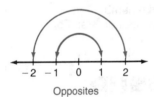

$-2 \quad -1 \quad 0 \quad 1 \quad 2$

Opposites

(a) $9 - (-7)$
     $= 9 + 7$
     $= 16$

(b) $-3 - 12$
     $= -3 + (-12)$
     $= -15$

(c) $15 + (-8) - 3$
     $= 15 + (-8) + (-3)$
     $= 7 + (-3)$
     $= 4$

If $x, y \in I$, $x - y = x + (-y)$

Check $15 + (-8) - 3$ on a calculator.

Press | C | 1 | 5 | + | 8 | +/- | − | 3 | = |

The display is | 0 | 1 | 15 | 15 | 8 | −8 | 7 | 3 | 4 |

EXERCISE 3.3

1. State the opposite of each of the following integers.

(a) 3   (b) −56   (c) 19
(d) 0   (e) −1   (f) −15
(g) −(−2)   (h) −(−5)   (i) −(+4)

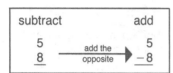

2. Subtract.

(a) 24   −19   (b) 18   18   (c) 5   8   (d) −7   3

(e) 12   −8   (f) 3   −7   (g) −5   −8   (h) 10   −4

(i) 0   −5   (j) −2   −2   (k) −8   −1   (l) −7   0

3. Simplify.

(a) 12 − 9   (b) 5 − (−2)
(c) 7 − (−1)   (d) −5 − (−9)
(e) −8 − 7   (f) 11 − 18
(g) 0 − (−5)   (h) −6 − 9
(i) −10 − (−10)   (j) 13 − (−8)
(k) −15 − (−3)   (l) −1 − 1
(m) −3 − 11   (n) 20 − 17
(o) 4 − (−5)   (p) −5 − 7

4. Simplify.

(a) 23 − (−7)   (b) −9 − (−12)
(c) 15 − (−8)   (d) 19 − 27
(e) 51 − 2   (f) −8 − (−8)
(g) 27 − (−30)   (h) 45 − 52
(i) −32 − (−3)   (j) −9 − 12
(k) −16 − 10   (l) −31 − 9
(m) −18 − 18   (n) −17 − 21
(o) −49 − 4   (p) −18 − (−24)

5. Simplify.

(a) 20 + (−7) − 10
(b) −53 + 3 − 50
(c) 36 − (−4) + (−8)
(d) −12 − (−3) + (−5)
(e) −56 + (−4) − (−60)
(f) −11 − 5 + (−3)
(g) −9 − 15 − (−10)

(h) −3 − 5 − 7
(i) −4 − 10 − 8
(j) −3 − (5 − 8)
(k) 10 + (−3 − 12)
(l) (15 − 21) + (−3 + 1)
(m) (6 − 2) − (−1 − 3)
(n) 8 + (4 − 9) − (−3 − 8)

6. The stock market report shows the net change in value of a stock from the previous day's closing price. Calculate the net change for the two days in each case below.

Stock	Net Change		
	Thursday	Friday	
Neonex	+47	−23	This is the net
Nordeen	−18	+30	change in
Normick P	−25	+11	value for each
Redstone	−10	−27	share in cents.
Rolland	+9	−15	
Superior A	−8	−19	

C 7. Complete the tables in your notebook.

(a)

x	−x
2	
1	
0	
−1	
−2	
−3	

(b)

x	7 − x
4	
2	
0	
−2	
−4	
−6	

(c)

x	x − 5
10	
5	
0	
−5	
−10	
−15	

(d)

x	−x − 2
2	
1	
0	
−1	
−2	
−3	

3.4 MULTIPLICATION OF INTEGERS

Multiplication of integers, as with whole numbers, is based on repeated addition. The following examples lead us to make the first two general statements.

$3 \times (+5) = (+5) + (+5) + (+5)$ $= +15$	The product of two positive integers is a positive integer. $\qquad (+a)(+b) = +ab$
$3 \times (-4) = (-4) + (-4) + (-4)$ $= -12$	The product of a positive integer and a negative integer is a negative integer. $\qquad\qquad (+a)(-b) = -ab$ and $\qquad (-a)(+b) = -ab$

Using these sign rules, we investigate the following patterns.

$3 \times 3 = 9$	$3 \times 3 = 9$	Note the	$(-5) \times 3 = -15$	$3 \times (-5) = -15$
$3 \times 2 = 6$	$2 \times 3 = 6$	pattern	$(-5) \times 2 = -10$	$2 \times (-5) = -10$
$3 \times 1 = 3$	$1 \times 3 = 3$	in the	$(-5) \times 1 = -5$	$1 \times (-5) = -5$
$3 \times 0 = 0$	$0 \times 3 = 0$	products.	$(-5) \times 0 = 0$	$0 \times (-5) = 0$
$3 \times (-1) = -3$	$(-1) \times 3 = -3$		$(-5) \times (-1) = 5$	$(-1) \times (-5) = 5$
$3 \times (-2) = -6$	$(-2) \times 3 = -6$	Continue	$(-5) \times (-2) = 10$	$(-2) \times (-5) = 10$
$3 \times (-3) = -9$	$(-3) \times 3 = -9$	the	$(-5) \times (-3) = 15$	$(-3) \times (-5) = 15$
$3 \times (-4) = \blacksquare$	$(-4) \times 3 = \blacksquare$	pattern.	$(-5) \times (-4) = \blacksquare$	$(-4) \times (-5) = \blacksquare$

The product of two integers with opposite signs is negative. $\qquad (+a)(-b) = -ab$ $\qquad (-a)(+b) = -ab$	The product of two integers with the same sign is positive. $\qquad (-a)(-b) = +ab$ $\qquad (+a)(+b) = +ab$

EXAMPLE. Perform the following computations using a calculator.
(a) $15 \times (-18)$
(b) 12×16
(c) $(-14) \times (+15)$

SOLUTION:
(a) $15 \times (-18)$

Press ▮C▮ ▮1▮ ▮5▮ ▮×▮ ▮1▮ ▮8▮ ▮+/−▮ ▮=▮

The display is `-270`

(b) 12×16

Press ▮C▮ ▮1▮ ▮2▮ ▮×▮ ▮1▮ ▮6▮ ▮=▮

The display is `192`

(c) $(-14) \times (+15)$

Press ▮C▮ ▮1▮ ▮4▮ ▮+/−▮ ▮×▮ ▮1▮ ▮5▮ ▮=▮

The display is `-210`

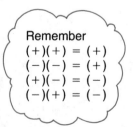

Remember
$(+)(+) = (+)$
$(-)(-) = (+)$
$(+)(-) = (-)$
$(-)(+) = (-)$

EXERCISE 3.4

1. Multiply.

(a) $(+3)(+5)$ (b) $2(-6)$ (c) $(-3)(+12)$
(d) $(-4)(-2)$ (e) $0 \times (-3)$ (f) $-4(-7)$
(g) 3×7 (h) $5(-7)$ (i) $-7(5)$
(j) $(-2)(-2)$ (k) 5×0 (l) $(-3)(10)$
(m) $(-8)(-7)$ (n) $12(-5)$ (o) $-9(-11)$
(p) -4×2 (q) -8×0 (r) $-1 \times (-6)$

2. Simplify.

(a) $(-20)(-1)(2)$ (b) $(-2)(-3)(-4)$
(c) $12(-1)(-3)$ (d) $-5 \times 2 \times 3$
(e) $(-2)(-2)(-2)$ (f) $-5 \times 3 \times (-4)$
(g) $0(-3)(-5)$ (h) $(-15)(-3)(-1)$
(i) $(-1)(-1)(-1)$ (j) $2 \times 7 \times (-2)$

3. Simplify.

(a) 5^2 (b) $(-4)^2$
(c) $(-1)^3$ (d) $(-3)^2$
(e) $(-3)^3$ (f) $(-2)^4$
(g) $(-2)^2 \times (-5)$ (h) $(-1) \times 6^2$
(i) $(-2)^3 \times (-3)$ (j) $(-1)^5 \times (-1)^4$

4.

(a) To show that
$-3(-7 + 8) = (-3)(-7) + (-3)(8)$,
evaluate (i) $-3(-7 + 8)$
       (ii) $(-3)(-7) + (-3)(8)$
(b) Show that $5(-3 + 8) = 5(-3) + 5(8)$
(c) Show that
$-8[4 + (-10)] = (-8)(4) + (-8)(-10)$
The results in problem 4 illustrate the
distributive property in I.

> If a, b, c ∈ I, then a(b + c) = ab + ac.

5. Use the distributive property to simplify the following expressions.

(a) $5(-3 + 7)$ (b) $-2(8 + 6)$
(c) $-3(9 + 2)$ (d) $-1(11 + 9)$
(e) $-5(-3 + 8)$ (f) $3[-2 + (-6)]$
(g) $7(-5 - 3)$ (h) $-4(-2 - 10)$
(i) $-1(-8 - 6)$ (j) $-2(-4 + 4)$

6. Use the correct order of operations to simplify the following problems.

(a) $(-3)(-5) + 2$ (b) $5(-3 + 7)$
(c) $-8(-2 - 7)$ (d) $4(12 - 18)$
(e) $(5 - 3)(7 - 11)$ (f) $10 + (-5)(-2)$

(g) $6 - (-2)(7)$ (h) $4 - 3(-6)$
(i) $12 - 5(-2)$ (j) $8 + (-3)(5)$
(k) $(-5)^2 + (-3)^2$ (l) $-2 - (-4)^2$
(m) $5(-3)(-2) - (-5)(2)$
(n) $-2(-5)^2 + 3(-1)$

C 7. Complete the tables in your notebook.

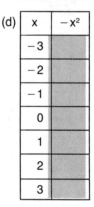

(a)

x	2x
-2	
-1	
0	
1	
2	
3	

(b)

x	-3x
-3	
-2	
-1	
0	
1	
2	

(c)

x	x³
-3	
-2	
-1	
0	
1	
2	

(d)

x	-x²
-3	
-2	
-1	
0	
1	
2	
3	

8. Evaluate for x = -5.

(a) $3x$ (b) $-2x$
(c) $-x$ (d) x^2
(e) $(-x)^2$ (f) $(-x)^3$
(g) $-4x^2$ (h) $(-4x)^2$

9. Evaluate for x = -4, y = 3.

(a) xy (b) $-xy$
(c) $5xy$ (d) $-3xy$
(e) $(xy)^2$ (f) x^2y
(g) xy^2 (h) $-2x^2y$
(i) $(-xy)^2$ (j) x^2y^2
(k) $(x^2y)^2$ (l) $-2(xy)^2$
(m) $x(-y)^2$ (n) $-x(2y)^2$
(o) $y(-2x)^2$ (p) $(-3x)(-4y)$

3.5 DIVISION OF INTEGERS

We use the fact that multiplication and division are inverse operations to derive rules for dividing positive and negative numbers.

$$4 \times 5 = 20 \text{ so that } 20 \div 5 = 4$$

same signs → positive quotient

$$(-10) \times (-3) = -30 \text{ so that } -30 \div (-3) = +10$$

Using inverses, the following tables demonstrate the rules for dividing integers.

Multiplication	Division		Multiplication	Division
$+3 \times (+5) = +15$	$\dfrac{+15}{+5} = +3$		$-6 \times (-3) = +18$	$\dfrac{+18}{-3} = -6$
$+4 \times (-3) = -12$	$\dfrac{-12}{-3} = +4$		$-4 \times (+7) = -28$	$\dfrac{-28}{+7} = -4$
$+18 \times (-2) = -36$	$\dfrac{-36}{-2} = +18$		$-4 \times 9 = -36$	$\dfrac{-36}{+9} = -4$
$+8 \times 6 = 48$	$\dfrac{+48}{+6} = +8$		$-4 \times (-11) = 44$	$\dfrac{+44}{-11} = -4$

> The quotient of two integers with the same sign is positive.
> $$\frac{+ab}{+a} = +b$$
> $$\frac{-ab}{-a} = +b$$

> The quotient of two integers with opposite signs is negative.
> $$\frac{-ab}{+a} = -b$$
> $$\frac{+ab}{-a} = -b$$

EXAMPLE. Perform the following computations using a calculator.
(a) $-360 \div (-15)$
(b) $-378 \div 21$
(c) $384 \div 32$

SOLUTION:
(a) $-360 \div (-15)$

Press `C` `3` `6` `0` `+/-` `÷` `1` `5` `+/-` `=`

The display is `24`

(b) $-378 \div 21$

Press `C` `3` `7` `8` `+/-` `÷` `2` `1` `=`

The display is `-18`

(c) $384 \div 32$

Press `C` `3` `8` `4` `÷` `3` `2` `=`

The display is `12`

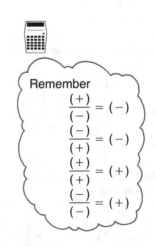

Remember
$$\frac{(+)}{(-)} = (-)$$
$$\frac{(-)}{(+)} = (-)$$
$$\frac{(+)}{(+)} = (+)$$
$$\frac{(-)}{(-)} = (+)$$

EXERCISE 3.5

A 1. Simplify.

(a) $\dfrac{18}{-9}$ (b) $\dfrac{-15}{3}$ (c) $\dfrac{12}{6}$

(d) $\dfrac{-36}{-9}$ (e) $\dfrac{45}{-9}$ (f) $\dfrac{56}{-7}$

(g) $\dfrac{48}{16}$ (h) $\dfrac{-21}{-3}$ (i) $\dfrac{7}{-7}$

(j) $\dfrac{72}{-8}$ (k) $\dfrac{-38}{-19}$ (l) $\dfrac{0}{-2}$

(m) $\dfrac{-60}{-4}$ (n) $\dfrac{120}{-40}$ (o) $\dfrac{-48}{16}$

B 2. Simplify.

(a) $25 \div (-5)$ (b) $-8 \div 8$
(c) $35 \div 7$ (d) $-63 \div (-7)$
(e) $-56 \div 2$ (f) $34 \div (-2)$
(g) $-44 \div (-11)$ (h) $45 \div 5$
(i) $65 \div (-13)$ (j) $-100 \div 5$
(k) $98 \div (-2)$ (l) $-69 \div (-3)$
(m) $0 \div (-1)$ (n) $-121 \div 121$
(o) $-73 \div (-73)$ (p) $-48 \div 16$

3. Simplify.

(a) $(-3)(8) \div 6$ (b) $\dfrac{5(-4)}{-10}$

(c) $\dfrac{2 \times 3}{-6}$ (d) $\left(\dfrac{27}{-3}\right)\left(\dfrac{5}{-1}\right)$

(e) $\dfrac{15(-2)}{(-3)(-1)}$ (f) $-5 + \left(\dfrac{12}{-4}\right)$

(g) $\dfrac{-8 + 2}{11 + (-5)}$ (h) $\dfrac{4 - 12}{3 - (-5)}$

(i) $\dfrac{42}{-7} - \dfrac{18}{2}$ (j) $(-3)^2 + \dfrac{27}{-9}$

(k) $-15 + 36 \div 4$
(l) $(3 - 5 - 6) \div (-4)$
(m) $0 - (-8) + 12 - 21$
(n) $\dfrac{-8 + 3 - 12 - 9}{-2}$

(o) $\dfrac{18 + (-12) \div 3}{20 \div (-2) - (-3)}$

(p) $\dfrac{8(-2)(-3)}{32 \div (-1 - 1)}$

(q) $\dfrac{4(-9 - 7)}{(-70 - 2) \div 9}$

(r) $54 \div (-3)(2) - (-1)$

Use integers to solve the following problems.

4. In a 7 d period, the temperature dropped a total of 21°C. Find the average temperature drop per day.

5. During one week in January, the daily temperatures in Montreal were recorded in the table.

Day	Temperature
Sun.	$-2°C$
Mon.	$-3°C$
Tues.	$-3°C$
Wed.	$-1°C$
Thurs.	$4°C$
Fri.	$0°C$
Sat.	$-2°C$

(a) Find the difference between the highest and lowest temperature.
(b) Find the average temperature for the week.

6. From sea level to the stratosphere, the temperature drops from approximately 15°C to -63°C.
(a) Find the difference between these temperatures.
(b) If the height of the stratosphere from the earth is approximately 27 km, find the average temperature drop per kilometre.

7. At 20:00 the temperature in Halifax was 3°C. Over the next 4 h, the temperature drop was 2°C/h.
(a) Express the drop in temperature per hour as an integer.
(b) Find the total drop in temperature in the four hours.
(c) Find the temperature at midnight.

3.6 APPLICATION OF INTEGERS: THE STOCK MARKET

The stock market report makes use of integers in showing daily changes in the value of stocks. In the examples selected below, the prices and changes are in cents.

Company Name	Number of shares sold	High	Low	Close	Net change from previous closing price
Stock	Sales	High	Low	Close	Change
Adanac M	1 000	24	24	24	−2
Advocate	800	380	360	360	−15
Am Eagle	5 500	56	55	56	+5
Bart C	5 642	165	150	155	+10
Biltmore 1	600	295	295	295	−5
Bl Hawk	1 000	12	11	11	−2
Black P A	800	460	440	450	−15
Blakwod A	6 700	340	320	330	−10
Bankeno	18 810	203	190	200	+9
Barex	300	7	7	7	
Bartaco	1 600	220	205	220	+5
Bary Expl	800	70	70	70	−5
Brinco	5 385	425	400	400	
CM Yachts	676	350	340	340	+25

Highest price paid per share   Lowest price paid per share   Value of each share when stock market closed

EXERCISE 3.6

Answer the following questions using the chart above.

B 1. Which stock showed the greatest gain in price?

2. Which stock showed the greatest loss in price?

3. Find the difference between the greatest gain and the greatest loss in price?

4. What integer could be used to show the net change of value of the Brinco shares?

5. Find the sum of the net changes for all of the stocks shown.

6. Find the gain or loss in value of the following for the day listed above.
(a) 800 shares of Advocate
(b) 5500 shares of Am Eagle
(c) 600 shares of Biltmore 1
(d) 300 shares of Barex
(e) 800 shares of Bary Expl
(f) 676 shares of CM Yachts

7. What is the change in value between 2000 shares of Bart C and 3000 shares of Blakwod A?

8. What is the change in value between 1000 shares of Adanac M, 1000 shares of Bl Hawk, and 1200 shares of Bartaco?

3.7 INTEGERS IN ALGEBRAIC EXPRESSIONS

In many expressions and formulas, the replacement set for the variables is the set of integers.

EXAMPLE 1.   Evaluate the following expressions if $x = -3$ and $y = 2$.
(a) $-5xy$ (b) $6y - 3x$
(c) $2x^2 - (x - y)$

SOLUTION:

(a) $-5xy = -5(-3)(2)$
$\qquad = 15 \times 2$
$\qquad = 30$

(b) $6y - 3x = 6(2) - 3(-3)$
$\qquad = 12 - (-9)$
$\qquad = 12 + 9$
$\qquad = 21$

(c) $2x^2 - (x - y) = 2(-3)^2 - (-3 - 2)$
$\qquad = 2(-3)(-3) - (-5)$
$\qquad = 2(9) - (-5)$
$\qquad = 18 + 5$
$\qquad = 23$

EXAMPLE 2.   Evaluate $E(-5)$ for the expressions
(a) $E(x) = 3x^2$ (b) $E(x) = -(2 - x)$

SOLUTION:

(a) $E(-5) = 3(-5)^2$
$\qquad = 3 \times (-5) \times (-5)$
$\qquad = 3 \times 25$
$\qquad = 75$

(b) $E(-5) = -[2 - (-5)]$
$\qquad = (-1) \times (2 + 5)$
$\qquad = (-1) \times 7$
$\qquad = -7$

EXAMPLE 3.   A formula for the addition of negative integers, $(-1) + (-2) + (-3) + (-4) + \ldots$ is

$$S = -\frac{n(n + 1)}{2}$$

where n is the number of integers to be added. Find the sum of the thousand integers from -1 to -1000.

SOLUTION:

$S_n = -\dfrac{n(n + 1)}{2}$ and $n = 1000$.

$S_n = -\dfrac{1000(1000 + 1)}{2}$
$\qquad = -500(1001)$
$\qquad = -500\ 500$

$\therefore (-1) + (-2) + (-3) + \ldots + (-999) + (-1000) = -500\ 500$

EXERCISE 3.7

A 1. If x = −2, evaluate

(a) 5x (b) x + 5 (c) x − 6 (d) x²
(e) − 2x (f) x³ (g) 3 − x (h) 2x²

2. If x = −8 and y = 2, evaluate

(a) xy (b) 3xy (c) x + y
(d) x − y (e) y − x (f) − 2xy
(g) $\dfrac{x}{y}$ (h) x + y + 8 (i) − 3x
(j) 2(x + y) (k) xy + 2 (l) 3 + x

3. If x = 5 and y = −3, evaluate

(a) − x (b) − y
(c) − xy (d) − (y + x)
(e) − (y − x) (f) − (x − y)
(g) − x² (h) − y²

4. If E(x) = 2x + 1, evaluate

(a) E(2) (b) E(− 2) (c) E(0)
(d) E(5) (e) E(− 10) (f) E(− 20)

B 5. If w = −7, evaluate

(a) − 3w (b) 2(w + 1) (c) − w
(d) 5(w + 3) (e) − (7 + w) (f) − 2(w + 8)
(g) − (w + 9) (h) 1 − w (i) 5 − 2w
(j) 3w + 9 (k) − w − 9 (l) − 3(8 − w)

6. If x = −3, evaluate

(a) x² + 1 (b) x² − 12
(c) 3x − 5 (d) (2x)²
(e) − 3x² (f) − x² + 10
(g) (5 − x)² (h) (x + 1)³
(i) − (x − 2)² (j) 3 − x²

7. Complete the tables in your notebook.

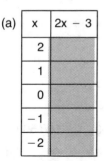

(a)

x	2x − 3
2	
1	
0	
− 1	
− 2	

(b)

x	x³
2	
1	
0	
− 1	
− 2	

(c)

x	x² − 5
2	
1	
0	
− 1	
− 2	

(d)

x	2 − x²
2	
1	
0	
− 1	
− 2	

8. If y = x² − 5x + 1, find the value of y when

(a) x = 2 (b) x = 1
(c) x = 0 (d) x = − 1
(e) x = − 2 (f) x = 4

9. If x = 2 and y = −4, evaluate

(a) x² + y (b) 3x + 2y
(c) x² + y² (d) 5x − 2y + 7
(e) x²y (f) xy²
(g) (xy)² (h) x(y − 2)
(i) (x + y)³ (j) (x + 2)(y + 1)
(k) x + y² − 2xy (l) 2x² − 3y

10. M represents the mean, or average, of the four values. Using the formula

$$M = \frac{a + b + c + d}{4}$$

calculate M, when
(a) $a = 5$, $b = -7$, $c = 12$, and $d = 6$
(b) $a = -9$, $b = -8$, $c = 3$, and $d = -10$

11. A formula for adding a series of numbers is

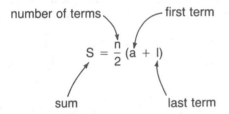

number of terms — first term

$$S = \frac{n}{2}(a + l)$$

sum — last term

(a) Calculate S for the series
$2 + 4 + 6 + 8 + 10 + 12 + 14 + 16 + 18$, when $n = 9$, $a = 2$, and $l = 18$.
(b) Calculate S when $n = 14$, $a = -50$, and $l = 15$.
(c) Calculate S for the series
$1 + 2 + 3 + \ldots + 98 + 99 + 100$.
(d) Calculate S for the series
$(-1) + (-2) + (-3) + \ldots + (-49) + (-50)$.

12. A paper dart is thrown from a second floor window and follows a path as shown.

The formula for the path of the flying dart is

$$h = -t^2 + 3t + 4$$

where h is the height in metres and t is the time in seconds. Explain the result for $t = 4$.

13. The velocity of the dart in question 12 is determined by the formula

$$v = 3 - 2t$$

where v is the velocity in metres per second (m/s) and t is the time in seconds (s).
(a) Complete the table in your notebook for the times given.

t	v
0	
1	
2	
3	
4	

(b) Why are some velocities negative?

C 14. If $x = -2$, and $y = -3$, show that
(a) $x^2 + y^2 - 2xy = (x - y)^2$
(b) $x^2 + y^2 + 2xy = (x + y)^2$
(c) $x^2 + y^2 = (x - y)^2 + 2xy$
(d) $x^2 + y^2 = (x + y)^2 - 2xy$
(e) $x^3 + y^3 = (x + y)(x^2 - xy + y^2)$
(f) $x^3 - y^3 = (x - y)(x^2 + xy + y^2)$
(g) $(2x + 3y)^2 = 4x^2 + 12xy + 9y^2$
(h) $(3x - 2y)^2 = 9x^2 - 12xy + 4y^2$
(i) $(x + y)(x - y) = x^2 - y^2$

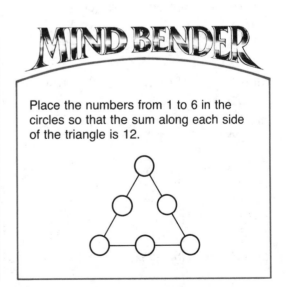

MIND BENDER

Place the numbers from 1 to 6 in the circles so that the sum along each side of the triangle is 12.

3.8 ADDING AND SUBTRACTING MONOMIALS

EXAMPLE 1. Simplify.

(a) $-5x + 7x$

(b) $3a^2 - 8a^2$

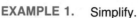
$-5x$ and $7x$ are like terms

SOLUTION:

(a) $-5x + 7x = (-5 + 7)x$
$\qquad = 2x$

(b) $3a^2 - 8a^2 = (3 - 8)a^2$
$\qquad = -5a^2$

When evaluating, it is often convenient to simplify the expression or formula before substituting values for the variables.

EXAMPLE 2. (a) Simplify the expression $-5x - 4y^2 + 9x + y^2$.
(b) Evaluate the expression when $x = -3$ and $y = 5$.

SOLUTION:

(a) $-5x - 4y^2 + 9x + y^2 = -5x + 9x - 4y^2 + y^2$
$\qquad = (-5 + 9)x + (-4 + 1)y^2$
$\qquad = 4x + (-3)y^2$
$\qquad = 4x - 3y^2$

(b) $4x - 3y^2 = 4(-3) - 3(5)^2$
$\qquad = -12 - 3(25)$
$\qquad = -12 - 75$
$\qquad = -87$

EXERCISE 3.8

A 1. Add.

(a) $\begin{array}{r} 8x \\ 11x \\ \hline \end{array}$

(b) $\begin{array}{r} 3x^2 \\ 5x^2 \\ \hline \end{array}$

(c) $\begin{array}{r} 2y \\ y \\ \hline \end{array}$

(d) $\begin{array}{r} -3xy \\ -5xy \\ \hline \end{array}$

(e) $\begin{array}{r} 12x^2 \\ -9x^2 \\ \hline \end{array}$

(f) $\begin{array}{r} -20y \\ 9y \\ \hline \end{array}$

(g) $\begin{array}{r} -8y \\ -9y \\ \hline \end{array}$

(h) $\begin{array}{r} -6z \\ 18z \\ \hline \end{array}$

(i) $\begin{array}{r} -12xy \\ 0 \\ \hline \end{array}$

(j) $\begin{array}{r} 18y^3 \\ -9y^3 \\ \hline \end{array}$

(k) $\begin{array}{r} wx \\ 9wx \\ \hline \end{array}$

(l) $\begin{array}{r} -12x \\ -x \\ \hline \end{array}$

2. Subtract.

(a) $\begin{array}{r} 12x \\ 7x \\ \hline \end{array}$

(b) $\begin{array}{r} 8x^2 \\ -5x^2 \\ \hline \end{array}$

(c) $\begin{array}{r} 3y \\ y \\ \hline \end{array}$

(d) $\begin{array}{r} 2z \\ 9z \\ \hline \end{array}$

(e) $\begin{array}{r} 4x^2 \\ 7x^2 \\ \hline \end{array}$

(f) $\begin{array}{r} -22x \\ 3x \\ \hline \end{array}$

(g) $\begin{array}{r} 0 \\ 3x \\ \hline \end{array}$

(h) $\begin{array}{r} -15xy^2 \\ 3xy^2 \\ \hline \end{array}$

(i) $\begin{array}{r} 8z \\ 8z \\ \hline \end{array}$

(j) $\begin{array}{r} -4x \\ 0 \\ \hline \end{array}$

(k) $\begin{array}{r} 0 \\ -9x \\ \hline \end{array}$

(l) $\begin{array}{r} -8y^2 \\ -8y^2 \\ \hline \end{array}$

(m) $\begin{array}{r} -5x \\ -9x \\ \hline \end{array}$

(n) $\begin{array}{r} 3z^2 \\ -9z^2 \\ \hline \end{array}$

(o) $\begin{array}{r} -18xy \\ -3xy \\ \hline \end{array}$

3. Simplify.

(a) $7x + 3x$

(b) $5y + (-8y)$

(c) $11z - 8z$

(d) $-5x + 4x$

(e) $6x^2 - 5x^2$

(f) $-4w + w$

(g) $3y - 5y$

(h) $-12xy + (-3xy)$

(i) $-24x - (-x)$

(j) $0 - (-5w)$

(k) $-13p - 8p$

(l) $4x^2y - (-3x^2y)$

(m) $8x - 19x$

(n) $-4w - w$

(o) $-12x - (-12x)$

(p) $-7x + (-3x)$

B 4. Simplify.

(a) $3x + 9x - 5y$

(b) $5xy + 7 + 10xy - 5$

(c) $4x + 9 - (-10) + 6x$

(d) $4y^2 - 3y^2 + 12y^2 - 15y^2$
(e) $3xyz - 5xy - 2xy - 7xyz$
(f) $12z - 5y + 14z - 5y$
(g) $14x^2 - 5x^2 + 3 - (-10)$
(h) $6x - 5y + 3x + 7y - 12x$
(i) $15x - 12z + 9x - 11z$
(j) $3 - 10x^2 + 5 + 7x^2 - 10 - 3x^2$

5. Simplify the given expressions, then evaluate when $x = -3$.
(a) $5x + 3x - 2x$
(b) $2x^2 + 3x$
(c) $-4x - (-5x)$
(d) $-2x^2 - 3x + 3x^2 + 5x$
(e) $15x - (-2x) + 3x - 10x$
(f) $x^2 - (-5x) + 2x^2 - x$
(g) $4x + 5x^3 - (-x) - 4x^3$
(h) $3x - 5x - 6x + 8x$

6. Simplify the given expressions and evaluate when $x = -2$, $y = 3$, and $z = -1$.
(a) $4xy - 3x + xy$
(b) $12x^4 + 2y - 8x^4 + y - 4x^4$
(c) $-4xyz - (-5xyz)$
(d) $-2x^2 - 3xy + 3x^2 + 5xy$
(e) $15x - (-2y) + 3z - 12x - z$
(f) $2yz - 5y^2 + (-3yz) - (-4y^2)$

7. (a) Write an expression for the perimeter of the rectangle.
(b) Evaluate the expression when $x = 7$.

8. (a) Write an expression for the perimeter.
(b) Evaluate the expression when $x = 5$.

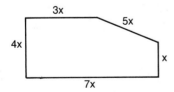

9. If the perimeter of the triangle is 56x, find the length of the third side.

10. The length of each side of the pentagon is $3 - 2x$.

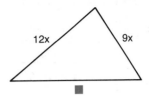

(a) Find the perimeter if $x = 1$.
(b) Find the perimeter if $x = 0$.
(c) Find the perimeter if $x = -1$.

Bob has a rectangular piece of canvas as shown.

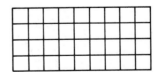

How can he cut it into two pieces so that he can sew it back together in the shape of a square?

3.9 MULTIPLYING AND DIVIDING MONOMIALS

In this section we extend our earlier work on multiplication and division of monomials to include integers. In working with the numerical coefficients, we use the sign rules of multiplication and division of integers.

Rules for Multiplication	Rules for Division
$(+a)(+b) = +ab$	$\dfrac{+ab}{+a} = +b$
$(+a)(-b) = -ab$	$\dfrac{-ab}{+a} = -b$
$(-a)(+b) = -ab$	$\dfrac{+ab}{-a} = -b$
$(-a)(-b) = +ab$	$\dfrac{-ab}{-a} = +b$

EXAMPLE. Simplify.

(a) $(-8x)(-2y^2)$

(b) $-20xyz^2 \div (+5xy)$

SOLUTION:

(a) $(-8x)(-2y^2) = [(-8)(-2)]xy^2$
$= [+16]xy^2$
$= 16xy^2$

(b) $-20xyz^2 \div (+5xy) = \dfrac{-20xyz^2}{+5xy}$

$= \left(\dfrac{-20}{+5}\right)\left(\dfrac{xyz^2}{xy}\right)$

$= -4z^2$

EXERCISE 3.9

B 1. Simplify.

(a) $(-5x)(+6y)$
(b) $3w(-2x)$
(c) $(-11y)(+7z)$
(d) $(-12xy)(-6z^2)$
(e) $\dfrac{+16xyz}{-8yz}$
(f) $\dfrac{-63xyz^2}{-9z^2}$
(g) $\dfrac{-28wxyz}{+4wz}$
(h) $\dfrac{45x^3y}{-9x^3}$

2. Multiply.

(a) $-8x$
$+3y$
(b) $-12wx$
$-4yz$
(c) $-9xy$
$-4z$
(d) $+2x$
$-5yz$

3. Divide.

(a) $\dfrac{+35xyz}{-5xz}$
(b) $\dfrac{-69z^2x}{23z^2}$
(c) $\dfrac{+50xyz^2}{+25xz^2}$
(d) $\dfrac{-55x^2yz}{+5x^2z}$
(e) $\dfrac{-48prs}{-6ps}$
(f) $\dfrac{+32xy^3z}{-8xz}$

4. Simplify.

(a) $(-17x)(+5y)$
(b) $32w(-4xy)$
(c) $(-11xy)(-15z)$
(d) $(-13w)(-17xy)$
(e) $(-27x^2)(-9y)$
(f) $(45x^3y)(-15z^2)$
(g) $(-17r)(-14s^2)$
(h) $-24rs(-12t^3)$

5. Simplify.

(a) $\dfrac{-48xy}{-8x}$
(b) $\dfrac{-125xyz}{-25x}$
(c) $\dfrac{+350xyz}{-25xz}$
(d) $\dfrac{+244wxy}{+61xy}$
(e) $\dfrac{-957z^2y}{-33z^2}$
(f) $\dfrac{-1470wx^2y}{+35x^2}$
(g) $\dfrac{-1536pqr}{-48r}$
(h) $\dfrac{+185x^3y^2}{-37x^3}$

6. Simplify.

(a) $\dfrac{(-12x)(+3y)}{+9y}$
(b) $\dfrac{(-17xy)(-15z^2)}{+5yz^2}$
(c) $\dfrac{-112xy}{(-7x)(8y)}$
(d) $\dfrac{(+16x^2y)(-9z)}{-12x^2yz}$

3.10 SIMPLIFYING ALGEBRAIC EXPRESSIONS

The simplification of algebraic expressions often involves multiplication and division. This requires the sign rules for integers.

EXAMPLE 1. Simplify.
(a) $-3(x + 9)$
(b) $-(2x - 5)$

SOLUTION:

(a)
$$\begin{aligned} -3(x + 9) &= (-3)(x) + (-3)(9) \\ &= -3x + (-27) \\ &= -3x - 27 \end{aligned}$$

> −1 is understood in front of the bracket.

(b)
$$\begin{aligned} -(2x - 5) &= (-1)(2x - 5) \\ &= (-1)(2x) + (-1)(-5) \\ &= -2x + 5 \end{aligned}$$

EXAMPLE 2. Simplify.
(a) $2(x + 5) - 3(x - 7)$
(b) $7x - (2x + 3)$

SOLUTION:

(a)
$$\begin{aligned} 2(x + 5) - 3(x - 7) &= (2)(x) + (2)(5) + (-3)(x) + (-3)(-7) \\ &= 2x + 10 + (-3x) + 21 \\ &= 2x + (-3x) + 10 + 21 \\ &= -x + 31 \end{aligned}$$

(b)
$$\begin{aligned} 7x - (2x + 3) &= 7x + (-1)(2x + 3) \\ &= 7x + (-1)(2x) + (-1)(3) \\ &= 7x + (-2x) + (-3) \\ &= 5x - 3 \end{aligned}$$

EXAMPLE 3. Evaluate $-3(x - 2) + 2(4 - x)$, for
(a) $x = 2$
(b) $x = -3$

SOLUTION:
Simplify the expression first.

$$\begin{aligned} -3(x - 2) + 2(4 - x) &= (-3)(x) + (-3)(-2) + (2)(4) + (2)(-x) \\ &= (-3x) + (6) + (8) + (-2x) \\ &= -3x + 6 + 8 - 2x \\ &= -5x + 14 \end{aligned}$$

(a) for $x = 2$,
$$\begin{aligned} -5x + 14 &= -5(2) + 14 \\ &= -10 + 14 \\ &= 4 \end{aligned}$$

(b) for $x = -3$,
$$\begin{aligned} -5x + 14 &= -5(-3) + 14 \\ &= 15 + 14 \\ &= 29 \end{aligned}$$

EXERCISE 3.10

A 1. Simplify.
(a) $3(x + 2)$
(b) $5(x - 2)$
(c) $4(2 - x)$
(d) $6(-6 + x)$
(e) $3(x + y)$
(f) $2(x - 3y)$
(g) $-3(x + 1)$
(h) $-2(-x + 3)$
(i) $-2(-x - 4)$
(j) $-4(-3 - x)$

2. Simplify.
(a) $3(2x + 6)$
(b) $5(-3y + 7)$
(c) $-3(x + y)$
(d) $-2(3x - 2)$
(e) $-(x + 5)$
(f) $4(x^3 + 5)$
(g) $12(x + 2y)$
(h) $-3(2x + 6)$
(i) $-(3x + 5)$
(j) $-8(x^2 + 1)$
(k) $-(-4x + 3)$
(l) $-4(3x^2 - 5)$

3. Simplify.
(a) $3(x - 2) + 5(x + 1)$
(b) $-2(x + 3) + 2(x - 4)$
(c) $4(x - 2) + 3(2 - x)$
(d) $-3(x + 4) - 5(x + 2)$
(e) $-6(x - 7) - 5(4 - x)$
(f) $4(6 - x) - 2(x + 4)$
(g) $4(x - 5) + 5(x - 2)$
(h) $-3(x + 3) - 2(x + 2)$
(i) $4(x - 3) + 3(x - 3)$
(j) $-5(4 - x) - 2(4 - x)$

B 4. Simplify.
(a) $3(x^2 + 2x - 5)$
(b) $5(2x^2 - 5x + 3)$
(c) $4(-3x^2 - 4x + 1)$
(d) $-2(x^2 - 2x + 4)$
(e) $-6(-x^2 + x - 1)$
(f) $-7(-2x^2 - 5x + 3)$
(g) $-5x^2 - 3(-x^2 + 2)$

5. Simplify.
(a) $\dfrac{12x - 6x + 2}{2}$
(b) $\dfrac{15x + 5 - 10x}{2}$
(c) $\dfrac{24x - 8x + 12}{4}$
(d) $\dfrac{-18x + 24x - 30}{-3}$
(e) $\dfrac{25x - 15 + 10x}{-5}$

6. Simplify, then evaluate when $x = -2$.
(a) $4(x - 2) + 7$
(b) $3x + 2(4x + 3)$
(c) $3(2x - 5) + 15$
(d) $12x^2 + (3x^2 + 7)$
(e) $3(x + 2) + 5(x - 1)$
(f) $4(3x^3 + 2) + 5(x^3 - 2)$
(g) $2(x + 5) + 7(3x - 1)$
(h) $6(x + 3) + 8(x + 2)$

7. Simplify.
(a) $4(x - 3) - 2(x + 5)$
(b) $2(y - 5) - 5(y + 2)$
(c) $5(x - y) - 2(x + y)$
(d) $5(x - 1) - 2(-3x + 4)$
(e) $4z^2(3z + 1) - 2z^3$
(f) $3x(y - 5) - 6x(5 - 2y)$
(g) $2x(5y - 2) - 3y(3 - x)$
(h) $6x - 3(x + 5)$
(i) $4xy - 2(xy - 7)$
(j) $8z - 10(3 - z)$

8. Simplify.
(a) $5x - (x + 2)$
(b) $3y - 5 - (2y - 3)$
(c) $(2x - 3) - (5x + 2)$
(d) $5(3y + 2) - (y + 7)$
(e) $(-3y^2 - 2) - (4y^2 + 3)$
(f) $7x^2(2x - 3) - x^2(3x^2 + 2)$
(g) $5(x + 2) - (-3x + 7)$
(h) $-(x + 6) + (5x - 9)$
(i) $-2(x - 3) - (-3x + 7)$
(j) $-(8y^2 - 1) - (7 - 9y^2)$

9. Develop an algebraic expression in simplest form to represent the area in

(a)

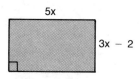

5x

3x − 2

(b)

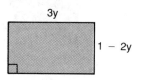

3y

1 − 2y

10. In the figure below, find an expression for
(a) the area of the large rectangle.
(b) the area of the small rectangle.
(c) the total area of the figure.

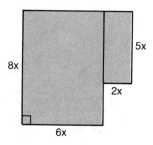

5x

8x

2x

6x

11. Find the total area in the figure.

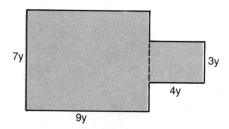

7y

3y

4y

9y

12. Find an expression for the area of the shaded portions in each figure.

(a)

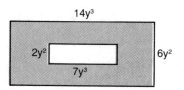

14y³

2y²

6y²

7y³

(b)

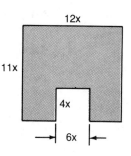

12x

11x

4x

6x

(c)

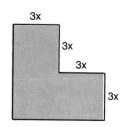

3x

3x

3x

3x

13. In the figure below, find an expression for
(a) the area of the large rectangle.
(b) the area of the small rectangle.
(c) the area of the shaded portion.

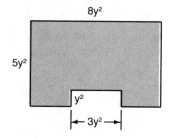

8y²

5y²

y²

3y²

MIND BENDER

Six water glasses are lined up in a row. The first three are full and the last three are empty.

Line up the glasses so that full glasses and empty glasses alternate by moving only one glass.

3.11 FLOW CHARTS

The order in which steps are performed to solve a problem or carry out a plan can be shown in a flow chart. The following symbols are used to represent the various parts of a flow chart.

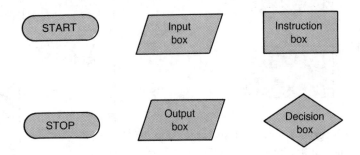

EXAMPLE 1. Follow the steps in the following flow chart to determine whether the year 2002 is a leap year.

SOLUTION:

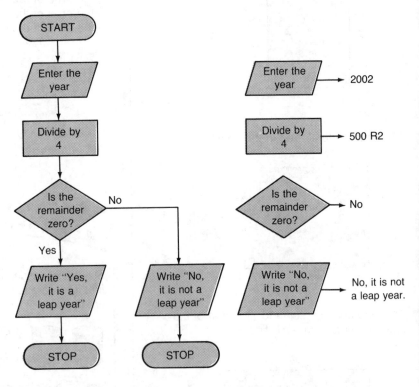

∴ the year 2002 is not a leap year.

The decision box can also be used to form loops that will provide several values for an expression as in the following example.

EXAMPLE 2. Find the output of the flow chart.

SOLUTION:
Working through the flow chart for x = 1,
the output is 1, 3.

Increasing x by 1, x = 2.
Working through the flow chart for x = 2,
the output is 2, 4.

Increasing x by 1, x = 3.
Working through the flow chart for x = 3,
the output is 3, 5.

This process is continued until x = 5,
making the output 1, 3
          2, 4
          3, 5
          4, 6
          5, 7

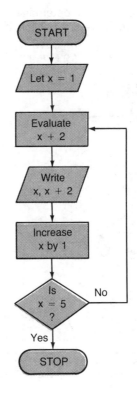

EXAMPLE 3. Arrange the following symbols to form a flow chart whose output is
49, 31, 17, 7, 1, −1, 1, 7, 17, 31, 49, when the input is −5.

START   Evaluate $2x^2 - 1$ Write $2x^2 - 1$ Is x = 5 ?

STOP   Increase x by 1   Let x = −5

SOLUTION:

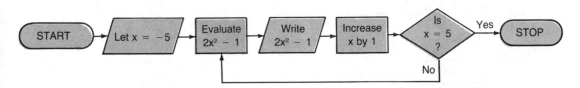

EXERCISE 3.11

B 1. Use the flow chart to determine which of the following numbers are divisible by 3.

(a) 2163　　　　　(b) 5216
(c) 46 509　　　　(d) 638 923

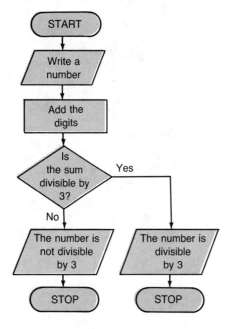

2. Write the output for the following flow charts.

(a)

(b)

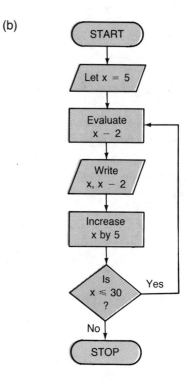

(c)

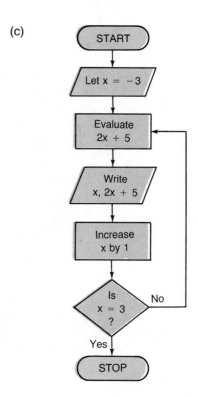

3. Write the output for the following flow charts.

(a)

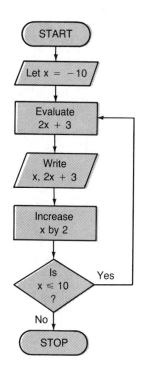

(b)

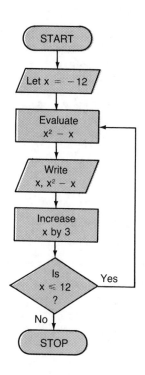

4. Arrange these symbols into a flow chart so that an input of -6 gives the output 34, 14, 2, -2, 2, 14, 34.

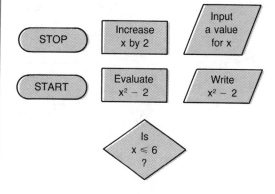

C 5. Draw flow charts to perform the following tasks.

(a) Evaluate $3x + 2$ for
$x = 0, 1, 2, 3, ..., 10$
(b) Evaluate $5 + 2x$ for
$x = -2, -1, 0, 1, 2, 3, 4$
(c) Evaluate $x^2 + 2x$ for
$x = -6, -4, -2, ..., 6$
(d) Evaluate $x(x - 2)$ for
$x = -10, -5, 0, 5, 10$
(e) Evaluate $3x^2 - 2$ for
$x = -6, -4, -2, ..., 8$
(f) Evaluate $x^3 - x^2 + x$ for
$x = -3, -2, -1, 0, 1, 2, 3, 4$

6. Draw flow charts to demonstrate the method for each of the following.

(a) Writing the squares of all the integers from -5 to 5.
(b) Writing the even integers from -10 to 10.
(c) Adding two numbers on a calculator.
(d) Making a telephone call from a pay phone, including when the line is busy.
(e) Depositing and withdrawing money from an automatic teller machine at a bank.

The year 1900 is divisible by 4 yet it is not a leap year. Why not?

3.12 BASIC COMPUTER LANGUAGE

BASIC is an acronym for Beginner's All-purpose Symbolic Instruction Code. It is a computer language that can be used to program a computer. The following chart gives the BASIC notation for the operations we use in mathematics.

Operation	Mathematics	BASIC
Addition	+	+
Subtraction	−	−
Multiplication	×	*
Division	÷	/
Raising to an exponent	exponent	∧ or ↑

EXAMPLE 1. Write these expressions in BASIC notation.
(a) 12.3 + 4.6
(b) 3.8^5
(c) x ÷ y
(d) ℓ × w

SOLUTION:

Expression	BASIC notation
(a) 12.3 + 4.6	12.3 + 4.6
(b) 3.8^5	3.8 ↑ 5
(c) x ÷ y	x / y
(d) ℓ × w	ℓ * w

When an expression contains more than one operation, the computer follows BEDMAS for the order of operations. The order of operations performed on a computer is the same as in mathematics.

In expressions like 7(6 + 8), where multiplication is understood, it is necessary to insert the * symbol when writing the expression in BASIC notation. Hence, the expression in BASIC is 7 * (6 + 8).

EXAMPLE 2. Write these expressions in BASIC notation.
(a) xy^3

(b) $\dfrac{x + y}{x - y}$

SOLUTION:

Expression	BASIC notation
(a) xy^3	x * y ↑ 3
(b) $\dfrac{x + y}{x - y}$	(x + y) / (x − y)

> Expressions with fractions are written on one line.

EXERCISE 3.12

1. Evaluate these expressions.
   (a) 5 * 3
   (b) 24 / 3
   (c) 2.4 − 8.4
   (d) 6 ↑ 2
   (e) (−2) ↑ 3
   (f) −2 ↑ 3
   (g) 2.5 * 2
   (h) 3 * (4 + 6)

2. Write these expressions in BASIC.
   (a) 5 × 6.3
   (b) − 12.3 ÷ 3
   (c) 2.4^2
   (d) 1.7 + 4.9
   (e) 6.2 ÷ 12.7
   (f) 2.5^3
   (g) 3.7 × 2.8

3. Write these expressions in BASIC.
   (a) 2.4(6.5 + 2.9)
   (b) (7.1 + 2.4)(3.7 − 6.3)
   (c) $(2.4 − 1.8)^2$
   (d) $(−1.6)^2 + 7.23$
   (e) $\dfrac{(−3.8)^2}{2.1 \times 4.3}$
   (f) (6.7 × 2.4)3.6

4. Evaluate these expressions.
   (a) 5 * 3 + 2
   (b) 5 + 3 * 2
   (c) 5 ↑ 2 + 2 ↑ 5
   (d) (5 + 7) ↑ 2
   (e) (2.7 + 3.3) * (5.5 − 2.5)
   (f) (6.3 − 5.7) ↑ 2 / (−0.5) + 1.4

5. Which is greater?
   (a) 2.5 − 3 ↑ 2   or   (2.5 − 3) ↑ 2
   (b) 7 ↑ 3 − 2   or   7 ↑ (3 − 2)
   (c) 11.5 − 3 ↑ 2   or   (11.5 − 3) ↑ 2
   (d) (3 * 2) ↑ 2   or   3 ↑ 2 * 2
   (e) 3.6 / 0.4   or   0.4 ↑ 2
   (f) 5 ↑ 2   or   2 ↑ 5
   (g) (2.1 + 3.9) ↑ 2   or   2.1 ↑ 2 + 3.9 ↑ 2

6. Write the following algebraic expressions in BASIC notation.
   (a) x + y   (b) x × y
   (c) 3.2x   (d) $x^2 + y^2$
   (e) $(x + y)^2$ (f) x × y ÷ z
   (g) x(x − y)   (h) $xy − x^2$

7. Write the following expressions in BASIC notation.
   (a) ℓw   (b) 2(ℓ + w)
   (c) 0.5bh   (d) 3.14d
   (e) $3.14r^2$ (f) (a + b)h ÷ 2
   (g) s^3 (h) 4s
   (i) a + b + c   (j) prt

8. Evaluate the following expressions for x = 2.3, y = 4.7, z = −4.4
   (a) x * y
   (b) (x + y) ↑ 2
   (c) x ↑ 2 + y ↑ 2
   (d) (x + y + z) ↑ 2
   (e) x ↑ 2 + y ↑ 2 + z ↑ 2
   (f) x * y − z
   (g) (x + y + 1.8) / z

What are the remaining numbers in the following list?

1 1 2 1 3 ... 12

3.13 "PRINT" AND "END" STATEMENTS

A program is a set of instructions that the computer carries out in a definite order. It is the purpose of a program to get data into the computer as input and to get information out as output. Each line of a program is numbered to tell the computer the order in which the instructions are to be carried out. Program lines or statements are usually numbered 10, 20, 30, ... so that other lines can be inserted if necessary, and numbered accordingly ... 11, 12 and so on.

The following program instructs the computer to print the result of multiplying 12.7 × 15.8.

```
NEW
10 PRINT 12.7*15.8
20 END
RUN
```

Before the program is keyed in, we type NEW and press the return key to clear away any other programs that may be in the memory of the computer. Line 10 is a PRINT statement that tells the computer to compute the product 12.7 × 15.8. Every program should finish with an END statement, as in line 20. After the program is keyed in, we type RUN and press Enter (or Return) to tell the computer to execute the program. There is no line number for the RUN command.

EXAMPLE 1. Write a program to compute $3.25^2 + 6.75^2$.

SOLUTION:
First we write the expression in BASIC notation.

$3.25^2 + 6.75^2$ is 3.25 ↑ 2 + 6.75 ↑ 2

The program is

RUN the program and check the answer.

```
NEW
10 PRINT 3.25↑2+6.75↑2
20 END
RUN
```

EXAMPLE 2. Write a program to compute $3.14 × 3.75^2$.

SOLUTION:
In BASIC notation

$3.14 × 3.75^2$ is 3.14 * 3.75 ↑ 2

The program is

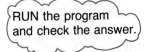
3.14*3.75↑2
is equivalent to
3.14*3.75*3.75

```
NEW
10 PRINT 3.14*3.75↑2
20 END
RUN
```
and the computer displays 44.15625.

EXERCISE 3.13

A 1. Explain what each of the following tells the computer to do.
   (a) NEW
   (b) RUN
   (c) PRINT
   (d) END

B 2. What is the output of each of the following programs?

(a) NEW
```
10 PRINT 3.14*78.5
20 END
RUN
```

(b) NEW
```
10 PRINT (-15)↑3
20 END
RUN
```

(c) NEW
```
10 PRINT (-2)↑4+4↑2
20 END
RUN
```

(d) NEW
```
10 PRINT (5-1)↑2/2↑3
20 END
RUN
```

(e) NEW
```
10 PRINT (2.4+4.8)/(1.2*3)
20 END
RUN
```

(f) NEW
```
10 PRINT 3.14*2.5↑2*12
20 END
RUN
```

(g) NEW
```
10 PRINT 3.5*(2.8+6.7)
20 END
RUN
```

(h) NEW
```
10 PRINT 2.7/0.3↑2+6.4/0.4↑3
20 END
RUN
```

3. Write a program to compute each of the following.
   (a) 5.6×7.8 (b) $64.7 - 21.9$
   (c) 736.3×0.675 (d) 1.065^5

4. Write a program to compute each of the following.
   (a) $\dfrac{5.75 + 3.68}{2.5}$
   (b) $\dfrac{6.8 \times 5.9}{3.57 \div 0.7}$
   (c) 3.14×6.2^2
   (d) $6.28 \times 4.25 \div 15.275$

5. (a) Use the given computer program to determine whether $(3.25 + 9.58)^2$ is greater than, equal to, or less than $3.25^2 + 9.58^2$.

```
NEW
10 PRINT (3.25+9.58)↑2-
   (3.25↑2+9.58↑2)
20 END
RUN
```

(b) Explain how you arrived at your conclusion?

6. Write computer programs to assist you in determining whether the first expression is less than, equal to, or greater than the second.
   (a) $(6.75 + 9.64)(6.75 - 9.64)$ and $6.75^2 - 9.64^2$
   (b) $5.25^2 + 4.15^2$ and $(5.25 + 4.15)^2$
   (c) $(3.2 - 1.4)(3.2^2 + 3.2 \times 1.4 + 1.4^2)$ and $3.2^3 - 1.4^3$
   (d) $(11.35 - 4.38)^2$ and $11.35^2 - 4.38^2$

7. Write computer programs to evaluate $E = 3x^3 - 2x^2 + 7x - 2.675$ for $x =$
   (a) 3.4
   (b) 6.8

Arrange these numbers in pairs so that all pairs have the same total.

21, 35, 26, 27, 33, 15, 39, 28, 19, 27

3.14 LET STATEMENT

A value can be assigned to a variable by using a LET statement.
Any letter of the alphabet can be used as a variable. In the following
program

```
NEW
10 LET X=-3
20 PRINT X↑2
30 END
RUN
```

line 10 is the LET statement. The computer will replace X by -3 in
the program. When the program is executed, the output is 9. In a LET
statement, the equal sign tells the computer to assign the value or
expression on the right to the variable on the left. LET statements can
be used to assign values to several variables.

EXAMPLE 1. Write a program to compute
$x^2 + y^2 + z^2$ for x = 3.8, y = 4.7, and z = 8.3.

SOLUTION:
First we write the expression in BASIC notation.

$$x^2 + y^2 + z^2 \text{ is } x↑2 + y↑2 + z↑2.$$

The program is

```
NEW
10 LET X=3.8
20 LET Y=4.7
30 LET Z=8.3
40 PRINT X↑2+Y↑2+Z↑2
50 END
RUN
```

Type NEW before
entering a new program.

The LET statement is another way to enter data into a program. In
most uses of the BASIC computer language, the word LET is optional
in statements. If we LET S = $x^2 + y^2 + z^2$, then the program in
Example 1 becomes

```
NEW
10 X=3.8
20 Y=4.7
30 Z=8.3
40 S=X↑2+Y↑2+Z↑2
50 PRINT X,Y,Z,S
60 END
RUN
```

EXAMPLE 2. Write a program to compute the volume of a cylinder
given

V = 3.14r²h, r = 6.75, and h = 9.54.

SOLUTION:
Writing the expression in BASIC,

$$V = 3.14r^2h \text{ is } V = 3.14 * r↑2 * h$$

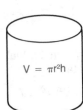

$V = \pi r^2 h$

The program is
```
NEW
10 R=6.75
20 H=9.54
30 V=3.14*R↑2*H
40 PRINT R,H,V
50 END
RUN
```

EXERCISE 3.14

1. Explain how a LET statement is used in writing computer programs.

2. What is the output of each of the following programs?

(a)
```
NEW
10 X=8
20 PRINT X+5
30 END
RUN
```

(b)
```
NEW
10 X=3.75
20 PRINT X,10*X
30 END
RUN
```

(c)
```
NEW
10 X=2.5
20 PRINT X,X↑2
30 END
RUN
```

(d)
```
NEW
10 X=3.5
20 Y=4.8
30 Z=X+Y
40 PRINT X,Y,Z
50 END
RUN
```

(e)
```
NEW
10 A=12
20 B=13
30 C=A-B
40 PRINT A,B,C
50 END
RUN
```

(f)
```
NEW
10 A=5
20 B=12
30 C=A↑2+B↑2
40 PRINT A,B,C
50 END
RUN
```

(g)
```
NEW
10 X=15
20 Y=25
30 Z=3X-Y
40 PRINT X,Y,Z
50 END
RUN
```

3. Write programs to compute the following.
(a) $x + 4$ for $x = 7.5$
(b) x^3 for $x = 8.2$
(c) $x - 12$ for $x = 9$
(d) y^6 for $y = 1.035$
(e) $5x^2$ for $x = 2.6$
(f) $2x - 3$ for $x = 1.8$
(g) $3.14r^2$ for $r = 2.5$

4. Write programs to compute the following.
(a) $x + y$ for $x = 7.5$, $y = 2.7$
(b) $(x + y)^2$ for $x = 3.5$, $y = 2.4$
(c) $(x - y)^2$ for $x = 5.75$, $y = 4.23$
(d) $x + y + z$ for $x = 7.87$, $y = 4.35$, $z = 7.12$
(e) $x^2 + y^2 + z^2$ for $x = 3.25$, $y = 4.65$, $z = 5.55$
(f) $(x + y + z)^2$ for $x = 3.2$, $y = 5.7$, $z = 9.3$

5. Write programs to compute the following.
(a) $x^3 + x^2 + 1$ for $x = 3$
(b) $2x^2 + 3x - 7$ for $x = 5$
(c) $2x^2 - 3x + 7.25$ for $x = 4.5$
(d) $x^3 + 3x^2 + 3x + 1$ for $x = 3.3$
(e) $(x + 3)^3$ for $x = 3.3$
(f) $(x + 1)^2 - (x^2 + 1)$ for $x = 5.8$

6. Write a program to determine whether $(x + y - z)^2$ is less than, equal to, or greater than $x^2 + y^2 + z^2$ for $x = 5.6$, $y = 2.3$, $z = 1.2$.

3.15 INPUT STATEMENT

An advantage in using computers is that we can perform the same calculation over again using different numbers. This is done using the INPUT statement.

When we execute a program with the statement

```
10 INPUT X
```

the computer will display a ?_ prompt and wait for the user to input a value for X. When the value for X has been entered the computer continues to the next instruction in the program. The following program will evaluate $E = 3x^2 - 2x + 7$ for values of x that you INPUT.

```
NEW
10 INPUT X
20 E=3*X↑2-2*X+7
30 PRINT X,E
40 END
RUN
```

The INPUT statement in line 10 tells the computer that a value for X will be inserted. When the program is executed by typing RUN, a prompt appears, ?_. After all INPUT values have been entered the computer continues to the end of the program.

EXAMPLE. (a) Write a program to evaluate $(x + y)^2 - 2xy$.
(b) RUN the program and find the value of the expression for
(i) x = 3.5, y = 2.7
(ii) x = 1.25, y = 3.75

SOLUTION:
(a) Writing the expression in BASIC

$(x + y)^2 - 2xy$ is $(x + y)↑2 - 2 * x * y$

The program is

```
NEW
10 INPUT X
20 INPUT Y
30 E=(X+Y)↑2-2*X*Y
40 PRINT E
50 END
RUN
```

(b) (i) When the program is RUN, and 3.5 and 2.7 are entered, the computer displays 19.54.
(ii) The program is executed again by typing RUN and entering 1.25 and 3.75 for x and y. The computer displays 15.625.

In order to avoid having to type RUN when we want to repeat the program, we can make the program reiterative by inserting the following lines in the program.

```
RUN
? 3.5
? 2.7
19.54
ANOTHER QUESTION?
Y OR N? Y
? 1.25
? 3.75
15.625
ANOTHER QUESTION?
Y OR N?
```

```
44 PRINT"ANOTHER QUESTION?"
45 INPUT"Y OR N";Z$
46 IF Z$="Y" THEN 10
```

EXERCISE 3.15

1. Explain how an INPUT statement is used in a program.

2. What is the output of each of the following programs?

(a) NEW
```
10 INPUT X
20 E=X↑2+5
30 PRINT X,E
40 END
RUN
```

Use the following values.
- (i) x = 3.5
- (ii) x = −5
- (iii) x = 11.2
- (iv) x = −12

(b) NEW
```
10 INPUT X
20 INPUT Y
30 E=5*X*Y-2*X-3*Y
40 PRINT X,Y,E
50 END
RUN
```

Use the following values.
- (i) x = 4, y = 5
- (ii) x = 3.5, y = 4.2
- (iii) x = −7, y = −9

(c) NEW
```
10 INPUT X
20 INPUT Y
30 INPUT Z
40 E=2*X-3*Y+4*Z
50 PRINT E
60 END
RUN
```

Use the following values.
- (i) x = 5.65, y = 1.25, z = 7.35
- (ii) x = −24, y = −18, z = 25
- (iii) x = −15, y = −12, z = −72

(d) NEW
```
10 INPUT X
20 INPUT Y
30 S=(X+Y)↑2
40 PRINT S
50 END
RUN
```

Use the following values.
- (i) x = 5, y = −3
- (ii) x = 6.25, y = 3.75
- (iii) x = 0.025, y = 0.045

3. Write programs to compute the following.

(a) $3x^2 + 5x + 3$ for the following values.
- (i) x = 8
- (ii) x = −5
- (iii) x = 2.5
- (iv) x = 1.25

(b) $5x^2 − 2x + 7$ for the following values.
- (i) x = 7
- (ii) x = −5
- (iii) x = 6.5
- (iv) x = 6.25

(c) $(x + y)^2$ for the following values.
- (i) x = 7, y = 9
- (ii) x = −5, y = −11
- (iii) x = 6.8, y = 3.7
- (iv) x = 1.25, y = 4.96

4. (a) Write a computer program to evaluate $E = x^2 − 4x − 1$.

(b) Use repeated trials and the program in (a) to find the smallest possible value of E for $−5 < x < 5$. Show your results in a table.

x	E
−5	
−4	

5. (a) Write a computer program to evaluate $E = −x^2 − 2x + 3$.

(b) Use repeated trials and the program in (a) to find the largest possible value of E for $−5 < x < 5$.

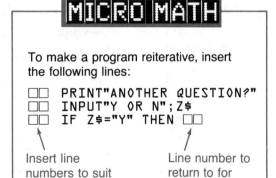

To make a program reiterative, insert the following lines:

```
□□  PRINT"ANOTHER QUESTION?"
□□  INPUT"Y OR N";Z$
□□  IF Z$="Y" THEN □□
```

Insert line numbers to suit the program.

Line number to return to for reiteration.

3.16 FOR—NEXT STATEMENTS

Computers are very helpful in printing out tables of values for algebraic expressions. The FOR—NEXT statement in a program permits us to print these tables for expressions, E(x), at regular values of x. The following program will print the positive integers from 1 to 12.

```
NEW
10 FOR X=1 TO 12
20 PRINT X
30 NEXT X
40 END
RUN
```

> Unless otherwise stated, the value of X is increased by 1.

When the computer reads line 10 the first time, X is assigned the value 1. At line 30, the computer returns to line 10, and increases the value of X by 1. This continues until the value of X reaches 12, when the computer goes to line 40.

EXAMPLE 1. Write a program to print the numbers from 1 to 15 and their squares.

SOLUTION:
The squares of the integers from 1 to 15 can be found using the expression $y = x^2$, for $x = 1, 2, 3, ..., 15$.
Writing in BASIC $y = x^2$ is $y = x \uparrow 2$.
The program is

```
NEW
10 FOR X=1 TO 15
20 Y=X↑2
30 PRINT X,Y
40 NEXT X
50 END
RUN
```

EXAMPLE 2. Write a program to evaluate $E = 2x^2 - 3x + 5$, for $x = -10, -8, -6, ..., 10$.

SOLUTION:
Writing E in BASIC, $E = 2x^2 - 3x + 5$ is $E = 2 * x \uparrow 2 - 3 * x + 5$

The program is

```
NEW
10 FOR X=-10 TO 10 STEP 2
20 E=2*X↑2-3*X+5
30 PRINT X,E
40 NEXT X
50 END
RUN
```

Adding STEP 2 to the FOR statement causes X to vary in increments of 2.

x RUN	E
-10	235
-8	157
-6	95
-4	49
-2	19
0	5
2	7
4	25
6	59
8	109
10	175

When no STEP is indicated in a FOR statement, the variable changes in increments of 1. Any other increment can be specified. These STEPS can be fractions or decimals such as $\frac{1}{2}$ or 0.5. Change the program in Example 2 so that the increment is 0.5.

EXERCISE 3.16

1. What will the following statements cause a program to do when combined with a NEXT statement?

(a) `10 FOR X=1 TO 7`
(b) `10 FOR X=-5 TO 3 STEP 2`
(c) `10 FOR X=-2 TO 2 STEP 0.5`
(d) `10 FOR X=-2 TO 2 STEP 0.25`

2. Insert FOR—NEXT statements to make the following program print the value for X and E with X ranging in value from -5 to 5 in increments of 2.
```
NEW
□□ E=2*X-5
□□ PRINT X,E
□□ END
RUN
```

3. (a) Find the output for the following program.
```
NEW
10 FOR X=-5 TO 5
20 E=X↑2-5*X-6
30 PRINT X,E
40 NEXT X
50 END
RUN
```
(b) For what values of X is E $= 0$?

4. (a) Find the output for the following program.
```
NEW
10 FOR X=-3 TO 3 STEP 0.5
20 E=2*X↑2-3*X-5
30 PRINT X,E
40 NEXT X
50 END
RUN
```
(b) For what values of X is E $= 0$?

5. Write programs to compute the following.
(a) the positive integers from 1 to 12
(b) the cubes of the integers from 1 to 12
(c) the even integers from 2 to 20
(d) the odd integers from 1 to 19

6. (a) Write a program to compute the values of E $= x^2 - 4x - 1$ for $-3 \leqslant x \leqslant 5$.
(b) What is the smallest value of E in the output?

7. Write programs to compute the following values. Use increments of 1 for x.
(a) E $= x^2 - 1$, for $-4 \leqslant x \leqslant 3$
(b) E $= 2x^2 - 5x - 3$, for $-5 \leqslant x \leqslant 3$
(c) E $= (x - 1)^3$, for $-3 \leqslant x \leqslant 3$
(d) E $= 3x^3 - 2x$, for $-2 \leqslant x \leqslant 3$

8. Write a program to compute the values of E $= 3x^2 - 5x + 7$ for $-10 \leqslant x \leqslant 10$ with x in increments of 10.

9. Write a program to compute the values of E $= (2x - 1)^2$ for $-2 \leqslant x \leqslant 3$ with x in increments of 0.5.

10. Write a program to compute the values of E $= x(x - 2)$ for x in increments of 0.5 from -2 to 4.

11. (a) Write a program to compute the following for $0 \leqslant x \leqslant 1$ with x in increments of 0.1.
  (i) y $= x^2$
  (ii) y $= x^4$
(b) For what values of x in the interval from 0 to 1 does $x^2 = x^4$?

12. (a) Find the output for the following program.
```
NEW
10 FOR X=1 TO 12
20 FOR Y=X TO 12
30 Z=X+Y
40 PRINT X,Y,Z
50 NEXT Y
60 NEXT X
70 END
RUN
```
(b) Explain the output of this program.
(c) Modify line 30 in the program to print a multiplication table from 1 × 1 to 12 × 12.

3.17 INTERNATIONAL STANDARD BOOK NUMBERS

All books now receive a coded 10-digit numerical label called an International Standard Book Number (ISBN). An ISBN is assigned to publishers for their books. This provides an easy way of ordering books and maintaining inventories. An ISBN is divided into four groups of numbers. The following is a typical ISBN.

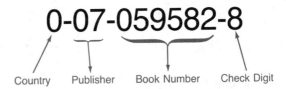

The first group of numbers indicates where the book is published (0 for English-speaking countries, 2 for French-speaking countries, 3 for German-speaking countries ...). The second group identifies the publisher (07 is the McGraw-Hill Ryerson number). The third group of digits (059582) is chosen by the publisher to identify the book. The final digit in the ISBN is the check digit. The check digit is either 1, 2, 3, 4, 5, 6, 7, 8, 9, or X (X stands for 10), and it is used to confirm that the other 9 digits are recorded correctly.

To determine the check digit, multiply the first 9 digits by 10, 9, 8, 7, 6, 5, 4, 3, and 2 respectively and add the products.

$$10(0) + 9(0) + 8(7) + 7(0) + 6(5) + 5(9) + 4(5) + 3(8) + 2(2) = 179$$

The check digit is chosen so that when added to the total, 179, the result is a multiple of 11. Therefore the check digit is 8.

EXERCISE 3.17

1. Determine if the following ISBNs are correct.

(a) 0-06-385445-6
(b) 0-8299-0087-X
(c) 0-673-13101-7
(d) 0-395-18978-2
(e) 0-07-082529-7

2. Determine the check digit for the following ISBNs.

(a) 0-07-082529-■
(b) 0-8129-0624-■
(c) 0-396-07451-■
(d) 0-201-05420-■
(e) 0-395-24579-■

3.18 UNIVERSAL PRODUCT CODE

The vertical bars on many products form the Universal Product Code. These bars in the UPC are scanned by an electronic reader and the signal is sent to a computer. The computer searches its memory for the name and price of the item, then prints these on the sales slip. Adjustments are also made to the list of inventory in the computer memory. The digits in the code are formed by patterns using 0 and 1, where 0 is a blank and 1 is a black bar.

The number system character, 0, indicates that the item is a standard supermarket item. Numbers are placed under the bars for reading by people. Not shown in the "human-readable" form, is the check digit. The check digit confirms that the other 11 digits have been scanned correctly. To find the check digit, we proceed as follows, using the example at the right.

1. Add the 2nd, 4th, 6th, 8th, and 10th digits.
$$1 + 3 + 5 + 7 + 9 = 25$$

2. Multiply the sum of the 1st, 3rd, 5th, 7th, 9th, and 11th digits by 3.
$$3 \times (0 + 2 + 4 + 6 + 8 + 0) = 60$$

3. Add. $25 + 60 = 85$

4. The check digit is the number that you add to 85 to give a multiple of 10. Since we add 5 to 85 to give 90, the check digit is 5.

EXERCISE 3.18

The check digit pattern has been cut off each of the following Universal Product Codes. Determine the check digit for each.

1. 0 ? 21120 05152

2. 0 ? 38000 41021

3. 0 ? 46000 09001

4. 0 ? 52600 11275

3.19 PROBLEM SOLVING

1.

You have five brass discs that have masses of 1 g, 2 g, 4 g, 8 g, and 16 g. How many different masses can you balance on the scale using one or more of the brass discs?

2. Name the wheels that are turning counter-clockwise.

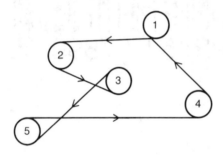

3. The stock market report on Stopco is shown below.

Stock	Sales	High	Low	Close	Ch'ge
StopC	19 300	155	120	120	−35

(a) If Mr. Good's shares decreased in value by a total of $112.00, how many shares did he have?
(b) Mr. Wood sold all of his shares at the highest price per share, for a total of $775.00.
   (i) How many shares did he sell?
   (ii) How much money did he gain by not selling at the low price?

4. A golfer shot four rounds of golf with an average score of 2 under par per round.

(a) How many strokes below par is the golfer after 4 rounds?
(b) If par is 71, what is the total score after the four rounds?

5. The commuter train arrived at Astor station where 7 people got on and 6 people got off. At Belleville station, 12 people got on and 11 people got off. At Carlisle station, 18 people got on and 7 got off. When the train left Carlisle station, there were 56 passengers on it. How many passengers were on the train when it originally arrived at Astor station?

6. If you pick a number, add 12, multiply by 5, and finally subtract 11, you get 124. What is the number?

7. In how many ways can a group of 4 be seated at a round table?

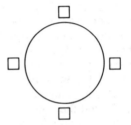

8. The sum of two consecutive integers is +25. Find the integers.

9. Find two consecutive integers whose product is +20.

10. A computer monitor and printer together cost $1125. One of these items costs $150 more than the other.

(a) Can you tell which of the items costs more?
(b) What is the difference in price?
(c) What are the individual prices of the items?

11. The following are the first four triangular numbers.

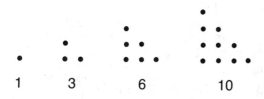

| 1 | 3 | 6 | 10 |

The mathematician Gauss thought that every positive integer could be written as the sum of, at most, three triangular numbers. Write the following numbers as the sum of, at most, three triangular numbers.

(a) 34   (b) 73   (c) 88

12. The following chart shows the average daily high and average daily low for selected Canadian locations during the month of March.

Location	Average High	Average Low
Calgary, Alberta	3	−10
Churchill, Manitoba	−16	−27
Halifax, Nova Scotia	3	−5
Thunder Bay, Ontario	−1	−11
Vancouver, B.C.	10	3
Yellowknife, N.W.T.	−12	−24

(a) What is the difference between the high and low in Calgary?
(b) What is the difference between the average daily high in Calgary and Halifax?
(c) What is the difference between the average daily high in Churchill and Vancouver?
(d) Which location has the warmest temperature?
(e) Which location has the coldest temperature?
(f) What is the difference between the highest average and the lowest average temperatures given in the chart?
(g) What is the difference between the average daily low in Calgary and Vancouver?

13. The width of a rectangle is one-half of the length. The perimeter of the rectangle is 120 cm. Find the length and width.

14. It takes 800 tiles measuring 1 cm by 1 cm to form a rectangle. There are 116 tiles around the outer edge of the rectangle. What are the dimensions of the rectangle?

15. The length of a rectangle is 3 more than twice the width. The perimeter of the rectangle is 150 cm. What are the dimensions of the rectangle?

16. The sum of two integers is 24. One of the integers is −11. What is the other integer?

17. Using only the digits
    1, 2, 3, 4, 5, 6
write two three-digit numbers that will give the greatest product.

18. A photograph 20 cm by 26 cm is to be surrounded by a 3 cm border called a mat. What are the dimensions of the glass that must be used to cover the photograph and mat?

19. The elevation of the entrance to the Consolidated Northern Basin gold mine is 486 m above sea level. The shaft is 2142 m deep. What is the elevation of the bottom of the shaft?

Put the numbers from 1 to 9 in the spaces to make the statements true. (Add brackets if necessary.)

■ + ■ ÷ ■ = 3

■ − ■ ÷ ■ = 3

■ − ■ − ■ = 3

3.20 REVIEW EXERCISE

1. Add.

(a) 15
   −3

(b) −8
   −2

(c) −7
   1

(d) −11
   8

(e) 0
   −9

(f) −9
   9

(g) 5x
   3x

(h) −7x²
   2x²

(i) −9xy
   −3xy

(j) 2x³
   −3x³

(k) 4y
   −3y

(l) 0
   −5x³

2. Subtract.

(a) 10
   12

(b) −12
   5

(c) −3
   2

(d) −1
   −4

(e) 0
   −2

(f) 8
   −6

(g) 14x
   9x

(h) −18y
   2y

(i) 3y²
   −5y²

(j) 4xy
   11xy

(k) −5w²
   −3w²

(l) −8y
   −15y

3. Simplify.

(a) $3(-6)$

(b) $(-5)(-6)$

(c) $(-8)^2$

(d) $0(-8)$

(e) $(-7) \times 2$

(f) -8×7

(g) $(-9)^2(-1)$

(h) $(-3)^3$

(i) $\dfrac{24}{-8}$

(j) $\dfrac{-28}{-7}$

(k) $\dfrac{-65}{5}$

(l) $-\dfrac{48}{3}$

(m) $42 \div (-7)$

(n) $(-72) \div (-9)$

(o) $(-99) \div 9$

(p) $120 \div (-40)$

4. Simplify.

(a) $5 - 8 + 12$
(b) $-7 + 2 + 10$
(c) $8 - 9 - 3$
(d) $7 + (-3) - 1$
(e) $4 - (-7)$
(f) $0 - (-9) + 7$
(g) $11 - (-7 + 2)$
(h) $3 - 8 - 7$
(i) $-9 - 4 - 3$
(j) $0 - 4 - 3$
(k) $1 - 5 - 7 + 12$
(l) $(-3 + 1) - (-8 + 2)$

5. Simplify.

(a) $6 + 3(-3)$

(b) $1 - 2(5)$

(c) $-(-8 + 2)$

(d) $(-7 - 5) \div 4$

(e) $3(-2 + 6) - (-8)$

(f) $(-8 + 1)(3 - 10)$

(g) $(-5)(-3) - 2(8)$

(h) $5 - 2(-1)$

(i) $\dfrac{(-8)(-2) - (-5)}{-3}$

(j) $\dfrac{4(-12) - 2}{10}$

(k) $\dfrac{5(-2) - 3(5)}{(-1)(-5)}$

(l) $\dfrac{4(-8 - 7)}{-15}$

(m) $\dfrac{3(-1 - 7) - (-4)}{2(-5)}$

(n) $\dfrac{(-3)^2(-5)}{3}$

(o) $\dfrac{(-2)^3 - 10}{(-3)^2}$

(p) $\dfrac{5 - (-7)^2}{-11}$

6. Graph the following sets.

(a) $\{x \mid x < -2, x \in I\}$
(b) $\{y \mid y \leq 3, y \in I\}$
(c) $\{w \mid w \geq -2, w \in I\}$
(d) $\{x \mid -1 \leq x < 3, x \in I\}$
(e) $\{y \mid -4 < y < 5, y \in I\}$
(f) $\{y \mid y < 0 \text{ or } y > 4, y \in I\}$
(g) $\{x \mid x \geq -2, x \in I\} \cap \{x \mid x < 1, x \in I\}$

7. If $x = -5$ and $y = 2$, evaluate the following expressions.

(a) $x + 2y$ (b) $3x - y$ (c) $5x^2$
(d) $7x - 3y$ (e) $2(y + x)^2$ (f) $x^2 - 3y^2$

8. If $E(x) = 2x^3 - 3x + 1$, find

(a) $E(2)$ (b) $E(0)$ (c) $E(-1)$
(d) $E(3)$ (e) $E(5)$ (f) $E(-3)$

9. Complete the tables in your notebook.

(a)

x	5 − x
3	
1	
0	
−1	
−3	
−5	

(b)

x	2x² − 4
2	
1	
0	
−1	
−2	
−3	

10. Simplify.
(a) $4x - x$
(b) $7y - 12y$
(c) $-5w + 3w$
(d) $4xy + 7xy - 12xy$
(e) $6x - 10 + 4x + 2$
(f) $14y^2 - 11y^2 - 3y^2$
(g) $15 - 2x - 8 + 5x$
(h) $5y - 7x + 3y - 2x$
(i) $-3xy - 2xy - xy$
(j) $15xy^2 - 2y + 10y - 6xy^2$
(k) $8x - x + 10x - 15x$
(l) $5x^2 + 6 - 5x - 7x + 3x^2$
(m) $4x - 7x + 15x - 12x$
(n) $4y - 3 - 6y - 7$

11. Simplify.
(a) $(-3x)(5y)$
(b) $(-2x)(-4x^3)$
(c) $(5x^2)(-3x^3)$
(d) $-1(-3x^2)$
(e) $(-3xy)(2x)$
(f) $(8x^2y^3)(-3x^2y^2)$
(g) $(-3x)(-2y)(-5y)$
(h) $(7x^2)(-3x^5)$
(i) $(3y)(5y)(-2y^3)$
(j) $(xy)(-xy)$
(k) $-12w(-6w)$
(l) $(5xy)(xy^3)$

12. Simplify.
(a) $\dfrac{-48x^2}{6}$
(b) $\dfrac{27x^2y}{-9y}$
(c) $\dfrac{-15w}{-3w}$
(d) $\dfrac{-18x^5}{18x}$
(e) $\dfrac{8t^2}{-8t}$
(f) $\dfrac{33x^2y^5}{-11x^2y}$
(g) $\dfrac{56xyz}{-7xy}$
(h) $\dfrac{15x^{10}y^2}{-15x^{10}y^2}$
(i) $(-9x^4) \div (-3x^2)$
(j) $(8x^{10}) \div (-2x^6)$
(k) $(-32w^3) \div (8w)$
(l) $(-48x^5yz^2) \div (16xyz)$

13. Simplify using the distributive property.
(a) $8x + 2(x + 5)$
(b) $5(x + 7) - 2x + 3$
(c) $4(w + 2) + 3(w - 5)$
(d) $3x^2 + 5x(x + 2)$
(e) $5y + 2 + 3(2y - 5)$
(f) $-2x(x + 1) - 3x^2 + 7x$
(g) $-4(x + 7) + 2(2x + 1)$
(h) $3(2y + 7) - 5(x + 2)$
(i) $-(3xy + 5) + 2(5 - 3xy)$
(j) $2(x - 3) - 3(1 - 2x)$
(k) $2x(1 - 2x) - x(3x - 2)$
(l) $3(2x - 5) - (5x + 2)$
(m) $4(3y - 2) - (5 + 3y)$

14. Evaluate these expressions.
(a) $3 * (5 - 2) \uparrow 2$
(b) $3 \uparrow 2 - 2 \uparrow 3$
(c) $5 * 3 \uparrow 2$
(d) $12 / 3 * 2$
(e) $5 + 2 * 2 + 3$
(f) $(3.6 / 0.4) \uparrow 2$

15. Evaluate $x \uparrow 2 - 2 * x * y$ for $x = 2$, $y = -3$.

16. What is the output of the following program?
```
NEW
10 X=2.5
20 Y=1.6
30 Z=2*X-3*Y
40 PRINT X,Y,Z
50 END
RUN
```

17. Write a program to compute the value of
$$\frac{4.5^2 + 3.85}{2.6 \times 5.7}$$

18. (a) Write a program that will compute a value of $E(x) = 5x^2 - 7x$.
(b) Find.
   (i) $E(-3)$
   (ii) $E(0)$
   (iii) $E(5)$
   (iv) $E(-7)$

19. Write a program to print the squares of 2, 4, 6, 8, 10.

20. Write a program to compute the values of $E = 2x^2 - 8x + 7$ for $x = 1, 2, 3, ..., 11$.

21. Write a program to compute the values of $E = 1 - x^3$ for $-1 \leqslant x \leqslant 1$ in increments of 0.5.

Complete the table.

2	3	4	5	5	7		10
1	2	4	4	6	12	10	

3.21 CHAPTER 3 TEST

1. Graph the following set on an integer line.
$$\{x \mid -3 < x \leqslant 3, x \in I\}$$

2. Simplify.
(a) $(+3)(-9)$
(b) $(-7)(-4)$
(c) $(-5)(+8)$
(d) $\dfrac{-24}{-6}$
(e) $\dfrac{18}{-3}$
(f) $\dfrac{-30}{5}$
(g) $(-9)(3)$
(h) $\dfrac{-20}{-5}$
(i) $-12(-5)$
(j) $-3 + (-5)$
(k) $-4 - (-11)$
(l) $(+3) + (-7)$
(m) $(-5) + (+12)$
(n) $-7 - (-4)$
(o) $-8 - (-12)$

3. Simplify.
(a) $+12 + (-25) + (+11)$
(b) $-15 - (+12) - (-7)$
(c) $(-3)(-8) \div (+2)$
(d) $(-36) \div (+9) \times (-3)$
(e) $-3[2 + 4(5 - 7)]$
(f) $(+4) - 2[(12 - 15) \div 3]$

4. If $E(x) = 2x - 7$, find
(a) $E(2)$
(b) $E(0)$
(c) $E(-3)$

5. Evaluate $S = \dfrac{n}{2}[2a + (n - 1)d]$ for $a = 2, d = -3, n = 24$.

6. Simplify.
(a) $11x - 15x$
(b) $3x^2 - 5x + 4x^4 + 2x$
(c) $5x - 2y - 5x - 2y$
(d) $5x - 3 + 7 - 8x^2$

7. Simplify.
(a) $-5(2x - 3)$
(b) $(-3x)(5y)$
(c) $4(2x + 3) - (2x - 1)$
(d) $\dfrac{(-3y)(4x)}{-24xy}$

8. Evaluate $3 \uparrow 2 * 5 / 15 * 2$.

9. Write a program to compute the values of $E = x(x - 5)$ for $x = -5, -4, -3, ..., 5$.

RATIONAL NUMBERS

CHAPTER

That vast book which stands forever open before our eyes. I mean the universe cannot be read until we have learned the language. It is written in mathematical language, and its characteristics are triangles, circles and other geometric figures, without which it is humanly impossible to comprehend a single word; without these one is wandering about a dark labyrinth.

Galileo

REVIEW AND PREVIEW TO CHAPTER 4

COMMON FRACTIONS

EXERCISE

1. Complete the following to form true statements.

(a) $\frac{1}{3} = \frac{\blacksquare}{12}$

(b) $\frac{3}{8} = \frac{\blacksquare}{16}$

(c) $\frac{20}{30} = \frac{\blacksquare}{3}$

(d) $5 = \frac{5}{\blacksquare}$

(e) $3 = \frac{\blacksquare}{2}$

(f) $10 = \frac{100}{\blacksquare}$

(g) $\frac{\blacksquare}{8} = \frac{21}{24}$

(h) $\frac{7}{\blacksquare} = \frac{21}{30}$

(i) $3\frac{1}{2} = \frac{\blacksquare}{2}$

(j) $4\frac{3}{5} = \frac{\blacksquare}{5}$

(k) $1\frac{2}{3} = \frac{\blacksquare}{3}$

(l) $\frac{\blacksquare}{5} = \frac{28}{35}$

2. Replace $\blacksquare$ with $>$ or $<$ to form a true statement.

(a) $\frac{2}{5} \blacksquare \frac{3}{5}$

(b) $3\frac{1}{3} \blacksquare 3\frac{1}{2}$

(c) $\frac{1}{2} \blacksquare \frac{3}{8}$

(d) $\frac{2}{3} \blacksquare \frac{5}{6}$

(e) $\frac{4}{5} \blacksquare \frac{7}{10}$

(f) $\frac{3}{5} \blacksquare \frac{3}{4}$

(g) $\frac{11}{8} \blacksquare 1\frac{1}{2}$

(h) $\frac{7}{12} \blacksquare \frac{3}{8}$

3. Perform the indicated operation. All answers should be expressed in lowest terms.

(a) $\frac{2}{5} + \frac{1}{5}$

(b) $\frac{6}{7} - \frac{3}{7}$

(c) $\frac{2}{5} + \frac{3}{10}$

(d) $\frac{5}{9} - \frac{5}{18}$

(e) $\frac{3}{4} + \frac{1}{2}$

(f) $\frac{5}{8} - \frac{1}{2}$

(g) $2\frac{1}{3} - \frac{2}{3}$

(h) $1\frac{3}{4} + \frac{1}{2}$

(i) $\frac{5}{12} - \frac{1}{3}$

(j) $2\frac{1}{4} - \frac{5}{8}$

(k) $1\frac{5}{6} + \frac{2}{3}$

(l) $3\frac{1}{2} - 2\frac{3}{4}$

(m) $1\frac{3}{4} + \frac{1}{2}$

(n) $3\frac{5}{8} - 1\frac{1}{4}$

(o) $4\frac{1}{2} - \frac{9}{2}$

(p) $2\frac{1}{8} - \frac{1}{2}$

(q) $3\frac{1}{3} - \frac{5}{6}$

(r) $4\frac{3}{4} - 2\frac{7}{8}$

4. Simplify.

(a) $\frac{1}{3} + \frac{2}{5} - \frac{1}{6}$

(b) $1\frac{1}{2} + \frac{2}{3} - \frac{3}{4}$

(c) $2\frac{1}{2} - \frac{3}{5} + \frac{1}{4}$

(d) $\frac{2}{3} + \frac{5}{6} - \frac{1}{2}$

(e) $\frac{1}{3} + \frac{3}{8} - \frac{1}{6}$

(f) $5\frac{1}{3} + \frac{3}{10} - 1\frac{1}{6}$

(g) $\frac{2}{5} - \frac{1}{7} + 1$

(h) $\frac{7}{8} + 1\frac{1}{4} + \frac{2}{3}$

5. Simplify.

(a) $\frac{3}{5} \times \frac{2}{7}$

(b) $\frac{1}{4} \times \frac{1}{2}$

(c) $\frac{3}{4} \times \frac{1}{3}$

(d) $\frac{5}{6} \times \frac{2}{3}$

(e) $3 \times \frac{1}{4}$

(f) $1\frac{1}{2} \times \frac{1}{2}$

(g) $3\frac{1}{2} \times 2$

(h) $2\frac{1}{3} \times \frac{15}{16}$

(i) $-\frac{1}{3} \times 5\frac{1}{4}$

(j) $\frac{1}{2} \times 3\frac{1}{2}$

(k) $1\frac{1}{2} \times 3\frac{1}{5}$

(l) $2\frac{1}{4} \times 1\frac{1}{3}$

6. Simplify.

(a) $\frac{2}{3} \div \frac{1}{5}$

(b) $\frac{3}{5} \div \frac{1}{2}$

(c) $\frac{1}{9} \div \frac{1}{3}$

(d) $\frac{5}{12} \div \frac{3}{4}$

(e) $1\frac{1}{2} \div 3$

(f) $2 \div \frac{1}{2}$

(g) $\frac{1}{2} \div 2$

(h) $\frac{2}{5} \div 2$

(i) $\frac{1}{12} \div 2\frac{1}{3}$

(j) $13 \div 3\frac{1}{4}$

(k) $9 \div 1\frac{1}{2}$

(l) $1 \div 1\frac{1}{2}$

7. Simplify.

(a) $5\frac{1}{2} \times \frac{3}{11} \times \frac{4}{5}$

(b) $\frac{3}{4} \times (\frac{1}{3} + \frac{1}{4})$

(c) $1\frac{1}{4} \div (\frac{3}{4} \times \frac{1}{2})$

(d) $4 \times \frac{3}{4} \div 3$

(e) $3 \times \frac{5}{6} \div 1\frac{1}{3}$

(f) $(\frac{2}{5} + \frac{1}{10}) \times (1\frac{1}{2} - \frac{5}{12})$

(g) $\frac{1}{5} + \frac{2}{3} \times 1\frac{3}{4}$

(h) $\frac{3}{5}(\frac{2}{3} + \frac{1}{4})$

8. Simplify.

(a) $(\frac{2}{5})^3$

(b) $\frac{4}{3} \div (\frac{2}{3})^2$

(c) $(\frac{5}{8} \times \frac{4}{15})^2(\frac{3}{2})^3$

(d) $(\frac{1}{2} - \frac{5}{12})^2 \div (\frac{1}{6})^2$

(e) $(\frac{3}{4} - \frac{1}{2})^2 \div 1\frac{1}{3}$

(f) $(\frac{1}{2} + \frac{1}{3})^2 - (\frac{1}{2})^2 - (\frac{1}{3})^2$

(g) $(\frac{2}{3} \times \frac{1}{2})^2 + (\frac{2}{3} \div \frac{1}{2})^2$

9. Find.

(a) $\frac{2}{3}$ of 12   (b) $\frac{3}{4}$ of 16

(c) $\frac{3}{4}$ of 12   (d) $\frac{2}{3}$ of 15

(e) $\frac{5}{8}$ of 16   (f) $\frac{5}{8}$ of 24

(g) $\frac{1}{10}$ of 200   (h) $\frac{3}{10}$ of 200

10. Find the amount.

(a) $\frac{1}{2}$ of $30   (b) $\frac{1}{4}$ of $60

(c) $\frac{1}{3}$ of $60   (d) $\frac{1}{8}$ of $200

(e) $\frac{1}{5}$ of $20   (f) $\frac{1}{5}$ of $50

(g) $\frac{1}{10}$ of $400   (h) $\frac{1}{100}$ of $400

(i) $\frac{1}{100}$ of $4000   (j) $\frac{1}{10}$ of $4000

11. Arrange in order from smallest to largest.

(a) $\frac{3}{7}, \frac{5}{7}, \frac{4}{7}, \frac{1}{7}, \frac{6}{7}, \frac{2}{7}$

(b) $\frac{1}{2}, \frac{3}{4}, \frac{5}{8}, \frac{1}{4}, \frac{1}{8}, \frac{7}{8}$

(c) $\frac{1}{2}, \frac{2}{3}, \frac{5}{6}, \frac{1}{3}, \frac{3}{2}, \frac{1}{6}, \frac{7}{6}$

(d) $\frac{1}{5}, \frac{1}{10}, \frac{1}{2}, \frac{3}{10}, \frac{7}{10}, \frac{4}{5}, \frac{2}{5}, \frac{9}{10}$

(e) $1\frac{1}{2}, 2\frac{1}{2}, \frac{4}{3}, 1\frac{1}{4}, 1\frac{3}{4}, 1\frac{5}{8}, 1\frac{2}{3}$

(f) $2\frac{1}{2}, 2\frac{3}{4}, 3\frac{1}{5}, 2\frac{3}{8}, 3\frac{1}{10}, 2\frac{7}{8}$

12. Which is greater?

(a) $\frac{2}{3}$ of 12   or $\frac{3}{4}$ of 16

(b) $\frac{5}{8}$ of 16   or $\frac{1}{2}$ of 24

(c) $\frac{2}{3}$ of 18   or $\frac{1}{3}$ of 15

(d) $\frac{7}{8}$ of 24   or $\frac{3}{4}$ of 28

(e) $\frac{3}{5}$ of 15   or $\frac{1}{3}$ of 30

(f) $\frac{1}{10}$ of 100   or $\frac{1}{5}$ of 25

13. There are 150 boys and 175 girls in grade nine. $\frac{2}{3}$ of the boys have blue eyes and $\frac{2}{5}$ of the girls have blue eyes. How many of the students have blue eyes?

14. One hundred fifty of 450 students rode bicycles to school. What fraction of the students rode bicycles to school?

WORD LADDER

Start with the word POST and change one letter at a time to form a new word until you reach MAIL. The best solution has the fewest steps.

P O S T

_ _ _ _

_ _ _ _

_ _ _ _

_ _ _ _

M A I L

4.1 RATIONAL NUMBERS AND EQUIVALENT FORMS

From the set of integers,

$$I = \{... -3, -2, -1, 0, 1, 2, 3, ...\}$$

we can construct a new set of numbers called the rational numbers. They are called rational numbers because they can be expressed in the form of a ratio of two integers.

$$\frac{-2}{5} \qquad \frac{3}{-1} \qquad \frac{3}{4} \qquad \frac{16}{3} \qquad \frac{10}{-2} \qquad \frac{0}{3}$$

Since the fractional form $\frac{a}{b}$ suggests division, it is usual to denote this set by the letter Q, the first letter in the word quotient.

$$Q = \left\{ \frac{a}{b} \,\middle|\, a, b \in I, b \neq 0 \right\}$$

Why must we state that $b \neq 0$? Recall that division is the inverse operation of multiplication.

$$\frac{6}{3} = 2 \text{ since } 2 \times 3 = 6$$

With this in mind, the problem of division by zero is illustrated in the following way.

$$\frac{5}{0} = \blacksquare \text{ implies that } \underbrace{\blacksquare \times 0 = 5}$$

no value of $\blacksquare$ will make
this statement true.

Since there is no answer to this problem, we make the following statement.

> Division by zero is not defined.

As with other sets of numbers, rational numbers may be located on a number line.

In this way, every rational number may be associated with a point on a number line. Recall that numbers increase in numerical value from left to right on the number line. Thus $-2\frac{1}{4}$ is smaller than -2.

It is possible to write an equivalent form of any rational number. Recall that $\frac{7}{7} = \frac{10}{10} = 1$. Similarly $\frac{-2}{-2} = \frac{-15}{-15} = 1$.

EXAMPLE 1. Express each rational number in an equivalent form.

(a) $\frac{3}{-5}$ (b) $-\frac{-10}{-12}$ (c) $\frac{-4}{5}$ (d) -5

SOLUTION:

(a) $\frac{3}{-5} = \frac{3}{-5} \times 1$

$\quad = \frac{3}{-5} \times \frac{-2}{-2}$

$\quad = \frac{-6}{10}$

(b) $-\frac{-10}{-12} = -\frac{-10}{-12} \times 1$

$\quad = -\frac{-10}{-12} \times \dfrac{\frac{1}{2}}{\frac{1}{2}}$

$\quad = -\frac{5}{6}$

> 1 is the identity element under multiplication.

(c) $\frac{-4}{5} = \frac{-4}{5} \times 1$

$\quad = \frac{-4}{5} \times \frac{-1}{-1}$

$\quad = \frac{4}{-5}$

(d) $-5 = -5 \times 1$

$\quad = -5 \times \frac{3}{3}$

$\quad = \frac{-15}{3}$

The results of Example 1 suggest the following general statement.

$$\frac{-a}{b} = \frac{a}{-b} = -\frac{a}{b} = -\frac{-a}{-b}, \text{ where } b \neq 0$$

Rational numbers can be compared using the lowest common denominator (LCD).

EXAMPLE 2. Which is smaller, $\frac{-9}{13}$ or $\frac{-3}{4}$?

SOLUTION:
The LCD of 13 and 4 is 52.

> < less than
> > greater than

$\frac{-9}{13} \times \frac{4}{4} = \frac{-36}{52}$ | $\frac{-3}{4} \times \frac{13}{13} = \frac{-39}{52}$

$\therefore \frac{-3}{4} < \frac{-9}{13}$

EXERCISE 4.1

1. State two equivalent forms for each of the following rational numbers.

(a) $\frac{2}{5}$ (b) $\frac{-1}{3}$ (c) $3\frac{1}{2}$

(d) $\frac{9}{13}$ (e) $\frac{7}{-8}$ (f) $-1\frac{1}{5}$

(g) -2 (h) 4 (i) $\frac{-6}{-7}$

(j) $-\frac{5}{7}$ (k) $\frac{9}{4}$ (l) $\frac{-5}{11}$

2. Mark the location of each of the following rational numbers on a suitable number line.

$-1\frac{3}{4}, \frac{7}{8}, \frac{-6}{-2}, \frac{5}{3}, \frac{6}{-10}, \frac{-8}{3}$

3. Arrange the following lists of rational numbers in order from largest to smallest.

(a) $\frac{1}{2}, \frac{3}{4}, 1\frac{1}{5}, -\frac{2}{3}, \frac{-7}{4}, \frac{17}{10}, -1, 2$

(b) $\frac{2}{3}, \frac{-3}{-4}, \frac{3}{4}, 0, -\frac{4}{5}, \frac{7}{10}, \frac{-2}{5}$

(c) $\frac{7}{3}, \frac{5}{8}, \frac{-5}{2}, \frac{6}{5}, \frac{-3}{8}, \frac{11}{9}, \frac{-13}{15}$

(d) $\frac{2}{3}, \frac{5}{8}, \frac{-3}{4}, \frac{3}{4}, \frac{-1}{2}, \frac{2}{5}$

(e) $1\frac{1}{2}, 1\frac{3}{4}, \frac{7}{3}, \frac{5}{2}, 1\frac{7}{8}, \frac{9}{7}$

(f) $-\frac{3}{4}, \frac{-5}{8}, -\frac{2}{3}, -\frac{1}{2}, -\frac{3}{7}, \frac{-2}{5}$

4.2 MULTIPLICATION OF RATIONAL NUMBERS

All operations involving rational numbers may be compared to previous operations with integers and common fractions.

$$\frac{2}{3} \times \frac{4}{5} = \frac{2 \times 4}{3 \times 5} \qquad \frac{-3}{4} \times \frac{1}{2} = \frac{-3 \times 1}{4 \times 2}$$

$$= \frac{8}{15} \qquad\qquad = \frac{-3}{8}$$

EXAMPLE. Simplify.

(a) $\frac{-5}{4} \times (-3)$ (b) $\frac{-3}{-5} \times \frac{1}{-6}$ (c) $\left(-2\frac{1}{2}\right)\left(\frac{3}{5}\right)\left(-\frac{2}{9}\right)$

SOLUTION:

(a) $\frac{-5}{4} \times (-3)$

$= \frac{-5}{4} \times \frac{-3}{1}$

$= \frac{(-5) \times (-3)}{4 \times 1}$

$= \frac{15}{4}$

(b) $\frac{-3}{-5} \times \frac{1}{-6}$

$= \overset{1}{\underset{}{\cancel{\frac{-3}{5}}}} \times \frac{1}{\underset{-2}{\cancel{-6}}}$

$= \frac{1}{-10}$

(c) $\left(-2\frac{1}{2}\right)\left(\frac{3}{5}\right)\left(-\frac{2}{9}\right)$

$= \overset{-1}{\underset{1}{\cancel{\frac{-5}{2}}}} \times \overset{1}{\underset{1}{\cancel{\frac{3}{5}}}} \times \overset{-1}{\underset{3}{\cancel{\frac{-2}{9}}}}$

$= \frac{(-1) \times 1 \times (-1)}{1 \times 1 \times 3}$

$= \frac{1}{3}$

$$\text{If } \frac{a}{b}, \frac{c}{d} \in Q, \text{ then } \frac{a}{b} \times \frac{c}{d} = \frac{ac}{bd}$$

EXERCISE 4.2

A 1. Simplify.

(a) $\frac{3}{4} \times \frac{1}{7}$ (b) $\frac{1}{2} \times \frac{2}{3}$

(c) $\frac{-3}{2} \times \frac{1}{5}$ (d) $\frac{2}{-5} \times \frac{-1}{3}$

(e) $2 \times \frac{3}{5}$ (f) $-\frac{3}{11} \times \frac{2}{5}$

(g) $\frac{1}{5} \times \left(-\frac{2}{11}\right)$ (h) $\frac{4}{-3} \times \frac{-3}{4}$

(i) $0 \times \left(-\frac{1}{5}\right)$ (j) $\frac{3}{4} \times \frac{-12}{5}$

(k) $\left(-\frac{1}{2}\right)\left(-\frac{1}{3}\right)$ (l) $3\left(-\frac{1}{2}\right)$

B 2. Find the products.

(a) $1\frac{1}{4} \times \frac{2}{3}$ (b) $3\frac{1}{2} \times \frac{-3}{14}$

(c) $\frac{-2}{5} \times 5\frac{1}{6}$ (d) $\frac{3}{-7} \times 1\frac{5}{9}$

(e) $-1\frac{1}{3} \times 1\frac{1}{2}$ (f) $-3\left(4\frac{1}{3}\right)$

(g) $\left(-1\frac{1}{3}\right)\left(-4\frac{1}{2}\right)$ (h) $-3\left(5\frac{2}{3}\right)$

(i) $\left(\frac{-1}{-4}\right)\left(-3\frac{1}{5}\right)$ (j) $\frac{-4}{5} \times \left(-1\frac{1}{4}\right)$

(k) $\left(\frac{-5}{3}\right)\left(\frac{-2}{-15}\right)$ (l) $\left(-2\frac{1}{4}\right)\left(\frac{4}{5}\right)$

3. Simplify.

(a) $\frac{1}{-3} \times \frac{7}{8} \times \frac{1}{2}$ (b) $\frac{5}{6} \times 1\frac{2}{3} \times \frac{-3}{10}$

(c) $\left(-1\frac{1}{5}\right)\left(\frac{-2}{3}\right)\left(\frac{5}{12}\right)$ (d) $2\frac{1}{5} \times \frac{-3}{4} \times 0$

(e) $\left(1\frac{4}{5}\right)\left(\frac{-1}{3}\right) \times 3$ (f) $\left(\frac{-5}{3} \times \frac{3}{10}\right)(-2)$

(g) $\left(-\frac{3}{5}\right)\left(1\frac{7}{10}\right)\left(-\frac{5}{3}\right)$ (h) $\frac{-1}{10} \times \frac{3}{-5} \times \frac{5}{9}$

4. Simplify.

(a) $\left(\frac{3}{4}\right)^2$ (b) $\left(\frac{-1}{2}\right)^2$ (c) $\left(\frac{-4}{5}\right)^2$

(d) $\left(\frac{1}{10}\right)^3$ (e) $\left(-\frac{1}{3}\right)^3$ (f) $5 \times \left(-\frac{1}{5}\right)^2$

(g) $\left(\frac{1}{3}\right)^3(-3)$ (h) $\left(\frac{-2}{3}\right)^2\left(\frac{1}{2}\right)^3$ (i) $\left(\frac{3}{-4} \times \frac{2}{9}\right)^2$

5. Calculate the areas of the rectangles.
(a)

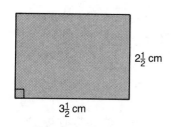

$2\frac{1}{2}$ cm

$3\frac{1}{2}$ cm

(b)

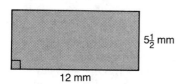

$5\frac{1}{2}$ mm

12 mm

(c)

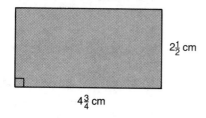

$2\frac{1}{2}$ cm

$4\frac{3}{4}$ cm

6. The average person spends $\frac{1}{3}$ of a lifetime in sleep.
(a) How many hours will a person sleep in 30 d?
(b) How many hours will be spent sleeping in $7\frac{1}{2}$ d?

7. Outboard motor oil is to be mixed with gasoline in the ratio 36 mL of oil per litre of gasoline. How many millilitres should be added to $5\frac{1}{2}$ L of gasoline?

8. The distance that an object falls is determined by the time that it is in the air. We use the formula

$$d = 490t^2$$

distance in centimetres ↗   ↖ time in seconds

Calculate the distance fallen in the following times.

(a) $\frac{1}{10}$ s   (b) $\frac{3}{10}$ s

(c) $\frac{3}{20}$ s   (d) $\frac{7}{10}$ s

9. Calculate the area of the shaded figures.
(a)

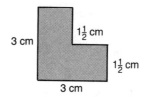

3 cm
$1\frac{1}{2}$ cm
$1\frac{1}{2}$ cm
3 cm

(b)

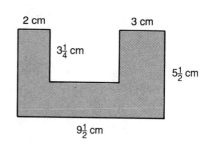

2 cm   3 cm
$3\frac{1}{4}$ cm
$5\frac{1}{2}$ cm
$9\frac{1}{2}$ cm

(c)

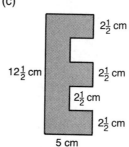

$2\frac{1}{2}$ cm
$12\frac{1}{2}$ cm
$2\frac{1}{2}$ cm
$2\frac{1}{2}$ cm
$2\frac{1}{2}$ cm
5 cm

These 12 coins look the same, but one is heavier than the others. Describe the method that involves the least number of weighings to detect the counterfeit coin.

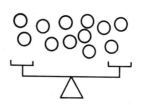

4.3 DIVISION OF RATIONAL NUMBERS

Multiplication and division are related in the same way as addition and subtraction, that is, they are inverse operations. In subtraction, we found that we could add the opposite to find the answer.

$$5 - (-3) = 5 + (+3)$$
$$= 8$$

Verify. $8 + (-3) = 5$

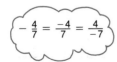
-3 and 3 are opposites (additive inverses)

In division, a similar idea may be used; we can multiply by the reciprocal.

> Two numbers are said to be reciprocals or multiplicative inverses of each other if their product is 1.

Thus, $\frac{1}{2} \div \frac{2}{3} = \frac{1}{2} \times \frac{3}{2}$

$$= \frac{3}{4}$$

Verify. $\overset{1}{\underset{2}{\cancel{\frac{3}{4}}}} \times \overset{1}{\underset{1}{\cancel{\frac{2}{3}}}} = \frac{1}{2}$

$\frac{3}{2}$ is the reciprocal of $\frac{2}{3}$ because $\frac{2}{3} \times \frac{3}{2} = 1$

> If $\frac{a}{b}, \frac{c}{d} \in Q$ and $b, c, d \neq 0$, then $\frac{a}{b} \div \frac{c}{d} = \frac{a}{b} \times \frac{d}{c} = \frac{ad}{bc}$

EXAMPLE 1. State the reciprocals of the following rational numbers, and check by multiplication.

(a) $\frac{3}{-5}$ (b) $-1\frac{3}{4}$

SOLUTION:

(a) The reciprocal of $\frac{3}{-5}$ is $\frac{-5}{3}$.

Check.

$$\overset{1}{\underset{1}{\cancel{\frac{3}{-5}}}} \times \overset{1}{\underset{1}{\cancel{\frac{-5}{3}}}} = 1$$

(b) Since $-1\frac{3}{4} = -\frac{7}{4}$, the reciprocal of $-1\frac{3}{4}$ is $-\frac{4}{7}$.

Check.

$$(-1\tfrac{3}{4})(-\tfrac{4}{7}) = (-\tfrac{7}{4})(-\tfrac{4}{7})$$

$$= \overset{1}{\underset{1}{\cancel{\frac{7}{4}}}} \times \overset{1}{\underset{1}{\cancel{\frac{4}{7}}}}$$

$$= 1$$

$-\frac{4}{7} = \frac{-4}{7} = \frac{4}{-7}$

EXAMPLE 2. Simplify.

(a) $\frac{3}{-5} \div 1\frac{3}{5}$ (b) $1\frac{1}{2} \div (-5)$ (c) $(-\frac{1}{2})(\frac{1}{5}) \div (-2\frac{1}{2})$

SOLUTION:

(a) $\quad \frac{3}{-5} \div 1\frac{3}{5}$

$\quad = \frac{3}{-5} \div \frac{8}{5}$

$\quad = \frac{3}{\overset{-1}{\underset{}{-5}}} \times \frac{\overset{1}{\cancel{5}}}{8}$

$\quad = -\frac{3}{8}$

(b) $\quad 1\frac{1}{2} \div (-5)$

$\quad = \frac{3}{2} \div \frac{-5}{1}$

$\quad = \frac{3}{2} \times \frac{1}{-5}$

$\quad = -\frac{3}{10}$

(c) $\quad (-\frac{1}{2})(\frac{1}{5}) \div (-2\frac{1}{2})$

$\quad = \frac{-1}{2} \times \frac{1}{5} \div \frac{-5}{2}$

$\quad = \frac{-1}{\underset{1}{\cancel{2}}} \times \frac{1}{5} \times \frac{\overset{1}{\cancel{2}}}{-5}$

$\quad = \frac{-1}{-25}$

$\quad = \frac{1}{25}$

EXERCISE 4.3

1. State the reciprocal of each of the following.

(a) $\frac{2}{3}$ (b) $\frac{5}{6}$ (c) $\frac{-3}{4}$

(d) $-\frac{2}{5}$ (e) $1\frac{1}{2}$ (f) $3\frac{1}{7}$

(g) $-5\frac{1}{2}$ (h) 5 (i) -3

(j) 1 (k) $\frac{7}{-8}$ (l) $-1\frac{1}{10}$

2. Which rational number does not have a reciprocal? Explain your answer.

3. Simplify.

(a) $\frac{1}{4} \div \frac{1}{2}$ (b) $\frac{2}{3} \div (-2)$ (c) $-3 \div \frac{1}{3}$

(d) $\frac{-2}{3} \div \frac{-2}{3}$ (e) $\frac{1}{-2} \div 2$ (f) $1\frac{1}{3} \div (-1\frac{1}{3})$

(g) $\frac{7}{8} \div \frac{1}{-4}$ (h) $\frac{3}{5} \div \frac{7}{10}$ (i) $\frac{5}{6} \div \frac{1}{-3}$

(j) $-9 \div \frac{3}{2}$ (k) $-\frac{1}{5} \div \frac{-1}{4}$ (l) $\frac{-2}{5} \div \frac{3}{-4}$

4. Simplify.

(a) $2\frac{1}{4} \div \frac{1}{2}$ (b) $\frac{-4}{3} \div \frac{8}{9}$

(c) $(-1\frac{1}{2}) \div \frac{2}{3}$ (d) $1 \div \frac{5}{6}$

(e) $4\frac{1}{3} \div 5\frac{1}{5}$ (f) $2\frac{2}{5} \div (-\frac{3}{10})$

(g) $(-1\frac{3}{4}) \div (-\frac{2}{3})$ (h) $7 \div 2\frac{1}{3}$

(i) $2 \div 1\frac{3}{5}$ (j) $1 \div \frac{-3}{5}$

(k) $\frac{3}{4} \div (-2\frac{3}{4})$ (l) $\frac{-15}{8} \div \frac{3}{-16}$

5. Simplify.

(a) $\frac{-1}{8} \times \frac{2}{3} \div \frac{1}{-3}$ (b) $(3\frac{1}{4}) \div \frac{-3}{2} \times 1\frac{1}{3}$

(c) $1\frac{1}{2}(\frac{3}{5} \div \frac{-3}{10})$ (d) $3\frac{1}{4} \times 1\frac{1}{5} \div \frac{-13}{6}$

(e) $\frac{-6}{25} \times \frac{7}{16} \div \frac{3}{8}$ (f) $\frac{-8}{15} \times (5\frac{1}{4} \div 2\frac{1}{2})$

6. The distance from Hamilton to Toronto is approximately 69 km. If the trip takes $\frac{3}{4}$ h, calculate the average speed for the trip.

7. At the end of a 300 km trip, a motorist finds that she has used half a tank of gasoline.
(a) If the tank holds 75 L, how much fuel has been used.
(b) What distance can she drive on 1 L of gasoline?

8. The pattern for a dress calls for $1\frac{1}{2}$ m of material. How many patterns can be cut from a piece of material 11 m long?

9. The area of the rectangle is $5\frac{1}{4}$ cm². If the length is $3\frac{1}{2}$ cm, calculate the width.

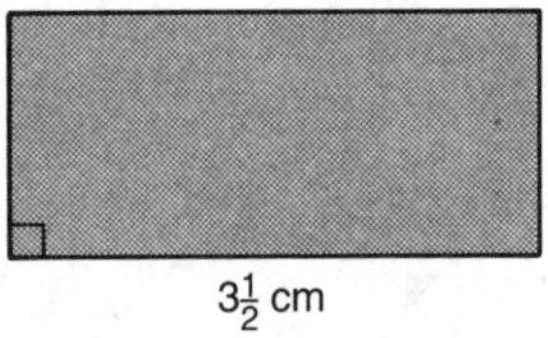
3½ cm

10. If the area of the two rectangles is to be the same, calculate the missing dimension.

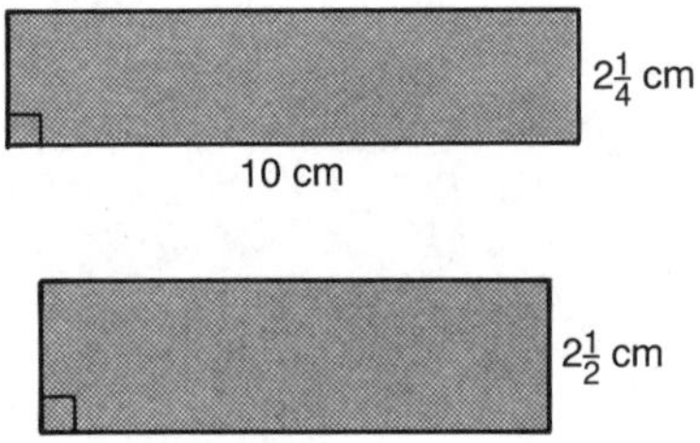
2¼ cm
10 cm
2½ cm

C 11. This section from a stock market report shows rational numbers used to represent values and changes in stock prices. The values are in cents unless a $ sign appears in front of the price.

In the following problems, use the stock market information shown.

(a) How much would be received from the sale of 140 shares of Imasco at
  (i) the highest price
  (ii) the lowest price

(b) A total of 480 shares of Indal were bought at the lowest price and sold at the highest. How much money was earned?

(c) Calculate the change in value of the following stocks and indicate whether there is an increase or decrease.
  (i) 1050 shares of Innopac
  (ii) 1600 shares of Inco
  (iii) 50 shares of Inglis
  (iv) 355 shares of Hy Zels

(d) Ms. Rossini earned $2400 for the sale of her shares of Intercan at the high price. How many shares did she sell?

(e) Mr. Larose's Inca o stock decreased in value by $1500. How many shares did he own?

(f) Mr. Williams' Imp Oil A stock increased by $360. How many shares did he own?

Stock	Div.	Bid or High	Ask or Low	Last Price	Chge	Vol.	Last 52 wks. High	Lo
HBC A p	1.80	$19⅛	19	19⅛	+⅛	5564	20	17¾
HBC Hp	1.87	$24	23⅞	24		21720	25¼	22⅛
Huksy Oil	.20	$11½	11⅜	11⅜		55875	11⅝	7
Hy Zels		$10½	10½	10½	−⅛	2300	10⅞	7½
Hydra Ex o		135	120	120	−10	33145	145	30
ICG Util p	1.50	$20¼	20½	20½		nt	21⅛	18¼
ICG Ont 260	2.60	$31	32½	31½		nt	35	30¾
ICG Ont 270	2.70	$33	35	34¼		nt	36½	34
ICG Ont 785	1.96	$25	25	25		550	25	23½
ISG Tec o		330	315	360	+50	26700	5⅞	250
ITL Ind		$6	5¾	6	+⅜	2400	11¼	475
ITL Ind 1p	1.20	$12	12⅛	11⅝		nt	12	11
ITL 775 p	.77½	$9	8⅞	9	+¼	7300	12½	8
ITT Can 1p	2.25	$26¾	26¾	26¾		7000	27½	26¼
ITT Can 2p	1.80	$25⅜	25½	25⅜		nt	25¾	24⅞
IU Intl	a .60	$22½	22½	22½	+¼	100	24½	17
Icor o		65	65	65	+3	2000	95	50
Imasco	.96	$37⅞	37¼	37⅝	+⅛	56200	40	27¾
Imasco A p	.29¼	400	400	400		4000	400	340
Imasco C p	1.84	$25¾	25⅝	25⅝		40500	25¾	25⅛
I Life III	1.84	$25⅝	25⅞	25¾		nt	26½	25⅛
Imp Metal		120	120	120		1700	145	95
Imp Oil A	1.60	$62⅛	60⅝	61⅞	+1⅛	67598	62⅛	34¾
Imp Oil B	y1.60			53¾		nt	60	35¾
Inca o		185	175	180	−5	4700	235	125
Inco	a.20	$20¾	19⅛	20⅝	+1¼	423617	23⅝	14¾
Inco 10	2.50	$26¾	26⅝	26¾		13150	28¼	25¼
Indal	.40	$15¾	15¼	15¾	+¾	7700	18¼	11½
Inglis	.24	$21⅝	22	21⅝		nt	25	19½
Inland Gas	.68	$13¼	13	13¼	+¼	10951	13⅞	11
Inland G p	1.00	$12¼	12¼	12¼		100	13½	10⅜
Inlnd G 10p	2.50	$27½	28½	27½		nt	27¾	25½
Innopac	.24	$14	13¼	13¾	+¼	32650	20⅛	11¾
Innotech	.06	440	450	445		nt	445	425
Inspiratn		$7⅞	7⅞	7⅞		3076	8⅞	5⅞
Inter Cabl		205	205	205		650	220	135
Inter Cabl p	1.00	$10	10½	10		nt	11¼	8⅞
Inter-City	.60	$18	17¾	18	+¼	22350	18¼	14
Inter C A p	1.30	$16	16	16	−½	300	17	15
Inter C B p	1.50	$19½		19½		nt	19¾	17
Inter C C p	2.12	$33¾	33	33	−¼	2150	34	29½
Int Div		$5	5¼	5		nt	5½	350
Intercan	.25	$6	6	6	−¼	1000	6½	475
Intrmetco	.28	$9½	10	9½		nt	12¾	9
I Amco A		110	120	120		nt	145	90
IBM	a4.40	$190	188¾	190	+¾	877	221¾	159

MIND BENDER

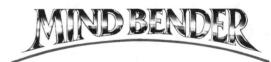

Arrange the digits 0, 1, 2, 3, 4, 5, 6, 7, 8, and 9 in fractional form so that

$$\frac{\blacksquare\blacksquare\blacksquare\blacksquare\blacksquare}{\blacksquare\blacksquare\blacksquare\blacksquare\blacksquare} = 9$$

4.4 ADDITION AND SUBTRACTION OF RATIONAL NUMBERS

Using equivalent rational numbers, the operations of addition and subtraction correspond to the same operations with integers and common fractions.

EXAMPLE 1. Simplify.

(a) $\frac{3}{4} + \frac{-1}{4}$

(b) $\frac{7}{-2} + \left(-1\frac{1}{3}\right)$

SOLUTION:

> For simplification, use the negative sign in the numerator.

(a) $\frac{3}{4} + \frac{-1}{4} = \frac{3 + (-1)}{4}$

$= \frac{2}{4}$

$= \frac{1}{2}$

(b) $\frac{7}{-2} + \left(-1\frac{1}{3}\right) = \frac{-7}{2} + \frac{-4}{3}$

$= \frac{-21}{6} + \frac{-8}{6}$

$= \frac{-21 - 8}{6}$

$= -\frac{29}{6}$

EXAMPLE 2. Simplify.

(a) $\frac{-5}{12} - \frac{3}{-4}$

(b) $-2 - 1\frac{2}{5}$

SOLUTION:

(a) $\frac{-5}{12} - \frac{3}{-4} = \frac{-5}{12} - \frac{-9}{12}$

$= \frac{-5 - (-9)}{12}$

$= \frac{-5 + 9}{12}$

$= \frac{4}{12}$

$= \frac{1}{3}$

(b) $-2 - 1\frac{2}{5} = \frac{-10}{5} - \frac{7}{5}$

$= \frac{-10 - 7}{5}$

$= -\frac{17}{5}$

If $\frac{a}{b}, \frac{c}{d} \in Q$, then $\frac{a}{b} + \frac{c}{d} = \frac{ad + bc}{bd}$

and $\frac{a}{b} - \frac{c}{d} = \frac{ad - bc}{bd}$

EXERCISE 4.4

Express all answers in simplest form.

1. Simplify.

(a) $\frac{5}{3} + \frac{-2}{3}$

(b) $\frac{3}{4} + \frac{-1}{4}$

(c) $\frac{-3}{8} + \frac{5}{8}$

(d) $1\frac{1}{4} + \frac{-3}{4}$

(e) $\frac{-1}{6} + \frac{1}{6}$

(f) $-\frac{7}{8} + \left(-\frac{1}{8}\right)$

(g) $\frac{-5}{10} + \frac{1}{10}$

(h) $\frac{-5}{6} + \frac{1}{-6}$

(i) $\frac{-4}{5} + \left(-\frac{1}{5}\right)$

2. Simplify.

(a) $\frac{5}{7} - \frac{2}{7}$

(b) $\frac{3}{5} - \frac{-1}{5}$

(c) $\frac{-3}{4} - \frac{1}{4}$

(d) $\frac{3}{-2} - \frac{1}{2}$

(e) $\frac{-3}{7} - \frac{-5}{7}$

(f) $\frac{1}{3} - \frac{-2}{3}$

(g) $-\frac{1}{5} - \left(-\frac{1}{5}\right)$

(h) $-1\frac{1}{2} - \frac{1}{2}$

(i) $0 - \frac{-1}{2}$

B **3.** Simplify.

(a) $2\frac{1}{3} + \frac{-5}{3}$ (b) $\frac{-3}{5} + 2$

(c) $\frac{-2}{3} + \frac{3}{-4}$ (d) $\frac{5}{6} - \frac{-3}{5}$

(e) $1\frac{1}{3} - \frac{-5}{12}$ (f) $\frac{4}{3} - \left(-\frac{3}{5}\right)$

(g) $\frac{1}{5} - \left(-1\frac{1}{10}\right)$ (h) $3\frac{1}{8} + \frac{5}{-4}$

(i) $\frac{-3}{10} - 1$ (j) $-\frac{3}{4} + \left(-1\frac{1}{2}\right)$

(k) $\frac{2}{5} - \frac{-3}{-10}$ (l) $-1 + \left(\frac{-3}{5}\right)$

4. Simplify.

(a) $1\frac{1}{2} + \frac{-5}{6} + \frac{1}{3}$ (b) $\frac{-7}{8} + \frac{-1}{2} - 2\frac{1}{8}$

(c) $1\frac{1}{8} - \frac{-5}{2} + \frac{-5}{6}$ (d) $\frac{3}{8} + \frac{1}{-6} - \left(-1\frac{1}{3}\right)$

(e) $3\frac{1}{10} - \frac{-3}{100} + 1$ (f) $\frac{-5}{8} - \frac{-1}{4} + \left(-1\frac{1}{2}\right)$

5. Calculate the total length of the shaft shown below.

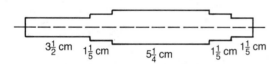

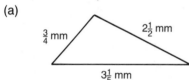

$3\frac{1}{2}$ cm $1\frac{1}{5}$ cm $5\frac{1}{4}$ cm $1\frac{1}{5}$ cm $1\frac{1}{5}$ cm

6. Calculate the perimeter of each figure.

(a)

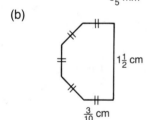

$\frac{3}{4}$ mm $2\frac{1}{2}$ mm

$3\frac{1}{5}$ mm

(b)

$1\frac{1}{2}$ cm

$\frac{3}{10}$ cm

7. To make three pant suits, the following lengths of material are needed.

size 4 — $2\frac{1}{2}$ m

size 8 — $3\frac{1}{5}$ m

size 10 — $3\frac{2}{5}$ m

If $10\frac{1}{2}$ m of material are available, how much will be left over?

8. Calculate the missing dimension in the crankshaft below.

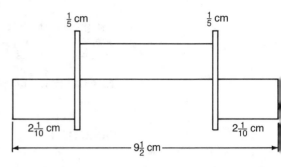

$\frac{1}{5}$ cm $\frac{1}{5}$ cm

$2\frac{1}{10}$ cm $2\frac{1}{10}$ cm

$9\frac{1}{2}$ cm

9. Calculate the area of the shaded region.

(a)

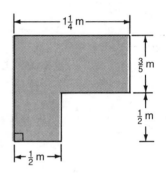

$1\frac{1}{4}$ m

$\frac{3}{5}$ m

$\frac{1}{2}$ m

$\frac{1}{2}$ m

(b)

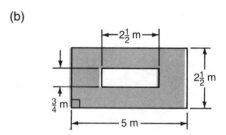

$2\frac{1}{2}$ m

$2\frac{1}{2}$ m

$\frac{3}{4}$ m

5 m

10. Big Sam's T-shirt shop advertised T-shirts for sale at $\frac{1}{3}$ of the list price. If the list price of a T-shirt was $7.59, what is the sale price?

11. If a sale advertised $\frac{1}{3}$ off the list price, what would be the sale price of an article listed at $6.90?

12. (a) Find the sum of the rational numbers.

$-\frac{1}{4}, \quad \frac{3}{8}, \quad -2 \quad -1\frac{1}{2}, \quad 3.$

(b) Find the average of the five numbers in (a).

13. Use the stock market information shown in the following problems.

(a) Find the difference between the high and low price per share of Coseka R.
(b) Find the difference between the net changes for CLife I A and Courvan o.
(c) Find the difference between the net changes for Crestbrk and CLife.
(d) List two pairs of companies which have opposite net changes.
(e) Find the average net change for the following stocks: Cuvier o, Costain Ltd, and CLife.

Stock	Div.	Bid or High	Ask or Low	Last Price	Chge	Vol.	Last 52 wks. High	Last 52 wks. Lo
Corby B f	.68	\$18	18	18		500	20½	14¾
Cor Mark f		290	275	275	−15	153226	8⅞	220
Cor Mrk A	1.87	\$16¾	16½	16½		2100	29¼	15½
Core Mrk w		62	61	61	−8	32100	410	50
Corp Food	x .80	\$30¼	29⅞	30		1200	33	22
C Falcon C	p .10	\$21½	21	21	−¼	5221	22	15½
Coseka R		64	62	63	−1	18000	190	57
Coseka 7 p	r .70	190	200	195		nt	420	125
Costain Ltd	p .20	\$14¼	14⅛	14¼	+¼	1600	16½	11½
Costain A p	v2.04	\$25¾	25⅞	26		nt	26½	25½
Costain w		\$5½	5⅜	5½		5800	9¼	475
Cott Bev		\$8⅛	8	8	−¼	3100	8¼	7
Counsel	.10	\$19½	18⅜	19½	+1¼	18265	19½	11½
Counsel w		\$7¾	7¼	7¾	+½	23000	7¾	375
Courvan o		40	40	40	+5	5000	46	28
Crain RL f	.38	\$10⅝	10⅜	10⅜	−⅛	6900	11¼	8¼
Crestbrk		\$25½	23½	25⅜	+2	92554	25½	9½
CLife I A	2.28	\$26⅜	26⅜	26⅜	+⅛	400	27⅝	25¾
Crownx	.40	\$22¼	22	22¼	+¼	1900	33¾	21½
Crownx A f	.30	\$9¾	9⅝	9¾	−⅛	34537	15¾	9
Crownx 1 p	2.00	\$31⅝	31½	31⅝	+⅜	4500	40½	28½
Crownx 2 p	v2.34	\$26⅜	26⅛	26⅜	+⅛	5300	27⅜	25
Crownx 3 p	1.87	\$23¾	24	23⅞		nt	24⅞	22¾
Crownx A w		\$5¾	5⅝	5⅝	−⅛	2600	15½	340
Crownx B w		\$15¼	15⅛	15⅛	+⅛	22450	16½	14⅝
Cuvier o		40	38	40	+2	8500	60	18
Cymric o		37	37	37		500	75	34

MIND BENDER

Determine the pattern.
Find the missing number.

42	7	5	30
55	11	7	35
36	9	8	32
24	3	5	

CALCULATOR MATH

FRACTION KEY

Some calculators have a fraction key, [a b/c]. To enter a fraction such as $3\frac{4}{5}$,

Press [C] [3] [a b/c] [4] [a b/c] [5] [a b/c]

The display is 3⌟4⌟5

EXAMPLE. Add. $2\frac{1}{3} + \frac{5}{6}$

SOLUTION:

Press	Display
[C] [2] [a b/c] [1] [a b/c] [3] [a b/c]	2⌟1⌟3
[+] [5] [a b/c] [6]	5⌟6
[=]	3⌟1⌟6

$\therefore 2\frac{1}{3} + \frac{5}{6} = 3\frac{1}{6}$

To obtain the answer in decimal form
Press [=] [a b/c]

Press	Display
[C] [4] [a b/c] [5]	4⌟5
[=] [a b/c]	0.8

Fractions are reduced to lowest terms by pressing [=].

Press	Display
[C] [4] [a b/c] [8]	4⌟8
[=]	1⌟2

EXERCISE

1. Calculate.

(a) $3\frac{1}{3} + 4\frac{2}{5}$

(b) $5 - 1\frac{5}{8}$

(c) $2\frac{1}{2} \times 4\frac{1}{4}$

(d) $5\frac{3}{4} \div 1\frac{1}{2}$

(e) $2\frac{1}{3} - 1 + 1\frac{3}{4}$

4.5 ORDER OF OPERATIONS WITH RATIONAL NUMBERS

Several of the basic operations with rational numbers are often combined in problems.

EXAMPLE 1. Simplify.

(a) $\frac{1}{3} \times (\frac{1}{4} - \frac{5}{8})$

(b) $\frac{2}{3} + \frac{-3}{5} \div 1\frac{1}{5}$

SOLUTION:

(a) $\frac{1}{3} \times (\frac{1}{4} - \frac{5}{8}) = \frac{1}{3} \times (\frac{2}{8} - \frac{5}{8})$

$\qquad = \frac{1}{3} \times \frac{-3}{8}$

$\qquad = -\frac{1}{8}$

(b) $\frac{2}{3} + \frac{-3}{5} \div 1\frac{1}{5} = \frac{2}{3} + \frac{-3}{5} \times \frac{5}{6}$

$\qquad = \frac{2}{3} + \frac{-1}{2}$

$\qquad = \frac{4}{6} + \frac{-3}{6}$

$\qquad = \frac{1}{6}$

EXAMPLE 2. Simplify. $\dfrac{\frac{-3}{5} + \frac{4}{3}}{\frac{-5}{6}}$

SOLUTION:
There are two methods of simplification.

METHOD I

$\dfrac{\frac{-3}{5} + \frac{4}{3}}{\frac{-5}{6}} = \dfrac{\frac{-9}{15} + \frac{20}{15}}{\frac{-5}{6}}$ simplify the numerator and denominator independently

$\qquad = \dfrac{\frac{11}{15}}{\frac{-5}{6}}$

$\qquad = \frac{11}{15} \times \frac{6}{-5}$

$\qquad = -\frac{22}{25}$

METHOD II

$\dfrac{\frac{-3}{5} + \frac{4}{3}}{\frac{-5}{6}} = \dfrac{(\frac{-3}{5} + \frac{4}{3}) \times 30}{\frac{-5}{6} \times 30}$ 30 is the lowest common denominator of all the rational numbers. (5, 3, 6)

$\qquad = \dfrac{(\frac{-3}{5})30 + \frac{4}{3}(30)}{(-\frac{5}{6})30}$

$\qquad = \dfrac{-18 + 40}{-25}$

$\qquad = -\frac{22}{25}$

EXERCISE 4.5

1. Simplify.

(a) $\frac{1}{2} + \frac{1}{3} - \frac{1}{4}$

(b) $\frac{1}{2} \times \frac{1}{3} - \frac{1}{4}$

(c) $\frac{1}{2} - \frac{1}{3} + \frac{1}{4}$

(d) $\frac{1}{2} \div \frac{1}{3} + \frac{1}{4}$

(e) $\frac{1}{2} - \frac{1}{3} \div \frac{1}{4}$

(f) $\frac{1}{2} - \frac{1}{3} \times \frac{1}{4}$

(g) $\frac{1}{2} + \frac{1}{3} \div \frac{1}{4}$

(h) $\frac{1}{2} + \frac{1}{3} \times \frac{1}{4}$

(i) $\frac{1}{2} + \frac{1}{3} + \frac{1}{4}$

(j) $\frac{1}{2} \times \frac{1}{3} \times \frac{1}{4}$

(k) $\frac{1}{2} \times \frac{1}{3} + \frac{1}{4}$

2. Simplify.

(a) $-\frac{2}{3} - \frac{1}{4} + \frac{1}{2}$

(b) $-\frac{2}{3} - \frac{1}{4} - \frac{1}{2}$

(c) $\left(-\frac{2}{3}\right) \times \left(-\frac{1}{4}\right) - \frac{1}{2}$

(d) $\left(-\frac{2}{3}\right) \div \left(-\frac{1}{4}\right) + \frac{1}{2}$

(e) $-\frac{2}{3} \times \left(-\frac{1}{4}\right) \div \left(-\frac{1}{2}\right)$

(f) $-\frac{2}{3} - \left(-\frac{1}{4}\right) \times \left(-\frac{1}{2}\right)$

(g) $-\frac{2}{3} + \left(-\frac{1}{4}\right) \div \left(-\frac{1}{2}\right)$

(h) $\left(-\frac{2}{3}\right) \div \left(-\frac{1}{4}\right) \div \left(-\frac{1}{2}\right)$

(i) $\left(-\frac{2}{3}\right) \times \left(-\frac{1}{4}\right) \times \left(-\frac{1}{2}\right)$

3. Simplify.

(a) $\frac{3}{-4} \times \frac{2}{3} + \frac{-3}{4}$

(b) $\frac{3}{5}\left(\frac{-2}{3} + \frac{1}{2}\right)$

(c) $\frac{3}{4} + \frac{-2}{3} \times 1\frac{1}{2}$

(d) $\left(1\frac{1}{4} - \frac{-2}{3}\right) \div 12$

(e) $\left(\frac{-1}{2} + \frac{1}{3}\right)\left(\frac{2}{5} + \frac{1}{2}\right)$

(f) $\frac{1}{2} \times \frac{-3}{4} + \frac{1}{2} \times \frac{5}{6}$

(g) $\left(-2\frac{1}{5} + \frac{-3}{4}\right) + \frac{2}{3} \times \frac{1}{5}$

(h) $\left(\frac{1}{2} - \frac{-2}{5}\right) - \left(\frac{-1}{2} - 2\right)$

(i) $\left(5 - \frac{1}{-3}\right) - \left(\frac{2}{3} - 2\right)$

4. Simplify.

(a) $\dfrac{\frac{-2}{5} + \frac{3}{4}}{\frac{1}{2}}$

(b) $\dfrac{\frac{1}{3} - \frac{1}{2}}{\frac{2}{3} + \frac{1}{5}}$

(c) $\dfrac{\frac{-7}{8} + 1\frac{1}{4}}{\frac{-2}{5} \times 1\frac{2}{3}}$

(d) $\dfrac{1\frac{1}{3} \times \frac{3}{5}}{\frac{-3}{4} \div \frac{1}{8}}$

(e) $\dfrac{\frac{5}{6} - \frac{-1}{3}}{-4}$

(f) $\dfrac{\frac{1}{2} + \frac{-3}{5} - \frac{2}{3}}{\frac{1}{15} \times (-3)}$

C 5. (a) $\dfrac{\left(1\frac{1}{2} + 2\frac{1}{2}\right) \times 3\frac{1}{2}}{\frac{5}{8} - 2\frac{3}{8}}$

(b) $\left(\frac{-3}{4} - \frac{2}{3}\right) \div \frac{5}{6} + \frac{1}{-8}$

6. Simplify.

(a) $\dfrac{1}{1 - \dfrac{1}{1 - \frac{1}{2}}}$

(b) $\dfrac{2\frac{1}{2}}{1 - \dfrac{2\frac{1}{2}}{1 - 2\frac{1}{2}}}$

Place the digits 1, 2, 3, 4, 5, 6, 7, 8, 9 in the square so that the sum of each row, column, and diagonal is the same.

4.6 CHANGING FRACTIONS TO DECIMALS

Rational numbers of the form $\frac{a}{b}$, $b \neq 0$ may be expressed in a decimal form by dividing the numerator by the denominator.

EXAMPLE. Determine the decimal equivalent for each of the following.

(a) $\frac{5}{8}$ (b) $\frac{2}{11}$ (c) $-\frac{4}{15}$

SOLUTION:

(a) Press   (b) Press   (c) Press

| C | 5 | ÷ | 8 | = | | C | 2 | ÷ | 1 | 1 | = | | C | 4 | +/− | ÷ | 1 | 5 | = |

The display is   The display is   The display is

0.625 0.18181818 -0.26666666

Terminating Decimal   Non-terminating Repeating Decimal

$\frac{5}{8} = 0.625$ $\frac{2}{11} = 0.1818...$ $-\frac{4}{15} = -0.266...$

The repeating decimal 0.1818 ... is also written $0.\overline{18}$.

the period is 18   the length of the period is 2

Every terminating decimal can also be expressed as a repeating decimal with 0 repeating.

$$\frac{5}{8} = 0.625\ 000\ ...$$

or $0.625\overline{0}$

The period is 0 and the length of the period is 1.

EXERCISE 4.6

1. Express each of the following rational numbers as a terminating decimal.

(a) $\frac{1}{50}$ (b) $\frac{1}{20}$ (c) $\frac{-3}{5}$

(d) $\frac{3}{16}$ (e) $-\frac{5}{8}$ (f) $\frac{7}{25}$

(g) $\frac{19}{16}$ (h) $\frac{17}{-40}$ (i) $\frac{-11}{32}$

2. Express each of the following rational numbers as a repeating decimal. State the period and length of the period in each case.

(a) $\frac{1}{3}$ (b) $\frac{7}{11}$ (c) $\frac{-1}{22}$

(d) $\frac{11}{18}$ (e) $-\frac{5}{3}$ (f) $\frac{8}{-9}$

(g) $\frac{87}{100}$ (h) $-\frac{13}{11}$ (i) $-\frac{7}{30}$

(j) $\frac{-3}{7}$ (k) $\frac{17}{3}$ (l) $\frac{-5}{13}$

3. Convert each of the following rational numbers to decimals, then list them in order from smallest to largest.

$$\frac{-4}{45}, \quad -\frac{3}{28}, \quad \frac{-1}{10}, \quad \frac{-47}{495}, \quad \frac{-1}{11}$$

4. Find the period and length of the period for these rational numbers.

(a) $\frac{1}{17}$ (b) $\frac{5}{23}$

MICRO MATH

```
NEW
100 REM THIS PROGRAM CONVERTS FRACTIONS
    TO DECIMALS
110 INPUT"NUMERATOR =";N
120 INPUT"NON-ZERO DENOMINATOR =";D
130 IF D=0 THEN 120
140 R=N/D
150 PRINT N;"DIVIDED BY";D;"IS";R
160 INPUT"ANOTHER QUESTION?(Y OR N)";A
170 IF A$="Y" THEN 110
180 END
RUN
```

Statement 100 in the program above should be entered on one line.

EXERCISE

1. Find the decimal equivalent.

(a) $\frac{1}{7}$ (b) $\frac{2}{7}$

(c) $\frac{3}{7}$ (d) $\frac{4}{7}$

(e) $\frac{5}{7}$ (f) $\frac{6}{7}$

Examine these decimal equivalents to determine a pattern.

GOTTFRIED WILHELM LEIBNIZ (1646–1716)

Born in Leipzig, Germany, Gottfried Leibniz became a major influence in such fields as logic, mathematics, and theology. His eagerness to learn emerged early; he taught himself Latin and Greek by the age of twelve. He entered the University of Leipzig at the age of fifteen, receiving a master's degree three years later. He received a doctorate in law at Altdorf in 1667. From 1672 to 1676 he lived in Paris. This was a crucial period for his scientific discoveries and for the development of his philosophy. His work shared the distinction with that of Sir Isaac Newton for being the first theories of integral and differential calculus. In 1679 Leibniz developed the binary (base 2) number system, which has become the basis of much of the computer technology in use today.

The binary system is similar to the decimal system except that instead of ten symbols there are only two (0 and 1).

Decimal:	0	1	2	3	4	5	6	7	8	9	10
Binary:	0	1	10	11	100	101	110	111	1000	1001	1010

4.7 CHANGING DECIMALS TO FRACTIONS

Repeating decimals such as $0.\overline{18}$ and terminating decimals such as 0.36 may be written as fractions in the form $\frac{a}{b}$, $b \neq 0$ as in the following examples.

EXAMPLE 1. Express the terminating decimal 0.36 in the following form.

$$\frac{a}{b}, b \neq 0$$

SOLUTION:

$$0.36 = \frac{36}{100}$$
$$= \frac{9}{25}$$

Answers should be written in the simplest form.

EXAMPLE 2. Express these repeating decimals in the following form.

$$\frac{a}{b}, b \neq 0$$

(a) 0.666 ...   (b) 0.1818 ...   (c) 0.324 24 ...

SOLUTION:
In each case, represent the repeating decimal by p. The method is to eliminate the repeating portion of the decimal by subtraction.

(a)
$$p = 0.666 \ldots$$
$$10p = 6.666 \ldots$$
but
$$p = 0.666 \ldots$$
Subtract.
$$9p = 6$$
$$p = \frac{6}{9}$$
$$= \frac{2}{3}$$

(b)
$$p = 0.1818 \ldots$$
$$100p = 18.1818 \ldots \longleftarrow$$ The identical repeating portion
but
$$p = \ \ 0.1818 \ldots$$ is eliminated.
Subtract.
$$99p = 18$$
$$p = \frac{18}{99}$$
$$= \frac{2}{11}$$

(c)
$$p = 0.324 \ 24 \ldots$$
$$1000p = 324.242 \ 4 \ldots \longleftarrow$$ note the 3 does not repeat
and
$$10p = \ \ \ \ 3.242 \ 4 \ldots$$
Subtract.
$$990p = 321$$
$$p = \frac{321}{990}$$
$$= \frac{107}{330}$$

EXERCISE 4.7

B 1. Express each terminating decimal as a rational number in the form $\frac{a}{b}$, $b \neq 0$.

(a) 0.3   (b) 0.25   (c) −0.6
(d) −1.5   (e) 3.75   (f) 0.125
(g) −1.875   (h) 0.18   (i) 5.15
(j) −100.1   (k) 2.36   (l) 0.0225

2. Complete the table in your notebook.

Repeating Decimal p	10 × p	100 × p	1000 × p
0.666 ...	6.66 ...		
0.1818 ...		18.1818 ...	
0.356 356 ...	3.563 56 ...		
2.333 ...			2333.33 ...
0.324 24 ...	3.2424 ...		324.2424 ...
	15.66 ...		
0.352 22 ...			

3. Express each repeating decimal in the form $\frac{a}{b}$, $b \neq 0$.

(a) 0.333 ...   (b) 0.$\overline{4}$ (c) 0.$\overline{13}$
(d) 0.$\overline{36}$ (e) 0.555 ...   (f) 0.2$\overline{6}$
(g) 0.1$\overline{5}$ (h) 0.2$\overline{93}$ (i) 3.$\overline{16}$
(j) 0.5252 ...   (k) 1.2$\overline{3}$ (l) 0.0$\overline{648}$

4. (a) Express the following in the form $\frac{a}{b}$, $b \neq 0$.

     (i) 0.3$\overline{9}$ (ii) 0.4$\overline{9}$
    (iii) 0.7$\overline{9}$ (iv) 0.8$\overline{9}$
     (v) 0.52$\overline{9}$ (vi) 0.53$\overline{9}$

(b) From your results in (a) write a general rule for the case of decimals with a period of 9.

(c) Check your rule using
     (i) 0.5$\overline{9}$ (ii) 0.$\overline{9}$

Simplify.

$$\cfrac{1}{1 + \cfrac{1}{2 + \cfrac{1}{3 + \cfrac{1}{4 + \cfrac{1}{3}}}}}$$

4.8 ROUNDING AND ESTIMATING

In this section we extend the rounding rules for a stated place value to rounding to a number of significant digits. The same rules for discarding digits apply in these examples. The following chart shows how we used the rules for rounding to a given place value in our earlier work.

Rules	Numbers	Required Place	Key Digit	Rounded Number
If the key digit is less than 5 round down.	7.374 427 5483	0.001 1000	7.374 427 5483	7.374 5000
If the key digit is greater than 5, or if it is a five followed by digits other than zero, round up.	6.628 64 0.524 504 52 764	0.001 0.001 100	6.628 64 0.524 504 52 764	6.629 0.525 52 800
If the key digit is 5, followed only by zeros, round to the nearest even digit.	8500 7500 65 000 7.35 4.085	1000 1000 10 000 0.1 0.01	8500 7500 65 000 7.35 4.085	8000 8000 60 000 7.4 4.08

The most significant digit (or figure) in a number is the first non-zero digit that you reach when reading a number from left to right.

In the following examples, the one most significant digit is shown in red.

4563,   75 006,   86,   0.036 78,   0.005 24,   3.14

When approximating to a stated number of significant digits, the rules for rounding are used on the last significant digit as in the following chart.

Given Number	Number of Significant Digits	Key Digit	Rounded Number
7462	two	7462	7500
0.004 207	one	0.004 207	0.004
3562.14	three	3562.14	3560
0.254 378 96	four	0.254 378 96	0.254 4
14 500 000	two	14 500 000	14 000 000
0.55	one	0.55	0.6
0.65	one	0.65	0.6

Rounding to a required place value or to a given number of significant digits depends upon the application and what is required in the question.

EXAMPLE 1. Round off the value 69.846525 to
(a) 3 significant digits.
(b) 2 significant digits.
(c) 5 significant digits.
(d) 7 significant digits.

SOLUTION:

(a) 69.846 525 ≐ 69.8
          ↑
    Key Digit < 5, round down

(b) 69.846 525 ≐ 70
          ↑
    Key Digit > 5, round up

(c) 69.846 525 ≐ 69.847
            ↑
    Key Digit not followed by zeros, round up

(d) 69.846 525 ≐ 69.846 52
          ↑
    Key Digit is followed by zeros only, round to the nearest even digit

The following example shows how rounding can be used to estimate answers in calculations.

EXAMPLE 2. Estimate the answer.

(a) 19.8×57.2
(b) $\dfrac{3.1 \times 76.2}{59}$

SOLUTION:

(a) $19.8 \times 57.2 \doteq 20 \times 60$
$= 1200$

(b) $\dfrac{3.1 \times 76.2}{59} \doteq \dfrac{3 \times 80}{60}$
$= \dfrac{240}{60}$
$= 4$

> **Estimating**
>
> Round all answers to one significant digit and calculate mentally.

EXERCISE 4.8

A 1. Round off the following values to three significant digits.

(a) 65.58   (b) 4856
(c) 958.73   (d) 1.072
(e) 7.925   (f) 12.8625
(g) 149.9   (h) 185 936
(i) 0.2355   (j) 6.006 7
(k) 879.6   (l) 699.7
(m) 0.065 38   (n) 0.001 987
(o) 0.000 659 8   (p) 19.8512

B 2. Estimate the answer.

(a) 7.1×6.3 (b) 4.91×21
(c) 61.2×9.8 (d) 1.958×30.41

(e) 193.5×5.31 (f) $\dfrac{194.7}{18.9}$

(g) $\dfrac{58.1}{4.74}$ (h) $\dfrac{292.32}{29.3}$

(i) $\dfrac{494}{96}$ (j) $4.8 \times 3.9 \times 5.1$

(k) $\dfrac{8.9 \times 2.9}{3.1}$ (l) $\dfrac{56 \times 2.1}{40.1}$

3. Using estimation, locate the decimal in each of the following answers.

(a) 7.35×12.98 ■ 954030
(b) 56.25×8.9 ■ 500625
(c) $4.1 \times 3.92 \times 5.06$ ■ 813243
(d) $\dfrac{46.83}{2.07}$ ■ 226231

(e) $\dfrac{182.04}{8.735}$ ■ 20840

(f) $\dfrac{7.98 \times 41.2}{18.9}$ ■ 173955

4. Estimate the areas of the following.
(a)

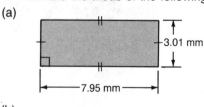
3.01 mm
7.95 mm

(b)

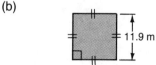
11.9 m

(c)

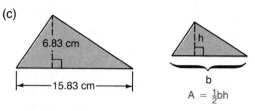
6.83 cm
15.83 cm
h
b
$A = \frac{1}{2}bh$

(d)

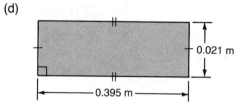
0.021 m
0.395 m

5. Estimate the area of the following using $\pi = 3$.

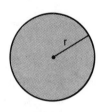
r
$C = 2\pi r$
$A = \pi r^2$

(a)

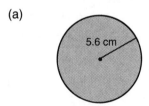
5.6 cm

(b)

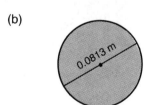
0.0813 m

(c)

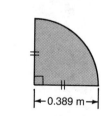
0.389 m

CALCULATOR MATH

ROUNDING OFF

Some calculators round off, while others truncate, or "chop off" the extra digits without rounding. The following exercise demonstrates how your calculator handles the extra digits. The displays from two different kinds of calculators are shown.

Press	Calculator #1 Display	Calculator #2 Display
C	0.	0.00
2	2.	2.
÷	2.	2.00
3	3.	3.
=	0.6666666	0.6666667
×	0.6666666	0.6666667
3	3.	3.
=	1.9999998	2

Notice that the two calculators give slightly different answers to the problem
$$2 \div 3 \times 3$$
The difference arises because Calculator #1 truncates and drops the digits after dividing. Calculator #2 does two things: (i) only the display is rounded off; (ii) digits are saved in the memory and not dropped off.

The solution is $2 \div 3 \times 3 = 2$ as we multiply and divide in order from left to right.

EXERCISE

1. Experiment with the following questions to determine whether the calculator you are using truncates, or rounds.

(a) $5 \div 3 \times 3$ (b) $6 \div 7 \times 7$
(c) $1 \div 6 \times 6$ (d) $2 \div 6 \times 6$
(e) $8 \div 3 \times 3$ (f) $3 \div 11 \times 11$

ACCEPTABLE ERROR

Suppose the two types of calculator were given the following calculation.

$$66\ 666.666\ \ldots$$
$$523\ 777.777\ \ldots$$
$$+\ 184\ 631.555\ \ldots$$

Calculator #1 truncates, so it would do the following.

$$66\ 666.666$$
$$523\ 777.777$$
$$+\ 184\ 631.555$$
$$\overline{775\ 075.998}$$

Calculator #2 saves the digits in its memory but rounds the display, so it would do as follows.

$$66\ 666.667$$
$$523\ 777.778$$
$$+\ 184\ 631.556$$
$$\overline{775\ 076.000}$$

In fact, the real calculation is

$$66\ 666.666\ \ldots$$
$$523\ 777.777\ \ldots$$
$$+\ 184\ 631.555\ \ldots$$
$$\overline{775\ 075.999\ \ldots}$$

In both cases there is a calculator error in the eighth significant digit, so the calculation is correct to seven significant digits. This degree of accuracy is sufficient for most calculations so the error is acceptable. However, in some very precise scientific calculations, a greater degree of accuracy is required.

Check the above calculation using the following BASIC computer program.

```
NEW
10 PRINT"ENTER THREE NUMBERS"
20 INPUT A
30 INPUT B
40 INPUT C
50 S=A+B+C
60 PRINT S
70 END
RUN
```

4.9 INTEGRAL EXPONENTS

In many expressions and formulas, exponents are used to simplify the writing of repeated multiplication.

When we write 3^4, we mean $3 \times 3 \times 3 \times 3$.

Similarly x^4 means $x \times x \times x \times x$.

In the following examples, we develop exponent laws for multiplication and division using numerical cases.

MULTIPLICATION

$$2^3 \times 2^2 = \underbrace{(2 \times 2 \times 2)}_{3 \text{ factors}} \times \underbrace{(2 \times 2)}_{2 \text{ factors}}$$

$$= \underbrace{2 \times 2 \times 2 \times 2 \times 2}_{5 \text{ factors}}$$

$$= 2^5$$

$$2^3 \times 2^2 = 2^{3+2}$$

$$= 2^5$$

$$x^3 \times x^2 = \underbrace{(x \times x \times x)}_{3 \text{ factors}} \times \underbrace{(x \times x)}_{2 \text{ factors}}$$

$$= \underbrace{x \times x \times x \times x \times x}_{5 \text{ factors}}$$

$$= x^5$$

$$x^5 \div x^3 = x^{5-3}$$

$$= x^2$$

The Exponent Law for Multiplication

$$x^m \times x^n = x^{m+n}, \; m, n, \in I$$

To multiply two powers of the same base, add the exponents.

EXAMPLE 1. Simplify. $x^3 \times x^{-7} \times x^{-1}$

SOLUTION:

$$x^3 \times x^{-7} \times x^{-1} = x^{3-7-1}$$

$$= x^{-5}$$

DIVISION

$$3^5 \div 3^3 = \frac{3^5}{3^3}$$

$$= \frac{\overbrace{3 \times 3 \times 3 \times 3 \times 3}^{5 \text{ factors}}}{\underbrace{3 \times 3 \times 3}_{3 \text{ factors}}}$$

$$= \overbrace{3 \times 3}^{2 \text{ factors}}$$

$$= 3^2$$

$$3^5 \div 3^3 = 3^{5-3}$$

$$= 3^2$$

$$x^5 \div x^3 = \frac{x^5}{x^3}$$

$$= \frac{\overbrace{x \times x \times x \times x \times x \times x \times x \times x \times x}^{5 \text{ factors}}}{\underbrace{x \times x \times x \times x \times x}_{3 \text{ factors}}}$$

$$= \overbrace{x \times x}^{2 \text{ factors}}$$

$$= x^2$$

$$x^3 \times x^2 = x^{3+2}$$

$$= x^5$$

The Exponent Law for Division

$$x^m \div x^n = \frac{x^m}{x^n} = x^{m-n}, \; x \neq 0, \; m, n \in I$$

To divide two powers of the same base, subtract the exponents.

EXAMPLE 2. Simplify.

(a) $x^{-1} \div x^{-5}$

(b) $z^5 \div z^{-2} \times z^{-12}$

SOLUTION:

(a) $x^{-1} \div x^{-5} = x^{-1-(-5)}$
$= x^4$

(b) $z^5 \div z^{-2} \times z^{-12} = z^{5-(-2)-12}$
$= z^{-5}$

ZERO EXPONENT

$5^3 \div 5^3 = 5^{3-3}$
$= 5^0$

$5^3 \div 5^3 = \dfrac{5^3}{5^3}$
$= 1$

$\left.\right\} 5^0 = 1$

$x^3 \div x^3 = x^{3-3}$
$= x^0$

$x^3 \div x^3 = \dfrac{x^3}{x^3}$
$= 1$

$\left.\right\} x^0 = 1$

For $x \neq 0$, $x^0 = 1$

NEGATIVE EXPONENT

$$7^2 = \frac{1}{7^2}$$

$$x^{-2} = \frac{1}{x^2}$$

$7^3 \div 7^5 = 7^{3-5}$
$= 7^{-2}$

$7^3 \div 7^5 = \dfrac{7^3}{7^5}$
$= \dfrac{7 \times 7 \times 7}{7 \times 7 \times 7 \times 7 \times 7}$
$= \dfrac{1}{7^2}$

$x^3 \div x^5 = x^{3-5}$
$= x^{-2}$

$x^3 \div x^5 = \dfrac{x^3}{x^5}$
$= \dfrac{x \times x \times x}{x \times x \times x \times x \times x}$
$= \dfrac{1}{x^2}$

For $x \neq 0$, $m > 0$, $x^{-m} = \dfrac{1}{x^m}$

EXAMPLE 3. Evaluate.

(a) $\left(-\frac{1}{2}\right)^0$

(b) $(-3)^{-1}$

(c) $\left(\frac{2}{3}\right)^{-2}$

(d) 10^{-4}

SOLUTION:

(a) $\left(-\frac{1}{2}\right)^0 = 1$

(b) $(-3)^{-1} = \dfrac{1}{(-3)^1}$
$= -\dfrac{1}{3}$

(c) $\left(\frac{2}{3}\right)^{-2} = \dfrac{1}{\left(\frac{2}{3}\right)^2}$
$= \dfrac{1}{\frac{4}{9}}$
$= \dfrac{9}{4}$

(d) $10^{-4} = \dfrac{1}{10^4}$
$= \dfrac{1}{10\ 000}$

EXERCISE 4.9

A 1. Simplify.

(a) $x^2 \times x^5$ (b) $y^{-3} \times y^9$
(c) $y^2 \times y^{-2}$ (d) $x^{-2} \times x^{-5}$
(e) $x^{-3} \times x^{-5}$ (f) $x \times x^0$
(g) $x \times x^{-3}$ (h) $x^{-1} \times x$
(i) $y^{-3} \times y^{-1}$ (j) $m^5 \times m^{-7}$

2. Simplify.

(a) $x^7 \div x^{-2}$

$$x^7 \div x^{-2} = x^{7-(-2)}$$
$$= \blacksquare$$

(b) $x^{12} \div x^8$ (c) $y^2 \div y^5$

(d) $y^6 \div y^6$ (e) $w^5 \div w^0$

(f) $x^0 \div x^5$ (g) $\dfrac{x^3}{x^7}$

(h) $\dfrac{y^0}{y^5}$ (i) $\dfrac{w^7}{w^{-3}}$

(j) $\dfrac{x^0}{x^{-3}}$ (k) $\dfrac{y^5}{y^{-1}}$

(l) $\dfrac{x^{-1}}{x}$ (m) $\dfrac{a^{-2}}{a^{-2}}$

3. Simplify.

(a) $10^5 \times 10^6$ (b) $10^0 \times 10^2$
(c) $10^{-8} \times 10^{10}$ (d) $10^8 \div 10^3$
(e) $10^2 \div 10^8$ (f) $10^{-3} \times 10^{-2}$
(g) $\dfrac{10^6}{10^3}$ (h) $\dfrac{10}{10^4}$

(i) $\dfrac{10^2}{10^5}$ (j) $\dfrac{10 \times 10^7}{10^{10}}$

(k) $\dfrac{10^{-3} \times 10^0}{10^{-3}}$ (l) $\dfrac{10^0}{10^{-6}}$

B 4. Evaluate the following.

(a) 5^0 (b) $(-2)^3$
(c) $(-1)^7$ (d) 10^{-2}
(e) 3^{-3} (f) 4^{-2}
(g) $(-2)^{-4}$ (h) 10^{-3}
(i) 10^3 (j) $(-2)^{-3}$
(k) 2^{-5} (l) $(-1)^{-5}$

5. Evaluate.

(a) $\left(\dfrac{5}{8}\right)^0$ (b) $\left(\dfrac{3}{4}\right)^2$

(c) $\left(-\dfrac{1}{5}\right)^2$ (d) $\left(\dfrac{1}{3}\right)^{-1}$

(e) $\left(\dfrac{1}{10}\right)^{-1}$ (f) $\left(\dfrac{1}{2}\right)^{-2}$

(g) $\left(\dfrac{2}{3}\right)^{-3}$ (h) $\left(-\dfrac{7}{8}\right)^0$

(i) $\left(\dfrac{1}{4}\right)^{-1}$ (j) $\left(-\dfrac{1}{2}\right)^3$

(k) $\left(-\dfrac{1}{8}\right)^{-1}$ (l) $\dfrac{1}{10^{-3}}$

6. Simplify.

(a) $x^{-3} \times x^{-2}$ (b) $y^5 \div y^{-2}$

(c) $\dfrac{w^{10}}{w^{-3}}$ (d) $\dfrac{x^0}{x^{-7}}$

(e) $y^{-3} \times y^5 \times y^{-1}$ (f) $x^{-7} \div x^{-5}$
(g) $z^{-3} + z^3$ (h) $x^{12} \div x^{15} \times x^{-3}$

(i) $\dfrac{x^{-5} \times x^3}{x^2}$ (j) $\dfrac{y^3 \times y^5}{y^{12}}$

(k) $(x^3 \times x) \div x^5$ (l) $\dfrac{1}{y^3} \times y^{-4}$

C 7. Evaluate.

(a) $3^0 + 3^{-1}$
(b) $5^{-1} + 2^{-1}$
(c) $(12^0 \times 3^{-1}) \times 4^{-2}$
(d) $\dfrac{2^{-1} + 3^{-1}}{3^0}$
(e) $2^{-3} + 3^{-2}$
(f) $\left(\dfrac{1}{2}\right)^{-3} + \left(\dfrac{1}{2}\right)^0$
(g) $\left(\dfrac{2}{3}\right)^{-2} \times \left(\dfrac{1}{4}\right)^{-1}$
(h) $\dfrac{1}{3^{-1}} + \dfrac{1}{2^{-1}}$

371

Simplify. $3^3 + 7^3 + 1^3 = 371$

Can you find another number like this?

4.10 SCIENTIFIC NOTATION: LARGE NUMBERS

Frequently, it is necessary to represent very large or very small quantities in numerical form.

The planet Pluto, at its closest point, is approximately 4 250 000 000 km from Earth. The mass of an electron is approximately 0.000 000 000 000 000 000 000 000 000 911 g.

Writing and working with numbers in this form becomes very awkward. In the next two exercises, we shall learn to express such numbers using powers of 10 in a form called scientific notation.

The distance to Pluto, when expressed in scientific notation, is 4.25×10^9 km.

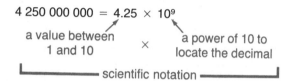

$$4\ 250\ 000\ 000 = 4.25 \times 10^9$$

a value between 1 and 10   ×   a power of 10 to locate the decimal

scientific notation

EXERCISE 4.10

B 1. Study the two complete examples, then complete the table in your notebook.

30	3×10	3×10^1
300	3×100	3×10^2
3 000	$3 \times$ ■	$3 \times$ ■
2 960	$2.96 \times$ ■	$2.96 \times$ ■
531	5.31×100	
72	■ $\times 10$	
75 000		$7.5 \times$ ■
2 600 000		
25.6	$2.56 \times$ ■	
1.73	$1.73 \times$ ■	
6.0		

2. Rewrite the following using scientific notation.

(a) 371
(b) 5600
(c) 18.2
(d) 173 000 000
(e) 4.5
(f) 290 000
(g) 596.2
(h) 8
(i) 800 000
(j) 3500.65
(k) 487
(l) 1 000 000 000 000

3. Express each of the following using scientific notation rounded to three significant digits.

(a) 5678
(b) 10 792
(c) 376 132
(d) 52 856
(e) 178 600 000
(f) 998 461
(g) 48.987
(h) 376.932

4. (a) Complete the table in your notebook.

Scientific Notation	Exponent of 10	Number
2.7×10	1	27
7.54×10^2	2	
4.35×10		
3.5×10^4		
1.325×10^3		
5.619×10^2		
8×10^6		

(b) To expand the number 1.73×10^6, how many places do you move the decimal point? In which direction?

4.11 SCIENTIFIC NOTATION: SMALL NUMBERS

The mass of an electron, as mentioned earlier, is approximately 0.000 000 000 000 000 000 000 000 000 911 g. It is expressed more conveniently in scientific notation as approximately 9.11×10^{-28} g.

EXERCISE 4.11

B 1. (a) Study the pattern in the table and fill in the missing values in your notebook.

Number	Scientific Notation	Exponent of 10
29 500	2.95×10^4	4
2 950	2.95×10^3	3
295	$2.95 \times \blacksquare$	2
29.5	$2.95 \times \blacksquare$	
2.95	$2.95 \times \blacksquare$	
0.295	$2.95 \times \blacksquare$	
0.029 5	$2.95 \times \blacksquare$	
0.002 95	$2.95 \times \blacksquare$	

(b) Rewrite the following in scientific notation.
(i) 0.0295   (ii) 0.5   (iii) 0.0082
(iv) 0.653   (v) 0.000 001   (vi) 0.632
(vii) 0.0102   (viii) 0.000 35   (ix) $0.\overline{79}$

2. (a) Complete the table in your notebook.

Scientific Notation	Exponent of 10	Number
3.5×10^{-1}	-1	0.35
1.7×10^{-3}	-3	
5.2×10^0		
7.35×10^{-2}		
1.0×10^{-5}		
5.932×10^{-1}		

(b) To expand the number 3.9×10^{-4}, how many places do you move the decimal point? In which direction?
(c) Expand the following numbers.
   (i) 5.79×10^{-1} (ii) 7.5×10^0
   (iii) 9.2×10^{-4} (iv) 1.03×10^{-9}
   (v) 6.9×10^{-3} (vi) 1×10^{-5}
   (vii) 4.2×10^{-7} (viii) 6×10^{-8}
   (ix) 7.53×10^{-2} (x) 3.51×10^{-6}

3. Express in scientific notation rounded to two significant digits.

(a) 0.001 872   (b) 0.3411
(c) 0.000 043 5   (d) 0.6
(e) 0.000 845   (f) $0.02\overline{5}$

4.12 ESTIMATING USING SCIENTIFIC NOTATION

The degree of accuracy is very important in some scientific calculations. To indicate clearly the number of significant digits, we use scientific notation.

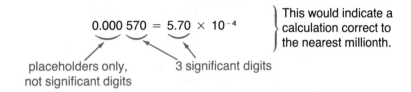

$$0.000\ 570 = 5.70 \times 10^{-4}$$

placeholders only, not significant digits

3 significant digits

This would indicate a calculation correct to the nearest millionth.

Scientific notation may be used to simplify estimation.

EXAMPLE. Estimate. 0.0073×0.0436

SOLUTION:

Round off to one significant digit, then calculate.

$$
\begin{aligned}
0.0073 \times 0.0436 &= 7.3 \times 10^{-3} \times 4.36 \times 10^{-2} \\
&\doteq 7 \times 10^{-3} \times 4 \times 10^{-2} \\
&= 28 \times 10^{-5} \\
&= 2.8 \times 10^{1} \times 10^{-5} \\
&= 2.8 \times 10^{-4}
\end{aligned}
$$

EXERCISE 4.12

1. Express in scientific notation rounded to three significant digits.

(a) 3 295 000
(b) 0.000 139 526
(c) 0.9568
(d) 0.039 728
(e) 9 998 235
(f) 0.590 623
(g) 0.000 049 22
(h) 28 499
(i) 70 841 162
(j) 0.505 663

2. Estimate the answer. (Answers may be left in scientific notation.)

(a) $3.2 \times 10^{-5} \times 2.3 \times 10^{8}$
(b) $5.1 \times 10^{-3} \times 3.2 \times 10^{6}$
(c) $7.8 \times 10^{-3} \times 12.03 \times 10$
(d) $4.86 \times 10^{8} \times 6.02 \times 10^{10}$
(e) $1\ 786\ 000 \times 611$
(f) 0.0091×83.5
(g) $489 \times 61 \times 90$
(h) 0.135×5280

(i) $\dfrac{5.8 \times 10^{12}}{1.95 \times 10^{3}}$

(j) $\dfrac{8.37 \times 10^{-3}}{4.2 \times 10^{2}}$

(k) $\dfrac{99.1 \times 10^{5}}{8.9 \times 10^{-2}}$

(l) $\dfrac{751.3}{0.03}$

(m) $\dfrac{0.059}{2.98}$

(n) $\dfrac{568 \times 34.8}{0.069}$

(o) $\dfrac{7500 \times 1798}{14\ 000\ 000}$

(p) $\dfrac{0.000\ 81 \times 0.0049}{0.13}$

4.13 APPLICATIONS OF DECIMALS

Rational numbers are often specified when working with algebraic expressions and formulas.

EXAMPLE 1. If $E(x) = 10x - 2$, determine $E(0.65)$.

SOLUTION:
$$E(0.65) = 10(0.65) - 2$$
$$= 6.5 - 2$$
$$= 4.5$$

In most formulas, the rational numbers appear in decimal form. Calculators are useful in the simplification involved.

EXAMPLE 2. The following formula is used for calculating the distance an object falls in time.

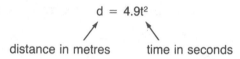

$$d = 4.9t^2$$

distance in metres   time in seconds

Calculate the distance, to the nearest tenth of a metre, that an object will fall in 2.5 s.

SOLUTION:

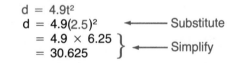

$$d = 4.9t^2$$
$$d = 4.9(2.5)^2 \longleftarrow \text{Substitute}$$
$$\left.\begin{array}{l} = 4.9 \times 6.25 \\ = 30.625 \end{array}\right\} \longleftarrow \text{Simplify}$$

∴ the object will fall 30.6 m. $\longleftarrow$ Statement

units must be shown

EXERCISE 4.13

A 1. If $E(x) = 3x$, determine
(a) $E(0.7)$ (b) $E(-1.25)$
(c) $E(-0.1)$ (d) $E(2.5)$

2. If $E(x) = x - 3$, determine
(a) $E(1.5)$ (b) $E(-0.5)$
(c) $E(-2.5)$ (d) $E(4.5)$

B 3. If $x = 1.3$ and $y = -3.2$, evaluate the following.
(a) $5x$ (b) $-3y$
(c) $2x + y$ (d) $x - y$
(e) $3x - 2y$ (f) $5y - x$
(g) $8x - 2$ (h) $-2x - 5y$
(i) x^2 (j) $3y^2$
(k) $x^2 + y^2$ (l) $3x^3 - y$

(m) $(x - y)^2$
(o) $x + y^2 - 2$
(n) $4x - 2y - 3$
(p) xy

4. Calculate the area of each circle. Use $\pi = 3.14$.

$A = \pi r^2$

(a)

5.0 m

(b)

3.0 mm

5. The volume of a cone is given by the formula

$$V = \tfrac{1}{3}\pi r^2 h$$

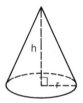

where V represents the volume, r represents the radius, and h represents the height. Calculate the volume in each case, correct to two significant digits.
(a) r = 2.0 cm, h = 4.5 cm, and $\pi = 3.14$
(b) r = 0.4 cm, h = 0.99 cm, and $\pi = 3.14$

6. The surface area of a cube is found from the formula

$$A = 6s^2$$

where A represents the area and s represents the length of each edge. Calculate the area in each case.
(a) s = 7.5 cm
(b) s = 0.8 mm

s

7. Calculate the shaded areas of each of the following.

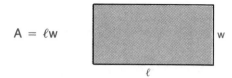
$A = \ell w$
w
ℓ

(a)

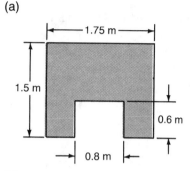
1.75 m
1.5 m
0.6 m
0.8 m

(b)

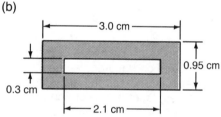
3.0 cm
0.95 cm
0.3 cm
2.1 cm

8. The stopping distance for a car under good conditions is given by the formula

$$D = 0.4s + 0.02s^2$$

where D represents the distance in metres and s is the speed in kilometres per hour. Calculate the stopping distance in each case.
(a) s = 50 km/h
(b) s = 75 km/h

MIND BENDER

Determine the pattern. Find the missing number.

15	5	7	17
22	12	13	23
21	11	4	

4.14 MATH GAMES

SPROUTS

The game of SPROUTS, a game for two players, was invented by two English mathematicians at Cambridge University.

RULES

1. Place 3 dots on a piece of paper.

2. The first player draws a path that joins 2 dots or that starts and ends at the same dot. Once the path is made, the player places a new dot on the path that was just drawn. Examples of some starting moves are shown below.

3. No dot can have more than 3 paths drawn from it.

4. No path can cross another path.

5. Players alternate turns. The last player to make a move is the winner.

The following is a sample game.

1st Player	2nd Player

1st Player	2nd Player

1st Player	2nd Player
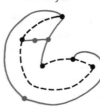	

1st Player

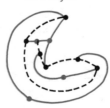

The second player cannot move. The first player wins.

3-D TIC-TAC-TOE

The game of Tic-Tac-Toe can be made more challenging by playing the game in 3 dimensions.

Three game boards are stacked as shown in the diagram.

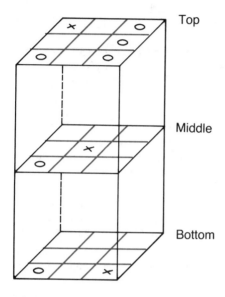

Top

Middle

Bottom

A winning row of Xs and two winning rows of Os are shown. Straight lines of Xs and Os do not have to be on the same level.

A simplified game board can be used as in the one shown here with the winning rows of Xs and Os from the previous diagram.

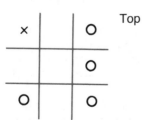

Top

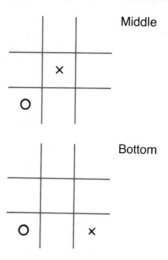

Middle

Bottom

The game proceeds, using either game board, with players alternating turns. The winner is the first player to get "3 Xs or Os in a row."

BRUSSELS SPROUTS

This is a variation of the game of SPROUTS. Instead of starting with 3 dots, the game begins with three crosses, as shown.

No cross can have more than 4 paths drawn from it. Players place a cross on the path they have drawn.

This action permits two other paths to come from the added cross. The play of BRUSSELS SPROUTS proceeds as in SPROUTS. Players alternate turns and the last player to make a move is the winner.

4.15 PROBLEM SOLVING

1. Place the numbers 10, 11, 12, 13, 14, 15, 16, and 17 in the boxes so that no two consecutive numbers are in boxes which touch at a point or a side.

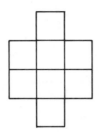

2. How old will you be when you have been alive for one billion seconds?

3. The state of Michigan is one of the states that touches Canada's border. What other states come into contact with the border?

4. Compact discs cost $12 wholesale. Seven of these are sold at $8, $8, $10, $18, $17, $14, and $9.
(a) Were the discs sold at a profit or loss?
(b) What was the profit (or loss) on the sale of the seven discs?

5. If you take a number, subtract 21, then add 5, and finally multiply by 8, you get 104. What is the number?

6. Which of the numbered wheels are turning clockwise?

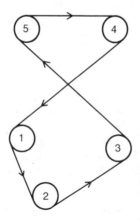

7. A section of the stock market report is shown below.

Stock	Sales	High	Low	Close	Ch'ge
BartC	600	210	200	200	−10
BaryE	3900	85	75	75	−17

Ch'ge is the change in value, in cents, for each share.
(a) If Mr. Martini owned 75 shares of BartC, what would be the net change in value of his holdings?
(b) If Mrs. Bacik owned 150 shares of BartC and 125 shares of BaryE, find the difference between the two net changes in value for her holdings.

8. Liberty bought two T-shirts at $13.75 each and four pairs of socks at $6.40 each. If the sales tax was 7%, how much change did she receive from a hundred dollar bill?

9. Sal is 14 a old. His mother is three times as old as he is. How old will Sal be when his mother is twice as old as he is?

10. Jane has 100 pennies in five piles.

The number of pennies in the first two piles is 52. The second and third piles contain 43 pennies; the third and fourth piles contain 34 pennies; and the fourth and fifth piles contain 30 pennies. How many pennies are in each pile?

11. The Arco Car Rental charges $37.75 per day plus $0.19/km. Doug rented a car for eleven days. When he left the Arco lot the odometer on the car read 12678.7 km. When he returned the odometer read 14998.8 km. How much money did he owe for the car?

12. The difference of the squares of two consecutive even numbers is 52. Find the numbers.

13. Eight students belong to the ski team. They decide to form committees of three to organize a downhill competition. How many different committees can be formed?

14. Frankie has 3 part-time jobs. Last week he worked 3 h at the video store where he earns $10.80/h. He worked 6 h at a variety store where he earns $8.35/h. He also worked 5 h at a gas station where he earns $11.50/h. How much did he earn last week?

15. For each of the following, make an assumption and find the next two terms.

(a) 17, 21, 26, 32, ■, ■
(b) 5, 10, 17, 26 37, 50, ■, ■
(c) 80, 40, 20, ■, ■

16.

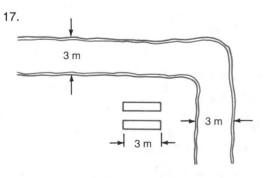

The opposite faces of a die all add up to 7. The die is placed on a 3 by 3 numbered grid as shown. Roll the die one-quarter turn to the right or down until you reach the 9 space. What number of dots will be showing on top of the die?

17.

How can you cross the 3 m of water using only 2 boards which are each 3 m long?

18. Each year, an automobile loses about 20% of its value due to depreciation. What is the value after 4 a, of an automobile that was purchased new for $22 500?

19. Find the missing digits in this multiplication.

MIND BENDER

State the output of the following flow chart.

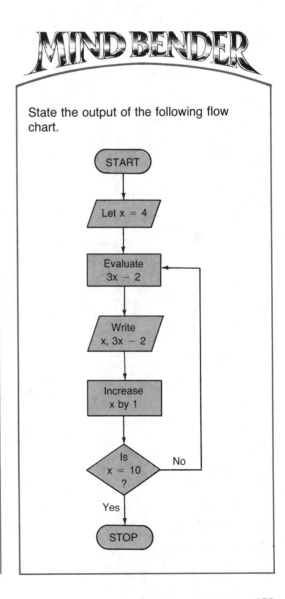

4.16 REVIEW EXERCISE

1. Define the set of rational numbers, Q.

2. Simplify.

(a) $\frac{15}{-18}$ (b) $\frac{-3}{6}$ (c) $\frac{4}{-2}$

(d) $\frac{-7}{-8}$ (e) $\frac{0}{-3}$ (f) $\frac{-12}{12}$

(g) $\frac{12}{-24}$ (h) $-\frac{2}{-6}$ (i) $\frac{-7}{49}$

3. State the reciprocal of each of the following.

(a) $\frac{2}{3}$ (b) 5   (c) $\frac{1}{2}$

(d) $\frac{-5}{3}$ (e) -6 (f) $-\frac{3}{10}$

(g) $-1\frac{1}{2}$ (h) $2\frac{3}{4}$ (i) $\frac{-11}{13}$

4. Express each of the following numbers using scientific notation.
(a) 13 600
(b) 3 562 000
(c) 0.56
(d) 37.5
(e) 0.000 856
(f) 0.000 02
(g) 0.01
(h) 0.000 000 21
(i) 758.17

5. Simplify.

(a) $\frac{3}{5} \times \frac{-5}{12}$

(b) $\frac{-1}{2} \times \frac{-1}{3}$

(c) $1\frac{1}{4} \times \frac{2}{3}$

(d) $\frac{4}{3} \times \frac{-12}{5}$

(e) $1\frac{1}{5} \times \left(-\frac{2}{3}\right)$

(f) $\frac{-3}{16} \times (-8)$

(g) $\left(-1\frac{1}{4}\right)\left(1\frac{1}{3}\right)$

(h) $-10\left(\frac{2}{5}\right)\left(-\frac{1}{2}\right)$

(i) $\frac{5}{-8} \times \frac{2}{3} \times \frac{-9}{10}$

(j) $\left(\frac{-3}{5}\right)\left(1\frac{7}{10}\right)\left(-\frac{5}{3}\right)$

(k) $\left(3\frac{1}{8}\right)\left(-3\frac{1}{5}\right)$

(l) $-3\left(6\frac{1}{3}\right)$

6. Simplify.

(a) $\frac{3}{5} \div \frac{-6}{7}$

(b) $\frac{-4}{3} \div \frac{8}{9}$

(c) $-1 \div \frac{2}{3}$

(d) $1\frac{1}{3} \div \frac{5}{9}$

(e) $\left(-2\frac{1}{4}\right) \div \frac{-3}{4}$

(f) $5 \div \left(-1\frac{1}{9}\right)$

(g) $\frac{6}{5} \div \frac{3}{-10}$

(h) $\frac{2}{3} \div (-3)$

7. Simplify.

(a) $\frac{5}{12} + \frac{-6}{12}$

(b) $\frac{-1}{8} + \frac{-6}{8}$

(c) $\frac{9}{10} - \frac{-1}{10}$

(d) $\frac{-3}{4} + \frac{2}{5}$

(e) $1\frac{3}{4} + \frac{-2}{3}$

(f) $\frac{-3}{4} - \frac{1}{6}$

(g) $1\frac{1}{8} - \frac{-2}{3}$

(h) $\left(-2\frac{1}{3}\right) - \left(-2\frac{1}{3}\right)$

(i) $1\frac{1}{2} + \frac{-5}{6} - \frac{1}{3}$

(j) $\frac{-7}{8} + \frac{-1}{2} - 2\frac{1}{8}$

(k) $1\frac{1}{3} - 2 + \frac{3}{4}$

(l) $-5 - 3 + 1\frac{3}{4}$

8. Simplify.

(a) $\frac{-3}{5} \times 1\frac{2}{3} + \frac{-5}{6}$

(b) $\left(\frac{-5}{7} \times 3\frac{1}{2}\right) \div \frac{1}{-4}$

(c) $\left(\frac{-2}{5} + \frac{3}{4}\right) \div \frac{1}{2}$

(d) $\frac{1}{2} \times \frac{-3}{4} + \frac{1}{2} \times \frac{5}{6}$

(e) $\left(\frac{-2}{3} + \frac{1}{8}\right) \div \left(-\frac{5}{12}\right)$

(f) $5\frac{1}{4} \div \left(\frac{-5}{8} - \frac{2}{3}\right)$

(g) $\left(\frac{-3}{4}\right)^2 + \frac{-3}{16}$

(h) $\left(\frac{1}{4}\right)^2 + \left(-\frac{1}{2}\right)^3$

(i) $\left(\frac{-15}{8} \div \frac{3}{-16}\right)\left(\frac{-2}{5}\right)$

(j) $\left(4\frac{2}{3} - 3\frac{7}{9}\right)^2$

9. If $x = -3.2$ and $y = 0.6$ evaluate the following expressions.

(a) $2xy$
(b) $2x - y$
(c) $3x - 5y$
(d) $5xy^2$
(e) $y^2 - x$
(f) $(x + y)^2$
(g) $\frac{x}{5} - y$
(h) $\frac{2}{3}x - 5y$
(i) $\frac{1}{2}y - \frac{x}{10}$

10. Simplify.

(a) $(x^5)(x^{-7})$
(b) $x \times x^0$
(c) $x^2 \times x^5$
(d) $y^{10} \times y^3 \times y^{-4}$
(e) $x^{-3} \times x^{-2}$
(f) $y^0 \times y^{-7}$
(g) $x^{12} \div x^4$
(h) $y^5 \div y^{10}$
(i) $x^9 \div x^{-2}$
(j) $x^{-3} \div x^{-5}$
(k) $y^{-5} \div y^0$
(l) $x^0 \div x^{-6}$

11. Evaluate.

(a) $\left(\frac{2}{3}\right)^0$ (b) $\left(\frac{1}{2}\right)^5$

(c) $\left(-\frac{1}{3}\right)^3$ (d) 3^{-2}

(e) 2^{-4} (f) $(-4)^0$

(g) $2^0 + 2^{-1}$ (h) $\left(\frac{1}{4}\right)^{-1}$

(i) $\left(\frac{3}{4}\right)^{-1}$ (j) $\left(\frac{1}{3}\right)^{-1} + 3^2$

(k) $\left(\frac{1}{2}\right)^{-2}$ (l) $\frac{1}{5^{-1}}$

12. Express each of the following values correct to three significant digits.

(a) 41.28   (b) 7.382   (c) 173
(d) 0.391 86   (e) 2.0648   (f) 5 729 000

(g) 1.798   (h) 0.002 189   (i) 0.2798

13. Express the following quantities in scientific notation.

(a) The mass of water in the world's oceans is approximately
6 950 000 000 000 000 000 000 kg.
(b) A single red cell of human blood contains approximately 270 000 000 hemoglobin molecules.
(c) The metric prefix nano means a multiplication factor of 0.000 000 001.
(d) The wave length of green light is approximately 0.000 05 cm.
(e) A human body contains approximately 5200 mL of blood.
(f) The diameter of a molecule of water is 0.000 000 028 cm.
(g) It is estimated that the sun will survive as an energy source for another 8 000 000 000 a.
(h) The distance from the earth to the sun is approximately 150 000 000 km.
(i) The mass of a proton is approximately 0.000 000 000 000 000 000 000 001 67 g.
(j) The metric prefix micro means a multiplication factor of 0.000 001.
(k) The circumference of the earth is approximately 40 000 km.

14. The formula for the surface area of a cylinder is

$$A = 2\pi r(h + r)$$

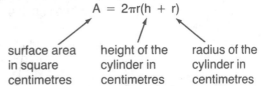

surface area in square centimetres   height of the cylinder in centimetres   radius of the cylinder in centimetres

Using $\pi = 3.14$, determine the surface area if $r = 5.25$ cm and $h = 10.0$ cm.

4.17 CHAPTER 4 TEST

1. List the rational numbers $-\frac{4}{5}$, $-\frac{8}{9}$, and $-\frac{13}{15}$ in order from smallest to largest by first writing them in equivalent forms having a lowest common denominator.

2. Simplify.

(a) $(\frac{4}{3})(1\frac{7}{8})(-\frac{7}{5})$

(b) $-\frac{3}{8} \div \frac{12}{7} \times -\frac{16}{5}$

(c) $-\frac{5}{6} + 1\frac{2}{3} - \frac{-3}{2}$

(d) $\dfrac{\frac{8}{9} - 1\frac{1}{4}}{\frac{1}{2} - \frac{37}{9}}$

3. (a) Write the following rational numbers as either terminating or repeating decimals.

(i) $\frac{51}{1000}$

(ii) $\frac{20}{27}$

(iii) $\frac{-5}{32}$

(b) For each repeating decimal in part (a) state the period and the length of the period.

4. Convert the following decimals to fractions in the form $\frac{a}{b}$, $b \neq 0$ and reduce to lowest terms.

(a) -0.6875

(b) $0.\overline{48}$

(c) $0.02\overline{4}$

5. Estimate. $\dfrac{689 \times 32.5}{458.1}$

6. Express in scientific notation.
(a) 482 000 000 000 000
(b) 0.000 000 079

7. Calculate the area of the shaded region.

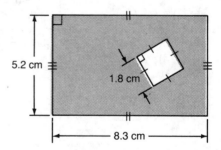

4.18 CUMULATIVE REVIEW FOR CHAPTERS 1 TO 4

1. Perform the indicated operation.
(a) $38\ 401 \times 64$
(b) $46\overline{)37\ 398}$
(c) $53\ 804 + 291\ 777 + 4863$
(d) $60\ 001 - 27\ 424$
(e) $567.49 + 34.125 + 813.4$
(f) $73.42 - 6.97$
(g) 47.5×0.76
(h) $165.032 \div 8.42$

2. Round off the following as indicated.
(a) 4672   (nearest hundred)
(b) 45 243   (nearest thousand)
(c) 750 000 (nearest ten thousand)
(d) 0.746   (nearest tenth)
(e) 1.85   (nearest tenth)
(f) 3.115   (nearest hundredth)

3. Simplify.
(a) $78 - (5 \times 1.1)^2$ (b) $6.6 \div 3 - 1.4$
(c) $1.4^2 \div 0.2 + 11.1$ (d) $7.6 \times 1.8 - 9.4$

4. If $r = 6$, $s = 4$, and $t = 3$ evaluate.
(a) $3r + 5s - 2t$
(b) $3r^2 - s - t$
(c) $(r + s)(s + t)$
(d) $4t^2 + 5rst$
(e) $\dfrac{r^2 + s^2 + t^2}{t}$
(f) $\dfrac{2rt - st + 4rs}{2}$

5. Simplify.
(a) $36x + 14y + 15x - 8y$
(b) $4x^2 + 6xy - x^2 - 3xy$
(c) $8r^2 + 5s^2 - 3s^2 + 7r^2$
(d) $21t^2 - 15t^2 + t^2 - 5s^2$

6. Substitute and find the value of the indicated variable.
(a) If $P = 2(\ell + w)$, find P when $\ell = 54.6$ m and $w = 18.7$ m.
(b) If $A = \frac{1}{2}bh$, find A when $b = 7.8$ cm and $h = 4.3$ cm.
(c) If $V = \ell wh$, find V when $\ell = 15.4$ m, $w = 5$ m, and $h = 9.5$ m.

7. Evaluate for $r = 4$ and $t = 3$.
(a) $10r + 3t - 4r + 5t$
(b) $2r^2 + 4rt - r^2 + 3rt$
(c) $6r^2 + 4t^2 - 2r^2 - 2t^2$

8. Carla wants to buy a pair of jeans that costs $42.56 and a jacket that costs $54.95. She has $72.50. Assuming there is no sales tax, how much more money does Carla need to buy the clothes?

9. The sum of four consecutive whole numbers is 230. Find the numbers.

10. Sam has three brass house numbers–a 5, a 6, and a 9. How many different three-digit house numbers can he make?

11. Justine had $235.89 in the bank. She made deposits of $45.00 and $56.90. She wrote cheques for $12.45, $21.89, and $61.23. What is her new bank balance?

12. David wants to catch the 09:15 ferry boat across the river. He should arrive ten minutes before the boat leaves to make sure he gets a ticket. It takes him forty minutes to get to the dock by bus and he lives five minutes from the bus stop. David decides to allow five extra minutes for delays. At what time should he leave his house?

13. Erica made a long-distance phone call that cost $8.32. The charges were $3.20 for the initial 3 min and $0.64 for each additional minute. How long was Erica's call?

14. What is the date and time in Halifax when it is 22:00 on January 3rd in Vancouver?

15. Each semester at Lee's school lasts twenty weeks. Lee decided to study mathematics for 1 min in the first week, 2 min in the second week, 4 min in the third week, and so on, doubling the time each successive week. During what week will Lee run out of time to study mathematics?

16. Add.

(a) $\begin{array}{r} -15 \\ 4 \\ \hline \end{array}$ (b) $\begin{array}{r} -7 \\ -9 \\ \hline \end{array}$ (c) $\begin{array}{r} 24 \\ -18 \\ \hline \end{array}$

(d) $\begin{array}{r} 3x^2 \\ -4x^2 \\ \hline \end{array}$ (e) $\begin{array}{r} -3xy \\ -9xy \\ \hline \end{array}$ (f) $\begin{array}{r} -2m^2 \\ 7m^2 \\ \hline \end{array}$

17. Subtract.

(a) $\begin{array}{r} -11 \\ 3 \\ \hline \end{array}$ (b) $\begin{array}{r} -15 \\ -16 \\ \hline \end{array}$ (c) $\begin{array}{r} 12 \\ -14 \\ \hline \end{array}$

(d) $\begin{array}{r} -6a \\ -7a \\ \hline \end{array}$ (e) $\begin{array}{r} 3a \\ -9a \\ \hline \end{array}$ (f) $\begin{array}{r} 6t^2 \\ 8t^2 \\ \hline \end{array}$

18. Simplify.

(a) $(-7)(-6)$ (b) $3(-2)$
(c) -9×6 (d) $(-16) \div (4)$
(e) $24 \div (-3)$ (f) $(-12) \div (-6)$
(g) $3 - 4 + 5$ (h) $6 - (-3) + 5$
(i) $(-2)^2 + 4$ (j) $3 - 5 - 9$
(k) $(-2)(-3) + 7$ (l) $1 - 3 - 4 + 7$

19. Simplify.

(a) $7x - 5x$
(b) $4y - 2 - 5y + 7$
(c) $15x^2 + 8xy + 3x^2 - 4xy$
(d) $(-3x)(-9y)$
(e) $-1(-4m^2)$

20. Simplify.

(a) $3x + 2(x - 2)$
(b) $4(t + 3) + 5(t - 2)$
(c) $2(x - 3) - 4(x - 6)$
(d) $7(2x - 1) - 6(3x + 2)$
(e) $2(5x^2 - 3) - 3(1 - 3x^2)$

21. If $E(x) = 3x^2 + 2x + 1$, find

(a) $E(2)$ (b) $E(3)$ (c) $E(0)$
(d) $E(-1)$ (e) $E(-2)$ (f) $E(-5)$

22. Write a computer program that will compute a value of $E = 2x^2 + 3x - 4$.

23. Express each of the following using scientific notation.

(a) 97 000 (b) 3 000 000 (c) 0.12
(d) 0.000 071 (e) 0.004 (f) 790 000

24. Simplify.

(a) $\frac{1}{3} \times \frac{-2}{5}$ (b) $1\frac{1}{3} \times \frac{-1}{4}$

(c) $-6 \times -1\frac{1}{3}$ (d) $\frac{1}{2} \div \frac{-2}{3}$

(e) $(-1\frac{1}{4}) \div \frac{-3}{5}$ (f) $2 \div \frac{-5}{6}$

(g) $\frac{-3}{8} \div 2$ (h) $1\frac{2}{5} \div \frac{1}{-2}$

25. Simplify.

(a) $\frac{3}{8} + \frac{-5}{8}$ (b) $\frac{-1}{6} + \frac{-5}{6}$

(c) $\frac{1}{4} - \frac{2}{5}$ (d) $2\frac{3}{4} - \frac{-3}{8}$

(e) $7 - \frac{-5}{6}$ (f) $1\frac{1}{2} - 2 + \frac{1}{3}$

26. Simplify.

(a) $x^7 \times x^6$ (b) $x^3 \times x^2 \times x$
(c) $x^{12} \div x^6$ (d) $x^9 \div x^2$

27. Evaluate.

(a) 2^{-3} (b) 4^0
(c) $(\frac{1}{3})^{-1}$ (d) $\frac{1}{4^{-1}}$
(e) $(\frac{1}{2})^{-2}$ (f) $3^0 + 3^{-1}$

28. Expand each of the following.

(a) 5×10^3 (b) 2.9×10
(c) 4.36×10^5 (d) 7.3×10^0
(e) 6.23×10^8 (f) 1.05×10^4
(g) 4.2×10^7 (h) 5.35×10^3
(i) 1.96×10^{12} (j) 6.018×10^6

29. Evaluate each of the following BASIC statements.

(a) $3 * 2 + 2 * 3$
(b) $3 * (2 + 2) * 3$
(c) $(3 * (2 + 2)) * 3$
(d) $3 \uparrow 2 + 2 \uparrow 3$
(e) $3 \uparrow 2 - 2 \uparrow 3$

30. What is the output for the following program?

```
NEW
10 FOR X=-4 TO 4
20 E=X↑2+X
30 PRINT X,E
40 NEXT X
50 END
RUN
```

RATIO AND PERCENT

CHAPTER

A good answer knows when to stop.
Italian proverb

REVIEW AND PREVIEW TO CHAPTER 5

DECIMALS AND FRACTIONS

EXERCISE

1. Multiply.
   (a) 3.2×2 (b) 5.2×3
   (c) 0.19×10 (d) 3.5×2
   (e) 0.03×100 (f) 4.3×3
   (g) 1.5×3 (h) 5×0.1
   (i) 7×0.2 (j) 9×0.5
   (k) 6.5×7 (l) 8×1.05
   (m) 7×0.01 (n) 4.4×0.5
   (o) 1.8×0.5 (p) 0.2×0.4
   (q) 0.9×0.3 (r) 0.2×0.01

2. Multiply.

   (a) 15.2 (b) 156.2
       $\times\ 3$ $\times\ 12$

   (c) 65.35 (d) 0.091
       $\times 0.96$ $\times 15.3$

   (e) 17.05 (f) 893.2
       $\times\ 11$ $\times\ 5.1$

   (g) 4.073 (h) 0.5692
       $\times 5.91$ $\times\ 3.1$

3. Divide.
   (a) $\dfrac{15.3}{3}$ (b) $\dfrac{4.2}{10}$ (c) $\dfrac{0.95}{5}$ (d) $\dfrac{3.2}{100}$

   (e) $\dfrac{0.3}{10}$ (f) $\dfrac{0.18}{10}$ (g) $\dfrac{0.36}{6}$ (h) $\dfrac{0.56}{8}$

   (i) $\dfrac{38}{1000}$ (j) $\dfrac{0.45}{15}$ (k) $\dfrac{1.25}{5}$ (l) $\dfrac{3.6}{9}$

   (m) $\dfrac{0.1}{1000}$ (n) $\dfrac{5.05}{5}$ (o) $\dfrac{4.97}{7}$ (p) $\dfrac{0.84}{12}$

4. Divide.
   (a) $2.4 \div 2$ (b) $18.9 \div 3$
   (c) $56 \div 100$ (d) $0.42 \div 7$
   (e) $0.3 \div 10$ (f) $7.5 \div 25$
   (g) $0.14 \div 7$ (h) $9.5 \div 5$
   (i) $3.2 \div 100$ (j) $0.27 \div 9$
   (k) $0.1 \div 100$ (l) $0.015 \div 15$

5. Divide.
   (a) $\dfrac{148}{8}$ (b) $\dfrac{71.12}{5.6}$

   (c) $\dfrac{0.5389}{17}$ (d) $\dfrac{55.3}{1.75}$

   (e) $\dfrac{12.985}{0.35}$ (f) $\dfrac{0.9933}{4.3}$

   (g) $\dfrac{0.209\ 61}{0.411}$ (h) $\dfrac{0.007\ 728}{0.069}$

   (i) $\dfrac{0.0819}{0.13}$ (j) $\dfrac{0.017\ 15}{2.5}$

   (k) $\dfrac{0.07}{56}$ (l) $\dfrac{0.004\ 56}{0.57}$

6. Simplify.
   (a) 43.56×5.002
   (b) 0.932×5.17
   (c) $(2.640 \div 1.5) \times 8.96$
   (d) $(83.06 + 1.532) \times 0.073$
   (e) $\dfrac{2.4 \times 0.075}{0.0005}$

   (f) $\dfrac{205.53}{0.85 \times 62}$

   (g) $0.756 \times (1.513 \div 0.89)$
   (h) $(17.3 \times 0.0728) \div 0.052$

7. Express as decimals.
   (a) $\frac{1}{8}$ (b) $\frac{1}{4}$ (c) $\frac{3}{8}$

   (d) $\frac{1}{2}$ (e) $\frac{5}{8}$ (f) $\frac{3}{4}$

8. Express as fractions in simplest form.
   (a) 0.25 (b) 0.4 (c) 0.35
   (d) 0.75 (e) 0.875 (f) 0.6
   (g) 0.375 (h) 0.2 (i) 0.08

9. Express as decimals to the nearest thousandth.

   (a) $\frac{1}{3}$ (b) $\frac{2}{3}$ (c) $\frac{3}{7}$

   (d) $\frac{7}{8}$ (e) $\frac{2}{11}$ (f) $\frac{5}{11}$

10. Express the following repeating decimals in the form $\frac{a}{b}$, $b \neq 0$.

EXAMPLE. $0.3\overline{25}$

SOLUTION:
Let $x = 0.325\ 252\ 5 \ldots$

① $\qquad 1000x = 325.252\ 5 \ldots$
② $\qquad\quad 10x = \quad 3.252\ 5 \ldots$
Subtract. $\quad 990x = 322$
① − ②. $\qquad\quad x = \frac{322}{990}$
$\qquad\qquad\qquad = \frac{161}{495}$

(a) $0.\overline{27}$ (b) $0.\overline{8}$ (c) $0.\overline{36}$
(d) $0.\overline{5}$ (e) $0.\overline{2}$ (f) $0.4\overline{2}$
(g) $0.\overline{324}$ (h) $0.4\overline{21}$ (i) $0.\overline{306}$

11. Write each group of fractions in order from smallest to largest.

(a) $\frac{3}{4}$, $\frac{5}{8}$, $\frac{1}{2}$, $\frac{3}{5}$, $\frac{5}{9}$

(b) $\frac{1}{3}$, $\frac{4}{9}$, $\frac{5}{11}$, $\frac{7}{12}$, $\frac{5}{12}$, $\frac{8}{19}$

(c) $\frac{5}{7}$, $\frac{3}{4}$, $\frac{10}{17}$, $\frac{5}{6}$, $\frac{2}{5}$

(d) $\frac{6}{7}$, $\frac{3}{4}$, $\frac{5}{6}$, $\frac{10}{13}$, $\frac{11}{12}$

(e) $\frac{15}{16}$, $\frac{12}{13}$, $\frac{17}{18}$, $\frac{18}{20}$, $\frac{20}{24}$

12. Simplify.

(a) $\frac{1}{5} + \frac{3}{5}$ (b) $\frac{1}{2} + \frac{1}{6}$

(c) $\frac{1}{6} + \frac{1}{3}$ (d) $\frac{2}{3} + \frac{1}{2}$

(e) $\frac{1}{2} + \frac{1}{5}$ (f) $\frac{3}{5} + \frac{2}{3}$

(g) $\frac{1}{2} + \frac{1}{3} + \frac{1}{5}$ (h) $\frac{1}{2} + \frac{2}{3} + \frac{3}{5}$

(i) $\frac{1}{2} + \frac{2}{3} + \frac{3}{4} + \frac{4}{5}$

13. Simplify.

(a) $2\frac{1}{2} + 3\frac{1}{8}$ (b) $5\frac{3}{4} + 2\frac{1}{2}$

(c) $3\frac{1}{3} + 2\frac{1}{2}$ (d) $5\frac{1}{4} + 2\frac{1}{3}$

(e) $5\frac{3}{4} - 2\frac{1}{2}$ (f) $6\frac{5}{8} - 2\frac{1}{4}$

(g) $6\frac{3}{4} - 3\frac{1}{2}$ (h) $5\frac{3}{4} + 2\frac{1}{2}$

14. Simplify.

(a) $5\frac{1}{4} - 1\frac{3}{4}$ (b) $6\frac{3}{8} - 2\frac{5}{8}$

(c) $8\frac{3}{8} - 2\frac{5}{8}$ (d) $5\frac{1}{3} - \frac{2}{3}$

(e) $9\frac{1}{2} - 2\frac{3}{4}$ (f) $5\frac{1}{4} - 2\frac{1}{2}$

(g) $8\frac{1}{3} - 4\frac{1}{2}$ (h) $6\frac{2}{3} - 1\frac{3}{4}$

15. Simplify.

(a) $\frac{1}{2} \times \frac{1}{3}$ (b) $\frac{3}{4} \times \frac{5}{8}$

(c) $\frac{3}{8} \times \frac{2}{5}$ (d) $\frac{4}{7} \times \frac{7}{8}$

(e) $\frac{1}{3} \times \frac{6}{7}$ (f) $\frac{3}{5} \times \frac{2}{5}$

(g) $\frac{3}{4} \times \frac{1}{2}$ (h) $\frac{2}{5} \times \frac{2}{3}$

16. Simplify.

(a) $\frac{1}{2}$ of 432   (b) $\frac{1}{4}$ of 515

(c) $\frac{2}{3}$ of 681   (d) $\frac{3}{4}$ of 2500

(e) $\frac{1}{5}$ of 3245   (f) $\frac{3}{5}$ of 6500

17. Simplify.

(a) $\frac{2}{3} \div \frac{1}{2}$ (b) $\frac{1}{2} \div \frac{2}{3}$

(c) $\frac{2}{3} \div \frac{1}{3}$ (d) $\frac{1}{3} \div \frac{2}{3}$

(e) $\frac{3}{4} \div \frac{1}{4}$ (f) $\frac{1}{4} \div \frac{3}{4}$

(g) $2\frac{1}{2} \div \frac{1}{5}$ (h) $5 \div 2\frac{1}{2}$

18. Simplify.

(a) $\frac{3}{4} + \frac{5}{8} - \frac{1}{2}$

(b) $2\frac{1}{2} + 3\frac{3}{4} - 1\frac{5}{8}$

(c) $6\frac{3}{4} \times 2\frac{1}{2} - 5\frac{7}{8}$

(d) $5\frac{1}{2} \times 3\frac{1}{3} - 7\frac{5}{6}$

(e) $3\frac{2}{3} \div 2 + 1\frac{1}{6}$

19. Which is larger?

(a) $\frac{2}{3}$ of 502   or $\frac{1}{2}$ of 670

(b) $\frac{5}{8}$ of 235   or $\frac{3}{4}$ of 200

5.1 RATIO AND RATE

> A ratio is a comparison of two or more quantities expressed in the same units.

A popular ratio of the chemical compounds nitrogen, phosphoric acid, and potassium oxide in lawn fertilizer is 12 : 4 : 8. This means that a 100 kg bag of fertilizer contains 12 kg of nitrogen, 4 kg of phosphoric acid, and 8 kg of potassium.

The ratio of wins to total number of baseball games for New York is 50 : 90.

| AMERICAN LEAGUE | | | |
| East | | | |
W	L	Pct.	GBL
Toronto 52	38	.578	—
Boston 50	37	.575	$\frac{1}{2}$
New York 50	40	.556	2
Cleveland 40	46	.465	10
Milwaukee 40	48	.455	11
Detroit 39	49	.443	12
Baltimore 33	56	.371	$18\frac{1}{2}$

The notation 50 : 90 is read "50 to 90" and forms a two-term ratio For calculations, a ratio is often written in fraction form.

$$50 : 90 \text{ is equivalent to } \frac{50}{90}$$

In this way the ratio may be simplified.

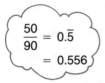

$$50 : 90 = \frac{50}{90} = \frac{5}{9} = 5 : 9$$

The ratio 50 : 90 is equivalent to 5 : 9.

(Certain ratios, such as the ratio of chemicals in fertilizers, should not be simplified. The terms of these ratios are also percents of a given mass or volume.)

EXAMPLE 1. Write a ratio in simplest form to compare each of the following.
(a) 36 m to 42 m
(b) 4 a to 6 months
(c) 5.4 cm to 0.6 cm

SOLUTION:

Divide each term of the ratio by the same value.

(a) $36 : 42 = \dfrac{\overset{6}{\cancel{36}}}{\underset{7}{\cancel{42}}}$

$\qquad\qquad = \dfrac{6}{7}$

$\qquad\qquad = 6 : 7$

(b) The quantities compared in a ratio must have the same units. Since there are 48 months in 4 a, the ratio is $48 : 6 = 8 : 1$.

(c) The decimal point is eliminated by multiplying each term by 10.

$$5.4 : 0.6 = 5.4 \times 10 : 0.6 \times 10$$
$$= 54 : 6$$
$$= 9 : 1$$

A rate is a comparison of two quantities with different units.

The following statements are examples of rates.

The car travelled at 65 km/h.

Harriet earns \$16.50/h.

Gasoline consumption was 12 L/100 km.

If a car travels 200 km in 4 h, then its rate of travel is 50 km/h or 1 km every $\frac{1}{50}$ h, or every 1.2 min.

 Press C 1 ÷ 5 0 × 6 0 =

The display is 1.2

If an employee earns \$540.00 in a 40 h work period, we express the rate of pay as an hourly rate.

 Press C 5 4 0 ÷ 4 0 =

The display is 13.5

We write the hourly rate of pay as \$13.50/h.

EXAMPLE 2. A secretary types a 936-word document in 12 min. Express this rate of typing in words per minute.

SOLUTION:

In 12 min the secretary types 936 words.

In 1 min the secretary types $\frac{936}{12}$ = 78 words.

The secretary's rate of typing is 78 words per minute.

EXERCISE 5.1

A 1. Express the following ratios in simplest form.

(a) 4 : 2   (b) 3 : 9   (c) 8 : 12
(d) 18 : 3   (e) 15 : 10   (f) 24 : 60
(g) 100 : 40   (h) 48 : 16   (i) 27 : 45
(j) 90 : 100   (k) 8 : 44   (l) 21 : 63

2. State an equivalent ratio for each of the following.

(a) 1 : 5   (b) 3 : 2   (c) 7 : 1
(d) 15 : 20   (e) 40 : 90   (f) 18 : 45
(g) 7 : 5   (h) 4 : 3   (i) 1 : 10

B 3. Express, in simplest form, a ratio for each of the following.

$$1 \text{ m} = 100 \text{ cm}$$
$$1 \text{ ha} = 10\ 000 \text{ m}^2$$

(a) 15 cm to 35 cm
(b) 5 m to 26 cm
(c) 75 pennies to 5 dimes
(d) 40 min to 30 min
(e) 18 min to 1 h
(f) 3 a to 15 months
(g) 300 m to 6 km
(h) 90 000 m² to 4 ha

4. Express each of the following rates as the rate for 1 unit.

(a) 480 m in 5 s
(b) $250.00 for 20 h
(c) 72 kg for $2.40
(d) 65 cm in $2\frac{1}{2}$ min
(e) 512 words in 6 min
(f) 862 km in $2\frac{1}{4}$ h

5. Simplify the ratios.

(a) 0.5 : 3.2   (b) 1.5 : 2.5   (c) 0.75 : 0.8
(d) 0.5 : 1   (e) 3.8 : 1   (f) 1 : 7.5

6. Calculate the ratio of the areas of the two rectangles below.

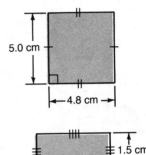

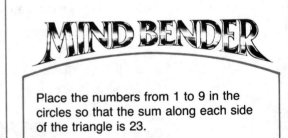

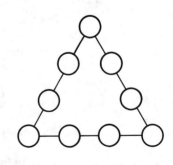

MIND BENDER

Place the numbers from 1 to 9 in the circles so that the sum along each side of the triangle is 23.

5.2 THREE-TERM RATIOS

Some applications of ratio require more than two terms.

EXAMPLE 1. A convenience store owner sold 124 L of 2% milk, 31 L of whole milk, and 62 L of skim milk in one day.
(a) What is the ratio sold in one day of skim milk to 2% milk to whole milk?
(b) Express this ratio in simplest form.

SOLUTION:
(a) The ratio of skim milk to 2% milk to whole milk is 62 : 124 : 31.
(b) If we examine the terms of the ratio, we see that

$$62 = 31 \times 2$$
$$124 = 31 \times 4$$
$$31 = 31 \times 1$$

The ratio in simplest form is 2 : 4 : 1.

When working with a ratio, the order in which the terms are stated is very important. Also, we must always ensure that the quantities being compared have the same units.

EXAMPLE 2. The ratio of cars to trucks is 7 : 9. The ratio of cars to motorcycles is 14 : 17. Find the ratio of cars to trucks to motorcycles.

SOLUTION:
The ratio of cars to trucks is 7 : 9 = 14 : 18.
The ratio of cars to motorcylces is 14 : 17.
The ratio of cars to trucks to motorcycles is 14 : 18 : 17.

EXERCISE 5.2

1. State the ratio of length to width to height in the following figures.

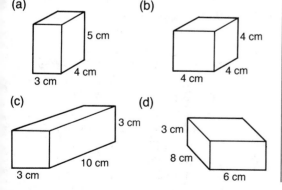

(a)

5 cm
4 cm
3 cm

(b)

4 cm
4 cm
4 cm

(c)

3 cm
10 cm
3 cm

(d)

3 cm
3 cm
8 cm
6 cm

B 2. There are 5 dimes, 12 quarters, and 15 nickels in a child's toy bank.

(a) What is the ratio of nickels to dimes to quarters?
(b) Express the ratio of the values of the dimes to the quarters to the nickels.
(c) What is the ratio of dimes to quarters to nickels?

3. At a recent school play, 36 student, 28 youth, and 60 adult tickets were sold.
(a) What is the ratio of student to youth to adult tickets sold?
(b) Express this ratio in simplest form.

5.3 PROPORTIONS

In a restaurant, 24 fried chicken dinners and 16 pasta dinners are served in 1 h. The ratio of chicken dinners to pasta dinners is 24 : 16. This means that there are three chicken dinners served to every two pasta dinners. Another way to write the ratio of chicken dinners to pasta dinners is 3 : 2.

24 : 16 and 3 : 2 are equivalent ratios

$$24 : 16 = 3 : 2 \quad \text{or} \quad \frac{24}{16} = \frac{3}{2}$$

Equivalent ratios represent the same comparison among the terms.

In the following example, we show how to test for equivalent ratios.

EXAMPLE 1. Determine whether 5 : 8 and 15 : 24 are equivalent ratios.

SOLUTION:
Express both ratios as fractions with a common denominator.

$$5 : 8 = \frac{5}{8} = \frac{5 \times 3}{8 \times 3} = \frac{15}{24} \quad \text{or} \quad 15 : 24 = \frac{15}{24} = \frac{15 \div 3}{24 \div 3} = \frac{5}{8}$$

∴ the ratios are 5 : 8 and 15 : 24 are equivalent.

When two ratios are equal the resulting equation is called a proportion.

A proportion is a statement of the equality of two ratios.	$\frac{a}{b} = \frac{c}{d}$ or $a : b = c : d$

EXAMPLE 2. Find the unknown term in the following proportions.

(a) $\dfrac{20}{8} = \dfrac{x}{40}$

(b) $\dfrac{15}{33} = \dfrac{10}{y}$

(c) $20 : m : 4 = 5 : 9 : n$

SOLUTION:

(a) $\dfrac{x}{40} = \dfrac{20}{8}$

$\phantom{\dfrac{x}{40}} = \dfrac{20 \times 5}{8 \times 5}$

∴ $\dfrac{x}{40} = \dfrac{100}{40}$

By comparison
$x = 100$

(b) $\dfrac{10}{y} = \dfrac{15}{33}$

$\dfrac{10 \times 3}{y \times 3} = \dfrac{30}{3y}$

$\dfrac{15 \times 2}{33 \times 2} = \dfrac{30}{66}$

By comparison
$3y = 66$
$y = 22$

(c) Write in fraction form.

$$\frac{20}{5} = \frac{m}{9} = \frac{4}{n}$$

$\dfrac{20}{5} = \dfrac{m}{9}$

$\dfrac{20 \times 9}{5 \times 9} = \dfrac{5 \times m}{5 \times 9}$

$\dfrac{180}{45} = \dfrac{5m}{45}$

$5m = 180$

$m = 36$

$\dfrac{4}{n} = \dfrac{20}{5} = \dfrac{4}{1}$

$\dfrac{4}{n} = \dfrac{4}{1}$

By comparison
$n = 1$

EXERCISE 5.3

A 1. Determine whether each pair of given ratios are equivalent ratios.

(a) $\frac{5}{8}, \frac{20}{30}$

(b) $\frac{12}{18}, \frac{16}{48}$

(c) $\frac{6}{11}, \frac{12}{33}$

(d) $\frac{15}{20}, \frac{30}{40}$

(e) $\frac{6}{8}, \frac{24}{32}$

(f) $\frac{48}{50}, \frac{24}{25}$

(g) $\frac{25}{5}, \frac{6}{1}$

(h) $\frac{4}{3}, \frac{36}{24}$

B 2. Write the following ratios in lowest terms.

(a) 12 : 3

(b) 15 : 3

(c) 5 to 20

(d) 27 to 3

(e) $\frac{5}{10}$

(f) $\frac{10}{4}$

(g) 19 : 36

(h) 64 : 12

(i) 9 : 6 : 15

(j) 8 : 15 : 24

(k) $\frac{32}{40}$

(l) $\frac{15}{24}$

3. Find the unknown value in each of the following proportions.

(a) $\dfrac{x}{50} = \dfrac{12}{100}$

(b) $\dfrac{x}{50} = \dfrac{32}{100}$

(c) $\dfrac{x}{10} = \dfrac{35}{50}$

(d) $\dfrac{x}{20} = \dfrac{56}{50}$

(e) x : 4 = 5 : 8

(f) 4 : x = 12 : 15

(g) 15 : 7 = x : 21

(h) 12 : 8 = 30 : x

(i) $\dfrac{4}{x} = \dfrac{32}{20}$

(j) $\dfrac{15}{24} = \dfrac{45}{x}$

4. Find the unknown value in each of the following proportions.

(a) $\dfrac{x}{7} = \dfrac{7}{21}$

(b) $\dfrac{7}{x} = \dfrac{15}{21}$

(c) 2 : 3 : 4 = 8 : x : y

(d) 5 : 6 : 10 = 10 : x : y

(e) 5 : x : 15 = 10 : 20 : y

(f) 33 : 12 : x = y : 8 : 20

(g) x : 6 : y = 24 : 24 : 36

5. The dimensions of a rectangle are in the ratio 4 : 7. The smaller dimension is 17 cm. What is the length of the rectangle?

6.

If 24 out of 200 people surveyed watched the news on the National TV network, how many people can be said to watch the news on this network in a city with a population of 320 000?

7. Construction companies bid for jobs through a process called tendering. The Blacktop Paving Company is successful in 7 out of every 20 bids that it submits for a job.

(a) How many jobs will this company get if it makes 100 bids?

(b) How many bids should this company have to make in order to get 100 jobs?

(c) In a total of 80 bids made, how many will be unsuccessful for this company?

8. The area of a square is 25 cm². What is the ratio of the sides?

9. The ratio of the lengths of the sides of two squares is 3 : 4. What is the ratio of the areas of the squares?

10. Ski jackets cost $100.00 and ski pants cost $80.00. The ratio of jackets sold to pants sold is 3 : 2.

(a) How many jackets are sold if there are 16 pants sold?

(b) What is the total amount of sales for jackets and pants if 16 pants are sold?

5.4 APPLICATIONS OF RATIO

In this section we look at problems that can be solved using ratios. Careful attention must be given to the READ step to identify how the parts are related.

READ

EXAMPLE 1. A punch is made with orange juice, lemonade, and ginger ale in the ratio 2 : 3 : 10. How much orange juice, lemonade, and ginger ale are needed to make 75 L of punch?

PLAN

SOLUTION:
Divide the 75 L into $2 + 3 + 10 = 15$ equal parts.
$$75 \div 15 = 5$$
1 part is 5 L

SOLVE

The amount of orange juice needed is
$$2 \times 5 = 10 \text{ L}$$
The amount of lemonade needed is
$$3 \times 5 = 15 \text{ L}$$
The amount of ginger ale needed is
$$10 \times 5 = 50 \text{ L}$$

The total needed is 10 L of orange juice, 15 L of lemonade, and 50 L of ginger ale to make 75 L of punch.
The ratio is 10 : 15 : 50 which is equivalent to 2 : 3 : 10.

Another method, using a simple equation, is as follows.
Let x represent the number of litres in each part.
$$2x + 3x + 10x = 75$$
$$15x = 75$$
$$x = 5$$

ANSWER

∴ each part is 5 L.

To find the amount of each ingredient, substitute the value of each part for x.
The amount of orange juice is $2 \times 5 = 10$ L.
The amount of lemonade is $3 \times 5 = 15$ L.
The amount of ginger ale is $10 \times 5 = 50$ L.

EXAMPLE 2. In a taste test, 14 out of every 17 people surveyed preferred unspiced salami to spiced salami. A total of 1500 kg of salami are being processed for sale. Find the amount of spiced and unspiced salami that should be processed to the nearest 10 kg.

SOLUTION:
Let the amount of unspiced salami be x kg.
$$\frac{x}{1500} = \frac{14}{17}$$
$$1500\left(\frac{x}{1500}\right) = \left(\frac{14}{17}\right)1500$$
$$x \doteq 1235.3$$
∴ the amount of unspiced salami is 1240 kg, and the amount of spiced salami is 260 kg to the nearest 10 kg.

EXERCISE 5.4

1. Elaine and Kasmir share a $1500 prize in the ratio 3 : 2. How much does each receive?

2. A piece of rope 1.5 m long is to be cut into 2 pieces in the ratio 2 : 3. How long is the shorter piece?

3. A hockey player has a record of 90 points earned, based on 1 point for each goal and 1 point for each assist. The ratio of goals to assists is 7 : 3. How many goals does this player have at this point in the season?

4. Three people share in a business in the ratio 4 : 3 : 1. They share in the profits of $450 000 in the same ratio. What is each person's share of the profits?

5. The school store orders track suits in sizes small, medium, and large in the ratio 2 : 5 : 4. How many of each size are there in an order of 396 track suits?

6. Construction companies bid for jobs through a process called tendering. The Buildright Construction Company is successful in getting 2 out of every 13 jobs that it tenders. How many tenders must the company submit in order to get 30 jobs?

7. Three people invest in a small business with $25 000, $12 000, and $12 500 respectively. They share in the profits in the ratio of the amounts invested.
(a) In what ratio should the profits be shared?
(b) How much should each receive from a profit of $150 000, to the nearest dollar?

8. A brass alloy contains copper and zinc in the ratio 20 : 7. How much copper is there in 200 kg of this alloy?

9. The ratio of nickels to dimes to quarters in a sum of money is 3 : 4 : 5. What is the value of the money if there are 144 coins?

10. One lap around the school track is 400 m. How many laps are required to run a 10 km race?

11. Francine walked 5 km in the same time that Lidwin ran 11 km. How far will Francine walk in the time it takes Lidwin to run 25 km? Give your answer to the nearest tenth of a kilometre.

12. An isosceles triangle has sides in the ratio of 3 : 3 : 5. The perimeter of the triangle is 121 cm. Find the length of each side of the triangle.

13. The monthly salaries of a plumber, mechanic, and accountant are in the ratio of 9 : 5 : 6. The sum of the monthly salaries for these three people is $5545.00. What is each person's monthly salary?

14. Jessie has some nickels, dimes, and quarters in the ratio of 3 : 8 : 4. The value of the coins is $13.65. How many nickels, dimes, and quarters does Jessie have?

Determine the pattern. Find the missing number.

1	2	3	8
2	1	1	3
5	2	3	16
4	2	1	░

5.5 APPLICATIONS OF RATE: UNIT PRICING

Products are often sold in different-sized containers and this can make it difficult for the consumer to know which size is the better value. In order to help consumers make comparisons, stores show unit prices for each item based on the size of the container. Unit rates and unit prices are found by calculating the rate for one.

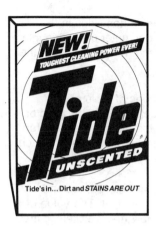

EXAMPLE 1. A large box of detergent costs $10.99 for 12 L. A small box of detergent costs $5.99 for 6 L. Which size is the better value?

SOLUTION:
The better value is found by calculating the unit price for each size and making a comparison.

LARGE		SMALL	
12 L cost	$10.99	6 L cost	$5.99
1 L costs	$10.99 ÷ 12	1 L costs	$5.99 ÷ 6
	≐ $0.9158		≐ $0.9983

The unit price is $0.9158/L.   The unit price is $0.9983/L.

Since 0.9158 < 0.9983, the large size is the better value.

EXAMPLE 2. The price of a 1 L bottle of syrup is $8.95. The price of a 750 mL bottle of syrup is $6.50.
(a) Express each price in terms of 100 mL units.
(b) Which size is the better value?

SOLUTION:
(a) LARGE   SMALL
   1 L costs $8.95   750 mL cost $6.50
   100 mL cost $8.95 ÷ 10   100 mL cost $6.50 ÷ 7.5
            = $0.895   ≐ $0.867
   The 100 mL cost is $0.895.   The 100 mL cost is $0.867

(b) Since 0.867 < 0.895, the better value is the 750 mL bottle.

EXERCISE 5.5

B 1. Calculate the unit price for each of the following.

(a) 750 mL of juice for $2.99
(b) 1.5 L of milk for $2.29
(c) 284 g of cheese for $2.25

2. Which is the better value?

(a) 750 mL for $1.29 or 500 mL for $0.85
(b) $66.00 per 8 h day or $8.25/h
(c) 20 kg for $24 or 50 kg for $65

MICRO MATH

The following program calculates unit prices.

```
NEW
10 PRINT"UNIT PRICING"
20 PRINT"ENTER THE PRICE OF THE ITEM"
30 INPUT P
40 PRINT"NUMBER OF UNITS IN THE ITEM"
50 INPUT N
60 PRINT"THE UNIT PRICE IS"
70 PRINT P/N
80 END
RUN
```

5.6 APPLICATIONS OF RATE: WORKING TOGETHER

In this section we use the reciprocal to solve rate problems that involve doing things together.

EXAMPLE. Jessie can cut a lawn in 3 h. It takes Sheila only 2 h to cut the same lawn. How long will it take Jessie and Sheila to cut the same lawn working together?

SOLUTION:

Step 1. Find the reciprocals.

Jessie takes 3 h to cut the lawn.

In 1 h Jessie cuts $\frac{1}{3}$ of the lawn.

Sheila takes 2 h to cut the lawn.

In 1 h Sheila cuts $\frac{1}{2}$ of the lawn.

Step 2. Add the reciprocals.

Working together, in 1 h they cut

$\frac{1}{3} + \frac{1}{2} = \frac{2}{6} + \frac{3}{6}$

$= \frac{5}{6}$ of the lawn.

Step 3. Find the reciprocal of the sum.

If they cut $\frac{5}{6}$ of the lawn in 1 h,

they can cut the whole lawn in $\frac{6}{5}$ h.

∴ Jessie and Sheila can cut the lawn in 1 h 12 min by working together.

EXERCISE 5.6

1. Kevin and Jason, working together, can do $\frac{1}{4}$ of a job in 1 h. How long will it take them to do the whole job?

2. Terry and Miguel, working together, can plough $\frac{2}{3}$ of their farm in 1 d. How many days will it take them to plough the whole farm?

3. Julio and Michelle operate automatic splitters for fireplace wood. Julio's machine can split a pile of wood in 4 d. Michelle's machine can do the same job in 3 d. They work 8 h/d. How long will it take them to split the pile of wood using both machines?

4. Elsie can line the football field in 2 h, while Carey can do the job in 1.5 h. How long will it take them to line the field working together?

5. Drain A will empty a tank in 5 h. Drain B will empty the tank in 6 h. How long will it take to empty the tank using both drains?

6. It takes 10 min to fill a bathtub with the tap turned on full. It takes 15 min to drain the same bathtub with the plug pulled out. How long will it take to fill the bathtub with the tap turned on full and the plug pulled out?

5.7 APPLICATIONS OF RATE: THE RULE OF THREE

A rate is a comparison of quantities with different units. Examples of rate are km/h, 35¢/kg, and 15 L/min.

In order to solve problems involving rate, we establish the Rule of Three, so-called because it involves three steps.

EXAMPLE 1. Find the cost of 11 golf balls if 3 golf balls cost $5.61.

SOLUTION:
Step 1.   Statement of Fact.

3 golf balls cost $5.61

Step 2.   Rate for 1.

1 golf ball costs $\dfrac{\$5.61}{3}$

Step 3.   Multiply.

11 golf balls cost $11 \times \dfrac{\$5.61}{3} = \$20.57$

EXAMPLE 2. A car travels 315 km on 45 L of gasoline.
(a) How far will it travel on 37 L of gasoline?
(b) How many litres will it take to travel 280 km?

SOLUTION:
(a) Step 1.   Statement of Fact.

45 L will allow 315 km of driving.

Step 2.   Rate for 1.

Divide by 45 to find the distance for 1 L.

1 L will allow $\dfrac{315}{45}$ km of driving.

Step 3.   Multiply.

37 L will allow $37 \times \dfrac{315}{45} = 259$ km of driving.

(b) Step 1.   Statement of Fact.

315 km takes 45 L of gasoline.

Step 2.   Rate for 1.

1 km takes $\dfrac{45}{315}$ L of gasoline.

Step 3.   Multiply.

Multiply by 280 to find the number of litres.

280 km takes $280 \times \dfrac{45}{315} = 40$ L of gasoline.

EXERCISE 5.7

B 1. If 10 calculators cost $179.50, how much do 17 calculators cost?

2. How far will a car travel on 11 L of gasoline if it travels 300 km on 40 L of gasoline?

3. A Boeing 747 burns 6 t of fuel in 3 h.
(a) How much fuel is used in 6.5 h?
(b) How long can the plane fly on 9 t of fuel?

4. Fred earns $75.15 for 9 h of work.
(a) How much will he earn for 28 h of work?
(b) How long must he work to earn $342.35?

5. If 3 m of material costs $20.94,
(a) what is the cost of 11 m of material?
(b) how much material could you buy for $272.22?

6. If twenty shares of stock give a dividend of $38.80,
(a) what is the dividend on 33 shares?
(b) how many shares would you need to receive a dividend of $292.94?

7. The moon revolves around the earth 4 times in 118 d.
(a) How long does it take the moon to revolve 15 times round the earth?
(b) How many times does the moon revolve round the earth in nine years?

8. A jet travels 2400 km in 3 h.
(a) How far does it travel in 7.5 h?
(b) How long would it take to fly 5800 km?

9. John can cut 2000 m² of grass in 4 h.
(a) How long will it take him to cut 6250 m² of grass?
(b) How many square metres of grass can he cut in 7.25 h?

10. Fifty-five air filters cost $1713.90.
(a) How much do 33 air filters cost?
(b) How many air filters can you buy for $396?

11. A drain can lower the water level of a pool 17 cm in 2 h.
(a) How long will it take the drain to lower the water level 40 cm?
(b) If the drain is opened for 6 h, by how much will the water level be lowered?

12. If you eat 2 pieces of apple pie you absorb about 2400 kJ of energy. How many kilojoules of energy would you absorb if you ate 3 pieces of apple pie?

13. If you climb a five-storey stairway you expend about 7.5 kJ of energy. If two golf balls are lifted through a height of 1 m then 1 J of work has been done.
(a) How much energy would be expended in climbing an eight-storey stairway?
(b) How much energy would be expended in climbing the Empire State building which has 102 stories?

14. The amount of energy required to melt 16 g of ice is about 5.3 kJ.
(a) How much energy is required to melt 50 g of ice?
(b) How many grams of ice can be melted with 30 kJ of energy?

15. It takes a radio signal approximately 1.3 s to travel from the earth to the moon, a distance of 374 000 km.
(a) How far into space will a radio signal travel in 15 s?
(b) How long will it take a radio signal to reach the sun which is 150 000 000 km away?

16. In one day approximately 432 billion litres of water flow over Niagara Falls. (Billion here means a thousand million, or 10^9. In some countries, a billion means a million million, or 10^{12}, which North Americans usually call a trillion.)
(a) How much water flows over the falls in 19 h?
(b) How long will it take 2268 billion litres to flow over the falls?

5.8 PERCENT

A ratio such as 51 : 100 is known as a percent since the value 51 is being compared to 100. The symbol, %, is used when working with a ratio in this form.

$$51 : 100 = \frac{51}{100} = 51\%$$

A ratio such as 1 : 4 can be expressed as a percent by changing it to an equivalent ratio having 100 as the second term. 1 : 4 = 25 : 100 or 25%.

EXAMPLE 1. Express each ratio as a percent.
(a) 3 : 25   (b) 9 : 5   (c) 3 : 8

SOLUTION:

(a) $3 : 25 = \frac{3}{25} \times \frac{4}{4}$ (b) $9 : 5 = \frac{9}{5} \times \frac{20}{20}$

$\qquad = \frac{12}{100}$ $\qquad = \frac{180}{100}$

$\qquad = 12\%$ $\qquad = 180\%$

(c) $3 : 8 = \frac{3}{8}$

Since it is not easy to determine the factor that multiplies by 8 to equal 100, we first express $\frac{3}{8}$ as a decimal by division.

$$3 : 8 = \frac{3}{8}$$

$\qquad = 0.375$ Press $\boxed{C}\ \boxed{3}\ \boxed{\div}\ \boxed{8}\ \boxed{\times}\ \boxed{1}\ \boxed{0}\ \boxed{0}\ \boxed{=}$

$\qquad = \frac{375}{1000}$ The display is $\boxed{37.5}$

$\qquad = \frac{37.5}{100}$

$\qquad = 37.5\%$

EXAMPLE 2. Express each percent as a decimal.
(a) 82%   (b) 5.75%   (c) 125%

SOLUTION:

82% = 0.82
5.75% = 0.0575
125% = 1.25
──────────→
Divide by 100.

(a) $82\% = \frac{82}{100}$ (b) $5.75\% = \frac{5.75}{100}$ (c) $125\% = \frac{125}{100}$

$\qquad = 0.82$ $\qquad = 0.0575$ $\qquad = 1.25$

EXAMPLE 3. Edna earns $680 per week working in a bank and receives a raise of $95. What is her percentage increase in pay?

SOLUTION:
The ratio of the amount of the raise to the amount previously earned is $\frac{95}{680}$.

$$\frac{95}{680} = 0.1397$$
$$\doteq 13.97\%$$
$$\doteq 14\%$$

Press [C] [9] [5] [÷] [6] [8] [0]
[×] [1] [0] [0] [=]

The display is `13.9705882`

∴ Edna's pay has increased 14%.

EXERCISE 5.8

1. Complete the following table in your notebook.

n ÷ 100	n	n × 100
	95	
	18.5	
	0.36	
	5.75	
	1.23	
	0.8	
	0.05	
	0.0065	

2. Express the ratios as a percent.
(a) 3 : 20   (b) 3 : 5
(c) 90 : 1000   (d) $\frac{49}{50}$
(e) $\frac{3}{2}$ (f) $\frac{5}{8}$
(g) $\frac{1}{8}$ (h) $\frac{1}{16}$
(i) $\frac{15}{16}$ (j) $\frac{6}{15}$

3. Express the following percents in decimal form.

(a) 35%   (b) 10%   (c) 3%   (d) $5\frac{1}{2}$%
(e) 1%   (f) 125%   (g) 6.75% (h) 0.1%

4. There are 32 students and 8 of them are girls.
(a) What percentage of the students are girls?
(b) What percentage of the students are boys?

5. In a shipment of 55 000 light bulbs, 425 were tested and found to be defective. What percentage of the light bulbs was defective?

6. The list price of a car that sold for $21 000 was raised by $750. What was the percentage increase in price?

7. The regular price of a jacket is $129.95. The jacket is put on sale for $100. Express the reduction in price as a percent.

CALCULATOR MATH

Some calculators have a [%] key. In order to use this key to find what percent 25 is of 40

Press [C] [2] [5] [÷] [4] [0] [%]

The display is `62.5`

The answer is 62.5%.

What percent is 16 of 24?

5.9 PERCENTS AND PROPORTIONS

Many percent problems are solved using proportions. A percent is a ratio with the second term 100.

EXAMPLE 1. Calculate 85% of $21.50.

SOLUTION:

METHOD I

$$\frac{85}{100} = \frac{x}{21.50}$$

$$21.50\left(\frac{85}{100}\right) = \left(\frac{x}{21.50}\right)21.50$$

$$x = 18.275$$

METHOD II

85% of 21.50 = 0.85 × 21.50
           = 18.275

∴ 85% of $21.50 is $18.28.

EXAMPLE 2. The Via Rail passenger train has the capacity to carry 288 passengers. It is estimated that 65% of the seats must be sold in order to meet expenses and start operating at a profit. What is the least number of seats that must be sold to operate at a profit?

SOLUTION:
We need to find 65% of 288.

METHOD I

$$\frac{65}{100} = \frac{x}{288}$$

$$288\left(\frac{65}{100}\right) = \left(\frac{x}{288}\right)288$$

$$x = 187.2$$

METHOD II

65% of 288 = 0.65 × 288
          = 187.2

> Due to the context of the question we round up.

The least number of seats that must be sold to operate at a profit is 188.

EXAMPLE 3. In the 1933 film, *King Kong* appeared to be about 15 m tall. The model used to make the film was really only 0.46 m tall. What percentage of the apparent height was the real model?

SOLUTION:

METHOD I

$$\frac{0.45}{15} = \frac{x}{100}$$

$$100\left(\frac{0.46}{15}\right) = \left(\frac{x}{100}\right)100$$

$$x \doteq 3.067$$

METHOD II

$$\frac{0.46}{15} = 0.46 \div 15$$

$$\doteq 0.030\ 667$$

$$\doteq 3\%$$

∴ the model of King Kong was about 3% of the apparent height.

EXERCISE 5.9

1. Calculate the following.
(a) 10% of 25
(b) 25% of 24
(c) 50% of 60
(d) 75% of 12
(e) 100% of 53
(f) 20% of 40
(g) 30% of 60
(h) 90% of 40

2. (a) What percent of 300 is 30?
(b) What percent of 450 is 90?
(c) What percent of 200 is 10?
(d) What percent of 50 is 50?
(e) What percent of 60 is 12?
(f) What percent of 150 is 10?
(g) What percent of 80 is 20?
(h) What percent of 90 is 30?

3. Calculate the following.
(a) 25% of $100
(b) 10% of $136.50
(c) 18% of $50.75
(d) 1.5% of $100
(e) 0.75% of $3560
(f) 8.5% of $25 000
(g) 6.5% of $35 000
(h) 12.5% of $42 500

4. During a survey of 75 drivers at a gas service station, the following data were recorded. 36 of the drivers ordered a full tank of gasoline and 45 drivers purchased regular unleaded gasoline. All of the others bought the higher octane premium gasoline.

(a) What percentage of the drivers in the survey ordered full tanks of gasoline?
(b) What percentage of the drivers bought the higher octane premium gasoline?

5. In a class survey, it was found that 35% of the students watched more than 2 h of television each day. Fourteen students said they watched more than 2 h of television each day. How many students are in the class?

6. The Royals basketball team took 48 shots in a basketball game and made 20 baskets. The Pirates basketball team took 64 shots and made 25 baskets.
(a) Express each team's ratio of number of baskets to number of shots taken as a percent.
(b) Which team had the better percentage?

7. A property was purchased for $80 000 and later sold for $100 000.
(a) Express the increase in value as a percentage of the purchase price.
(b) Express the selling price as a percentage of the purchase price.

8. Juanita operates a designer dress shop. Last year, her sales were $2 500 000. This year her sales were 115% of the sales last year. What were the sales for this year, to the nearest ten thousand?

9. Last year, the Micro Electronics company had a 2.7 million dollar profit. What is this year's profit if there is an increase of 125% over last year?

10. A car that sold for $18 500 in 1985, now sells for $25 000. Express the increase in price as a percent.

A, B, and C all play each other once in hockey. A partial table of results follows.

	G	W	L	T	Goals For	Goals Against
A	2	1			4	
B	2				3	0
C	2			1	2	

Find the score in each game.

5.10 APPLICATIONS OF PERCENT: SALES TAX

Sales tax is a very common application of percent. The amount of sales tax depends on the amount of the purchase and the rate of tax. The rate of sales tax for each province is determined by each provincial government.

EXAMPLE. A portable stereo costs $249.95. The rate of sales tax is 7%.

(a) What is the amount of sales tax?
(b) What is the cost of the stereo, including tax?

SOLUTION:
(a) 7% of $249.95 $= 0.07 \times$ $249.95
$$\doteq \$17.50$$

∴ the sales tax is $17.50
(b) $249.95 + $17.50 = $267.45
∴ the total cost of the stereo is $267.45

EXERCISE 5.10

B 1. Calculate.
(a) 7% of $24.95   (b) 7% of $89.95
(c) 7% of $24 500   (d) 8% of $34.50
(e) 8% of $69.95   (f) 8% of $21 700
(g) 7% of $495   (h) 8% of $49.50

2. Hanna buys the following items: paper at $3.50, pen at $16.95, and envelopes at $1.99.

(a) What is the total purchase?
(b) Calculate the sales tax at 7%.
(c) What is the total cost of the purchase including tax?

3. Calculate the sales tax at 6% for each of the following purchases.

(a) a new car listed at $19 995
(b) a ten-speed bicycle priced at $449
(c) three baseballs at $4.95 each

4. Calculate the total cost, including sales tax of 7%, on each of the following purchases.

(a) new skates at $225
(b) tennis racquet at $79.95
(c) 3 cassette tapes at $2.25 each

5. The cost of a sweater, including 7% sales tax, is $42.75. What is the price of the sweater?

6. The cost of a new automobile, including 8% sales tax, is $18 900. What is the price of the automobile?

7. The cost of a jacket, including sales tax, is $200. Find the selling price of the jacket if the rate of sales tax is

(a) 6%   (b) 7%   (c) 8%

MICRO MATH

The following program computes the amount of sales tax and the total amount when you enter the rate of tax and the amount of the purchase.

```
NEW
10 PRINT"SALES TAX CALCULATOR"
20 PRINT"ENTER THE PERCENT TAX RATE"
30 INPUT R
40 PRINT"ENTER THE AMOUNT OF PURCHASE"
50 INPUT P
60 PRINT"SALES TAX","TOTAL"
70 PRINT R*P/100,R*P/100+P
80 END
RUN
```

5.11 APPLICATIONS OF PERCENT: DISCOUNT

When a store or business reduces the price of an item, the amount of the reduction is called the discount.

sale price = original price − discount	rate of discount = $\dfrac{\text{discount}}{\text{original price}} \times 100$

EXAMPLE 1. A television set that sells for $399.95 is sold at a 15% discount.
(a) What is the amount of the discount in dollars?
(b) What is the new sale price?

SOLUTION:
(a) 15% of $399.95 = 0.15 × 399.95
$\qquad\qquad\qquad\doteq 59.99$
The discount is $59.99.
(b) $399.95 − $59.99 = $339.96
The sale price is $339.96.

EXAMPLE 2. The price of a desk has been reduced from $149.95 to $99.50. What is the rate of discount?

SOLUTION:
The amount of discount is
$\qquad$ $149.95 − $99.50 = $50.45.
The rate of discount is
$\qquad \dfrac{50.45}{149.95} \times 100 \doteq 0.336\,445 \times 100$
$\qquad\qquad\qquad \doteq 0.336 \times 100$
$\qquad\qquad\qquad = 33.6\%$

EXERCISE 5.11

1. A golf store advertises the following sale.

(a) Find the discount on each of the following.
$\qquad$ (i) a golf glove listed at $14.95
$\qquad$ (ii) a set of clubs at $725
$\qquad$ (iii) a golf bag at $129.50
$\qquad$ (iv) a dozen golf balls at $29.95

(b) Find the amount paid for each item in (a).

2. Long-distance telephone calls are discounted at certain times of the day. What is the cost of a telephone call that regularly costs $9.80 if the discount is
(a) 50%$\qquad$ (b) 60%$\qquad$ (c) 35%

3. What is the rate of discount on a $50 shirt that is reduced to $38?

4. What is the rate of discount on a new car that lists for $19 575 and is reduced by $2500?

5. What is the rate of discount on a radio with an original price of $149.50 and a sale price as follows?
(a) 125\qquad$ (b) 99.95\qquad$ (c) $74.95

A storekeeper bought a blanket for $50.00 and tried to sell it for 30% more. The blanket did not sell so the selling price was reduced by 30%.

1. Did the storekeeper
(a) make money$\qquad$ (b) lose money
(c) "break even"

2. Express any difference in Question 1 as a percent.

5.12 APPLICATIONS OF PERCENT: SIMPLE INTEREST

When money is deposited in a bank account, a certain amount of money, called interest, is paid to the depositor. When money is borrowed from the bank, interest is charged to the borrower.

The formula to determine simple interest is
$$I = Prt$$
where I is the interest
P is the principal (amount deposited or invested)
r is the rate of interest per year
t is the time in years

EXAMPLE 1. Dean borrowed $6000 for 225 d at a rate of 8%.
(a) What is the simple interest to be charged?
(b) How much is required to repay the loan?

SOLUTION

(a) P = $6000   r = 8%   t = 225
$$= 0.08 \qquad = \frac{225}{365}$$

$$I = Prt$$
$$I = 6000(0.08)\left(\frac{225}{365}\right)$$
$$\doteq 295.89$$

∴ the simple interest on the loan is $295.89.

(b) The amount to be repaid is $6000.00 + $295.89 = $6295.89.

The total value, when interest is added to the principal, is called the amount.
$$A = P + I$$
If we replace I by $I = Prt$, $A = P + Prt$
$$= P(1 + rt)$$

EXAMPLE 2. What is the amount when $1500 is invested for 124 d at 10% per annum?

SOLUTION:
$$A = P(1 + rt)$$
where P = 1500,   r = 0.01, $t = \frac{124}{365}$

$$A = 1500\left(1 + 0.01 \times \frac{124}{365}\right)$$
$$\doteq 1500(1.003\ 397)$$
$$\doteq 1505.10$$

∴ the amount is $1505.10.

The formula to determine the amount is
$$A = P(1 + rt)$$
where P is the principal
r is the rate of interest per year
t is the time in years

EXERCISE 5.12

A 1. Express the following percents as decimals.

(a) 7%   (b) 5%   (c) 8%
(d) 12%   (e) 10%   (f) 22%
(g) 0.5% (h) 14%   (i) 6%

2. Express as a fraction of a year.

(a) 6 months   (b) 30 d
(c) 1 month   (d) 100 d
(e) 24 d   (f) 400 d
(g) 9 months   (h) 300 d

B 3. Find the simple interest earned on each of the following investments.

(a) $7000 invested for 3 a at 5% annual interest
(b) $8000 invested for 5 a at 6% annual interest
(c) $12 000 invested for 6 months at 7% annual interest
(d) $10 000 invested for 7 a at 8% annual interest
(e) $700 invested for 3.5 a at 7% annual interest
(f) $10 000 invested for 5 a at 6% annual interest

4. Find the simple interest charged for each of the following loans.

(a) $300 for 60 d at 9%
(b) $2000 for 6 months at 8%
(c) $2500 for 90 d at 10%
(d) $4000 for 180 d at 9%
(e) $3500 for 30 d at 8%

5. After four years, Wayne had earned $720 on money invested at 7% annual interest. How much was his investment?

6. After two years, Bonita had earned $900 interest on money invested at 8% annual interest. How much was her investment?

7. To help pay college expenses, Marc borrowed $6000 from his mother for five years. The interest rate was 3% annual interest. How much did Marc owe his mother after five years?

MICRO MATH

The following program computes the simple interest for

principal	P ($)
rate	r (%)
time	t (days)

```
NEW
10 PRINT"SIMPLE INTEREST"
20 PRINT"ENTER THE PRINCIPAL"
30 INPUT P
40 PRINT"ENTER THE RATE"
50 INPUT R
60 PRINT"ENTER THE TIME"
70 INPUT T
80 I=P*0.01*R*T/365
90 PRINT"THE INTEREST IS ";I
100 END
RUN
```

EXERCISE

1. What is the interest on $2495 for 61 d at 7%?

2. Use repeated trials to find the interest rate that will produce $100 interest on $2000 in 6 months.

3. Use repeated trials to find the number of days required for an investment of $6000 at 9% to produce $200 interest.

5.13 APPLICATIONS OF PERCENT: COMPOUND INTEREST

When money is invested for a longer period, the interest is added to the principal, and new interest is calculated at the end of each interest period. This is called compound interest.

READ

EXAMPLE 1. $2000 is invested at 9% compounded annually. Find the amount after 3 a.

PLAN

SOLUTION:
We use the amount formula $A = P(1 + rt)$. When $t = 1$, $A = P(1 + r)$ for 1 a.
In order to keep track of our calculations, we use a table.

SOLVE

Year	P	r	A = P(1 + r)
1	2000.00	0.09	A = 2000(1 + 0.09) = 2000.00(1.09) = 2180.00
2	2180.00	0.09	A = 2180.00(1 + 0.09) = 2180.00(1.09) = 2376.20
3	2376.20	0.09	A = 2376.20(1 + 0.09) = 2376.20(1.09) ≐ 2590.06

> The amount at the end of year 1 is the principal at the beginning of year 2.

When we examine our calculations, we see that we get the same result if we multiply

$$A = 2000(1.09)(1.09)(1.09)$$
$$= 2000(1.09)^3$$

Principal   rate   years

Using a calculator and the y^x key

Press C 2 0 0 0 × 1 · 0 9 y^x 3 =

The display is `2590.058`

ANSWER

∴ the amount after 3 a is $2590.06.

The formula for the amount under compound interest is

$$A = P(1 + r)^n$$

where P is the principal
r is the rate
n is the number of years

EXAMPLE 2. $2500 is invested at 11.5% compounded annually. Find the amount after 5 a.

SOLUTION:

Using the formula for compound interest
$$A = P(1 + r)^n$$

where $P = 2500, \quad r = 0.115, \quad n = 5$

$$A = 2500(1.115)^5$$

Using a calculator and the y^x key

Press [C] [2] [5] [0] [0] [×] [1] [.] [1] [1] [5] [y^x] [5] [=]

The display is   4308.383417

∴ when $2500 is invested at 11.5% compounded annually, the amount after 5 a is $4308.38.

EXERCISE 5.13

B 1. Find the amount of the following.
(a) $2000 at 7% per annum for 3 a compounded annually
(b) $5000 at 8% per annum for 4 a compounded annually
(c) $6000 for 5 a at 9% per annum compounded annually
(d) $4500 for 4 a at 8% per annum compounded annually

2. Find the amount of each of the following loans compounded annually.
(a) $3000 at 12% per annum for 4 a
(b) $3500 at 8% per annum for 4 a
(c) $6800 at 9% per annum for 3 a
(d) $7500 at 10% per annum for 5 a

3. Allain invested $1000 at 9% per annum compounded annually for 3 a. What is the compound amount?

4. When Julian was born, his grandparents invested $100 for him at 9% per annum compounded annually. What is the amount after 18 a?

5. Which of the following gives the greater amount compounded annually?
(i) $100 invested at 8% per annum for 4a, or
(ii) $100 invested at 4% per annum for 8a?

6. Mary Jo invests $1000 at 8% per annum compounded annually. After 3 a the interest rate rises to 10% per annum. What is the amount after 5 a?

7. A credit card company charges interest on the unpaid balance at a rate of 1.5% per month. To find the amount which is owed, multiply the balance by $(1.015)^n$, where n is the number of months. What amount is owed if a balance of $575 is not paid after 3 months?

MICRO MATH

The following program computes an amount under compound interest.

```
NEW
10 PRINT"COMPOUND INTEREST"
20 PRINT"WHAT IS THE PRINCIPAL ?
30 INPUT P
40 PRINT"WHAT IS THE RATE (%)"
50 INPUT R
60 PRINT"HOW MANY YEARS"
70 INPUT N
80 A=P*(1 + 0.01*R)↑N
90 PRINT"THE COMPOUND AMOUNT IS ";A
100 END
RUN
```

5.14 APPLICATIONS OF PERCENT: RELATIONSHIPS OF LENGTH AND AREA

In this section we consider the effect of the relationships of length and area.

READ

EXAMPLE. A rectangle is 8 cm by 12 cm. The length and width are increased by 50%. What is the percentage increase in area?

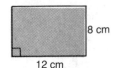

PLAN

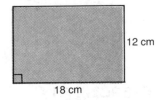

SOLUTION:
The area of the original rectangle is
$$A = \ell w$$
$$A = 12 \times 8$$
$$= 96 \text{ cm}^2$$

E=mc²

SOLVE

The dimensions of the larger rectangle are
$$8 + 50\% \text{ of } 8 = 8 + 4 = 12$$
$$12 + 50\% \text{ of } 12 = 12 + 6 = 18$$

The area of the enlarged rectangle is
$$A = \ell w$$
$$A = 18 \times 12$$
$$= 216 \text{ cm}^2$$

The increase in area as a percentage is
$$\frac{216 - 96}{96} = \frac{5}{4} \longleftarrow \times \frac{25}{25}$$
$$= \frac{125}{100}$$
$$= 125\%$$

ANSWER

When the lengths of the sides of the rectangle are increased by 50%, the area is increased by 125%.

EXERCISE 5.14

B 1. The sides of a square are 16 cm. Each side is increased by 25%. What is the percentage increase in area?

2. The sides of a rectangle are 10 cm by 15 cm. Each side is increased by 10%. What is the percentage increase in area?

3. The sides of a square are 40 cm. The length of each side is reduced by 25%.
(a) What are the dimensions of the reduced square?
(b) What is the percentage change in area of the square?

4. The sides of a rectangle are 20 cm and 25 cm. The length is increased by 100% and the width is increased by 50%. What is the percentage increase in area?

5. The sides of a rectangle are 40 cm by 60 cm. The lengths of the sides are reduced by 50%.
(a) What are the dimensions of the reduced rectangle?
(b) What is the percentage change in the area of the rectangle?

5.15 SCALE DRAWING: MAPS

A map is a scale drawing. The scale on a map is the ratio of the distance on the map to the actual distance on the earth. The scale on the given map is 1 : 7 500 000. This means that 1 cm on the map represents 7 500 000 cm or 75 km on the earth.

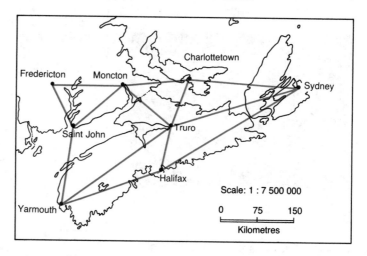

EXAMPLE 1. Find the distance by air from Halifax to Fredericton.

SOLUTION:
The distance on the map is 3.8 cm by measurement.
1 cm on the map represents 75 km on the earth.
3.8 cm on the map represent 3.8 × 75 km on the earth.

The distance from Halifax to Fredericton is approximately 285 km by air.

EXERCISE 5.15

1. Use the map and a scale of 1 cm represents 75 km to complete the distance chart in your notebook.

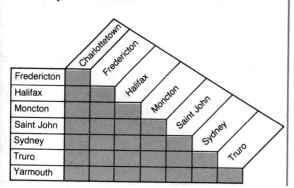

2. Enlarge the following map in the ratio of 3 : 1.

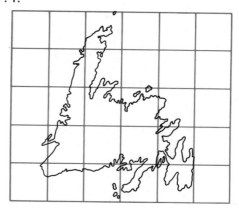

5.16 *CATS*

EXERCISE 5.16

1. The show *Cats* was the most successful Canadian stage production ever. It ran for just over two years at the Elgin Theatre in Toronto. There were 844 performances with an average attendance of 1200 at an average ticket cost of $40. About how much did *Cats* gross in the two years?

2. The Elgin Theatre seats 1600 people. How much more money would have been earned if the show had been a sellout for every performance?

3. If you had invested $100 000 in *Cats* you would have earned $300 000 by the end of the two years. What annual rate of interest did the investment earn?

4. One of the play's characters, Old Deuteronomy, signed about 85 000 autographs during intermissions. How long would it take you to sign your name 85 000 times?

5. *Cats* opened on March 4, 1985, and closed on March 14, 1987. How many days was the show at the theatre? Why were there more performances than days?

5.17 RACING THE BAY

North America's oldest road race takes place every year in Hamilton, Ontario. The race is run around the Hamilton Harbour and is 30 km long.

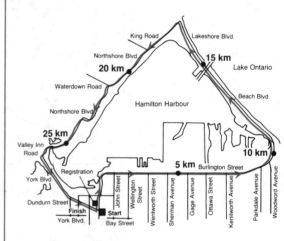

EXERCISE 5.17

1. What scale was used to draw the map?

2. The fastest time for a woman was set in 1984 by Anne-Marie Malone. Her time was 1 h, 46 min, and 29 s. What was her rate of running in km/h?

3. The fastest time for a man was set in 1967 by Fergus Murray. His time was 1 h, 33 min, and 28 s. Express his rate of running in km/h.

4. The first race was run on December 25, 1894. How many days ago was that?

5. If the race has been run every year, how many races have there been?

5.18 THE MÖBIUS STRIP

Topologists study odd shapes and strange objects. One of the most interesting of these is the one-sided surface introduced by the German mathematician and astronomer August Möbius. He discovered a contradiction to something that had always been taken for granted – every two dimensional surface has two sides. Möbius discovered a surface with one side.

If you join the two ends of a strip of paper with tape, a cylinder with two sides is formed.

To make a one-sided surface, take a strip of paper about 30 cm long.

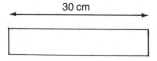

30 cm

Turn one end of the paper to form a half-twist.

Then tape the two ends together. This is the Möbius strip.

To show that the strip has only one side draw a line around the middle of the strip starting at the tape. Compare this to drawing a line around the middle of a paper cylinder.

Cutting the strip in Half
Cut a Möbius strip around the middle and describe the resulting shape.

Cutting the strip in Thirds
Cut a Möbius strip one-third of the way from its edge. The scissors will make two complete trips around the strip. Describe your results.

Another German mathematician, Felix Klein, followed Möbius' lead and designed a bottle which has an outside but no inside. No one will ever see a Klein bottle because it exists only in topoligsts' imaginations. However, if you ever find a Klein bottle, cut it in half. It will fall into two Möbius strips.

5.19 PROBLEM SOLVING

1. Place the numbers from 31 to 39 in the circles so that the sum along each side is 140.

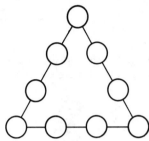

2. What 3-digit whole numbers satisfy all the following conditions.
(a) all 3 digits are odd numbers
(b) all 3 digits are different
(c) the product of the digits is greater than 30
(d) the ones digit is greater than the sum of the tens and hundreds digits.

3. The solid is made up of 60 cubes.

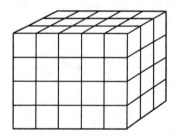

If you painted the solid, how many of the cubes would be
(a) painted on 3 sides?
(b) painted on 4 sides?
(c) painted on 2 sides?
(d) not painted at all?

4. Find a 4-digit number such that when you divide by 10, the remainder is 9; when you divide by 9, the remainder is 8; when you divide by 8, the remainder is 7; when you divide by 7, the remainder is 6; when you divide by 6, the remainder is 5; when you divide by 5, the remainder is 4; when you divide by 4, the remainder is 3; when you divide by 3, the remainder is 2; when you divide by 2, the remainder is 1.

5. A ball is dropped from a height of 100 m. It bounces one-half the distance from which it was dropped. How far will the ball have travelled when it strikes the ground for the fifth time?

6. If New Year's Day falls on a Tuesday
(a) how many more Tuesdays are there in the year?
(b) on what day of the week will St. Valentine's Day fall?

7. A radio station is heard at 980 AM on the radio dial. What does the 980 mean?

8. Caroline bought a sweater for $64 and paid for it with 10 bills. What denominations did she use?

9. The usual amount of tip on a meal in a restaurant is 15%. How much tip should you leave for a meal that costs $45.80?

10. Gail started a foot race 60 steps ahead of Charles. Charles took 2 steps to every 3 taken by Gail. Charles' stride covered as much ground in 3 steps as Gail covered in 7 steps. How many steps did Charles take in order to catch up to Gail?

11. If you take a number, multiply its square by 2, then subtract 10, you get 152. What is the number?

12. Divide the front and back of a sheet of paper as shown. The 2 is on the back of the 1.

Front

3	6	1
10	7	12

Back

2	5	4
11	8	9

Fold the paper so that the sections are arranged from 1 to 12 like the pages in a 12-page book.

13. (a) Jessica opened a book where the product of the two page numbers was 7832. At what pages did she open the book?
(b) Is it possible to open your math book so that the product of the two page numbers will be 6320?

14. The number 7 is a prime number because it has only two factors, itself and 1. The numbers 5 and 7 are called twin primes. Twin primes differ by 2.

There are 7 other pairs of twin primes among the first 100 numbers. What are they?

15. Name the wheels that are turning clockwise.

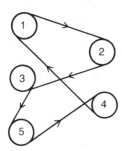

16.

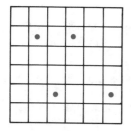

Four red dots are located on a 6 by 6 square grid. Cut the grid along the lines into two identical pieces having the same size and shape, with each piece containing two of the dots.

17. Driving at a constant speed, Mary can travel 150 km on 20 L of gasoline.
(a) How many litres of gasoline will she require to travel 400 km?
(b) How far can she drive on 35 L of gasoline?

18. There are twenty-one glasses. Seven glasses are full of water, seven glasses are half-full of water, and seven glasses are empty. How would you divide the glasses into three groups so that each group contains the same number of full, half-full, and empty glasses?

19. How would you plant 10 trees so there are 5 rows with 4 trees in each row?

20. There are some red and some black marbles in three boxes that are all labelled wrong. One box contains only red marbles, another box contains only black marbles, and the third box contains both black and red marbles.

| Black | Red and Black | Red |

Develop a plan to label the boxes correctly drawing only one marble from one box.

Determine the pattern. Find the missing number.

5	14	12	28
9	22	17	
8	20	15	34
13	30	19	42

5.20 REVIEW EXERCISE

1. Express each of the following as a ratio in simplest form.
(a) 20 m to 35 m
(b) 1 h 15 min to 45 min
(c) 24 min to 1 h
(d) 500 m to 2 km
(e) 3 a to 4 months
(f) 45 nickels to 25 dimes
(g) 4 quarters to 1 dollar

2. Express the following rates as a rate for 1 unit.
(a) 90 m in 15 s
(b) 144 kg for $3.60
(c) 240 km in 3 h
(d) 980 m in 20 min
(e) $350.00 in 7 h
(f) 1.5 L for $1.89
(g) $1.89 for 1.5 L

3. There are 15 pennies, 5 nickels, and 3 quarters.
(a) What is the ratio of pennies to nickels to quarters?
(b) What is the ratio of the value of the quarters to the value of the nickels to that of the pennies?
(c) What is the total value of the coins?

4. Find the unknown value in each of the following proportions.
(a) $\dfrac{x}{4} = \dfrac{5}{8}$
(b) $\dfrac{x}{4} = \dfrac{8}{15}$
(c) $\dfrac{6}{x} = \dfrac{12}{7}$
(d) $\dfrac{15}{19} = \dfrac{3}{x}$

5. The ratio of the length to the width to the height of a rectangular solid is 12 : 6 : 4. The width of the solid is 18 cm. Find the other two dimensions.

6. In a taste test the number of people who preferred brand A cookies to brand B cookies was 7 : 1.
(a) How many people selected brand A if there were 288 people in the test?
(b) How many people selected brand B in the test?

7. The ratio of the length to the width for a rectangle is 8 : 5. The perimeter is 52 cm. What are the dimensions of the rectangle?

8. A fruit basket that sells for $39.95 contains 3 bananas, 5 apples, and 5 oranges along with some cheeses and grapes.
(a) What is the ratio of apples to oranges?
(b) What is the ratio of bananas to apples to oranges?
(c) How many bananas and oranges are required to make up the baskets if there are 125 apples?

9. Three people invest $45 000, $65 000, and $75 000 in a small business. The business is sold for $250 000, and the money from the sale is divided among the three investors in the same ratio as the original investment. How much does each receive?

10. Calculate the unit price for each of the following.
(a) 1.5 L of juice for $3.95
(b) 350 g of meat for $8.75
(c) 150 g of chopped walnuts for $1.65

11. Which is the better value?
(a) 1.5 kg for $9.95 or 800 g for $5.50
(b) $13.85/h or $110.00 for an 8 h day

12. Jerome takes 2.5 h to paint a trailer. Ivan can paint the trailer in 2 h. How long will they take to paint the same trailer if they work together?

13. Calculate each of the following.
(a) 3% of $79.95
(b) 5% of $125.50
(c) 7% of $49.95
(d) 11% of $59.95
(e) 107% of $299
(f) 12.5% of $64
(g) 75% of $32.50

14. Calculate each of the following.
(a) What percentage is 50 of 32?
(b) What percentage of 125 is 25?

(c) What percentage of 20 is 25?
(d) What percentage of 65 is 13?
(e) What percentage of 80 is 50?
(f) What percentage of 32 is 50?

15. Calculate to the nearest tenth.
(a) 35 is 10% of what number?
(b) 65 is 15% of what number?
(c) 32 is 25% of what number?
(d) 65 is 18% of what number?
(e) 56 is 125% of what number?
(f) 145 is 110% of what number?

16. 234 of the 654 students at Richvale High School ate at least one sandwich for lunch. What percentage of the students ate a sandwich for lunch?

17. A new car which lists at $24 348 was sold for $22 450. Express the discount as a percent to the nearest tenth.

18. Greta earns $16.50/h and receives a raise of 4.2%.
(a) What is the hourly raise in pay?
(b) What is the new hourly rate of pay?

19. In a curb check of 375 cars it was found that 21 had unsafe brakes. What percentage (to the nearest tenth) of the cars checked had unsafe brakes?

20. The Big Sound Audio Store had sales of $2 525 000 last year. This year, the sales are expected to increase by 14.7%. What is the expected sales figure for this year?

21. Jeremy bought a calculator for $29.95 and some computer paper for $24.50 at the same store. Sales tax is calculated at 5%. What did Jeremy pay for the calculator and paper, including tax?

22. Glenda bought a pair of downhill ski poles for $39.95 plus sales tax of 7%. How much did she pay for the poles, including tax?

23. Tom borrows $1250 from the bank for 63 d at an annual rate of 9%. Calculate the interest.

24. A record album which regularly sells for $14.95 is on sale at a discount of 20%. How much would you pay for the record, including the sales tax of 11%?

25. Ludmilla deposits $2400 at the Credit Union and earns interest at the annual rate of 5.5%. What is the interest after 6 months?

26. Andrew had a student loan of $4500. The simple interest on the loan was charged at a rate of 6.25%. What is the interest for 1 d?

27. The dimensions of a rectangle are 20 cm by 16 cm. The length and width are increased by 25%.
(a) What are the new dimensions of the rectangle?
(b) What is the percentage increase in area?

A ruler is placed on top of two round pencils at the 5 cm and the 15 cm mark.

The ruler is rolled over the pencils until the pencils are at the 15 cm and 25 cm mark

How far has the ruler advanced?
How far have the pencils advanced?

5.21 CHAPTER 5 TEST

1. There are 8 nickels and 3 quarters. What is the ratio of the value of the quarters to the value of the nickels?

2. In 1 h, 32 trucks, 56 vans, and 128 cars passed through an intersection. What is the ratio, in simplest form, of cars to trucks to vans?

3. Solve for x in the following proportions.

(a) $\dfrac{x}{8} = \dfrac{12}{20}$ (b) $\dfrac{15}{x} = \dfrac{24}{32}$

4. The ratio of the length of the sides of two squares is 5 : 8. What is the ratio of their areas?

5. Three people invest in a small business with $45 000, $60 000, and $75 000 respectively. They share in the profits of the business in the ratio of the amount invested.
(a) In what ratio should the profit be shared?
(b) How much should each receive from a profit of $12 000?

6. A leak in the bottom of a tank will lower the water level 8 cm in 2 min. How long will it take to lower the level in the tank 50 cm?

7. Express the following to the nearest tenth.
(a) What is 15% of $25.00
(b) What percentage is 12 of 32?
(c) 65 is 13% of what number?

8. A shirt costs $39.95. Sales tax is charged at a rate of 7%. What is the cost of the shirt, including sales tax?

9. A pair of gloves which regularly sell for $32.50 are sold at a discount of 30%. What is the sale price of the gloves?

10. What is the simple interest charged on a loan of $2500 for 90 d at 11%?

POWERS AND SQUARE ROOTS

CHAPTER

6

Concentration is the price the modern student pays for success.
William Osler

REVIEW AND PREVIEW TO CHAPTER 6

EXPONENT LAWS

The following summarizes the exponent laws.

Multiplication

$$2^{-2} \times 2^5 = 2^{-2+5}$$
$$= 2^3$$

$$x^a \times x^b = x^{a+b}, a, b \in I$$

Division

$$2^{-5} \div 2^3 = 2^{-5-3}$$
$$= 2^{-8}$$

$$x^a \div x^b = x^{a-b}, a, b \in I$$

Power of a Power

$$(2^{-4})^3 = 2^{-4} \times 2^{-4} \times 2^{-4}$$
$$= 2^{-4 \times 3}$$
$$= 2^{-12}$$

$$(x^a)^b = x^{a \times b}$$
$$= x^{ab}$$

Zero Exponent

For $x \neq 0$, $x^0 = 1$

Negative Exponent

For $x \neq 0$, $x^{-a} = \dfrac{1}{x^a}$

EXERCISE

1. Simplify.
(a) $3^5 \times 3^3 \times 3$ (b) $5^5 \times 5^{17}$
(c) $2^8 \div 2^3$ (d) $4^9 \div 4^9$
(e) $(3^4)^2$ (f) 7^0
(g) $4^7 \div 4^3 \times 4^2$ (h) $3^9 \times 3^{10} \div 3^{17}$

2. Simplify.
(a) $2^3 \times 2^{-5}$ (b) $2^4 \div 2^6$
(c) $(3^{-5})^2$ (d) 4^{-3}
(e) 5^0 (f) $(-2)^{-2}$

3. Simplify.
(a) $10^2 \times 10^3 \times 10^{-5}$
(b) $10^4 \div 10^{-2}$
(c) $(10^{-3})^2$
(d) 10^0
(e) $\dfrac{1}{10^{-4}}$
(f) $10^{-4} \times 10^{-3} \times 10^9$

4. Simplify.
(a) $\left(\frac{1}{2}\right)^{-1}$ (b) $\left(\frac{2}{3}\right)^{-3}$
(c) $\left(-\frac{1}{4}\right)^2$ (d) $\left(-\frac{3}{5}\right)^0$
(e) $2^{-3} \times 3^{-2}$ (f) $\dfrac{1}{2^{-3}} \times \dfrac{1}{3^{-2}}$
(g) $\dfrac{1}{2^{-3}} + \dfrac{1}{3^{-2}}$ (h) $3^{-4} \div \dfrac{1}{3^2}$

5. Simplify.
(a) $x^3 \times x^4 \times x^7$
(b) $y^5 \div y^{-2}$
(c) $m^4 \div m^2 \times m^5$
(d) $x^{-2} \times x^7 \times x^{-1}$
(e) $a^{-2} \times a^{-3} \div a^{-5}$
(f) $t^5 \div t^2 \times t^{-2}$
(g) $(x^{-3})^2$
(h) $(y^4)^{-5}$
(i) m^0
(j) $(n^{-7})^{-2}$

6. Which is larger
$$2^{-3} + 3^{-2} \text{ or } 2^{-3} \times 3^{-2} ?$$

POWERS OF TEN

EXERCISE

1. Calculate.
(a) 1000×23 (b) 0.01×78
(c) 100×5.7 (d) 0.1×123
(e) $10\ 000 \times 56$ (f) 0.001×7300
(g) 100×0.003 (h) 10×0.056
(i) $100\ 000 \times 0.02$ (j) 1000×43.9
(k) 0.001×6000 (l) 100×0.025

2. Calculate.

(a) $34 \div 100$ (b) $0.67 \div 1000$
(c) $1.9 \div 0.1$ (d) $0.06 \div 100$
(e) $4000 \div 0.001$ (f) $360 \div 0.01$
(g) $999 \div 10\ 000$ (h) $2300 \div 0.01$
(i) $0.08 \div 0.1$ (j) $99 \div 10$
(k) $0.08 \div 100$ (l) $0.025 \div 0.01$

MENTAL MATH

EXERCISE

Perform the following calculations mentally.

1. (a) $123 - 20$ (b) $234 + 101$
(c) $200 \div 10$ (d) 202×4
(e) $1000 - 888$ (f) $1234 + 66$
(g) $330 \div 11$ (h) 555×2
(i) $101 - 92$ (j) $434 + 121$
(k) $848 \div 4$ (l) 1001×5

2. (a) $456 - 31$ (b) $789 + 11$
(c) $642 \div 2$ (d) 43×3
(e) $789 - 121$ (f) $444 + 323$
(g) $606 \div 6$ (h) 323×3
(i) $750 - 21$ (j) $707 + 101$
(k) $5500 \div 5$ (l) 432×100

3. (a) $666 \div 111$ (b) $700 - 444$
(c) $650 \div 5$ (d) 123×3
(e) $765 + 111$ (f) $9900 - 99$
(g) $320 \div 8$ (h) 2200×4
(i) $444 + 212$ (j) $888 - 424$
(k) $1001 \div 3$ (l) 242×2

4. Calculate.

(a) $7 - 5 - 6$
(b) $23 + 31 + 10$
(c) $44 - 22 + 5$
(d) $55 \div 5 - 6$
(e) $33 \div 3 - 2$
(f) $7 \times 9 - 1$
(g) $1000 - 900 + 34$
(h) $600 + 56 - 11$
(i) $23 \times 2 - 3$
(j) $1010 + 505$
(k) $6400 \div 8 + 3$
(l) $111 \times 2 - 1$
(m) $120 - 19 - 1 - 10$

EQUATIONS

EXERCISE

1. Solve.

(a) $x + 7 = 10$
(b) $t - 3 = 5$
(c) $4 = w + 1$
(d) $3 = y - 4$
(e) $6 = 3 + x$
(f) $7 + s = 20$

2. Solve.

(a) $3 + x = 9$
(b) $2 + x = 0$
(c) $5 - x = 3$
(d) $x + 8 = 12$
(e) $x - 7 = -3$
(f) $x - 3 = 10$

NUMBER LINES

EXERCISE

1. Graph on a number line.

(a) $\{x \mid x < 5, x \in W\}$
(b) $\{x \mid x > 0, x \in I\}$
(c) $\{x \mid x \leqslant 3, x \in I\}$
(d) $\{x \mid x \geqslant -2, x \in I\}$
(e) $\{x \mid x < 4, x \in W\}$
(f) $\{x \mid x \geqslant -1, x \in I\}$

2. Write a defining statement for each of the following.

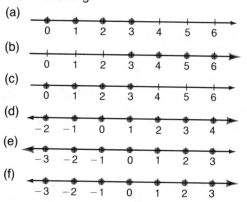

6.1 PERFECT SQUARES

The number 16 is called a perfect square because it can be represented as a square.

 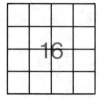

To get the perfect square numbers we square the whole numbers.

$$1^2 = 1 \qquad 2^2 = 4 \qquad 3^3 = 9 \qquad 4^2 = 16$$
$$5^2 = 25 \qquad 6^2 = 36 \qquad 7^2 = 49 \qquad 8^2 = 64$$

Another way to generate perfect squares is to add the consecutive odd numbers starting with 1.

$1 = 1$

$1 + 3 = 4$

$1 + 3 + 5 = 9$

$1 + 3 + 5 + 7 = 16$

$1 + 3 + 5 + 7 + 9 = 25$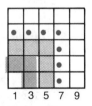

The following diagrams illustrate the first five triangular numbers.

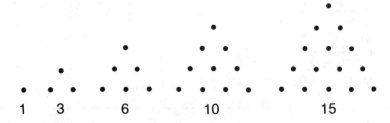

1   3   6   10   15

The sum of any two consecutive triangular numbers will always give a perfect square.

$$3 + 6 = 9$$
$$6 + 10 = 16$$
$$10 + 15 = 25$$

EXERCISE 6.1

1. What is the second triangular number that is also a perfect square?

2. Augustus De Morgan, a mathematician of the nineteenth century once said:

'I was [x] years old in the year $[x^2]$."

(a) What year does x represent?
(b) In what year was De Morgan born?
(c) In what year would a twentieth century mathematician have to be born in order to make the same statement as De Morgan?
(d) What is the only year that is a perfect square in the twenty-first century?

3. The number 196 is a perfect square since $14^2 = 196$.

(a) Starting with 1, what consecutive odd numbers when added give 196?
(b) What two consecutive triangular numbers when added give 196?

4. What two consecutive triangular numbers when added give the perfect square 324?

5. A famous problem in mathematics is Fermat's four-square problem. Fermat stated that any whole number can be written as the sum of, at most, four perfect squares. For example

$$1 = 1^2$$
$$2 = 1^2 + 1^2$$
$$3 = 1^2 + 1^2 + 1^2$$
$$4 = 2^2$$
$$5 = 2^2 + 1^2$$
$$6 = 2^2 + 1^2 + 1^2$$
$$7 = 2^2 + 1^2 + 1^2 + 1^2$$
$$8 = 2^2 + 2^2$$
$$9 = 2^2 + 2^2 + 1^2$$
$$10 = 2^2 + 2^2 + 1^2 + 1^2$$

No matter how large the number, we can write it as the sum of, at most, four perfect squares.

Write each of the following numbers as the sum of, at most, four perfect squares.
(a) 21   (b) 36   (c) 126   (d) 143
(e) 280   (f) 351   (g) 5053   (h) 1000

BLAISE PASCAL (1623–1662)

Pascal was born in Clermont-Ferrand, France. He was a person of frail health and his father, a mathematician, actually kept mathematics books from his son, in an attempt to conserve his energy. Pascal persisted, however, making many geometrical discoveries by the age of twelve. At the age of eighteen, he developed the first calculating machine. Pascal is said to have made significant discoveries in the geometry of conics as the result of a toothache — claiming he needed something to occupy his thoughts and keep his mind off the pain. He later expanded his interests to philosphy and theology, and became a monk in 1654.

One of Pascal's contributions to mathematics is the number triangle that bears his name.

6.2 SQUARE ROOTS

7 is called a square root of 49 since

$$7 \times 7 = 49$$

-6 is called a square root of 36 since

$$(-6) \times (-6) = 36$$

> The square root of a whole number is a number which, when multiplied by itself, gives the whole number.

In ancient Greece, the followers of Pythagoras discovered the existence of irrational numbers during their investigations of right-angled triangles. The solution of the equation

$$x^2 = 2$$

could not be expressed in the form $\frac{a}{b}$. The symbol, $\sqrt{2}$, was assigned to this value, and was called the square root of 2. Mathematicians have since shown that the value for $\sqrt{2}$ is an irrational number (a non-terminating, non-repeating decimal).

The radical sign, $\sqrt{}$, is used to represent the square root of any number.

EXAMPLE 1. Evaluate.
(a) $\sqrt{36}$ (b) $\sqrt{225}$

SOLUTION:

(a) $\sqrt{36} = 6$ since $6^2 = 36$

(b) $\sqrt{225} = \sqrt{9 \times 25}$
$= \sqrt{3 \times 3 \times 5 \times 5}$
$= \sqrt{(3 \times 5) \times (3 \times 5)}$
$= \sqrt{15^2}$
$= 15$

The equation $x^2 = 25$ may be seen to have two solutions.

$$(5)^2 = 25 \text{ and } (-5)^2 = 25$$

To avoid the confusion of a symbol representing two values, mathematicians agree that the radical sign, $\sqrt{}$, represents only the positive square root (called the principal square root).

$\sqrt{4} \times \sqrt{4} = 2 \times 2 = 4$ $\sqrt{9} \times \sqrt{9} = 9$	If $x \geq 0$, then $\sqrt{x} \times \sqrt{x} = x$

An expression, such as $\sqrt{2}$, which does not have a rational value is called a radical.

n	$\sqrt{n}$	n	$\sqrt{n}$
1	1.000	51	7.141
2	1.414	52	7.211
3	1.732	53	7.280
4	2.000	54	7.349
5	2.236	55	7.416
6	2.450	56	7.483
7	2.646	57	7.550
8	2.828	58	7.616
9	3.000	59	7.681
10	3.162	60	7.746
11	3.317	61	7.810
12	3.464	62	7.874
13	3.606	63	7.937
14	3.742	64	8.000
15	3.873	65	8.062
16	4.000	66	8.124
17	4.123	67	8.185
18	4.243	68	8.246
19	4.359	69	8.307
20	4.472	70	8.367
21	4.583	71	8.426
22	4.690	72	8.485
23	4.796	73	8.544
24	4.899	74	8.602
25	5.000	75	8.660
26	5.099	76	8.718
27	5.196	77	8.775
28	5.292	78	8.832
29	5.385	79	8.888
30	5.477	80	8.944
31	5.568	81	9.000
32	5.657	82	9.055
33	5.745	83	9.110
34	5.831	84	9.165
35	5.916	85	9.220
36	6.000	86	9.274
37	6.083	87	9.327
38	6.164	88	9.381
39	6.245	89	9.434
40	6.325	90	9.487
41	6.403	91	9.539
42	6.481	92	9.592
43	6.557	93	9.644
44	6.633	94	9.695
45	6.708	95	9.747
46	6.782	96	9.798
47	6.856	97	9.849
48	6.928	98	9.900
49	7.000	99	9.950
50	7.071	100	10.000

EXAMPLE 2. Simplify.
(a) $\sqrt{7} \times \sqrt{7}$
(b) $5 \times \sqrt{3} \times 2 \times \sqrt{3}$
(c) $\sqrt{5} \times \dfrac{2}{\sqrt{5}}$

SOLUTION:
(a) By definition,
$$\sqrt{7} \times \sqrt{7} = 7$$

(b) $5 \times \sqrt{3} \times 2 \times \sqrt{3} = 5 \times 2 \times \sqrt{3} \times \sqrt{3}$
$$= 10 \times 3$$
$$= 30$$

(c) $\sqrt{5} \times \dfrac{2}{\sqrt{5}} = \dfrac{\overset{1}{\sqrt{5}} \times 2}{\underset{1}{\sqrt{5}}}$
$$= 2$$

To determine the square root of a number you can use a table of square roots or a calculator.

EXAMPLE 3. Evaluate to the nearest tenth.
(a) $\sqrt{88}$
(b) $5\sqrt{10} + \sqrt{6}$

$5\sqrt{10}$ means $5 \times \sqrt{10}$

SOLUTION:
(a) USING THE TABLE
$$\sqrt{88} \doteq 9.381$$
$$\doteq 9.4$$

USING A CALCULATOR

Press C 8 8 √ =

Display 9.3808315

$\sqrt{88} \doteq 9.4$

(b) USING THE TABLE
$$5\sqrt{10} + \sqrt{6} \doteq 5(3.162) + 2.450$$
$$\doteq 15.810 + 2.450$$
$$\doteq 18.26$$
$$\doteq 18.3$$

USING A CALCULATOR

Press C 1 0 √ × 5 + 6 √ =

Display 18.260878

$5\sqrt{10} + \sqrt{6} \doteq 18.3$

EXERCISE 6.2

A 1. Complete the following.
  (a) $\sqrt{64} = \blacksquare$ (b) $\sqrt{36} = \blacksquare$ (c) $\sqrt{100} = \blacksquare$
  (d) $\sqrt{1} = \blacksquare$ (e) $\sqrt{\blacksquare} = 4$ (f) $\sqrt{\blacksquare} = 12$
  (g) $\sqrt{\blacksquare} = 0$ (h) $\sqrt{\blacksquare} = 11$ (i) $\sqrt{\dfrac{16}{25}} = \blacksquare$

  (j) $\sqrt{\dfrac{1}{4}} = \blacksquare$ (k) $\sqrt{\blacksquare} = \dfrac{2}{3}$ (l) $\sqrt{\blacksquare} = \dfrac{1}{3}$

B 2. Simplify.
  (a) $\sqrt{3} \times \sqrt{3}$ (b) $\sqrt{17} \times \sqrt{17}$
  (c) $2 \times \sqrt{49}$ (d) $5 \times \sqrt{100}$
  (e) $9 \times \sqrt{81}$
  (f) $\sqrt{3} \times \sqrt{3} \times \sqrt{3} \times \sqrt{3}$
  (g) $4 \times \sqrt{6} \times \sqrt{6}$
  (h) $(\sqrt{5})^2$
  (i) $(\sqrt{31})^2$
  (j) $7 \times (\sqrt{2})^2$
  (k) $3 \times \sqrt{2} \times 7 \times \sqrt{2}$

  (l) $\sqrt{\dfrac{2}{3}} \times \sqrt{\dfrac{2}{3}}$

  (m) $\sqrt{\dfrac{5}{6}} \times \sqrt{\dfrac{5}{6}}$

  (n) $\sqrt{6} \times \dfrac{5}{\sqrt{6}}$

  (o) $\dfrac{\sqrt{2}}{\sqrt{3}} \times \dfrac{\sqrt{2}}{\sqrt{3}}$

3. Evaluate.
  (a) $\sqrt{400}$ (b) $\sqrt{625}$
  (c) $\sqrt{121} + \sqrt{36}$ (d) $\dfrac{\sqrt{100} + \sqrt{4}}{\sqrt{36}}$
  (e) $\sqrt{10\,000}$ (f) $(\sqrt{100})^2$
  (g) $\dfrac{\sqrt{49}}{14}$ (h) $\dfrac{\sqrt{25} \times \sqrt{81}}{\sqrt{15} \times \sqrt{15}}$
  (i) $\sqrt{1\frac{9}{16}}$ (j) $\sqrt{8 + 8}$
  (k) $\sqrt{16 + 9}$ (l) $\sqrt{500 - 100}$

4. Evaluate to the nearest tenth.
  (a) $2\sqrt{5}$ (b) $5\sqrt{20}$
  (c) $\dfrac{\sqrt{40}}{3}$ (d) $\sqrt{4} + \sqrt{13}$
  (e) $\sqrt{20} - \sqrt{3}$ (f) $\dfrac{\sqrt{56}}{4}$

  (g) $2\sqrt{3} + \sqrt{5}$ (h) $\dfrac{\sqrt{18}}{7}$
  (i) $5\sqrt{7} + 5\sqrt{7}$ (j) $10\sqrt{7}$
  (k) $3\sqrt{5} - \sqrt{35}$ (l) $\dfrac{5\sqrt{3}}{2}$

5. Calculate the perimeter of each, to the nearest tenth.
  (a)

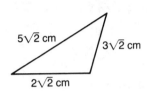

5√2 cm   3√2 cm   2√2 cm

  (b)

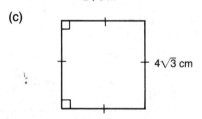

3√5 m   2√5 m

  (c)

4√3 cm

C 6. Evaluate to the nearest tenth.
  (a) $5\sqrt{3} - 4\sqrt{3}$
  (b) $3\sqrt{2} + 7\sqrt{2} - 8\sqrt{2}$
  (c) $2\sqrt{45} + \sqrt{5}$
  (d) $\sqrt{18} + 3\sqrt{18}$
  (e) $2\sqrt{3} + \sqrt{12} - \sqrt{75}$
  (f) $5\sqrt{2} - 3\sqrt{10} + \sqrt{2} + 3\sqrt{10}$
  (g) $\sqrt{32} - 3\sqrt{2}$
  (h) $\sqrt{3}(2\sqrt{3} + \sqrt{2})$
  (i) $3\sqrt{2}(\sqrt{8} + \sqrt{2})$
  (j) $4\sqrt{3} + 7\sqrt{2} - \sqrt{3} + \sqrt{2}$
  (k) $\sqrt{45} + 3\sqrt{10} - 2\sqrt{5} - \sqrt{90}$
  (l) $\dfrac{5\sqrt{3} - 3\sqrt{3}}{2}$
  (m) $\dfrac{\sqrt{18} + \sqrt{32}}{3}$

6.3 SQUARE ROOTS BY OTHER MEANS

SUBTRACTION

The following steps illustrate a way to find the root of a perfect square.

1. Start with 1 and subtract the odd numbers, in increasing order, from the perfect square until the result is 0.

2. The number of subtractions is the square root of the perfect square.

EXAMPLE. Find the square root of 49.

SOLUTION:

$$
\begin{array}{r}
49 \\
-1 \\
\hline
48
\end{array}
\quad
\begin{array}{r}
48 \\
-3 \\
\hline
45
\end{array}
\quad
\begin{array}{r}
45 \\
-5 \\
\hline
40
\end{array}
\quad
\begin{array}{r}
40 \\
-7 \\
\hline
33
\end{array}
\quad
\begin{array}{r}
33 \\
-9 \\
\hline
24
\end{array}
\quad
\begin{array}{r}
24 \\
-11 \\
\hline
13
\end{array}
\quad
\begin{array}{r}
13 \\
-13 \\
\hline
0
\end{array}
$$

We have made 7 subtractions.

The $\sqrt{49} = 7$.

NEWTON'S METHOD

The following method was devised by Sir Isaac Newton.

Since $\sqrt{36} = 6$, then $\dfrac{36}{6} = 6$.

To find $\sqrt{19}$, we can estimate $\sqrt{19} \doteq 4.5$.

$$\frac{19}{4.5} \doteq 4.2 \quad\longleftarrow\quad \text{4.2 is too small}$$
$$\text{4.5 is too large}$$

The average of 4.5 and 4.2 is a better estimate.

$$\frac{4.5 + 4.2}{2} = 4.35$$
$$\sqrt{19} \doteq 4.35 \text{ is better}$$

Repeating this process estimate $\sqrt{19} \doteq 4.35$

$$\frac{19}{4.35} \doteq 4.37$$

The average is

$$\frac{4.35 + 4.37}{2} = 4.36$$

Dividing again

$$\frac{19}{4.36} \doteq 4.36$$
$$\therefore \sqrt{19} \doteq 4.4$$

(to the nearest tenth)

EXERCISE 6.3

B 1. Find the square root of the following, by subtraction.

(a) 144
(b) 256
(c) 324
(d) 625

2. Find the square root, by subtraction.

(a) 441
(b) 529
(c) 676
(d) 841
(e) 961
(f) 1024

B 1. Use Newton's method to evaluate to the nearest tenth.

(a) $\sqrt{15}$
(b) $\sqrt{68}$
(c) $\sqrt{190}$
(d) $\sqrt{250}$

2. Use Newton's method to evaluate each of the following to the nearest tenth.

(a) $\sqrt{340}$
(b) $\sqrt{480}$
(c) $\sqrt{640}$
(d) $\sqrt{800}$
(e) $\sqrt{1400}$
(f) $\sqrt{1800}$

6.4 APPLICATIONS OF SQUARE ROOTS

There are many formulas that have a square root calculation built into them. The following are some examples.

EXAMPLE 1. When you are high above the ground, the distance you can see to the horizon is given by the formula

$$d = 3.6\sqrt{h}$$

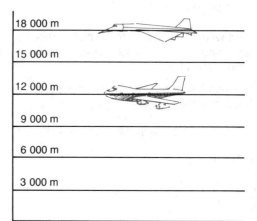

18 000 m

15 000 m

12 000 m

9 000 m

6 000 m

3 000 m

where d represents the distance you can see in kilometres and h represents your height in metres. Using the diagram, determine how much farther you could see from a window in the Concorde than from a window in the 747.

SOLUTION:

From the Concorde

$$d = 3.6\sqrt{h}$$
$$d = 3.6\sqrt{18\ 000}$$
$$\doteq 3.6 \times 134.2$$
$$\doteq 483 \text{ (nearest km)}$$

From the 747

$$d = 3.6\sqrt{h}$$
$$d = 3.6\sqrt{12\ 000}$$
$$\doteq 3.6 \times 109.54$$
$$\doteq 394 \text{ (nearest km)}$$

You could see about 89 km farther from the window in the Concorde.

EXAMPLE 2. The water at the surface of a river moves faster than the water near the bottom. The formula that relates these two speeds is

$$\sqrt{b} = \sqrt{s} - 1.3$$

where b is the speed near the bottom in km/h and s is the speed at the surface.
(a) Find the speed near the bottom if the speed on the surface is 16 km/h.
(b) Find the speed on the surface if the speed near the bottom is 6 km/h.

SOLUTION:

(a) $\sqrt{b} = \sqrt{s} - 1.3$
$\sqrt{b} = \sqrt{16} - 1.3$
$\quad = 4 - 1.3$
$\quad = 2.7$
$\quad b = 7.3 \text{ (nearest tenth)}$

The speed near the bottom is about 7.3 km/h.

(b) $\quad\sqrt{b} = \sqrt{s} - 1.3$
$\quad\sqrt{6} = \sqrt{s} - 1.3$
$\quad 2.4 = \sqrt{s} - 1.3$
$2.4 + 1.3 = \sqrt{s}$
$\quad 3.7 =$
$\quad 13.7 = s$

The speed on the surface is 13.7 km/h.

EXERCISE 6.4

B 1. The time for an object to fall a distance h is found by using the formula

$$t = 0.45\sqrt{h}$$

where h is the height in metres and t is the time in seconds.

(a) Find the time it would take a stunt artist to fall to the ground from a hot air balloon which is 380 m high?

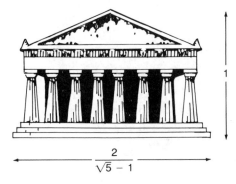

(b) How much longer would it take the stunt artist to fall to the ground from the top of the CN Tower which is 550 m high?

2. The design of the Parthenon, in Greece, is based on a figure called the golden rectangle.

The front of the Parthenon fits into a golden rectangle.

$$\frac{2}{\sqrt{5} - 1}$$

We can show that the length of a golden rectangle is $\dfrac{2}{\sqrt{5} - 1}$ times as long as its width. How many times longer is that?

3. The time for a pendulum to make one complete swing is found from the formula

$$t = 2\pi \sqrt{\frac{\ell}{9.8}}$$

where t is the time in seconds and ℓ is the length of the pendulum in metres. Calculate the time to the nearest tenth of a second when

(a) $\ell = 49$ m
(b) $\ell = 122.5$ m

4. The area of a triangle can be found by using Heron's formula

$$A = \sqrt{s(s - a)(s - b)(s - c)}$$

where a, b, and c are the lengths of the sides and

$$s = \frac{a + b + c}{2}$$

Calculate the area of each triangle.

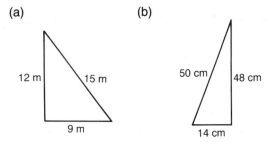

(a)

12 m 15 m

9 m

(b)

50 cm 48 cm

14 cm

C 5. For a satellite to stay in orbit it must have a speed of

$$s = \sqrt{\frac{4 \times 10^{14}}{d}}$$

where s represents the speed in m/s and d represents the distance, in metres, of the satellite from the centre of the earth.

(a) Find the radius of the earth in metres and state the reference.

(b) If a satellite is put in an orbit 35 900 km above the earth, it will circle the earth at the same speed as the earth is rotating. It will appear to hover over a spot on the earth. At what speed will this happen?

6.5 THE PYTHAGOREAN THEOREM

The triangle at the right is a right triangle because it has a 90° angle.

The longest side of the triangle, c, is opposite the right angle and it is called the hypotenuse.

The other two sides, a and b, are called legs.

Around 500 B.C. the Pythagoreans discovered that if they constructed any right triangle and then constructed squares on each of the sides, the area of the square on the hypotenuse is equal to the sum of the areas of the squares drawn on the legs. The diagram illustrates the property using a triangle with sides 5 cm, 4 cm, and 3 cm.

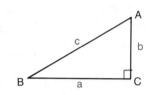

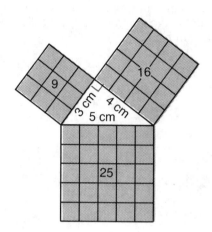

Pythagorean Theorem

For a right triangle ABC with sides a, b, and c, and $\angle C = 90°$

$$c^2 = a^2 + b^2$$

EXAMPLE. Calculate the length of the unknown side, to the nearest tenth of a metre.

(a)

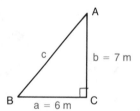

(b)

R s = 13 m T

t

r = 15 m

S

SOLUTION:

(a) In △ABC

$$c^2 = a^2 + b^2$$
$$c^2 = 6^2 + 7^2$$
$$= 36 + 49$$
$$c^2 = 85$$
$$c = \sqrt{85}$$
$$\doteq 9.2$$

The length of c is 9.2 m.

(b) In △RST

$$r^2 = s^2 + t^2$$
$$15^2 = 13^2 + t^2$$
$$625 = 169 + t^2$$
$$625 - 169 = t^2$$
$$456 = t^2$$
$$\sqrt{456} = t$$
$$21.4 \doteq t$$

The length of t is 21.4 m.

EXERCISE 6.5

A 1. State the Pythagorean Theorem for each triangle.

(a)

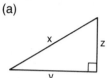

(b)

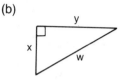

(c)

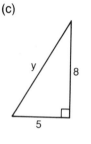

(d)

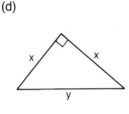

(e)

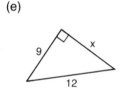

(f)

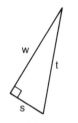

(g)

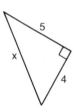

(h)

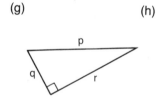

B 2. Calculate the length of each unknown side.

(a)

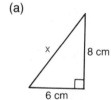

(b)

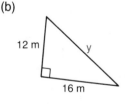

(c)

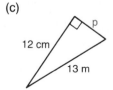

(d)

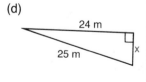

3. Calculate the length of each unknown side, to the nearest tenth.

(a)

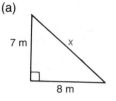

(b)

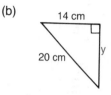

(c)

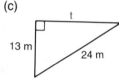

(d)

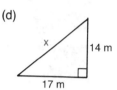

(e)

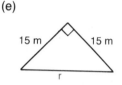

(f)

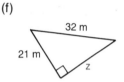

PROVING THE PYTHAGOREAN THEOREM

Figure A and Figure B are squares with the same area.

Figure A   Figure B

Figure A is made up of 4 identical triangles and a square. The square is drawn on the hypotenuse of each of the triangles.

Figure B is made up of 4 triangles, identical to those in Figure A, and 2 squares. The squares are drawn on the legs of two of the triangles.

Why does the area of the red square in Figure A equal the sum of the areas of the two red squares in Figure B?

6.6 APPLYING THE PYTHAGOREAN THEOREM

Applications of the Pythagorean Theorem occur in many situations.

READ

EXAMPLE 1. A 4 m ladder is placed 1.5 m from the base of a wall. To what height does the ladder reach on the wall?

PLAN

$E=mc^2$

SOLUTION:
Draw a diagram and use the Pythagorean Theorem. Let h represent the height up the wall.

SOLVE

$$4^2 = 1.5^2 + h^2$$
$$16 = 2.25 + h^2$$
$$h^2 = 16 - 2.25$$
$$h^2 = 13.75$$
$$h = \sqrt{13.75}$$
$$h \doteq 3.708$$

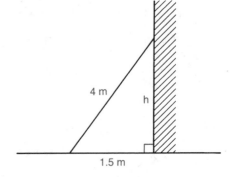

4 m

h

1.5 m

ANSWER

The ladder will reach a height of 3.7 m on the wall.

EXAMPLE 2. A diving tower is 29 m high. It is supported by 4 wires attached 4 m below the top of the tower and 10 m from the base of the tower. What is the total length of the support wires?

SOLUTION:
Use the Pythagorean Theorem to calculate the length of one supporting wire and then multiply by 4.

$E=mc^2$

Let ℓ represent the length of one of the supporting wires.

$$\ell^2 = 25^2 + 10^2$$
$$\ell^2 = 625 + 100$$
$$= 725$$
$$\ell = \sqrt{725}$$
$$\doteq 26.93$$

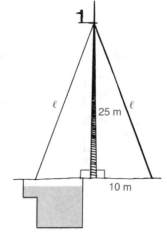

1

ℓ

ℓ

25 m

10 m

Each support wire is 26.9 m long.
The total length of the wires is $4 \times 26.9 = 107.6$ m.

EXERCISE 6.6

B 1. A vacant lot measures 50 m by 60 m. What distance is saved by walking diagonally across the lot from A to B instead of walking around the outside? (Express your answer to the nearest tenth of a metre.)

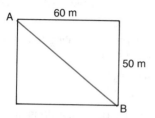

2. A 6 m fence is to be constructed as shown in the diagram.

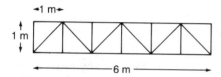

How many metres of lumber are needed?

3. The front of an A-frame ski chalet is in the shape of an equilateral triangle. The base of the chalet is 8 m.

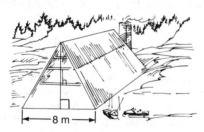

How high is the front of the chalet?

4. The size of a TV screen is usually given in terms of its diagonal. Find the diagonal length of the screen shown in the diagram, to the nearest tenth of a centimetre.

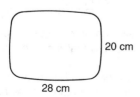

5. Stainless steel wires, called shrouds, are used to support the mast of a sailboat. To one decimal place, calculate the total length of wire needed for the shrouds.

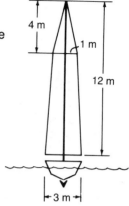

MICRO MATH

```
NEW
10 PRINT"FINDING THE HYPOTENUSE"
20 PRINT"ENTER THE SIDES"
30 INPUT A, B
40 C = SQR(A*A + B*B)
50 PRINT"THE HYPOTENUSE IS";C
60 END
RUN

NEW
10 PRINT"FINDING A SIDE"
20 PRINT"ENTER THE HYPOTENUSE"
30 INPUT C
40 PRINT"ENTER A SIDE"
50 INPUT B
60 A = SQR(C*C - B*B)
70 PRINT"THE SIDE IS";A
RUN
```

EXERCISE

1. Calculate the length of the unknown side.

(a)

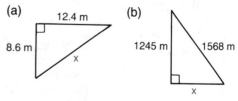

6.7 REAL NUMBERS

In Chapter 4, we saw that rational numbers can be expressed as either terminating decimals or non-terminating repeating decimals.

$$\frac{3}{4} = 0.75$$

terminating decimal

$$\frac{2}{11} = 0.181\ 818\ ...$$
$$= 0.\overline{18}$$

non-terminating, repeating decimal

There are also numbers that are neither terminating nor repeating. Compare the patterns in the following numbers

$$0.181\ 818\ 181\ ...$$
$$0.181\ 181\ 118\ ...$$

Although the second number displays a pattern, it does not terminate or repeat. It is a non-terminating, non-repeating decimal and cannot be expressed as a fraction or ratio. Such numbers are called irrational numbers.

> The set of irrational numbers is denoted by the symbol $\overline{Q}$.

We can construct an irrational number between any two rational numbers. For example, the irrational number 1.515 115 111 ... lies between the rational numbers 1.5 and 1.6.

$$1.5 < 1.515\ 115\ 111\ ... < 1.6$$

There are many other instances of irrational numbers. In working with circles, the ratio of circumference to diameter is represented by the symbol π. This ratio is a constant value for all circles, and has been proven to be an irrational number. The first 24 decimal places of π are shown below.

$$\pi = 3.141\ 592\ 653\ 589\ 793\ 238\ 462\ 643\ ...$$

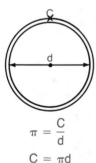

$$\pi = \frac{C}{d}$$
$$C = \pi d$$

In Section 6.2, we saw that numbers such as $\sqrt{2}$ and $\sqrt{3}$ are irrational numbers. In Section 4.1, we noted that every rational number had a position on the number line. Since we can construct an irrational number between any two rational numbers, there must be gaps or holes between rational numbers. If we join the rational numbers and the irrational numbers, we can fill the number line.

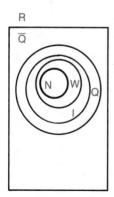

> The set of real numbers, R, is the union of the set of rational numbers, Q, and irrational numbers, $\overline{Q}$.
>
> $$R = Q \cup \overline{Q}$$

In the graphing of subsets of the real numbers, a solid line is used rather than a series of dots. This indicates that the number line is complete in two ways:
(i) to each point on the number line there corresponds a real number.
(ii) to each real number there corresponds a point on the number line.

EXAMPLE. Graph.
(a) $\{x \mid x \geqslant -2, x \in R\}$
(b) $\{x \mid -1 \leqslant x < 5, x \in R\}$
(c) $\{x \mid x > -2, x \in R\} \cap \{x \mid x \leqslant 1, x \in R\}$

SOLUTION:
(a)

This point is included   This solid line indicates that
(closed dot)   all points are included.

(b)

This point is not included
(open dot)

(c) If the two sets are graphed, the intersection is easily seen.

$x > -2$

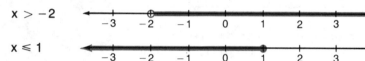

$x \leqslant 1$

Therefore the graph of the intersection is

EXERCISE 6.7

1. Determine
(a) a rational number and
(b) an irrational number between each pair of real numbers.
(i) 1 and 2
(ii) 0.5 and 0.6
(iii) 0.633 and 0.635
(iv) 0.222 ... and 0.255 ...

2. Throughout history, many approximations have been used for π. If $\pi = 3.141\,592\,65$, correct to nine significant digits, calculate, by division, the number of correct digits in each of the following approximations.

(a) $\frac{32}{9}$ (b) $\frac{22}{7}$ (c) $\frac{1178}{375}$

3. Graph.

(a) $\{x \mid x \geqslant 1, x \in R\}$
(b) $\{y \mid y < 4, y \in R\}$
(c) $\{w \mid w \leqslant -1, w \in R\}$
(d) $\{x \mid x > -5, x \in R\}$

(e) $\{y \mid y < 0, y \in R\}$
(f) $\{x \mid x \neq -2, x \in R\}$
(g) $\{w \mid w \geqslant -3, w \in R\}$
(h) $\{y \mid y > -10, y \in R\}$

4. Graph.
(a) $\{y \mid y \geqslant 2 \text{ or } y < -1, y \in R\}$
(b) $\{x \mid x < 0 \text{ and } x \geqslant -6, x \in R\}$
(c) $\{x \mid -2 \leqslant x \leqslant 3, x \in R\}$
(d) $\{w \mid 1 < w \leqslant 4, w \in R\}$
(e) $\{t \mid -3 < t < 0, t \in R\}$
(f) $\{x \mid 2 < x < 2, x \in R\}$
(g) $\{y \mid y > -1 \text{ or } y < -1, y \in R\}$

5. Graph.
(a) $\{x \mid x > -3, x \in R\} \cap \{x \mid x < 3, x \in R\}$
(b) $\{y \mid y > 0, y \in R\} \cup \{y \mid y < -2, y \in R\}$
(c) $\{x \mid x \leqslant -1, x \in R\} \cap \{x \mid x \geqslant -5, x \in R\}$
(d) $\{w \mid -1 < w \leqslant 3, w \in R\} \cap$
    $\{w \mid w \geqslant 1, w \in R\}$
(e) $\{x \mid x > -1, x \in R\} \cup \{x \mid x \leqslant 5, x \in R\}$
(f) $\{t \mid t > 0, t \in R\} \cap \{t \mid t < -1, t \in R\}$

6.8 THE SOLAR SYSTEM

The table gives the approximate circumference of the sun, the earth, and the moon.

	Circumference (km)
Sun	4 373 000
Earth	40 000
Moon	11 000

At a steady jogging pace of 10 km/h, how many days would it take you to jog around each?

In one year the earth travels about 940 000 000 km during its voyage around the sun.
(a) Calculate the speed of the earth in km/s.
(b) Compare the speed of the earth to the speed of a commercial jet flying at 1000 km/h.

There are 9 planets that circle our sun. Their approximate diameters are given in the table.

Planet	Diameter (km)
Mercury	4000
Venus	12 000
Earth	13 000
Mars	7000
Jupiter	143 000
Saturn	120 000
Uranus	52 000
Neptune	50 000
Pluto	6000

Using a scale of 1 cm = 10 000 km, draw circles to represent the planets. Start with Jupiter and draw the other circles (planets) inside Jupiter.

Our ancestors studied the motion of the sun, the moon, and the stars. They divided the stars into groups called constellations. The zodiac group of constellations received special attention. There are 12 constellations in the zodiac. Zodiac means "ring of animals."

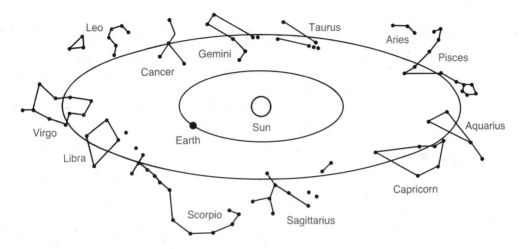

As the earth orbits around the sun, it makes the sun appear to pass through each of the zodiacal constellations in turn. At different times in the year, the sun will appear to be in different constellations.

EXERCISE 6.8

1. The sun appears to stay an equal amount of time in each constellation. How many days is that?

2. The table lists the constellations with their symbols. What symbols have line symmetry?

3. In what constellation does the sun appear in the following months.
(a) December
(b) June

4. If the sun appears to be in Taurus, where would the earth be to someone standing on the sun?

5. The path that the sun appears to follow through the constellations is called the ecliptic. Why is it impossible to calculate the circumference of the ecliptic?

Constellation	Symbol	
Aries	ram	♈
Taurus	bull	♉
Gemini	twins	♊
Cancer	crab	♋
Leo	lion	♌
Virgo	virgin	♍
Libra	scales	♎
Scorpio	scorpion	♏
Sagittarius	archer	♐
Capricorn	goat	♑
Aquarius	water-bearer	♒
Pisces	fish	♓

6.9 PROBLEM SOLVING

1. Evaluate.

(a) $\dfrac{1}{1 \times 2} = \blacksquare$

(b) $\dfrac{1}{1 \times 2} + \dfrac{1}{2 \times 3} = \blacksquare$

(c) $\dfrac{1}{1 \times 2} + \dfrac{1}{2 \times 3} + \dfrac{1}{3 \times 4} = \blacksquare$

(d) $\dfrac{1}{1 \times 2} + \dfrac{1}{2 \times 3} + \dfrac{1}{3 \times 4} + \dfrac{1}{4 \times 5} = \blacksquare$

(e) $\dfrac{1}{1 \times 2} + \dfrac{1}{2 \times 3} + \dfrac{1}{3 \times 4} + \cdots \dfrac{1}{97 \times 98}$
$+ \dfrac{1}{98 \times 99} = \blacksquare$

2. The product of two numbers is 900 and the sum of the two numbers is 61. Find the numbers.

3. One number is 32 more than another. The sum of the two numbers is 48. Find the numbers.

4. (a) Place the digits 2, 3, 4, 5, and 6 in the boxes so that the product is a maximum.

(b) Place the digits 2, 3, 4, 5, and 6 in the boxes so that the product is a minimum.

5. In one year, the National Basketball Association uses 1150 basketballs.
(a) How high would these balls reach if they were stacked one on top of the other?
(b) How many balls would be left over if you made a pyramid with one ball on top, four balls in the second layer, nine balls in the third layer, and so on?

6. Paper cups can be bought in packages of 25 or 50. Melissa bought 325 cups in ten packages. How many packages of 25 did she buy?

7. If you divide a number by 3, then add 4, and finally multiply by 7 you get 77. What is the number?

8. A block of cheese has dimensions of 6 cm by 5 cm by 6 cm. The cheese is covered in wax and then cut into one-centimetre cubes. How many cubes will not have wax on them?

9. Name the wheels that are turning counter-clockwise.

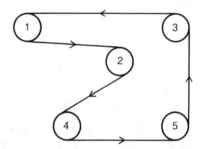

10. The average monthly temperatures for Ottawa are shown in the table.

Month	Temperature
Jan.	−11°C
Feb.	−11°C
Mar.	−4°C
Apr.	5°C
May	12°C
June	18°C
July	20°C
Aug.	19°C
Sept.	13°C
Oct.	8°C
Nov.	0°C
Dec.	−9°C

(a) Find the difference between the highest and lowest temperature.

(b) Find the change in temperature from
   (i) January to February
   (ii) February to March
   (iii) March to April
   (iv) January to June
(c) Find the average temperature for the six coldest months.
(d) Find the average annual temperature.
(e) Find the amount above or below the annual average for
   (i) January
   (ii) July

11. Jane has $10 in dimes. The dimes are in five piles, such that the value of the dimes in the first and second piles is $5.20. The value of the dimes in the second and third piles is $4.30, while the value of the dimes in the third and fourth piles is $3.40. There is $3.00 in dimes in the fourth and fifth piles.

How many dimes are in each pile?

12. Arrange 12 toothpicks as shown. Move 3 toothpicks to form 3 squares all the same size.

13. What point on the globe is diametrically opposite (through the earth) to 49°N, 72°W?

14. How many different times are all the digits on a digital clock the same during a twenty-four hour period?

15. If your heart makes its millionth beat of September at noon on September 10, what is your average heartbeat per minute?

16. Approximately how high would a stack of one million pennies be?

17. Here are the first three tetrahedral numbers.

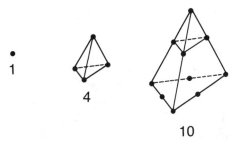

What are the next three tetrahedral numbers?

18. Amanda bought three shirts at $23.49 each and two sweaters at $67.50 each. How much change should she receive from $190.00?

19. The number 90 can be written as the sum of consecutive even numbers as follows.

$$14 + 16 + 18 + 20 + 22 = 90$$

Find four other ways to write 90 as the sum of consecutive even numbers.

6.10 REVIEW EXERCISE

1. Complete the following.
   (a) $\sqrt{81}$ = ■ (b) $\sqrt{■}$ = 10 (c) $\sqrt{0}$ = ■
   (d) $\sqrt{■}$ = 1   (e) $\sqrt{169}$ = ■ (f) $\sqrt{400}$ = ■
   (g) $\sqrt{\dfrac{9}{16}}$ = ■ (h) $\sqrt{■}$ = $\frac{1}{2}$ (i) $\sqrt{■}$ = 25

2. Simplify.
   (a) $\sqrt{5} \times \sqrt{5}$ (b) $3 \times \sqrt{81}$
   (c) $\sqrt{16} \times \sqrt{4}$ (d) $\dfrac{\sqrt{81}}{\sqrt{1}}$
   (e) $\dfrac{1}{\sqrt{9}}$ (f) $\dfrac{\sqrt{64}}{2}$
   (g) $\sqrt{\dfrac{1}{4}} \times \sqrt{64}$ (h) $\sqrt{4} + \sqrt{81}$
   (i) $5\sqrt{49}$ (j) $\sqrt{2\frac{1}{4}}$
   (k) $\dfrac{\sqrt{100} + \sqrt{4}}{\sqrt{49}}$ (l) $\sqrt{1\frac{7}{9}}$

3. Evaluate to the nearest tenth.
   (a) $\sqrt{76}$ (b) $\sqrt{201}$
   (c) $2\sqrt{5}$ (d) $8\sqrt{7}$
   (e) $\sqrt{12} + \sqrt{17}$ (f) $2\sqrt{13} + \sqrt{21}$
   (g) $5\sqrt{39} - \sqrt{6}$ (h) $10\sqrt{92} - 2\sqrt{41}$

4. Calculate the length of the unknown side to the nearest tenth.
   (a)

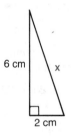

6 cm x 2 cm

   (b)

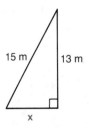

15 m   13 m   x

   (c)

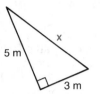

5 m   x   3 m

   (d)

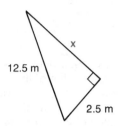

12.5 m   x   2.5 m

5. Calculate the length of AD to the nearest tenth of a centimetre.

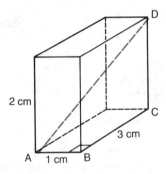

2 cm   3 cm   A   1 cm   B   C   D

6. Find the length of AB to the nearest tenth of a centimetre.

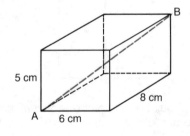

5 cm   8 cm   A   6 cm   B

7. Find the length of AB to the nearest tenth of a metre.

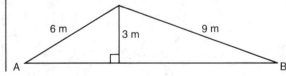

6 m   3 m   9 m   A   B

8. Find the length of XY to the nearest tenth of a metre.

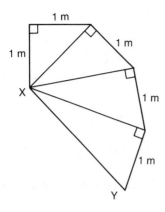

9. From a lighthouse, the distance you can see to the horizon is given approximately by the formula

$$d = 3.6\sqrt{h}$$

distance in kilometres — height of the lighthouse in metres

Calculate the distance visible from a lighthouse 46 m high.

10. The velocity of sound may be found from the formula

$$V = 20\sqrt{273 + t}$$

velocity in metres per second — temperature in °C

Calculate the velocity of sound when the temperature is
(a) −10°C
(b) 16°C
(c) 35°C

11. The bottom of a pencil box is 8 cm by 15 cm.

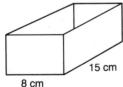

What is the length of the longest pencil that can be placed in the bottom of the box?

SQUARE ROOTS FROM A GRAPH

A graph can be used to estimate square roots.

To find $\sqrt{30}$, locate 30 on the vertical axis. Move horizontally to the curve, then vertically down to the horizontal axis.

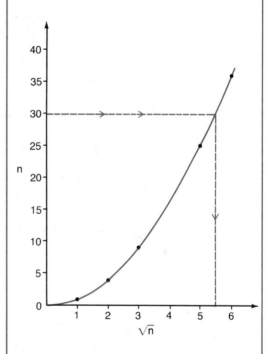

$$\sqrt{30} \doteq 5.5$$

EXERCISE

1. Use the graph to estimate the square root of each of the following.
(a) 20   (b) 35
(c) 12   (d) 7

6.11 CHAPTER 6 TEST

1. Simplify.
   (a) $\sqrt{4} \times \sqrt{4}$

   (b) $2 \times \sqrt{3} \times 3 \times \sqrt{3}$

   (c) $\sqrt{144} + \sqrt{36}$

   (d) $\sqrt{5} \times \dfrac{3}{\sqrt{5}}$

2. Evaluate to the nearest tenth.
   (a) $3\sqrt{7}$

   (b) $\sqrt{9} + \sqrt{3}$

   (c) $\dfrac{\sqrt{19}}{6}$

   (d) $4\sqrt{2} + 3\sqrt{5}$

3. The formula for the distance you can see to the horizon when above ground is

$$d = 3.6\sqrt{h}$$

where d is measured in kilometres and h is your height above ground in metres. Calculate the distance you can see from a height of 144 m.

4. Calculate the length of each unknown side to the nearest tenth.

(a)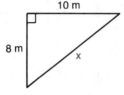

(b)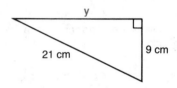

5. Find the length of AB to the nearest tenth of a metre.

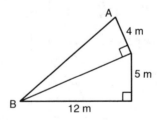

ALGEBRA

CHAPTER

7

To understand the theory which underlies all things is not sufficient. Theory is but the preparation for practice.

James Stephens

REVIEW AND PREVIEW TO CHAPTER 7

SIMPLIFYING ALGEBRAIC EXPRESSIONS

EXERCISE

Simplify the following.

1. (a) $3x + 5 - 6x + 2$
(b) $5x^2 + 3x - 6 + 4x^2$
(c) $5y - 6 + 11y - 12y + 7$
(d) $-6t + 5 - 3t - 11$

2. (a) $-5xy + 4x - 3xy - 7x$
(b) $5x^2 - x + 4 - 3x + 10 + x^2$
(c) $6xy - xy + 3x - y - 4x$
(d) $5x^2 - 3x - 5x + 10x^2 + 5x$

3. (a) $12x - 3xy - 6x + 7$
(b) $7y - 13 - 6 + 15y - 14$
(c) $7y^2 - 6y - 11y^2 - 5y - y^2$
(d) $-3 + 2y - 7 - 11y + 15$

4. (a) $-6y^2 + 2y - 7 - 11y^2 - 6y$
(b) $5x^3 - 7x^2 + 6 - 4x^3 - 9x^2 + 16$
(c) $12xy - 6yz + 4xy - 11yz - 7xz$
(d) $6y^2 - y - 7 - 5y + 8 - y^2$

5. (a) $4xy + 3y^2 - xy - 5y^2 + 6xy$
(b) $6t - 5s - 7 - 7t + 3s + 16$
(c) $4x^2 - 6x + 2x - 5x + 11x^2$
(d) $0 - 5x - 6y + 11x - 7y + 1$

Simplify using the distributive property.

6. (a) $2(x - 7)$
(b) $4(2x^2 - 3x + 1)$
(c) $4(x^2 - 3x + 2)$
(d) $7(6x - 2y + 3)$

7. (a) $3(-4x + 6y - 1)$
(b) $(-3 + 2x - 4y)8$
(c) $8(x - y - 6)$
(d) $(4x - 3y) - 5(x + 2y)$

8. (a) $11(2x - 6y - 1)$
(b) $3(x^2 - 5x) - (x - 1)$
(c) $2(x - 5) + 3(x + 2)$
(d) $5(x - 5) + 3(x + 2)$

9. (a) $3(3x - 4y) + 6(x + 6y)$
(b) $2(s - 3t) - (4s - 6t) - 3(2s + 2t)$
(c) $(2xy - 6z) + 5(3xy + 4z) + 6$
(d) $(3x - 5y) - 2(4y - 6x)$

10. (a) $7(3x - 2z) + 6 - 4(x + 7)$
(b) $2(2x + 6 - y) + 3(4x - 6y)$
(c) $3(2s + 6t + 3) - 16$
(d) $4(3x - 7y) + (4x - 2b)$

AREA

EXERCISE

Calculate the area of each of the following.

1.

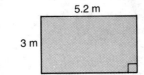

3 m, 5.2 m

2.

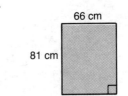

66 cm, 81 cm

3.

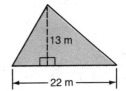

13 m, 22 m

4.

8 m
6 m

5.

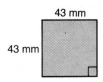

18.1 m
18.1 m

6.

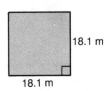

43 mm
43 mm

7.

r = 9 m

8.

6 m

9.

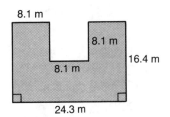

8.1 m
8.1 m
8.1 m
16.4 m
24.3 m

10.

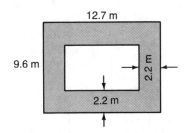

12.7 m
9.6 m
2.2 m
2.2 m

VOLUME

EXERCISE

Calculate the volume of each of the following.

1.

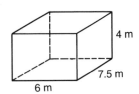

4 m
7.5 m
6 m

2.

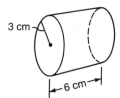

3 cm
6 cm

3.

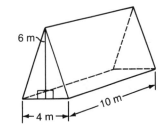

6 m
4 m
10 m

4.

3 m
2 m
2 m
2 m
12 m
10 m

7.1 POLYNOMIALS

A monomial is a number, a variable, or a product of numbers and variables. Each of the following expressions for area is an example of a monomial.

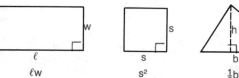

ℓw s^2 $\frac{1}{2}bh$ πr^2

A polynomial is a monomial or a sum of monomials. Algebraic expressions such as $x^2 - 5x + 6$, $3x^2 + 2$, and $4xy$ are all polynomials. Polynomials with two and three terms are called binomials and trinomials respectively.

Polynomial	Number of Terms	Name
4xy	one term	monomial
$3x^2 - 7$	two terms	binomial
$x^2 - 5x + 6$	three terms	trinomial

mono rail
bi cycle
tri athalon

Monomial   3 factors

4xy

1 term

Trinomial   2x + 5y − 7

3 terms

The degree of a monomial is the sum of the exponents of its variables.

Monomial	Degree
$4x^3$	3
$5a^2bc^4$	$2 + 1 + 4 = 7$
6	0

The degree of a polynomial in one variable is the highest power of the variable in any one term.

$5x^2 - 7x$ is a polynomial of degree two
$x^5 - 7x^2 + 4$ is a polynomial of degree five

The degree of a polynomial in two or more variables is the largest sum of the exponents in any one term.

$3x^2 - 2x^2y^2 + x^3$ is a polynomial of degree four
$3x^2y^3 - 2y^4 + 3x^3y^3$ is a polynomial of degree six

The terms of a polynomial are usually arranged so that the powers of one variable are either in descending or ascending order.

Descending Order	Ascending Order
$x^3 + 2x^2 - 3x + 1$ (in x) $4x^2 + 3xy + 2y^2$	$1 - 3x + 2x^2 + x^3$ (in x) $2y^2 + 3xy + 4x^2$

Polynomials are essential parts of equations. To solve many equations, it is often necessary to combine polynomials or to factor them. To build mathematical models, it is also often necessary to combine polynomials or to factor them. In following sections, we shall learn to factor polynomials. In this chapter we shall learn to combine polynomials.

EXERCISE 7.1

1. Identify each of the following as a monomial, binomial, or trinomial.
(a) 3abc
(b) $4x^2 + 7$
(c) $2a + 7b - 6c$
(d) $-6m$
(e) 8
(f) $1 - 5t^2 - 3t$
(g) $25x^5y^3$
(h) $4 - 11y^2$

2. State the degree of each monomial.
(a) 80x
(b) $27y^2$
(c) 13
(d) $4x^3y^4$
(e) $-2a^3b$
(f) $-9p^2q^3r$
(g) 4xyz
(h) m^7n^3p

3. State the degree of each polynomial.
(a) $6a^2b + 7a^3b^3$
(b) $4xyz - 5$
(c) $4m - 3s + 2t$
(d) $2x^2 - 2x^5$
(e) $a + a^2 + a^3 + a^4$
(f) $-6x^3y^2 + 5x^5y^6$
(g) $5 + 7x - 11a + 13t$
(h) $6a^4b^5c^6$
(i) $7mn^2p - 11x^5$
(j) $3^3a^2 - 5$

4. The expression for the perimeter of a rectangle, $2\ell + 2w$, is a binomial. Write two other expressions for measurement that are binomials or trinomials

5. Arrange the terms in each polynomial so that the powers of x are in descending order.
(a) $1 + x^2 + x^5 - x^3$
(b) $3 + 5x^2 - 4x$
(c) $6a^2 - 3ax + 4x^2$
(d) $24px^2 - 11p^2x + p^4x^3 + x^4$
(e) $-3mx + 4m^2x^3 - 5m^3x^2 - 4x^6$

6. Arrange the terms in each polynomial so that the powers of x are in ascending order.
(a) $x^5 + x + 1 - x^2 - x^3$
(b) $2x^4 + x^3 - x + 4$
(c) $3x^2y - 4xy^2 + 3x^3 + 5$
(d) $3x^3y^4 - 2xy - 5x^2y^4 + 7x^4$
(e) $0.4x^3 - 1.5x^2 + 1.7 - 0.3x$
(f) $x + y$

7. Use the polynomial $2\ell w + 2\ell h + 2wh$ to calculate the surface area of a box with the given dimensions.

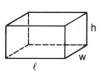

(a) $\ell = 20$ cm, $w = 5$ cm, $h = 10$ cm
(b) $\ell = 5.2$ cm, $w = 2.5$ cm, $h = 4$ cm

8. What is the volume of the space in a lead rectangular container if the outside dimensions are 20 cm by 20 cm by 15 cm and the walls are 1 cm thick?

7.2 ADDING POLYNOMIALS

To simplify a polynomial we collect and then combine like terms.

$$3x + 7y + 5x + 8y = 3x + 5x + 7y + 8y$$
$$= 8x + 15y$$

A polynomial is in simplest form when it contains no like terms.
To add polynomials we collect and then combine like terms.

EXAMPLE 1. Add. $(x^2 + 2x + 2) + (3x^2 - x - 6)$

SOLUTION:
$$(x^2 + 2x + 2) + (3x^2 - x - 6) = x^2 + 2x + 2 + 3x^2 - x - 6$$
$$= x^2 + 3x^2 + 2x - x + 2 - 6$$
$$= 4x^2 + x - 4$$

EXAMPLE 2. Add. $(3m^2 - 6m - 6) + (m^2 + 5)$

SOLUTION:
$$(3m^2 - 6m - 6) + (m^2 + 5) = 3m^2 - 6m - 6 + m^2 + 5$$
$$= 3m^2 + m^2 - 6m - 6 + 5$$
$$= 4m^2 - 6m - 1$$

Polynomials can also be added in column form.

EXAMPLE 3. Add in column form.
$$(3m^2 - 9m - 6) + (4m^2 + 6m + 1)$$

SOLUTION:
Rewrite in column form.

$$
\begin{array}{r}
3m^2 - 9m - 6 \\
4m^2 + 6m + 1 \\
\hline
7m^2 - 3m - 5
\end{array}
$$

EXAMPLE 4. Add in column form.
$$(5y^2 + 3y^2 - 2y - 11) + (8 - 2y - 6y^2)$$

SOLUTION:
Write the terms in descending order and align like terms.

$$
\begin{array}{rcl}
5y^2 + 3y^3 - 2y - 11 & \rightarrow & 3y^3 + 5y^2 - 2y - 11 \\
8 - 2y - 6y^2 & \rightarrow & \underline{ - 6y^2 - 2y + 8} \\
& & 3y^3 - y^2 - 4y - 3
\end{array}
$$

EXERCISE 7.2

B 1. Add.

(a) $(3x + 2) + (2x - 1)$
(b) $(2x^2 - 7x + 3) + (x^2 - 5x + 2)$
(c) $(y^2 - 2y - 6) + (3 - 2y - y^2)$
(d) $(x^2 - 2x) + (3x^2 + 5x)$

2. Add.

(a) $\begin{array}{l} x + 2 \\ \underline{3x + 5} \end{array}$

(b) $\begin{array}{l} 2x^2 + x - 3 \\ \underline{3x^2 + 4x - 5} \end{array}$

(c) $\begin{array}{l} 3x - 2y + 7 \\ \underline{2x - 5y - 4} \end{array}$

(d) $\begin{array}{l} 2x^2 - x + 3 \\ \underline{x^2 + 3x - 5} \end{array}$

3. Simplify.

(a) $(x^3 + 6) + (x + 3)$
(b) $(x^2 + 2x) + (-7x + 2)$
(c) $(y^3 + 2y^2 + 3) + (4y^2 - 3y - 1)$
(d) $(2z + 3) + (10 - 13z + z^2)$
(e) $(x^2 + xy) + (xy + y^2)$
(f) $(3y^3 + 10) + (5 - 2y^2)$
(g) $(m + n + x) + (-x - y - z)$
(h) $(3x^3 - 2x^2 + 3x + 4) + (6x^3 + x)$

4. Add in column form.

(a) $(3x^2 - 7x + 4) + (x^2 - x - 1)$
(b) $(2y^2 - y - 5) + (y^2 - y - 6)$
(c) $(m^2 - 3m - 1) + (2m^2 - 6m + 7)$
(d) $(3t^2 + 7 - 4t) + (5 - 2t - 3t^2)$
(e) $(6s^2 + 11) + (1 + 8s + 5s^2)$
(f) $(d^2 - 5 - 4d) + (8 - 6d + d^2)$

5. Simplify.

(a) $(3x^2 + 2xy + y^2) + (x^2 - xy + y^2)$
(b) $(6t^2 - st + s^2) + (8t^2 - 3st - s^2)$
(c) $(8y^2 - y - 5t) + (6t - 3y + 7y^2)$
(d) $(8a^2b + 6ab^2 - 4a^2b^2) + (2a^2b + a^2b^2)$
(e) $(-x^2 - 1 - x) + (7 - x - x^2)$
(f) $(3s^2t - 4st + 5st^2) + (s^2t + st^2)$

6. Simplify.

(a) $(2x^2 + 3x + 7) + 2x^2 + 4$
(b) $(5t^2 - t - 4) + 3t - 7$
(c) $(2x^2 - 3xy - y^2) + x^2 + y^2$
(d) $(3m^2 + 5mn + 7n^2) + 4n^2 - 5mn$

7. Find the perimeter of the following.

(a)

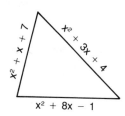

(b)

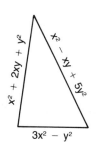

(c)

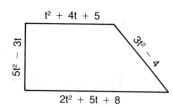

C 8. Simplify.

(a) $(\frac{1}{2}x^2 + \frac{1}{3}x + \frac{1}{4}) + (\frac{1}{2}x^2 + \frac{1}{3}x + \frac{3}{4})$
(b) $(\frac{3}{4}t^2 + \frac{5}{3}t + \frac{1}{2}) + (\frac{5}{4}t^2 + \frac{2}{3}t + \frac{3}{2})$
(c) $(\frac{5}{8}m^2 - \frac{3}{4}m - \frac{1}{2}) + (\frac{1}{8}m^2 - \frac{1}{4}m + 1)$
(d) $(0.6t^2 - 0.3t + 1.4) + (0.2t^2 - 0.1t + 0.5)$
(e) $(1.9y^2 + 1.3y + 5.2) + (0.9y^2 + 6.4)$
(f) $(2.4x^2 - 5) + (1.6x^2 - 0.7x - 8)$

MIND BENDER

Find the missing number.

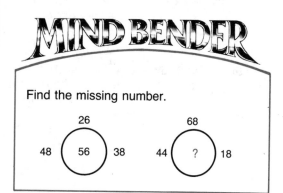

7.3 SUBTRACTING POLYNOMIALS

An integer such as 5 and its opposite -5 are called additive inverses We subtract an integer by adding its additive inverse.

$$5 - (-6) = 5 + (+6) = 11$$

We subtract a polynomial by adding its additive inverse.

Polynomial	Additive Inverse
$x + 4$	$-x - 4$
$3x - y$	$-3x + y$
$2x^2 - 2x - 3$	$-2x^2 + 2x + 3$

EXAMPLE 1. Subtract. $(3x^2 + 5x + 7) - (x^2 + 2x + 1)$

SOLUTION:

$$\begin{aligned}
(3x^2 + 5x + 7) - (x^2 + 2x + 1) &= (3x^2 + 5x + 7) + (-x^2 - 2x - 1) \\
&= 3x^2 + 5x + 7 - x^2 - 2x - 1 \\
&= 3x^2 - x^2 + 5x - 2x + 7 - 1 \\
&= 2x^2 + 3x + 6
\end{aligned}$$

Polynomials can also be subtracted in column form.

EXAMPLE 2. Subtract in column form. $(2t^2 - 3t + 5) - (5t^2 + 6t - 8)$

SOLUTION:

$$\begin{array}{ll}
\;\; 2t^2 - 3t + 5 & \\
(-) \;\; \underline{5t^2 + 6t - 8} & \qquad -5t^2 - 6t + 8 \qquad
\end{array}$$

additive inverse

$$\begin{array}{l}
2t^2 - 3t + 5 \\
\underline{-5t^2 - 6t + 8} \\
-3t^2 - 9t - 3
\end{array}$$

EXAMPLE 3. Subtract and check by addition. $(5x^3 - 3x - 5) - (2x^2 + 3x + 1)$

SOLUTION:

$$\begin{array}{ll}
\;\; 5x^3 \phantom{{}- 2x^2} - 3x - 5 & \\
(-) \;\; \underline{ 2x^2 + 3x + 1} & \qquad -2x^2 - 3x - 1
\end{array}$$

additive inverse

$$\begin{array}{l}
5x^3 \phantom{{}- 2x^2} - 3x - 5 \\
\underline{ -2x^2 - 3x - 1} \\
5x^3 - 2x^2 - 6x - 6
\end{array}$$

Check.

$$\begin{array}{ll}
\;\; 5x^3 - 2x^2 - 6x + 6 & \leftarrow \text{difference} \\
(+) \;\; \underline{\; 2x^2 + 3x + 1} & \leftarrow \text{second polynomial} \\
\;\; 5x^3 \phantom{{}- 2x^2}\; - 3x - 5 & \leftarrow \text{first polynomial}
\end{array}$$

EXERCISE 7.3

B 1. Subtract.
(a) $(6x - 3) - (7x + y)$
(b) $(5x + 7) - (2x + 3)$
(c) $(3x - 2) - (2x - 1)$
(d) $(x - y + 3) - (x + y + 3)$
(e) $(5x^2 - 7x + 2) - (3x^2 - 2x + 4)$
(f) $(13x^3 - 3x^2 - xy) - (13y^3 - 3y^2 - xy)$
(g) $(7y^2 - xy) - (8x^2 + xy)$

2. Subtract.
(a) $-4x^2 - 7x + 3$
$\ -3x^2 + 5x - 4$

(b) $-6x^2 + 5$
$\ \ 9x^2 - 11$

(c) $3 - 4x - 5x^2$
$\ -2 + 3x - 6x^2$

(d) $x^2 - 4x - 13$
$\ 5x^2 - 7x + 2$

(e) $-9x^2 + 12x - 13$
$\ \ \ 5 \ \ + 3x^2 - 4x$

(f) $20x + 15x^2 - 4$
$\ 13x^2 - 5x + 6$

3. Subtract in column form.
(a) $(5t^2 - 4t + 7) - (3t^2 - t - 1)$
(b) $(8y^2 + 5y - 1) - (3y^2 + 8)$
(c) $(7x^2 - x - 2) - (1 + x + 3x^2)$
(d) $(3m^3 - m + 5) - (3 + m^2)$
(e) $(4x^2 - 1) - (5x^2 - 3x + 4)$
(f) $(4t^3 + t^2 - 2) - (2t^3 - 7)$

4. Subtract.
(a) $2x + x - 7$ from $5x^2 + 6x + 1$
(b) $3m^2 - 4$ from $8m^2 - m - 4$
(c) $9t^2 + 9t + 1$ from $t^2 - 5$
(d) $2x^2 - 3xy + y^2$ from $x^2 + xy + y^2$
(e) $7m^2 - mn + 2n^2$ from $3m^2 - n^2$

5. Simplify.
(a) $3x^2 + 8 - (5x^2 + 2x - 4)$
(b) $5t - 3 - (4t^2 - 2t - 11)$
(c) $6m^3 - 5m^2 - (2m^2 - m - 5)$
(d) $5r^2 + 7r - (1 - 3r + 6r^2)$
(e) $3p^2 - 4pq - (p^2 + 2pq - 3q^2)$

6. Simplify.
(a) $(3x^2 + 2x - 1) + (x^2 - 7x - 1)$
(b) $(6t^2 - 3st + s^2) - (5t^2 - st - s^2)$
(c) $(9m^2 - 3m - 7) + (4m^2 + 11)$
(d) $(8x^2 - 3y^2) - (2x^2 - xy - y^2)$
(e) $(a^2b + 3ab + ab^2) + (2a^2b - 3ab^2)$
(f) $(9c^2 - 3cd + d^2) - (5c^2 - 7d^2)$

7. Find the length of BC.

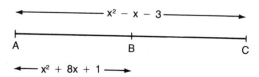

8. Given P, the perimeter, and the length of two sides, find the length of the third side.
(a)

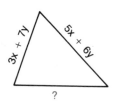

$P = 11x - 3y$

(b)

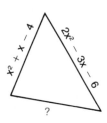

$P = 5x^2 - 6x + 12$

C 9. Simplify.
(a) $(\frac{1}{2}x^2 - \frac{1}{4}x + 2) - (\frac{5}{2}x^2 - \frac{1}{4}x - 5)$
(b) $(0.7y^2 - 0.6y + 1.3)$
$\ - (1.4y^2 + 0.7y + 0.2)$
(c) $(\frac{2}{3}x^2 - \frac{7}{8}) - (\frac{1}{3}x^2 + \frac{1}{2}x - \frac{5}{8})$
(d) $(0.4t^2 - 2.7t + 3.1)$
$\ - (0.6t^2 + 1.5t + 2.4)$
(e) $(\frac{5}{8}x^3 + \frac{3}{2}x^2 - 4) - (\frac{1}{4}x^2 + 3\frac{1}{2})$

7.4 MULTIPLYING MONOMIALS BY MONOMIALS

When we write x^4 we mean $x \times x \times x \times x \times x$. Similarly x^3 means $x \times x \times x$.

Therefore,

$$x^4 \times x^3 = \underbrace{\overbrace{(x \times x \times x \times x \times x)}^{\text{4 factors}} \times \overbrace{(x \times x \times x \times x)}^{\text{3 factors}}}_{\text{7 factors}}$$

$$= x \times x \times x \times x \times x \times x \times x \times x \times x \times x \times x \times x \times x$$
$$= x^7$$
$$= x^{4+3}$$

This result is generalized in the exponent rule for multiplication.

Product of Powers

> To find the product of powers with the same base, add the exponents.
> $$x^m \times x^n = x^{m+n}$$

EXAMPLE 1. Simplify. $(3x^2)(5x^4)$

SOLUTION:
$$(3x^2)(5x^4) = 3 \times 5 \times x^2 \times x^4$$
$$= 3 \times 5 \times x^{2+4}$$
$$= 15x^6$$

EXAMPLE 2. Simplify. $(-4x^2y)(5x^3y^4)$

SOLUTION:
$$(-4x^2y)(5x^3y^4) = -4 \times 5 \times x^2 \times x^3 \times y \times y^4$$
$$= -4 \times 5 \times x^{2+3} \times y^{1+4}$$
$$= -20x^5y^5$$

EXAMPLE 3. Simplify. $(-3s^2t^3)(-2s^5)(5s^6t^3)$

SOLUTION:
$$(-3s^2t^3)(-2s^5)(5s^6t^3) = -3 \times -2 \times 5 \times s^2 \times s^5 \times s^6 \times t^3 \times t^3$$
$$= 30s^{2+5+6} \times t^{3+3}$$
$$= 30s^{13}t^6$$

EXERCISE 7.4

A 1. Express in exponential form.
 (a) $2 \times 2 \times 2 \times 2 \times 2 \times 2$
 (b) $3 \times 3 \times 3 \times 3 \times 3$
 (c) $t \times t \times t \times t \times t \times t$
 (d) $(-3) \times (-3) \times (-3) \times (-3)$

B 2. Verify each product by multiplication.
 (a) $2^2 \times 2^3 = 2^5$ (b) $3^1 \times 3^3 = 3^4$
 (c) $2^4 \times 2^3 = 2^7$ (d) $5^2 \times 5^3 = 5^5$

3. Simplify.
 (a) $(x^4)(x^5)$ (b) $w^3 \times w^7$
 (c) $t \times t^6$ (d) $s^6 \times s^7$
 (e) $m^3 \times m^4 \times m^6$ (f) $t^3 \times t \times t^{10}$
 (g) $2^4 \times 2^6$ (h) $3^5 \times 3^7$
 (i) $(x^4)(w^5)$ (j) $5^4 \times 5^3 \times 5$
 (k) $r^{16} \times r^{13} \times r$ (l) $x \times x \times x^6$
 (m) $4^3 \times 4^2$ (n) $x^6 \times y^7$
 (o) 2×2^{14} (p) $3^2 \times 2^3$

4. Simplify.
 (a) $(2x^2)(x^3)$
 (b) $(3w^2)(-6w^4)$
 (c) $(9m^4)(5m^8)$
 (d) $(-16x^8)(-3x^9)$
 (e) $(4x^2)(3x^3)(5x)$
 (f) $(-7w^3)(3w^4)(2w^5)$
 (g) $(7t)(4t^3)(5t)$
 (h) $(8s^2)(4s^4)(-2s)$
 (i) $(-9x^5)(3x^2)(2x^4)(3)$
 (j) $(-3t^2)(-5t)(-6t^3)$

5. Simplify.
 (a) $(3x^2y)(4xy^4)$
 (b) $(7s^4t^3)(5st^2)$
 (c) $(16x^4y)(-5x^3)(-2x)$
 (d) $(-14w^3x)(5w^4y)$
 (e) $(26w^4x^6)(5w^6xy)$
 (f) $(19m^2n^4)(3m^6n)$
 (g) $(9w^7x^3y)(5w^4x)$
 (h) $(-14s^3t^8)(-3s^5t^4)$
 (i) $(9xy^7)(-4x^5y)(-5y)$
 (j) $(-7x^4y^3)(x^6y^7)(-xy)$
 (k) $(9m^7n)(2m^3n)(3mn)$
 (l) $(4x^4)(3y^3)(7xy)$
 (m) $(8x^2)(3y^3)(7x^2y)$
 (n) $(-5wx)(6x^3)(7wx^2)$
 (o) $(8r)(7s^3)(3r^2s^3)$
 (p) $(-7a)(-3a^2b)(-4a^3b^3)$

6. Calculate the area of each figure.
 (a)

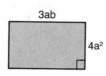

 (b)

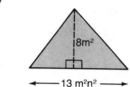

 (c)

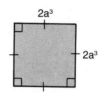

 (d)

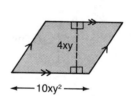

C 7. Simplify.
 (a) $(6x^2y^3)(\frac{1}{2}x^4y^5)$

 (b) $(-\frac{1}{4}xy)(-2x^3y^4)$

 (c) $(\frac{3}{4}a^3b^4)(-\frac{4}{5}ab^6)$

 (d) $6s^2t^3(-\frac{1}{2}st)$

 (e) $20abc(-2ab)(-\frac{1}{5}ab)$

 (f) $-9p^2q^3(\frac{1}{3}pq^5)$

8. Simplify.
 (a) $x^3 \times x^6$
 (b) $m^{a+1} \times m^3$
 (c) $(y^{x-4})(y^{x+3})$
 (d) $(x^{a-4})(x^{2a+3})$

7.5 POWERS OF MONOMIALS

In the expression $(a^3)^4$, a^3 is called the power; the expression $(a^3)^4$ is called a power of a power.

The rule for evaluating a power of a power is shown in the following examples.

$$(5^2)^3 = (5^2) \times (5^2) \times (5^2)$$
$$= 5^{2+2+2}$$
$$= 5^6$$

$$(a^3)^4 = (a^3) \times (a^3) \times (a^3) \times (a^3)$$
$$= a^{3+3+3+3}$$
$$= a^{12}$$

The examples suggest the following rule.

Power of a Power

> To find the power of a power, multiply the exponents.
>
> $$(x^m)^n = x^{mn}$$

$(a^3)^4$ is called a power of a power. $(ab)^4$ is called a power of a product.

$$(ab)^4 = (ab) \times (ab) \times (ab) \times (ab)$$
$$= a \times a \times a \times a \times b \times b \times b \times b$$
$$= a^4b^4$$

Power of a Product

> To find the power of a product, find the power of each factor.
>
> $$(xy)^m = x^m y^m$$

These two rules are now combined to find the power of a monomial.

$$(a^2b^3)^4 = (a^2)^4 \times (b^3)^4$$
$$= a^{2 \times 4}b^{3 \times 4}$$
$$= a^8b^{12}$$

Power of a Monomial

> The rule for finding a power of a monomial is stated as follows
>
> $$(x^m y^n)^p = x^{mp} y^{np}$$

EXAMPLE 1. Simplify.
(a) $(2x^2y^3)^3$

(b) $(-3a^2b^3)^4$

SOLUTION:
(a) $(2x^2y^3)^3 = (2^1x^2y^3)^3$
$$= (2^1)^3(x^2)^3(y^3)^3$$
$$= 2^3x^6y^9$$
$$= 8x^6y^9$$

(b) $(-3a^2b^3)^4 = (-3)^4(a^2)^4(b^3)^4$
$$= 81a^8b^{12}$$

EXAMPLE 2. Simplify.

(a) $(-5abc^2)^2$ (b) $(2x^2y^4)^3(-4x^3y^2)^2$

SOLUTION:

(a) $(-5abc^2)^2 = (-5a^1b^1c^2)^2$
$= (-5)^2(a^1)^2(b^1)^2(c^2)^2$
$= 25a^2b^2c^4$

(b) $(2x^2y^4)^3(-4x^3y^2)^2 = (2)^3(x^2)^3(y^4)^3(-4)^2(x^3)^2(y^2)^2$
$= 8 \times x^6 \times y^{12} \times 16 \times x^6 \times y^4$
$= 128x^{12}y^{16}$

EXERCISE 7.5

1. Simplify.
(a) $(x^2)^3$ (b) $(x^3)^2$
(c) $(y^5)^2$ (d) $(z^3)^3$
(e) $(x^3)^5$ (f) $(y^5)^4$
(g) $(z^3)^1$ (h) $(x^4)^6$
(i) $(3^2)^2$ (j) $(2^2)^2$
(k) $(2^3)^2$ (l) $(3^3)^3$

2. Simplify.
(a) $(xy)^4$ (b) $(pq)^6$
(c) $(ab)^7$ (d) $(2x)^3$
(e) $(-3abc)^2$ (f) $(5mn)^4$
(g) $(4rst)^3$ (h) $(-2xy)^2$

3. Simplify.
(a) $(x^3y^2)^4$ (b) $(m^2n^6)^3$
(c) $(rs^2t^3)^5$ (d) $(a^2bc^4)^2$
(e) $(m^3n^2p^3)^6$ (f) $(def^3)^3$

4. Simplify.
(a) $(2a^2b^2)^3$ (b) $(5x^3y^4)^2$
(c) $(6mn^2)^5$ (d) $(3r^2s^3t^4)^4$
(e) $(-2x^3y^4)^2$ (f) $(-7a^3b^4c)^3$
(g) $(-4m^6n^2p^3)^4$ (h) $(-5a^3b^2c^6)^3$
(i) $(-r^3s^4t^2)^5$ (j) $(9d^2e^3f)^2$
(k) $(-xyz^3)^3$ (l) $(-2a^4b^5c^6)^5$

5. Simplify.
(a) $(2x^2y^3)^2(5x^2y)^3$
(b) $(3a^2bc)^3(4a^2b^2c)^3$
(c) $(-4d^2e^3)^2(-d^3e^4)^4$
(d) $(2x^3y)^2(-3x^4y^2)^2$
(e) $(4xy)^3(-2x^2y)^4$
(f) $(2x^4y^3)^5(-x^4y^2)^3$

6. Simplify.
(a) $(2xy^3)^2(3xy^2)^2(x^3y)^4$
(b) $-6x^3y^2(-3xy^2)^3$
(c) $10a^2b^3(-2ab^2)^3(ab^2)^3$

7. Simplify.
(a) $(0.4x^3y)^2$
(b) $(\frac{1}{2}x^4y^3)^3$
(c) $(-\frac{2}{3}m^4n)^4$
(d) $(0.2r^3s^2t)^3$
(e) $(0.5x^2y^4)^2(10x^4y^3)^3$
(f) $(-\frac{1}{2}x^4y^5)^3(-2x^3y)^4$

Use the digits from 1 to 6 and fill each box to make the multiplication true. There is only one solution.

7.6 MULTIPLYING A POLYNOMIAL BY A MONOMIAL

In this section we use the distributive property
$$a(b + c) = ab + ac$$
to multiply a polynomial by a monomial.

For example
$$4(3x + 2) = 4(3x + 2)$$
$$= 12x + 8$$

The product $4(3x + 2)$ can be interpreted geometrically if we use a rectangle with sides 4 and $(3x + 2)$. The area of the rectangle can be expressed in two ways $4(3x + 2)$ and $12x + 8$. Therefore, $4(3x + 2) = 12x + 8$.

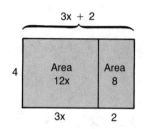

Multiplying
by
Monomials

> To multiply a polynomial by a monomial, use the distributive property to multiply each term of the polynomial by the monomial.

When given an expression in brackets, we assume the unwritten factor to be 1. For example

$$(3x - 2) = 1(3x - 2) = 3x - 2$$

This method is also used when the bracket is preceded by a negative sign. For example

$$-(2x - 5) = -1(2x - 5) = -2x + 5$$

EXAMPLE 1. Expand and simplify. $3(2x + 5) + 2(3x - 1)$

SOLUTION:
$$3(2x + 5) + 2(3x - 1) = 3(2x + 5) + 2(3x - 1)$$
$$= 6x + 15 + 6x - 2$$
$$= 12x + 13$$

EXAMPLE 2. Expand and simplify. $0.4(m + 2n) - 0.2(2m - 3n)$

SOLUTION:
$$0.4(m + 2n) - 0.2(2m - 3n) = 0.4(m + 2n) - 0.2(2m - 3n)$$
$$= 0.4m + 0.8n - 0.4m + 0.6n$$
$$= 1.4n$$

EXERCISE 7.6

A 1. Expand each of the following.
(a) $3(x + 2)$
(b) $-2(t - 3)$
(c) $-2(x - y)$
(d) $3(4b - 7)$
(e) $x(x - 2)$
(f) $-x(3x - 5)$
(g) $-3x(2x - 5)$
(h) $2x^2(3x - 2)$
(i) $xy(x + y)$
(j) $-xy(x - y)$

B 2. Expand and simplify.
(a) $3(x + 2) + 2(x - 5)$
(b) $4(x - 1) - 2(x + 1)$
(c) $(3t - 2) - (2t + 3)$
(d) $3(s - 2) - 2(2s - 1)$
(e) $5(3x - 2) + 2(x - 3)$
(f) $4(3x - 1) + 2(1 - 2x)$
(g) $-3(y - 3) - 2(4 - y)$
(h) $5(3x - 2) - 4(3x - 2)$
(i) $3(x - 5) + (x + 4)2$
(j) $-5(3x - 4) - (3 - x)4$

3. Expand and simplify.
(a) $3(2x - 5) + 2(x + 3) + 4(x - 4)$
(b) $3(t - 4) - 5(t + 1) + 4(2t + 3)$
(c) $(3y - 5) - (2y + 3) + 4(y - 2)$
(d) $x(2a - 1) + 3(a^2 + x) + 7a$
(e) $-(x^2 + 1) - 2x(x + 3) - 2x + 1$
(f) $3(x + y - z) + 2(x - y + z)$
(g) $3(x^2 - 2x + 3) + 5(x^2 - x - 1)$
(h) $5(n - 3) - 3(2n + 1) + 2(n - 5)$
(i) $-2(3w - 1) + 5(w - 2) - 7(w + 1)$
(j) $3x(x - 2) + 5x^2 + 4x(x + 2)$

4. Expand and simplify.
(a) $2x(3x - 7y) - 2y(x + 3y) + (x^2 + y^2)$
(b) $3x(x + y + 1) + 2y(x - y - 2)$
    $+ (x - y)$
(c) $5y(1 - x - y) - 3x(2 - 3x + 5y)$
    $+ 20xy$
(d) $2xy(x - y) - xy(2x + 3y)$
(e) $x^2y(x - 2y) + 2x^2y(y - 2x)$
(f) $(xy + 1)x - xy(x + 1) - x$
(g) $3x^2y(x + 2y) - x^2y(x + y)$
(h) $3xy^2(x - 3y) - 2xy^2(y - 2x)$

5. Expand and simplify.
(a) $0.5(4x - 6y) + 0.2(10x - 15y)$
(b) $0.3(x + y) - 0.4(2x - 3y)$
(c) $0.3(0.2x - 0.5y) + 0.4(0.7x + 0.3y)$
(d) $1.5(2x - 3y) + 0.5(2x + 3y)$
(e) $0.5x(0.4x - 0.6y) - 0.2y(0.5x - 1.5y)$

6. Expand and simplify.
(a) $\frac{1}{2}(2x - 6y) - \frac{1}{3}(3x + 12y)$
(b) $\frac{x}{2}(6x - 4y) - \frac{2x}{3}(3x - 6y)$
(c) $\frac{x}{5}(10x - 15y) + \frac{1}{2}(2x^2 + 4y^2)$
(d) $\frac{2}{3}(6x - 9y) + \frac{4}{3}(3x + 12y)$
(e) $\frac{3x}{5}(15x + 10y) - \frac{2x}{3}(9x - 12y)$

7. Calculate the area.
(a)

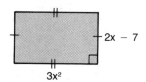

$2x - 7$

$3x^2$

(b)

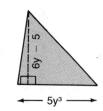

$6y - 5$

$5y^3$

8. Calculate the volume.

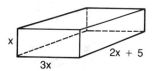

x

$3x$

$2x + 5$

C 9. Expand and simplify.
(a) $5[x - 2(x + 3)] + 3[x + 2(x - 1)]$
(b) $3x[x + 4(1 - x)] - 2x[3(x - 2) + 2x]$
(c) $-3x[2x - 4(x - 2)] + 4[x - 2x(x + 3)]$
(d) $2x[5x - 3(x - 2)] - 3x[3x - 5(x - 1)]$
(e) $-[2x - 5x(x + 2)] + [-3x + 2x(x - 3)]$

7.7 DIVIDING MONOMIALS BY MONOMIALS

In this section we use the following exponent rules to divide monomials by monomials.

Power of a Quotient

> To find the power of a quotient with the same base, subtract the exponents.
>
> $$x^m \div x^n = x^{m-n}$$

Zero Exponent
$x^0 = 1, x \neq 0$

Negative Exponents
$x^{-n} = \dfrac{1}{x^n}, x \neq 0$

EXAMPLE 1. Simplify. $\dfrac{20a^4b^3}{5a^2b^2}$

SOLUTION:

$$\frac{20a^4b^3}{5a^2b^2} = \left(\frac{20}{5}\right)\left(\frac{a^4}{a^2}\right)\left(\frac{b^3}{b^2}\right)$$
$$= 4a^{4-2}b^{3-2}$$
$$= 4a^2b$$

To simplify a quotient of monomials, write an expression that has positive exponents and fractions in lowest terms.

EXAMPLE 2. Simplify.

(a) $\dfrac{-6x^3y^8}{2x^5y^5}$

(b) $\dfrac{40m^2n^{-4}}{30m^7n^{-3}p^{-2}}$

SOLUTION:

(a) $\dfrac{-6x^3y^8}{2x^5y^5} = \left(\dfrac{-6}{2}\right)\left(\dfrac{x^3}{x^5}\right)\left(\dfrac{y^8}{y^5}\right)$

$$= -3x^{-2}y^3$$
$$= \frac{-3y^3}{x^2}$$

(b) $\dfrac{40m^2n^{-4}}{30m^7n^{-3}p^{-2}} = \left(\dfrac{40}{30}\right)\left(\dfrac{m^2}{m^7}\right)\left(\dfrac{n^{-4}}{n^{-3}}\right)\left(\dfrac{1}{p^{-2}}\right)$

$$= \frac{4}{3}m^{-5}n^{-1}p^2$$
$$= \frac{4p^2}{3m^5n}$$

EXAMPLE 3. Find the length of the rectangle.

SOLUTION:

$$\ell = \frac{A}{w}$$

$$\ell = \frac{60w^7y^5}{5x^2y^3}$$

$$= 12x^5y^2$$

The length is $12x^5y^2$.

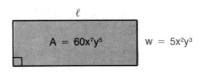

$$A = 60x^7y^5 \qquad w = 5x^2y^3$$

EXERCISE 7.7

Throughout the exercise, assume that no denominator is equal to zero.

1. Simplify.

(a) $\dfrac{6x^6}{3x^6}$

(b) $\dfrac{15t^5}{5t^4}$

(c) $\dfrac{20m^7}{-4m^3}$

(d) $\dfrac{-28s^8}{7s^3}$

(e) $\dfrac{-10x^4}{-5x^2}$

(f) $\dfrac{14a^3b^4}{2ab}$

(g) $\dfrac{18x^4y^5}{-2x^3y}$

(h) $\dfrac{-30m^6n^7}{10m^4n^7}$

(i) $\dfrac{-24d^6e^6}{-6d^5e^2}$

(j) $\dfrac{16a^2b^3c}{-2a^2b^2}$

2. Simplify.
(a) $5x^3y^6 \div x^2y^2$
(b) $-12a^3b^4 \div ab$
(c) $36m^6n^7 \div -9m^4$
(d) $-20x^6y^{10} \div -4x^2y$
(e) $10a^3b^2c \div -10ab$
(f) $-8x^2y^7 \div -2xy^6$

3. Simplify.

(a) $\dfrac{10a^4b^3}{5a^6b^2}$

(b) $\dfrac{-15x^6y^7}{-5x^5y^8}$

(c) $\dfrac{-12m^3n^2}{4m^6n^2}$

(d) $\dfrac{22x^2y^3z}{-11xy^4z^3}$

(e) $\dfrac{20a^4b^6c}{15a^4b^6c}$

(f) $\dfrac{-18x^5y^6}{12x^3y^8}$

(g) $\dfrac{25r^3s^3t^3}{-30r^2s^4t^5}$

(h) $\dfrac{-14m^4n^2}{21m^8n^5}$

4. Simplify.

(a) $\dfrac{10x^5y^3}{5x^3y^{-1}}$

(b) $\dfrac{12a^4b^{-3}}{3a^2b^{-5}}$

(c) $\dfrac{-16m^7n^{-2}}{4m^8n^3}$

(d) $\dfrac{-9x^{-4}y^3}{-3x^{-5}y^2}$

(e) $\dfrac{24x^{-5}y^{-2}}{18x^{-6}y^{-3}}$

(f) $\dfrac{11a^3b^{-1}c^2}{-a^{-2}b^3c^2}$

(g) $\dfrac{m^4n^{-3}}{-6m^{-6}n^4}$

(h) $\dfrac{-2r^{-3}st^{-1}}{-8r^{-3}s^{-1}t^{-2}}$

(i) $\dfrac{30x^{-2}y^7}{40x^2y^7z^{-2}}$

(j) $\dfrac{-18xyz}{-27x^2y^2z^{-1}}$

5. Find the missing dimension in each rectangle.

(a)

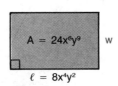

$$A = 24x^6y^9 \qquad w$$

$$\ell = 8x^4y^2$$

(b)

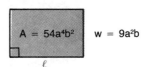

$$A = 54a^4b^2 \qquad w = 9a^2b$$

$$\ell$$

6. Evaluate each expression for $x = 2$, $y = -1$, $z = -2$.

(a) $\dfrac{12x^3y^2}{-6xy}$

(b) $\dfrac{-20x^5y^4z^2}{5x^4y^3z}$

(c) $\dfrac{9x^{-3}y^{-2}}{-3x^{-5}y^{-4}}$

(d) $\dfrac{-14xy^{-3}z^{-2}}{-2x^{-1}y^{-4}z^{-2}}$

7.

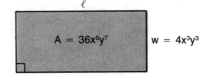

$$A = 36x^5y^7 \qquad w = 4x^3y^3$$

Find the perimeter of the rectangle.

7.8 DIVIDING POLYNOMIALS BY MONOMIALS

By definition, multiplication distributes over addition and subtraction. For example

$$2(x + 3) = 2x + 6 \quad \text{and} \quad 3(x - 4) = 3x - 12$$

Division also distributes over addition and subtraction.

$$\frac{1}{2}(x + 3) = \frac{x}{2} + \frac{3}{2} \quad \text{and} \quad \frac{x + 3}{2} = \frac{x}{2} + \frac{3}{2}$$

This property is used to divide a polynomial by a monomial.

The area of the rectangle is $4x^3 + 6x^2 + 8x$.
The width is $2x$.
To determine the length we divide the area by the width.

$2x$ A = $4x^3 + 6x^2 + 8x$

ℓ

> We state the restriction $x \neq 0$ since division by zero is not defined.

$$\frac{4x^3 + 6x^2 + 8x}{2x} = \frac{4x^3}{2x} + \frac{6x^2}{2x} + \frac{8x}{2x}$$
$$= 2x^2 + 3x + 4, x \neq 0$$

The length is $2x^2 + 3x + 4$.

Dividing by Monomials

> To divide a polynomial by a monomial, divide each term of the polynomial by the monomial.

EXAMPLE 1. Divide. $(6m^3 - 9m^2 - 12m) \div 3m$ Check.

SOLUTION:

$$\frac{6m^3 - 9m^2 - 12m}{3m} = \frac{6m^3}{3m} - \frac{9m^2}{3m} - \frac{12m}{3m}$$
$$= 2m^2 - 3m - 4, m \neq 0$$

Check.
$$3m \times (2m^2 - 3m - 4) = 6m^3 - 9m^2 - 12m$$

EXAMPLE 2. Simplify. $\dfrac{5x^4y^2 - 15x^3y^3 + 30xy}{-5xy}$

SOLUTION:

$$\frac{5x^4y^2 - 15x^3y^3 + 30xy}{-5xy} = \frac{5x^4y^2}{-5xy} - \frac{15x^3y^3}{-5xy} + \frac{30xy}{-5xy}$$
$$= -x^3y + 3x^2y^2 - 6, x, y \neq 0$$

EXERCISE 7.8

A 1. Simplify.

(a) $\dfrac{12xy}{3y}$

(b) $\dfrac{8xy}{2x}$

(c) $\dfrac{5x^2y}{5x}$

(d) $\dfrac{12xy}{6xy}$

(e) $\dfrac{-12stu}{2st}$

(f) $\dfrac{-16x^2y}{-8xy}$

(g) $\dfrac{20x^2y}{-5xy}$

(h) $\dfrac{12xyz}{-6xz}$

B 2. Simplify the following, state restrictions, and check.

(a) $\dfrac{3x + 3y}{3}$

(b) $\dfrac{5xy + 5x}{5}$

(c) $\dfrac{4y^2 - 4}{4}$

(d) $\dfrac{2x + 4}{2}$

(e) $\dfrac{5x + 10y}{5}$

(f) $\dfrac{4xy - 2y}{2y}$

(g) $\dfrac{3x - 6x^2}{3x}$

(h) $\dfrac{5x^2y - 10xy^2}{5xy}$

3. Simplify, state restrictions, and check.

(a) $\dfrac{7x^2 - 14x}{7x}$

(b) $\dfrac{4x^3 - 6x^2 + 2x}{2x}$

(c) $\dfrac{16xyz + 4xy - 8xz}{-2x}$

(d) $\dfrac{12x^3 + 6x^2 - 18x}{6x}$

(e) $\dfrac{4x^4 - 16x^2 + 12x}{4x}$

(f) $\dfrac{12xy - 4ax}{-4x}$

4. Given the area and one side of a rectangle, find the other side.

(a)

5. Divide. Assume no denominator is equal to zero.

(a) $\dfrac{12x^3y - 9x^2y^2}{3xy}$

(b) $\dfrac{20m^3n^2 - 10mn^3 - 30m^2n^2}{-5mn}$

(c) $\dfrac{6a^4b^3 + 8a^2b^2 - 4ab^3}{2ab^2}$

(d) $\dfrac{-18x^3y^3 - 6x^2y^2 - 3xy}{-3xy}$

(e) $\dfrac{-7xyz + 14x^2yz - 21xy^2z^3}{-7xy}$

(f) $\dfrac{18a^3b^2c - 12a^2b^3c + 24a^2b^2c^2}{6a^2b^2c^2}$

(g) $\dfrac{x^5 - x^4 + x^3 - x^2 - x}{-x}$

C 6. Simplify. Express solutions with positive exponents.

(a) $\dfrac{5x^2 + 15x}{5x^2}$

(b) $\dfrac{8m^2 - 4m - 12}{-4m}$

(c) $\dfrac{6m^3n - 12m^2n^2 - 18mn^3}{3m^3}$

7. Simplify.

(a) $\dfrac{4a + 8b}{4} + \dfrac{2a - 6b}{2}$

(b) $\dfrac{3x^2 - 6x}{3x} + \dfrac{8x^2 + 16x}{4x}$

7.9 GREATEST COMMON FACTOR — GCF

Factoring is the reverse of multiplication. We can write 12 as the product of factors in several ways.

$$12 = 3 \times 4 \qquad 12 = 2 \times 6 \qquad 12 = 2 \times 2 \times 3$$

In the last case the factors 2 and 3 cannot be factored further. This is true because the only factors of 2 are 2 and 1, and the only factors of 3 are 3 and 1. The numbers 2 and 3 are called prime numbers.

> A prime number is a whole number greater than 1 whose only whole number factors are itself and 1.

The prime numbers less than 30 are 2, 3, 5, 7, 11, 13, 17, 19, 23, and 29.

A composite number is any positive integer that is not prime. The first few composite numbers are 4, 6, 8, 9, 10, 12, and 14.

When a composite number is expressed as the product of factors that are all prime, the number is said to be prime factored.

Prime factoring 20 gives $2 \times 2 \times 5$.
Prime factoring 30 gives $2 \times 3 \times 5$.

To prime factor a negative integer, it is first expressed as the product of -1 and a positive integer.

$$-210 = -1 \times 210$$
$$= -1 \times 2 \times 3 \times 5 \times 7$$

The numbers 20 and 30 have factors in common, namely 2, 5, and 2×5 or 10. The greatest of these is 10 which is called the Greatest Common Factor (GCF).

> The Greatest Common Factor of two or more integers is the greatest of the factors common to both.

The Greatest Common Factor of two or more monomials is the product of their common factors when each monomial is expressed in factored form.

EXAMPLE 1. Find the GCF of 90, 225, and 60.

SOLUTION:

$$90 = 2 \times 3 \times 3 \times 5$$
$$225 = 3 \times 3 \times 5 \times 5$$
$$60 = 2 \times 2 \times 3 \times 5$$

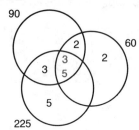

The GCF of 90, 225, and 60 is 3×5, or 15.

EXAMPLE 2. Find the GCF of $20d^2e$ and $18d^2e^2f$.

SOLUTION:

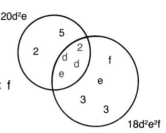

$$20d^2e = 2 \times 2 \times 5 \times d \times d \times e$$
$$18d^2e^2f = 2 \times 3 \times 3 \times d \times d \times e \times e \times f$$

The GCF of $20d^2e$ and $18d^2e^2f$ is $2d^2e$.

EXERCISE 7.9

A 1. Factor each expression. Do not use exponents.

(a) $4x^2y$ (b) $-24a^3b^2$
(c) $36x^2y^3z$ (d) $-18a^2b^2c$
(e) $-32x^4y^2z^2$ (f) $16a^2bc$

B 2. Find the GCF of each pair of numbers.

(a) 6, 15   (b) 12, 16   (c) 30, 20
(d) 72, 80   (e) 60, 90   (f) 56, 63

3. Find the GCF of each set of numbers.

(a) 4, 6, 8   (b) 16, 24, 28
(c) 18, 30, 36   (d) 24, 84, 144
(e) 8, 22, 32   (f) 24, 36, 40

4. Find the GCF for each of the following.

(a) $12x$, $8x$ (b) $6ab$, $10abc$
(c) $-15x^2y$, $18x^3y$ (d) $21a^2b$, $28a^3b^2$
(e) $14a^2x^3y$, $16a^2x$ (f) $32xyz$, $42abc$

5. Find the GCF of each of the following.

(a) $12abc$, $18ab$, $6ac$
(b) $8x^2$, $10x^3$, $20x$
(c) $10x^2y$, $15xy^2$, $25xyz$
(d) $14a^2b$, $21a^2b^2c$, $35ab^2c$
(e) $12mn$, $16m^3n$, $20mnp$
(f) $28rst$, $32r^2s$, $36rs^2t$
(g) $3abc$, $6def$, $9rst$

6. Find the missing factor.

(a) $2ab(\blacksquare) = 2a^2b^2$
(b) $3xy(\blacksquare) = 6x^2y^3$
(c) $4mn(\blacksquare) = 4m^3n^n$
(d) $5x^2y(\blacksquare) = 20x^2y$
(e) $3abc(\blacksquare) = -9a^2b^2c$

(f) $-2xy(\blacksquare) = -8x^3yz$
(g) $-mn(\blacksquare) = 3mnp$
(h) $7a^2b(\blacksquare) = -21a^3b^3c^3$
(i) $-5p^3q(\blacksquare) = 5p^3q^2$
(j) $6xy^3z(\blacksquare) = -30xy^4z$
(k) $(\blacksquare)2xy = 16x^2y$
(l) $(\blacksquare)x^2y^2z = -7x^3y^2z$

DIVISIBILITY RULES

I.   If the ones digit of a number is 0, 2, 4, 6, or 8, the number is divisible by 2.
II.   If the ones digit is 0 or 5, the number is divisible by 5.
III.   If the sum of the digits is divisible by 3, the number is divisible by 3.

EXERCISE

1. Determine whether each of the following is divisible by 2, 3, or 5.

(a) 66   (b) 75   (c) 130   (d) 401

2. Using the above rules, determine the divisibility rules for dividing by 4, 6, and 9.

7.10 COMMON MONOMIAL FACTORS

The distributive property has been used to multiply a polynomial by a monomial. The distributive property can also be used in reverse to write a polynomial as the product of a common monomial factor and another expression.

Multiplying	Factoring
$5(x - 2) = 5x - 10$	$5x - 10 = 5(x - 2)$
$2x(3x - 7) = 6x^2 - 14x$	$6x^2 - 14x = 2x(3x - 7)$

EXAMPLE 1. Factor. $2a^2 + 6a$

SOLUTION:

Step 1. Find the GCF of $2a^2$ and $6a$.
$$2a^2 = 2 \times a \times a$$
$$6a = 2 \times 3 \times a$$

The GCF is $2a$.

Step 2. Express the terms as products with the GCF as one of the factors.
$$2a^2 + 6a = 2a(a) + 2a(3)$$

Step 3. Use the distributive property in reverse.
$$2a(a) + 2a(3) = 2a(a + 3)$$

3·2·1

Once the GCF has been determined, the other factor can also be found by division.

$$2a^2 + 6a = 2a\left(\frac{2a^2}{2a} + \frac{6a}{2a}\right)$$
$$= 2a(a + 3)$$

EXAMPLE 2. Factor.
(a) $5x^2y + 15xy$ (b) $3x - 6x^2 + 9x^3$

SOLUTION:
(a) The GCF of $5x^2y$ and $15xy^2$ is $5xy$.
$$5x^2y + 15xy^2 = 5xy(x) + 5xy(3y)$$
$$= 5xy(x + 3y)$$
(b) The GCF of $3x - 6x^2 + 9x^3$ is $3x$.
$$3x - 6x^2 + 9x^3 = 3x(1) - 3x(2x) + 3x(3x^2)$$
$$= 3x(1 - 2x + 3x^2)$$

It is always possible to factor out something. For example

$$2x + 7 = \tfrac{1}{2}(4x + 14) \quad \text{and} \quad 2x + 7 = \tfrac{1}{3}(6x + 21)$$

Because of this feature of the distributive property, we will only factor polynomials over the integers.

> To factor a polynomial over the integers is to express it as a product of polynomials whose terms have integral coefficients.

EXAMPLE 3. Factor by grouping.
(a) $3xy - 6x + 5y - 10$
(b) $8xy + 2x - 12y - 3$

SOLUTION:

(a) $3xy - 6x + 5y - 10 = (3xy - 6x) + (5y - 10)$
$= 3x(y - 2) + 5(y - 2)$
$= (y - 2)(3x + 5)$

(b) $8xy + 2x - 12y - 3 = (8xy + 2x) + (-12y - 3)$
$= 2x(4y + 1) - 3(4y + 1)$
$= (4y + 1)(2x - 3)$

EXERCISE 7.10

A 1. Expand.

(a) $3(x + 5)$ (b) $2(y - 7)$
(c) $3x(x - 1)$ (d) $5x(1 - 2x)$
(e) $3x(1 - 2x + x^2)$ (f) $-2y(4 - 3y)$

2. State the common factor in each of the following.

(a) $3x + 6 = \blacksquare(x + 2)$
(b) $5y + 10 = \blacksquare(y + 2)$
(c) $2z^2 + 6z = \blacksquare(z + 3)$
(d) $7xy - 14x = \blacksquare(y - 2)$
(e) $8y^2 - 12y = \blacksquare(2y - 3)$
(f) $6x^2 - 9x = \blacksquare(2x - 3)$
(g) $3x^2 + 6xy + 12x = \blacksquare(x + 2y + 4)$
(h) $bx + by = \blacksquare(x + y)$
(i) $3x^2y - 5xy^2 = \blacksquare(3x - 5y)$
(j) $11st + 33tu = \blacksquare(s + 3u)$

B 3. Write the remaining factor in each of the following.

(a) $3x^2 + 12 = 3(\blacksquare)$
(b) $7y + 21 = 7(\blacksquare)$
(c) $2x^2 - 10 = 2(\blacksquare)$
(d) $12x + 3y = 3(\blacksquare)$
(e) $xy + yz = y(\blacksquare)$
(f) $3ax + 3ay = 3a(\blacksquare)$
(g) $3x^2 + 9x = 3x(\blacksquare)$
(h) $3x^3 - x^2 = x^2(\blacksquare)$
(i) $16x^2 - 4x = 4x(\blacksquare)$
(j) $8x^2y^2 - 12xy = 4xy(\blacksquare)$

4. Expand.

(a) $3x(2x - 7)$ (b) $4x^2(x - y)$
(c) $2x(7x - 3y)$ (d) $5xy(y + x^2)$
(e) $3x(x - xy)$ (f) $7s(2s - 3t)$
(g) $7x^2y(y + 1)$ (h) $2xy(yz + 2)$
(i) $3x(x + y - xy)$ (j) $5y(2y^2 - 3y + 5)$

5. Factor if possible.

(a) $5x - 10$ (b) $6x^2 + 8x$
(c) $6xy + 18y$ (d) $7y^2 + 21y$
(e) $5z^3 + 10z^2$ (f) $3x^4 - 6x^3$
(g) $8xyz - 12wxy$ (h) $7x^2yz + 14yz^3$
(i) $35y^2 - 18y^3$ (j) $3x^2 + 5y^2$
(k) $24xy^2c + 12x^2yc^2$ (l) $2x^3 - 3yz$

6. Factor if possible.

(a) $3x^2 + 2xy + x$
(b) $6xy + 5xz + 3x$
(c) $4xy + 2xz + 6ax$
(d) $x + 3y - 5z$
(e) $3xy - 6x^2y + 12xy^2$
(f) $12xy - 9x^2 + 6z^2$
(g) $x^2 + 1$
(h) $15x^2y + 5xy - 20xy^2$
(i) $5x^2t^2 - 10xt^2 + 15x^2t$
(j) $7x^2 - 5y^2 + xy$

7. Factor.

(a) $(a + b)x + (a + b)y$
(b) $(x - 2)x + (x - 2)3$
(c) $5(2x - 3) - x(2x - 3)$
(d) $3x(x + y) + 2y(x + y)$
(e) $3x(2x + 1) - 2(2x + 1)$
(f) $(x - 2y)3x + (x - 2y)9y$

8. Factor by grouping to get a common factor.

(a) $xy + 6x + 3y + 18$
(b) $2xy - 6x + y - 3$
(c) $xy + x - y - 1$
(d) $xy - 2x - 7y + 14$
(e) $10xy + 20x + 9y + 18$
(f) $xy + 2x + 2y + 4$
(g) $xy - 2x + 3y - 6$
(h) $xy + 4x - 2y - 8$

7.11 PRODUCT OF BINOMIALS

The distributive property is used to multiply a monomial by a polynomial.

$$2x(3x - 5) = 2x(3x - 5)$$
$$= 6x^2 - 10x$$

The distributive property can also be used to find the product of two binomials.

EXAMPLE. Multiply. $(x + 2)(x + 3)$

SOLUTION:
Let $m = (x + 2)$
Then $(x + 2)(x + 3) = m(x + 3)$

Using the distributive property
$$m(x + 3) = m \times x + m \times 3$$
Substituting $(x + 2)$ for m
$$m \times x + m \times 3 = (x + 2) \times x + (x + 2) \times 3$$
$$= x^2 + 2x + 3x + 6$$
$$= x^2 + 5x + 6$$

The product $(x + 2)(x + 3)$ can be interpreted geometrically as the area of a rectangle with sides $(x + 2)$ and $(x + 3)$.

$$(x + 2)(x + 3) = x^2 + 2x + 3x + 6$$
$$= x^2 + 5x + 6$$

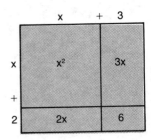

The same result is obtained when each term in the first binomial is multiplied by each term in the second binomial.

$$(x + 2)(x + 3) = (x + 2)(x + 3)$$
$$= x^2 + 3x + 2x + 6$$
$$= x^2 + 5x + 6$$

An easy way to remember how to multiply binomials is based on the acronym FOIL.

First terms   Last terms   F   O   I   L

$$(2a + 5)(3a + 7) = (2a + 5)(3a + 7) = 2a \times 3a + 2a \times 7 + 5 \times 3a + 5 \times 7$$
$$= 6a^2 + 14a + 15a + 35$$
$$= 6a^2 + 29a + 35$$

Inner terms

Outside terms

EXERCISE 7.11

B 1. Multiply.

(a) $(x + 2)(x + 5)$ (b) $(x + 4)(x + 3)$
(c) $(x + 1)(x + 2)$ (d) $(x - 3)(x - 2)$
(e) $(x - 4)(x - 2)$ (f) $(x - 5)(x - 3)$

2. Expand.

(a) $(x + 4)(x - 1)$ (b) $(t + 5)(t - 3)$
(c) $(x + 6)(x - 2)$ (d) $(x - 5)(x + 3)$
(e) $(p - 4)(p + 1)$ (f) $(x - 5)(x + 4)$
(g) $(q + 3)(q - 7)$ (h) $(x - 2)(x + 5)$
(i) $(r - 3)(r + 4)$ (j) $(t - 7)(t - 11)$

3. Multiply.

(a) $(x + 7)(x + 2)$ (b) $(x + 7)(x - 2)$
(c) $(x - 7)(x + 2)$ (d) $(x - 6)(x + 3)$
(e) $(x + 5)(x - 5)$ (f) $(x + 7)(x + 6)$
(g) $(x - 4)(x + 3)$ (h) $(x + 5)(x - 4)$
(i) $(x - 3)(x + 2)$ (j) $(x + 8)(x + 10)$

4. Multiply.

(a) $(x - 8)(x + 2)$ (b) $(x - 5)(x + 4)$
(c) $(x - 4)(x - 2)$ (d) $(x + 3)(x - 5)$
(e) $(x - 3)(x + 7)$ (f) $(x + 7)(x - 3)$

5. Expand.

(a) $(3x + 1)(2x + 3)$ (b) $(5y + 2)(3y + 1)$
(c) $(3x + 5)(2x - 7)$ (d) $(3z - 4)(2z - 7)$
(e) $(3y - 8)(2y + 5)$ (f) $(x + 11)(3x - 2)$
(g) $(2x + 7)(3x - 5)$ (h) $(5z - 2)(5z + 2)$
(i) $(3x - 5)(2x + 7)$ (j) $(3 + 5y)(2 - 7y)$
(k) $(4z - 3)(2z - 5)$ (l) $(2x - 11)(3x + 1)$
(m) $(5x - 3)(x + 5)$ (n) $(3x - 8)(2x + 5)$

6. Calculate the area of each of the following.
(a)

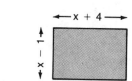

(b)

(c)

C Expand and simplify.

7. (a) $3(2x - 3)(5x + 4)$
(b) $4(3x - 1)(3x + 1)$
(c) $-2(3 - x)(4 + x)$
(d) $5(3 - 2x)(4 - x)$

8. (a) $\frac{1}{2}(2x + 6)(x - 5)$

(b) $0.5(3x + 2)(4x + 6)$
(c) $-3(x + 4)(x - 5)$
(d) $(3x - 1)(1 + 3x)3$
(e) $5(x + 3)(2x - 5)$
(f) $4(x + 0.5)(x - 0.5)$

9. Find the area of each of the following figures.
(a)

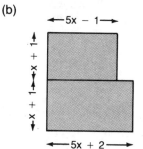

$r = (3x - 2)$

$\pi = 3.14$

(b)

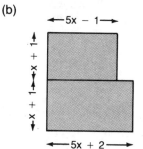

(c)

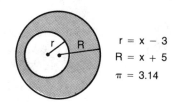

$r = x - 3$
$R = x + 5$
$\pi = 3.14$

7.12 FACTORING TRINOMIALS: $x^2 + bx + c$

Trinomials such as $x^2 + 5x + 6$ can sometimes be factored into the product of two binomials. The following expansions show a pattern for factoring.

the sum of these numbers is here

$$(x + 2)(x + 3) = x^2 + 5x + 6$$
$$(x - 2)(x - 4) = x^2 - 6x + 8$$
$$(x - 5)(x + 3) = x^2 - 2x - 15$$
$$(x + 5)(x - 3) = x^2 + 2x - 15$$

the product of these numbers is here

3·2·1

Expanding two general binomials gives

$$(x + m)(x + n) = x^2 + nx + mx + mn$$
$$= x^2 + mx + nx + mn$$
$$= x^2 + (m + n)x + mn$$

Comparing the results to the general trinomial $x^2 + bx + c$

$$x^2 + \quad bx \quad + c$$
$$x^2 + (m + n)x + mn$$
$$b = m + n \quad \text{and} \quad c = mn$$
$$\therefore x^2 + bx + c = x^2 + (m + n)x + mn$$
$$= (x + m)(x + n)$$

EXAMPLE. Factor.
(a) $x^2 + 7x + 12$ (b) $x^2 - 3x - 28$

SOLUTION:
(a) $x^2 + 7x + 12$

We want $m + n$ to equal 7 and mn to equal 12.

$m = 3$ and $n = 4$

$x^2 + 7x + 12 = x^2 + (3 + 4)x + (3)(4)$
$\qquad\qquad\qquad = (x + 3)(x + 4)$

Factors of 12	Sum of factors
1, 12	13
$-1, -12$	-13
2, 6	8
$-2,\ -6$	-8
3, 4	7
$-3,\ -4$	-7

(b) $x^2 - 3x - 28$

We want $m + n$ to equal -3 and mn to equal -28. This means that one value is negative and the other positive.

$m = -7$ and $n = 4$

$x^2 - 3x - 28 = x^2 + (-7 + 4)x + (-7)(+4)$
$\qquad\qquad\qquad = (x - 7)(x + 4)$

Factors of -28	Sum of factors
1, -28	-27
$-1,$ 28	27
4, -7	-3

EXERCISE 7.12

A 1. State values for m and n to satisfy the given conditions.

(a)

Sum m + n	Product mn
11	30
7	12
8	15
13	12
18	77
− 7	10
− 8	15
− 10	25
− 7	12
− 7	6

(b)

Sum m + n	Product mn
− 1	− 12
1	− 12
− 3	− 40
2	− 15
25	150
35	250
4	− 5
− 1	− 42
− 7	− 60
2	− 48

B 2. State each of the following in factored form.

(a) $x^2 + (3 + 5)x + (3)(5)$
(b) $x^2 + [5 + (-3)]x + (5)(-3)$
(c) $x^2 + (-3 - 2)x + (-3)(-2)$
(d) $x^2 + (-7 + 8)x + (-7)(8)$
(e) $x^2 + (5 + 5)x + (5)(5)$
(f) $x^2 + (-3 - 3)x + (-3)(-3)$

3. State the remaining factors.

(a) $x^2 + 7x + 10 = (x + 2)(\blacksquare)$
(b) $x^2 + 3x + 2 = (x + 1)(\blacksquare)$
(c) $x^2 + 7x + 12 = (x + 3)(\blacksquare)$
(d) $x^2 + 5x + 4 = (x + 4)(\blacksquare)$
(e) $x^2 + 11x + 18 = (\blacksquare)(x + 2)$
(f) $x^2 - 6x + 5 = (\blacksquare)(x - 1)$
(g) $x^2 - 5x + 6 = (x - 2)(\blacksquare)$
(h) $x^2 - 8x + 7 = (x - 7)(\blacksquare)$
(i) $x^2 - x - 20 = (x - 5)(\blacksquare)$
(j) $x^2 + x - 20 = (\blacksquare)(x - 4)$
(k) $x^2 + x - 12 = (x + 4)(\blacksquare)$
(l) $x^2 + 2x - 8 = (x + 4)(\blacksquare)$

4. Factor if possible.

(a) $a^2 + 7a + 12$ (b) $t^2 + 5t + 4$
(c) $b^2 - 5b + 6$ (d) $x^2 - 4x + 3$
(e) $x^2 + 3x + 2$ (f) $x^2 - 8x + 7$
(g) $x^2 + 9x + 8$ (h) $a^2 - 6a + 8$
(i) $a^2 - 10a + 9$ (j) $y^2 - 12y + 20$
(k) $x^2 - 6x + 5$ (l) $y^2 - 6y + 7$

5. Factor if possible.

(a) $m^2 + 2m - 3$ (b) $t^2 - 2t - 3$

(c) $x^2 - x - 2$ (d) $x^2 + x - 2$
(e) $a^2 + a + 2$ (f) $a^2 - a - 12$
(g) $x^2 + x - 12$ (h) $x^2 - x - 20$
(i) $x^2 + x - 42$ (j) $y^2 + y + 42$
(k) $y^2 + 2y - 15$ (l) $x^2 + 3x - 88$

6. Factor if possible.

(a) $y^2 + y - 30$ (b) $t^2 - 6t - 7$
(c) $b^2 + 5b + 6$ (d) $x^2 + 5x - 6$
(e) $x^2 + 7x - 30$ (f) $x^2 - 7x - 8$
(g) $x^2 + 11x + 33$ (h) $y^2 - 4y - 21$
(i) $a^2 + 3a - 40$ (j) $y^2 - 22y + 121$
(k) $a^2 + 25a + 150$ (l) $x^2 - 5x - 84$

C 7. Factor fully.

(a) $3y^2 - 21y + 36$
(b) $5x^2 - 35x + 30$
(c) $5x^2 + 15x + 10$
(d) $6x^2 + 12x - 90$
(e) $y^3 + y^2 - 12y$
(f) $5x^2 - 5x - 100$
(g) $ax^2 - 28ax + 75a$
(h) $5ax^2 + 40ax + 75a$
(i) $2x^4 + 16x^3 + 24x^2$
(j) $3x^3 + 15x^2 - 18x$
(k) $3x^2 + 30x + 72$
(l) $3bx^2 + 12bx + 12b$

8. Find the value of k to make each of the following a true statement.

(a) $(x + 2)(x + 3) = x^2 + (k + 1)x + 6$
(b) $(x - 4)(x - 3) = x^2 + (k - 2)x + 12$
(c) $(x - 5)(x + 2) = x^2 - 3x + k$
(d) $(x - 11)(x + 1) = x^2 + 2(k + 4)x - 11$

9. Factor as trinomials.

(a) $(2x)^2 + 4(2x) + 3$
(b) $(3y)^2 - 5(3y) + 4$
(c) $(2x)^2 - 7(2x) + 12$
(d) $(a + b)^2 - 5(a + b) + 6$

7.13 FACTORING TRINOMIALS: $ax^2 + bx + c$

3·2·1

In the previous section, trinomials in the form $ax^2 + bx + c$, a = 1, or $x^2 + bx + c$, were factored. In this section, trinomials where the value of a is not 1 will be factored. The problem solving technique of working backwards will be used to determine a pattern for factoring.

Expanding $(3x + 2)(5x + 1)$

$$(3x + 2)(5x + 1) = (3x + 2)(5x + 1)$$

$$= 15x^2 + 3x + 10x + 2$$

At this point in the expansion the product of the middle coefficients is the same as the product of the outer coefficients.

$$3 \times 10$$
$$15 \times 2$$

$$= 15x^2 + 13x + 2$$

We shall now take $5x^2 + 23x + 12$ and work backwards to obtain the original factors.

$$5x^2 + 23x + 12 = 5x^2 + 3x + 20x + 12$$

The middle term, $+23x$, has been replaced by $+3x + 20x$. The two numbers 3 and 20 are chosen because their sum is 23 and their product is 60, which is also the product of 5 and 12. We can now factor the trinomial by grouping.

$$5x^2 + 23x + 12 = 5x^2 + 3x + 20x + 12$$
$$= (5x^2 + 3x) + (20x + 12)$$
$$= x(5x + 3) + 4(5x + 3)$$
$$= (5x + 3)(x + 4)$$

This method is called decomposition of the middle term.

EXAMPLE 1. Factor. $8x^2 + 26x + 15$

SOLUTION:

We must decompose 26x, the middle term, into two terms so we can group to obtain a common factor.

$$25x + x$$
$$24x + 2x$$
$$\cdots$$
$$8x^2 + 26x + 15 = 8x^2 + 20x + 6x + 5 \qquad \text{These are the possibilities to decompose 26x}$$
$$\cdots$$
$$13x + 13x$$
$$\cdots$$
$$x + 25x$$

The product of the coefficient of x^2 and the constant term is $8 \times 15 = 120$. We now need two numbers whose sum is 26 and whose product is 120. The numbers are 20 and 6.

$$8x^2 + 26 + 15 = 8x^2 + 20x + 6x + 15$$
$$= (8x^2 + 20x) + (6x + 15)$$
$$= 4x(2x + 5) + 3(2x + 5)$$
$$= (2x + 5)(4x + 3)$$

EXAMPLE 2. Factor.
(a) $15x^2 + 49x + 40$
(b) $21x^2 - 41x + 10$
(c) $15x^2 - 23x - 28$

SOLUTION:

$15 \times 40 = 600$
$600 = 25 \times 24$
$49 = 25 + 24$

(a) $15x^2 + 49x + 40 = 15x^2 + 24x + 25x + 40$
$\qquad\qquad\qquad\quad = 3x(5x + 8) + 5(5x + 8)$
$\qquad\qquad\qquad\quad = (5x + 8)(3x + 5)$

$21 \times 10 = 210$
$210 = (-35)(-6)$
$-41 = (-35) + (-6)$

(b) $21x^2 - 41x + 10 = 21x^2 - 35x - 6x + 10$
$\qquad\qquad\qquad\quad = 7x(3x - 5) - 2(3x - 5)$
$\qquad\qquad\qquad\quad = (3x - 5)(7x - 2)$

$(15)(-28) = -460$
$-460 = (12)(-35)$
$-23 = (12) + (-35)$

(c) $15x^2 - 23x - 28 = 15x^2 + 12x - 35x - 28$
$\qquad\qquad\qquad\quad = 3x(5x + 4) - 7(5x + 4)$
$\qquad\qquad\qquad\quad = (5x + 4)(3x - 7)$

We can also factor trinomials by analysis and trial. Let us factor $5x^2 + 23x + 12$ using this method.

Since $5x^2 = (5x)(x)$ the first terms in each binomial factor are $5x$ and x. All signs are positive in the given trinomial so both signs in the binomial factors will be positive. The second terms in the binomial factors must have a product of 12. The correct pair of binomial factors must be the one that gives a cross product of $23x$.

$5x + 6$	$5x + 2$	$5x + 4$	$5x + 3$	$5x + 12$	$5x + 1$
$x + 2$	$x + 6$	$x + 3$	$x + 4$	$x + 1$	$x + 12$
$16x$	$32x$	$19x$	$23x$	$17x$	$61x$

$23x$ is the required cross product.

$$5x^2 + 23x + 12 = (5x + 3)(x + 4)$$

Factoring $8x^2 + 26x + 15$ from Example 1 by analysis and trial,

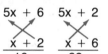

$4x$	$8x + 15$	1	5	3
$2x$	$x + 1$	15	3	5

Again the factors are $(4x + 3)(2x + 5)$.

Factoring Example 2(c) by analysis and trial, we have the possibilities

$5x$	$3x$	x	$15x + 28$	1	14	2	7	4
$3x$	$5x$	$15x$	$x - 1$	28	2	14	4	7

$(5x + 4)(3x - 7)$ is the combination that gives $-23x$.

EXERCISE 7.13

B 1. Find pairs of numbers to satisfy the given conditions.

(a)

Sum m + n	Product mn	Numbers m,n
13	42	
1	− 42	
− 1	− 42	
14	33	
− 2	− 120	

(b)

Sum m + n	Product mn	Numbers m,n
− 17	72	
5	− 66	
− 7	− 44	
5	− 36	
17	60	

2. Complete the factoring.
(a) $(5x + 2)3x + (5x + 2)4$
(b) $(3x − 7)2x + (3x − 7)3$
(c) $4x(2x − 5) + 3(2x − 5)$
(d) $3x(x + 4) − 2(x + 4)$
(e) $6x(2x + 3) + 5(2x + 3)$
(f) $3a(x + y) − 2b(x + y)$
(g) $5x(3x + 4) + 2(3x + 4)$
(h) $2x(x − 3) − 5(x − 3)$

3. Factor.
(a) $9x^2 + 19x + 10$ (b) $10x^2 + 11x + 3$
(c) $2x^2 − 11x + 12$ (d) $6x^2 − 19x + 10$
(e) $15x^2 + 26x + 8$ (f) $6x^2 − 17x + 5$
(g) $12x^2 + 17x + 6$ (h) $15x^2 − 32x + 16$
(i) $6x^2 + 19x + 10$ (j) $16x^2 − 16x − 5$

4. Factor.
(a) $6x^2 + 11x − 10$ (b) $8x^2 − 10x − 3$
(c) $8x^2 + 2x − 21$ (d) $20x^2 − 3x − 9$
(e) $15x^2 + 14x − 8$ (f) $9x^2 − 12x + 4$
(g) $12x^2 − 4x − 5$ (h) $4x^2 − 4x − 15$
(i) $20x^2 + 9x − 18$ (j) $20x^2 + 11x − 4$

5. Factor if possible.
(a) $2x^2 + x − 15$ (b) $7x^2 + 51x + 14$
(c) $2x^2 − 19x + 45$ (d) $10x^2 + 21x − 10$
(e) $3x^2 − 5x − 28$ (f) $8x^2 − 11x + 15$
(g) $3x^2 − 5x + 7$ (h) $10x^2 + 19x − 15$
(i) $6x^2 − 19x − 11$ (j) $16x^2 + 14x − 15$

6. Factor if possible.
(a) $6x^2 − 11x + 4$ (b) $21x^2 + 52x + 32$
(c) $14x^2 + 41x + 15$ (d) $20x^2 + 17x − 24$
(e) $15x^2 + 17x − 18$ (f) $10x^2 − 11x − 6$
(g) $3x^2 − 10x − 8$ (h) $18x^2 − 19x − 12$
(i) $36x^2 + 9x − 10$ (j) $25x^2 + 25x + 6$

7. Factor if possible.
(a) $2x^2 + 23x + 45$ (b) $14x^2 + 31x − 10$
(c) $18x^2 − 9x − 35$ (d) $8x^2 − 46x + 45$
(e) $14x^2 − 15x − 9$ (f) $3x^2 − 31x + 56$
(g) $3x^2 + 29x + 40$ (h) $2x^2 − 29x + 60$

C 8. Factor fully if possible.
(a) $4x^2 + 2x − 30$
(b) $12x^2 + 28x − 24$
(c) $14x^2 − 74x + 20$
(d) $12x^2 + 12x − 9$
(e) $10x^2 − 25x + 10$
(f) $7x^2 + 21x + 14$
(g) $36x^2 + 66x − 60$
(h) $40x^2 + 184x − 80$
(i) $6x^2 + 3x − 45$
(j) $63x^2 − 33x − 6$
(k) $40x^2 − 22x − 105$
(l) $24x^2 − 68x − 180$

MIND BENDER

Determine the pattern. Find the missing number.

4	7	8	5
3		3	4
2	5	7	3
2	3	5	2

7.14 SPECIAL PRODUCT: (a + b)(a − b)

The example illustrates a pattern for the product of two binomials that are identical except for the signs in the middle.

EXAMPLE. Expand.
(a) $(x + 5)(x − 5)$ (b) $(3x + 5)(3x − 5)$ (c) $(5 − 2x)(5 + 2x)$

SOLUTION:

(a) $(x + 5)(x − 5) = (x + 5)(x − 5)$

$$= x^2 − 5x + 5x − 25$$
$$= x^2 − 25$$

(b) $(3x + 5)(3x − 5) = 9x^2 − 15x + 15x − 25$
$$= 9x^2 − 25$$

(c) $(5 − 2x)(5 + 2x) = 25 + 10x − 10x − 4x^2$
$$= 25 − 4x^2$$

We generalize the results of Example 1 by expanding

$$(a + b)(a − b) = (a + b)(a − b)$$
$$= a^2 − ab + ab − b^2$$
$$= a^2 − b^2$$

where $(a + b)$ is the sum and $(a − b)$ is the difference. This is a special case of the product of two binomials called the difference of squares.

$$(a + b)(a − b) = a^2 − b^2$$

EXERCISE 7.14

1. Expand.

(a) $(x − 2)(x + 2)$ (b) $(y + 1)(y − 1)$
(c) $(r + 5)(r − 5)$ (d) $(s − 6)(s + 6)$
(e) $(v − 10)(v + 10)$ (f) $(w + 12)(w − 12)$
(g) $(5x + 1)(5x − 1)$ (h) $(3x − 1)(3x + 1)$
(i) $(1 + x)(1 − x)$ (j) $(t + 6)(t − 6)$
(k) $(z − 3)(z + 3)$ (l) $(1 + 4x)(1 − 4x)$
(m)$(4 − t)(4 + t)$ (n) $(1 + 2x)(1 − 2x)$
(o) $(3 + x)(3 − x)$ (p) $(5 − m)(5 + m)$

2. Expand.

(a) $(2x + 3)(2x − 3)$
(b) $(3x + 7)(3x − 7)$
(c) $(5y + 6)(5y − 6)$
(d) $(5x + 3y)(5x − 3y)$
(e) $(2t − 7)(2t + 7)$
(f) $(3r − 2s)(3r + 2s)$
(g) $(11x + 5y)(11x − 5y)$
(h) $(5p + 12q)(5p − 12q)$

(i) $(4s − 13t)(4s + 13t)$
(j) $(7x − 8v)(7x + 8v)$
(k) $(10x − 15y)(10x + 15y)$
(l) $(9x − 11y)(9x + 11y)$
(m)$(xy + 2)(xy − 2)$

C 3. Expand and simplify.

(a) $(x^2 + 1)(x + 1)(x − 1)$
(b) $(x^2 − 3)(x^2 + 3)$
(c) $2(x + 1)(x − 1)$
(d) $5(x − 2)(x + 2)$
(e) $3(3 + y)(3 − y)$
(f) $x(x + y)(x − y)$
(g) $(x^2 + 9)(x − 3)(x + 3)$
(h) $5s(2s − 5)(2s + 5)$
(i) $(x^2 + 20)(x^2 − 20)$
(j) $3z(5 − 2z)(2z + 5)$
(k) $(x + 2)(x^2 + 4)(x − 2)$
(l) $3x^2(3x + 1)(3x − 1)$

7.15 FACTORING THE DIFFERENCE OF SQUARES: $a^2 - b^2$

$$\xrightarrow{\text{expanding}}$$
$$(a + b)(a - b) = a^2 - b^2$$
$$\xleftarrow{\text{factoring}}$$

EXAMPLE 1. Factor.
(a) $x^2 - 9$ (b) $4x^2 - 25$ (c) $49x^2 - 64y^2$

SOLUTION:
(a) $x^2 - 9 = x^2 - 3^2 = (x + 3)(x - 3)$
(b) $4x^2 - 25 = (2x)^2 - 5^2 = (2x + 5)(2x - 5)$
(c) $49x^2 - 64y^2 = (7x)^2 - (8y)^2 = (7x - 8y)(7x + 8y)$

EXAMPLE 2. Factor.
(a) $x^4 - 1$ (b) $(x - 2y)^2 - (3x + y)^2$

SOLUTION:
(a) $x^4 - 1 = (x^2 + 1)(x^2 - 1)$
           $= (x^2 + 1)(x + 1)(x - 1)$
(b) $(x - 2y)^2 - (3x + y)^2 = [(x - 2y) + (3x + y)][(x - 2y) - (3x +$
                     $= [x - 2y + 3x + y][x - 2y - 3x - y]$
                     $= [4x - y][-2x - 3y]$
                     $= -[4x - y][2x + 3y]$

EXERCISE 7.15

A 1. Find the remaining factors.
(a) $x^2 - 16 = (x + 4)(\blacksquare)$
(b) $4x^2 - 1 = (2x + 1)(\blacksquare)$
(c) $x^2 - 36 = (\blacksquare)(x - 6)$
(d) $9y^2 - 4 = (3y + 2)(\blacksquare)$
(e) $x^2 - 25 = (\blacksquare)(x + 5)$
(f) $25 - x^2 = (5 + x)(\blacksquare)$
(g) $x^2 - y^2 = (x - y)(\blacksquare)$
(h) $s^2 - t^2 = (s + t)(\blacksquare)$

B 2. Factor.
(a) $x^2 - 81$ (b) $81 - y^2$
(c) $x^2 - 100$ (d) $x^2 - 121$
(e) $y^2 - 144$ (f) $x^2 - 4y^2$
(g) $100x^2 - 1$ (h) $1 - 121y^2$

3. Factor if possible.
(a) $9x^2 - 25$ (b) $4y^2 - 49$
(c) $25x^2 - 36$ (d) $100x^2 - 81$
(e) $64x^2 + 81$ (f) $9x^2 - 16$
(g) $5x^2 - 16$ (h) $121x^2 - 100$

4. Factor if possible.
(a) $x^2y^2 - 1$ (b) $9 - x^2y^2$
(c) $25 - 16x^2y^2$ (d) $36x^2y^2 - 1$
(e) $x^2y^2 + 49$ (f) $100s^2 - t^2x^2$
(g) $16x^2 - 25t^2y^2$ (h) $16x^2 - 39y$

5. Factor if possible.
(a) $4x^2 - 64$ (b) $3x^2 - 3$
(c) $x^4 - 16$ (d) $x^4 - 81$
(e) $81x^4 - 25y^4$ (f) $(x - 3)^2 - 9$
(g) $(x + y)^2 - (x - y)^2$
(h) $(x + y)^2 - z^2$
(i) $x^2 - (x - 3)^2$

6. Factor as a difference of squares and find the value of the following.
(a) $60^2 - 40^2$ (b) $125^2 - 25^2$
(c) $112^2 - 111^2$ (d) $252^2 - 248^2$
(e) $70^2 - 30^2$ (f) $55^2 - 45^2$
(g) $93^2 - 7^2$ (h) $68^2 - 32^2$

7.16 SPECIAL PRODUCTS: PERFECT SQUARES $(a + b)^2$ AND $(a - b)^2$

$(x + 3)^2$ is called a perfect square. The expansion can be illustrated using a diagram.

$$(x + 3)^2 = (x + 3)(x + 3)$$
$$= x^2 + 3x + 3x + 9$$
$$= x^2 + 6x + 9$$

The same result is obtained using FOIL.

$(x + 3)^2 = (x + 3)(x + 3)$

$$= x^2 + 3x + 3x + 9$$
$$= x^2 + 6x + 9$$

	x	+ 3
x	x^2	3x
+ 3	3x	9

In general,

$(a + b)^2 = (a + b)(a + b)$	$(a - b)^2 = (a - b)(a - b)$
$= a^2 + ab + ab + b^2$	$= a^2 - ab - ab + b^2$
$= a^2 + 2ab + b^2$	$= a^2 - 2ab + b^2$

EXAMPLE. Expand and simplify. $3(x - 5)^2$

SOLUTION:
$$3(x - 5)^2 = 3(x^2 - 10x + 25)$$
$$= 3x^2 - 30x + 75$$

Note that the three is not squared because only the polynomial in the bracket is squared. We square the bracket first and then multiply by the factor.

EXERCISE 7.16

A 1. Expand.

(a) $(x + 1)^2$ (b) $(x + 3)^2$ (c) $(x + 5)^2$
(d) $(y - 2)^2$ (e) $(y - 4)^2$ (f) $(y - 5)^2$
(g) $(x + y)^2$ (h) $(x - y)^2$ (i) $(1 + 2y)^2$
(j) $(5 - s)^2$ (k) $(3 + t)^2$ (l) $(7 + z)^2$
(m) $(a + x)^2$ (n) $(x - 9)^2$ (o) $(r + 5)^2$
(p) $(3 - y)^2$ (q) $(2x - 1)^2$ (r) $(3z + 1)^2$
(s) $(1 - 3x)^2$ (t) $(1 + 5y)^2$ (u) $(v - 6)^2$

B 2. Expand.

(a) $(2x + 3)^2$ (b) $(5x - 2)^2$
(c) $2(5x + 3)^2$ (d) $(2y - 5)^2$
(e) $(4 - y)^2$ (f) $3(2 - 5y)^2$
(g) $(3z + 7)^2$ (h) $(2z - 5)^2$
(i) $4(5 - 2z)^2$ (j) $(3t + 8)^2$
(k) $(7 + 4s)^2$ (l) $-2(2r - 9)^2$

3. Expand.

(a) $(xy + 1)^2$ (b) $(st - 3)^2$
(c) $5(pq + 2)^2$ (d) $(3xy + 1)^2$
(e) $(yz + 7)^2$ (f) $3(5y - xz)^2$
(g) $(2xy - 3)^2$ (h) $(5xz + 8)^2$
(i) $4(3xy + 4)^2$ (j) $(5x + 7yz)^2$
(k) $(2xy - 9)^2$ (l) $-(5rs + 2t)^2$

4. Rewrite in the form $(a + b)^2$ or $(a - b)^2$.

(a) $x^2 + 18x + 81$
(b) $x^2 - 14x + 49$
(c) $9t^2 + 12t + 4$
(d) $25m^2 - 70m + 49$
(e) $100t^2 - 20t + 1$
(f) $64m^2 + 112m + 49$

7.17 PRODUCTS OF POLYNOMIALS

We can multiply polynomials using the distributive property.

$$(x^2 + 2x + 3)(x + 2) = (x^2 + 2x + 3)(x + 2)$$
$$= (x^2 + 2x + 3)x + (x^2 + 2x + 3)2$$
$$= x^3 + 2x^2 + 3x + 2x^2 + 4x + 6$$
$$= x^3 + 4x^2 + 7x + 6$$

The same result is obtained when each term of the first factor multiplies each term in the second factor as follows.

$$(x + 2)(x^2 + 2x + 3) = (x + 2)(x^2 + 2x + 3)$$

$$= x^3 + 2x^2 + 3x + 2x^2 + 4x + 6$$
$$= x^3 + 4x^2 + 7x + 6$$

EXAMPLE 1. Expand. $(2x - 3)(x^2 - 5x + 2)$

SOLUTION:

$$(2x - 3)(x^2 - 5x + 2) = (2x - 3)(x^2 - 5x + 2)$$

$$= 2x^3 - 10x^2 + 4x - 3x^2 + 15x - 6$$
$$= 2x^3 - 13x^2 + 19x - 6$$

Multiplication of polynomials may also be done in a vertical arrangement as follows.

EXAMPLE 2. Multiply.

(a) $2x + 3$
　　$x - 5$

(b) $3x^2 - 5x + 2$
　　$2x + 3$

SOLUTION:

(a) $2x + 3$
　　$x - 5$
　　$2x^2 + 3x$
　　$\quad - 10x - 15$
　　$2x^2 - 7x - 15$

(b) $3x^2 - 5x + 2$
　　$2x + 3$
　　$6x^3 - 10x^2 + 4x$
　　$\quad\quad 9x^2 - 15x + 6$
　　$6x^3 - x^2 - 11x + 6$

Check the results of Example 2 using the horizontal arrangement described in Example 1.

EXAMPLE 3. Simplify. $(x + 3)(x + 5) - 2(x - 5)$

SOLUTION:

$$(x + 3)(x + 5) - 2(x - 5) = (x + 3)(x + 5) - 2(x - 5)$$

$$= x^2 + 5x + 3x + 15 - 2x + 10$$
$$= x^2 + 6x + 25$$

EXERCISE 7.17

1. Multiply.

(a) $\begin{array}{r} 2x + 3 \\ x - 1 \end{array}$

(b) $\begin{array}{r} x + 7 \\ x - 2 \end{array}$

(c) $\begin{array}{r} 2x + 5 \\ 3x - 7 \end{array}$

(d) $\begin{array}{r} 3x + 5 \\ 4x + 3 \end{array}$

2. Multiply.

(a) $\begin{array}{r} x^2 - 5x + 2 \\ x - 2 \end{array}$

(b) $\begin{array}{r} 3x^2 - 7x + 1 \\ x + 4 \end{array}$

(c) $\begin{array}{r} 2x^2 + x - 2 \\ 3x - 5 \end{array}$

(d) $\begin{array}{r} x^2 - 5x + 3 \\ 2x + 5 \end{array}$

(e) $\begin{array}{r} x^2 - 5x + 3 \\ x^2 + x - 2 \end{array}$

(f) $\begin{array}{r} x^2 + 3x - 2 \\ x^2 - x + 5 \end{array}$

(g) $\begin{array}{r} 2x^2 - 7x + 5 \\ 3x^2 + x - 2 \end{array}$

(h) $\begin{array}{r} 3x^2 - 8x + 1 \\ 2x^2 - 5 \end{array}$

3. Expand and simplify.

(a) $(x^2 + 3x + 1)(x + 1)$
(b) $(2x^2 - 5x + 3)(x - 2)$
(c) $(3x^2 - 2x + 7)(x + 3)$
(d) $(2y^2 - 5y + 3)(y + 3)$
(e) $(3y^2 - 5y + 3)(y - 3)$
(f) $(3x^2 + 5)(2x + 3)$

4. Expand and simplify.

(a) $(2s^2 - 5s + 3)(3s - 2)$
(b) $(3t - 5t^2 + 2)(3 - 2t)$
(c) $(5x^2 - 3x)(x + 4)$
(d) $(4 - 3t + t^2)(2 - 3t)$
(e) $(v^2 - 3v + 5)(2v - 7)$
(f) $(3r^2 - 5r + 7)(2r + 3)$
(g) $(3x^2 - 1)(2x + 1)$

5. Find the area of each of the following rectangles.

(a)

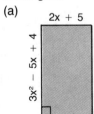

(b)

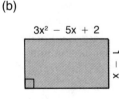

6. Expand and simplify.

(a) $2(x + y) + 3(x - y)$
(b) $2(3y - 7) - (y + 2)$
(c) $3(x^2 - x + 2) - 2(x + 3)$

(d) $-2(x - 5) + 3(x^2 + x + 2)$
(e) $(x + 2)(x - 3) + (x + 4)(x + 3)$
(f) $(y - 3)(y + 2) + (y + 1)(y + 5)$

7. Expand and simplify.

(a) $3(x + 1)(x + 3) - (x - 5)(x + 7)$
(b) $2(x + 1)(x + 6) - 3(x - 4)(x - 2)$
(c) $(3y + 1)(y + 2) - 2(2y - 1)(y + 3)$
(d) $3(2x - 3)(x + 5) - 4(x - 4)(x + 6)$

8. Expand and simplify.

(a) $-(3x + 5)(2x - 7) + (x + 4)(5x - 3)$
(b) $(7 - 2x)(x - 5) + (3 - 2x)(4 + 3x)$
(c) $(8 - 3x)(5 - 2x) - (2x + 3)(3x - 5)$
(d) $5(x + 2)(x - 7) + 3(x + 1)(x - 1)$

9. Expand and simplify.

(a) $2(x - 5)^2 + (x - 2)(x + 2)$
(b) $3(x - 3)^2 - 2(x - 2)^2$
(c) $3(x + 5)(x - 5) - 2(x + 6)(x - 6)$
(d) $3(2x^2 - 6x + 1) - (3x + 2)(2x - 5)$
(e) $5(2x - 3)^2 - 2(x + 4)^2$
(f) $-3(5 - 2x)^2 + 3(2x + 7)^2$

10. Expand and simplify.

(a) $(x + 1)^3$
(b) $(x + 2)^3$
(c) $(x + 3)^3$
(d) $3(x^2 - 5x + 2)(x + 3)$
(e) $-4(x^2 + x - 3)(x - 2)$

11. Expand and simplify.

(a) $(3x + 2y)^2 - (2x + 3y)^2$
(b) $5(x + 3)^2 - 2(x - 5)^2$
(c) $(3x - 4)^2 - (2x + 3)^2$
(d) $3(x - 7)^2 + 2(x + 4)^2$
(e) $(x + 3y)^2 - (2x + y)^2$
(f) $2(x - y)^2 + 3(x + 2y)^2$
(g) $(2x + 5)^2 - (5x + 2)^2$
(h) $5(x - 3)^2 - 4(x + 1)^2$
(i) $(x + 3)^2 - (x + 6)^2$
(j) $3(2x - 3)^2 - 2(3x + 1)^2$

C 12. Simplify.

(a) $(x^2 - 5x + 3)(2x - 1)$
$- (x + 3)(x^2 - 5x + 2)$
(b) $(y^2 + 3y - 1)(3y + 2)$
$- (y + 4)(y^2 - 6y + 2)$

7.18 PROBLEM SOLVING

1. How many days are there in one million seconds?

2. What is the greatest three-digit number that is a perfect square?

3. The price of an item was reduced by 10%, then later reduced by 20%. What single percent reduction gives the same result as the two reductions?

4. Find three consecutive numbers whose sum is 117.

5. Determine a formula for the area of the figure.

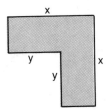

6. Caroline attends a university where an academic year consists of two semesters of 16 weeks each. Caroline budgeted $800 for transportation for the year. After three weeks of school she had spent $100 for transportation. If she continues to spend at the same rate will her budget for transportation be adequate? If not, when will her transportation funds be exhausted and how much more will she need to complete the year?

7. A group of friends plans to bicycle across Manitoba in 5 d on their 10-speed bikes. Is this a reasonable goal?

8. If you take a number, multiply it by 4, subtract 10, and finally add 11, you get 33. What is the number?

9. The sum of the digits of an odd two-digit prime number is 11. The ones digit is less than the tens digit. What is the number?

10. Three students are to be chosen to work in the Legislative Assembly. The five candidates are Al, Beth, Corrine, David, and Terry.
(a) How many different combinations of three students can be selected?
(b) How many different combinations can be selected if Terry has to be one of the students chosen?

11. The numbers in the sequence
$$1, 1, 2, 3, 5, 8, \ldots$$
are called the Fibonacci numbers. To write the numbers in the Fibonacci sequence you start with 1, 1. Other numbers are found by adding the two preceding numbers. Find the sum of the squares of the first fifteen Fibonacci numbers.

12. Sandra had $945.56 in the bank for the dance expenses. She wrote cheques for $23.89, $265.78, and $625. What was the new balance?

13. The formula for the surface area of a rectangular solid is
$$SA = 2(\ell h + wh + \ell w)$$
Use the formula to calculate the surface area of the following solid.

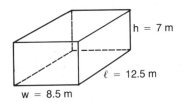

14. Place the numbers from 1 to 9 in the circles so that the sum of each row is 23.

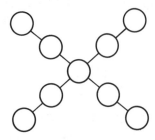

15. (a) How many games are necessary in a twenty-team league if each team is to play every other team twice — once at home and once away?
(b) How many games are required if the league has n teams?

16. Together Sam and Cory walked 43 km. Cory walked 11 km more than Sam. How far did each walk?

17. A rectangular field measures 45 m by 255 m.

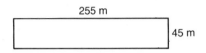
255 m
45 m

A fence is to be constructed around the field so that the fence posts are 5 m apart. How many fence posts are needed?

18. What is the next number in the following sequence?

2, 5, 7, 10, 12, . . .

19. Justine bought two shirts at $33.78 each and three pairs of socks at $3.56 a pair. How much change did she receive from $80?

20. A 40 m board is cut into two pieces. The long piece is 8 m longer than the short piece. How long is each piece?

21. ABCD is a square.
GC = 3 m
AH = 7 m
The area of the shaded region is 39 m².

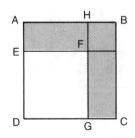
A   H   B
E   F
D   G   C

What is the area of EFGD?

22. How many 1 m squares are needed to make a border around the shaded square which has 9 m sides?

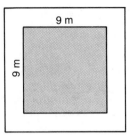
9 m
9 m

23. Name the wheels that are turning clockwise.

A Pythagorean triple is a set of 3 numbers such that the sum of the squares of the first two numbers is equal to the square of the third number.

3, 4, 5 is a Pythagorean triple because
$$3^2 + 4^2 = 5^2$$

Find a Pythagorean triple in which each number is less than 100, and all 3 numbers begin with the same digit.

7.19 REVIEW EXERCISE

1. Write the degree of each polynomial.
(a) $5a^2b + 6ab^3c - 12$
(b) $7xyz - 3x^2 + 2y$
(c) $9r^2s^2t^3 - 4r^2t^2 + 3r^2s^3t$

2. Simplify.
(a) $(2x^2 + 3x - 7) + (4x^2 - 2x - 5)$
(b) $(2y^2 + 3y - 6) + (6y^2 - 4y - 9)$
(c) $(1 - 2m - 3m^2) + (5m^2 - 2m - 8)$
(d) $(4t - 3t^2 + 13) + (1 - 5t - t^2)$

3. Simplify.
(a) $(2x^2 + 3x + 7) - (x^2 - 5x - 9)$
(b) $(3t^2 - 6t - 9) - (7t^2 + 6t + 6)$
(c) $(1 - 3m - 2m^2) - (4m + 6 - 5m^2)$
(d) $(4y^2 - 4y - 1) - (5 - 3y - 6y^2)$

4. Simplify.
(a) $(4x^2y^3)(5x^3y^2)$
(b) $(-3m^2nt)(2m^3)$
(c) $(-11r^2st)(-9r^3s^2t^3)$
(d) $(12x^2y)(-4x^3)(-x^2)$

5. Calculate the area of each figure.
(a)

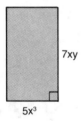

$7xy$

$5x^3$

(b)

$5x^2y$

$5x^2y$

6. Simplify.
(a) $(4x^2yz)^3$
(b) $(3r^3st^4)^5$
(c) $(-2mn^2p)^4$
(d) $(-d^3e^2f^4)^3$
(e) $(-5x^3y^2)^2(-3x^2y^4)^3$
(f) $(2x^2y^3z)^3(-xy^3z^4)^2$

7. Expand and simplify.
(a) $2(x + 3) - 5(x + 1) + 2(x - 5)$
(b) $3(2y + 5) + 2(y + 3) - 4(y - 4)$
(c) $-(x^2 - 1) + 2x(x + 3) - (3x - 1)$
(d) $2(2x - 3y) - 4(3x + 2y)$

8. Expand and simplify.
(a) $2x(4x - 3) - 5x(x + 1)$
(b) $5t(3t - 4s) - 2t(5t - 6s)$
(c) $3xy(2x - 5y) + 2xy(x - 3y)$
(d) $3mn(m - 5n) - mn(3m + 2n)$
(e) $x^2y(x + y) - xy^2(x - y)$

9. Simplify. Assume no denominator is equal to zero.
(a) $\dfrac{8t^4}{2t^3}$
(b) $\dfrac{20x^6y^3}{-4x^2y}$
(c) $\dfrac{-15m^4n^6}{-3mn}$
(d) $\dfrac{-80r^3t^2}{5rt}$
(e) $\dfrac{18a^3b^2}{9a^4b^6}$
(f) $\dfrac{9a^{-1}b^2c^{-3}}{-3a^2b^2c^{-1}}$
(g) $\dfrac{60x^{-3}y^{-1}z^4}{-25xy^{-3}z^{-2}}$
(h) $\dfrac{-4r^{-2}s^3t^4}{-2r^2s^{-3}t^{-2}}$

10. Divide. Assume no denominator is equal to zero.
(a) $\dfrac{6x^3y^2 - 4x^2y^3}{2xy}$
(b) $\dfrac{15m^3n^3 - 5m^2n}{-5m^2n}$
(c) $\dfrac{21a^3b^2c - 14ab^2c^2 - 35a^2b^2c^2}{-7ab^2c}$
(d) $\dfrac{x^7 - x^6 + x^5 - x^4 + x^3 - x^2}{-x}$

11. Find an expression for ℓ.

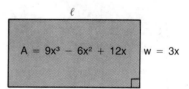

ℓ

$A = 9x^3 - 6x^2 + 12x$ $w = 3x$

12. Find the GCF of the following.
(a) $14xyz,\ 7xy,\ 21yz$
(b) $10a^2b,\ 15ab^2,\ 25a^2b^2$
(c) $24r^2st,\ 28rs^2t,\ 32rst^2$

13. Find the missing factor.

(a) $2xy(\blacksquare) = 4x^3y^2$
(b) $5mn(\blacksquare) = 20m^2n^2p$
(c) $-3xy(\blacksquare) = 12x^4y^2$
(d) $8a^2b(\blacksquare) = -24a^2b^4c$

14. Factor.

(a) $3m^2n + 6mn$
(b) $8xy + 4xz + 2x$
(c) $20x^3y^2 + 15x^2y^2 - 5xy^3$
(d) $14rt - 7r + 21rs$

15. Expand and simplify.

(a) $(x - 3)(x + 5)$　　(b) $(x + 2)(x - 3)$
(c) $(2y - 1)(3y - 2)$　(d) $(2x + 1)(2x - 1)$
(e) $(3z - 2)(3z - 2)$　(f) $(2t + 1)(5t + 3)$

16. Factor.

(a) $x^2 - x - 6$　　　(b) $x^2 - 13x + 42$
(c) $m^2 + 6m - 27$　(d) $t^2 + 18t + 80$
(e) $s^2 - 14s + 33$　(f) $x^2 + 2x - 35$
(g) $m^2 - 13m + 12$　(h) $t^2 - 2t - 24$
(i) $t^2 - 20t + 99$　　(j) $r^2 + 6r - 16$

17. Factor.

(a) $2x^2 + 5x - 3$　　(b) $20t^2 + 11t - 3$
(c) $9r^2 + 24r + 7$　　(d) $10m^2 - 29m + 10$
(e) $40s^2 + 17s - 12$　(f) $21y^2 + 25y - 4$
(g) $25x^2 + 20x + 4$　(h) $14b^2 - 11b + 2$
(i) $6m^2 - 23m + 15$　(j) $4y^2 + 5y - 9$

18. Expand.

(a) $(x - 7)(x + 7)$　　(b) $(m + 5)(m - 5)$
(c) $(2x - 3)(2x + 3)$　(d) $(4t + 5)(4t - 5)$
(e) $(2m - 1)(2m + 1)$　(f) $(x - y)(x + y)$

19. Factor.

(a) $x^2 - 100$　　(b) $a^2 - 81$
(c) $m^2n^2 - 64$　(d) $1 - 36t^4$
(e) $25x^2 - 4y^2$　(f) $16a^2 - 9b^2$

20. Expand.

(a) $(2x - 1)^2$　　(b) $(3m + 4)^2$
(c) $(5m + 7)^2$　　(d) $(4t - 3)^2$
(e) $(6x - y)^2$　　(f) $(9b - 2w)^2$

21. Expand and simplify.

(a) $(x^2 - 2x - 2)(2x - 1)$
(b) $(3z^2 - 2z + 1)(2z - 1)$
(c) $(2y^2 - 3y - 4)(y + 2)$

22. Simplify.

(a) $(x - 7)(x - 2) - (x - 4)(x + 1)$
(b) $3(y - 2)(y - 3) - (y - 5)(y + 2) + 7$
(c) $2(x - 3)(2x + 1) - 2(3x - 1)(x + 1)$
(d) $4(z^2 - 2z - 2) + 2(z^2 - 9z + 2)$

23. Expand and simplify.

(a) $(x^2 - 3x - 2)(2x - 1)$
(b) $(y^2 + y + 1)(y - 2)$
(c) $2(z - 3)(2z - 1) - 3(3z - 1)(z + 2)$
(d) $(3x^2 - 2x - 2)(x + 1)$

24. There are 24 fence posts spaced evenly around a rectangular field. The posts are 2 m apart. Eight posts form the length.

(a) How many posts form the width?
(b) What is the area of the field?

25. What number times itself is 65 536?

26. What is the maximum number of times four straight lines can intersect?

A sports store has a number of bicycles, tricycles, and wagons for sale. There are an equal number of tricycles and wagons. There is a total of 60 pedals and 180 wheels. How many bicycles, tricycles, and wagons are there in the store?

7.20 CHAPTER 7 TEST

1. Simplify.
   (a) $(2x^2 + 3x - 7) + (7x^2 - 5x - 4)$
   (b) $(3t^2 - 2t + 5) - (1 - t - 4t^2)$
   (c) $(5x^2y^4)(-4xy^5)$
   (d) $\dfrac{-60x^5y^2}{-10x^3y^2}$

2. Expand and simplify.
   (a) $2(x - 4) - (2x + 3)$ (b) $2xy(2x - y) - 3xy(x - 2y)$

3. Divide. $\dfrac{4x^3y^2 - 6x^2y^3 + 4x^2y^2}{2xy}$

4. Factor.
   (a) $2xy - 6yz + 8y$ (b) $20m^3n^2 - 5m^2n^3 + 10mn^2$

5. Expand and simplify.
   (a) $(3x - 1)(2x + 5)$ (b) $(5t - 1)^2$

6. Factor.
   (a) $x^2 + x - 20$ (b) $9x^2 - 16$
   (c) $2t^2 + 9t - 5$ (d) $6m^2 - 23m + 21$

7. Expand and simplify.
   (a) $(2x^2 - 3x - 1)(x + 2)$
   (b) $2(x - 1)(x + 1) - 3(2x + 5)(3x - 1)$

EQUATIONS
AND
INEQUALITIES
CHAPTER

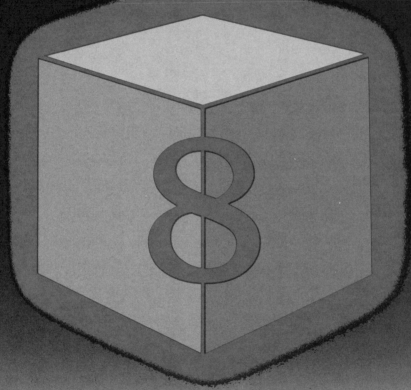

It's strange that thoughts often sound silly when you
try to put them into words.
Edwin R. Procunier

REVIEW AND PREVIEW TO CHAPTER 8

ALGEBRA, EQUATIONS, AND INEQUALITIES

EXERCISE

1. Simplify.
(a) $12x + 33x$
(b) $13x + 35x + 12x$
(c) $21y - 14y + 37y$
(d) $13xy - 24xy + 53xy$
(e) $14x^2 - 22x^2 - 11x^2$
(f) $53t + 47t - 61t$
(g) $42x + 13y - 17x + 84y$
(h) $24x^2 + 13x + 62x^2 - 47x$
(i) $63x - 16x^2 + 24x^2 - 31x + 3$
(j) $47 - 42s + 67t - 11s + 54 - 19t$
(k) $45 - 16x + 81y - 43x + 62$
(l) $97 - 88z + 61x^2 - 19z - 39 + x^2$
(m) $24xy - 13x^2 + 19xy - 61x^2$
(n) $114 - 53x^2 + 24x^3 - 9x + 17x^3$
(o) $-xy + 19x - 49y + 82x - xy$
(p) $321x + 482y - 163x - 594y + 2$
(q) $147x + 381y - 242x + 333x$
(r) $31.4x + 67.8y - 84.2x - 91.9y$
(s) $17.5x^2 - 49.8x^2 - 31.2y + 78.5y$

2. Simplify.
(a) $91.9t - 43.7s - 51.5s + 38.4t$
(b) $107.4 - 39.4t - 51.9t - 483.7$
(c) $46.3x^3 - 21.9x + 68.5x - 58.3x^3$
(d) $0.92x + 0.87y - 1.43x + 9.99x$
(e) $39.7 + 84.6x - 81.3 + 51.4x$
(f) $6.2x - 3.75x + 4.8x - 9.7x$
(g) $64.7x - 23.6x^2 + 51.2x - 18.7x^2$
(h) $6.37x^3 - 2.45x + 6.84x^2 + 3.61x$
(i) $3.26y - 5.45y + 2.68y^2 + 3.75y^2$
(j) $0.25x + 3.75x^2 + 6.14x - 2.68x^2$
(k) $1.125x + 2.375x + 0.5x - 2x$

3. Expand.
(a) $5(x + 4)$
(b) $13(3x - 7)$
(c) $-(3x^2 - 9x - 14)$
(d) $-9(8t - 7s + 51)$
(e) $-4(13x^2 - 51x - 11)$
(f) $19(3x^3 - 4x^2 - 8x + 6)$
(g) $-13(4y - 31x - 11)$
(h) $52(5x^2 - 11x + 16)$
(i) $-34(5 - 7x^2 + 33x)$
(j) $0.4(8x^3 - 7x^2 + 13x)$
(k) $-9.2(6x + 13y - 5)$
(l) $1.4(5.3t - 5.2s + 9.5)$

4. If $x = 3$, $y = 2$, and $z = 1$, evaluate the following.
(a) $x + y - z$
(b) $x^2 - y^2 + 2z$
(c) $4xy - 3x^2 + 5z^2$
(d) $13 - 4x^2 - 3y - x$
(e) $5xy - 2x^2y + 7$
(f) $2x^2 - y - 5z$
(g) $4y^2 - 3z^3 + 2xy$
(h) $3 - 5xy^2 - 4x - 17$
(i) $13z^4 - 8xyz + 4yz$
(j) $3x^2 - 2xz + xyz$

5. If $x = -3$, $y = -2$, and $z = 2$, evaluate the following.
(a) $3x - 4y + 5z$
(b) $7x + 7y - 5z$
(c) $14y - x + 3z$
(d) $x^2 + y^2 + z^2$
(e) $4xy - 3yz + 4xz$
(f) $13 - 5xy^2 + 3x^2z^2$
(g) $8xyz - 3xy + 5yz$
(h) $z - x - y$
(i) $15xy^2 - 3x^2y + 5z^2$
(j) $-2xy^2 + 5yz - xyz$

6. If $I = Prt$, find the value of I when
(a) $P = 4000$, $r = 8\%$, $t = 2$
(b) $P = 1500$, $r = 4\%$, $t = 0.5$
(c) $P = 3000$, $r = 12\%$, $t = 6$
(d) $P = 1800$, $r = 7.5\%$, $t = 30$
(e) $P = 2100$, $r = 8.4\%$, $t = 3$
(f) $P = 900$, $r = 0.5\%$, $t = 2.5$
(g) $P = 2000$, $r = 2\%$, $t = 2$
(h) $P = 1500$, $r = 2.5\%$, $t = 3$

7. Solve the following equations by inspection.

(a) $x + 3 = 10$ (b) $x + 12 = 20$
(c) $x - 5 = 7$ (d) $x - 4 = 18$
(e) $2x = 20$ (f) $5x = 40$
(g) $3x = 21$ (h) $4x = -16$
(i) $7x = -56$ (j) $-2x = 14$
(k) $-5x = 10$ (l) $-6x = -18$
(m) $-3x = -15$ (n) $-x = 5$
(o) $-x = -7$ (p) $\frac{1}{2}x = 8$

8. Solve the following equations by inspection.

(a) $\frac{1}{3}x = 7$ (b) $2x + 1 = 15$
(c) $2x - 1 = 9$ (d) $3x + 2 = 11$
(e) $10x - 2 = 98$ (f) $2x - 5 = 45$
(g) $7x - 1 = 20$ (h) $9 - x = 2$
(i) $5x - 2 = 22$ (j) $2x - 5 = 23$
(k) $23 - 2x = 5$ (l) $-3x + 7 = 16$
(m) $9 - 2x = 21$ (n) $-2x - 21 = 9$
(o) $3x + 5 = 26$ (p) $2 - 4x = 14$

GRAPHING ON A NUMBER LINE

EXERCISE

$N = \{1, 2, 3, ...\}$
$I = \{..., -3, -2, -1, 0, 1, 2, 3, ...\}$

1. Graph the following on a number line.

(a) $\{x \mid x < 5, x \in N\}$
(b) $\{x \mid x \leqslant 6, x \in N\}$
(c) $\{x \mid x > 3, x \in N\}$
(d) $\{x \mid x \geqslant -2, x \in I\}$
(e) $\{x \mid 1 < x \leqslant 7, x \in N\}$
(f) $\{x \mid -3 \leqslant x < 2, x \in I\}$
(g) $\{x \mid 3x > 6, x \in I\}$
(h) $\{x \mid 2x < 0, x \in I\}$
(i) $\{x \mid -2 \leqslant x \leqslant 5, x \in I\}$
(j) $\{x \mid -3 < x < 6, x \in I\}$
(k) $\{x \mid 2 \leqslant x - 3 \leqslant 5, x \in N\}$
(l) $\{x \mid x + 2 < 8, x \in N\}$
(m) $\{x \mid -x > 2, x \in I\}$
(n) $\{x \mid -3 < x - 1 \leqslant 4, x \in I\}$
(o) $\{x \mid -2 \leqslant x + 2 \leqslant 2, x \in I\}$

FLOW CHARTS

EXERCISE

1. Write the output for the following flow charts.

(a)
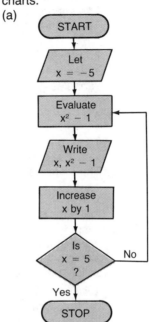

(b)
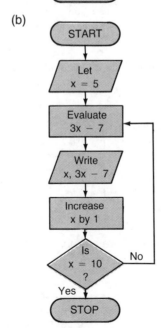

8.1 OPEN SENTENCES: EQUATIONS AND INEQUALITIES

We can identify the following sentences as either true or false.

The number 12 is even.
$4 \times 5 = 20$
The square of 5 is not 25.
The square root of 7 is less than 3.

In the open sentences that follow, it is not possible to say whether the statement is true or false, until some replacement is made for the variables.

$x + 4 = 7$
$x - 3 > 2$
There are x provinces in Canada.
$x < 5, x \in W$
The length is twice the width.

$x + 4 = 7$ is true if x is replaced by 3. Other replacements for x make the statement false. Therefore, 3 is called a solution of the sentence. The open sentence $x + 4 = 7$ is called an equation. A value of a variable that converts an open sentence into a true statement is called a solution or root of the equation. It is said to satisfy the equation.

$x < 5, x \in W$ is true if we replace x by any number from the set $\{0, 1, 2, 3, 4\}$. The set of all solutions of an open sentence is called the solution set of the sentence over that domain. An open sentence is solved when we can state its solution, that is, its root, or roots, or the solution set.

EXAMPLE. Use systematic trial to find the solution set; $x \in W$.
(a) $x + 6 = 9$ (b) $x + 2 < 5$ (c) $x + 1 \neq 4$

SOLUTION:
In each example, replace x by 0, 1, 2, 3, 4, ...

(a) $x + 6 = 9$	(b) $x + 2 < 5$	(c) $x + 1 \neq 4$
$1 + 6 = 9$ False	$1 + 2 < 5$ True	$1 + 1 \neq 4$ True
$2 + 6 = 9$ False	$2 + 2 < 5$ True	$2 + 1 \neq 4$ True
$3 + 6 = 9$ True	$3 + 2 < 5$ False	$3 + 1 \neq 4$ False
$4 + 6 = 9$ False	$4 + 2 < 5$ False	$4 + 1 \neq 4$ True
$x = 3$	$x \in \{1, 2\}$	$x \in \{1, 2, 4, 5, ...\}$

In part (c) of the example, we are able to generalize that all values of x larger than 5 will also be solutions of the open sentence.

> Open sentences with an equal sign, $=$, are called equations.
> Open sentences containing $<$, $>$, $\leq$, $\geq$, or $\neq$, are called inequalities.

An equation is called inconsistent if the solution, S, is the empty set. The solution of a consistent equation is not the empty set.

Inconsistent Equations	Consistent Equations
$7x = -21, x \in N; S = \phi$ $x^2 = -16, x \in R; S = \phi$ $10x = 5, x \in I; S = \phi$ $2x + 1 = 2x, x \in R, S = \phi$	$7x = -21, x \in I; S = \{-3\}$ $x^2 = 16, x \in I; S = \{4, -4\}$ $10x = 5, x \in R; S = \{\frac{1}{2}\}$ $2x + x = 3x, x \in I; S = I$

EXERCISE 8.1

1. If $x \in \{1, 2, 3, 4\}$, state the solution set for each of the following open sentences.

(a) $x + 1 = 3$ (b) $x - 1 = 4$
(c) $2x = 4$ (d) $x \div 2 = 3$
(e) $x + 1 \neq 2$ (f) $x - 1 \neq 2$
(g) $x + 1 > 3$ (h) $x - 2 < 4$
(i) $2x \geq 4$ (j) $x + 3 \leq 5$

2. Determine whether each of the following equations is consistent or inconsistent.

(a) $x + 5 = 15, x \in I$
(b) $2x = -16, x \in N$
(c) $3x + x = 4x, x \in N$
(d) $2x - 1 = 2x, x \in R$
(e) $6x = 3, x \in R$
(f) $12x = 4, x \in I$

3. If $x \in \{1, 2, 3, 4\}$, write the solution of each of the following.

(a) $x + 3 = 5$ (b) $x - 1 = 2$ (c) $x + 1 > 3$
(d) $x - 2 < 2$ (e) $x + 1 \neq 3$ (f) $6 - x = 2$

4. If $x \in \{1, 2, 3, 4, 5, 6, 7, 8\}$, write the solution set for each of the following open sentences.

(a) $x + 7 = 12$ (b) $3x = 9$
(c) $2 + x = 6$ (d) $x \div 3 = 2$
(e) $x + 5 \neq 6$ (f) $x \div 2 = 5$
(g) $x^2 = 4$ (h) $5 - x \neq 2$
(i) $x^3 = 8$ (j) $3 + x = x$
(k) $x + x = 6$ (l) $x^2 = 100$
(m) $12 \div x = 4$ (n) $\frac{1}{2}x = 4$
(o) $x + 1 = 0$ (p) $x > 5$

5. If $x \in I$, write the solution set for each of the following.

(a) $2x + 1 = 5$ (b) $3x - 1 = 11$

(c) $12 - 3x \neq 6$ (d) $2x + 3 > 14$
(e) $x + (-3) = 8$ (f) $2x + 1 \neq 7$
(g) $10 \div x + 3 = 5$ (h) $3x - 1 \geq 10$

MICRO MATH

The following program is used to solve equations by systematic trial. To solve an equation we find the value of x that makes LS − RS = 0, where LS is the left side and RS is the right side of the equation.
Notice how 2, 3, 2.5, 2.8, and 2.7 are used in the input of the program.
Solve. $2(x - 1.8) = 5x - 11.7$

```
NEW
10 INPUT X
20 LET LS=2*(X-1.8)
30 LET RS=5*X-11.7
40 LET D=LS-RS
50 PRINT"X=";X ;"AND D=";D
60 IF D=0 THEN 80
70 IF D<>0 THEN 10
80 PRINT "THE ROOT IS ";X
90 END
RUN
? 2
X=2 AND D=2.1
? 3
X=3 AND D=-.9000001
? 2.5
X=2.5 AND D=.5999999
? 2.8
X=2.8 AND D=-.3000002
? 2.7
X=2.7 AND D=0
THE ROOT IS 2.7
```

Solve the following equations.
(a) $24x - 53 = 17x - 32$
(b) $5(x - 6) = 18 - x$

8.2 SOLVING EQUATIONS WITH INVERSE FLOW CHARTS

Many equations in our earlier work were solved easily by inspection. Where the solution was not immediately evident, systematic trial was used. Equations can also be solved using flow charts.

Consider the equation $3x - 5 = 7$. The following flow chart can be used to build the LEFT SIDE of the equation.

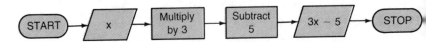

To solve $3x - 5 = 7$, it is necessary to isolate the variable, x, on one side of the equation. We do this by reversing the steps in the flow chart used to build the left side.

LEFT SIDE

START → $3x - 5$ → Add 5 → Divide by 3 → x → STOP

These reversed steps are now applied to the RIGHT SIDE of the equation.

RIGHT SIDE

START → 7 → $7 + 5 = 12$ → $12 \div 3 = 4$ → $x = 4$ → STOP

This result can be checked by substituting in the original equation.

Check.

L.S. = $3(4) - 5$ R.S. = 7
     = $12 - 5$
     = 7

Since L.S. = R.S., the root of the equation is 4.

EXAMPLE. (a) Complete the following flow chart.

START → $5.2(x + 2.1)$ → ? → ? → x → STOP

(b) Use the flow chart to solve $5.2(x + 2.1) = 29.12$

SOLUTION:

(a)

START → $5.2(x + 2.1)$ → Divide by 5.2 → Subtract 2.1 → x → STOP

(b)

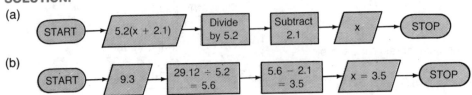

EXERCISE 8.2

A 1. Find the result of each flow chart.

(a)

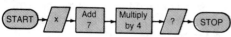

(b)

START → x → Multiply by 5 → Subtract 3 → ? → STOP

(c)

START → x → Divide by 3 → Add 6 → ? → STOP

(d)

START → x → Subtract 3 → Multiply by 5 → ? → STOP

(e)

START → x → Add 4 → Square → ? → STOP

(f)

START → x → Subtract 12 → Divide by 4 → ? → STOP

2. Complete the following flow charts.

(a)

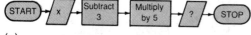

(b)

START → 3(x − 2) → ? → ? → x → STOP

(c)

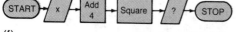

(d)

START → 4(x + 3) → ? → ? → x → STOP

(e)

(f)

START → 1 − ½x → ? → ? → x → STOP

B 3. Determine the result of each flow chart.

(a)

START → 8 → Add 7 → Multiply by 4 → ? → STOP

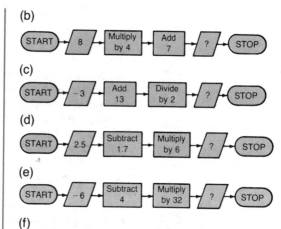

(b)

START → 8 → Multiply by 4 → Add 7 → ? → STOP

(c)

START → −3 → Add 13 → Divide by 2 → ? → STOP

(d)

START → 2.5 → Subtract 1.7 → Multiply by 6 → ? → STOP

(e)

START → −6 → Subtract 4 → Multiply by 32 → ? → STOP

(f)

START → 7.8 → Multiply by 1.3 → Add 6.25 → ? → STOP

4. Solve the following equations using flow charts.

(a) $3x - 5 = 13$
(b) $3(x - 5) = 24$
(c) $6 - x = 11$
(d) $5x + 3 = 43$
(e) $4 - 2x = 20$
(f) $3(x - 4) = 36$
(g) $2.3x - 5.7 = 3.5$
(h) $1.6(x + 2.8) = 6.4$
(i) $3.5x + 6.23 = 11.48$

5. Solve the following equations using flow charts.

(a) $\dfrac{x}{2} + 4 = 5$

(b) $\dfrac{x}{3} - 7 = 6$

(c) $3\left(\dfrac{x}{4} + 4\right) = 12$

(d) $2\left(\dfrac{x}{5} - 3\right) = 14$

(e) $4\left(7 - \dfrac{x}{3}\right) = 20$

(f) $3(x + 2) - (x - 3) = 5$

8.3 SOLVING EQUATIONS BY ADDITION AND SUBTRACTION

Equations have been solved by inspection and the use of inverse flow charts. In the sections which follow, a set of rules will be established so that more complex equations can be transformed into equivalent equations with solutions that can be found by inspection.

Equivalent equations are equations that have the same solution set. There are four rules or axioms of equality that are used to solve equations. The addition and subtraction rules for equations are introduced here by using inverse flow charts to examine solutions.

We can solve $x - 5 = 7$ using flow charts.

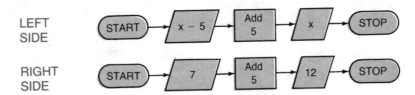

LEFT SIDE

RIGHT SIDE

Adding 5 to both the LEFT SIDE and the RIGHT SIDE of the equation gives the result, $x = 12$. We can use this strategy to establish the addition rule for equations.

Addition Rule for Equations	
Equality is preserved if the same number is added to each side of the equation.	
Since $5 = 5$, then $5 + 3 = 5 + 3$	If $x = y$, then $x + a = y + a$

Similarly, $x + 6 = 14$ can be solved using inverse flow charts.

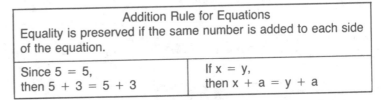

LEFT SIDE

RIGHT SIDE

Subtracting 6 from the LEFT SIDE and the RIGHT SIDE of the equation gives the result, $x = 8$. This strategy is used to establish the subtraction rule for equations.

Subtraction Rule for Equations	
Equality is preserved if the same number is subtracted from each side of the equation.	
Since $7 = 7$, then $7 - 9 = 7 - 9$	If $x = y$, then $x - a = y - a$

EXAMPLE 1. Solve and check. $\quad x - 9 = 35, x \in I$

SOLUTION:

$$x - 9 = 35$$
$$x - 9 + 9 = 35 + 9 \quad \longleftarrow \quad \text{Add}$$
$$x = 44$$

Check.

L.S. $= x - 9$ | R.S. $= 35$
$\quad = 44 - 9$ |
$\quad = 35$ |

∴ 44 is the solution of the equation.

By using the rules to form equivalent equations, we get the variable terms on one side of the equation and the constant terms on the other.

EXAMPLE 2. Solve. $\quad 5x + 54 = 4x - 41, x \in I$

SOLUTION:

$$5x + 54 = 4x - 41$$
$$5x + 54 - 54 = 4x - 41 - 54 \quad \longleftarrow \quad \text{Subtract}$$
$$5x = 4x - 95 \quad \longleftarrow \quad \text{Simplify}$$
$$5x - 4x = 4x - 4x - 95 \quad \longleftarrow \quad \text{Subtract}$$
$$x = -95 \quad \longleftarrow \quad \text{Simplify}$$

∴ the root of the equation is -95.

EXAMPLE 3. Solve and check. $\quad 4(x - 2) = 3(x - 4) - 5, x \in I$

SOLUTION:

$$4(x - 2) = 3(x - 4) - 5$$
$$4x - 8 = 3x - 12 - 5 \quad \longleftarrow \quad \text{Distributive property}$$
$$4x - 8 = 3x - 17 \quad \longleftarrow \quad \text{Simplify}$$
$$4x - 8 + 8 = 3x - 17 + 8 \quad \longleftarrow \quad \text{Add}$$
$$4x = 3x - 9 \quad \longleftarrow \quad \text{Simplify}$$
$$4x - 3x = 3x - 3x - 9 \quad \longleftarrow \quad \text{Subtract}$$
$$x = -9 \quad \longleftarrow \quad \text{Simplify}$$

Check.

L.S. $= 4(x - 2)$ | R.S. $= 3(x - 4) - 5$
$\quad = 4(-9 - 2)$ | $\quad = 3(-9 - 4) - 5$
$\quad = 4(-11)$ | $\quad = 3(-13) - 5$
$\quad = -44$ | $\quad = -39 - 5$
| $\quad = -44$

∴ -9 is the root of the equation.

EXERCISE 8.3

A 1. Solve the following.
(a) $x + 5 = 7$
(b) $x - 1 = 5$
(c) $x - 4 = 11$
(d) $5 + y = 25$
(e) $10 + t = 12$
(f) $14 = x + 7$
(g) $8 = y - 5$
(h) $z + 8 = -2$
(i) $12 = -4 + x$
(j) $35 = x + 15$
(k) $27 + x = 28$
(l) $y - 3 = -13$
(m) $x - 8 = -15$
(n) $t - 9 = -14$
(o) $-12 = x - 8$
(p) $-20 = t - 25$
(q) $31 + x = -42$
(r) $21 + t = -9$
(s) $-13 = x - 15$
(t) $15 = m + 24$

B 2. Solve and check the following. Variables have domain I.
(a) $x + 47 = 59$
(b) $x - 26 = 34$
(c) $x + 31 = -16$
(d) $x - 33 = -18$
(e) $3x + 14 = 2x - 9$
(f) $7t - 18 = 6t + 34$
(g) $18 + 6y = 5y - 11$
(h) $-22 + 9x = -37 + 8x$
(i) $16t + 24 = 15t - 18$
(j) $-16 + 12x = -11 + 11x$
(k) $75 + 8x = -13 + 7x$
(l) $-63 + 15s = 14s + 18$

3. Solve and check the following. Variables have domain I.
(a) $5x + 14 - 3x = x + 21$
(b) $7t + 41 - 11 = 5t - 15 + t$
(c) $14 - 3t + 7t = 15 + 3t - 24$
(d) $13x + 15 - 12x + 25 = 0$
(e) $43 + 7t = 8t + 61 - 2t$
(f) $29 + 9y + 46 = 31 + 2y + 6y$
(g) $21y = 53 + 31y - 11y$
(h) $-74 + 6z + 8 = 8z - 3z$
(i) $17x - 65 + 8x = 20x - 13 + 4x$
(j) $18x - 8x + 42 = 7x + 2x - 13$

4. Solve and check the following. Variables have domain I.
(a) $3(x - 5) - 1 = 2x + 6$
(b) $2(3x - 4) - 8 = 5x - 17$
(c) $17 + 3(2x - 1) = 7x - 18 - 2x$
(d) $13x - 18 = 4(3x - 1) + 5$
(e) $4(2x - 3) - 5 = 7x + 9$
(f) $5(x - 3) + 2x = 2(x - 4) + 4x$
(g) $3(2x - 7) - 5x = 13$
(h) $15x = 2(7x - 5) - 13$
(i) $21 + 3x + 4(x + 2) = 6x - 17$
(j) $7(x - 3) - 152 = 6(x - 1)$
(k) $4(y - 3) - 18 = 3y + 62$
(l) $5(2t + 3) + 4(2t - 1) = 17t$

C 5. Solve the following. Variables have domain R.
(a) $x + 13.4 = 16.5$
(b) $x - 0.75 = 1.76$
(c) $-13.3 + t = 7.4$
(d) $-9.73 + y = -11.62$
(e) $4x + 0.81 = 3x - 0.72$
(f) $7s - 1.57 = 6x - 5.02$
(g) $2(x - 3.1) = x + 8.5$
(h) $5(2x - 1.8) = 9x - 11.9$
(i) $3(2x - 0.7) + 1.9 = 5(x - 8.4)$
(j) $0.75 - 1.82 + 5x = 4(x - 1.61)$
(k) $10.9 + 7y = 6(y - 1.4)$
(l) $0.065 + 3x = 2x - 1.013 + 5.106$

Some cuts of steak require 12 min to cook on a barbecue, 6 min per side. If the barbecue grill is just big enough for two steaks, what is the minimum time required to cook three steaks?

8.4 SOLVING EQUATIONS BY DIVISION

To solve $5x = -30$ using inverse flow charts, we have:

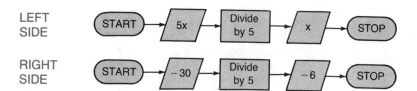

LEFT SIDE

RIGHT SIDE

Dividing both the LEFT SIDE and the RIGHT SIDE of the equation by 5 gives the result, $x = -6$. This result is generalized in the division rule for equations.

Division Rule for Equations
Equality is preserved when both sides of an equation are divided by the same non-zero number.
Since $12 = 12$, then $\frac{12}{-3} = \frac{12}{-3}$ If $x = y$, then $\frac{x}{a} = \frac{y}{a}$, $a \neq 0$

Using the division rule

$$5x = -30$$
$$\frac{5x}{5} = \frac{-30}{5}$$
$$x = -6$$

$\therefore$ the root of the equation is -6.

EXAMPLE 1. Solve and check.

$$4x + 5 + 3x = 5x + 17, x \in I$$

SOLUTION:

$$4x + 5 + 3x = 5x + 17$$
$$7x + 5 = 5x + 17 \qquad \longleftarrow \text{Simplify}$$
$$7x + 5 - 5 = 5x + 17 - 5 \qquad \longleftarrow \text{Subtract}$$
$$7x = 5x + 12 \qquad \longleftarrow \text{Simplify}$$
$$7x - 5x = 5x - 5x + 12 \qquad \longleftarrow \text{Subtract}$$
$$2x = 12 \qquad \longleftarrow \text{Simplify}$$
$$\frac{2x}{2} = \frac{12}{2} \qquad \longleftarrow \text{Divide}$$
$$x = 6$$

Check.

L.S. $= 4x + 5 + 3x$
$= 4(6) + 5 + 3(6)$
$= 24 + 5 + 18$
$= 47$

R.S. $= 5x + 17$
$= 5(6) + 17$
$= 30 + 17$
$= 47$

$\therefore$ 6 is the root of the equation.

EXAMPLE 2. Solve. $3(x - 2) - 4 = 6x + 2$
Unless otherwise stated, the domain of the variable is R.

SOLUTION:

METHOD I

$$3(x - 2) - 4 = 6x + 2$$
$$3x - 6 - 4 = 6x + 2$$
$$3x - 10 = 6x + 2$$
$$3x - 10 + 10 = 6x + 2 + 10$$
$$3x = 6x + 12$$
$$3x - 6x = 6x - 6x + 12$$
$$-3x = 12$$
$$\frac{-3x}{-3} = \frac{12}{-3}$$
$$x = -4$$

METHOD II

$$3(x - 2) - 4 = 6x + 2$$
$$3x - 6 - 4 = 6x + 2$$
$$3x - 10 = 6x + 2$$
$$3x - 3x - 10 = 6x + 2 - 3x$$
$$-10 = 3x + 2$$
$$-10 - 2 = 3x + 2 - 2$$
$$-12 = 3x$$
$$\frac{-12}{3} = \frac{3x}{3}$$
$$-4 = x$$

The solution is -4.

EXAMPLE 3. Solve and check. $3(2x - 1) - 4 = 3x - 6, x \in R$

SOLUTION:

$$3(2x - 1) - 4 = 3x - 6$$
$$6x - 3 - 4 = 3x - 6$$
$$6x - 7 = 3x - 6$$
$$6x - 7 + 7 = 3x - 6 + 7$$
$$6x = 3x + 1$$
$$6x - 3x = 3x - 3x + 1$$
$$3x = 1$$
$$\frac{3x}{3} = \frac{1}{3}$$
$$x = \frac{1}{3}$$

Check.

L.S. $= 3(2x - 1) - 4$
$= 3(2 \times \frac{1}{3} - 1) - 4$
$= 3(\frac{2}{3} - 1) - 4$
$= 3(-\frac{1}{3}) - 4$
$= -1 - 4$
$= -5$

R.S. $= 3x - 6$
$= 3(\frac{1}{3}) - 6$
$= 1 - 6$
$= -5$

$\therefore$ the solution is $\frac{1}{3}$.

EXERCISE 8.4

A 1. Solve the following.

(a) $3x = 15$
(b) $4x = 20$
(c) $2x = 14$
(d) $5x = 30$
(e) $6y = -42$
(f) $21 = 7t$
(g) $-2s = 16$
(h) $-3z = 15$
(i) $-10x = -20$
(j) $-5y = -40$
(k) $3x = 0$
(l) $-4 = -4t$
(m) $-6x = -72$
(n) $-3y = 27$
(o) $-x = -4$
(p) $30 = 10t$
(q) $-12s = 108$
(r) $20y = 80$
(s) $-39 = -13x$
(t) $-17x = 34$

B 2. Solve and check the following. Variables have domain I.

(a) $3x + 12 = 39$
(b) $2x - 18 = 54$
(c) $25 + 5x = 135$
(d) $4t + 64 = -128$
(e) $111 + 3t = 0$
(f) $172 = 2x + 38$
(g) $78 - 6t = 144$
(h) $37 - x = -208$
(i) $140 = -7t - 91$
(j) $143 = 39 - x$
(k) $253 = 22 - 11y$
(l) $325 - 5x = -105$

3. Solve and check.

(a) $7x - 14 = 5x + 42$
(b) $5x + 31 = 73 + 3x$
(c) $2x - 15 = 201 - 4x$
(d) $3x - 57 = 5x - 83$
(e) $10x - 7 = 14x - 9$
(f) $21y + 4 - 6y = 9$
(g) $21t - 205 + 75 = 47t$
(h) $8x + 13 - 3x = -26 + 2x$
(i) $-7 + 40y = 35y - 6$
(j) $35x - 14 + 17x - 90 = 0$
(k) $-53 = 7x - 14 + 6x$
(l) $15s + 52 - 7s = -5s$

4. Solve and check.

(a) $3(x - 7) - 4 = -19$
(b) $2(x + 4) = 7(x - 3) + 34$
(c) $5(y - 3) = 2(y + 6)$
(d) $3(t - 6) + 8 = 4(t + 7)$
(e) $3 + 5(x - 1) = 2(x - 6) + 1$
(f) $3(x + 4) + 3x = 0$
(g) $5(2x - 1) - 7 = 3(1 - 2x) + 17$
(h) $3(2 - 3x) + 4 = 5(x + 2)$
(i) $7(2x + 5) - 77 = 0$
(j) $4(2x + 1) - 3(1 - 4x) = -9$
(k) $6 - (x - 4) = 3x + 70$
(l) $4(2 - 3x) + 6 = (7 - 6x) + 5$

C 5. Solve.

(a) $7x - 1.4 = 5x + 3.8$
(b) $6x + 1.71 = 8x - 1.23$
(c) $4(x - 0.3) = x + 1.5$
(d) $13x + 3.6 = 7x - 8.4$
(e) $5(3x - 7) + 0.5 = -30$
(f) $7(1 - 3x) - 3.5 = 0.5 - 24x$
(g) $0.2x + 5.8 = 7.4$
(h) $1.7x - 0.2 = 1.4x + 2.5$
(i) $0.5(3x - 1.2) = 0.5x$

If you write the whole numbers out fully, as in

> zero,
> one,
> two,
> three,
> four,
> etc.,

what is the first number that contains the letter "a"?

8.5 SOLVING EQUATIONS BY MULTIPLICATION

The equation $\dfrac{x}{2} = \dfrac{x}{5} + 3$ can be solved by subtracting from both sides to find an equivalent equation.

$$\frac{x}{2} - \frac{x}{5} = \frac{x}{5} + 3 - \frac{x}{5}$$

$$\frac{5x}{10} - \frac{2x}{10} = 3$$

$$\frac{3x}{10} = 3$$

Using an inverse flow chart

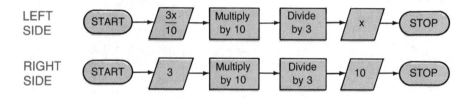

Multiplying both the LEFT SIDE and the RIGHT SIDE of the equation by 10, gives an equivalent equation. Notice that 10 is the lowest common denominator (LCD) of the fractions in the equation. This result is generalized in the multiplication rule for equations.

Multiplication Rule for Equations
Equality is preserved when both sides of an equation are multiplied by the same number.

Since $4 = 4$, then $4 \times (-3) = 4 \times (-3)$	If $x = y$, then $a \times x = a \times y$

Using the multiplication rule

$$\frac{3x}{10} = 3$$

$$10\left(\frac{3x}{10}\right) = 10(3)$$

$$3x = 30$$

$$x = 10$$

Multiplying both sides of the original equation by the lowest common denominator (LCD), 10, results in an equivalent equation without fractions.

$$\frac{x}{2} = \frac{x}{5} + 3$$

$$10\left(\frac{x}{2}\right) = 10\left(\frac{x}{5} + 3\right) \qquad \longleftarrow \quad \text{Multiply both sides by 10}$$

$$5x = 2x + 30$$

$$5x - 2x = 2x - 2x + 30 \qquad \longleftarrow \text{Subtract}$$

$$3x = 30$$

$$\frac{3x}{3} = \frac{30}{3} \qquad \longleftarrow \text{Divide}$$

$$x = 10$$

The solution is 10.

EXAMPLE. Solve and check. $\dfrac{x + 1}{3} - 7 = \dfrac{x - 1}{2}$

SOLUTION:

$$\frac{x + 1}{3} - 7 = \frac{x - 1}{2}$$

The division bar is also a grouping symbol.

$$\frac{(x + 1)}{3} - 7 = \frac{(x - 1)}{2}$$

The LCD for 3 and 2 is 6.

$$6 \times \left[\frac{(x + 1)}{3} - 7\right] = 6 \times \frac{(x - 1)}{2} \qquad \longleftarrow \text{Multiply}$$

$$2(x + 1) - 42 = 3(x - 1)$$

$$2x + 2 - 42 = 3x - 3$$

$$2x - 40 = 3x - 3$$

$$2x - 40 + 40 = 3x - 3 + 40 \qquad \longleftarrow \text{Add}$$

$$2x = 3x + 37 \qquad \longleftarrow \text{Simplify}$$

$$2x - 3x = 3x - 3x + 37 \qquad \longleftarrow \text{Subtract}$$

$$-x = 37$$

$$(-1)(-x) = (-1)(37) \qquad \longleftarrow \text{Multiply}$$

$$x = -37$$

Check.

$$\text{L.S.} = \frac{x + 1}{3} - 7 \qquad\qquad \text{R.S.} = \frac{x - 1}{2}$$

$$= \frac{-37 + 1}{3} - 7 \qquad\qquad = \frac{-37 - 1}{2}$$

$$= \frac{-36}{3} - 7 \qquad\qquad = \frac{-38}{2}$$

$$= -12 - 7 \qquad\qquad = -19$$

$$= -19$$

$\therefore$ the solution is -37.

EXERCISE 8.5

A 1. Solve the following.

(a) $\dfrac{x}{2} = 7$

(b) $\dfrac{x}{5} = 3$

(c) $\dfrac{t}{7} = 6$

(d) $\frac{1}{2}x = 8$

(e) $\frac{1}{3}y = 11$

(f) $\dfrac{x}{4} = -5$

(g) $\dfrac{x}{7} = -2$

(h) $\dfrac{s}{6} = 0$

2. Check whether the given value is a root of the equation.

(a) $\dfrac{x - 1}{3} = \dfrac{1}{2}, 2$

(b) $\dfrac{2x + 3}{4} = 2\frac{1}{4}, 3$

(c) $\dfrac{5 - x}{2} = \dfrac{1}{2}, 4$

(d) $\dfrac{2x - 4}{5} = \dfrac{x}{5}, 4$

(e) $\dfrac{3 - 2x}{2} = \dfrac{x + 1}{4}, 2$

(f) $\dfrac{4 - 2x}{3} = \dfrac{x + 2}{3}, 2$

B 3. Solve and check.

(a) $\dfrac{x}{2} = \dfrac{x}{3} + 5$

(b) $\dfrac{x}{4} = \dfrac{x}{5} - 1$

(c) $\dfrac{x}{6} + 1 = \dfrac{x}{7}$

(d) $\dfrac{s}{4} - 3 = \dfrac{s}{3} + \dfrac{1}{2}$

(e) $\dfrac{x}{6} + 3 = \dfrac{x}{4} + 4$

(f) $\frac{1}{7}x - 1 = \frac{1}{5}x + 1$

(g) $\frac{1}{6}x - \frac{1}{8}x = 1$

(h) $\dfrac{3x}{5} - 5 = \dfrac{x}{2} - 8$

(i) $\dfrac{4x}{3} - \dfrac{5x}{2} = \dfrac{7}{6}$

4. Solve and check.

(a) $\dfrac{x + 1}{4} = 7$

(b) $\dfrac{x - 3}{2} = 5$

(c) $\dfrac{x - 1}{3} = \dfrac{x}{6}$

(d) $\dfrac{2x - 1}{3} = 5$

(e) $\dfrac{1 - 3x}{5} = -1$

(f) $\dfrac{x + 1}{4} = \dfrac{x}{2} + 7$

C 5. Solve.

(a) $\dfrac{x - 1}{4} = \dfrac{3x + 2}{6}$

(b) $\dfrac{x - 7}{6} + 3 = \dfrac{x + 1}{2}$

(c) $\dfrac{x + 7}{6} + \dfrac{1}{2} = \dfrac{x - 2}{4}$

(d) $\dfrac{2 - 3x}{4} = \dfrac{6 - x}{5}$

(e) $\dfrac{2x + 7}{4} - \dfrac{x}{3} = -\dfrac{1}{3}$

(f) $\dfrac{2(3x - 1)}{5} + \dfrac{x + 2}{2} = 4$

MIND BENDER

WORD LADDER

Start with the word ROPE and change one letter at a time to form a new word until you reach LINE. The best solution has the fewest steps.

R O P E

_ _ _ _

_ _ _ _

_ _ _ _

_ _ _ _

L I N E

8.6 EQUATIONS INVOLVING POLYNOMIALS

In this section we combine the rules for solving equations with the methods of simplifying polynomials, to solve equations involving polynomials.

EXAMPLE 1. Solve for x, and check.
$$2(2x - 1) - (2x + 3) = 3(x - 2)$$

SOLUTION:

$$
\begin{aligned}
2(2x - 1) - (2x + 3) &= 3(x - 2) \\
4x - 2 - 2x - 3 &= 3x - 6 \qquad \text{Remove brackets}\\
2x - 5 &= 3x - 6 \qquad \text{Simplify}\\
2x - 3x - 5 &= 3x - 3x - 6 \qquad \text{Subtract}\\
-x - 5 &= -6 \qquad \text{Simplify}\\
-x - 5 + 5 &= -6 + 5 \qquad \text{Add}\\
-x &= -1 \qquad \text{Simplify}\\
(-1)(-x) &= (-1)(-1) \qquad \text{Multiply}\\
x &= 1
\end{aligned}
$$

Check.

L.S. $= 2(2x - 1) - (2x + 3)$	R.S. $= 3(x - 2)$
$= 2[2(1) - 1] - [2(1) + 3]$	$= 3(1 - 2)$
$= 2(1) - (5)$	$= 3(-1)$
$= 2 - 5$	$= -3$
$= -3$	

$\therefore$ 1 is the root of the equation.

EXAMPLE 2. Solve for y.
$$2(y - 3)(y + 2) - 5 = (2y - 1)(y + 2)$$

SOLUTION:

$$
\begin{aligned}
2(y - 3)(y + 2) - 5 &= (2y - 1)(y + 2) \\
2(y^2 + 2y - 3y - 6) - 5 &= (2y^2 + 4y - y - 2) \\
2(y^2 - y - 6) - 5 &= (2y^2 + 3y - 2) \\
2y^2 - 2y - 12 - 5 &= 2y^2 + 3y - 2 \\
2y^2 - 2y - 17 &= 2y^2 + 3y - 2 \\
2y^2 - 2y^2 - 2y - 3y - 17 + 17 &= 2y^2 - 2y^2 + 3y - 3y - 2 + 17 \\
-5y &= 15 \\
y &= -3
\end{aligned}
$$

$\therefore$ the root of the equation is -3.

EXERCISE 8.6

B 1. Solve the following equations.

(a) $2(x - 3) + 3(x + 2) = 10$

(b) $4(2x - 1) - 3(2x + 2) = 0$

(c) $5(3x - 1) + 12 = 4(2x + 3) + 9$

(d) $3(2y - 5) - 7(y + 1) = 2(y + 1)$

(e) $3(2y - 4) - 7(y + 2) = (y - 3) - 1$

(f) $3(y - 7) + 41 = 5(y + 2)$

(g) $-2(2m - 3) + 5(m + 7) = 40$

(h) $2(3x - 1) + 7 = 4(2x + 3) + 1$

(i) $2(y^2 - 3y + 1) = 2(y^2 + y - 4) - 6$

(j) $2(x^2 + 3x + 2) - (2x^2 + 3x - 7) = 17$

C 2. Solve the following equations.

(a) $(x - 3)(x + 4) = (x - 1)(x + 5) - 1$

(b) $(y - 3)(y + 4) = (y + 2)(y + 1) - 16$

(c) $(x - 1)(x + 2) = (x + 3)(x + 2)$

(d) $(2x - 3)(x - 1) = 6 + 2(x + 2)(x + 3)$

(e) $(y - 1)(y - 2) - 2[y - (3y + 2)] = y^2$

(f) $(x - 3)(2x + 1) - 2x^2 = 2$

(g) $(x - 2.5)(x + 3.6) = x^2 - 3.28$

(h) $x(x + 3) = x^2 + 11.7$

(i) $(x + 2.3)(x - 3.4) = x(x + 1.4) - 19.07$

(j) $3.2(x + 5.1) + 4.7(x - 3.8) = 35.59$

(k) $x(x - 3.7) - x(x + 6.3) = 4.5$

(l) $3.4(x - 3.1) + 2.7(x + 2.4) = 13.02$

(m) $5.2(2.1x - 5.8) + 3.7x = 59.022$

(n) $(2.1x - 5.7)(x + 3.6) = 2.1x^2 - 8.43$

(o) $3.2[x - 5.7(x + 3.6)] = -136.352$

(p) $(x + 2.5)^2 - 46.54 = (x + 4.2)(x - 3.7)$

MIND BENDER

Identify the pattern and complete the chart.

2.4	3.7	4.2	5.7	6.1
9.5	2.7	7.7		

MICRO MATH

This program solves equations. Type in the left side of your equation in place of (left side) in statement 20. Type in the right side of your equation in place of (right side) in statement 30.

```
NEW
10 FOR X=0 TO 1
20 L=(left side)
30 R=(right side)
40 F(X)=L-R
50 NEXT X
60 A=F(0)/(F(0)-F(1))
70 PRINT"X=";A
80 END
RUN
```

EXAMPLE. Solve for x.

$3.2(x - 2.5) = 2.7(x + 3.6) - 14.02$

SOLUTION:

```
NEW
10 FOR X=0 TO 1
20 L=3.2*(X-2.5)
30 R=2.7*(X+3.6)-14.02
40 F(X)=L-R
50 NEXT X
60 A=F(0)/(F(0)-F(1))
70 PRINT"X=";A
80 END
RUN
```

$x = 7.4$

∴ the root of the equation is 7.4.

EXERCISE

1. Solve the following equations.

(a) $10(2x + 3) + 8 = 6x - 4$

(b) $5 - 4(x + 6) = 5 - 8x$

(c) $2.5x - 2.1(x + 2.7)$
$= 4.2x + 5.73$

(d) $4.1(2.3x - 1.5) - 3.7x$
$= 6.1x - (3.4x + 1.2)$

(e) $(x - 2.5)(2x + 3.6) = 2x^2 + 5.8$

8.7 EQUATIONS WITH LITERAL COEFFICIENTS

Equations in x such as $ax + b = c$, where variables take the place of numerical coefficients are called literal equations. We say that we have solved the above equation when we can state x explicitly in terms of a, b, and c.

For example

$$ax + b = c$$
$$ax + b - b = c - b$$
$$ax = c - b$$
$$\frac{ax}{a} = \frac{c - b}{a}$$
$$x = \frac{c - b}{a}, \qquad a \neq 0$$

EXAMPLE. Solve for x. $\quad a(x - b) = b(x + a)$

SOLUTION:

$$a(x - b) = b(x + a)$$
$$ax - ab = bx + ab$$
$$ax - bx - ab + ab = bx - bx + ab + ab$$
$$ax - bx = 2ab$$
$$(a - b)x = 2ab$$
$$x = \frac{2ab}{a - b}, \qquad a \neq b$$

EXERCISE 8.7

B 1. Solve the following equations for x.

(a) $ax - b = c$
(b) $ab - x = a$
(c) $ax + ab = bx - ab$
(d) $ax - bx = a + b$
(e) $ax - bx = (a - b)$
(f) $abx = ab + ab$
(g) $bx - ac = ax + ac$
(h) $a(x - a) = b(x - b)$
(i) $b(a - x) = ab + bx$
(j) $\dfrac{x}{a} - \dfrac{x}{b} = \dfrac{a - b}{ab}$

2. Solve each of the following for the indicated variable.

(a) $E = IR$, R
(b) $I = Prt$, r
(c) $C = \pi d$, d

3. Solve each of the following for the indicated variable.

(a) $C = 2\pi r$; r
(b) $y = mx + b$; x
(c) $y = m(x - a)$; x
(d) $A = \frac{1}{2}bh$; h
(e) $A = \frac{1}{2}h(a + b)$; h
(f) $v = ut + \frac{1}{2}at^2$; a
(g) $A = P + I$; I
(h) $D = ST$; S
(i) $P = 2(\ell + w)$; ℓ
(j) $y = m(x - a)$; a
(k) $s = \dfrac{n}{2}(a + I)$; a
(l) $t = a + (n - 1)d$; n

8.8 WORKING WITH FORMULAS

The ability to solve equations is very useful when working with formulas.

EXAMPLE 1. The following formula indicates the number of hours of sleep, h, a young person n years old should have each day.

$$h = \tfrac{1}{2}(18 - n) + 8$$

(a) How many hours of sleep should a ten year-old have?
(b) How old is someone who should have 13 h of sleep?

SOLUTION:

(a) $h = \tfrac{1}{2}(18 - n) + 8$

$h = \tfrac{1}{2}(18 - 10) + 8$

$= \tfrac{1}{2}(8) + 8$

$= 4 + 8$

$= 12$

∴ a ten year-old should have 12 h of sleep each day.

(b) $\qquad h = \tfrac{1}{2}(18 - n) + 8$

$\qquad 13 = \tfrac{1}{2}(18 - n) + 8$

$\qquad 13 = 9 - \tfrac{1}{2}n + 8$

$\qquad 13 = 17 - \tfrac{1}{2}n$

$13 - 17 = 17 - 17 - \tfrac{1}{2}n$

$\qquad -4 = -\tfrac{1}{2}n$

$(-2)(-4) = (-2)(-\tfrac{1}{2}n)$

$\qquad 8 = n$

∴ an eight year-old should have 13 h of sleep each day.

In the formula $P = 2(\ell + w)$, P is called the subject of the formula. In situations where repeated calculations are required to determine the value of one of the other variables, say w, it is convenient to solve the formula for this variable before substituting.

EXAMPLE 2. Given $P = 2(\ell + w)$, solve for w.

SOLUTION:

$$P = 2(\ell + w)$$
$$P = 2\ell + 2w \qquad \longleftarrow \text{Distributive property}$$
$$P - 2\ell = 2w \qquad \longleftarrow \text{Subtract}$$
$$\frac{P - 2\ell}{2} = w \qquad \longleftarrow \text{Divide}$$
$$w = \frac{P - 2\ell}{2}$$

Now w has become the subject of the formula.

This form of the formula is convenient when we wish to find w given P and ℓ. For example, if P = 318 m and ℓ = 121 m, then

$$w = \frac{P - 2\ell}{2}$$

$$w = \frac{318 - 2(121)}{2}$$

$$= \frac{318 - 242}{2}$$

$$= \frac{76}{2}$$

$$= 38 \text{ m}$$

EXERCISE 8.8

B 1. An object is said to be in uniform motion if it moves without changing its speed. The formula relating distance, rate, and time is

$$\text{Distance} = \text{Rate} \times \text{Time}$$
$$D = RT$$

(a) How far can a car travel in 7 h at 65 km/h?
(b) How long will it take to fly from Los Angeles to Montreal, a distance of 3900 km, at 600 km/h?
(c) It is 8808 km from Chicago to Moscow. How fast must you fly in order to make the trip in 12 h?
(d) Terry drove from Toronto to Phoenix, a distance of 3800 km, at 70 km/h. He then drove to Seattle, a distance of 2400 km, at 60 km/h. How many hours did he spend driving?
(e) Saturn is about 1 250 000 000 km from the earth. How long would it take you to fly to Saturn at 1000 km/h? (Express your answer in years.)

(f) Solve the given formula for R.

2. The speed of an aircraft is affected by the wind.

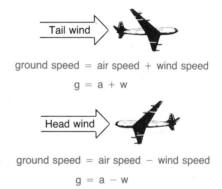

ground speed = air speed + wind speed
$$g = a + w$$

ground speed = air speed − wind speed
$$g = a - w$$

(a) Determine the ground speed if the air speed is 500 km/h and there is a tailwind of 50 km/h.
(b) Determine the ground speed if the air speed is 600 km/h and there is a headwind of 37 km/h.
(c) If the ground speed is 530 km/h, and the air speed is 575 km/h, determine the speed of the headwind.
(d) The air speed of a 747 jetliner is 625 km/h. The ground speed is 670 km/h. Determine the speed of the tailwind.
(e) How long will it take an aircraft to fly from Chicago to Miami, a distance of 1980 km, if the air speed is 550 km/h and there is a tailwind of 50 km/h?
(f) How long will it take to fly from Toronto to San Francisco, a distance of 3800 km, if the air speed is 540 km/h and there is a headwind of 65 km/h?
(g) Solve the given formulas for a.

3. Food supplies energy. During World War II, it was determined that the amount of food energy required by a soldier per day depended on the temperature. This can be expressed in the formula

$$E_f = -125t + 15\ 250$$

where E_f represents the food energy required, in kilojoules, and t is the temperature in degrees Celsius.
(a) How much food energy is required per day by a soldier stationed in the tropics where the temperature averages 40°C?
(b) How much food energy is needed per day at a northern radar station where the average temperature is −10°C?
(c) Solve the given formula for t.
(d) Explain why more food energy is required in colder temperatures.

4. A car rental agency charges $19.95/d plus $0.24/km to rent a car. The cost to rent a car can be expressed as

$$C = 19.95d + 0.24k$$

where d represents the number of days, and k represents the number of kilometres driven.
(a) Determine the cost if you rent a car for 6 d and drive 950 km.
(b) Determine the cost if you have the car for 9 d and drive 1375 km.
(c) If you rented the car for 8 d and the charge was $271.92, how many kilometres did you drive?
(d) If you drove 152 km, and the charge was $96.33, how many days did you have the car?
(e) Solve the given formula for k.

5. The following formula relates mass in kilograms and height in centimetres for young adults.

$$m = \frac{6(h - 90)}{7}$$

(a) Frank is 180 cm tall. What should Frank's mass be?
(b) Terry has a mass of 70 kg. How tall should Terry be?
(c) Solve the given formula for h.

6. The following formula relates the distance an object will fall during the time it falls.

$$d = 4.9t^2$$

where d is in metres and t is in seconds.
(a) It takes a sandbag 3.33 s to reach the ground when dropped from the top of the Leaning Tower of Pisa. What is the height of the Tower?
(b) A ball dropped from the Sears Tower in Chicago will take 9.5 s to reach the ground. How high is the Tower?
(c) How long will it take an object to fall 313.6 m?
(d) Solve the given formula for t^2.

7. The speed of sound in metres per second through any given temperature of air is given by the formula

$$V = \frac{332\sqrt{273 + t}}{16.5}$$

where t is the temperature in °C. Determine the speed of sound when the temperature is
(a) 27°C
(b) 0°C

8. If a baseball pitcher has an earned run average (ERA) of 2.00, it means that the opposing team will score an average of 2 runs for every 9 innings pitched. The formula for calculating the ERA is

$$ERA = \frac{9r}{i}$$

where r represents the total earned runs charged to a pitcher and i represents the total number of innings pitched. The ERA is calculated to the nearest hundredth (2 decimal places).
(a) In 1901, Cy Young pitched 371 innings and gave up 67 runs. Determine his ERA.
(b) Sandy Koufax pitched twelve years for the Dodgers. During that time, he gave up 713 runs in 2324 innings. Calculate his ERA.
(c) In 1916, Babe Ruth pitched 324 innings for Boston. He had an ERA of 1.75. How many runs did he give up?
(d) Solve the given formula for i.

8.9 DEVELOPING FORMULAS

Formulas can be developed by taking measurements and making tables. It is important to look for patterns and to find the relationship among the variables. For example, the following table shows the relationship between the diameter and radius of some familiar circular objects (to the nearest thousandth).

Item	Diameter	Circumference	Circumference / Diameter
Lamp shade	32 cm	100 cm	3.125
Juice can	8.7 cm	27.3 cm	3.140
Bicycle tire	66 cm	207 cm	3.136
Dinner plate	25 cm	78.5 cm	3.14
Computer disk	13.3 cm	41.8 cm	3.143
Quarter	2.4 cm	7.5 cm	3.125
Telephone dial	7.5 cm	23.6 cm	3.147

If we take the average of all values in the fourth column, the result is 3.14. This is the familiar value of π, pronounced "pi." Taking the circumference as C, and the diameter as d, we have $\frac{C}{d} \doteq 3.14$ which simplifies to $C = 3.14d$ which is the formula for the circumference of a circle.

$\pi = 3.14$

EXERCISE 8.9

1. The cost of printing signs for the school play is based on a fixed amount to prepare the silk screen, plus a variable amount based on the number of signs. Find a formula that relates the number of signs, n, and the total cost in dollars, c, using the values given in the following table.

n	c
0	10
10	15
20	20
50	35
100	60

2. (a) Draw five squares with sides, s, as indicated in the chart.
(b) Measure the diagonal of the square, and record the result.
(c) Find a formula that relates the side length of a square, s, and the length of the diagonal, d.

Side s (cm)	Diagonal d (cm)
4	
5	
6	
8	
10	

8.10 SOLVING INEQUALITIES BY ADDITION AND SUBTRACTION

On a number line, the graph of -4 is left of the graph of 3. So -4 is less than 3.

$-4 < 3$

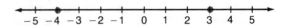

If you move 5 units from the graph of -4 and also 5 units in the same direction from the graph of 3 you arrive at points in the same order on the line as the graphs of -4 and 3.

$$-4 < 3$$
$$-4 + 5 < 3 + 5$$
$$1 < 8$$

$$-4 < 3$$
$$-4 - 5 < 3 - 5$$
$$-9 < -2$$

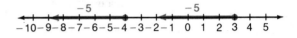

These statements suggest the following properties of order.

Addition Property of Order
The sense of inequality is preserved when the same number is added to both sides of an inequality.

Since $8 > -2$	If $x > y$
then $8 + 4 > -2 + 4$	then $x + a > y + a$
Since $5 < 9$	If $x < y$
then $5 + 7 < 9 + 7$	then $x + a < y + a$

Subtraction Property of Order
The sense of inequality is preserved when the same number is subtracted from both sides of an inequality.

Since $8 > -2$	If $x > y$
then $8 - 4 > -2 - 4$	then $x - a > y - a$
Since $5 < 9$	If $x < y$
then $5 - 6 < 9 - 6$	then $x - a < y - a$

EXAMPLE 1. Solve and graph the solution set.
$$3x - 4 < 2x - 1, x \in I$$

SOLUTION:

$$3x - 4 < 2x - 1$$
$$3x - 4 + 4 < 2x - 1 + 4 \quad \longleftarrow \text{Add}$$
$$3x < 2x + 3$$
$$3x - 2x < 2x - 2x + 3 \quad \longleftarrow \text{Subtract}$$
$$x < 3$$
$$\{x \mid x < 3, x \in I\}$$

EXAMPLE 2. Graph the solution set.
$$5x + 4 \geqslant 4x - 3, x \in R$$

SOLUTION:

$$5x + 4 \geqslant 4x - 3$$
$$5x + 4 - 4 \geqslant 4x - 3 - 4 \qquad \longleftarrow \text{Subtract}$$
$$5x \geqslant 4x - 7$$
$$5x - 4x \geqslant 4x - 4x - 7 \qquad \longleftarrow \text{Subtract}$$
$$x \geqslant -7$$
$$\{x \mid x \geqslant -7, x \in R\}$$

The dot on -7 means that -7 is included in the solution set.

EXAMPLE 3. Graph the solution set.
$$3(x - 3) < 2x - 5, x \in R$$

SOLUTION:

$$3(x - 3) < 2x - 5$$
$$3x - 9 < 2x - 5$$
$$3x - 9 + 9 < 2x - 5 + 9$$
$$3x < 2x + 4$$
$$3x - 2x < 2x - 2x + 4$$
$$x < 4$$

The circle on 4 means that 4 is not included in the solution set.

EXERCISE 8.10

A 1. State the solution set of each of the following, $x \in R$.

(a) $x + 3 > 7$ (b) $x - 1 < 4$
(c) $x + 2 > -2$ (d) $x - 3 < -5$
(e) $x + 6 \geqslant 1$ (f) $x - 2 \leqslant -8$
(g) $x + 9 < 2$ (h) $x + 8 \geqslant -3$
(i) $5 + x < -6$ (j) $-4 + x \geqslant -3$
(k) $x - 1 \leqslant -5$ (l) $x + 15 > 16$
(m) $x - 3 \leqslant 0$ (n) $x + 6 > -11$
(o) $-7 + x < -6$ (p) $x - 10 \leqslant -13$

B 2. Solve and graph the solution set of the following. Variables have domain R.

(a) $5x - 4 < 4x + 3$
(b) $7x + 6 \geqslant 6x - 5$
(c) $4t - 11 \leqslant 3t - 10$
(d) $9s + 15 > 8s - 3$
(e) $7 + 6y \leqslant -4 + 5y$
(f) $-11 + 9w > 8w - 31$

3. Solve and graph the solution set of the following. Variables have domain R.

(a) $3(x - 2) > 2x + 5$
(b) $4(y + 1) \leqslant 3(y - 4)$
(c) $3(2x - 1) > 5x - 16$
(d) $4(x - 1) - 2x \geqslant x - 9$
(e) $7x - 2(x - 1) < 4(x - 3) + 5$
(f) $13x - 21 \leqslant 3(2x - 1) + 6x$
(g) $7w - 3(2w - 13) < 42$
(h) $42 - 5(w + 3) + 6w \geqslant 93$
(i) $7(3w - 9) - 10(2w + 5) < 0$

C 4. Solve and graph the solution set. Variables have domain R.

(a) $5x - 7.4 > 4x - 8.5$
(b) $8y + 11.3 \leqslant -9.2 + 7y$
(c) $2(x - 1.3) + 3x \leqslant 4(x - 1.2)$
(d) $3(x - 0.72) \geqslant 2(x - 0.63) + 1$

8.11 SOLVING INEQUALITIES BY DIVISION

If $\qquad 12 > -16$

then $12 \div (4) > -16 \div (4)$

or $\qquad 3 > -4$

It appears that the sense of inequality is preserved if both sides of the inequality are divided by the same number.

However, when both sides are divided by the same negative number the sense of inequality is reversed.

$$12 > -16$$
but $\qquad 12 \div (-4) \not> -16 \div (-4)$
since $\qquad -3 < 4$

Division Property of Order
The sense of inequality is preserved if both sides of an inequality are divided by a positive number and reversed if divided by a negative number.

Since $5 > 3$, then $\frac{5}{2} > \frac{3}{2}$	If $x > y$ and $c > 0$, then $\frac{x}{c} > \frac{y}{c}$
Since $-5 < 3$, then $-\frac{5}{3} < \frac{3}{3}$	If $x < y$ and $c > 0$, then $\frac{x}{c} < \frac{y}{c}$
Since $5 > 3$, then $\frac{5}{-2} < \frac{3}{-2}$	If $x > y$ and $c < 0$, then $\frac{x}{c} < \frac{y}{c}$
Since $-5 < 3$, then $\frac{-5}{-2} > \frac{3}{-2}$	If $x < y$ and $c < 0$, then $\frac{x}{c} > \frac{y}{c}$

EXAMPLE 1. Graph the solution set.
$\qquad 6x - 5 < 4x + 3, x \in R$

SOLUTION:

$$6x - 5 < 4x + 3$$
$$6x - 5 + 5 < 4x + 3 + 5 \qquad \longleftarrow \text{Add}$$
$$6x < 4x + 8$$
$$6x - 4x < 4x - 4x + 8 \qquad \longleftarrow \text{Subtract}$$
$$2x < 8$$
$$\frac{2x}{2} < \frac{8}{2} \qquad \longleftarrow \text{Divide}$$
$$x < 4$$

EXAMPLE 2. Graph the solution set.

$$3(x - 2) \leq 5x + 2$$

SOLUTION:

$$3(x - 2) \leq 5x + 2$$
$$3x - 6 \leq 5x + 2$$
$$3x - 6 \;-5x + 6\leq 5x + 2 \;- 5x + 6 \qquad \left\{ \begin{array}{l} \text{Add} \\ \text{Subtract} \end{array} \right.$$
$$-2x \leq 8$$
$$\frac{-2x}{(-2)} \geq \frac{8}{(-2)} \qquad \longleftarrow \quad \text{Divide by } (-2)$$
$$x \geq -4$$

$$
\begin{array}{ccccccccccc}
-6 & -5 & -4 & -3 & -2 & -1 & 0 & 1 & 2 & 3 & 4
\end{array}
$$

EXERCISE 8.11

A 1. State the solution set of each of the following, t, x, y, z $\in$ R.

(a) $2x > 6$
(b) $3y < 12$
(c) $4t \leq 20$
(d) $5z \geq 10$
(e) $3x \leq -9$
(f) $-2x > -8$
(g) $-y < 10$
(h) $6t \geq -12$
(i) $-4z > 12$
(j) $-3x \leq -18$
(k) $4x > -8$
(l) $-4t < 4$

B 2. Solve and graph the solution set of the following. Variables have domain R.

(a) $5x + 3 \leq 3x + 7$
(b) $4y - 1 > y + 8$
(c) $3z - 5 < 7 - z$
(d) $3x - 7 > x - 15$
(e) $2x - 3 < 5 - 2x$
(f) $3x + 10 \geq 5x - 16$
(g) $3x - 5 \leq 5x + 7$
(h) $3 - 4x + 12 \leq 2x - 9$
(i) $3y - 7 > 6y + 11$
(j) $12 < 5x - 6 - 2x$
(k) $7 - 2t + 3 \geq 4t + 10$
(l) $8x - 63 < 6x + 95$

3. Solve and graph the solution set. Variables have domain R.

(a) $2(t - 1) \leq 3(t + 4)$
(b) $3(2x - 2) > 2(1 - 2x) + 4$
(c) $6(x - 2) + 5 \geq 8(x - 3) - 1$
(d) $2x + 3(x - 7) < 9(x - 1)$
(e) $5(4x + 3) - 7(3x - 4) > 10$
(f) $3(2z + 3) - (3z + 2) > 12$
(g) $5y + 7(1 - y) \leq -2(y - 5)$
(h) $3(x + 12) > 6(x - 4)$
(i) $4(x + 1) - 2(x + 3) \geq 4(x - 1)$
(j) $5(x - 4) - (x + 2) < 4(x - 4) - 6$

If a train one kilometre long travels at the rate of one kilometre per minute through a tunnel that is two kilometres long, how long will it take the train to pass completely through the tunnel?

8.12 SOLVING INEQUALITIES BY MULTIPLICATION

If $\qquad$ $8 > -4$

then $\qquad$ $8 \times 2 > -4 \times 2$

or $\qquad$ $16 > -8$

When multiplying both sides by (-2)

$$8 > -4$$

but $\qquad$ $8 \times (-2) \not> -4 \times (-2)$

or $\qquad$ $-16 < 8$

The following are the properties of order for multiplication and division.

<table>
<tr><td colspan="2" align="center">Multiplication Property of Order</td></tr>
<tr><td colspan="2">The sense of inequality is preserved if both sides of an inequality are multiplied by a positive number and reversed if multiplied by a negative number.</td></tr>
<tr><td>Since $6 > 4$,
then $3(6) > 3(4)$</td><td>If $x > y$ and $c > 0$,
then $cx > cy$</td></tr>
<tr><td>Since $-6 < 4$,
then $3(-6) < 3(4)$</td><td>If $x < y$ and $c > 0$,
then $cx < cy$</td></tr>
<tr><td>Since $6 > 4$,
then $-3(6) < -3(4)$</td><td>If $x > y$ and $c < 0$,
then $cx < cy$</td></tr>
<tr><td>Since $-6 < 4$,
then $-3(-6) > -3(4)$</td><td>If $x < y$ and $c < 0$,
then $cx > cy$</td></tr>
</table>

EXAMPLE 1. Solve and graph the solution set.

$$\frac{x}{3} - \frac{1}{2} > \frac{1}{6}$$

SOLUTION:

$$\frac{x}{3} - \frac{1}{2} > \frac{1}{6}$$

$$6\left[\frac{x}{3} - \frac{1}{2}\right] > \left[\frac{1}{6}\right]6 \qquad \longleftarrow \text{Multiply}$$

$$2x - 6 > 1 \qquad \longleftarrow \text{Add}$$

$$2x > 7 \qquad \longleftarrow \text{Divide}$$

$$x > \frac{7}{2}$$

$$x > 3.5$$

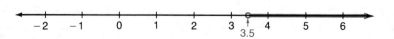

EXAMPLE 2. Solve and graph the solution set.

$$\frac{2x}{5} - 3 \geq \frac{3x}{4} + 4$$

SOLUTION:

$$\frac{2x}{5} - 3 \geq \frac{3x}{4} + 4$$

$$20\left[\frac{2x}{5} - 3\right] \geq \left[\frac{3x}{4} + 4\right]20 \qquad \left\{\begin{array}{l}\text{Multiply} \\ \text{by 20}\end{array}\right.$$

$$8x - 60 \geq 15x + 80$$

$$8x - 60 - 15x + 60 \geq 15x + 80 - 15x + 60 \qquad \left\{\begin{array}{l}\text{Add} \\ \text{Subtract}\end{array}\right.$$

$$-7x \geq 140$$

$$\frac{-7x}{(-7)} \leq \frac{140}{(-7)} \qquad \longleftarrow \qquad \begin{array}{l}\text{Divide} \\ \text{by } (-7)\end{array}$$

$$x \leq -20$$

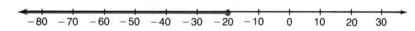

EXERCISE 8.12

1. State the solution set, t, x, z ∈ R.

(a) $\frac{x}{2} > 8$

(b) $\frac{x}{3} < 5$

(c) $\frac{t}{4} \leq -1$

(d) $\frac{z}{5} \geq -2$

(e) $-\frac{x}{3} < 1$

(f) $-\frac{t}{5} \geq -1$

(g) $\frac{z}{6} \leq 0$

(h) $-\frac{x}{4} > -3$

(i) $-\frac{x}{2} \geq -6$

(j) $\frac{x}{6} < -3$

(k) $-\frac{t}{3} \leq -1$

(l) $-\frac{x}{5} > 3$

2. Solve and graph the solution set, x ∈ R.

(a) $\frac{x}{3} - 1 < -2$

(b) $\frac{x}{2} + 3 \geq \frac{3}{4}x - 1$

(c) $\frac{x}{3} - \frac{x}{2} < \frac{1}{3} - \frac{x}{4}$

(d) $\frac{3}{2} - \frac{2}{3}x > \frac{3}{4} - \frac{x}{6}$

(e) $3 < \frac{2}{3}x + 4$

(f) $\frac{x}{3} \geq \frac{x}{2} - 3$

(g) $\frac{3}{5}x - \frac{1}{4} > 1 + \frac{x}{10}$

(h) $\frac{x}{8} - 2 \leq \frac{x}{4}$

(i) $\frac{3}{5}x - \frac{1}{3} > \frac{1}{5} - \frac{1}{3}x$

(j) $0 \geq \frac{2}{3}x - \frac{1}{6}$

(k) $\frac{3}{2}x + \frac{1}{6} \geq \frac{7}{6}$

(l) $\frac{x}{3} + \frac{1}{6} < \frac{3x}{2} - 1$

C 3. Graph the solution set, x ∈ R.

(a) $\frac{x + 1}{3} > \frac{x - 2}{4}$

(b) $\frac{x - 3}{5} + 1 \leq \frac{x + 4}{3}$

(c) $\frac{x - 3}{2} + \frac{x}{4} \geq \frac{x - 2}{6}$

(d) $\frac{2x - 3}{6} + \frac{1}{8} < \frac{3x + 1}{4}$

(e) $3 + \frac{x - 3}{6} \leq x$

(f) $\frac{x + 1}{2} - \frac{x + 1}{3} > 8$

(g) $\frac{x - 4}{3} - 2 + \frac{x + 1}{2} \geq 4x - \frac{x - 1}{6}$

Change one dollar into exactly 50 coins using at least one penny, nickel, dime, and quarter.

8.13 SOLVING LINEAR INEQUALITIES

In this section we combine the rules for solving linear inequalities with the methods for simplifying polynomials.

EXAMPLE 1. Graph the solution set.
$$3(1 - 2x) \geqslant -2x + 11, x \in R$$

SOLUTION:

$$3(1 - 2x) \geqslant -2x + 11$$
$$3 - 6x \geqslant -2x + 11$$
$$3 - 3 - 6x \geqslant -2x + 11 - 3 \qquad \longleftarrow \text{Subtract}$$
$$-6x \geqslant -2x + 8$$
$$-6x + 2x \geqslant -2x + 2x + 8 \qquad \longleftarrow \text{Add}$$
$$-4x \geqslant 8$$
$$\frac{-4x}{-4} \leqslant \frac{8}{-4} \qquad \longleftarrow \text{Divide}$$
$$x \leqslant -2$$

EXAMPLE 2. Graph the solution set.
$$\frac{x}{3} + \frac{1}{2} < \frac{2}{3}x - \frac{5}{2}, x \in R$$

SOLUTION:

$$\frac{x}{3} + \frac{1}{2} < \frac{2}{3}x - \frac{5}{2}$$

The LCD for 2 and 3 is 6.

$$6 \times \left[\frac{x}{3} + \frac{1}{2}\right] < 6 \times \left[\frac{2}{3}x - \frac{5}{2}\right]$$
$$2x + 3 < 4x - 15$$

The solution continues in either of the following ways.

METHOD I
$$2x + 3 < 4x - 15$$
$$2x + 3 - 3 < 4x - 15 - 3$$
$$2x < 4x - 18$$
$$2x - 4x < 4x - 4x - 18$$
$$-2x < -18$$
$$\frac{-2x}{-2} > \frac{-18}{-2}$$
$$x > 9$$

METHOD II
$$2x + 3 < 4x - 15$$
$$2x + 3 + 15 < 4x - 15 + 15$$
$$2x + 18 < 4x$$
$$2x - 2x + 18 < 4x - 2x$$
$$18 < 2x$$
$$\frac{18}{2} < \frac{2x}{2}$$
$$9 < x$$

EXERCISE 8.13

B 1. Simplify and graph the solution set.

(a) $12(x - 1) \geqslant 3x$

(b) $\frac{1}{16} < 1 - \frac{3}{8}x$

(c) $2x \leqslant 12(x - 15)$

(d) $\frac{3}{4}(x - 2) < x + \frac{1}{2}$

(e) $\frac{1}{2}(x + 10) - 3x \leqslant 0$

(f) $5(5 + x) - 3(3 - x) > 0$

(g) $2(x - 2) + 1 < 3(x + 3) - 3$

(h) $2(x - 2) - 2 \leqslant 3(x + 1) + 5$

(i) $2(x - 2) - 3(x - 3) \leqslant -2x - 14$

(j) $2(x - 3) - x \geqslant 3(x + 1) - 3$

(k) $3(2x - 1) - 3x > 2(x + 1) + 8$

Four more than the larger of two positive consecutive odd integers is five less than, or equal to, twice the smaller integer. What are the integers?

Consecutive odd integers: x, $x - 2$
Let x be the larger consecutive odd integer, and $x - 2$ the smaller consecutive odd integer.

Four more than the larger:
$\quad x + 4$
Five less than twice the smaller:
$\quad 2(x - 2) - 5$
The inequality is
$\quad x + 4 \leqslant 2(x - 2) - 5$

$$x + 4 \leqslant 2(x - 2) - 5$$
$$x + 4 \leqslant 2x - 4 - 5$$
$$x + 4 \leqslant 2x - 9$$
$$x + 4 - x + 9 \leqslant 2x - 9 - x + 9$$
$$13 \leqslant x$$
$$x \geqslant 13$$
$$x - 2 \geqslant 11$$

Check using a table.

x	x − 2	Four more than x	Five less than twice x − 2	Check
*	*	*	*	*
17	15	21	25	✓
15	13	19	21	✓
13	11	17	17	✓
11	9	15	13	No
9	7	13	9	No
*	*	*	*	*

∴ the consecutive odd integers are 11 and 13, 13 and 15, 15 and 17, ...

1. The sum of two positive consecutive odd integers is at most 22. Find the integers.

2. The larger of two consecutive integers is greater than six more than half the smaller. Find the integers.

8.14 PROBLEM SOLVING

1. Maria is 15 a old. Her mother is three times as old. How many times older than Maria was her mother five years ago?

2. Name the wheels that turn clockwise.

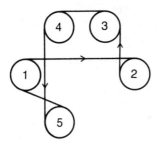

3. Melanie has $1.40 in nickels, dimes and quarters. How many of each does she have?

4. Gold Key accounts at the bank cost $3.00 per month plus $0.25 for each cheque written for service. What is the service charge for one month if 7 cheques are written?

5. A Blue Chip account at a bank has a service charge of $0.50 for each cheque written. What is the service charge for one month if 11 cheques are written?

6. Find the digit or digits in each of the following.

$$2^4 = 1x$$
$$2^{10} = 102x$$
$$2^{16} = 65\ 53x$$
$$2^{22} = 4\ 194\ 30x$$

7. Arrange 25 coins into 3 groups so there is an odd number of coins in each group.

8. Players on teams often shake hands with their team-mates before the start of a game. Find the total number of handshakes made by the players on each of the following teams.
(a) two people on a mixed doubles badminton team
(b) four people on a relay team
(c) five players on the starting line-up of a basketball team

(d) nine players on the starting line-up of a baseball team

9. How many times between one-thirty in the afternoon and ten-thirty at night will the hands of a clock cross?

10. How many ways can one make change for fifty cents using only nickels, dimes, and quarters?

11. 25, 26, 27, 28, 29 are consecutive numbers. Find five consecutive numbers with a sum of 265.

12. The product of two integers is 96, and the sum is less than 26. How many possible solutions are there?

13. For each of the following, make an assumption about the pattern and state the next three numbers.

(a) 3, 6, 9, 12, ...
(b) 12, 10, 7, 3, ...
(c) 1, 3, 7, 15, ...
(d) 2, 5, 10, 17, ...
(e) 3, 3, 3, 3, ...

14. How many days are there from today to the following.

(a) Christmas vacation
(b) July 1
(c) your birthday

15. A small quantity of nickels and dimes has a value of $2.25. There are three more nickels than there are dimes. How many of each are there?

16. The value of 34 coins is $2.25. The coins are nickels and dimes. How many of each are there?

17. There are 28 more nickels than there are dimes. The number of nickels is three times the number of dimes. What is the total value of the nickels and dimes?

18. Place the digits 1, 2, 3, 4, 5, 6, and 7 in the circles so that the sum of each line of connected circles is the same.

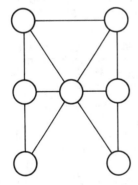

19. Each year, an antique automobile increases in value by about 12%. How many years will it take a $30 000 antique car to double in value?

20. The sum of three consecutive numbers is 219. Find the numbers.

21. The school basketball team played a total of 32 games. The team receives 2 points for each game won, 1 point for each tie, and 0 points for a loss. The team has 36 points.
(a) What is the greatest possible number of games that have been won?
(b) What is the greatest possible number of ties?

22. How many page numbers in this book have at least one digit that is a 3?

CALCULATOR MATH

Perform the following calculations on a calculator without using the 7 or 8 keys.

1. 4572 + 2863

2. 483 256 − 297 638

3. 785 × 268

4. 77 284 ÷ 278

8.15 REVIEW EXERCISE

1. Determine whether each of the following equations is consistent or inconsistent.
(a) $x + 3 = 2$, $x \in N$ (b) $5x = 15$, $x \in I$
(c) $8x = 4$, $x \in R$ (d) $8x = 4$, $x \in I$
(e) $x + 4 = x$, $x \in I$ (f) $x^2 = 9$, $x \in I$

2. State the solution set of each of the following.
(a) $2x = 6$ (b) $x + 5 = 11$
(c) $t - 9 = -7$ (d) $5 + x = -4$
(e) $-4x = -12$ (f) $7x = -42$
(g) $17 = x + 4$ (h) $-5x = 0$
(i) $40 = 5y$ (j) $-17t = 0$
(k) $-x = 5$ (l) $-x = -7$
(m) $5 = -x$ (n) $-13 = x - 7$
(o) $7 + x = 17$ (p) $-30 = -20 + x$
(q) $\dfrac{x}{2} = 5$ (r) $\dfrac{x}{3} = -4$
(s) $\frac{1}{2}x = 7$ (t) $\dfrac{t}{5} = 0$

3. State the solution set of each of the following, $x \in R$.
(a) $x + 1 > 4$ (b) $t - 1 < 7$
(c) $y + 2 \leqslant -4$ (d) $2x \geqslant 8$
(e) $-3 + x > -4$ (f) $-4x < 12$
(g) $-3x \geqslant -21$ (h) $\dfrac{x}{2} < -9$
(i) $-\dfrac{x}{3} \geqslant 5$ (j) $x + 4 > -11$
(k) $-x < 1$ (l) $-\dfrac{t}{3} \geqslant -4$
(m) $14 > 2x$ (n) $13 < x - 4$
(o) $-5 \geqslant y - 5$ (p) $-2x > 0$
(q) $-10 \leqslant 5x$ (r) $5 > \dfrac{x}{2}$
(s) $0 < -3x$ (t) $-1 \geqslant \dfrac{x}{3}$

4. Solve and check the following.
(a) $2x - 13 = 53$
(b) $5x + 11 = 91$
(c) $3x - 11 = 58$
(d) $35 - 4t = -85$
(e) $307 + x = 451$
(f) $181 = 2x - 27$
(g) $7x - 19 = 6x + 53$
(h) $6x - 13 = 4x - 43$

(i) $10x - 27 = 7x + 54$
(j) $7t - 31 = 43 + 9t$
(k) $8w - 19 + 3w = 4w + 30$
(l) $4x + 71 = 10 - 2x - 11$
(m) $4w - 53 + 5w = -73 + 11w$
(n) $13 - t + 25 = 14 - 9t$
(o) $5m - 43 - 6m = 85 - 3m$

5. Solve and check.
(a) $2(t - 3) - 5 = 7$
(b) $3(x + 4) + 2(x - 7) = 38$
(c) $46 = 4(1 - 2x) + x$
(d) $5(3x - 4) - (1 - 3x) = -75$
(e) $5 - (w + 3) = 3(w + 2)$
(f) $5(t + 4) - 3t = 2t$
(g) $\dfrac{x}{4} - \dfrac{x}{5} = \dfrac{1}{2}$
(h) $\dfrac{2x + 1}{3} = 5$
(i) $\dfrac{x + 1}{2} - \dfrac{x}{3} = 7$
(j) $\dfrac{x + 2}{5} = \dfrac{x - 3}{4} + 2$
(k) $\dfrac{x + 2}{4} - \dfrac{x - 3}{3} = \dfrac{1}{2}$
(l) $\frac{1}{2}(x + 2) + \frac{1}{3}(x - 1) = 4$

6. How long will it take an aircraft to fly from Los Angeles to New Orleans, a distance of 2700 km, if the air speed is 580 km/h and there is a headwind of 80 km/h?

7. The formula $Q = 10t + 40$ gives the quantity of water in a tank originally containing 40 L when water is running in at the rate of 10 L/min.
(a) How much water will be in the tank after
     (i) 7 min?   (ii) 26 min?
(b) If the tank has a capacity of 600 L, how long will it take to fill the tank?

8. The formula $Q = -15t + 900$ gives the quantity of water in a tank initially holding 900 L and draining at the rate of 15 L/min.
(a) How much water will be in the tank after
     (i) 5 min?   (ii) 49 min?
(b) How long will it take the tank to empty?

9. One of the best predictors of vital capacity (maximum amount of expirable air) for young people is height cubed. For males, the formula for vital capacity is

$$V = 0.95H^3 - 0.13$$

where V is the capacity in litres and H is the height in metres. For females, the formula is

$$V = 0.75H^3 + 0.45$$

(a) Determine the vital capacity of a boy 1.6 m tall.
(b) Determine the vital capacity of a girl 1.5 m tall.
(c) What is the difference in vital capacities for a boy and girl who are both 1.4 m tall?

10. Solve and graph the solution set. Variables have domain R.

(a) $4x + 7 \geqslant 15$
(b) $3t - 4 > -16$
(c) $5 \leqslant 1 - 2x$
(d) $3x - 4 < 2x + 5$
(e) $5t + 4 \geqslant 3t + 10$
(f) $5t - 7 < 8t - 13$
(g) $5t - 7 + 3t > 10t + 13$
(h) $11w + 33 - 5w < w - 2$
(i) $6 - 3(s + 4) \geqslant 0$

11. Solve and graph the solution set, $x \in R$.

(a) $5(x + 6) > 2(x - 1) + 2$
(b) $5 - 2(x + 4) \leqslant 11$
(c) $3(2x + 1) + 4(x - 5) \geqslant -67$
(d) $4(x - 5) - (x + 1) \leqslant 3$
(e) $-49 > 2(3 + x) - 7(1 + 2x)$
(f) $1 > 7 - 3(2x - 5) - x$

12. Solve.

(a) $7x - 0.4 = 5x + 5.2$
(b) $5(t - 0.4) + 3t = 6$
(c) $0.2(8w - 3) + 0.1w = w + 0.8$
(d) $4.2x - 0.4 = 2(1.1x - 1)$
(e) $\dfrac{2x + 1}{3} - \dfrac{x + 4}{5} = 7$
(f) $\dfrac{x}{2} - \dfrac{1 - 3x}{5} + 2 = \dfrac{x}{10}$

13. Solve each of the following for the indicated variable.

(a) $P = 2(\ell + w)$; w

(b) $A = \frac{1}{2}h(a + b)$; b

(c) $t = a + (n - 1)d$; d

(d) $S = \dfrac{n}{2}(a + l)$; l

14. Graph the solution set, $x \in R$.

(a) $\dfrac{x - 1}{3} - \dfrac{x + 2}{4} < 1$

(b) $\dfrac{x + 5}{3} - \dfrac{x - 4}{2} \geqslant -1$

(c) $\dfrac{2x + 1}{3} \leqslant x - \dfrac{x}{5} - 1$

(d) $\dfrac{5x + 3}{2} - 3 > 2(x + 1)$

MIND BENDER

Which of the following figures can you draw without lifting your pencil, crossing any line, or going over any line twice?

1.

2.

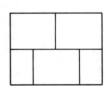

3.

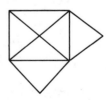

8.16 CHAPTER 8 TEST

1. Complete the following flow chart.

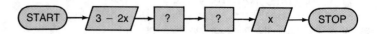

2. Solve and check.
(a) $2(3x - 5) - 2 = 4(x - 1)$
(b) $18 - 2x = 44$
(c) $\dfrac{x}{2} + \dfrac{x}{3} = 10$

3. Solve and graph.
(a) $3x - 2 \geqslant 2x - 3$, $x \in R$
(b) $-5x + 7 < 2$, $x \in R$
(c) $5 - \dfrac{x}{2} \geqslant 3$, $x \in R$

4. Solve, $x \in R$.
(a) $(x - 2)(x - 1) = x(x + 2) - 2(x + 3) + 2$
(b) $(2x - 3)(2x + 3) = (4x - 2)(x + 1) + 1$
(c) $2x(x - 3) + 4 \leqslant (2x + 1)(x - 2)$
(d) $\dfrac{x - 3}{4} + \dfrac{x(x + 2)}{8} \leqslant \dfrac{x - 4}{3} + \dfrac{x^2}{8}$

5. (a) Solve for x. $ax = b(1 - x)$
(b) Solve for h. $A = \frac{1}{2}(a + b)h$

6. The formula $n = \dfrac{c - 45}{1.5}$ gives the number of home-coming badges, n, you can purchase for a given cost, c, in dollars.
(a) How many badges can be purchased for $3000?
(b) Solve for c.
(c) What is the cost of 1600 badges?

8.17 CUMULATIVE REVIEW FOR CHAPTERS 5 TO 8

1. Express the following ratios in simplest form.
(a) 12 : 8
(b) 35 : 20
(c) 3 : 6 : 9
(d) 12 : 15 : 45

2. Find the unknown value in each of the following proportions.

(a) $\dfrac{x}{12} = \dfrac{15}{48}$

(b) $\dfrac{x}{18} = \dfrac{48}{108}$

(c) $\dfrac{24}{x} = \dfrac{96}{144}$

(d) $\dfrac{18}{32} = \dfrac{24}{x}$

(e) 2 : 3 : x = 8 : y : 24
(f) x : 10 : 15 = 5 : y : 30

3. If 36 out of 144 students ate chicken fingers for lunch, while the others ate chicken nuggets, what is the ratio of students who ate nuggets to those that ate fingers?

4. The length of a rectangle is 4 cm more than the width. The perimeter of the rectangle is 32 cm. What is the ratio of the length to the width?

5. The ratio of wins to losses to ties for the school basketball team over the past ten years is 8 : 3 : 1. The total number of games played in the ten-year period was 288. How many games did the basketball team win during the ten-year period?

6. Which is the better value for orange juice: 750 mL for $1.49 or 500 mL for $0.99?

7. Six golf balls cost $13.95. What is the cost of ten of these golf balls?

8. (a) What is 15% of 24?
(b) 12 is what percentage of 60?
(c) 32 is 40% of what number?

9. In a check of three year-old used cars, it was found that 5 out of 450 cars had defective steering parts. What percentage of the cars checked had defective steering parts?

10. A blue blazer sells at a regular price for $125. It is sold at a discount of 20%. What is the sale price of the blazer?

11. A new car with a sticker price of $24 500 has been reduced by 8%. What is the sale price of the car?

12. Janice receives a commission of 3% on the sale of real estate. Her commission on the sale of a small service station was $11 400. What was the sale price of the service station?

13. Jennifer bought a calculator for $19.50. Sales tax is charged at a rate of 7%. How much did Jennifer pay for the calculator, including tax?

14. Harry paid $18.73 for a teapot, including sales tax which is charged at a rate of 7%. What is the price of the teapot before sales tax?

15. Three people invest in a small business with $30 000, $40 000, and $60 000 respectively. A profit of $54 250 is to be divided in the same ratio as the original investment. How much is each share of the profit?

16. A rectangle is 40 cm by 50 cm. The length and width are both increased by 10%.
(a) What is the larger area?
(b) What is the increase in area as a percentage?

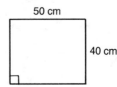
50 cm
40 cm

17. Evaluate.
(a) 3^2 (b) 2^3 (c) $(-3)^2$
(d) -3^2 (e) 4^2 (f) -4^2
(g) $(-4)^2$ (h) 0.1^3 (i) 0.01^2

18. Simplify.
(a) $2^2 \times 3^2$ (b) $4^2 \times 2^3$
(c) $(x^4)(x^3)$ (d) $(x^5)(x^{-2})$
(e) $\dfrac{x^5}{x^2}$ (f) $\dfrac{x^2}{x^{-3}}$
(g) $(-2x^2)(5x^3)$ (h) $(-2x^2)^3$
(i) $(-3x^2)(-4x^3)$ (j) $(3x^3)(5x^2)$

19. Evaluate.
(a) $3x^2$ for $x = -2$
(b) $-2x^3$ for $x = 4$
(c) $(3x^2)(2x^3)$ for $x = -2$
(d) $(-2x^2)(-3x^3)$ for $x = -1$

20. Evaluate the following square roots.
(a) $\sqrt{1156}$ (b) $\sqrt{2704}$ (c) $\sqrt{3969}$

21. Evaluate the following square roots to the nearest tenth.
(a) $\sqrt{521}$ (b) $\sqrt{6.8}$ (c) $\sqrt{60}$

22. Find the length of the hypotenuse in each of these right triangles.
(a)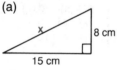
(b)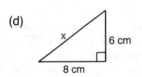
(c)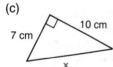
(d)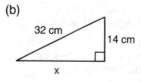

23. Find the length of the unknown side to the nearest tenth.
(a)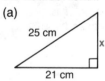
(b)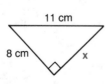
(c)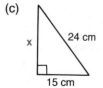
(d)

24. Simplify.
(a) $(3x^2 + 2x - 5) + (2x^2 - 5x + 7)$
(b) $(-2x^2 - 3x + 4) - (4x^2 + 7x - 6)$
(c) $2(2x + 3) + 3(x - 4) + 4(2x + 1)$
(d) $3(2x - 3) - 4(3x - 2)$
(e) $x(3x - 5) + 4x - 2x(x + 3)$

25. Expand.
(a) $(x + 3)(x - 5)$ (b) $(y + 3)(y - 3)$
(c) $(x - 5)(x - 6)$ (d) $(z + 1)(z - 7)$
(e) $(2x + 1)(2x - 1)$ (f) $(4 - x)(4 - x)$
(g) $(3x - 2)^2$ (h) $(4x + 5)^2$
(i) $(5 - 3x)(5 + 3x)$ (j) $(5x + 2)^2$

26. Factor.
(a) $x^2 - x - 12$ (b) $x^2 + x - 20$
(c) $x^2 + 8x + 15$ (d) $x^2 - 7x + 12$
(e) $x^2 - 5x + 6$ (f) $x^2 + 3x - 10$
(g) $x^2 + 3x - 28$ (h) $x^2 + 3x - 4$
(i) $x^2 - 25$ (j) $x^2 - 49$
(k) $x^2 - 121$ (l) $x^2 - 12x + 36$

27. Expand and simplify.
(a) $(x^2 - 2x + 3)(x + 4)$
(b) $(x^2 + x + 1)(x - 1)$
(c) $(x + 2)^3$

28. Solve and check.
(a) $3x - 14 = 7$
(b) $5x + 2 = 4x - 3$
(c) $2(x + 3) = 14$
(d) $3(x + 1) = x + 1$
(e) $4(x - 5) = 3 + (x + 1)$
(f) $x(x + 5) = x^2 - 2x + 14$
(g) $(x - 2)(x + 3) = (x + 2)(x + 4) - 5$

29. Solve and graph the solution set.
(a) $2x + 3 < 11, x \in R$
(b) $3x - 5 > 2, x \in R$
(c) $5x + 2 < 3x - 4, x \in I$
(d) $3(x - 2) > 2(5 - x) + 4, x \in I$
(e) $4(x + 1) - 3 > 3(x - 2) + 2x, x \in I$

30. Solve each of the following for the indicated variable.
(a) $y = mx + b$; solve for m
(b) $v = u + at$; solve for u
(c) $P = 4s$; solve for s
(d) $\ell = \frac{1}{2}(P - 2w)$; solve for P
(e) $A = P(1 + rt)$; solve for P

PROBLEM SOLVING
WITH EQUATIONS

CHAPTER

9

It isn't that they can't see the solution; it is that they can't see the problem.
G.K. Chesterton

REVIEW AND PREVIEW TO CHAPTER 9

EQUATIONS AND INEQUALITIES

EXERCISE

1. Solve.
   (a) $x - 5 = 7$
   (b) $x - 2 = 15$
   (c) $m + 3 = 11$
   (d) $y + 5 = 7$
   (e) $n + 1 = 1$
   (f) $z - 11 = 4$
   (g) $3x = 15$
   (h) $5y = 20$
   (i) $4m - 8 = 0$
   (j) $3x + 18 = 0$
   (k) $\dfrac{x}{3} = \dfrac{4}{6}$
   (l) $\dfrac{y}{8} = \dfrac{3}{12}$

2. Solve.
   (a) $x + 3.6 = 5.7$
   (b) $y - 2.7 = 4.3$
   (c) $x = 5.2 + 3.8$
   (d) $3x = 42.3$
   (e) $4x = 6.4$
   (f) $x - 3.2 = 1.6$
   (g) $5.2x - 3.8 = 1.4$
   (h) $4.8x + 2.7 = 1.4 + 3.7$
   (i) $x + 2.4x = 5.8 - 2.4x$

3. Solve.
   (a) $x - 2 < 3$
   (b) $x + 3 < 7$
   (c) $y + 1 \leqslant 7$
   (d) $n - 4 \geqslant 2$
   (e) $x - 1 \geqslant 0$
   (f) $3x > 6$
   (g) $-x < 2$
   (h) $-x > -2$
   (i) $x - 1 \leqslant -2$
   (j) $3x \geqslant 12$
   (k) $\dfrac{x}{2} > \dfrac{3}{4}$
   (l) $\dfrac{x}{5} < -\dfrac{4}{3}$
   (m) $\dfrac{-x}{3} \leqslant \dfrac{3}{2}$
   (n) $\dfrac{-x}{-2} \geqslant \dfrac{-2}{3}$

4. Solve.
   (a) $2(y - 1) = 4$
   (b) $3(x + 4) = 15$
   (c) $4(m - 2) = m + 1$
   (d) $2(y - 3) = 3(y + 1)$
   (e) $5 - 2(x + 1) = 3$
   (f) $3 - (2x - 3) = 0$
   (g) $3(y + 2) - 4 = -1$
   (h) $5(x + 1) - 5 = 20$

5. (a) Round to the nearest thousand.
   (i) 325 125
   (ii) 165 500
   (iii) 23 565
   (iv) 3 206 500
   (b) Round to the nearest tenth.
   (i) 25.625
   (ii) 0.550
   (iii) 5.656 35
   (iv) 12.459 85
   (c) Round to the nearest unit.
   (i) 465 923.65
   (ii) 45.500
   (iii) 324.575
   (iv) 4.500

6. The formula to add the natural numbers $1 + 2 + 3 + \ldots + (n - 1) + n$

   is $\qquad S = \dfrac{n(n + 1)}{2}$

   where S is the sum and n is the number of natural numbers in the sum.

   (a) Find the sum of the natural numbers from 1 to 1000.
   (b) Find the sum of the natural numbers $1200 + 1201 + 1202 + \ldots + 2000 + 2001$.

FRACTIONS

EXERCISE

1. Simplify.

(a) $1\frac{1}{2} + 2\frac{2}{3}$

(b) $3\frac{1}{4} - 2\frac{5}{8}$

(c) $3\frac{3}{4} + 2\frac{1}{2}$

(d) $1\frac{5}{8} - \frac{3}{8}$

(e) $3\frac{2}{3} - 1\frac{3}{4}$

(f) $4\frac{3}{4} - 2\frac{2}{3}$

(g) $3\frac{5}{8} + 1\frac{1}{2}$

2. Simplify.

(a) $\frac{2}{3} \times \frac{3}{4}$

(b) $1\frac{1}{2} \times 2\frac{2}{3}$

(c) $3\frac{3}{4} \div 3\frac{1}{4}$

(d) $2\frac{5}{8} \div 1\frac{2}{3}$

(e) $3\frac{1}{4} \times 1\frac{1}{4}$

(f) $(2\frac{1}{2})^2$

(g) $3\frac{1}{2}(1\frac{1}{4} + \frac{3}{8})$

3. Express the following fractions as decimals, rounded to the nearest thousandth if possible.

(a) $\frac{5}{8}$ (b) $\frac{7}{11}$ (c) $\frac{12}{15}$ (d) $\frac{8}{9}$

(e) $\frac{7}{12}$ (f) $\frac{5}{12}$ (g) $\frac{5}{6}$ (h) $\frac{1}{6}$

4. Express as fractions in the form $\frac{a}{b}$.

(a) 0.75   (b) 0.35

(c) 0.48   (d) 0.09

(e) $0.\overline{5}$ (f) $0.\overline{36}$

(g) $0.\overline{72}$ (h) $0.0\overline{6}$

(i) $0.\overline{235}$ (j) $0.4\overline{24}$

(k) $0.4\overline{9}$ (l) $0.2\overline{9}$

PERIMETER

EXERCISE

1. Find the perimeter.

(a)

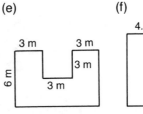

2.6 cm, 3.5 cm, 3.2 cm

(b)

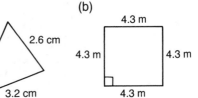

4.3 m, 4.3 m, 4.3 m, 4.3 m

(c)

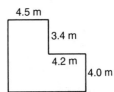

4.7 m, 3.8 m, 3.8 m, 4.7 m

(d)

2.4 m, 2.4 m, 2.4 m, 2.4 m, 2.4 m

(e)

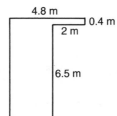

3 m, 3 m, 3 m, 6 m, 3 m

(f)

4.5 m, 3.4 m, 4.2 m, 4.0 m

(g)

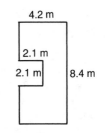

4.8 m, 0.4 m, 2 m, 6.5 m

(h)

4.2 m, 2.1 m, 2.1 m, 8.4 m

(i)

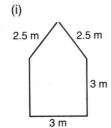

2.5 m, 2.5 m, 3 m, 3 m

(j)

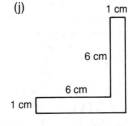

1 cm, 6 cm, 6 cm, 1 cm

9.1 WORD PHRASES INTO ALGEBRAIC EXPRESSIONS

In this chapter we apply the READ—PLAN—SOLVE—ANSWER model to solve problems that would be difficult to solve without the use of algebra. Many problems can be represented as algebraic equations. These equations can then be solved using the methods of the preceding chapter.

However, before attempting to solve these problems, it is helpful to become familiar with the technique of representing words by algebraic expressions. The PLAN stage of the model involves the introduction of a variable and the translation of the information from words into an algebraic expression.

READ

EXAMPLE. A rectangle is 7 m longer than it is wide. Find an expression for the area of the rectangle.

PLAN

SOLUTION:

Introduce a variable.
Make a diagram.
Translate the words into an expression.

SOLVE

Let x represent the width in metres (m).

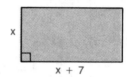

x

$x + 7$

ANSWER

The area of the rectangle is $x(x + 7)$.

EXERCISE 9.1

A 1. Represent each of the following as an algebraic expression.

(a) x increased by seven
(b) twice a number
(c) the sum of y and eight
(d) five times a number
(e) six added to x
(f) a number multiplied by four
(g) x diminished by three
(h) 2 less than a number
(i) the product of nine and a number
(j) a number decreased by eleven
(k) x divided by six
(l) fifteen more than a number
(m) Sean's age three years from now
(n) Nadine's age two years ago
(o) the number of cents in n quarters
(p) the number of cents in y dimes
(q) the number of days in x weeks
(r) the difference when eight is subtracted from x
(s) the difference when x is subtracted from eight

2. Represent the following as algebraic expressions.

(a) five times a number, increased by three
(b) double the speed, less thirteen
(c) three times the height, increased by two
(d) four less than six times a number

(e) Sam's age plus twice his age
(f) six times the price, less five
(g) the sum of two consecutive integers
(h) the product of two consecutive integers
(i) half the diameter, increased by seven
(j) twice Linda's age three years from now
(k) five times Jean's age two years ago

3. Complete the tables.
(a) The length of a rectangle is three times the width.

Width (m)	16	47	257	x	7y	68z
Length (m)						

(b) Marisa is twice as old as Luis.

Marisa's age				24	10m	34w
Luis' age	7	18	x	19y		

(c) There are 120 times as many houses as apartment buildings.

Number of houses					2280w
Number of apt. buildings	36	59	x	13y	

4. In each of the following statements there are two unknowns. Represent each unknown in terms of the same variable.

(a) One number is six times a second number.
(b) Paul is three times as old as his sister.
(c) A jet travels nine times as fast as a car.
(d) The length of a rectangle is five times the width.
(e) The population of the U.S.A. is ten times the population of Canada.
(f) There are eight times as many radio stations as TV stations.
(g) Angel Falls in Venezuela is twenty times as high as Niagara Falls.

(h) There are half as many pistons as valves in an engine.
(i) The altitude of a triangle is one-third the base.

5. Complete the tables.
(a) One number is 17 more than a second number.

First number						75	w
Second number	8	57	x	3y	4n		

(b) Marty is three years younger than Terry.

Marty's age		19		w		7m	
Terry's age	26		x		5y		6t + 5

(c) The selling price is $47 more than the cost price.

Cost price ($)	191	354			x		5w
Selling price ($)			86	252		y	

6. In each of the following statements there are two unknowns. Represent each unknown in terms of the same variable.

(a) John is three years older than Susan.
(b) Bill is six years younger than Bob.
(c) The length is fifteen metres longer than the width.
(d) The selling price is thirteen dollars more than the cost price.
(e) The Amazon River is 1335 km shorter than the Nile.
(f) A train travels 20 km/h faster than a bus.
(g) The Saturn I launch vehicle was 53 m shorter than Saturn V.

9.2 FORMULAS FROM PRACTICAL SITUATIONS

In this section we develop mathematical formulas by examining the relationships among the variables. In the PLAN step, we express the relationship among the variables as a formula using an equation.

READ

EXAMPLE. To determine the selling price of a diamond a jeweller multiplies his cost price by 1.8.

(a) Determine a formula for selling price in terms of cost price.
(b) Find the selling price for diamonds that have the following cost prices,
  (i) $500
  (ii) $800
  (iii) $1550

PLAN

$E=mc^2$

SOLUTION:
(a) Let CP represent the cost price. Then the selling price, SP, may be expressed as

$$SP = 1.8CP$$

SOLVE

ANSWER

(b) $SP = 1.8CP$
  (i) $SP = 1.8(500) = \$900$
  (ii) $SP = 1.8(800) = \$1440$
  (iii) $SP = 1.8(1550) = \$2790$

EXERCISE 9.2

B 1. The distance at which you can see an object is approximately 3440 times the height of the object.

(a) Determine a formula for distance in terms of height.
(b) Find the distance at which you could see objects with the following heights.
  (i)   5 cm
  (ii) 10 m
  (iii) 183 cm
  (iv) 1065 m

2. To determine the list price of a new car a dealer multiplies his cost price by 1.25.

(a) Determine a formula for list price in terms of cost price.
(b) Find the list price for cars that have the following cost prices.
  (i) $8760
  (ii) $9830
  (iii) $10 730
  (iv) $19 400

3. The distance a spacecraft travels (in kilometres) is 40 200 times the length of time it has been travelling (in hours).

(a) Determine a formula for distance travelled in terms of time.
(b) Find the distance travelled for the following times.
  (i)   7 h
  (ii) 80 h
  (iii) 176.5 h
  (iv) 946.25 h

4. Sue earns $8.75/h selling shoes.

(a) Determine a formula for her salary in terms of the number of hours worked.
(b) Find her earnings if she worked the following number of hours.
  (i)   10
  (ii) 30
  (iii) 37.5
  (iv) 51.5

5. It has been determined that the shoreline of Lake Erie is receding at the rate of eleven centimetres per year.

(a) Determine a formula for the amount of land lost in terms of years.

(b) Find the amount of land that would be lost after the following number of years.
- (i)   20
- (ii) 100
- (iii) 1000
- (iv) 2500

6. Sound travels at a speed of 330 m/s.

(a) Determine a formula for your distance from a storm in terms of the time interval between when you see the lightning and when you hear the thunderclap.

(b) Find your distance from a storm if the time interval between lightning flash and thunderclap is
- (i)   2 s
- (ii) 7 s
- (iii) 13.5 s

7. Bruce sells cars and earns $250/week plus 5% commission on all sales.

(a) Determine a formula for his weekly earnings in terms of salary plus commission.

(b) Find his weekly salary if his sales for a given week were as follows.
- (i) $124 723
- (ii) $61 900
- (iii) $88 330

8. As a computer salesperson, Mary earns $300/week plus 6% of all sales over $300 000/a.

(a) Determine a formula for her annual earnings in terms of salary plus commission.

(b) Find her annual salary if her sales for a given year were as follows.
- (i) $850 000
- (ii) $525 000
- (iii) $298 700
- (iv) $746 940

C 9. In Canada, motor vehicle accidents causing injury occur at the rate of one every four minutes.

(a) Determine a formula for the number of accidents in terms of time (in minutes).

(b) Determine the approximate number of accidents causing injury.
- (i)   per day
- (ii) per week
- (iii) per month
- (iv) per year

10. In the U.S.A., motor vehicle accidents causing injury occur at the rate of one every eighteen seconds.

(a) Determine a formula for the number of accidents in terms of time (in seconds).

(b) Determine the approximate number of accidents causing injury.
- (i)   per day
- (ii) per week
- (iii) per month
- (iv) per year

MIND BENDER

Find the missing numbers in this multiplication.

```
      ■ 5 ■
  ×    ■ 5
  ■ ■ ■ ■ 5
  ■ ■ 5 9
  ■ ■ ■ ■ 5 5
```

9.3 MATHEMATICAL SENTENCES

A variety of methods and strategies have been established to solve problems. While this chapter concentrates on using equations to solve problems, many of the other strategies will be used. In the work that follows, the Guess and Check strategy leads to the use of equations in problem solving. In this section, we convert mathematical word sentences into equations.

Consider the following number problem.

> A certain number, increased by eight,
> is equal to twice the number decreased by 1.

This number problem can be solved using GUESS AND CHECK.

Guess	Number increased by 8	Twice the number decreased by 1	Check
5	5 + 8 = 13	2(5) − 1 = 10 − 1 = 9	13 ≠ 9 The number is not 5.
10	10 + 8 = 18	2(10) − 1 = 20 − 1 = 19	18 ≠ 19 The number is not 10.
9	9 + 8 = 17	2(9) − 1 = 18 − 1 = 17	17 = 17 The number is 9.
x	x + 8	2x − 1	x + 8 must equal 2x − 1

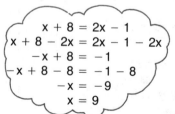

$$x + 8 = 2x - 1$$
$$x + 8 - 2x = 2x - 1 - 2x$$
$$-x + 8 = -1$$
$$-x + 8 - 8 = -1 - 8$$
$$-x = -9$$
$$x = 9$$

Representing an unknown number by x in our Guess and Check strategy gives us two expressions, $x + 8$ and $2x - 1$, that are equal. Setting these expressions equal to each other gives the equation

$$x + 8 = 2x - 1$$

In order to use a variable to represent a number, it must be properly introduced before writing the equation. The next example shows how to introduce a variable to represent a number and then write the equation.

EXAMPLE. Lake Ontario is four times as deep as Lake Erie. The sum of their depths is 300 m. Write an equation to find their depths.

SOLUTION:
Let x be the depth of Lake Erie in metres. Then 4x can represent the depth of Lake Ontario.

$$\underset{\text{depth}}{\text{Lake Erie}} + \underset{\text{depth}}{\text{Lake Ontario}} = 300 \text{ m}$$
$$x + 4x = 300$$
$$5x = 300$$

Lake Erie   Lake Ontario
  x   4x

An equation to find the depths of the lakes is 5x = 300.

EXERCISE 9.3

A 1. Express each sentence as a mathematical equation.

(a) Five times a number is equal to fifteen.
(b) Twice Mary's age is thirty.
(c) A number increased by seven is equal to thirteen.
(d) A number decreased by two is equal to eleven.
(e) Six less than a number is equal to fourteen.
(f) Bill's age two years ago was ten.
(g) Nicole's age five years from now will be twenty-one.

2. The perimeter of each rectangle is 24 cm. Write an equation to find the dimensions for each.

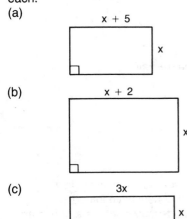

(a) x + 5, x

(b) x + 2, x

(c) 3x, x

B 3. Translate the following into mathematical equations.

(a) Eight more than five times a number is sixty-three.
(b) The sum of 15 and three times a number is 75.
(c) Eleven pens cost $6.93.
(d) Sam is three years younger than Phil and the sum of their ages is 33.
(e) Six times a number decreased by 3 is 93.
(f) Paul is ten years older than Beth and the sum of their ages is 36.
(g) The Blue Jays scored 3 more runs than the Yankees. There were 13 runs scored in the game.
(h) Kate has twice as much money as Meg. Together they have $78.
(i) Lake Erie is 77 km longer than Lake Ontario. Their lengths total 698 km.
(j) David is five years older than Tracey and the sum of their ages is nineteen.
(k) The St. Lawrence River is 24 km longer than the Rio Grande. The sum of their lengths is 6090 km.
(l) The area of the Atlantic Ocean is one-half the area of the Pacific Ocean. Their areas total 250 000 000 km².
(m) In 1927, Babe Ruth and Lou Gehrig hit a total of 107 home runs. Ruth hit 13 more than Gehrig.
(n) The diameter of the sun is 110 times the diameter of the Earth. The sum of their diameters is 1 405 000 km.

9.4 SOLVING PROBLEMS USING ONE VARIABLE — PART I

In this section we solve word problems using the planning skills developed in previous sections with the techniques for solving equations.

READ	Determine what information is given. Identify what is asked. Determine the number of unknowns.
PLAN	Introduce a variable. Express other unknowns in terms of the same variable. Write an equation using the condition supplied in the problem.
SOLVE	Solve the equation. Find the required values.
ANSWER	Check your solution with the words in the problem. State the solution in words.

READ

EXAMPLE 1. Angel Falls, in Venezuela, is 20 times as high as Niagara Falls. The sum of their heights is 1050 m. Find the height of each.

PLAN

$E=mc^2$

SOLUTION:
Let x represent the height of Niagara Falls in metres.
Then 20x is the height of Angel Falls.

Height of Niagara Falls	plus	Height of Angel Falls	is	1050 m

SOLVE

$$x \qquad + \qquad 20x \qquad = \qquad 1050$$

$$x + 20x = 1050$$
$$21x = 1050$$
$$x = 50$$

ANSWER

$$20x = 1000$$

Check.
Angel Falls is 20 times as high as Niagara Falls.
$$1000 = 20 \times 50$$
The sum of their heights is 1050.
$$1000 + 50 = 1050$$
Niagara Falls is 50 m high.
Angel Falls is 1000 m high.

If you count by ones from any integer, you obtain consecutive integers. For example, 6, 7, 8 are three consecutive integers. Similarly, $-5, -4, -3, -2$, are four consecutive integers. If n is an integer, then n, n + 1, n + 2, are consecutive integers.

If n is an even integer, write expressions for the next three even integers.

n, ▇▇▇, ▇▇▇, ▇▇▇

If n is an odd integer, write expressions for the next three odd integers.

n, ▇▇▇, ▇▇▇, ▇▇▇

EXAMPLE 2. Find four consecutive integers, with a sum of 106.

SOLUTION:
Let n represent the smallest integer.
Then the other integers are $n + 1$, $n + 2$, and $n + 3$.
The sum of the integers is 106.

$$n + (n + 1) + (n + 2) + (n + 3) = 106$$
$$n + n + 1 + n + 2 + n + 3 = 106$$
$$4n + 6 = 106$$
$$4n = 100$$
$$n = 25$$

$$n + 1 = 26, n + 2 = 27, n + 3 = 28$$

Check.
25, 26, 27, 28, are consecutive integers.

$$25 + 26 + 27 + 28 = 106$$

The integers are 25, 26, 27, and 28.

READ

EXAMPLE 3. Find the dimensions of a rectangle with a perimeter of 240 m, if the length is 4 m longer than the width.

PLAN

SOLUTION:
Let x represent the width in metres.
Then the length is $x + 4$.
The perimeter of the rectangle is twice the width plus twice the length.

x

x + 4

$E=mc^2$

Four more than x
is $x + 4$

SOLVE

ANSWER

$$P = 2x + 2(x + 4)$$

Therefore

$$x + 2(x + 4) = 240$$
$$2x + 2x + 8 = 240$$
$$4x + 8 = 240$$
$$4x = 232$$
$$x = 58$$
$$x + 4 = 62$$

Check.
$$58 + 62 + 58 + 62 = 240$$
The perimeter is 240 m.

$62 - 58 = 4$. The length is 4 m longer than the width. The rectangle is 62 m long and 58 m wide.

EXERCISE 9.4

B 1. Five times a number, increased by 3, is 85. Find the number.

2. Seven times a number, decreased by 11, is 129. Find the number.

3. Eight times a number, increased by 13, is 133. Find the number.

4. Four times a number, increased by 56, is 24. Find the number.

5. Don is three times as old as David and the sum of their ages is 52. Find their ages.

6. Sue's mother is 22 a older than Susan and the sum of their ages is 60. Find their ages.

7. Pete is twice as old as Mary. Seven years ago the sum of their ages was 31. Find their ages.

8. The length of a rectangle is 4 m longer than the width. If the perimeter of the rectangle is 128 m, what are the dimensions of the rectangle?

9. Find three consecutive integers with a sum of 246.

10. Find four consecutive integers with a sum of 490.

11. Find five consecutive integers with a sum of −115.

12. Karen is twice as old as Lori. Three years from now the sum of their ages will be 42. How old is Karen?

13. Frank is eight years older than his sister. In three years he will be twice as old as she is. How old are they now?

14. The Mackenzie River is 437 km longer than the St. Lawrence River. The sum of their lengths is 3 011 km. How long is the Mackenzie?

15. John is three times as old as Mary and the sum of their ages is 24. Find their ages.

16. Lake Ontario is four times as deep as Lake Erie. The sum of their depths is 300 m. What is the depth of each lake?

17. Dave has six times as much money as Fred, and Bill has three times as much as Fred. Together they have $550. How much does each have?

18. The Suez Canal is 80.3 km longer than the Panama Canal. The sum of their lengths is 243.5 km. Find the length of each.

19. To find the length of a certain rectangle you must triple the width and add 5 m. If the perimeter of the rectangle is 74 m, find the dimensions.

20. Find three consecutive even numbers with a sum of 252.

21. Find four consecutive odd numbers with a sum of 376.

22. Sam is one-half as old as Mary. Bill is one-third as old as Mary. The sum of their ages is 44 a. How old is Sam?

23. One-half of John's age two years from now plus one-third of his age three years ago is 20 a. How old is John?

24. In a certain isosceles triangle, to find the length of one of the equal sides you must double the base and subtract 3 cm. If the perimeter of the triangle is 79 cm, what are the dimensions of the triangle?

25. A famous television star, unwilling to give his age, posed the following problem to a fan magazine reporter. "I have a dog called Eight Ball. Four years ago I was eleven times as old as Eight Ball. Now I am six times as old." How old is he?

9.5 SOLVING PROBLEMS USING ONE VARIABLE — PART II

In the PLAN step, it is necessary to identify how the quantities are related to each other. For example, if the sum of two numbers is 18 and one number is x, then the numbers are x and (18 − x).

READ

PLAN

$E=mc^2$

The numbers are x and 26 − x.

SOLVE

ANSWER

EXAMPLE 1. The sum of two numbers is 26. Twice one number plus three times the other is 64. Find the numbers.

SOLUTION:
Let x represent the first number.
Then (26 − x) can represent the second number.

Twice one number plus three times the other is 64.

$$2x \quad + \quad 3(26 - x) \quad = 64$$

$$2x + 3(26 - x) = 64$$
$$2x + 78 - 3x = 64$$
$$-x + 78 = 64$$
$$-x = -14$$
$$x = 14$$
$$26 - x = 12$$

Check.

$$14 + 12 = 26$$

$$2(14) + 3(12) = 64$$

The numbers are 14 and 12.

Example 1 did not specify which number should be doubled and which one multiplied by three. In the PLAN step, the equation could have been

$$2(26 - x) + 3x = 64$$

Solving, we get

$$52 - 2x + 3x = 64$$
$$52 + x = 64$$
$$x = 12$$

and
$$26 - x = 14$$

Twice one number   Three times the other
2x   +   3(26 − x)
2(26 − x) +   3x

Again the numbers are 14 and 12.

READ

EXAMPLE 2. A vending machine contains $27.70 made up of dimes and quarters. If there are 199 coins in all, how many dimes and quarters are there?

PLAN

SOLVE

SOLUTION:
Let x represent the number of dimes.
Then (199 − x) can represent the number of quarters.

In this type of problem it is easiest to work in cents. If there are x dimes, there are 10x cents. Similarly (199 − x) quarters results in 25(199 − x) cents. The problem states that the total value of the coins is $27.70 or 2770 cents.

Coins	Value	
x dimes	10x	¢
199 − x quarters	25(199 − x)	¢
Total	2770	¢

$$10x + 25(199 - x) = 2770$$
$$10x + 4975 - 25x = 2770$$
$$4975 - 15x = 2770$$
$$-15x = -2205$$
$$x = 147$$
$$199 - x = 52$$

ANSWER

Check.

$$147(\$0.10) + 52(\$0.25) = \$27.70$$

The total value is $27.70.

$$147 + 52 = 199$$

∴ there are 199 coins.

There are 147 dimes and 52 quarters.

The following exercises provide practice in setting up problems where the sum of two unknowns is given.

EXERCISE 9.5

A 1. Complete the tables.

(a) The sum of two numbers is 20.

First number	13	9			x	
Second number			7	14		y

(b) There were 800 students at the concert.

Number of girls	450		x			4r
Number of boys		520		y	3w	

(c) The cash register contained 70 nickels and dimes.

Number of nickels	30		43			5w	7n
Number of dimes		51		x	y		

2. In each of the following statements there are two unknowns. Represent each unknown in terms of the same variable.
(a) The sum of two numbers is 35.
(b) The sum of two numbers is 87.
(c) The length and width of a rectangle total 200 m.
(d) There are a total of 34 boys and girls in the class.
(e) The salesman sold a total of 16 cars and vans.
(f) In 1961, Mantle and Maris hit a total of 115 home runs.
(g) The soft drink machine contained a total of 257 dimes and quarters.
(h) Our solar system has a total of 63 moons and planets.

B 3. The sum of two numbers is 73. Twice one number plus the other is 104. Find the numbers.

4. The sum of two numbers is 85. Twice one number plus four times the other is 218. Find the numbers.

5. Our solar system has a total of 63 moons and planets. Three times the number of moons minus four times the number of planets is 126. How many planets are there?

6. At a carnival shooting gallery you get five points for hitting a destroyer and three points for hitting a submarine. Dawn scored 36 points with 10 hits. How many submarines did she hit?

7. The sum of two numbers is 125. Five times one number minus three times the other is 41. Find the numbers.

8. Sam sells cookies and milk at the exhibition. He has $10.65 made up of dimes and quarters. If there are 54 coins in all, how many dimes are there?

9. A bill of $2.35 was paid in dimes and nickels. If there were 32 coins in all, how many dimes were there?

10. Mary bought a radio for $120. She paid for it with two-dollar bills and five-dollar bills. If there were 30 bills in all, how many were there of each?

C 11. Dave travelled a total of 20 km by walking and running. One-third of the distance he walked equalled one-half the distance he ran. How far did he walk?

12. The sum of two numbers is 80. One-fifth of one of them plus one-quarter of the other is 17. Find the numbers.

9.6 RATE OF WORK PROBLEMS

In this section we use equations to solve problems involving the rate of doing things. We use the following concept which was developed in Section 5.6.

In 4 h John can clean the stadium seats.

In 1 h John can clean $\frac{1}{4}$ of the seats.

In x h John can clean $\frac{x}{4}$ of the seats.

READ

EXAMPLE. If it takes John 4 h to clean the stadium seats and Pete 3 h to clean the seats, how long would it take them to clean the stadium seats together?

PLAN

SOLUTION:

$E=mc^2$

Let x represent the number of hours for John and Pete to clean the seats together.

Then $\frac{x}{4}$ represents the part cleaned by John.

SOLVE

Similarly $\frac{x}{3}$ represents the part cleaned by Pete.

Part cleaned by John + Part cleaned by Pete = Whole stadium

$$\frac{x}{4} \qquad + \qquad \frac{x}{3} \qquad = \qquad 1$$

$$\frac{x}{4} + \frac{x}{3} = 1$$

$$12 \times \left[\frac{x}{4} + \frac{x}{3} \right] = 12 \times 1 \qquad \text{The LCD is 12.}$$

$$3x + 4x = 12$$

$$7x = 12$$

$$x = \frac{12}{7}$$

ANSWER

$$= 1\frac{5}{7}$$

Check.

In $\frac{12}{7}$ h John cleans $\frac{1}{4}(\frac{12}{7}) = \frac{3}{7}$ of the stadium.

In $\frac{12}{7}$ h Pete cleans $\frac{1}{3}(\frac{12}{7}) = \frac{4}{7}$ of the stadium.

$$\frac{3}{7} + \frac{4}{7} = 1$$

It takes $1\frac{5}{7}$ h for John and Pete to clean the stadium.

$$\boxed{\begin{array}{c} \text{Work Formula} \\ \dfrac{\text{Time for A and B together}}{\text{Time for A alone}} + \dfrac{\text{Time for A and B together}}{\text{Time for B alone}} = 1 \end{array}}$$

EXERCISE 9.6

B 1. It takes drain A two hours to drain a water tank. It takes drain B four hours to drain the same tank. How long will it take to drain the tank with both drains open?

2. One pipe can fill a tank in four hours. It takes another pipe six hours to fill the same tank. How long will it take to fill the tank with both pipes filling together?

3. It takes John eight hours to paint a two-bedroom apartment. It takes Mary ten hours to paint the same size apartment. How long will it take them to paint a two-bedroom apartment together?

4. Sue takes eight minutes to wash a car. It takes Bob six minutes to do the same job. How long will it take them to wash a car together?

5. Al can complete a job in thirty minutes. His brother can do it in one-half the time. How long will it take them to complete the job working together?

6. Working by himself, it takes Mike one hour to tape the ankles of the players on the school football team. It takes Mark forty minutes to do the same job. Bob can do it in thirty minutes. How long would it take them to complete the job working together?

7. Ralph takes forty minutes to type the weekly pay cheques for the Pizza Place. It takes Jane thirty minutes to type them. How long would it take to type the pay cheques if Ralph and Jane were both typing?

8. It takes Fred eight hours to prepare the stadium field for a football game. He earns $10/h. It takes Sam twelve hours to do the same job and he gets paid $7/h. If the stadium manager is not concerned with the time factor, only expenses, how should he get the field prepared:
 (i) hire Fred only?
 (ii) hire Sam only?
 (iii) hire Fred and Sam?

9. It takes spillway A six hours to lower the water level in a reservoir by one metre. It takes spillway B twelve hours and it takes spillway C twenty-four hours. How long would it take to lower the water level by one metre if all three spillways are opened together?

10. Dean, Paul, and Brenda work for a decorator installing wall-to-wall carpet in the apartments of a new high-rise building. It takes Dean ten hours to install the carpet in a one-bedroom apartment. Paul takes fifteen hours and Brenda twelve hours to do the same job. If they worked together, how long would it take them to install the carpet in one apartment?

C 11. Corporal Jones takes 12 h to complete a planned maintenance check on an anti-submarine helicopter. Jones had been working on a helicopter for 4 h when Sergeant Marco arrived to help him finish the job. They completed the check in 2 h. How long would it have taken Sergeant Marco to complete the job alone?

9.7 MOTION PROBLEMS

In this section we shall solve uniform motion problems. An object is in uniform motion if it moves without changing its speed. The formula we use in solving such problems is

$$D = RT$$

where D represents distance, R, rate or speed, and T, time.

READ

EXAMPLE 1. A plane flew from Cleveland to Denver at 500 km/h and returned at 400 km/h. If the total trip took 9 h, how far is it from Cleveland to Denver?

PLAN

SOLUTION:
Let x represent the distance, in kilometres, from Cleveland to Denver.

SOLVE

	D (km)	R (km/h)	T (h)
Cleveland to Denver	x	500	$\dfrac{x}{500}$
Denver to Cleveland	x	400	$\dfrac{x}{400}$

Time (Cleveland to Denver) + Time (Denver to Cleveland) = 9

$$\underbrace{\dfrac{x}{500}} + \underbrace{\dfrac{x}{400}} = 9$$

$$\dfrac{x}{500} + \dfrac{x}{400} = 9$$
$$4x + 5x = 18\,000 \qquad \text{The LCD is 2000.}$$
$$9x = 18\,000$$
$$x = 2000$$

ANSWER

Check.
$$\text{Time (Cleveland to Denver)} = \dfrac{2000}{500}$$
$$= 4 \text{ h}$$
$$\text{Time (Denver to Cleveland)} = \dfrac{2000}{400}$$
$$= 5 \text{ h}$$
$$\text{Total time} = 4 + 5$$
$$= 9 \text{ h}$$

∴ it is 2000 km from Cleveland to Denver.

The following is an alternate solution to Example 1.

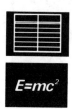

Let x represent the time to fly from Cleveland to Denver, in hours. Then (9 − x) represents the time to fly from Denver to Cleveland.

	D (km)	R (km/h)	T (h)
Cleveland to Denver	500x	500	x
Denver to Cleveland	400(9 − x)	400	9 − x

Distance (Cleveland to Denver) = Distance (Denver to Cleveland)
$$500x = 400(9 - x)$$
$$500x = 3600 - 400x$$
$$900x = 3600$$
$$x = 4$$
$$\therefore 500x = 500(4)$$
$$= 2000$$

∴ it is 2000 km from Cleveland to Denver.

READ

EXAMPLE 2. A jet left Toronto for Berlin, a distance of 6300 km, at a speed of 800 km/h. At the same time, a jet left Berlin for Toronto at a speed of 600 km/h. How long after take-off will the jets pass each other?

PLAN

SOLUTION:
Let x be the time in hours from take-off to "passing."

	D (km)	R (km/h)	T (h)
Toronto to "passing"	800x	800	x
Berlin to "passing"	600x	600	x

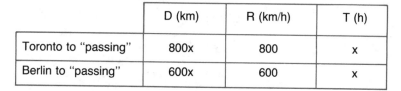

SOLVE

The sum of the distances is 6300 km.

$$800x + 600x = 6300$$
$$1400x = 6300$$
$$x = 4.5$$

ANSWER

Check.

$$800 \times 4.5 = 3600 \text{ km}$$
$$600 \times 4.5 = 2700 \text{ km}$$
$$3600 \text{ km} + 2700 \text{ km} = 6300 \text{ km}$$

The jets will pass each other 4.5 h after take-off.

EXAMPLE 3. After leaving a service centre, a car travelled at 80 km/h on the highway. Fifteen minutes later a police cruiser left the same service centre at 120 km/h, in pursuit of the car. How long will it take the cruiser to overtake the car?

E=mc²

SOLUTION:
Let x represent the time required to overtake the car.
The car was 20 km down the highway when the cruiser left the service centre.

	D (km)	R (km/h)	T (h)
Car	80x	80	x
Cruiser	120x	120	x

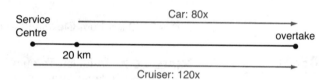

The difference in the distance travelled is 20 km.

$$120x - 80x = 20$$
$$40x = 20$$
$$x = 0.5$$

Check.

Car's distance $= 20 + 80 \times 0.5 = 20 + 40$
$= 60$ km
Cruiser's distance $= 120 \times 0.5$
$= 60$ km

The cruiser will overtake the car in 0.5 h.

EXERCISE 9.7

A 1. (a) How far will you travel in 4 h at 60 km/h?

(b) How long will it take to travel 600 km at 50 km/h?

(c) How fast are you driving if you travel 200 km in 2 h?

(d) How far will you travel in 6 h at 70 km/h?

(e) How long will it take to travel 350 km at 100 km/h?

B2. Complete the following table.

	D (km)	R (km/h)	T (h)
(a)		75	x
(b)	x	60	
(c)		80	0.5x
(d)	270x	90	

3. Complete the following table.

	D (km)	R (km/h)	T (h)
(a)	510		6
(b)		80	7.5
(c)	840	60	
(d)		75	12.5
(e)	779		8.2
(f)	506	92	

4. The winner of the 24 h Grand Prix d'Endurance (also known as the twenty-four hours of Le Mans) is the car that covers the greatest distance in 24 h. A Porsche team drove 5334 km. What was the average speed in kilometres per hour? What is the present distance record for Le Mans?

5. The fastest automobile race in the world is the NASCAR Grand National 200 km event held on the Daytona International Speedway. Cale Yarborough set a record by covering the distance in 40 min 55 s. What was his average speed in kilometres per hour?

6. The world's fastest animal is a bird called the spine-tailed swift. It can fly 1 km in 0.35 min. Determine its speed in kilometres per hour.

7. A jet flew from Toronto to Paris at 800 km/h and returned at 700 km/h. If the total trip, not including stopover time, took 15 h, how far is it from Toronto to Paris?

8. A jet left Kansas City for San Francisco, a distance of 2550 km, at a speed of 800 km/h. At the same time, a jet left San Francisco for Kansas City at a speed of 900 km/h. How long after take-off will the jets pass each other?

9. After robbing the bank in Yuma City, the Dalton brothers galloped away at 24 km/h. Fifteen minutes later the posse left at 28 km/h. How long did it take the posse to overtake the Daltons?

10. A jet left Regina for Moscow at 600 km/h. Fifteen minutes later a second jet left Regina for Moscow at 700 km/h. How long after take-off can the second jet expect to overtake the first?

11. Sally drove from Buffalo to Boston at 90 km/h and returned at 80 km/h. If her total driving time was 17 h, how far is it from Buffalo to Boston?

12. A jet left Winnipeg for Halifax at 900 km/h. At the same time a jet left Halifax for Winnipeg at 700 km/h. If the distance between Winnipeg and Halifax is 2800 km, how long after take-off will the jets pass each other?

13. Pierre drove from Ottawa to London, a distance of 575 km, in 8 h. Part of the trip was spent driving on a four-lane highway where he averaged 100 km/h. The remainder of the trip was spent on a two-lane highway where he averaged 50 km/h. How much time was spent driving on the four-lane highway?

14. A secret agent left Washington for Montreal, a distance of 950 km, driving at 100 km/h. At the same time another agent left Montreal for Washington driving at 90 km/h. How far from Montreal will the agents meet in order to exchange their information?

C 15. A cost guard patrol boat cruises at 30 km/h in still water. The rate of the current in the river to be patrolled is 5 km/h. Each patrol lasts 6 h. The captain of the boat is ordered to patrol upstream as far as possible and then return to base. How far upstream should he travel?

9.8 REVIEW EXERCISE

1. Represent each of the following as an algebraic expression.
(a) seven times a number
(b) a number increased by nine
(c) Kristine's age three years ago
(d) four less than a number
(e) Mark's age six years from now
(f) the number of cents in y nickels
(g) seven times a number decreased by four
(h) five less than three times a number
(i) the sum of three consecutive integers

2. Express each sentence as a mathematical equation.
(a) A number increased by ten is sixty-three.
(b) Mike's age five years ago was thirteen.
(c) A number decreased by seven is six.
(d) Six times a number increased by four is forty.
(e) Twice a number decreased by three is seven.

3. Six times a number increased by 5 is 263. Find the number.

4. Nine times a number decreased by 14 is 175. Find the number.

5. Fifteen times a number decreased by 27 is 168. Find the number.

6. The length of a rectangle is 7 m longer than the width. If the perimeter of the rectangle is 210 m, what are the dimensions of the rectangle?

7. If you multiply the number of touchdowns scored against the Chicago Bears in 1932 by 20 and add 41 you get 161. How many touchdowns were scored?

8. If you multiply the record number of days for staying in a cave by three and add four you get 1393. What is the record?

9. If you multiply the length of the tunnel in Tsugara, Japan, by four and add seven, the result is 220 km. How long is the tunnel?

10. Find the three consecutive integers with a sum of 291.

11. During his major league career, Hank Aaron hit 31 more home runs than Babe Ruth. Together they hit 1459 home runs. How many home runs did Babe Ruth hit?

12. As a major league baseball player, Ty Cobb had 482 more hits than Hank Aaron. Together they had 7900 hits. How many hits did Ty Cobb have?

13. The sum of two numbers is 117. Seven times one number plus three times the other is 623. Find the numbers.

14. Bob has $21.90 made up of dimes and quarters. If there are 117 coins in all, how many quarters are there?

15. Jeff has $3.15 made up of nickels and dimes. If he has five times as many nickels as dimes, how many dimes does he have?

16. The denominator of a fraction is five greater than two times its numerator, and the reduced value of the fraction is $\frac{1}{3}$. Find the numerator.

17. It takes Frances 2 h to paint a car. It takes Phil 1 h to do the same job. How long will it take them to paint a car working together?

18. Mary and Paul share a paper route. It takes Mary 70 min to deliver all the papers. It takes Paul 80 min. How long would it take them to deliver the papers working together?

19. A Boeing 747 left Thunder Bay for Victoria, a distance of 3000 km, at a speed of 800 km/h. At the same time another 747 left Victoria for Thunder Bay at a speed of 700 km/h. How long after take-off will the jets pass each other?

20. A jet flew from Toronto to Phoenix at 900 km/h. Due to a strong headwind the return trip was made at 600 km/h. If the round trip took 7.5 h, how far is it from Toronto to Phoenix?

21. After starting a car race, team 1 drove away at 160 km/h. Nine minutes later, team 2 began the chase at 180 km/h. How long will it take team 2 to overtake team 1?

22. It takes spillway A 2 h to lower the water level in a reservoir by 2 m. It takes spillway B 3 h and spillway C 4 h to lower the level by 2 m. How long will it take to lower the water level by 4 m if all three spillways are opened together?

23. The captain of a coast guard boat is ordered to travel upstream as far as possible and then return to base. The total time of the patrol is to be 6 h. If the boat travels upstream at 24 km/h and downstream at 30 km/h, how far upstream should the boat go?

24. Two cyclists, 90 km apart, started riding toward each other at the same time. The speed of one of the cyclists is twice as fast as the other. Find their speeds if they meet after 2 h.

MARIA GAETANA AGNESI (1718-1799)

Born in Milan, Italy, Maria Agnesi became well-known for her active role in promoting higher education for women of her time. Her early studies were encouraged by her family who loved to show off her mathematical ability and flair for languages. At the age of twenty, Agnesi published *Analytical Institutions*. Considered to be the first comprehensive calculus text, it contained a discussion of the curve known as the *versiera*. When translated into English, *versiera* became "witch." As a result, the curve became known as the "Witch of Agnesi."

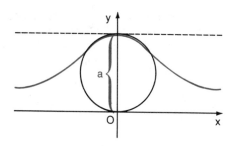

$$x^2y = a^2(a - y)$$

In 1762 Agnesi abandoned her work in mathematics, devoting her life to helping the poor and the sick, turning her own home into a refuge.

9.9 CHAPTER 9 TEST

1. If x is one number, write the other numbers in terms of x under each of the following conditions.
(a) the sum of the numbers is 25
(b) one number is three more than the other
(c) one number is three times the other
(d) one number is two less than five times the other
(e) three consecutive integers
(f) three consecutive odd numbers

2. To find the price of a television set, a dealer multiplies the cost price by 1.32.
(a) Find a formula for the selling price in terms of the cost price.
(b) What is the selling price of a television set that has a cost price of $371.17?

3. Write an equation for each of the following statements. Do not solve the equation.
(a) Twice a number added to three less than the number is twelve. Find the number.
(b) Jane is five years older than Jason. In three years, the sum of their ages will be thirty-four. What are their ages?
(c) A train travelled from Calgary to Edmonton at 75 km/h, and returned at 100 km/h. The total trip took 7 h. How far is it from Calgary to Edmonton?

4. The sum of three consecutive odd numbers is 111. Find the numbers.

5. It takes 6 h to drain a tank using only valve A. Valve B can drain the tank in 12 h, while it would take valve C a total of 24 h to drain the tank. How long will it take to drain the tank using all three valves?

6. A freight train left Thunder Bay for Vancouver, a distance of 3045 km, travelling at an average rate of 92 km/h. Two hours later a passenger train leaves Thunder Bay for Vancouver travelling at an average rate of 110 km/h. How long will it take for the passenger train to catch up to the freight train?

PROBABILITY AND STATISTICS

CHAPTER

A reasonable probability is the only certainty.
E.W. Howe

REVIEW AND PREVIEW TO CHAPTER 10

PERCENT

EXERCISE

1. Express each of the following as decimals.

(a) 25%   (b) 10%
(c) 40%   (d) 45%
(e) 65%   (f) 100%
(g) 63%   (h) 5%
(i) 1%   (j) 25.5%
(k) 7.6% (l) $12\frac{1}{2}$%
(m) 12.4% (n) 109%
(o) 230% (p) $7\frac{3}{4}$%
(q) 153% (r) 9.9%
(s) $3\frac{1}{3}$% (t) $66\frac{2}{3}$%

2. Express each of the following as a percent.

(a) $\frac{3}{4}$ (b) $\frac{1}{2}$
(c) $\frac{7}{10}$ (d) $\frac{3}{20}$
(e) $\frac{7}{50}$ (f) 0.25
(g) 0.1   (h) 0.67
(i) 0.08 (j) 0.81
(k) 3.2   (l) 1.5

3. Evaluate the following.

(a) 50% of 60   (b) 30% of 140
(c) 15% of 900 (d) 21% of 700
(e) 63% of 45   (f) $6\frac{1}{2}$% of 80
(g) 8.5% of 500 (h) 110% of 250
(i) $7\frac{3}{4}$% of 240 (j) 15.2% of 800
(k) 0.5% of 80 (l) 0.02% of 1000

4. What percent of 24 is 8?

5. What percent of 30 is 6?

6. What percent of 50 is 5?

7. 7 is what percent of 42?

8. 30 is what percent of 210?

9. What percent of 12 is 24?

10. What percent of 14 is 52?

11. If 10% of a number is 18, what is the number?

12. If 5% of a number is 6, what is the number?

13. If 17% of a number is 51, what is the number?

14. A school has a daily absence rate of 4%. If there are 1200 students registered, how many are absent each day?

15. What would you pay for a $65 sweater if the rate of sales tax is 7%?

16. Monica is a salesperson and is paid a 6% commission on all of her sales. If her total sales for a week are $4200, what is her pay for the week?

17. Find the commission for each salesperson.

Sales-person	Total Weekly Sales	Rate of Commis-sion	Weekly Commis-sion
Chang	$16 000	6%	
Klein	$19 000	7%	
Jackson	$13 000	$7\frac{1}{2}$%	
Giardino	$18 500	$5\frac{1}{2}$%	

18. Frank earns $400/week plus a commission of 2% of his sales. If his sales for one week are $3600, what is his total pay for the week?

19. Find the total weekly pay for each salesperson.

	Buchner	McDade	Bethune	Florio
Weekly Sales	$15 000	$27 500	$18 700	$29 800
Rate of Commission	2%	3%	$2\frac{1}{2}$%	3.5%
Commission				
Regular Weekly Salary	$300	$330	$395	$415
Total Weekly Pay				

20. Vehicles enter an intersection by route A. 40% of the vehicles then follow route B. 25% take route C. During one twenty-four hour period 15 000 vehicles followed route D.
(a) How many vehicles took route C?
(b) How many vehicles took route B?
(c) How many vehicles entered the intersection at A?

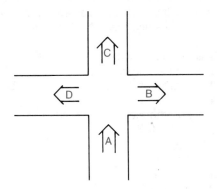

21. A commission of 6% is charged for listing and selling a house. The 6% is divided as follows:
(a) 3% to the broker who listed the property
  (i) $1\frac{1}{2}$% to the company
  (ii) $1\frac{1}{2}$% to the agent listing
(b) 3% to the broker representing the buyer
  (i) $1\frac{1}{2}$% to the company
  (ii) $1\frac{1}{2}$% to the agent

Complete the following chart.

	Selling Price of House			
	165 000	257 000	174 000	268 300
Total Commission				
Listing broker's share				
Listing agent's share				
Buyer agent's share				

22. To get a good estimate of the daily vehicular traffic flow through an intersection, a statistician will count the number of vehicles passing through the intersection during a "rush-hour." This figure represents 9% of the daily traffic. If the "rush-hour" count is 2340 vehicles, what is the estimated daily flow?

10.1 COLLECTING DATA

Number facts are called data. Statistics is the science of collecting, organizing, and interpreting data.

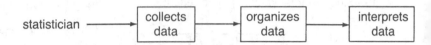

statistician → collects data → organizes data → interprets data

The group of people from whom data are gathered is called the population. If data are collected from each member of the population, the process is called a census. A sample is that part of the population who have provided the data.

Statisticians usually use samples in gathering data because:
(i) this method is less expensive than a census, and
(ii) samples give a "picture" of the population that is very close to that provided by a census.

For example, suppose a polling company is asked to determine the national popularity of a new TV show. The person in charge of the poll is not going to employ enough canvassers to survey every TV viewer. What the pollster does is take a sample.

A small group of viewers, the sample, are asked for their reaction to the new show. A well chosen sample of 1000 viewers will give an excellent indication of what the entire population thinks about the show.

The most important requirement of a sample is that it be chosen at random. A random sample is one where each individual in the population has an equal chance of being selected. If a sample is not random, it may not give a true picture of the population that it is supposed to represent. The facts collected by the canvassers are the data.

The data are then organized and interpreted. Inferences are then made about the popularity of the new TV show.

Statistical inference is the process of making statements about an entire population from data obtained from a sample of the population.

Pollsters must consider the population that the sample is supposed to represent. An election survey that includes elementary school students would lose some validity since these students are not eligible to vote.

The size of a sample is also very important. If a sample is too small then the individuals in the sample may not be typical of the population. On the other hand, when a sample is too large it becomes very costly to collect data.

There are many methods of gathering data. The primary ones are:
    (a) testing (of both people and things)
    (b) questionnaires
    (c) telephone surveys
    (d) personal interviews
    (e) measurement
    (f) encyclopedia, newspaper, and computer data bases

EXERCISE 10.1

A 1. State the method you would use to gather the following data.

(a) the heights of the ten tallest buildings in the world

(b) information on whether or not the headlights on new cars work properly

(c) the cost of travelling to Rome

(d) the popularity of a new video

(e) the area of the world's seven largest countries

(f) a list of the Canadian universities that offer degrees in medicine

(g) the most popular time for watching television in the home

(h) the choice of projects the citizens of a town would like to see undertaken by the town council

(i) the quality of new compact discs

(j) the brand names of the soaps used by families

(k) the speed of the cars passing in front of the school

(l) the popularity of various recreational activities for teenagers

B 2. A company that makes flares for sea rescue operations tests one out of every 1000 flares.

(a) Why is it not feasible to test all of the flares that are made?

(b) What kinds of industries would not be able to test 100% of their products?

(c) What kinds of industries would test 100% of their products?

3. When would you use a telephone survey to collect data as opposed to a mail survey?

4. Design a questionnaire to be used in determining the type of food to sell at a school dance and the best day of the week to hold the dance.

5. Who would you survey to get the community's reaction to a proposed opera house?

6. Discuss the validity of the following sampling techniques.

(a) To determine the popularity of an election candidate, every one hundredth person listed in the telephone book is phoned.

(b) A pollster surveys people getting off a subway train to determine the popularity of a new magazine.

(c) A survey dealing with the problems of the unemployed is conducted on a jet flying to Miami.

(d) The whole school is surveyed about this year's graduation plans.

C 7. Suppose you are responsible for conducting a survey about the radio listening habits of a city. You are instructed to use a questionnaire that you will mail out and ask people to return.

(a) How would you determine your sample?

(b) How would you get the names and addresses if you wanted each member of a family to complete a questionnaire?

(c) What could you do to encourage people to complete the questionnaire and return it?

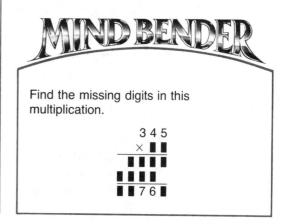

Find the missing digits in this multiplication.

```
    3 4 5
  × ■ ■
  ■ ■ ■ ■
  ■ ■ ■ ■
  ■ ■ 7 6 ■
```

10.2 MAKING PREDICTIONS USING SAMPLES

The city of Sandhurst has 150 000 eligible voters. The local radio station hired the Parr Polling Company to predict the outcome of the municipal election.

Five university students were hired to conduct a survey. Each student asked 50 eligible voters as to how they might vote in the upcoming election. Each opinion was registered in the tally column as a stroke (/). After 50 strokes, the results were totalled. The following is Maria's completed tally sheet.

Candidate	Tally	Frequency
E. EVANS	ℍℍ ℍℍ	10
M. SANTUCCI	ℍℍ ℍℍ ℍℍ |||	18
R. WONG	ℍℍ ℍℍ ℍℍ	15
T. KORCHAK	ℍℍ ||	7

The data gathered by the students were summarized as follows.

Candidate	Maria	Bob	Theo	Chris	Beth	Totals
E. EVANS	10	7	10	7	6	40
M. SANTUCCI	18	11	13	9	19	70
R. WONG	15	25	19	26	20	105
T. KORCHAK	7	7	8	8	5	35
Total Voters Surveyed						250

Using percentages, the Parr Polling Company made a prediction as to how the population of Sandhurst would vote.

Candidate	Ratio	Percent	Calculation	Predicted Votes
E. EVANS	$\frac{40}{250}$	16%	150 000 × 0.16 = 24 000	24 000
M. SANTUCCI	$\frac{70}{250}$	28%	150 000 × 0.28 = 42 000	42 000
R. WONG	$\frac{105}{250}$	42%	150 000 × 0.42 = 63 000	63 000
T. KORCHAK	$\frac{35}{250}$	14%	150 000 × 0.14 = 20 400	21 000

EXERCISE 10.2

B 1. There are five television stations within viewing distance of Fort Edwards. There are about 300 000 potential television viewers. Joe was asked to determine the number of people that watched the six o'clock news on each of the stations. To do this, Joe surveyed 100 viewers with the following results.

TELEVISION STATION VIEWERS

Station	Tally	Frequency
CHRT	ℍℍ ℍℍ ℍℍ ℍℍ ///	
CJLP	ℍℍ ℍℍ ℍℍ ℍℍ ℍℍ ℍℍ	
CBC	ℍℍ ℍℍ ℍℍ ℍℍ	
WXNT	ℍℍ ℍℍ ℍℍ /	
WRQT	ℍℍ ℍℍ /	

Use Joe's results to predict how many people watch the news on each of the stations.

2. The table gives the responses of fifty tourists in the town of Drew Beach when they were asked to name their favourite type of food.

```
I — Italian     C — Canadian
F — French      T — Chinese
```

```
T  C  C  C  F  F  F  I  I  C
C  C  T  I  F  C  C  T  F  F
C  I  F  C  C  T  C  F  T  I
F  C  I  I  C  C  F  T  C  F
C  T  I  F  C  F  F  C  C  I
```

(a) Construct a tally sheet for the information.
(b) If there are an estimated 500 000 tourists visiting Drew Beach each year, predict the number of people that would prefer each type of food.

3. Statistics can be abused. Analyse the following statements and state what is misleading.
(a) Most people have automobile accidents within 10 km of home. Therefore, it is safer to drive when you are farther than 10 km from home.

(b) Of the 10 people surveyed, 7 drank cola. Therefore, more people drink cola than any other type of soft drink.
(c) A recent survey showed that only 40% of the people will vote for the Free Party in the next election. This means that the Free Party will not win the next election.

4. Choose a sample paragraph from a novel and count the first 100 words. Count the number of letters in each word and record your results on a tally sheet. Repeat this procedure for another 100-word sample.

Word Length	Tally	Frequency
1 letter		
2 letters		
3 letters		

10 letters		
11 letters		
12 letters		
13+ letters		

(a) According to your sample, what length of word is most common?
(b) Out of 5000 words in the novel, how many would you predict to have the following?
    (i) 2 letters
    (ii) 3 letters
    (iii) 4 letters
(c) Conduct a similar survey using a newspaper as a source for words. Compare these results to the results obtained from the novel. Can you account for any difference?

5. Use samples from various sources to determine the frequency of occurrence of the letters in ordinary English.
(a) What is the most used letter?
(b) What is the least used letter?
(c) How would a code-breaker use this information?

10.3 RANDOM SAMPLING

In order for a sample to be useful, it must be a random one. A random sample is one where each member of the target population has an equal chance of being selected. If this is not true, the sample has a good chance of being biased.

The techniques for determining a random sample are quite simple. Suppose you were asked to select 100 students out of 1000 to participate in a ski-weekend. One way to select the sample is to place each student's name on a slip of paper and then put the 1000 pieces of paper in a container so that the slips can be mixed in a random fashion. Then 100 names are selected from the container without replacement. This method of selecting a random sample is called a draw.

Another way to select the 100 students is to assign each of the 1000 students a different three-digit number from 000 to 999. Then a method can be used to generate 100 three-digit numbers. One way to do this is to use a spinner with the digits 0 to 9 marked on it. By spinning the spinner three times and recording the number each time you will generate a random 3-digit number.

This method was given the code-name Monte Carlo by John von Neumann when he first applied it to some critical questions in physics.

The easiest way to select a sample in a random manner is to use random numbers. These can be obtained from a table of random numbers or they can be generated by a computer. A partial table of random numbers, or digits, is shown.

To select 100 students at random, assign each student a number from 000 to 999. Then start at the top of the table and record digits in groups of three horizontally. This method gives 952, 158, 639, 861, 040, and 741 as the first six numbers. Match the random numbers generated in this fashion to the numbers assigned to the students to complete the selection process.

Another way to use the random number table is to start at the top and record digits in groups of three vertically. This method gives 952, 741, 961, 089, 003, and 604 as the first six numbers. Match again to the students' assigned numbers to continue the selection process. If, in the process of selecting three-digit numbers, we find a certain number for the second time, we discard it and go on to the next number.

These are two of several ways that the table of random numbers can be used.

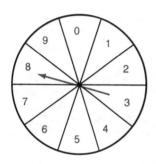

RANDOM NUMBERS

95215	86398	61040
74138	20631	87122
96173	44491	37337
08904	56728	41943
00326	85591	71671
60422	25943	03709
75412	33144	32837
03454	66762	87685
94409	63306	50349
20713	48833	02660
30999	64100	33331
00152	99655	56417

EXERCISE 10.3

B 1. List five common activities that use a draw to make a random selection.

2. List some precautions that must be taken when using a draw in order to be certain that the technique produces a random selection.

3. Four people own shares in a yacht. Pauline has a 10% share, David has a 20% share, Carl has a 30% share, and Peggy has a 40% share.

Each of them wants the yacht on July 1. They all agree to draw lots for it and they want their chances of winning to be equal to their fraction of ownership. Design a method for deciding who should get the yacht for July 1.

4. Using the random number table on the previous page, describe a procedure for selecting eight people out of a group of sixty people.

5. A polling company wants to use a telephone survey of 100 people to get public reaction to new long-distance telephone rates. Assume that the telephone directory has: 568 pages, 4 columns per page, and 100 names and numbers per column. Describe a method for selecting the 100 people at random to be surveyed.

6. Describe how a table of random numbers can be used to perform 10 trials of tossing a coin.

7. Describe how a table of random numbers can be used to perform 15 trials of rolling a die.

MICRO MATH

The following program generates lists of random numbers.

```
NEW
10 PRINT"RANDOM NUMBERS"
20 PRINT"HOW MANY NUMBERS?"
30 INPUT N
40 FOR I=1 TO N
50 X=RND(5)
60 PRINT INT(9*X)+1;
70 NEXT I
75 PRINT
80 PRINT"ANOTHER LIST? Y OR N"
90 INPUT Z$
100 IF Z$="Y" THEN 20
110 END
RUN
RANDOM NUMBERS
HOW MANY NUMBERS
? 100
2 6 8 7 8 1 5 5 1 9 7
5 4 1 7 5 6 7 6 3 5 2
7 2 2 7 7 7 9 3 5 5 2
5 7 4 1 4 8 9 5 2 8 6
5 9 3 9 9 5 6 7 7 7 7
5 1 4 6 9 3 6 9 4 9 8
5 6 2 3 8 6 8 2 1 1 2
8 2 9 6 6 7 8 4 3 1 4
9 3 4 4 5 4 2 7 7 5 9
6
ANOTHER LIST? Y OR N
?
```

MIND BENDER

Put the numbers from 1 to 9 in the spaces to make the statements true.

$\blacksquare \times \blacksquare + \blacksquare = 7$

$\blacksquare \div \blacksquare + \blacksquare = 7$

$\blacksquare + \blacksquare - \blacksquare = 7$

10.4 READING BAR GRAPHS AND BROKEN LINE GRAPHS

Graphs are used to display data in a visual way.

Bar Graphs

Bar graphs are used to compare similar things. The bar graph shown compares maximum speeds.

What is the approximate speed of each?

How many times faster than a man is a cheetah?

How long would it take a dolphin to swim 30 km?

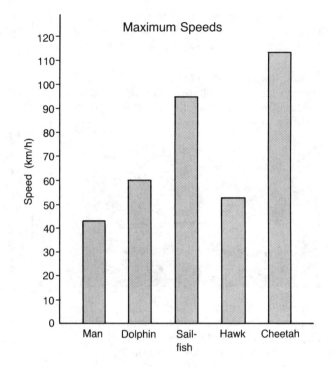

Broken Line Graphs

Broken line graphs are used to show how something changes. The broken line graph on ocean temperature shows how the average mid-ocean surface temperature changes at different latitudes.

What is the maximum temperature?

At what latitude does the maximum temperature occur?

At what latitudes does the temperature reach 0°C?

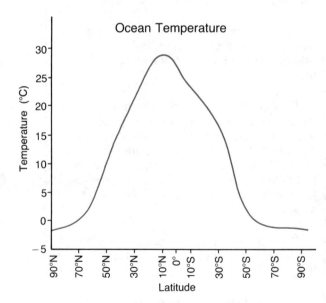

EXERCISE 10.4

B 1. The bar graph compares the length of the day in hours on several planets.

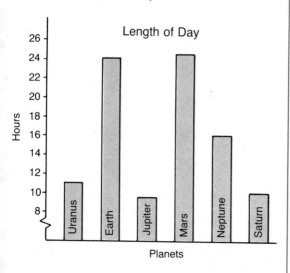

(a) What is the length of day on each planet?
(b) What planets have approximately the same day length?
(c) Approximately how many Jupiter days would it take to make 4 days on Mars?

2. The line graph shows the cassette sales for Sound City during one week.

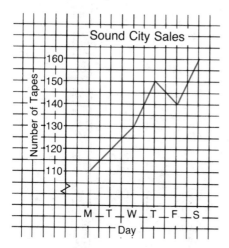

(a) How many cassettes were sold on each day?
(b) On which days were there more than 130 cassettes sold?

3. The line graph shows the amount of gasoline in the tank of a car at various times on a certain day.

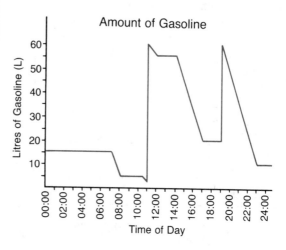

(a) At what time did the owner leave for work?
(b) If the car averages 7 km/L of gasoline, how far is it from the owner's home to her office?
(c) What was her average speed when driving from home to her office?
(d) How long did she spend at her office?
(e) After leaving the office, how far did she drive before having the tank filled?
(f) When did she have her lunch meeting?
(g) What was her average speed when driving to her meeting at 17:00?
(h) How long was this meeting?
(i) If she arrived home at 23:00, how far did she drive since her last meeting?
(j) How many litres of gasoline were used during the day?

What is the least number of pitches that must be thrown in a regulation baseball game if the visiting team wins?

10.5 DRAWING BAR GRAPHS

The table shown gives the lengths of the world's longest mountain ranges. This data compares similar things.

Mountain Range	Length (km)
Himalayas (Asia)	2500
Rockies (N. America)	4800
Great Dividing Range (Oceania)	3600
Andes (S. America)	8900
Trans-Antarctic (Antarctica)	3500

To display the data on a bar graph we proceed as follows.

1. Draw and label the horizontal and vertical axes.

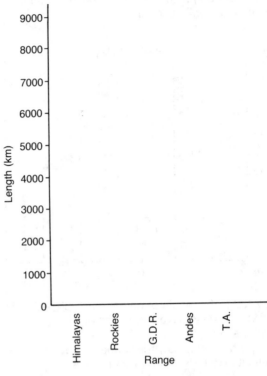

2. Draw the bars to show the length of each mountain range.

3. Give the graph a title.

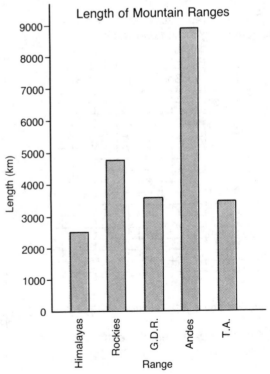

EXERCISE 10.5

1. Construct bar graphs to illustrate the following data.

(a) The maximum depth of each of the Great Lakes.

Lake	Depth (m)
Erie	65
Huron	230
Michigan	280
Ontario	235
Superior	390

(b) The daily newspapers by province.

Province	Number
Alberta	8
British Columbia	19
Manitoba	9
New Brunswick	4
Newfoundland	3
Nova Scotia	6
Ontario	46
Prince Edward Island	3
Quebec	11
Saskatchewan	4

(c) The boiling temperature of water in several places.

Place	Boiling Temp. (°C)
Dead Sea	101
Halifax	100
Mt. Everest (top)	71
Lhasa, Tibet	87

2. The Data Find Company conducted a survey to determine the participation of people between the ages of 12 and 20 in several recreational activities. Each person surveyed was allowed to select one activity.

The following table gives the results of the survey.

Activity	Participants
Swimming	75
Boating	25
Camping	30
Snow-skiing	45
Water-skiing	20
Sailing	20
Horseback riding	15
Bicycling	80
Ice Skating	90

(a) Display the results on a bar graph.

(b) Use your results to predict how many Canadians in this age group participate in each of these activities.
(c) Of what interest would this information be to the business community and to the government?

3. Conduct a survey in your class to determine the popularity of various fast food restaurants. Display the results on a bar graph.

10.6 DRAWING BROKEN LINE GRAPHS

The table shown gives the approximate number of daylight minutes for the first day of each month. This data shows how something changes.

To display the data on a broken line graph we proceed as follows.

Month	Daylight (min)
Jan.	550
Feb.	600
Mar.	675
April	750
May	850
June	900
July	900
Aug.	875
Sept.	800
Oct.	700
Nov.	625
Dec.	550

1. Draw and label the horizontal and vertical axes.

2. Plot the ordered pairs from the table.

3. Connect each pair of points with a line.

4. Give the graph a title.

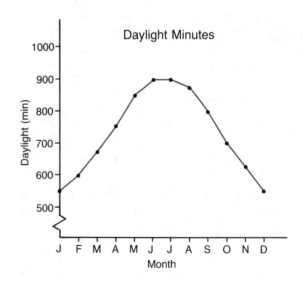

EXERCISE 10.6

B 1. The table gives the selling price of one share of Diamond Mines stock during one week. Display this information on a broken line graph.

Day	Selling Price
Monday	$2.50
Tuesday	$2.80
Wednesday	$2.40
Thursday	$2.30
Friday	$2.70

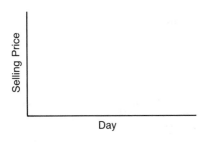

2. The winning distances for the gold medal in the discus throw in the Olympic games are given in the table.

Year	Distance (m)
1948	52.7
1952	55.1
1956	56.4
1960	59.2
1964	61.0
1968	64.8
1972	64.4
1976	67.6
1980	66.7
1984	66.6

Display this data on a broken line graph.

3. The table gives the average number of persons per Canadian household for several years.

Year	Average Size
1950	3.8
1955	3.3
1960	3.3
1965	3.2
1970	3.1
1975	3.0
1980	2.9
1985	2.7

Display this information on a broken line graph.

4. The table gives the average daily temperature in °C for each month of a year for three Canadian cities. Display this information on the same set of axes.

Month	London	Winnipeg	Calgary
Jan.	−7	−19	−12
Feb.	−6	−16	−7
Mar.	−1	−8	−4
April	6	3	3
May	12	11	9
June	18	17	14
July	20	20	16
Aug.	20	18	15
Sept.	15	12	11
Oct.	9	6	6
Nov.	3	−5	−3
Dec.	−4	−14	−8

10.7 READING AND DRAWING CIRCLE GRAPHS

Circle graphs are used to show how a quantity is divided. The circle graph shown gives the percentage of advertising revenue spent in various media.

If 10 billion dollars in total was spent on advertising, then mail advertising cost

$$15\% \text{ of } \$10\ 000\ 000\ 000 = 0.15 \times 10\ 000\ 000\ 000$$
$$= \$1\ 500\ 000\ 000$$

Which media received the most advertising dollars?
Which media received the least?
Which type of advertising would be included in "other"?

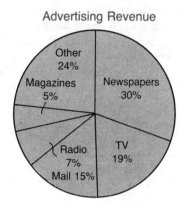

Advertising Revenue

EXAMPLE. The Roy family spends its income in the following way.

Shelter	$21 600
Food	$18 000
Clothing	$10 800
Savings	$ 7 200
Miscellaneous	$14 400
Total	$72 000

Construct a circle graph to show this information.

SOLUTION:

Step 1. Express each item as a percent of the total income.

Shelter: $\dfrac{21\ 600}{72\ 000} \times 100 = 30\%$

Food: $\dfrac{18\ 000}{72\ 000} \times 100 = 25\%$

Clothing: $\dfrac{10\ 800}{72\ 000} \times 100 = 15\%$

Savings: $\dfrac{7\ 200}{72\ 000} \times 100 = 10\%$

Miscellaneous: $\dfrac{14\ 400}{72\ 000} \times 100 = 20\%$

Total: 100%

Step 2. Write each percentage as a decimal and multiply by 360° to find the size of each central angle.

Shelter: $0.3 \times 360° = 108°$
Food: $0.25 \times 360° = 90°$
Clothing: $0.15 \times 360° = 54°$
Savings: $0.1 \times 360° = 36°$
Miscellaneous: $0.2 \times 360° = 72°$

Step 3. Draw a circle and construct each central angle. Label each section and write a title for the graph.

Roy Family Budget

EXERCISE 10.7

B 1. The circle graph shows how Allison Dalton's college expenses are divided.

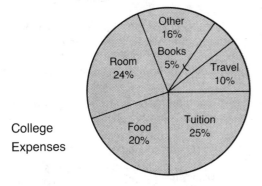

College Expenses

(a) if Allison's expenses are $12 000, what did she spend in each category.
(b) What expenses might be included under "other"?

2. The town of Sperry published a circle graph to show how the town's money was spent during the past year. If the total expenditure was $4 500 000, how much was spent for each category?

(a) education
(b) government
(c) public works
(d) protection
(e) sanitation
(f) recreation

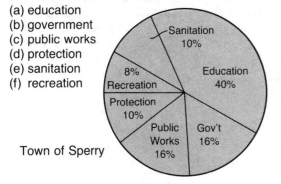

Town of Sperry

3. The circle graph shows the make-up of the human body.

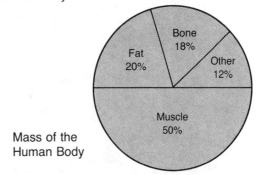

Mass of the Human Body

If Sam has a mass of 80 kg, how much of his body mass is made up of the following?
   (i) muscle   (ii) fat
   (iii) bone   (iv) other

4. Construct circle graphs to illustrate the following data.

(a) The student council raised $2000 selling chocolate bars and spent it as follows.

Dances	$700
Concerts	$300
Athletics	$500
School play	$100
Graduation	$400

(b) Franco's power boat expenses for last year are as follows.

Slip rental	$700
Gasoline	$2000
Maintenance	$500
Insurance	$800

(c) The television stations associated with a network.

Network	Number of Stations
CBC	62
NBC	236
CBS	277
ABC	1365

5. The circle graph shows retail sales by type of business. If the total retail sales last year were 130 billion dollars, how much was spent in each category?

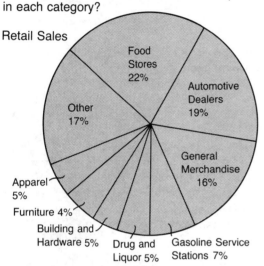

Retail Sales

6. The telephone company uses a circle graph to show how the day is divided for discounts on long-distance charges. Note that the central angle in these graphs is determined by the time of day and not by the amount of discount.

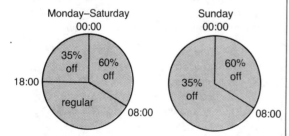

If the regular charge for a three-minute call to Vancouver is $4, what would you pay for the call if you made it at the following times.
(a) at 07:00 on Tuesday
(b) at 16:00 on Sunday
(c) at 09:00 on Wednesday

7. The circle graph shows household liabilities for Canadian households.
If the total liabilities for Canadian households are 210 billion dollars, how much is owed in each category?

Liabilities

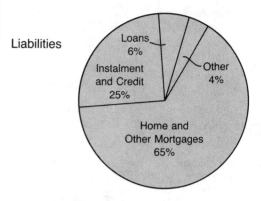

8. Use a circle graph to show how you spend your time during a typical weekday. Categories should include at least school time, sleeping time, and recreation time.

9. The circle graph shows how one hour of a radio station's time is divided.

One Hour of Radio

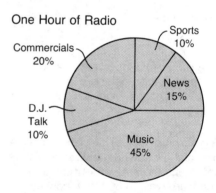

How many minutes are used in each category in one week if the station broadcasts for 24 hours a day, 7 days a week.

10.8 PICTOGRAPHS

Pictographs display data visually by using symbols that represent the data.

The pictograph on energy use shows the amount of energy used by someone in one hour for several activities. The amount of energy used is represented as the number of litres of water that could be brought to a boil using this energy.

How many litres of water could you boil with the energy you use in two hours of each activity?

How many hours of sleep does it take to burn the amount of energy used in one hour of running?

Energy Used (One Hour)	
Sleeping	⊔L
Sitting	⊔⊔L
Standing	⊔⊔⊔
Walking	⊔⊔⊔⊔⊔L
Running	⊔⊔⊔⊔⊔⊔⊔⊔⊔ ⊔⊔⊔⊔⊔
Each ⊔ represents 1 litre	

EXERCISE 10.8

1. The pictograph gives the capacities of different types of vehicles.

Vehicle Capacities	
Concorde jet	웃웃웃웃웃웃웃웃웃웃웃 웃웃웃웃웃
the Mayflower	웃웃웃웃웃웃웃웃웃웃웃 웃웃웃
a Gondola	⌐
Double-decker bus	웃웃웃웃웃웃웃웃
Each 웃 represents 10 people	

(a) What is the approximate capacity of each type of vehicle?

(b) How many gondolas are needed to transport the same number of passengers as the Mayflower?

(c) The ocean liner Queen Elizabeth II could carry 2900 passengers. Approximately how many Concorde jets would be needed to transport the same number of people across the Atlantic?

B 2. Display this information on a pictograph.

(a) The table gives the number of performances of several Broadway plays.

Play	No. of Performances
Grease	3388
The Music Man	1375
Oklahoma!	2212
South Pacific	1925
Cabaret	1165

(b) The table gives the approximate daily circulation for six Canadian newspapers.

Newspaper	Circulation
Calgary Herald	140 000
Winnipeg Free Press	180 000
Halifax Chronicle-Herald	80 000
Toronto Star	540 000
Ottawa Citizen	190 000
Regina Leader-Post	70 000

10.9 THE MEAN, MEDIAN, AND MODE

Graphical presentation alone does not always provide enough information about the data. In this section we shall introduce three measures of central tendency — mean, median, and mode — to describe the data further.

MEAN

The mean of a set of numbers, often called the average, is found by adding them and dividing the result by the number of values added.

EXAMPLE 1.   During a seven-day period, the following numbers of deer were tagged by the game warden.

$$7, 9, 8, 10, 11, 8, 10$$

Find the mean number of deer tagged.

SOLUTION:

$$\text{mean} = \frac{7 + 9 + 8 + 10 + 11 + 8 + 10}{7}$$

$$= \frac{63}{7}$$

$$= 9$$

∴ the mean is 9.

MEDIAN

If a set of numbers is arranged in order (smallest to largest) then the number that is in the middle is called the median. This occurs when there is an odd number of values. If the number of values is even, the median is the mean of the two middle values.

EXAMPLE 2.   Determine the median of the following.

$$3, 10, 7, 4, 8, 16, 21$$

SOLUTION:
Arrange the numbers in order.

$$3, 4, 7, 8, 10, 16, 21$$

The median is the middle value, 8.

EXAMPLE 3.   Determine the median of the following.

$$9, 8, 4, 7, 6, 12$$

SOLUTION:
Arrange the values in order.

$$4, 6, 7, 8, 9, 12$$

The middle two values are 7 and 8.

The median is $\dfrac{7 + 8}{2} = 7.5$

MODE

The mode of a set of numbers is the value that occurs most often. If every number occurs just once, there is no mode. A set of numbers may have more than one mode.

EXAMPLE 4. Determine the mode(s) of the following sets of data.
(a) 3, 5, 7, 4, 8, 7, 5, 7
(b) 18, 19, 24, 17, 13
(c) 9, 8, 15, 8, 6, 4, 6

SOLUTION:
(a) The mode is 7.
(b) There is no mode.
(c) The modes are 6 and 8.

EXERCISE 10.9

A 1. Determine the modes of the following sets of data.

(a) 9, 15, 24, 17, 9, 16, 5
(b) 43, 57, 19, 24, 35, 42
(c) 56, 24, 35, 59, 24, 31, 34
(d) 9, 18, 9, 24, 31, 56, 18, 12
(e) 33, 41, 26, 41, 33, 55, 24, 41
(f) 24, 55, 13, 19, 25, 6

B 2. Determine the mean, median, and mode for the following data.

(a) 7, 9, 10, 16
(b) 10, 9, 34, 24, 13
(c) 2, 4, 6, 8, 6, 4, 6, 4
(d) 86, 56, 33, 24, 35, 41, 61
(e) 51, 31, 23, 18, 37, 42, 63, 23
(f) 103, 108, 131, 142, 153, 113, 124, 103, 152, 153
(g) 7.3, 2.5, 11.3, 9.4, 4.6, 12.7, 8.2

3. Suzanne's final marks in eight subjects are as follows:

Math 94	English 86
Science 88	History 93
Art 73	Typing 74
Phys. Ed. 71	Electronics 71

Determine the mean of these marks.

4. Paul's median weekly salary for 5 weeks was $230. Was it necessary for Paul to earn exactly $230 in one of the weeks? Explain your answer.

5. Thirty-three students wrote a geography test. The median mark was 84. Alicia was the only student to get 84.

(a) How many students scored higher than Alicia?
(b) How many students scored lower?

6. Find Sam's bowling average at the end of three weeks.

Week	Game 1	Game 2	Game 3	Average
1	214	197	204	
2	182	183	220	
3	200	201	235	

MICRO MATH

```
NEW
100 PRINT"FIND THE MEAN"
110 PRINT"HOW MANY NUMBERS?"
120 INPUT N
130 PRINT"ENTER THE NUMBERS"
140 PRINT"ONE AT A TIME"
150 LET S=0
160 FOR I=1 TO N
170 INPUT X
180 LET S=S+X
190 NEXT I
200 LET A=S/N
210 PRINT"THE MEAN IS";A
220 END
RUN
```

10.10 MEAN, MEDIAN, OR MODE?

The word average has been used to refer to either mean, median, or mode, depending on the situation. All three are called measures of central tendency. Each of these measures gives some central or general trend of the data. One of them will usually prove to be more meaningful than the other two.

A law firm lists the salaries of its ten lawyers as follows.

$300 000	$130 000
$210 000	$130 000
$190 000	$130 000
$140 000	$130 000
$140 000	$130 000

The mean salary is $163 000.
The median salary is $135 000.
The mode is $130 000.

Which is the better indication of the lawyers' salaries? If you were earning $130 000 and looking for a raise, you might say: "The average salary is $163 000 and I'm earning $130 000."

If you were the head of the firm and earning $300 000, you might respond by saying "The average salary is $130 000 and you are already earning $130 000."

MEAN

The mean is affected by extreme values as we have seen in the example of the lawyers' salaries. However there are many situations where the mean is the appropriate measure. A few of them are

    (a) average yearly rainfall for an area
    (b) bowling averages
    (c) the litres of gasoline used by a car in one hundred kilometres

MEDIAN

The median is not affected by extreme values and it is the positional middle of the data. Half of the values are on either side of the median. Some appropriate uses of the median as a measure of central tendency are

    (a) salaries
    (b) days absent by employees
    (c) test marks

MODE

The mode is the most common of the values. The mode is always equal to a value of one of the observations, which is not necessarily true of the mean or median. Situations where the mode is used are

    (a) hat sizes
    (b) number of cylinders in engines
    (c) number of wheels on trucks

EXERCISE 10.10

A 1. What measure of central tendency would be best suited to the following situations?

(a) the shirt sizes that should be stocked in a store

(b) the goals scored on a goal-tender per game

(c) the salary of employees

(d) the number of school buses bought each year

(e) the amount of snowfall for an area each year

(f) the bat length in major league baseball

(g) the number of pills per bottle

(h) the number of meals sold in a cafeteria each day

(i) the class mark on a mathematics test

2. A dress manufacturer claims that the average size of dress sold is 10. Which average is being referred to, the mean, median, or mode?

3. If the mean age of people in one town is 40 and the mean age of people in a second town is 38, can you conclude that the mean age of both groups is 39? Explain.

4. The Ace Hat Company has received a Department of National Defence contract to manufacture hats for the entire military personnel. The company was given the following information about hat sizes.

mean hat size: $7\frac{1}{8}$

median hat size: $6\frac{7}{8}$

modal hat size: 7

Which of these figures is most important to the production planner? Why?

B 5. An athlete's official competition times for the 100 m dash over a season are as follows.

11.3, 10.9, 11.4, 11.2, 10.9, 11.1, 17.2

The 17.2 time occurred when the athlete tripped and fell.

(a) Determine the mean, median, and mode for the given times.

(b) Which measure is the best indication of the athlete's average ability in this event?

6. A car manufacturer is interested in knowing how often customers return their new cars to the dealer for repairs during the first year of ownership. A questionnaire was sent to 20 owners and the number of times each returned the car to the dealer was 4, 3, 2, 0, 7, 5, 3, 2, 1, 1, 2, 6, 4, 8, 3, 12, 4, 2, 0, 1.

(a) Find the mean, median, and mode for the data.

(b) What is the better indication of the frequency of repair?

7. The Kelsa Vegmart has decided to package its onions in bags. A decision has to be made as to how many onions should be put in each bag. Thirty customers purchased the following number of onions during a peak buying time: 1, 2, 3, 6, 10, 4, 4, 3, 2, 4, 5, 5, 4, 4, 3, 4, 3, 2, 1, 2, 4, 5, 6, 5, 3, 4, 3, 2, 3, 4. How many onions should be put in each bag?

8. Ten typists applied for a secretarial job and were tested for their typing speeds. The speeds which they attained in words per minute were as follows: 50, 52, 57, 59, 51, 62, 51, 48, 60, 54. Calculate the mean typing speed and determine how many typists attained a speed greater than the mean.

9. Fran purchased 25 shares of Apple Inc. at $10/share, 30 shares of Blue Inc. at $15/share, and 40 shares of Link Inc. at $8/share. Determine the following.

(a) mean price per share of stock

(b) median price per share of stock

10. The King Manufacturing Company employs 50 people. Last year the average number of overtime hours per employee was 200. Based on a 40 h week and a 50 week operating year, does the King Co. need any additional employees? If so, how many?

C 11. The lifetime of a certain brand of tires has a mean of 32 000 km and a median of 24 000 km. Describe the performance of these tires.

10.11 PROBABILITY — POSSIBLE OUTCOMES

Blaise Pascal

Pierre Fermat

A problem in probability is the opposite of a problem in statistical inference. In probability we start with a population about which we have total information and then proceed to make statements about a sample from the population. For example, the faces of a die are marked with dots from 1 to 6. The numbers 1, 2, 3, 4, 5, 6 constitute the total population under consideration. If we roll a die, the "number" that ends "face up" is the sample of the population. Probability theory is concerned with the statements which can be made about this sample since we know the total population.

Probability theory has long been associated with games of chance. The first book on the subject was written by the Italian mathematician Girolamo Cardano (1501–1576) who supported himself as a professional gambler for several years. Later the French mathematicians Blaise Pascal (1623–1662) and Pierre Fermat (1601–1665) founded modern probability theory.

When a single die is rolled, there are six equally likely outcomes which we can picture as a tree diagram.

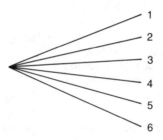

The set of possible outcomes 1, 2, 3, 4, 5, 6 is called the sample space

Now consider the more difficult problem of rolling a pair of dice. In order to better understand the problem, assume that one die is black and the other white. The possible outcomes are

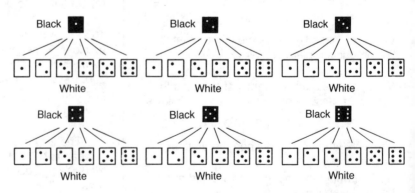

The sample space may also be written as follows.
{(1, 1), (1, 2), ..., (2, 1), ..., (3, 1), (3, 2), ..., (6, 6)}

INVESTIGATION

Usually we are interested in the total of a pair of dice. Complete the following table in your notebook.

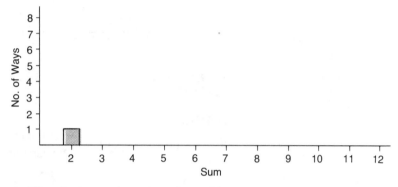

Complete the following bar graph in your notebook, taking data from the table.

1. What is the total number of possible outcomes when a pair of dice is rolled?

2. In how many ways can the dice total 6?

3. In how many ways can the dice total 9?

4. In how many ways can the dice total 7 or 11?

5. In how many ways can the dice total 2 or 12?

EXERCISE 10.11

B 1. List the sample space for each of the following experiments.

(a) A card is drawn from a deck of playing cards and you are interested in the colour of the suit.

(b) A card is drawn from a deck of playing cards and you are interested in the suit of the card.

(c) A coin is tossed and a die is rolled.

2. A bag contains four balls: one red, one blue, one green, and one yellow. List the sample space if you select in the following manner.

(a) one at a time
(b) two at a time
(c) three at a time
(d) four at a time

10.12 THE PROBABILITY FORMULA

The probability of an event E is often denoted by P(E).

When a die is rolled there is only one way in six for the die to turn up the number 5, and so we say that the probability of rolling a 5 is $\frac{1}{6}$. In symbols we write

$$P(5) = \frac{1}{6}$$

In general, if a sample space consists of N equally likely outcomes and if S of those outcomes are considered successful (or favourable) for an event E, then we define probability as follows.

$$\text{Probability of an event E} = \frac{\text{number of successful outcomes}}{\text{total number of possible outcomes}}$$

$$P(E) = \frac{S}{N}$$

EXAMPLE 1. What is the probability of a tossed coin landing heads?

SOLUTION:

$$P(H) = \text{Probability (head)} = \frac{\text{number of successful outcomes}}{\text{total number of possible outcomes}}$$

$$P(H) = \frac{1}{2}$$

This means that you could expect a head to occur one-half the number of times a coin is tossed.

EXAMPLE 2. What is the probability that the card you select from a deck of cards is a heart?

SOLUTION:

$$P(\text{heart}) = \text{Probability (heart)} = \frac{\text{number of hearts}}{\text{total number of cards}}$$

$$= \frac{13}{52}$$

$$= \frac{1}{4}$$

EXAMPLE 3. When a pair of dice is rolled what is the probability that the outcome is a 6? That the outcome is 11?

SOLUTION:

$$P(6) = \frac{\text{number of favourable outcomes}}{\text{total number of possible outcomes}} = \frac{5}{36}$$

$$P(11) = \frac{2}{36}$$

$$= \frac{1}{18}$$

EXERCISE 10.12

B 1. A card is drawn from a deck of cards. What is the probability that it is the following?

(a) a 4
(b) a face card
(c) a spade
(d) a red face card
(e) a club face card

2. Two decks of cards are thoroughly mixed. One card is selected. What is the probability that it is the following?

(a) a diamond
(b) an eight
(c) a face card
(d) the ace of spades

3. Use the results of Investigation from the previous section to determine the probability of the following sums when a pair of dice is rolled.

(a) P(11)　(b) P(3)　(c) P(6)　(d) P(8)
(e) P(7)　(f) P(9)　(g) P(1)　(h) P(10)

4. A drawer contains 6 black socks, 4 grey socks, 3 red socks, and 1 blue sock. If you select 1 sock from the drawer, what is the probability that it is the following?

(a) black　　(b) blue　　(c) red

5. A box contains 10 tickets. One ticket is drawn from the box and the person whose name is on the ticket wins a prize. What is the probability that Tom wins if his name is on the following?

(a) three tickets
(b) one ticket
(c) six tickets
(d) ten tickets
(e) none of the tickets

6. The data on the students in the computer club are as follows.

Age	Girls	Boys
13	3	2
14	5	6
15	8	9
16	1	3

If a student is selected at random what is the probability that the student is the following?

(a) a boy
(b) 15 years old
(c) a 13 year-old girl
(d) a 15 year-old boy
(e) less than 15 years old
(f) 17 years old

7. Two regular tetrahedrons (triangular pyramids) are made. Each has four faces. The faces are numbered 1, 2, 3, 4. If the tetrahedrons are treated as dice and rolled, make a bar graph to show the possible outcomes. Calculate the probability of the following.

(a) rolling 5
(b) rolling 7
(c) rolling 2
(d) rolling 9

8. If an event will never happen, what is its probability of occurring? If an event is certain to happen, what is its probability of occurring?

10.13 PROBABILITY FROM 0 TO 1

In the previous section it was possible to calculate the probability of a certain event since the sample space was made up of events that were equally likely. However, it is sometimes necessary to determine the probability of an event when possible outcomes are not equally likely.

For example, when a professional baseball player comes up to bat there are two possible outcomes.

(a) he gets a hit
(b) he doesn't get a hit

We cannot say that the probability that he gets a hit is $\frac{1}{2}$ since the possible outcomes are not equally likely. The probability that he will get a hit is determined experimentally. After many times at bat we determine the probability that he gets a hit. We call the result his batting average.

The probability of an event occurring can be marked on a scale starting at 0 and extending to 1. If an event is certain to happen, the probability of occurrence is 1. If an event can never happen, the probability of occurrence is 0.

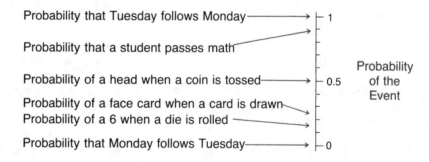

Probability that Tuesday follows Monday ⟶ ─ 1

Probability that a student passes math

Probability of a head when a coin is tossed ⟶ ─ 0.5   Probability of the Event

Probability of a face card when a card is drawn

Probability of a 6 when a die is rolled ⟶

Probability that Monday follows Tuesday ⟶ ─ 0

EXERCISE 10.13

B 1. In his last 150 times at bat Joe got 60 hits. What is the probability that he gets a hit on his next time at bat?

2. A magazine subscription service that solicits business by telephone has determined that for every 400 telephone calls made there will be 88 orders of which 80 are actually paid for.

(a) What is the probability that on any given call a solicitor will receive an order?
(b) What is the probability that a solicitor will receive an order that will be paid for?

3. Drop a handful of thumbtacks on a table and count the number of "points up" and "points down." Repeat the experiment several times. Using your data, calculate the probability of a thumbtack landing "point down" when tossed.

4. A quality controller at the Bright Light bulb manufacturing company tests a sample of the bulbs that come off the production line. Of the 120 bulbs tested, 3 were found to be defective.

(a) What is the probability of a bulb being defective?

(b) If 10 000 bulbs are produced each day, how many should be defective?

5. A biologist tested a new vaccine and found that for 1000 tests it was successful 990 times.
(a) What is the probability of the vaccine being successful?
(b) If the vaccine is used on 25 000 people, how many successes can be expected?

6. After one week the owner of an antique shop classified the customers in the following manner.

	Purchase	No Purchase	Total
Male	50	160	210
Female	60	190	250

(a) What is the probability that a customer is a male? a female?
(b) When a customer enters the store, what is the probability of a purchase?
(c) If a purchase is made, what is the probability that the purchaser is a female?

7. The following table gives the times at bat and number of hits for eight members of a baseball team.

Name	AB	Hits
Robinson	142	52
Kaline	163	65
Mantle	155	45
Ruth	134	35
Gehrig	146	41
Williams	122	42
Jackson	135	38
Carew	141	40

(a) Calculate the probability of each player getting a hit on the next time at bat (correct to 3 decimal places).
(b) What is the team batting average?

BUFFON'S NEEDLE PROBLEM

The problem which has made Buffon's name famous in the history of probability is his needle problem. It was originally performed with needles, but toothpicks will work just as well. On a piece of paper (or cardboard) construct a set of parallel lines with the distance between them equal to the length of the toothpicks.

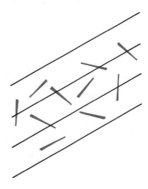

Now drop several toothpicks on the paper and count the number of toothpicks which land touching one of the lines. Repeat the experiment until you have dropped 200 toothpicks. Using this information, estimate the probability of a toothpick touching a line when it is dropped on the paper.

Buffon stated that $\pi = \dfrac{2}{P}$, where P is the probability of a toothpick touching a line. Using your value of P, calculate the value of π by this method.

10.14 PROBLEM SOLVING

1. How many numbers between 1 and 200 begin and end with a 3?

2. There are five students on the executive council of the judo club. They need to appoint a committee of 3 from the 5 to represent the club at the national meeting. How many different groups of 3 members are possible?

3. Each year a car loses one-fifth of its value in the previous year. Rick's three year-old sports car is worth $25 800. How much was the car worth new?

4. XY and YZ are diagonals on two faces of a cube.

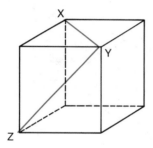

What is the measure of ∠XYZ.

5. If AO = OB; OC = CB, and AB = 20 cm, calculate the area of the shaded region to the nearest tenth. (Use π = 3.14.)

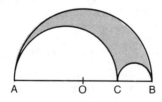

6. Adult tickets for the art show cost $5.50. Student tickets cost $4.25. The cash box contained a float of $210.75 before the ticket booth opened. If 146 student tickets were sold and the cash box contained $1986.25 when ticket sales were finished, how many adult tickets were sold?

7. Peter has written four history tests and his average is 78. What mark will he have to get on the next test to raise his average to 80?

8. Eight square sheets of paper, all the same size, have been arranged as shown.

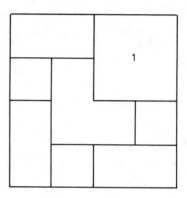

Number the squares in order from the top to the bottom.

9. Supply the missing information and solve the problem.
   On May 20, 1927, Charles Lindbergh left Roosevelt Field, N.Y., alone in the plane "Spirit of St. Louis." He landed at Le Bourget airfield in Paris 33.5 h later. What was the average speed of the flight?

10. A bank manager has eight gold coins. One of the coins is counterfeit and has a mass slightly less than each of the seven identical legal coins. The bank manager has a balance with two pans.

How can the counterfeit coin be identified with only two weighings?

11. A commuter train is operated by three people named Jones, Roberts, and Lee. They are the engineer, computer operator, and conductor, but not necessarily in that order. There are three passengers on the train named Dr. Jones, Dr. Roberts, and Dr. Lee.

(1) Dr. Roberts lives in Toronto.
(2) Dr. Jones earns exactly $80 000 a year.
(3) The conductor lives half-way between Toronto and Montreal.
(4) Lee beat the computer operator at chess.
(5) The conductor's next door neighbour, one of the passengers, earns exactly three times as much as the conductor.
(6) The passenger, whose name is the same as the conductor's, lives in Montreal.

What are the names of the engineer, computer operator, and conductor?

12. July 1 is on a Monday. How many more Mondays are there in the year?

13. Express the continued fraction in the form $\frac{a}{b}$:

$$1 + \cfrac{1}{1 + \cfrac{1}{3}}$$

14. How many triangles are there?

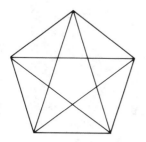

15. Find the missing number.

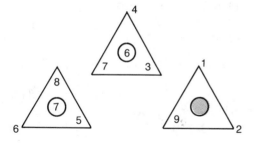

Can you walk through a playing card? You can by carefully cutting the card as shown.

1. Fold the card.

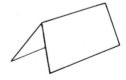

2. Cut the card.

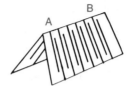

3. Cut the folded side from A to B as shown below.

Walk through the loop.

Put the numbers from 1 to 9 in the spaces to make the statements true.

$$\blacksquare - \blacksquare + \blacksquare = 4$$
$$\blacksquare + \blacksquare \div \blacksquare = 4$$
$$\blacksquare \times \blacksquare \div \blacksquare = 4$$

10.15 REVIEW EXERCISE

1. Draw graphs to display the following data.
(a) The number of home games by the days of the week played by the Toronto Blue Jays.

Day	Number of games
Monday	12
Tuesday	13
Wednesday	9
Thursday	5
Friday	14
Saturday	14
Sunday	14

(b) Babe Ruth's home run totals while playing for the New York Yankees.

Year	Home runs
1920	54
1921	59
1922	35
1923	41
1924	46
1925	25
1926	47
1927	60
1928	54
1929	46
1930	49
1931	46
1932	41
1933	34
1934	22

(c) The James family spends its income as follows.

Food	$14 000
Shelter	$12 000
Clothing	$ 4 000
Savings	$ 9 000
Car	$ 5 000
Misc.	$ 6 000
	$50 000

2. Take a random sample of thirty pages from this book. Record whether or not each page of the sample has a photograph on it. Use these results to estimate the number of pages in the book that have photographs on them.

3. The bar graph shows the favourite type of television show chosen by students at Westdale High School.

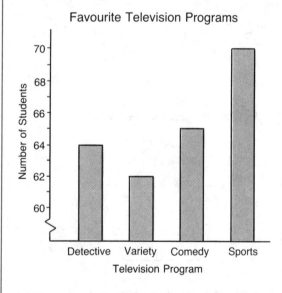

(a) How many students prefer the following?
   (i) detective programs
   (ii) variety shows
   (iii) comedy shows
   (iv) sports events
(b) How many students were surveyed?

4. Determine the mean, median, and mode of the following sets of data.
(a) 6, 8, 15, 7, 9, 6, 5

(b) 5, 10, 11, 23, 14, 7, 33, 14, 5, 1
(c) 33.5, 19.5, 53.2, 15.1, 35.1, 24.7, 16.4, 31.5, 46.4

5. The following are the number of goals scored per game on the goal-tender during the months of November and December.

2, 4, 3, 5, 6, 0, 1, 1, 3, 4, 5,

0, 1, 5, 1, 2, 2, 2, 0, 4, 3

(a) Determine the mean, median, and mode for the data.
(b) What measure is the best indication of the goal-tender's ability?

6. A card is drawn from a deck of cards. What is the probability that it is the following?

(a) a club
(b) a jack
(c) a red king

7. Basketball player Rick Barry attempted 3512 free throws and was successful on 3137. What was his probability of sinking a free throw?

8. An automobile insurance company compiled the following data for 7000 drivers.

Age Group	No Accidents	One Accident	Two or more Accidents	Total
16−20	935	45	20	1000
21−25	910	60	30	1000
26−30	885	74	41	1000
31−35	914	50	36	1000
36−40	903	62	35	1000
41−45	908	52	40	1000
46−50	905	60	35	1000

(a) What is the probability that a 16−20 year-old driver has had no accidents?
(b) What is the probability that 36−40 year-old driver has had one accident?
(c) What is the probability that a 46−50 year-old driver has had more than one accident?

(d) What percent of all drivers under 31 have had no accidents?
(e) What percent of all drivers over 25 have had more than one accident?
(f) What percent of all drivers between 26 and 40 have had one accident?

9. (a) How many possible ways can three people line up at a bus stop?
(b) If you are one of the people, what is the probability that you will be last in line?

MIND BENDER

Six pennies are arranged as shown in the diagram. Move three pennies to form a circle according to the following rules.

1. You can move one penny at a time.

2. You cannot pick up a penny.

3. When you complete a move, the penny you have moved must be touching at least 2 other pennies.

10.16 CHAPTER 10 TEST

1. The table gives the average noon temperature by month in Dry Creek for one year. Display this information on a broken line graph.

Month	J	F	M	A	M	J	J	A	S	O	N	D
Temp °C	18	20	21	22	25	26	30	29	28	20	19	17

2. The table gives the speed of several animals. Display this information on a bar graph.

Animal	Cheetah	Hyena	Bear	Lion	Horse
Speed (km/h)	110	70	50	85	80

3. Calculate the mean, median, and mode for each set of numbers.
(a) 8, 11, 9, 13, 12, 10, 9, 8, 11, 9
(b) 131, 153, 127, 144, 173, 166, 121

4. A bag contains 5 red cubes, 3 blue cubes, and 2 yellow cubes. One cube is selected from the bag. What is the probability of the following?
(a) the cube is red
(b) the cube is blue
(c) the cube is red or yellow

5. A penny, a nickel, and a dime are tossed at the same time. What is the probability of getting the following?
(a) three heads
(b) two heads and a tail

PERIMETER, AREA, AND VOLUME

CHAPTER

11

The secret of efficiency is to be well attuned with ourselves
and our surroundings.
Bliss Carman

LINEAR UNITS

The following table shows the set of linear metric units that are used frequently.

Quantity	Unit	Symbol	Relationship
length	kilometre metre centimetre millimetre	km m cm mm	1 km = 1000 m 1 m = 100 cm 1 cm = 10 mm

We can place the linear metric units on a place value chart.

kilometre	hectometre	decametre	metre	decimetre	centimetre	millimetre
km	hm	da	m	dm	cm	mm
1000 m	100 m	10 m	1 m	0.1 m	0.01 m	0.001 m

AREA UNITS

The following table shows the set of area metric units that are used frequently.

Quantity	Unit	Symbol	Relationship
area	square kilometre hectare square metre square centimetre square millimetre	km² ha m² cm² mm²	1 km² = 100 ha 1 ha = 10 000 m² 1 m² = 10 000 cm² 1 cm² = 100 mm²

We can place the area metric units on a place value chart.

square kilometre	square hectometre or hectare	square decametre or are	square metre	square decimetre	square centimetre	square millimetre
km²	ha	da²	m²	dm²	cm²	mm²
1 000 000 m²	10 000 m²	100 m²	1 m²	0.01 m²	0.000 1 m²	0.000 001 m²

VOLUME AND CAPACITY UNITS

The basic units for volume and capacity are the cubic metre (m^3) and the litre (L).
An object that has a capacity of one litre (1 L) holds 1000 cm^3.

The following table shows the units for volume and capacity.

Quantity	Unit	Symbol	Relationship
volume	cubic metre cubic decimetre cubic centimetre	m^3 dm^3 cm^3	1 m^3 = 1000 dm^3 1 dm^3 = 1000 cm^3
capacity	kilolitre litre millilitre	kL L mL	1 kL = 1000 L 1 L = 1000 mL

We can place the volume and capacity metric units on a place value chart.

cubic metre or kilolitre	cubic decimetre or litre	cubic centimetre or millilitre
m^3 or kL	dm^3 or L	cm^3 or mL
1000 L	1 L	0.001 L

MASS UNITS

The common units for mass are shown in the following table.

Quantity	Unit	Symbol	Relationship
mass	tonne kilogram gram milligram	t kg g mg	1 t = 1000 kg 1 kg = 1000 g 1 g = 1000 mg

We can relate the metric units for mass to a place value chart.

kilogram	gram	milligram
kg	g	mg
1000 g	1 g	0.001 g

EXERCISE

1. Express in metres.
(a) 4.4 km
(b) 7000 cm
(c) 0.6 km
(d) 350 cm

2. Express in centimetres.
(a) 1.3 m
(b) 450 mm
(c) 0.77 m
(d) 0.25 mm

3. Express in hectares.
(a) 75 000 m²
(b) 10 km²
(c) 0.5 km²
(d) 5 km²

4. Express in square metres.
(a) 1.2 km²
(b) 3 ha
(c) 0.7 km²
(d) 0.2 ha

5. Express in square centimetres.
(a) 0.8 m²
(b) 300 mm²
(c) 1500 mm²
(d) 0.25 m²

6. Express in litres.
(a) 3500 mL
(b) 0.6 mL
(c) 5.2 kL
(d) 0.25 kL

7. Express in kilograms.
(a) 8.4 t
(b) 8000 g
(c) 0.5 t
(d) 75 g

8. Light travels at a speed of 10^9 km/h. A light year is the distance light will travel in one year.
(a) Express this distance in kilometres.
(b) Express this distance in metres.

9. A parking space for a car has an area of 10 m². Canada has an area of about 9 976 000 km². How many cars could you park in Canada?

10. The area of a pin-head is 1 mm². How many pin-heads would fit in 1 cm²?

11. Lake Superior has an area of 82 414 km². Express this area in hectares.

12. The Pacific Ocean has a volume of about 700 000 000 km³. How many litres is that?

13. A blue whale has a mass of 138 000 kg. An African elephant has a mass of 6300 kg. How many times heavier is the whale?

14. An ant can lift objects that are 50 times its own mass. Suppose you were as strong as an ant. How many horses could you lift? (A horse has a mass of about 450 kg.)

In the universe there are objects known as black holes. A black hole results when a heavy star collapses under the force of its own gravity. The force of gravity is so intense that even light cannot escape, so it appears black.

The Earth has a mass of about 6×10^{24} kg.

 The black dot shows the actual size of a black hole with the same mass as the Earth.

PROBLEM SOLVING: SEARCH FOR A PATTERN

1. Find the missing numbers.

(a)

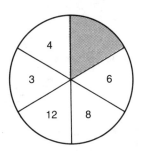

(b)

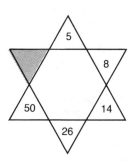

(c)

2	5	9	14	
4	8	13	19	

(d)

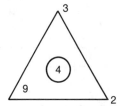

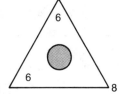

2. Find the missing numbers.

(a) 2, 5, 6, 8, 10, 11, ■, ■

(b)

9	81	90
8	64	72
5		

(c)

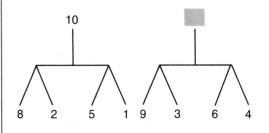

(d)

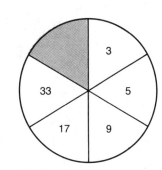

(e)

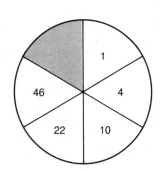

11.1 PERIMETER OF POLYGONS

A polygon is a closed figure formed by straight line segments. The perimeter of a polygon is found by adding the lengths of each side.

EXAMPLE 1. Find the perimeter of the polygon.

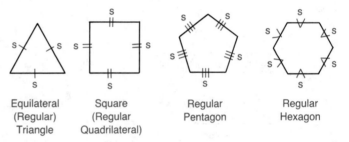

SOLUTION:
$$P = 8.6 + 9.1 + 10.3 + 7 + 6.6$$
$$= 41.6$$

The perimeter is 41.6 cm.

In a regular polygon, all sides have the same length and all angles are equal.

Equilateral (Regular) Triangle	Square (Regular Quadrilateral)	Regular Pentagon	Regular Hexagon

We can find the perimeter of a regular polygon by multiplying the number of sides (n) by the length of each side (s).

$$\boxed{\text{In a regular polygon, } P = n \times s}$$

EXAMPLE 2. Find the perimeter of the regular hexagon.

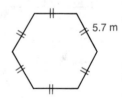

SOLUTION:
$$P = n \times s$$
$$P = 6 \times 5.7$$
$$= 34.2$$

The perimeter is 34.2 m.

One of the most common polygons is a rectangle.

The perimeter of a rectangle is
$$P = \ell + w + \ell + w$$
$$= 2\ell + 2w$$
$$= 2(\ell + w)$$

EXAMPLE 3. Use a calculator to calculate the perimeter of the rectangle.

SOLUTION:

$$P = 2(\ell + w)$$
$$P = 2(39.6 + 27.3)$$

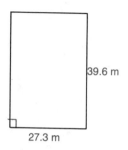

39.6 m

27.3 m

Press

| C | 3 | 9 | · | 6 | + | 2 | 7 | · | 3 |

| = | × | 2 | = |

The display is   133.8

The perimeter is 133.8 m.

EXERCISE 11.1

1. Find the perimeter of each regular polygon.

(a)

15.8 cm

(b)

36.54 m

(c)

146.8 km

(d)

80.4 cm

(e)

231.6 m

(f)

0.64 cm

2. Calculate the perimeter of each of the following.

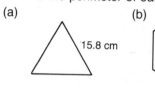

(a)

11.5 m   18.4 m

13.3 m   22.4 m

(b)

156.3 m   142.5 m

186.7 m

(c)

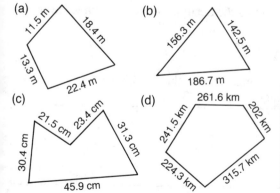

21.5 cm   23.4 cm

30.4 cm

45.9 cm

31.3 cm

(d)

261.6 km

241.5 km   202 km

224.3 km   315.7 km

3. Find the missing length in each of the following.

(a)

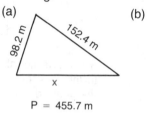

98.2 m   152.4 m

x

P = 455.7 m

(b)

0.65 cm

y

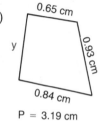

0.93 cm

0.84 cm

P = 3.19 cm

4. Each side of a regular octagon is 33.8 cm long. What would be the length of each side of a square having the same perimeter as the octagon?

5. Frank has been hired to put new trim around the inside of the windows of an office building. Each window measures 1.9 m by 2.8 m. There are 182 windows.

(a) How much trim will Frank need?
(b) The trim costs $8.99/m. How much will it cost to buy the trim?
(c) It takes Frank 1.5 h to complete one window. Frank earns $16.75/h. How much should he charge for the job, including the cost of the trim?

6. The distance between the bases on a major league baseball diamond is 27.45 m. What is the shortest distance a player must cover to score a run?

11.2 CIRCUMFERENCE OF A CIRCLE

The perimeter of a circle is called the circumference (C).

A straight line drawn through the centre of a circle is called the diameter (d).

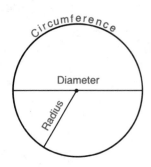

Half of the diameter is called the radius (r).

The ratio of the circumference to the diameter in a circle is a constant called pi (π).

$$\pi = \frac{\text{circumference}}{\text{diameter}} = 3.141\ 59\ ...$$

π is an irrational number, also known as a non-repeating, non-terminating decimal. The number of decimal places used depends on the desired accuracy.

APPROXIMATIONS OF π

$\pi = 3.141\ 592\ 653\ 5897\ ...$

Using a calculator when we press $\boxed{\text{C}}$ $\boxed{\pi}$

the display is $\boxed{3.1415926}$

The mixed number $3\frac{1}{7}$ is an approximation of π, accurate to the nearest hundredth, or to two decimal places.

$$3\tfrac{1}{7} = \tfrac{22}{7} = 3.142\ 857\ ...$$

Use a calculator to determine the accuracy of each of the following approximations of π.

1. $\dfrac{7604}{2420}$ 2. $\dfrac{4908}{1562}$ 3. $\dfrac{355}{113}$

When performing calculations without using the $\boxed{\pi}$ key on a calculator, it is customary to use $\pi = 3.14$.

The circumference of a circle is
$$C = \pi d$$

$$C = 2\pi$$

EXAMPLE. Use a calculator and π = 3.14 to calculate the circumference of the circles to the nearest tenth.

(a)

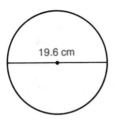

19.6 cm

(b)

413 m

SOLUTION:

(a) C = πd
    C = 3.14 × 19.6

Press C 3 · 1 4 × 1 9 · 6 =

Display 61.544

The circumference is 61.5 cm.

(b) C = 2πr
    C = 2 × 3.14 × 413

Press C 2 × 3 · 1 4 × 4 1 3 =

Display 2593.64

The circumference is 2593.6 m.

EXERCISE 11.2

B 1. Calculate the circumference of these circles to the nearest tenth. Use π = 3.14.

(a)

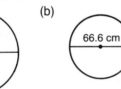

180 m

(b)

66.6 cm

(c)

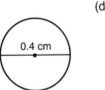

0.4 cm

(d)

18 m

2. The circumference of a circle is 357.96 cm. Use π = 3.14 and calculate the length of the diameter.

3. The circumference of a circle is 1186.92 m. Use π = 3.14 and calculate the length of the radius.

4. Calculate the perimeter.

(a)

|← 12 m →|

6 m

(b)

|← 8 cm →|

3 cm

5. (a) Calculate the circumference of the large circle.
(b) Calculate the total circumference of the three smaller circles.
(c) Draw a conclusion.

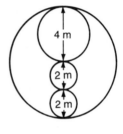

4 m

2 m

2 m

6. (a) The diameter of the earth at the equator is approximately 12 750 km. Use π = 3.14 and calculate the circumference of the earth to the nearest thousand.
(b) The closest the moon comes to the earth is about 357 000 km. How many planet Earths, placed side by side, would it take to reach the moon from the earth.

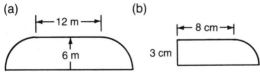

(c) The sun is approximately 150 000 000 km from the earth. How many planet Earths, placed side by side, would it take to reach the sun from the earth.

11.3 AREA OF RECTANGLES AND SQUARES

The area of a figure is a measure of the surface it covers.
The formula for the area of a rectangle can be shown in the following examples.
Each square is 1 cm by 1 cm.

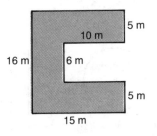

Rectangle	Area by Counting	Length	Width	Length × Width
A	20	5	4	5 × 4 = 20
B	28	7	4	7 × 4 = 28
C	45	15	3	15 × 3 = 45

Area of a rectangle = length × width

Area of a rectangle

$A = \ell w$

In the case of a square, all sides are equal.

Area of a square

$A = s^2$

EXAMPLE. Calculate the area.

10 m
5 m
16 m
6 m
5 m
15 m

SOLUTION:

Adding Areas

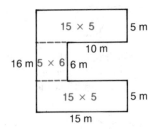

$A = 75\ m^2 + 30\ m^2 + 75\ m^2$
  $= 180\ m^2$

Subtracting Areas

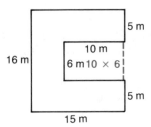

$A = 16\ m \times 15\ m - 10\ m \times 6\ m$
  $= 240\ m^2 - 60\ m^2$
  $= 180\ m^2$

EXERCISE 11.3

B 1. Find the area of each rectangle.

(a)
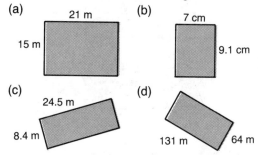
21 m
15 m

(b)
7 cm
9.1 cm

(c)
24.5 m
8.4 m

(d)
131 m
64 m

2. Find the area of each of these squares.

(a)
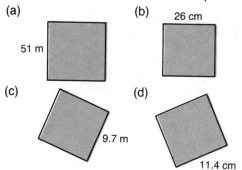
51 m

(b)
26 cm

(c)
9.7 m

(d)
11.4 cm

3. Find the area of each of these rectangular shapes.

(a)
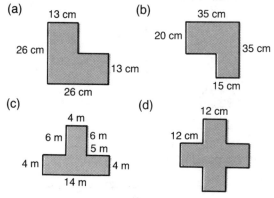
13 cm
26 cm
13 cm
26 cm

(b)
35 cm
20 cm
35 cm
15 cm

(c)
4 m
6 m   6 m
5 m
4 m   4 m
14 m

(d)
12 cm
12 cm
4 m

4. Find the area of each of the following rectangular shapes.

(a)
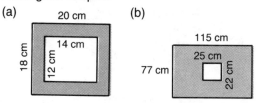
20 cm
14 cm
18 cm
12 cm

(b)
115 cm
25 cm
77 cm
22 cm

5. Calculate the area of a page from this book.

6. Carpeting costs $21.50/m². Find the cost of carpeting the hotel lobby.

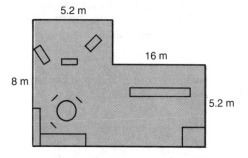
5.2 m
16 m
8 m
5.2 m

7. The base of the Pyramid of Khufu is a square with an area of 52 900 m². What is the length of each side of the square?

8. The Taj Mahal in India is built on a square piece of land that has an area of 9101.16 m². What is the length of each side of the square?

MIND BENDER

A large fountain in the centre of the fairground sits on a concrete pad 20 m by 30 m, which is surrounded by a moat 3 m wide. How can a worker cross the moat using only two planks measuring 3 m long each?

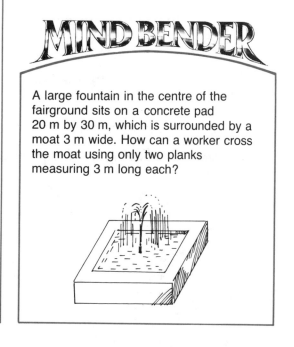

11.4 PARALLELOGRAMS, TRIANGLES, AND TRAPEZOIDS

PARALLELOGRAMS

We can write the dimensions of a rectangle in terms of base and height.

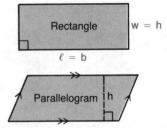

A parallelogram is a figure with opposite sides parallel. The diagram shows the base and height of a parallelogram.

The formula for area of a parallelogram is found by relating the figure to a rectangle. Slide triangle X to position Y.

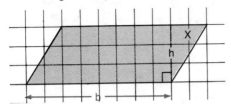

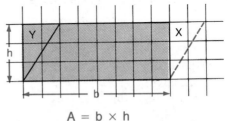

$A = b \times h$
$A = 8 \times 3$
$= 24$ square units

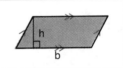

Area of a parallelogram
$A = bh$

TRIANGLES

For a triangle
$A = \frac{1}{2} \times b \times h$

We can show this relationship by drawing the diagonal of a parallelogram.

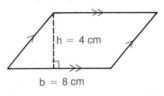

$h = 4$ cm

$b = 8$ cm

$A = b \times h$
$A = 8 \times 4$
$= 32$ cm²

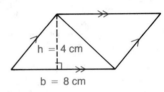

$h = 4$ cm

$b = 8$ cm

$A = \frac{1}{2} \times b \times h$
$A = \frac{1}{2} \times 8 \times 4$
$= 16$ cm²

TRAPEZOIDS

A trapezoid has only one pair of sides parallel. The formula for area of a trapezoid is found by dividing it into two triangles.

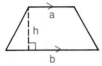

The height of the triangles, h, is the distance between the parallel lines.

Area of a trapezoid

$$A = \tfrac{1}{2}ah + \tfrac{1}{2}bh$$

$$= \tfrac{1}{2}(a + b)h$$

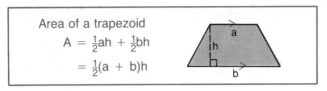

EXERCISE 11.4

1. Calculate the area.

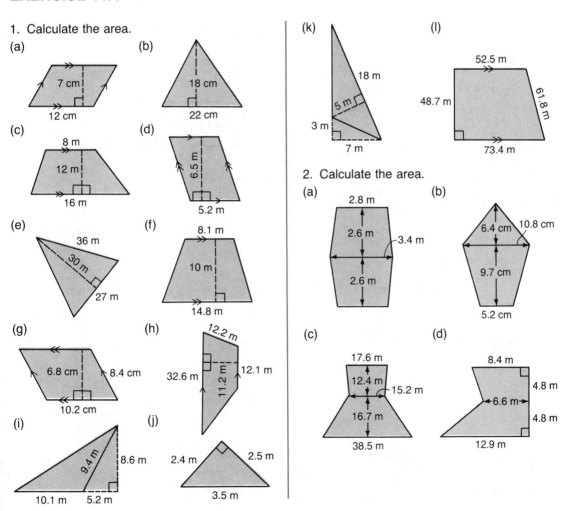

(a)

7 cm
12 cm

(b)

18 cm
22 cm

(c)

8 m
12 m
16 m

(d)

6.5 m
5.2 m

(e)

36 m
30 m
27 m

(f)

8.1 m
10 m
14.8 m

(g)

6.8 cm
8.4 cm
10.2 cm

(h)

12.2 m
32.6 m
11.2 m
12.1 m

(i)

9.4 m
8.6 m
10.1 m   5.2 m

(j)

2.4 m   2.5 m
3.5 m

(k)

18 m
5 m
3 m
7 m

(l)

52.5 m
48.7 m
61.8 m
73.4 m

2. Calculate the area.

(a)

2.8 m
2.6 m   3.4 m
2.6 m

(b)

6.4 cm   10.8 cm
9.7 cm
5.2 cm

(c)

17.6 m
12.4 m   15.2 m
16.7 m
38.5 m

(d)

8.4 m
4.8 m
6.6 m
4.8 m
12.9 m

11.5 AREA OF A CIRCLE

By transforming a circle into a parallelogram, the formula for the area of a circle can be found.

1. Divide the circle into sectors as shown.

Circumference
C = 2πr

2. Separate the circle along any diameter to form 2 semi-circles.

$\frac{1}{2}C = \frac{1}{2}(2\pi r)$
$= \pi r$

---

3. Open up each semi-circle and place the two sections together to form a parallelogram.

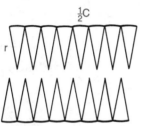

$\frac{1}{2}C$

r

height = r
base = πr

4. Find the area of the parallelogram.

b × h   or   πr × r

∴ the area of the circle, A, is

πr × r
= π × r × r
= πr²

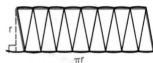

πr

The formula for the area of a circle can also be approximated by dividing a circle into n congruent triangles.
The area of each triangle is given by

$\frac{1}{2}b \times h$

For n triangles, we have

A (circle) = n($\frac{1}{2}$bh)

= $\frac{1}{2}$nbh

As the number of triangles increases, the sum of all the bases, nb, approaches the circumference 2πr.
The length of n approaches r.

A (circle) = $\frac{1}{2}$nbh

= $\frac{1}{2}$(2πr)r

= πr²

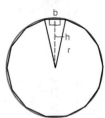

The area of a circle is
A = πr²

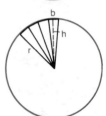

EXERCISE 11.5

1. Find the area of each of the following circles, to the nearest tenth.

(a)

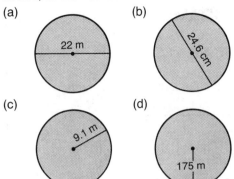

22 m

(b)

24.6 cm

(c)

9.1 m

(d)

175 m

2. Find the area of each figure to the nearest tenth. Use π = 3.14.

(a)

4.1 m

(b)

56 cm

(c)

14.3 m

(d)

7.9 cm

3. Calculate the area of the shaded region to the nearest tenth. Use π = 3.14.

(a)

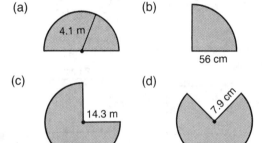

4 m

5.6 m

5.6 m

(b)

80 m

4. Calculate the area of the playing field.

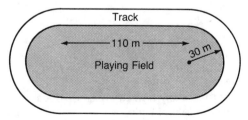

Track

110 m

Playing Field

30 m

5. Calculate the area.

(a)

◄10 m►

5 m

(b)

◄6 cm►

4 cm

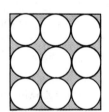

6. Sandria tied her dog with a rope to one corner of a shed. The shed is 8 m long and 6 m wide. The rope is 10 m long.

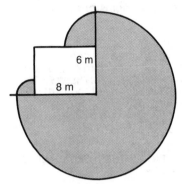

6 m

8 m

Calculate the area within the dog's reach.

7. Both squares have sides 2 m long. Calculate the area of the shaded regions. Express answers in terms of π.

(a)

(b)

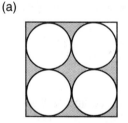

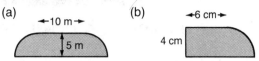

MIND BENDER

Determine the pattern. Find the missing number.

12	8	13	7
13	41	22	51
6	11	7	10
59	47	69	

MICRO MATH

11.6 PERIMETER COMPUTER PROGRAMS

The following programs can be used to compute the perimeters of plane figures.

The following program can be used to compute the perimeter of a polygon when the lengths of the sides are known.

```
NEW
10 PRINT"PERIMETER OF A POLYGON"
20 INPUT"HOW MANY SIDES?";N
30 PRINT"ENTER THE LENGTHS"
40 PRINT"ONE AT A TIME"
50 P=0
60 FOR I=1 TO N
70 INPUT S
80 P=P+S
90 NEXT I
100 PRINT"THE PERIMETER IS";P
110 END
RUN
```

The following program can be used to compute the perimeter of a rectangle when the length and width are known.

```
NEW
10 PRINT"PERIMETER OF A RECTANGLE"
20 INPUT"WIDTH IS";W
30 INPUT"LENGTH IS";L
40 P=2*(L+W)
50 PRINT"THE PERIMETER IS";P
60 END
RUN
```

The following program computes the circumference of a circle when the radius is known.

```
NEW
10 PRINT"CIRCUMFERENCE OF A CIRCLE"
20 INPUT"RADIUS IS";R
30 C=2*3.14*R
40 PRINT"THE CIRCUMFERENCE IS";C
50 END
RUN
```

To make any of these programs reiterative, insert the following statements in the program before the END statement.

```
PRINT"ANOTHER QUESTION? Y OR N"
INPUT Z$
IF Z$ ="Y" THEN 20
```

EXERCISE 11.6

1. Find the perimeter of each figure.

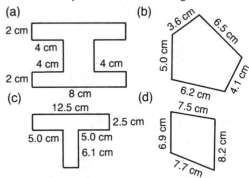

(a)

(b)

(c)

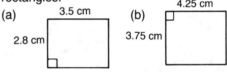

(d)

2. Find the perimeter of the following rectangles.

(a) 3.5 cm, 2.8 cm

(b) 4.25 cm, 3.75 cm

(c) ℓ = 3.6 m and w = 2.7 m
(d) ℓ = 5.125 m and w = 3.625 m

3. Calculate the circumference of each circle. Round answers to the nearest tenth.

(a) d = 246.5 m   (b) r = 47.8 cm
(c) d = 1048 km   (d) r = 157 m

4. Calculate the distance around the track to the nearest tenth.

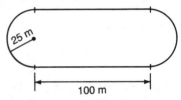

25 m

100 m

5. (a) Calculate the circumference of a 10-speed bicycle wheel.
(b) Approximately how many times does the tire rotate in 2 km?

MICRO MATH

11.7 AREA COMPUTER PROGRAMS

The following programs can be used to compute the areas of plane figures.

RECTANGLE

```
NEW
10 PRINT"AREA OF A RECTANGLE"
20 INPUT"LENGTH IS";L
30 INPUT"WIDTH IS";W
40 A=L*W
50 PRINT"THE AREA IS ";A
60 END
RUN
```

PARALLELOGRAM

```
NEW
10 PRINT"AREA OF A PARALLELOGRAM"
20 INPUT"BASE IS ";B
30 INPUT"HEIGHT IS ";H
40 A=B*H
50 PRINT"THE AREA IS ";A
60 END
RUN
```

TRIANGLE

```
NEW
10 PRINT"AREA OF A TRIANGLE"
20 INPUT"BASE IS ";B
30 INPUT"HEIGHT IS ";H
40 A=0.5*B*H
50 PRINT"THE AREA IS ";A
60 END
RUN
```

TRAPEZOID

```
NEW
10 PRINT"AREA OF A TRAPEZOID"
20 INPUT"BASE A IS ";A
30 INPUT"BASE B IS ";B
40 INPUT"HEIGHT H IS ";H
50 X=0.5*(A + B)*H
60 PRINT"THE AREA IS ";X
70 END
RUN
```

CIRCLE

```
NEW
10 PRINT"AREA OF A CIRCLE"
20 INPUT"RADIUS IS ";R
30 A=3.14*R*R
40 PRINT"THE AREA IS ";A
50 END
RUN
```

EXERCISE 11.7

1. Calculate the area of the following rectangles.
(a) ℓ = 52 m, w = 19 m
(b) ℓ = 24.7 m, w = 8.4 m
(c) ℓ = 375 m, w = 248 m

2. Calculate the area of each parallelogram, where
(a) b = 11.6 cm and h = 21.5 cm
(b) b = 21.6 cm and h = 15.7 cm
(c) b = 24.5 m and h = 36.7 m

3. Calculate the area of each triangle, where
(a) b = 30.4 cm and h = 14.6 cm
(b) b = 6.75 cm and h = 6.75 cm
(c) b = 20.0 m and h = 17.3 m

4. Calculate the area of each trapezoid, where
(a) a = 36.4 m, b = 29.8 m, h = 30.4 m
(b) a = 51.2 m, b = 45.5 m, h = 12.4 m
(c) a = 24.6 m, b = 18.4 m, h = 12.2 m

5. Calculate the area of the circles given the following information.
(a) r = 173 m   (b) r = 11.6 m
(c) d = 0.514 m   (d) d = 3892 km

6. Calculate the area of each of the following figures.

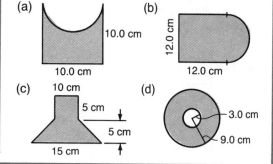

(a) 10.0 cm, 10.0 cm
(b) 12.0 cm, 12.0 cm
(c) 10 cm, 5 cm, 5 cm, 15 cm
(d) 3.0 cm, 9.0 cm

11.8 SURFACE AREA OF PRISMS

Polyhedra are three-dimensional objects with flat surfaces. A polyhedron has faces, edges, and vertices.

Faces are polygons.

Faces meet at edges.

Edges meet at vertices.

A right prism is a polyhedron whose faces are rectangles. The bases of a right prism are parallel congruent polygons. We use the bases to name prisms. Some examples of right prisms are:

| Cube or | Cuboid or | Triangular | Pentagonal |
| Square Prism | Rectangular Prism | Prism | Prism |

To find the surface area of a polyhedron, calculate the sum of the areas of each face.

EXAMPLE. Find the surface area of the right triangular prism.

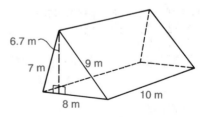

SOLUTION:

Area of Ⓐ $= \frac{1}{2} \times 8 \times 6.7 = 26.8$

Area of both Ⓐ $= \quad 53.6$

Area of Ⓑ $= 10 \times 7 = \quad 70$

Area of Ⓒ $= 10 \times 8 = \quad 80$

Area of Ⓓ $= 10 \times 9 = \underline{\quad 90}$

$\overline{\qquad 293.6}$

The surface area is 293.6 m².

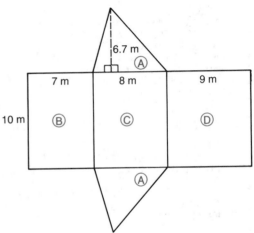

EXERCISE 11.8

B 1. Find the surface area of each of these right prisms.

(a)

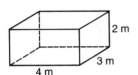
2 m
3 m
4 m

(b)

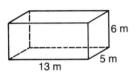
6 m
5 m
13 m

(c)

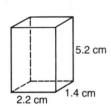
5.2 cm
1.4 cm
2.2 cm

(d)

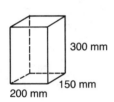
300 mm
150 mm
200 mm

2. Calculate the surface area of the right prisms.

(a)

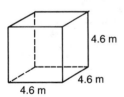
4.6 m
4.6 m
4.6 m

(b)

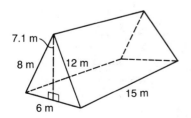
7.1 m
8 m
12 m
15 m
6 m

(c)

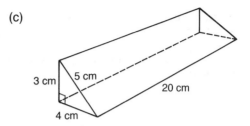
3 cm
5 cm
20 cm
4 cm

3. The dimensions of a mountain climber's tent are shown in the diagram.

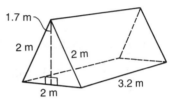
1.7 m
2 m
2 m
3.2 m
2 m

Tent material costs $21.75/m². How much will it cost for the materials to make this tent?

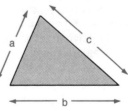

EXTRA

The Greek mathematician, Heron of Alexandria, developed the following formula to calculate the area of a triangle.

$$A = \sqrt{s(s - a)(s - b)(s - c)}$$

where

$$s = \frac{a + b + c}{2}$$

If a = 5 m, b = 6 m, and c = 7 m, then

$$s = \frac{5 + 6 + 7}{2}$$

$$= 9$$

and $A = \sqrt{9(9 - 5)(9 - 6)(9 - 7)}$

$$= \sqrt{9 \times 4 \times 3 \times 2}$$

$$= \sqrt{216}$$

$$\doteq 14.7 \text{ m}^2$$

1. Find the area of the triangles with the given sides.
(a) 6 m, 7 m, 8 m
(b) 24 m, 28 m, 33 m
(c) 421 km, 430 km, 456 km

11.9 SURFACE AREA OF CYLINDERS AND PYRAMIDS

CYLINDERS

The surface area of a right cylinder can be determined using the area formula for a circle and a rectangle.

EXAMPLE 1. Calculate the surface area to the nearest tenth.

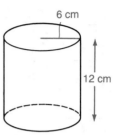

6 cm

12 cm

SOLUTION:

Surface Area = area of bases + area of side
$$= 2 \times (\pi r^2) + 2\pi r \times h$$
$$= 2 \times (3.14 \times 6^2) + (2 \times 3.14 \times 6 \times 12)$$
$$= 678.24$$

The surface area is 678.2 cm².

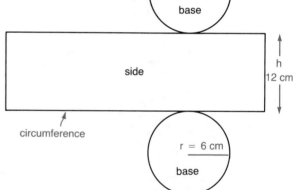

r = 6 cm

base

side

h
12 cm

circumference

r = 6 cm

base

PYRAMIDS

A pyramid has a polygon as base, and the sides are triangles with a common vertex. A right pyramid has a regular polygon as its base and the sides are congruent isosceles triangles.

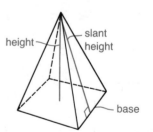

height — slant height

base

In each of the following figures, the base is a polygon. We use the base to name a pyramid.

Triangular
Pyramid

Square
Pyramid

Pentagonal
Pyramid

EXAMPLE 2. Calculate the surface area of the right pyramid.

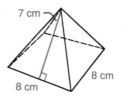

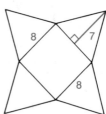

SOLUTION:

Area of base = 8 × 8
= 64

Area of sides = 4($\frac{1}{2}$ × 8 × 7)
= 112

The surface area is 176 cm².

EXERCISE 11.9

B 1. Calculate the surface area of each of the following cylinders to the nearest tenth.

(a)

8 cm

15 cm

(b)

6 m

4.6 m

(c)

7 cm

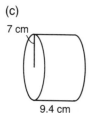

9.4 cm

(d)

20 cm

5 cm

(e)

11 m

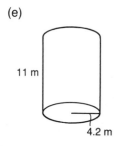

4.2 m

(f)

8.8 cm

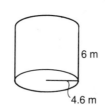

12 cm

2. Calculate the surface area of each right pyramid, to the nearest tenth.

(a)

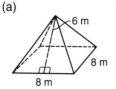

6 m

8 m

8 m

(b)

9 m

15.1 m

15.1 m

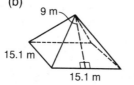

3. A road roller is 2 m wide and has a diameter of 1 m. How much area will it cover in 500 revolutions?

4. A skylight has the shape of a right pyramid. Each side is 2.5 m. The slant height is 1.4 m. Calculate the area of the glass in the skylight.

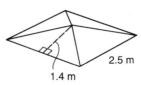

2.5 m

1.4 m

MICRO MATH

```
NEW
10 PRINT"TOTAL AREA"
20 PRINT"OF A CYLINDER"
30 INPUT"RADIUS IS ";R
40 INPUT"HEIGHT IS ";H
50 LET A=2*3.14*R↑2+2*3.14*R*H
60 PRINT"THE SURFACE AREA IS ";A
70 END
RUN
```

1. Calculate the surface area of each cylinder.
(a) r = 10.4 m, h = 22.1 m
(b) d = 46.6 cm, h = 81.7 cm
(c) r = 385 m, h = 764 m

11.10 VOLUME OF PRISMS

The area of a plane figure is measured with squares.
The volume of a polyhedron is measured with cubes.

A rectangular prism is 6 cm long, 3 cm wide,
and 4 cm high. When 1 cm cubes are placed
in the prism, each layer will contain 18 cubes.
The prism is 4 cm high so the prism will hold
4 layers. Since there are 18 cubes in each
layer, the prism will hold 18 × 4 or 72 cubes.
   By multiplying the area of the base (18 cm²)
by the height (4 cm) we can determine the
volume of the prism. (72 cm³)

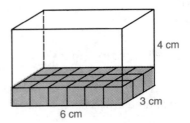

Volume of a prism = (area of base) × height	$V_{prism} = A_{base} \times h$

For a right prism, the area of the base is $\ell \times w$.

The volume of a right prism is

$$V = \ell \times w \times h$$

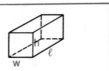

For a triangular prism, the area of the base is $\frac{1}{2} \times b \times h$.

The volume of a right triangular prism is

$$V = (\tfrac{1}{2} \times a \times b) \times h$$

EXAMPLE 1. Calculate the volume.

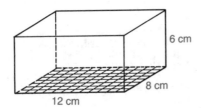

6 cm
8 cm
12 cm

SOLUTION:
$$V = (area\ of\ base) \times height$$
$$V = \ell \times w \times h$$
$$V = 12 \times 8 \times 6$$
$$= 576$$

The volume is 576 cm³.

EXAMPLE 2. Calculate the volume.

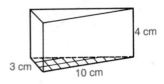

4 cm
3 cm
10 cm

SOLUTION:
$$V = (area\ of\ base) \times height$$
$$V = (\tfrac{1}{2} \times 10 \times 3) \times 4$$
$$= 15 \times 4$$
$$= 70$$

The volume is 70 cm³.

EXERCISE 11.10

1. Find the volume of each of the following rectangular solids.

(a)

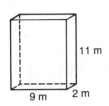

11 m

9 m   2 m

(b)

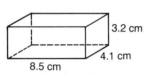

3.2 cm

4.1 cm

8.5 cm

(c)

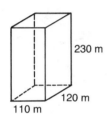

230 m

120 m

110 m

2. Calculate the volume of the rectangular solids.

(a)

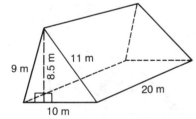

9 m   8.5 m   11 m

20 m

10 m

(b)

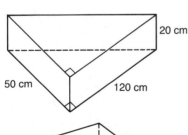

20 cm

50 cm   120 cm

(c)

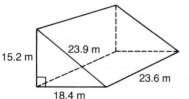

23.9 m

15.2 m

23.6 m

18.4 m

(d)

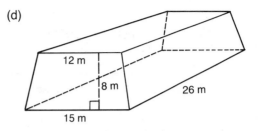

12 m

8 m

26 m

15 m

3. The diagram shows the side view of a pool.

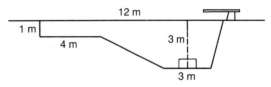

12 m

1 m

4 m   3 m

3 m

(a) The pool is 5 m wide. What is the volume of the pool?

(b) How many litres of water are in the pool? (1 m³ = 1000 L)

(c) A pump can remove 300 L of water per minute. How long would it take to drain the pool?

11.11 VOLUME OF CYLINDERS AND PYRAMIDS

CYLINDERS

To find the volume of a right cylinder, we use the same formula as for a prism.

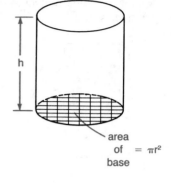

> Volume = (area of the base) × height

The base of a cylinder is a circle.

> A(of a circle) = πr^2

> Volume of a right cylinder
> $V = \pi r^2 h$

EXAMPLE 1. Calculate the volume of the cylinder to the nearest tenth.

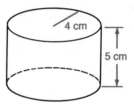

SOLUTION:

$V = \pi r^2 h$
$V = 3.14 \times (4)^2 \times 5$
$ = 251.2$

The volume is 251.2 cm³.

PYRAMIDS

The volume of a right pyramid is equal to one-third the volume of a right prism with the same base and height.

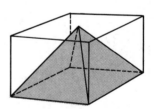

> $V_{prism} = A_{base} \times h$

> $V_{pyramid} = \frac{1}{3} \times A_{base} \times h$

EXAMPLE 2. Calculate the volume of the right triangular pyramid.

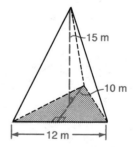

SOLUTION:

$V = \frac{1}{3}Ah$
$V = \frac{1}{3}(\frac{1}{2} \times 12 \times 10) \times 15$
$ = 300$

The volume is 300 m³.

EXERCISE 11.11

A 1. Complete the chart.

Solid	Height	Area of Base	Volume
Cylinder	100 m	20 m²	
Pyramid	30 cm	10 cm²	
Cylinder	60 m	30 m²	
Pyramid	90 m	12 m²	

B 2. Calculate the volume of the cylinders to the nearest tenth. Use π = 3.14.

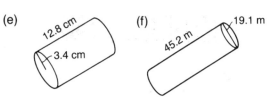

(a) 9 m, 12 m

(b) 8.4 m, 6.5 m

(c) 13.2 cm, 5.6 cm

(d) 965 m, 142 m

(e) 12.8 cm, 3.4 cm

(f) 45.2 m, 19.1 m

3. Calculate the volume of the right pyramids.

(a) 6.4 m, 5.1 m, 5.1 m

(b) 11.4 cm, 9.9 cm, 8.6 cm

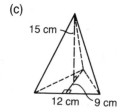

(c) 15 cm, 12 cm, 9 cm

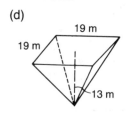

(d) 19 m, 19 m, 13 m

4. The box holds twelve cans. The dimensions of the box are shown. Calculate the total volume of the twelve cans.

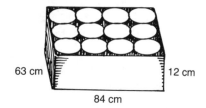

63 cm, 12 cm, 84 cm

5. When cannons were used to defend forts, the cannon-balls were stacked in the shape of a square pyramid. How many cannon-balls are there in a square pyramid when each side of the base has 6 balls?

MICRO MATH

```
NEW
10 PRINT"VOLUME OF A CYLINDER"
20 INPUT"RADIUS IS ";R
30 INPUT"HEIGHT IS ";H
40 V=3.14*R↑2*H
50 PRINT"VOLUME IS ";V
60 END
RUN
```

1. Calculate the volume of the following cylinders.
(a) r = 4.5 cm, h = 13.6 cm
(b) r = 0.56 cm, h = 11.5 cm

```
NEW
10 PRINT"VOLUME OF A"
20 PRINT"RECTANGULAR BASED PYRAMID"
30 INPUT"LENGTH OF BASE IS ";L
40 INPUT" WIDTH OF BASE IS ";W
50 INPUT"HEIGHT IS ";H
60 V=L*W*H/3
70 PRINT"VOLUME IS ";V
80 END
RUN
```

1. Calculate the volume of the following rectangular-based pyramids.
(a) ℓ = 15.4 cm, w = 8.6 cm, h = 11.5 cm
(b) ℓ = 596 m, w = 435 m, h = 707 m

11.12 SURFACE AREA AND VOLUME OF A CONE

The surface area of a right cone consists of the area of
the curved surface plus the area of the circular base.

S.A. = (area of base) + (area of curved surface)
S.A. = $\pi r^2 + \pi rs$
= $\pi r(r + s)$

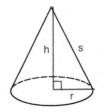

s: slant height

h: height

The volume of a right cone is equal to one-third the
volume of a cylinder with the same base and height.

$V_{cone} = \frac{1}{3} \times A_{base} \times h$

$V = \frac{1}{3} \times \pi r^2 \times h$

$= \frac{1}{3}\pi r^2 h$

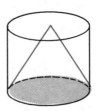

EXERCISE 11.12

B 1. Calculate the volume and surface area of
each right cone to the nearest tenth.

(a)
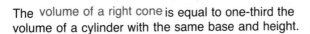
12 m

5 m

(b)
20 cm

12 cm

(c)
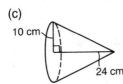
10 cm

24 cm

(d)
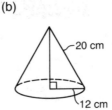
8 cm

6 cm

(e)
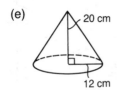
20 cm

12 cm

(f)
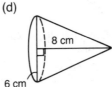
7 cm

24 cm

2. Find the volume of
the two cones inside
the right cylinder.

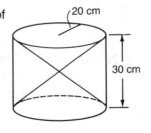
20 cm

30 cm

C 3. A square with 6 cm
sides is revolved about a
diagonal as an axis. Find
the volume.

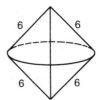
6 6

6 6

MICRO MATH

```
NEW
10 PRINT"SURFACE AREA OF A CONE"
20 INPUT"RADIUS IS ";R
30 INPUT"SLANT HEIGHT IS ";S
40 A=3.14*R*(R+S)
50 PRINT"THE SURFACE AREA IS ";A
60 END
RUN
```

```
NEW
10 PRINT"VOLUME OF A CONE"
20 INPUT"RADIUS OF BASE IS ";R
30 INPUT"HEIGHT IS ";H
60 V=3.14*R↑2*H/3
70 PRINT"VOLUME IS ";V
80 END
RUN
```

1. Calculate the surface area and
volume of each right cone.
(a) r = 9.6 m, s = 12.4 m
(b) r = 11.5 cm, h = 15.6 cm
(c) h = 15.6 cm, s = 20.4 m

11.13 SURFACE AREA AND VOLUME OF A SPHERE

A sphere is the set of all points that are a given distance from a given point.

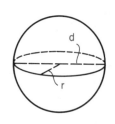

To find the area of a sphere we use this formula.

Area of a sphere
S.A. $= 4\pi r^2$

The formula for the volume of a sphere is

$$V = \tfrac{4}{3} \times \pi \times r^3 \quad \text{or} \quad V = \tfrac{4}{3}\pi r^3$$

EXERCISE 11.13

B 1. Calculate the surface area and volume of each sphere to the nearest tenth.

(a) 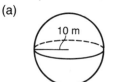 10 m

(b) 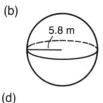 5.8 m

(c) 40 m

(d) 2.6 cm

(e) 34 m

(f) 128 cm

2. Calculate the surface area and volume of the solid.

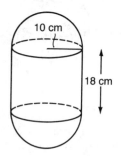
10 cm
18 cm

3. A cube whose edge is 20 cm is circumscribed about a sphere.
(a) Find the total surface area of the cube.
(b) Find the surface area of the sphere.
(c) Find the ratio of the area of the sphere to the area of the cube.

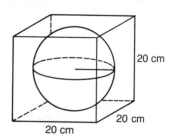
20 cm
20 cm
20 cm

MICRO MATH

```
NEW
10 PRINT"SURFACE AREA OF A SPHERE"
20 INPUT"RADIUS IS ";R
30 A=4*3.14*R↑2
40 PRINT"SURFACE AREA IS ";A
50 END
RUN

NEW
10 PRINT"VOLUME OF A SPHERE"
20 INPUT"RADIUS OF SPHERE IS ";R
30 V=3.14*R↑3/3
40 PRINT"VOLUME IS ";V
50 END
RUN
```

11.14 APPLICATIONS: PERIMETER, AREA, AND VOLUME

In this section perimeter, area, and volume formulas will be applied.

READ

EXAMPLE. The hot water tank is in the shape of a cylinder. The tank is to be insulated by covering the total surface area. The tank has a height of 4.4 m and a diameter of 1.8 m. Insulation material costs $2.40/m². How much will it cost for the insulation?

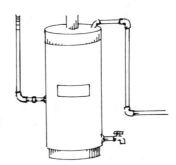

PLAN

SOLUTION:
Calculate the surface area.
Assume that insulation material must be bought in whole number units.
Calculate the cost.

SOLVE

S.A. = $2\pi r^2 \times 2\pi rh$
S.A. = $2(3.14)(0.9)^2 + 2(3.14)(0.9)(4.4)$
$\doteq 29.4 \text{ m}^2$

Cost = 2.40×30
= 72

ANSWER

It will cost $72.00 for the insulation.

EXERCISE 11.14

B 1. The Pentagon building in Washington, D.C. is a regular pentagon. Each side is 280 m long.

What is the perimeter of the Pentagon?

2. The sides of a wheelbarrow are in the shape of trapezoids. Calculate the volume of sand the wheelbarrow will hold when it is full, level with the top of the sides.

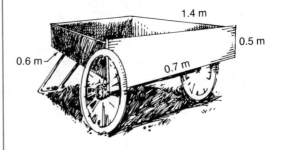

3. A round tower with a 12 m circumference is surrounded by a fence that is 2 m from the tower. How long is the fence?

4. The Cinesphere at Ontario Place in Toronto encloses a movie screen measuring 18 m by 24 m. The radius of the sphere is approximately 19 m.

(a) Calculate the area of the sphere.
(b) Calculate its volume.

5. Calculate the perimeter and area of the floor plan.

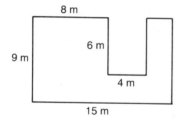

6. How many metres of chain-link fence are needed for an L-shaped field with the following dimensions: 72 m, 67 m, 40 m, 47 m, 32 m, 20 m.

7. A driveway is 25 m long and 4 m wide. Blacktop was spread over the driveway to an average depth of 5 cm. Approximate the volume of the blacktop used.

8. A pipe is 35 m long and has an inside diameter of 0.5 m. Find the number of cubic metres of oil it can hold.

9. An inflated balloon has a radius of 12 cm. If more air is added and the radius increases by 4 cm, what will be the increase in volume?

C 10. Find the area of the basketball free-throw key to the nearest tenth.

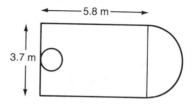

11. Find the area of the ice rink.

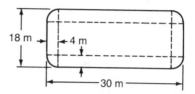

12. The large sprocket on the pedals of a bicycle has 50 teeth. The small sprocket on the rear wheel has 20 teeth. How many revolutions does the rear wheel make when the pedals make four complete revolutions?

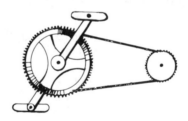

WORD LADDER

Start with the word "slow" and change one letter at a time to form a new word until you reach "fast." The best solution has the fewest steps.

11.15 PROBLEM SOLVING

1. Place the letters from A to P in the squares according to the following statements.

	H	F	
	L	O	

(a) H, O, F, and L have already been placed.
(b) B is in the top row.
(c) P is not in the top row.
(d) C is in a corner.
(e) M is in a corner.
(f) D is in the right column.
(g) J is in the right column.
(h) No row or column contains two consecutive letters of the alphabet.
(i) No row or column contains two vowels.

2. The following are the airline codes for several North American cities. Name the cities.

(a) YYZ	(b) LAX
(c) YBE	(d) YFC
(e) YYQ	(f) YVR
(g) YQM	(h) YUL
(i) YHM	(j) YHZ
(k) YWG	(l) YYC

3. Divide 28 into two parts so that the larger part is 3 times the smaller part.

4. Sharon Devereaux drove along the coast at 60 km/h for a distance of 240 km. She made the return trip the next day travelling the same 240 km at a speed of 40 km/h. Sharon's brother calculated her average speed for the whole trip to be 50 km/h.
(a) Where did her brother make the mistake in his calculation?
(b) What was Sharon's average speed for the trip?

5. The nine areas in the diagram have to be coloured so that no two areas bordering each other have the same colour. What is the least number of colours you will need?
(a) 2
(b) 3
(c) 4
(d) 5
(e) 6

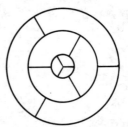

6. A rectangle and an equilateral triangle have the same perimeter. The length of the rectangle is twice its width. Each side of the triangle is 60 cm. What are the dimensions of the rectangle?

7. Six consecutive even numbers are written in order on a piece of paper. The sum of the first three numbers is 30. What is the sum of the last three?

8. The Pythagorean society flourished in the 5th century B.C. The members spent much of their time studying whole numbers. They placed a special significance on the numbers 220 and 284. These are called amicable numbers. All the whole number divisors of 220, except 220 itself, are 1, 2, 3, 4, 5, 10, 11, 20, 22, 44, 55, and 110. Their sum is 284.
Similarly, the whole number divisors of 284, except 284 itself, are 1, 2, 4, 71, and 142. Their sum is 220. Are 1210 and 1184 amicable numbers?

9. A mechanic charged $83.20 to replace a muffler. He worked for two hours. The muffler cost $33.10. How much did the mechanic charge per hour for labour?

10. In how many ways can seven books be divided among three people so that each person receives at least one book?

11. Which gives you more to eat: two pizzas each 25 cm in diameter or one pizza with a diameter of 40 cm?

12. Place the numbers 2, 3, 4, 5, 7, 8, and 9 in the circles so that each line of three numbers totals 18.

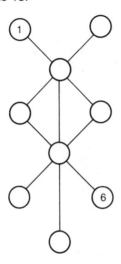

13. Make a table to show the number of different ways you can make change for one dollar.

50¢	25¢	10¢	5¢	1¢

14. Stephanie had a bank balance of $678.98. She wrote cheques for $12.45, $56.70, $87.93, and $101.30. What was her new balance?

15. The number of bacteria in a sample triples every hour. At 09:00 there were 81 000 bacteria. How many were there three hours before, at 06:00?

16. Make an assumption and determine the next number in the following sequence.

25, 23, 20, 18, 15, 13, 10,

YOUR APPROXIMATE BODY AREA

Height (cm)	Area (m²)	Mass (kg)
200		80
	2.1	75
190	2.0	
	1.9	70
180	1.8	65
170	1.7	60
	1.6	
160	1.5	55
150		50

This is a means of approximating the surface area of your body. A line joining your height on the left-hand scale to your mass (without clothing) on the right-hand scale cuts the centre scale at your body area.

1. If you grow 5 cm, how much will your body area change?

2. If you gain 5 kg, how much will your area change?

11.16 REVIEW EXERCISE

1. Calculate the perimeter of each of the following.

(a)

(b)

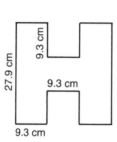

42 m

(c)

27.9 cm 9.3 cm 9.3 cm 9.3 cm

(d)

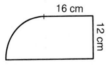

16 cm 12 cm

2. Calculate the area.

(a)

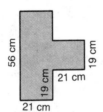

56 cm 19 cm 21 cm 19 cm 21 cm

(b)

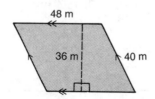

48 m 36 m 40 m

(c)

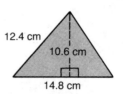

12.4 cm 10.6 cm 14.8 cm

(d)

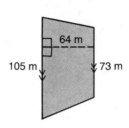

64 m 105 m 73 m

3. Calculate the area.

(a)

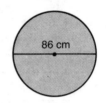

86 cm

(b)

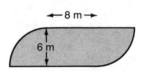

8 m 6 m

4. Calculate the surface area of the right prisms.

(a)

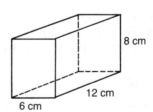

8 cm 12 cm 6 cm

(b)

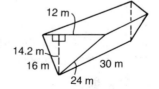

12 m 14.2 m 16 m 24 m 30 m

5. Calculate the surface area of each of the following, to the nearest tenth.

(a)

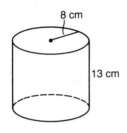

8 cm

13 cm

(b)

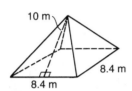

10 m

8.4 m

8.4 m

6. Calculate the volume of the rectangular solids.

(a)

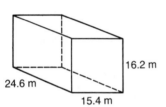

16.2 m

24.6 m

15.4 m

(b)

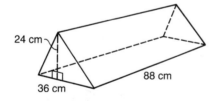

24 cm

88 cm

36 cm

7. Calculate the volume of the right pyramid.

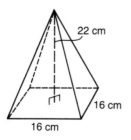

22 cm

16 cm

16 cm

8. Calculate the volume of the cylinder to the nearest tenth.

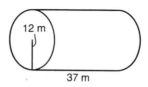

12 m

37 m

9. Calculate the volume and surface area of each.

(a)

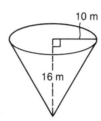

10 m

16 m

(b)

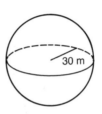

30 m

10. The tent shown in the diagram has a floor.

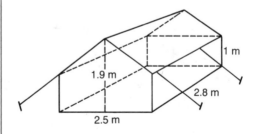

1 m

1.9 m

2.8 m

2.5 m

(a) Calculate the surface area of the tent.
(b) Calculate the floor area of the tent.
(c) A sleeping bag measures 0.7 m by 2 m. What is the maximum number of sleeping bags that can be placed on the floor if overlapping is not allowed?

11. (a) Calculate the volume of the earth and the moon.
(b) How many times the volume of the moon is the volume of the earth?

11.17 CHAPTER 11 TEST

1. Calculate the perimeter.

(a)

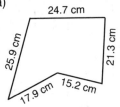
24.7 cm
25.9 cm
21.3 cm
17.9 cm   15.2 cm

(b)

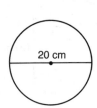
20 cm

2. Calculate the area.

(a)

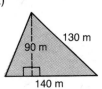
130 m
90 m
140 m

(b)

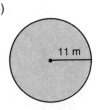
11 m

(c)

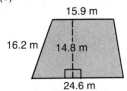
15.9 m
16.2 m   14.8 m
24.6 m

3. Calculate the surface area and volume of each.

(a)

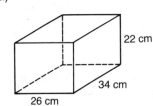
22 cm
34 cm
26 cm

(b)

22 m
60 m

(c)

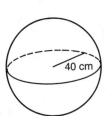
40 cm

(d)

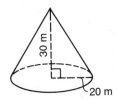
30 m
20 m

GEOMETRY

CHAPTER

12

Others will follow the path we have taken urged by our daring,
our dreams and our dangers.
A.H. Lambden

MEASURING, DRAWING, AND CLASSIFYING ANGLES

Angles are measured in degrees. A protractor is the instrument that measures the size of an angle. To determine how large an angle is, we measure how much one ray, or arm, has been rotated from the other.

One complete turn is 360 degrees and is written as 360°.

$\frac{1}{2}$-turn is $\frac{1}{2} \times 360°$ or 180°.

$\frac{1}{4}$-turn is $\frac{1}{4} \times 360°$ or 90°.

one complete turn

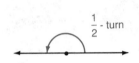
$\frac{1}{2}$ - turn

$\frac{1}{4}$ - turn

To measure an angle with a protractor, proceed as follows.

Place the centre point of the protractor on the vertex B of the angle with the baseline of the protractor along the ray BC.

Determine how much ray BA has been rotated from ray BC.

∠ABC = 120°

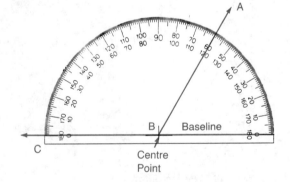

There are two scales on the protractor. To measure an angle, always start from 0 on one of the scales. The diagram shows how both scales of the protractor are used.

∠ABD = 30°
∠CBE = 41°
∠CBD = 150°
∠ABE = 139°

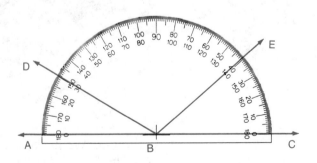

We classify angles according to their measures.

Straight Angle	Right Angle	Acute Angle	Obtuse Angle	Reflex Angle
180° O	90° O	O	O	O
If the arms of an angle form a straight line, then its measure is 180° and it is a straight angle.	A right angle is one-half of a straight angle and its measure is 90°.	An acute angle has a measure less than a right angle. That is, it is less than 90°.	An angle with measure greater than a right angle and less than a straight angle is an obtuse angle. That is, it is between 90° and 180°.	An angle with measure greater than a straight angle is a reflex angle. That is, it is greater than 180°, and less than 360°.

COMPLEMENTARY ANGLES

Two angles are complementary if the sum of their measures is 90°.

∠ABD and ∠DBC are complementary since
    ∠ABD + ∠DBC = 67° + 23°
                 = 90°
∠RST and ∠WXY are complementary since
    ∠RST + ∠WXY = 71° + 19°
                 = 90°

SUPPLEMENTARY ANGLES

Two angles are supplementary if the sum of their measures is 180°.

∠DBA and ∠DBC are supplementary since
    ∠DBA + ∠DBC = 131° + 49°
                 = 180°
∠PQR and ∠LMN are supplementary since
    ∠PQR and ∠LMN = 62° + 118°
                   = 180°

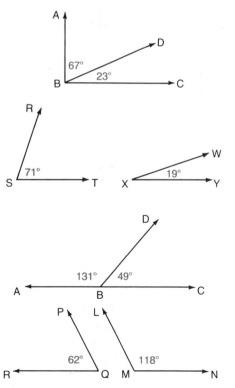

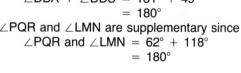

OPPOSITE ANGLES

When two lines intersect, two pairs of equal opposite angles are formed.

$$\angle AED = \angle BEC$$
$$\angle AEC = \angle DEB$$

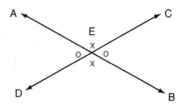

EXERCISE

1. Find the measure of the following angles on the protractor below.

(a) $\angle DCF$ (b) $\angle ICD$ (c) $\angle LCB$
(d) $\angle MCB$ (e) $\angle HCD$ (f) $\angle JCD$
(g) $\angle GCB$ (h) $\angle LCD$ (i) $\angle ECB$

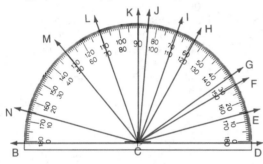

2. Find the measures of the following angles on the protractor below.

(a) $\angle NED$ (b) $\angle GEF$ (c) $\angle HEF$
(d) $\angle MED$ (e) $\angle KED$ (f) $\angle JEF$
(g) $\angle GED$ (h) $\angle LEF$ (i) $\angle IED$

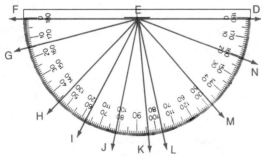

3. Draw the following angles.

(a) 45°   (b) 83°
(c) 107°   (d) 175°
(e) 210°   (f) 225°
(g) 310°   (h) 346°

4. What angle is complementary to each of the following angles?

(a) 41°   (b) 55°
(c) 84°   (d) 7°

5. What angle is supplementary to each of the following angles?

(a) 56°   (b) 106°
(c) 13°   (d) 94°
(e) 90°   (f) 179°

6. Classify the following angles as either straight, right, acute, obtuse, or reflex.

(a) $\angle AOB$ (b) $\angle AOC$
(c) $\angle AOD$ (d) $\angle AOE$
(e) $\angle BOC$ (f) $\angle COE$
(g) $\angle DOE$ (h) $\angle BOD$

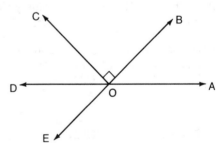

7. Find the measure of the unknown angles.

(a)   (b)

CLASSIFYING TRIANGLES

We classify triangles according to sides, angles, and lines of symmetry.

Sides	Angles	Lines of symmetry

Scalene	**Acute**	**Scalene**
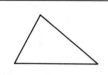		
No sides are equal in length.	All angles are acute.	There are no lines of symmetry.
Isosceles	**Right**	**Isosceles**
Two sides are equal in length.	One angle is a right angle.	There is one line of symmetry.
Equilateral	**Obtuse**	**Equilateral**
	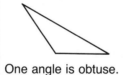	
All three sides are equal in length.	One angle is obtuse.	There are three lines of symmetry.

EXERCISE

1. Classify the following triangles according to their sides or angles.

(a)

(b)

(c)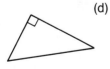

(d)

2. Classify the following triangles according to their lines of symmetry.

(a)

(b)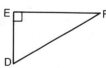

(c)

(d)

12.1 ANGLES AND TRIANGLES

The sum of the interior angles of a triangle is 180°.

$$\angle A + \angle B + \angle C = 180°$$

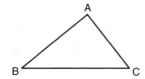

$\triangle$ABC is an isosceles triangle. If we "fold the triangle" through A so that AB falls along AC we see that $\angle B = \angle C$.

In an isosceles triangle, the angles opposite the equal sides are equal.

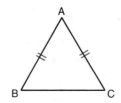

In an equilateral triangle, all sides and angles are equal. Since the sum of the interior angles is 180°, each angle of an equilateral triangle is 60°.

$\angle$ACD is an exterior angle of $\triangle$ABC. An exterior angle of a triangle is formed by extending one of the sides of a triangle.

Since $\angle ABC + \angle BCA + \angle BAC = 180°$
and $\angle BCA + \angle ACD = 180°$
then $\angle ABC + \angle BCA + \angle BAC = \angle BCA + \angle ACD$
and $\angle ABC + \angle BAC = \angle ACD$

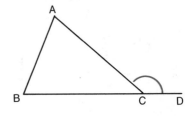

The exterior angle of a triangle is equal to the sum of the two interior and opposite angles.

EXERCISE 12.1

A 1. Find the value of the unknown angles.

(a)

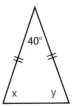

81°   x   35°

(b)

15°

y

14°

(c)

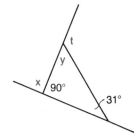

40°

x   y

(d)

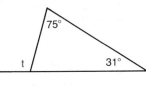

75°

t   31°

(d)

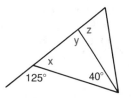

z

y

x

125°   40°

(e)

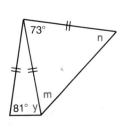

73°   n

m

81° y

3. Determine the sum of the interior angles of the following polygons by completing the chart.

Sides	Number of Diagonals from One Vertex	Number of Triangles Formed	Sum of Interior Angles
4	1	2	360°
5	2	3	540°
6			
7			
8			
9			
10			
11			
12			

B 2. Find the value of the unknown angles.

(a)

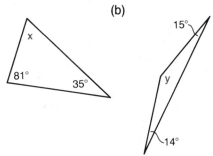

t

y

x   90°

31°

(b)

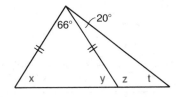

72°   56°

x

w   61°   y

(c)

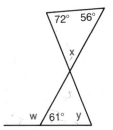

66°   20°

x   y   z   t

4. In a regular polygon, all sides have the same length and all angles are equal. What is the measure of each angle in the following?

(a) a regular quadrilateral
(b) a regular pentagon
(c) a regular hexagon

12.2 CONGRUENT TRIANGLES

Congruent triangles have the same size and shape. When triangles are congruent, one can be placed on top of the other and all parts will be equal.

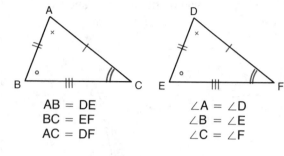

$$AB = DE$$
$$BC = EF$$
$$AC = DF$$

$$\angle A = \angle D$$
$$\angle B = \angle E$$
$$\angle C = \angle F$$

$$\triangle ABC \cong \triangle DEF$$

For two triangles to be congruent, it is necessary to have the three sides and three angles of one triangle respectively equal to the three sides and three angles of the second triangle. However, it is sufficient to have the following conditions in order to state that two triangles are congruent.

Case	Statement	Figures $\triangle ABC \cong \triangle DEF$
SSS	If the three sides of one triangle are respectively equal to the three sides of another triangle, then the triangles are congruent.	
SAS	If two sides and the contained angle of one triangle are respectively equal to two sides and the contained angle of another triangle, then the triangles are congruent.	
ASA	If two angles and a side of one triangle are respectively equal to two angles and a side of another triangle, then the triangles are congruent.	
HS	If the hypotenuse and one side of one right-angled triangle are respectively equal to the hypotenuse and one side of another right-angled triangle, the triangles are congruent.	

EXERCISE 12.2

1. (a) State the reason why the triangles are congruent.
(b) List the other equal parts as a result of the congruence.

(i)

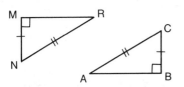

(ii)

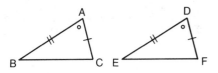

(iii)

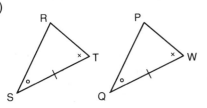

(iv)

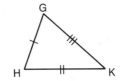

2. State the reason each of the following is a pair of congruent triangles and find the value of the missing dimensions.

(a)

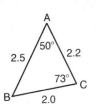

(b)

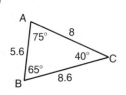

B 3. Complete the following.

(a)

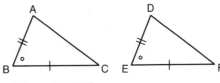

In △ABC and △DEF
AB = ■
∠ABC = ■
BC = ■
△ABC ≅ △DEF (■)

(b)

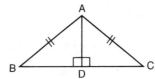

In △ABD and △ADC
∠ADB = ■
AB = ■
AD = ■
∴△ABD ≅ △ADC (■)

4. In each of the following
(a) state the reason why the triangles are congruent.
(b) list the other equal parts as a result of the congruence.

(i)

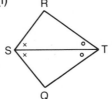

(ii)

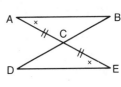

(iii)

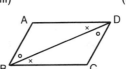

(iv)

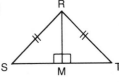

(v)

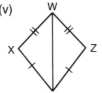

(vi)

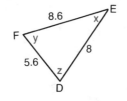

12.3 COPYING AND BISECTING AN ANGLE

In mathematics, an accurate construction is a drawing made with only a ruler and a compass.

To copy an angle

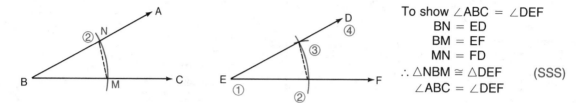

To show ∠ABC = ∠DEF
BN = ED
BM = EF
MN = FD
∴ △NBM ≅ △DEF   (SSS)
∠ABC = ∠DEF

To bisect an angle

The following diagrams show how to bisect an angle using a ruler and a compass. Describe each step.

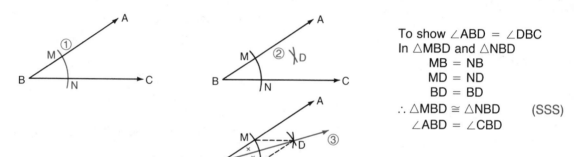

To show ∠ABD = ∠DBC
In △MBD and △NBD
MB = NB
MD = ND
BD = BD
∴ △MBD ≅ △NBD   (SSS)
∠ABD = ∠CBD

BD bisects ∠ABC.

EXAMPLE. Construct the bisectors of the angles of △ABC to find the incentre of the triangle.

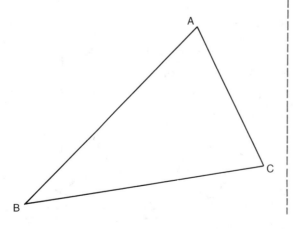

SOLUTION:
1. Bisect each angle of △ABC.
2. Label the point of intersection I.

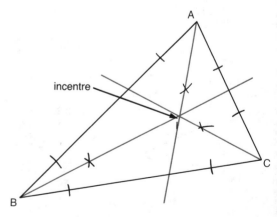

incentre

EXERCISE 12.3

B 1. (a) Using only a ruler and a compass, copy the following angles in your notes.

(i)   (ii)

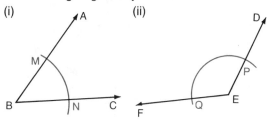

(iii)   (iv)

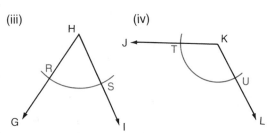

(b) Bisect each of the angles in part (a).

2. Using only a ruler and a compass, construct angles with the following measures.

(a) 90°   (b) 45°
(c) 22.5°   (d) 60°
(e) 30°   (f) 15°
(g) 135°   (h) 120°
(i) 67.5°   (j) 82.5°

3. The following figure shows the bisection of ∠PQR.

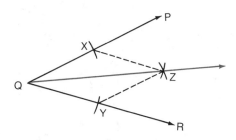

Use congruent triangles to show that QZ bisects ∠PQR.

4. (a) Using a protractor, draw an angle with a measure of 152°.
(b) Using the 152° angle and only a ruler and a compass, draw an angle with a measure of 38°.

5. Given

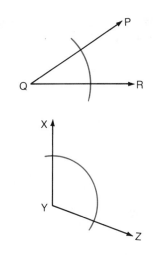

construct △ABC such that ∠ABC = ∠PQR, ∠ACB = $\frac{1}{2}$∠XYZ and BC = MN.

6. (a) Copy the following triangles.
(b) Bisect the three angles of each triangle to find the incentre.
(i)

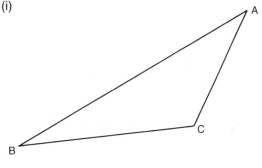

(ii)

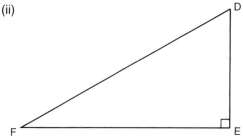

12.4 RIGHT BISECTOR

The right bisector of a line segment cuts the line segment into two equal parts, making an angle of 90°.

The following diagrams show how to construct a right bisector of a line segment using a ruler and a compass. Describe each step.

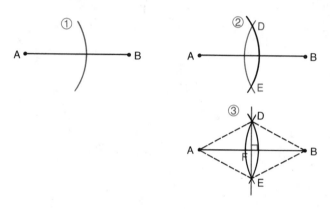

We can show F is the midpoint of AB and DE ⊥ AB.
In △AED and △BED,

$$DE = DE$$
$$AE = BE$$
$$AD = BD$$

∴ △AED ≅ △BED   (SSS)

$$∠ADF = ∠BDF$$
$$FD = FD$$
$$AD = BD$$

∴ △AFD ≅ △BFD   (SAS)
AF = BF and ∠AFD = ∠BFD
But ∠AFD + ∠BFD = 180°
∴ ∠AFD = ∠BFD = 90°

EXAMPLE. Construct the right bisectors of the three sides of △ABC to find the circumcentre of the triangle.

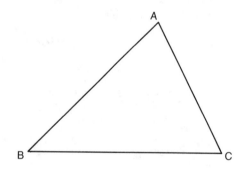

SOLUTION:
1. Bisect each side of △ABC.
2. Label the point of intersection J.
3. With centre J and radius JB, draw a circle.

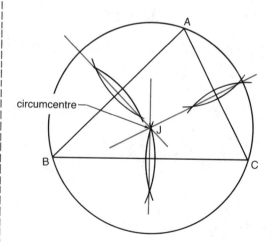

The circle which passes through the vertices of a triangle is called the circumcircle.

EXERCISE 12.4

Use only a ruler and a compass to complete the following constructions.

3 1. (a) Draw a line segment 10 cm long and label it AB.
(b) Construct XY, the right bisector of AB, to cut AB at M.
(c) With centre M and radius AM, draw a circle.
(d) Use the circle in (c) to determine whether M is the midpoint of AB.

2. (a) Draw a line segment 12 cm long and label it DE.
(b) Construct XY, the right bisector of DE, to cut DE at M.
(c) Construct JK, the right bisector of DM, to cut DM at L.
(d) Show that DE = 4 × DL

3. The following figure shows the right bisection of XY.

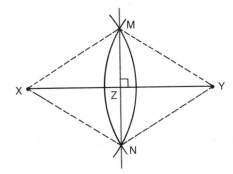

Use congruent triangles to show that MN is the right bisector of XY.

4. (a) Copy the following triangles.
(b) Construct the right bisectors of the three sides of each triangle to find the circumcentre.
(c) Draw the circumcircle.
(i)

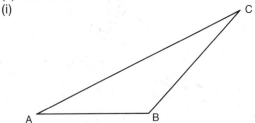

(ii)

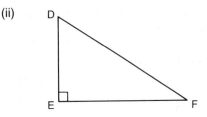

(iii)

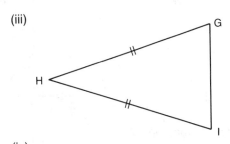

(iv)

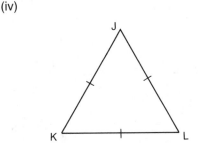

C 5. The median of a triangle is a line from a vertex of a triangle to the midpoint of the opposite side.

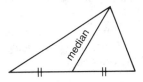

(a) Draw any acute triangle, and construct the three medians to find the centroid.
(b) Repeat (a) using
   (i)   an obtuse triangle
   (ii) a right triangle
   (iii) an equilateral triangle.
(c) Cut out a triangle from stiff cardboard. Find the centroid. Balance the triangle on the tip of a pencil located at the centroid.

12.5 PERPENDICULAR LINES

The following diagrams show how to construct perpendicular lines using a ruler and a compass. Describe each step.

Perpendicular at a point

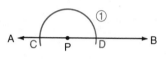

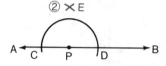

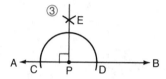

To show EP ⊥ AB,
∠EPC = ∠EPD = 90°
In △ECP and △EDP,
EC = ED
EP = EP
CP = DP
∴ △ECP ≅ △EDP (SSS)
∠EPC = ∠EPD
But ∠EPC + ∠EPD = 180°
∴ ∠EPC = ∠EPD = 90°

Perpendicular from a point

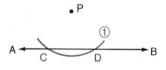

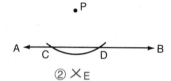

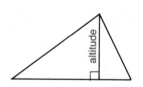

Show that
∠AFP = ∠BFP = 90°

An altitude of a triangle is the perpendicular distance from a vertex to the opposite side.

EXAMPLE. Construct the three altitudes of △ABC to find the orthocentre.

SOLUTION:
1. Draw perpendiculars from A to BC, B to AC, and C to AB.
2. Label the point of intersection O.

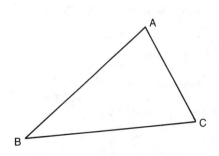

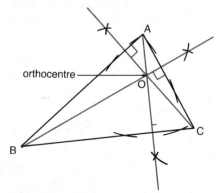

EXERCISE 12.5

B 1. (a) Copy line segment AB and point P.

(b) Construct the perpendicular to AB from P, to meet AB at N.
(c) Measure ∠PNB.

2. (a) Copy line segment DE and point P.

(b) Construct the perpendicular from P to DE, to meet DE extended at M.
(c) Measure ∠PME.

3. (a) Draw a line segment, AB, 7 cm long.
(b) Construct a square with AB as the base.

4. (a) Draw a line segment, PQ, 15 cm long.
(b) Construct a square with perimeter equal to PQ.

5. (a) Copy each of the following triangles.
(b) Draw an altitude for each triangle.
(i)

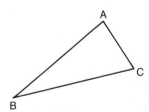

(ii)

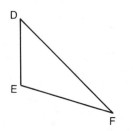

6. (a) Copy the following triangles.
(b) Draw the three altitudes of each triangle to find the orthocentre.
(i)

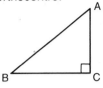

(ii)

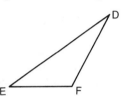

(iii)

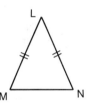

(iv)

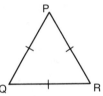

C 7. Using only a ruler and a compass, construct a perpendicular at B without extending the line.

A •————————————• B

8. (a) Copy △ABC.

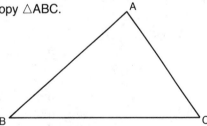

(b) Bisect the three angles to find the incentre, I.
(c) From I, construct a perpendicular to BC, meeting BC at D.
(d) With compass at centre I, and radius ID, draw the inscribed circle.

12.6 PARALLEL LINES

Parallel lines are lines which never meet when extended in either direction.

The following diagrams show how to construct parallel lines using a ruler and a compass.

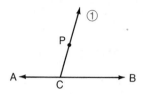 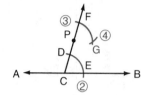 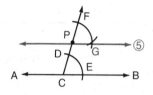

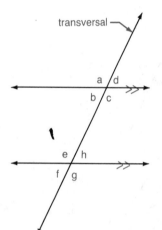

When a transversal intersects two parallel lines, we classify the pairs of angles formed as alternate, corresponding, or co-interior.

Alternate angles
form a ⟍ pattern
and are equal.

$\angle c = \angle e$
$\angle b = \angle h$

Corresponding angles
form an ⊏ pattern
and are equal.

$\angle a = \angle e$
$\angle b = \angle f$
$\angle d = \angle h$
$\angle c = \angle g$

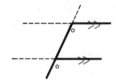

Co-interior angles
form a ⌐ pattern
and are supplementary.

$\angle b + \angle e = 180°$
$\angle c + \angle h = 180°$

EXAMPLE. Calculate the value of each unknown angle in the diagram.

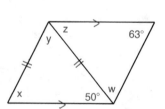

SOLUTION:

$$x = 50° \qquad \text{isosceles triangle}$$
$$x + y + 50° = 180° \qquad \text{sum of angles of a triangle}$$
$$50° + y + 50° = 180°$$
$$y + 100° = 180°$$
$$y = 180° - 100°$$
$$y = 80°$$
$$z = 50° \qquad \text{alternate angles}$$
$$z + w + 63° = 180° \qquad \text{sum of angles of a triangle}$$
$$50° + w + 63° = 180°$$
$$w + 113° = 180°$$
$$w = 180° - 113°$$
$$w = 67°$$

EXERCISE 12.6

B 1. Copy each diagram and construct a line through P parallel to AB.

(a)

•P

(b)

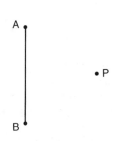

2. (a) Given △ABC,
   (i) construct a line through A, parallel to BC.
   (ii) construct a line through B, parallel to AC.
   (iii) construct a line through C, parallel to AB.

(b) Show that the triangle formed is four times the size of △ABC.

3. Calculate the value of the unknown angles.

(a)   (b)

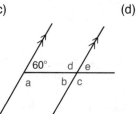

(c)   (d)

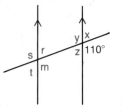

4. Calculate the value of the unknown angles.

(a)   (b)

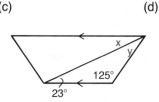

(c)   (d)

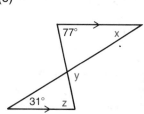

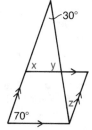

(e)   (f)

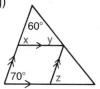

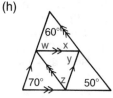

(g)   (h)

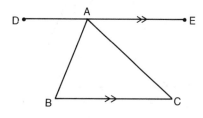

5. Use alternate angles to show that the sum of the interior angles of a triangle is 180°.

12.7 GEOMETRIC PROPERTIES

EXERCISE 12.7

B 1. Using only a ruler and a compass, construct the following triangles.

(a) △ABC, AB = 12 cm, ∠A = 60°, ∠B = 60°

(b) △DEF, ∠D = 90°, DE = 13 cm, ∠E = 45°

(c) △GHI, ∠H = 60°, GH = 10 cm, ∠I = 90°

(d) △JKL, ∠K = 120°, JK = 9 cm, KL = 9 cm

(e) △PQR, ∠P = 135°, PQ = 10 cm, ∠Q = 15°

2. (a) Construct △ABC with ∠A = 90°, AB = 8 cm, AC = 10 cm.

(b) Using a protractor, measure and find the value of ∠A + ∠B + ∠C.

(c) Measure BC. Determine whether
$BC^2 = AB^2 + AC^2$.

3. An aircraft travels from A in a direction N45°W for 600 km to B. Then it turns 60° in a clockwise direction and flies another 800 km to C.

(a) Using only a ruler and a compass, draw the course flown using the scale:
   1 cm represents 100 km.

(b) Join AC and measure.

(c) How far is the aircraft from its starting point?

4. (a) Copy △ABC with sides extended forming exterior angles.

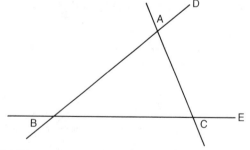

(b) Bisect the exterior angles ∠DAC and ∠ECA at A and C.

(c) Bisect the interior angle at B.

(d) In how many points do the bisectors meet?

(e) The point of intersection P lies outside △ABC, and is called an excentre of the triangle. From P, draw a perpendicular to meet AC at Q. With centre P and radius PQ, construct a circle. Such a circle is called an excircle of △ABC.

(f) Draw the other two excircles of the triangle.

5. (a) Draw any ∠ABC.

(b) Construct BD, the bisector of ∠ABC.

(c) Select three points P, Q, and R on the angle bisector BD, and construct perpendiculars:
PS ⊥ BC, QT ⊥ BC, and RU ⊥ BC.

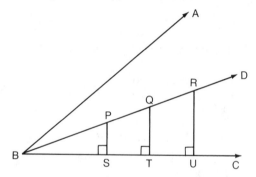

(d) Construct corresponding perpendiculars from P, Q, and R to AB.

(e) With centre P and radius PS, construct a circle. Repeat for points Q and R.

(f) Use symmetry to show:
   Any point on the angle bisector is equidistant from the arms of the angle.

6. (a) Draw any line segment AB.

(b) Construct the right bisector of AB.

(c) Select three points P, Q, and R on the right bisector.

(d) With centre P and radius AP, construct a circle. Repeat using centres Q and R.

(e) Use symmetry to show:
   Any point on the right bisector is equidistant from the ends of the segment.

12.8 REFLECTION GEOMETRY

The following diagrams show how to do geometric constructions using a semi-transparent mirror.

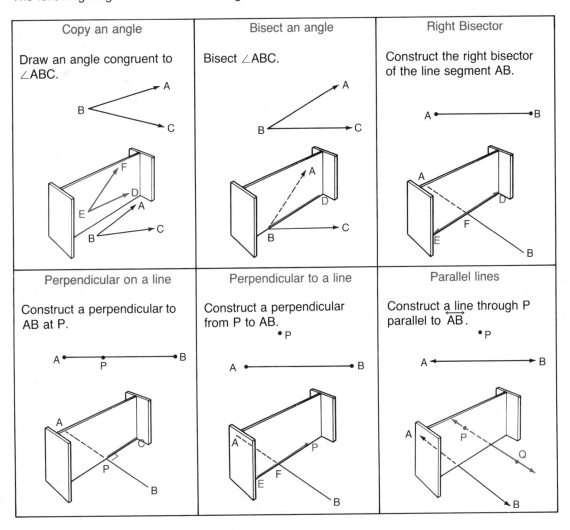

Copy an angle	Bisect an angle	Right Bisector
Draw an angle congruent to ∠ABC.	Bisect ∠ABC.	Construct the right bisector of the line segment AB.

Perpendicular on a line	Perpendicular to a line	Parallel lines
Construct a perpendicular to AB at P.	Construct a perpendicular from P to AB.	Construct a line through P parallel to $\overrightarrow{AB}$.

EXERCISE 12.8

B 1. Use a semi-transparent mirror to perform the following constructions.

(a) copy ∠ABC   (b) bisect ∠XYZ

(c) right bisect PO

2. Construct perpendiculars at P to AB.

(a)   (b)

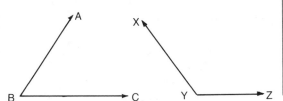

12.9 THE CIRCLE

The following diagrams illustrate the important parts of a circle.

Radius	Diameter	Chord	Circumference
OA is a radius.	AB is a diameter.	AB is a chord.	The circumference is the perimeter of a circle.

Sector	Segment	Arc	Semi-circle
A sector is a region bounded by 2 radii and an arc.	A segment is a region bounded by an arc and a chord.	AB is an arc (part of the circumference).	ABC is a semi-circle (half a circle).

EXERCISE 12.9

A 1. From the diagram, name
(a) a radius
(b) a diameter
(c) a chord
(d) an arc
(e) a sector
(f) a semi-circle

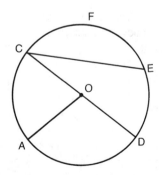

B 2. (a) Draw a circle with centre O.
  (b) Draw two non-parallel chords AB and CD.

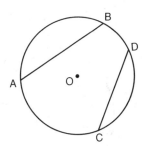

(c) Construct the right bisectors of AB and CD.
(d) Where do the right bisectors intersect?

3. (a) Draw a circle by tracing a circular object and leaving no centre mark.
(b) Draw two non-parallel chords AB and CD.
(c) Construct the right bisectors of AB and CD.
(d) Use your compass to show that the point of intersection is the centre of the circle.

C 4. Three hospitals are located as shown in the diagram.

How would you determine where to locate the Emergency Station so that it is the same distance from each hospital?

5. Archaeologists found part of the outside wall of a circular fort.

How could they determine the radius of the fort?

CALENDAR MATH

Select a month from a calendar.
Select any square of 16 days.

S	M	T	W	T	F	S
					1	2
3	4	5	6	7	8	9
10	11	12	13	14	15	16
17	18	19	20	21	22	23
24	25	26	27	28	29	30
31						

1. Find the sum of each diagonal.

2. Find the sum of the 4 corners.

3. Find the sum of the 4 inside numbers.

4. What is the pattern?

5. What other combinations of 4 numbers give the same sum?

6. Now draw a 4 by 4 grid.

n	n + 1		
n + 7			

Assume it is a grid with squares numbered in the same way as a calendar. If the upper left square is n, the one to its right is n + 1 and the one below it is n + 7, fill in the other squares of the grid.

7. Find the sum of each diagonal.

8. Find the sum of the 4 corners.

9. Find the sum of the 4 inside squares.

10. What is the pattern?

12.10 ANGLES IN A CIRCLE

The following diagrams illustrate the angles of a circle.

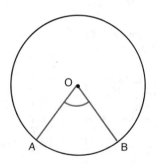

∠AOB is a central angle subtended by arc AB.

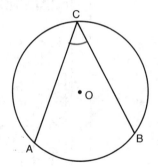

∠ACB is an inscribed angle subtended by arc AB.

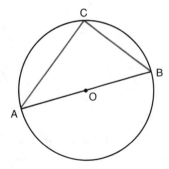

∠ACB is an angle inscribed in a semi-circle.

EXERCISE 12.10

B 1. Inscribed Angles

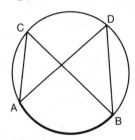

∠ACB and ∠ADB are subtended by the same arc AB.
(a) Draw a similar diagram in your notebook.
(b) Measure ∠ACB and ∠ADB.
(c) How are the angles related?
(d) Repeat the procedure for other inscribed angles subtended by the same arc.

2. Inscribed and Central Angles

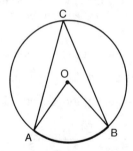

∠ACB and ∠AOB are an inscribed angle and a central angle subtended by the same arc AB.
(a) Draw a similar diagram in your notebook.
(b) Measure ∠ACB and ∠AOB.
(c) How are the angles related?
(d) Repeat the procedure for other central and inscribed angles subtended by the same arc.

3. Angles in a Semi-circle

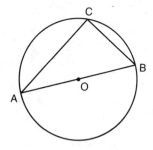

∠ACB is an angle inscribed in a semi-circle
(a) Draw a similar diagram in your notebook.
(b) Measure ∠ACB.
(c) Repeat the procedure for other angles in semi-circles.
(d) What is the measure of an angle inscribed in a semi-circle?

The following summarizes the properties of angles in circles.

Inscribed angles subtended by the same arc are equal.

The central angle is twice the inscribed angle subtended by the same arc.

Angles inscribed in semi-circles are right angles.

4. Find the value of the unknown angles. O is the centre of the circle.

(a)

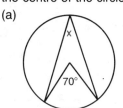

(b)

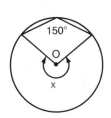

(c)

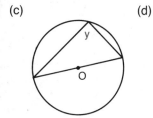

(d)

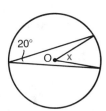

(e)

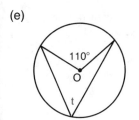

(f)

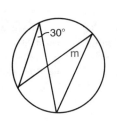

(g)

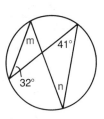

(h)

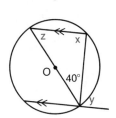

5. Find the value of the unknown angles.

(a)

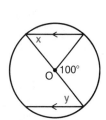

(b)

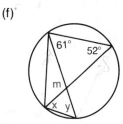

(c)

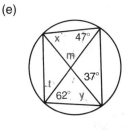

(d)

(e)

(f)

C 6. Show that central angles subtended by equal chords are equal.

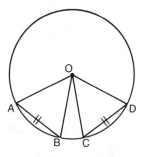

(a) Construct a circle with centre O, and chords AB = CD.
(b) Construct ∠AOB and ∠COD.
(c) Show △AOB ≅ △COD
   and ∠AOB = ∠COD

12.11 CYCLIC QUADRILATERALS

A cyclic quadrilateral is a quadrilateral whose vertices lie on the circumference of a circle.

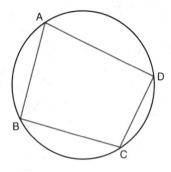

ABCD is a cyclic quadrilateral.

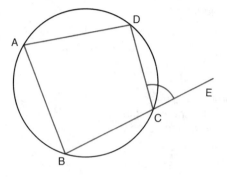

∠DCE is an exterior angle of the cyclic quadrilateral ABCD.

EXERCISE 12.11

B 1. PQRS is a cyclic quadrilateral.

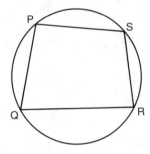

(a) Draw a similar diagram in your notebook.
(b) Measure ∠P and ∠R and find the sum of their measures.
(c) Measure ∠Q and ∠S and find the sum of their measures.
(d) Compare the sums of the angles in (b) and the angles in (c).
(e) Repeat the procedure for other cyclic quadrilaterals.

2. WXYZ is a cyclic quadrilateral and ∠WXQ is an exterior angle.

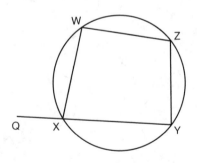

(a) Draw a similar diagram in your notebook.
(b) Measure ∠WXQ and ∠Z.
(c) How are the angles related?
(d) Repeat the procedure for other cyclic quadrilaterals and exterior angles.

The following summarizes the properties of cyclic quadrilaterals.

The opposite angles of a cyclic quadrilateral are supplementary.

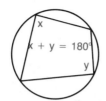

$x + y = 180°$

The exterior angle of a cyclic quadrilateral is equal to the interior and opposite angle.

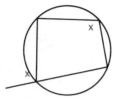

3. Find the value of the unknown angles.

(a)

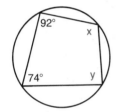

92°
x
74°
y

(b)

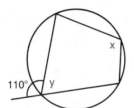

x
110°
y

(c)

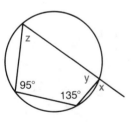

z
95°
y
x
135°

(d)

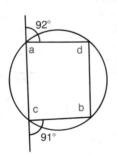

92°
a
d
c
b
91°

(e)

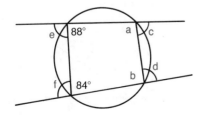

e
88°
a
c
d
b
f
84°

4. Find the value of the unknown angles.

(a)

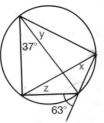

y
37°
x
z
63°

(b)

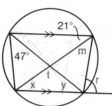

21°
47°
m
t
x
y
r

(c)

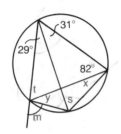

31°
29°
82°
t
x
y
s
m

Which of the following pieces of string will make a knot when the ends are pulled tight?

1.

2.

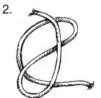

3.

4.

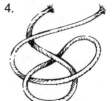

12.12 SIMILAR TRIANGLES

We have studied congruence, where lengths and angles are equal. In this section, we shall work with triangles where only the angles are equal.

1. Construct $\triangle ABC$, where AB = 8.0 cm, $\angle A = 35°$, $\angle B = 50°$.

2. Construct $\triangle DEF$, where DE = 12.0 cm, $\angle D = 35°$, $\angle E = 50°$.

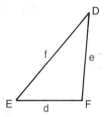

3. Measure the remaining angles and sides of the triangles and complete the following.

$$\angle A = \blacksquare \qquad \angle D = \blacksquare$$
$$\angle B = \blacksquare \qquad \angle E = \blacksquare$$
$$\angle C = \blacksquare \qquad \angle F = \blacksquare$$

$$a = \blacksquare \qquad d = \blacksquare \qquad \frac{a}{d} = \blacksquare$$

$$b = \blacksquare \qquad e = \blacksquare \qquad \frac{b}{e} = \blacksquare$$

$$c = \blacksquare \qquad f = \blacksquare \qquad \frac{c}{f} = \blacksquare$$

> If the angles of two triangles are respectively equal and the corresponding sides are in a constant ratio, then the triangles are similar and we write
> $$\triangle ABC \sim \triangle DEF$$

The statement $\triangle ABC \sim \triangle DEF$ sets up a one-to-one correspondence:

$$A \leftrightarrow D \qquad B \leftrightarrow E \qquad C \leftrightarrow F$$

which tells us that

$$\angle A = \angle D, \angle B = \angle E, \angle C = \angle F$$

and

$$\frac{a}{d} = \frac{b}{e} = \frac{c}{f}$$

where a, b, c, d, e, f are the measures of the sides opposite the vertices A, B, C, D, E, and F respectively.

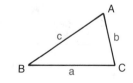

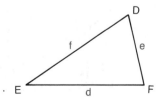

EXAMPLE 1. Given △ABC ~ △DEF, find the missing dimensions.

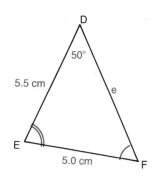

SOLUTION:

The correspondence between the two triangles is:

$$A \leftrightarrow D \qquad a \leftrightarrow d$$
$$B \leftrightarrow E \qquad b \leftrightarrow e$$
$$C \leftrightarrow F \qquad c \leftrightarrow f$$

$$\frac{a}{d} = \frac{b}{e} = \frac{c}{f}$$

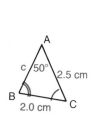

$$\therefore \frac{2.0}{5.0} = \frac{2.5}{e} = \frac{c}{5.5}$$

To find e,

$$\frac{2.0}{5.0} = \frac{2.5}{e}$$

Multiply both sides by 5.0e.

$$5.0e \times \frac{2.0}{5.0} = \frac{2.5}{e} \times 5.0e$$
$$2.0e = 2.5 \times 5.0$$
$$e = \frac{2.5 \times 5.0}{2.0}$$
$$e = 6.25$$

∴ the length of e is 6.3 cm.

To find c,

$$\frac{2.0}{5.0} = \frac{c}{5.5}$$

Multiply both sides by 5.5.

$$5.5 \times \frac{2.0}{5.0} = \frac{c}{5.5} \times 5.5$$
$$2.2 = c$$

∴ the length of c is 2.2 cm.

EXAMPLE 2. Given △PQR ~ △XYZ as in the diagram, find ∠Z and x.

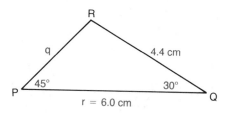

SOLUTION:

The correspondence is

$$P \leftrightarrow X \qquad\qquad p \leftrightarrow x$$
$$Q \leftrightarrow Y \qquad\qquad q \leftrightarrow y$$
$$R \leftrightarrow Z \qquad\qquad r \leftrightarrow z$$

$$\angle R = 180° - (45° + 30°)$$
$$= 180° - 77°$$
$$= 105°$$
$$\angle Z = 105°$$

$$\frac{x}{p} = \frac{z}{r}$$
$$\frac{x}{4.4} = \frac{2.0}{6.0}$$
$$x = \frac{2 \times 4.4}{6.0}$$
$$\doteq 1.5$$

∴ ∠Z = 105° and x = 1.5 cm.

EXERCISE 12.12

Use the correspondence in similar triangles to find the values of the variables in the following.

A 1.

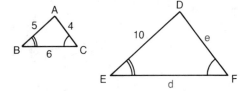

△ABC ~ △DEF

2.

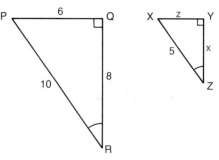

△PQR ~ △XYZ

3.

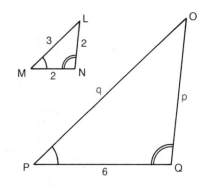

△LMN ~ △OPQ

B 4.

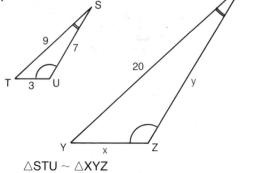

△STU ~ △XYZ

5.

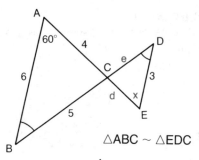

△ABC ~ △EDC

6.

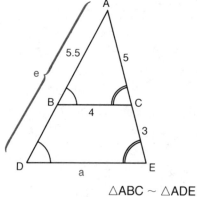

△ABC ~ △ADE

7.

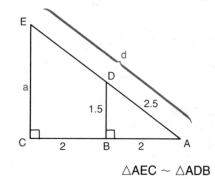

△AEC ~ △ADB

8.

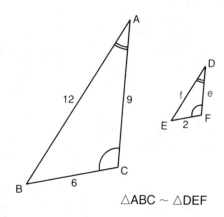

△ABC ~ △DEF

9. A flagpole casts a shadow 11.2 m long at a time when a vertical metre stick casts a shadow 0.9 m long, forming the similar triangles shown. Find the height of the flagpole, h.

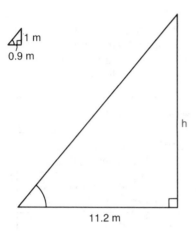

10. To find the distance across a river we can lay out two triangles as shown. Find the distance d.

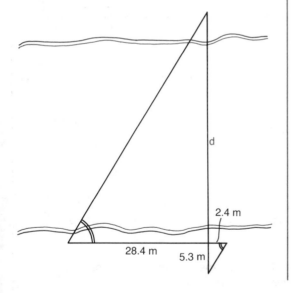

11. A surveyor takes a bearing on a marker and it is 105°. From a point 100 m due south the bearing is 70°. From a scale map where △ABC ~ △A′B′C′, the surveyor measures A′B′ = 6.7 cm and A′C′ = 11 cm. Find the real distance AC.

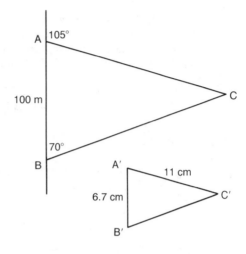

12. To estimate the distance to a building, Margaret holds a centimetre stick at arm's length, and sights on a door of the building. She holds the scale 60 cm from her eye. Find the distance to the building if the door is 2 m high and appears to be 2.8 cm on the scale.

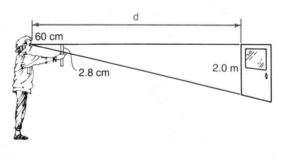

12.13 LOGO

LOGO is a high-level interactive computer language. It provides opportunities to study relationships and properties of geometric figures and to apply them in creative ways.

Figures are drawn on the screen by typing commands that move the "turtle" or "pencil." Some of the more fundamental commands are given in the table below.

■ represents a numerical value

Command	Meaning	Example	Explanation
FD ■	move forward	FD 100	The turtle moves 100 units forward.
BK ■	move backward	BK 75	The turtle moves 75 units backward.
RT ■	right turn	RT 90	The turtle turns 90° clockwise.
LT■	left turn	LT 45	The turtle turns 45° counter-clockwise.

EXAMPLE. Write the LOGO commands to draw a square with sides 75 units. RUN the program.

SOLUTION:
Since the angles in a square equal 90°, the turtle must turn 90°.

The commands are:

```
CS        ◄── CS means Clear the Screen
FD 75
RT 90
FD 75
RT 90
FD 75
RT 90
FD 75  }  The initial and final position
RT 90  }  of the turtle.
```

In the example, the commands FD 75 and RT 90 are repeated four times. The four pairs of commands can be shortened into one "repeat" command as follows.

REPEAT 4 [FD 75 RT 90]

number of repetitions

The group of commands to be repeated

EXERCISE 12.13

1. What will the following LOGO commands cause the turtle to do?

(a) RT 30
(b) LT 45
(c) RT 270
(d) FD 100
(e) BK 25
(f) LT 100

2. Identify the figures that are drawn by each of the following LOGO programs.

(a) CS
```
FD 100
RT 120
FD 100
RT 120
FD 100
RT 120
```

(b) CS
```
FD 100
RT 90
FD 50
RT 90
FD 100
RT 90
FD 50
RT 90
```

3. Enter the following LOGO programs into a computer. RUN the program and describe the figure.

(a) REPEAT 3 [FD 100 LT 120]
(b) REPEAT 60 [FD 2 RT 6]
(c) REPEAT 90 [FD 1 RT 4]
(d) REPEAT 120 [FD 1 RT 3]
(e) REPEAT 180 [FD 1 RT 2]
(f) REPEAT 360 [FD 1 RT 1]

4. The following program will begin by drawing a square with sides 80 units. RUN the program and describe the results.

```
TO SQUARE
REPEAT 4 [FD 80 RT 90]
END
CS
REPEAT 8 [SQUARE LT 45]
```

5. Total Turtle Turn Theorem

In a regular polygon, all the sides are equal and all the angles are equal. When drawing one of these with a LOGO program, each turn of the turtle has the same measure. The number of turns of the turtle is equal to the number of sides in the polygon. The total number of degrees turned is 360°. This is referred to as the Total Turtle Turn Theorem.

Complete the following table.

Figure	Number of sides and vertices	Degree measure of each turn	Total degrees turned	LOGO Command
Equilateral Triangle	3	120°	360°	REPEAT 3 [FD 100 RT 120]
Square	4	90°	360°	REPEAT 4 [FD 100 RT 90]
Regular Pentagon	5			
Regular Hexagon				
Regular Octagon				
Regular Polygon with n sides				

12.14 PROBLEM SOLVING

1. (a) What is the sum of the first 4 odd numbers?
(b) What is the sum of the first 5 odd numbers?
(c) What is the sum of the first 6 odd numbers?
(d) What is the sum of the first 7 odd numbers?
(e) What is the sum of the first 5634 odd numbers?
(f) What is the sum of the first n odd numbers?

2. The area of the outer square is 64 cm².

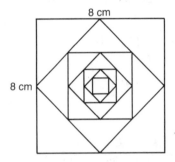

8 cm

8 cm

Each inside square is formed by joining the midpoints of the sides of the next larger square. What is the area of the smallest square?

3. AB ∥ CD

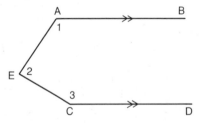

Find ∠1 + ∠2 + ∠3.

4. Sandra had twenty-three coins. She put them into three bags so that there was an odd number of coins in each bag. How many different possibilities are there?

5. If you divide a number by 5, then multiply it by 3, and finally subtract 21 from it you get 18. What is the number?

6. Dan is in a bowling league.

(a) In the first week he bowled games of 173, 180, and 169. What was his average after the first week?
(b) The second week he bowled games of 185, 191, and 140. What was his average after the second week?
(c) The third week he bowled games of 200, 184, and 171. What was his average after the third week?

7. What is the greatest amount of money you can have in coins and not be able to give change for a dollar?

8. A year has two consecutive months with Friday the thirteenth. Which months are they?

9. Paul wants to put a fence around his 10 m by 6 m rectangular swimming pool. He wants to leave a 4 m wide grass area between the pool and the fence.

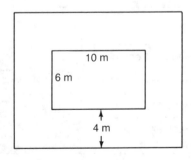

10 m

6 m

4 m

(a) How much fencing should Paul buy?

(b) If fencing costs $11.90/m, how much will the fencing cost, including sales tax of 7%?

(c) How many posts are required if there is to be a post every 2 m.

(d) Posts cost $15.50 each. How much will the posts cost, including sales tax of 7%?

(e) The cost of labour and materials for the job is $430. What is the total cost of installing the fence?

10. Divide 64 into four parts so that when you add 3 to the first part, subtract 3 from the second part, multiply the third part by 3, and divide the fourth part by 3, all the numbers are equal.

11. The number 131 is a palindrome; it reads the same forwards and backwards. The number 64 is a cubic number because $4^3 = 64$. Find a cubic number with more than one digit that is a palindrome.

12. Twenty-four boxes each measuring 8 cm by 6 cm by 3 cm will fit exactly into a large box which has a base measuring 12 cm by 12 cm. What is the height of the large box?

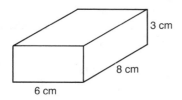

13. A piece of paper has been wrapped around a styrofoam cylinder.

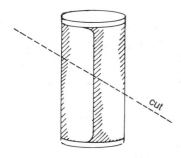

The cylinder is then cut through at a slant. Draw a picture of the paper after it has been unrolled.

14. The "glide to height" ratio for a jet airliner is 13 : 1. This means that for every kilometre of height, the aircraft can glide 13 km horizontally with the engines off.

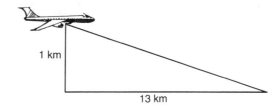

How far will a jetliner glide from a height of 9.7 km?

15.

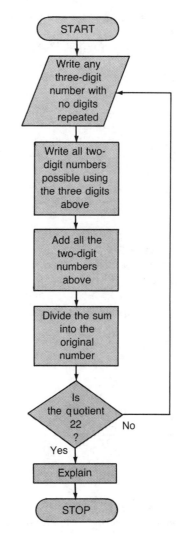

12.15 REVIEW EXERCISE

1. Using only a ruler and a compass, construct the following angles.

(a) 90°   (b) 270°
(c) 135°   (d) 22.5°
(e) 15°   (f) 120°

2.

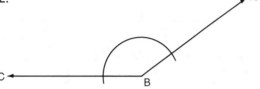

(a) Copy ∠ABC using a ruler and a compass.
(b) Bisect ∠ABC.
(c) Divide ∠ABC into four equal parts.

3. In the following figures, BD bisects ∠ABC.

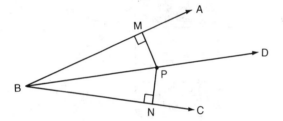

(a) Show that PM = PN.
(b) Show that any point on BD is equidistant from AB and CB.

4. In the following figure, CD is the right bisector of AB.

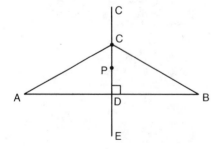

(a) Show that PA = PB.
(b) Show that any point on CD is equidistant from A and B.

5. Calculate the values of the variables.

(a)

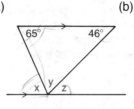

(b)

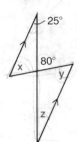

(c)

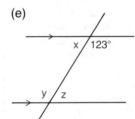

(d)

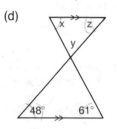

(e)

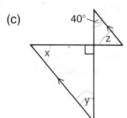

(f)

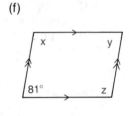

(g)

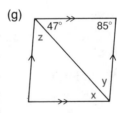

(h)

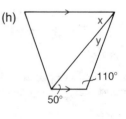

(i)

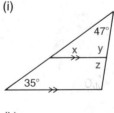

(j)

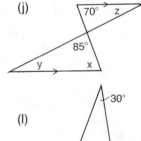

(k)

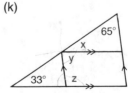

(l)

6. Find x, y, z, in each of the following.

(a)

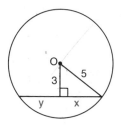

(b)

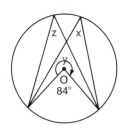

(c)

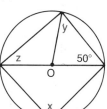

(d)

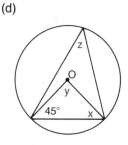

(e)

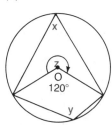

(f)

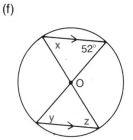

(g)

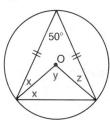

(h)

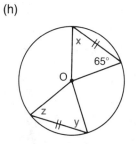

(i)

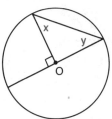

(j)

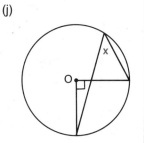

7. Find the values of the variables in the similar triangles.

(a)

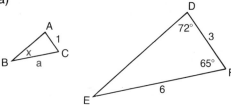

△ABC ~ △DEF

(b)

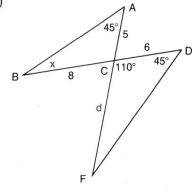

△ABC ~ △DFC

(c)

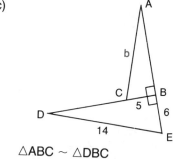

△ABC ~ △DBC

8. (a) Construct any triangle ABC.
(b) Bisect AB at D and construct DE ∥ BC.
(c) Measure AE, AC, DE, and BC, then calculate the ratios $\frac{AE}{AC}$, $\frac{AD}{AB}$ and $\frac{DE}{BC}$.

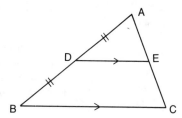

12.16 CHAPTER 12 TEST

1. Find the value of the unknown angles.

(a)

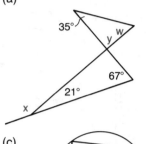

(b)

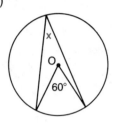

(c)

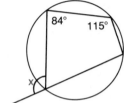

(d)

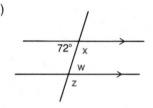

2. In each of the following,
(a) state the reason why the triangles are congruent.
(b) list the other equal parts as a result of the congruence.

(i)

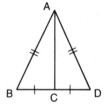

(ii)

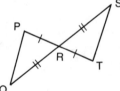

3. Given △ABC ~ △DEF, determine the missing dimensions.

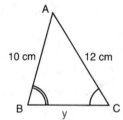

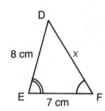

4. Use a ruler and a compass to perform the constructions.
(a) a 45° angle
(b) a 30° angle
(c) a line through P parallel to XY
(d) the incentre of △PQR

12.17 CUMULATIVE REVIEW FOR CHAPTERS 9 TO 12

1. Find four consecutive numbers with sum of 446.

2. Find the dimensions of a rectangle which has a perimeter of 266 m and a length 43 m longer than the width.

3. A baby's bank contains $2.75, made up of dimes and nickels. There are thirty-four coins in all. How many dimes are there?

4. Determine the simple interest earned on each of the following investments.
(a) $4000 invested at 7% annual interest for five years.
(b) $2000 invested at 6% annual interest for six months.

5. When the Canadian dollar was worth 75 cents in U.S. currency, a package of three golf balls was selling for $9.30 in Canada and for $7.50 in the United States. Which package of golf balls is the best bargain?

6. A plane flew from Thunder Bay to Niagara Falls at 400 km/h and returned at 300 km/h. The total trip took 7 h. How far is it from Thunder Bay to Niagara Falls by air?

7. A car, travelling at 100 km/h left Crow's Pass for Red Rock, a distance of 720 km. At the same time, a car left Red Rock for Crow's Pass at a speed of 80 km/h. How long after departure will the cars pass each other?

8. The table gives the responses to a survey which asked fifty people to name the media which has the most effective advertising.

R = radio   T = television   P = print

```
R  T  P  T  R  R  T  T  P  T
T  P  T  R  R  R  T  T  T  P
T  P  R  T  T  P  R  R  R  P
T  R  R  T  T  R  T  P  R  T
T  T  T  P  R  P  T  T  R  T
```

(a) Construct a tally sheet for the information.

(b) If there are 70 000 people in the population, how many think radio has the most effective advertising?
(c) Display this information on a graph.

9. When would you use a mail questionnaire survey as opposed to a telephone survey to gather information?

10. The table gives the type and number of movies rented on one weekend at World Video.

Type	Number
Horror	43
Suspense	31
Comedy	35
Drama	22
Musical	12
Action	48
Other	9

Display this information on a graph.

11. Calculate the mean, median, and mode of the following.
(a) 22, 24, 27, 29, 23, 23, 27, 32, 27
(b) 143, 165, 192, 201, 120, 151, 183, 213

12. A die is rolled and a coin is tossed. What is the probability of getting
(a) a tail and a 6?
(b) a tail and an odd number?

13. Calculate the perimeter.
(a)   (b)

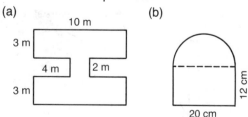

GEOMETRY   423

14. Calculate the area.

(a)

10 m

(b)

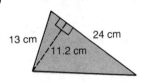

13 cm   24 cm
11.2 cm

(c)

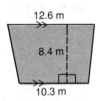

12.6 m
8.4 m
10.3 m

(d)

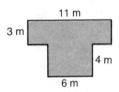

11 m
3 m
4 m
6 m

15. Calculate the surface area to the nearest tenth.

(a)

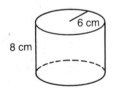

6 cm
8 cm

(b)

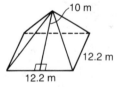

10 m
12.2 m
12.2 m

16. Calculate the volume to the nearest tenth.

(a)

8 cm
12 cm

(b)

50 cm

17. Calculate the values of the unknowns.

(a)

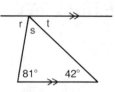

r   t
s
81°   42°

(b)

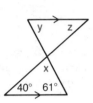

y   z
x
40° 61°

(c)

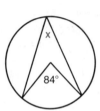

x
84°

(d)

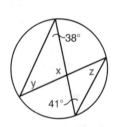

38°
x
z
y
41°

18. Find the missing dimensions.

(a)

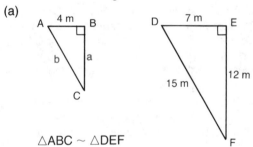

A   4 m   B   D   7 m   E
b   a
C
15 m   12 m

F

△ABC ~ △DEF

(b)

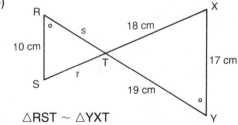

R   X
10 cm   s   18 cm
T   17 cm
S   r
19 cm
Y

△RST ~ △YXT

RELATIONS

CHAPTER

Mathematics is the science which uses easy words for hard ideas.
Edward Kasner and James R. Newman

REVIEW AND PREVIEW TO CHAPTER 13

SET NOTATION

EXERCISE

1. List the members of the set. The first one is done for you.

(a)

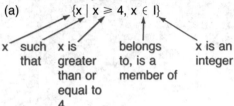

Solution {4, 5, 6, 7, ...}

(b) {x | x < 5, x ∈ W}
(c) {x | x ⩾ −1, x ∈ I}
(d) {x | x < 0, x ∈ I}
(e) {x | x < 5, x ∈ I}
(f) {x | 2 < x < 7, x ∈ W}
(g) {x | 0 < x ⩽ 8, x ∈ W}
(h) {x | −1 ⩽ x < 3, x ∈ I}
(i) {x | −5 < x ⩽ −1, x ∈ I}

GRAPHING

EXERCISE

1. Graph each of the following. The first one is done for you.

(a) x ⩽ 5, x ∈ R

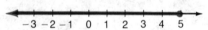

(b) x > 4, x ∈ R
(c) x ⩽ 2, x ∈ R
(d) x ⩾ −3, x ∈ R
(e) x < −1, x ∈ R
(f) 2 < x < 5, x ∈ R
(g) 0 ⩽ x ⩽ 6, x ∈ R
(h) −3 ⩽ x ⩽ 1, x ∈ R
(i) −5 ⩽ x < −2, x ∈ R

THE PYTHAGOREAN THEOREM

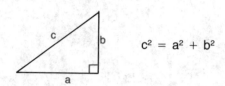

$$c^2 = a^2 + b^2$$

EXERCISE

1. Calculate the length of the unknown side to the nearest tenth.

(a)

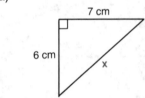

(b)

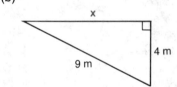

(c)

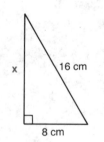

(d)

A "WORD" PROBLEM

Contained in the array below are over 60 words associated with mathematics. These words are written forward, backwards, diagonally, and upside down.

The word ROOT starts at coordinates (K, 2) and ends at coordinates (H, 5).

EXERCISE

1. (a) Find thirty words and record your answers using the coordinates. For example, ROOT: (K, 2) to (H, 5).

(b) Give a definition for each word.

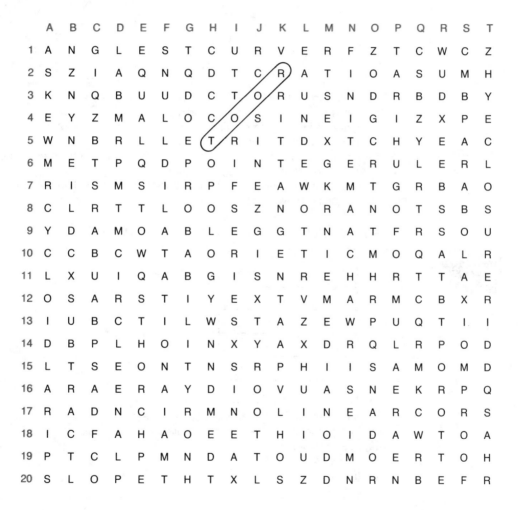

	A	B	C	D	E	F	G	H	I	J	K	L	M	N	O	P	Q	R	S	T
1	A	N	G	L	E	S	T	C	U	R	V	E	R	F	Z	T	C	W	C	Z
2	S	Z	I	A	Q	N	Q	D	T	C	R	A	T	I	O	A	S	U	M	H
3	K	N	Q	B	U	U	D	C	T	O	R	U	S	N	D	R	B	D	B	Y
4	E	Y	Z	M	A	L	O	C	O	S	I	N	E	I	G	I	Z	X	P	E
5	W	N	B	R	L	L	E	T	R	I	T	D	X	T	C	H	Y	E	A	C
6	M	E	T	P	Q	D	P	O	I	N	T	E	G	E	R	U	L	E	R	L
7	R	I	S	M	S	I	R	P	F	E	A	W	K	M	T	G	R	B	A	O
8	C	L	R	T	T	L	O	O	S	Z	N	O	R	A	N	O	T	S	B	S
9	Y	D	A	M	O	A	B	L	E	G	G	T	N	A	T	F	R	S	O	U
10	C	C	B	C	W	T	A	O	R	I	E	T	I	C	M	O	Q	A	L	R
11	L	X	U	I	Q	A	B	G	I	S	N	R	E	H	H	R	T	T	A	E
12	O	S	A	R	S	T	I	Y	E	X	T	V	M	A	R	M	C	B	X	R
13	I	U	B	C	T	I	L	W	S	T	A	Z	E	W	P	U	Q	T	I	I
14	D	B	P	L	H	O	I	N	X	Y	A	X	D	R	Q	L	R	P	O	D
15	L	T	S	E	O	N	T	N	S	R	P	H	I	I	S	A	M	O	M	D
16	A	R	A	E	R	A	Y	D	I	O	V	U	A	S	N	E	K	R	P	Q
17	R	A	D	N	C	I	R	M	N	O	L	I	N	E	A	R	C	O	R	S
18	I	C	F	A	H	A	O	E	E	T	H	I	O	I	D	A	W	T	O	A
19	P	T	C	L	P	M	N	D	A	T	O	U	D	M	O	E	R	T	O	H
20	S	L	O	P	E	T	H	T	X	L	S	Z	D	N	R	N	B	E	F	R

13.1 RELATIONS AND ORDERED PAIRS

In everyday life, the word relation has a familiar meaning.

Doug is the brother of Dave.
Karen is the cousin of Deane.

In mathematics, this idea is expanded to include a great variety of relationships between pairs of objects or numbers.

EXAMPLE. (a) Using the polygons shown, construct a table showing the number of sides and the number of non-intersecting diagonals.

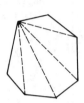

(b) From the pattern in the table, how many non-intersecting diagonals can be drawn for an eight-sided figure?
(c) State, in words, the relationship between the number of sides and the number of diagonals.
(d) If n represents the number of sides, write a formula for the number of non-intersecting diagonals.
(e) Use your formula to find the number of non-intersecting diagonals in a 12-sided polygon.

SOLUTION:

(a)

Number of sides	Number of diagonals
3	0
4	1
5	2
6	3
7	4

(b) 5 non-intersecting diagonals can be drawn.
(c) The number of non-intersecting diagonals is 3 less than the number of sides.
(d) $d = n - 3$
(e) If $n = 12$,
$$d = 12 - 3$$
$$= 9$$

There are 9 non-intersecting diagonals in a 12-sided polygon.
Values in a table are often expressed as a set of pairs of numbers.

$$\{(3, 0), (4, 1), (5, 2), (6, 3), (7, 4)\}$$

To avoid confusion, the numbers are written in the same order:

(number of sides, number of non-intersecting diagonals)

For this reason, each pair of numbers is called an ordered pair.

> A set of ordered pairs is called a relation.

EXERCISE 13.1

1. (a) Use the polygons shown to construct a table showing the number of sides and the number of triangles formed by drawing non-intersecting diagonals.

(b) Write the relationship as a set of ordered pairs.
(c) Write in words the relationship between the number of sides and the number of triangles.
(d) If n represents the number of sides, write an equation for the number of triangles.
(e) Use the equation to find the numbers of triangles formed in a 14-sided polygon by drawing all the non intersecting diagonals.

2. In the diagram shown, each small square has sides 1 cm in length, and an area of 1 cm².

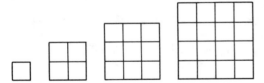

(a) Complete the tables in your notebook where, for the 3 larger groups of squares

    n represents the length of each side
    P represents the perimeter
    A represents the area

(i)

n	P

(ii)

n	A

(b) Write each relationship as a set of ordered pairs.
(c) Write an equation showing the relationship between n and P.
(d) Use the equation to find P when n = 21.
(e) Write an equation showing the relationship between n and A.
(f) Use the equation to find A when n = 19.

3. The table gives Paula's earnings for the number of hours worked.

h	2	3	4	5	6
E	$19.50	$29.25	$39.00	$48.75	$58.50

(a) Write an equation showing the relationship between E and h.
(b) Use the equation to determine Paula's earnings if she worked 23 h.
(c) How many hours would she have to work to earn $780?

4. For each table, make an assumption and write an equation showing the relationship between x and y.

(a)

x	y
2	8
4	6
6	4

(b)

x	y
5	3
7	5
11	9

(c)

x	y
1	1
2	4
3	9

(d)

x	y
5	4
7	6
8	7

13.2 REPRESENTING RELATIONS

A relation may be expressed in two additional ways:

(i) as an arrow diagram
(ii) in mapping notation

EXAMPLE 1. Express the relation $\{(-2, -4), (-1, -2), (0, 0), (1, 2)\}$
(a) as an arrow diagram
(b) in mapping notation.

SOLUTION:

(a)

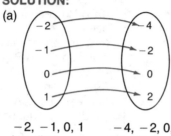

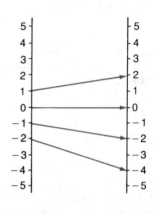

$-2, -1, 0, 1$
is called
the domain
of the
relation

$-4, -2, 0, 2$
is called
the range
of the
relation

(b) Note that the second number in each ordered pair is twice the first number. The mapping notation is

x is mapped onto 2x $x \rightarrow 2x,\ x \in \{-2, -1, 0, 1\}$ These are the values of x which must be used.

> The domain of a relation is the set of all first components from the ordered pairs in a relation. The range of a relation is the set of all second components from the ordered pairs in a relation.

EXAMPLE 2. For the mapping $x \rightarrow 2x - 1,\ x \in \{-4, -2, 0, 2, 4\}$
(a) construct a table of values
(b) state the range of the relation.

SOLUTION:

(a)

x	2x − 1
−4	−9
−2	−5
0	−1
2	3
4	7

When x = −4,

$2(-4) - 1 = -8 - 1$
$= -9$

(b) The range is $\{-9, -5, -1, 3, 7\}$ for this relation.

EXERCISE 13.2

A 1. State the domain for each relation.
(a) {(−2, 1), (−1, 2), (0, 3), (1, 4)}
(b) {(0, 0), (1, 1), (2, 4), (3, 9)}
(c) {(−2, 0), (−2, 1), (−2, 2), (−2, 3)}
(d)   (e)

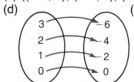   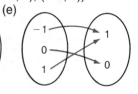

2. State the range for each relation.
(a) (1, 3), (2, 5), (3, 7), (4, 9)
(b) (−1, 2), (−2, 4), (−3, 6), (−4, 8)
(c) (2, 1), (3, 1), (4, 1), (−5, 1)
(d)   (e)

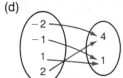   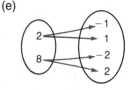

3. For the mapping x → 3x, x ∈ I, state the missing value in each ordered pair.
(a) (2, ■)   (b) (−1, ■)
(c) (■, 12)   (d) (■, 0)
(e) (−5, ■)   (f) (■, 45)
(g) (■, −18)   (h) (−7, ■)

4. For the mapping x → 2x + 1, x ∈ I, state the missing value in each ordered pair.
(a) (3, ■) (b) (0, ■) (c) (−1, ■)(d) (■, 7)
(e) (−4, ■)(f) (−2, ■) (g) (■, 9) (h) (■, −1)

B 5. Express each mapping shown
(a) as an arrow diagram
(b) as a set of ordered pairs.
(i)   x → 3x − 2, x ∈ {0, 1, 2, 3}
(ii) x → 1 − x, x ∈ {−2, −1, 0, 1, 2}
(iii) x → 2x², x ∈ {−1, 0, 1, 2, 3}
(iv) x → ¾x, x ∈ {0, 2, 4, 6, 8}
(v)   x → 0.2x, x ∈ {0, 5, 10, 15}

6. The relationship between numbers may be translated from words into a mapping.
Express each of the following relationships as a mapping in the form x → ■.
(a) The second value is five less than the first value.

(b) The second value is twice the first value.
(c) The second value is one third of the first value.
(d) The second value is three more than five times the first value.
(e) The second value is one less than one half of the first value.

7. Complete the mapping notation x → ■, x ∈ {■} for each relation shown.
(a) {(1, 3), (2, 6), (3, 9), (4, 12)}
(b) {(2, 0), (3, 1), (4, 2), (5, 3)}
(c) {(1, 1), (2, 4), (3, 9), (4, 16)}
(d) {(−2, −1), (−4, −2), (−6, −3), (−8, −4)}
(e)   (f)

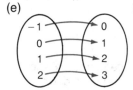   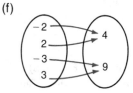

8. For the mapping x → 5x − 2, x ∈ {−1, 0, 1, 2, 3},
(a) construct a table of values
(b) state the range of the relation.

9. For the mapping x → ⅓x + 3, x ∈ {−6, −3, 0, 3, 6},
(a) construct a table of values
(b) state the range of the relation.

10. In your notebook, complete each table of values.

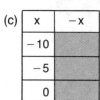

(a)
x	1 − 2x
−2	
−1	
0	

(b)
x	0.5x + 2
−4	
−2	
0	

(c)
x	−x
−10	
−5	
0	

(d)
x	x² + 1
−2	
−1	
0	

13.3 GRAPHING ORDERED PAIRS

In the 17th century, a French mathematician named Rene Descartes developed the Cartesian Plane, a grid for the graphing of ordered pairs of real numbers.

Two perpendicular number lines, which intersect at a point called the origin, form the basis for this grid. The first number in the ordered pair is called the horizontal coordinate, and the second number, the vertical coordinate.

Since unknown ordered pairs are usually represented by (x, y), the horizontal coordinate is called the x-coordinate, and the vertical coordinate is called the y-coordinate. For this reason the horizontal axis is called the x-axis and the vertical axis is called the y-axis.

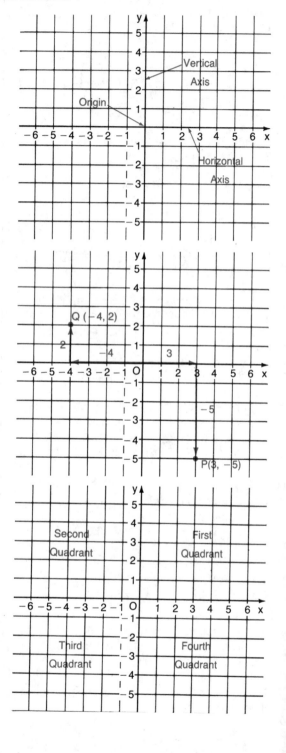

The point P(3, −5) is located three units to the right of the origin and five units down.

x-coordinate

(3, −5)

y-coordinate

The point Q(−4, 2) is located four units to the left of the origin and two units up.

The two axes divide the Cartesian Plane into four quadrants.

EXAMPLE. Plot the points A(5, 4), B(−3, 3), C(−4, 0), and D(2, −3). Join the points in the order A, B, C, D and name the polygon.

SOLUTION:
ABCD is a quadrilateral.

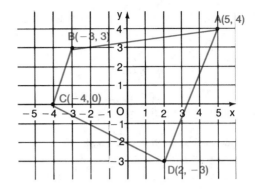

EXERCISE 13.3

A 1. (a) State the coordinates of the points A to P.
(b) Name two points in the second quadrant.
(c) Name four points on the y-axis.
(d) Name two points which have equal x-coordinates.

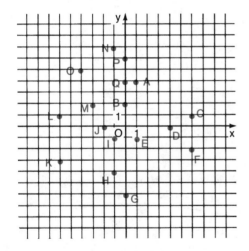

2. State three ordered pairs which lie on each line.
(a)

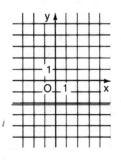

(b)

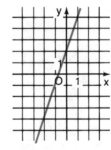

(c)

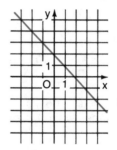

3. (a) State the length of each line segment.

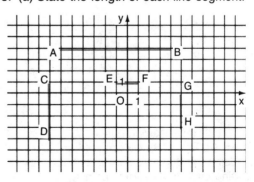

(b) State the coordinates of the midpoint of each line segment.

B 4. Find the letter for each ordered pair and decode the message.

$$(2, 3), (-1, -1), (5, 0),$$
$$(-4, -3), (0, 5), (0, 0), (4, 2)!$$

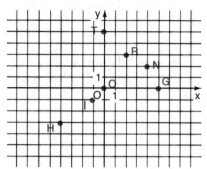

5. (a) Plot the following points.

$$A(-1, 1), B(-3, 0), C(1, 2), D(5, 4)$$

(b) State three other points on the same straight line.

6. Plot the following sets of points, and identify the figure formed when the points are joined in the order given:
(a) X(3, 1), Y(3, 5), Z(8, 4)
(b) R(-6, 2), S(0, 2), T(0, 7)
(c) D(1, 1), E(1, -2), F(-5, -2), G(-5, 1)
(d) A(6, 0), B(9, 1), C(9, -4), D(6, -5)
(e) J(-3, 0), K(0, -4), L(5, -4), M(8, 0), N(5, 4), T(0, 4)

7. (a) Plot the points A(-4, 2), B(-4, -2), and C(1, 2).
(b) State the coordinates of a fourth point which will form a rectangle with these three points.

8. (a) Plot the points R(-2, -3), S(0, 1), and T(4, -1).
(b) State the coordinates of a fourth point which will form a parallelogram with these three points. (There is more than one solution.)

9. (a) Plot the following points.
A(-5, 0), B(-4, 3), C(0, 5), D(4, 3), E(3, -4)
(b) Using the origin as centre, draw a circle passing through these five points.
(c) State the coordinates of four other points on this circle.

10. To get the message, plot each set of points and join them in the order they were plotted.
(a) (-14, 5), (-14, 9), (-12, 7), (-10, 9), (-10, 5).
(b) (-7, 5), (-6, 7), (-5, 9), (-4, 7), (-3, 5). Join (-6, 7) to (-4, 7).
(c) (0, 9), (4, 9). Join (2, 9) to (2, 5).
(d) (7, 5), (7, 7), (7, 9).
(e) (11, 5), (11, 7), (11, 9). Join (7, 7) to (11, 7).
(f) (-4, 2), (-4, -2).
(g) (2, 2), (-1, 2), (-1, 0), (2, 0), (2, -2), (-1, -2).
(h) (-6, -5), (-9, -5), (-9, -7), (-9, -9). Join (-9, -7) to (-7, -7).
(i) (-3, -5), (-3, -9), (0, -9), (0, -5).
(j) (3, -9), (3, -5), (6, -9), (6, -5).
(k) (-3, -13), (-3, -12), (1, -12), (1, -14), (-1, -15), (-1, -17).
(l) (-1, -19).

Determine the pattern. Find the missing number.

6	5	13	43
5	9	18	63
7	6	35	77
8	4	21	▨

13.4 GRAPHING RELATIONS FROM EQUATIONS

A relation described by the mapping notation

$$x \rightarrow 3x - 5, x \in \{0, 1, 2, 3, 4\}$$

will result in ordered pairs of the form (x, y) where $y = 3x - 5$.

This is called the defining equation of the relation. To graph a relation, we must find and plot these ordered pairs.

EXAMPLE 1. A relation is described by the mapping notation

$$x \rightarrow 2x + 1, x \in \{-2, -1, 0, 1, 2\}$$

(a) State the domain of the relation.
(b) State the defining equation of the relation.
(c) Construct a table of values for the relation.
(d) Graph the relation.
(e) How are the points related?

SOLUTION:
(a) The domain is $\{-2, -1, 0, 1, 2\}$.
(b) The defining equation is $y = 2x + 1$.
(c) The values of the y-coordinate may be found by substituting the values of x into the defining equation.

(d)

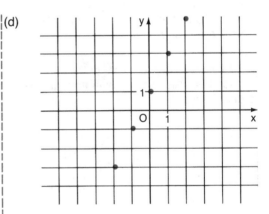

x	y = 2x + 1	y	(x, y)
-2	y = 2(-2) + 1 = -4 + 1 = -3	-3	(-2, -3)
-1	y = 2(-1) + 1 = -2 + 1 = -1	-1	(-1, -1)
0	y = 2(0) + 1 = 0 + 1 = 1	1	(0, 1)
1	y = 2(1) + 1 = 2 + 1 = 3	3	(1, 3)
2	y = 2(2) + 1 = 4 + 1 = 5	5	(2, 5)

(e) The points are in a straight line.

> A relation whose points are in a straight line is called a linear relation.

EXAMPLE 2.

(a) Graph $\{(x, y) \mid y = 2 - x, x \in I\}$

(b) If $x \in R$, what change is made in the graph?

SOLUTION:

(a) To graph a relation, a table of values is constructed.

x	y = 2 − x	y	(x, y)
−2	y = 2 − (−2)	4	(−2, 4)
0	y = 2 − (0)	2	(0, 2)
2	y = 2 − (2)	0	(2, 0)
4	y = 2 − (4)	−2	(4, −2)

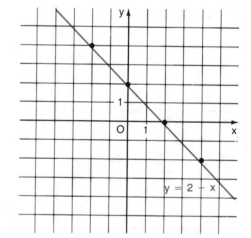

At least three ordered pairs should be determined.

Since the domain, I, is an infinite set, it is not possible to plot all of the points in the relation. This is a partial graph.

(b) If $x \in R$, all of the points in the line will be included. A solid line is drawn through the ordered pairs.

A relation may be described in any of the following ways.

    (i)   in words
    (ii)   as a set of ordered pairs
    (iii) by an arrow diagram
    (iv) in mapping notation
    (v)   by a table of values
    (vi) by a graph
    (vii) by set notation
    (viii) by a defining equation

EXERCISE 13.4

 A 1. If y = 4x + 2, state the missing value in each ordered pair.

(a) (2, ■)   (b) (0, ■)   (c) (−1, ■)

(d) (¼, ■)   (e) (■, 10)   (f) (■, 4)

2. For each relation, state an equation in the form y = ■x.

(a) {(2, 10), (3, 15), (4, 20), (5, 25)}
(b) {(−1, −3), (0, 0), (1, 3), (2, 6)}
(c) {(8, 4), (6, 3), (2, 1), (1, ½)}

B 3. State the equation for each of the following relations.

(a)   (b)

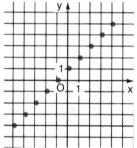

(c)   (d)

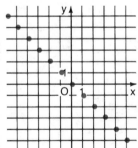

4. Complete the table of values in your notebook for each given equation.

(a) y = 3x − 2   (b) y = 5 − x

x	y
−1	
0	
1	
2	

x	y
−2	
−1	
0	
1	

(c) y = ½x + 1   (d) y = 2 − 3x

x	y
−2	
0	
2	
4	

x	y
−2	
−1	
0	
1	

(e) y = −½x + 1   (f) y = 2

x	y
0	
2	
4	
6	

x	y
−1	
0	
1	
2	

5. Construct a table of values and graph each relation.

(a) x → 5x − 1, ∈ I
(b) x → 1 − x, x ∈ I
(c) x → ⅔x, x ∈ {−6, −3, 0, 3, 6}
(d) x → x, x ∈ I
(e) x → 2x + 3, x ∈ R
(f) x → 3 − 5x, x ∈ R

6. Construct a table of values and graph the relation described by each equation.

(a) y = 3x + 1, x ∈ I
(b) y = 2(x − 1), x ∈ R
(c) y = 2, x ∈ {−3 −2, −1, 0, 1, 2}
(d) x = −1, y ∈ R
(e) y = ½x − 3, x ∈ {−4, −2, 1, 2, 4}
(f) y = −x, x ∈ {−2, −1, 0, 1, 2}

7. Construct a table of values and graph the relation in each case.

(a) {(x, y) | y = 3x, x ∈ R, y ∈ R}
(b) {(x, y) | y = 5 − 2x, x ∈ R, y ∈ R}
(c) {(x, y) | y = −2, x ∈ R}
(d) {(x, y) | y = ¼x + 3, x ∈ R, y ∈ R}
(e) {(x, y) | x + y = 7, x ∈ R, y ∈ R}
(f) {(x, y) | x = 3, y ∈ R}

13.5 INTERSECTING GRAPHS

EXAMPLE. Sarah and Earl are avid water-skiers. Every weekend they go to Lake Manitoulin. While taking a rest they calculated that the defining equations of their respective paths on the lake were $y = 2x + 6$ and $y = 5x + 3$.
(a) Graph the equations on the same set of axes.
(b) Locate the point at which they would meet.

SOLUTION:
(a) Before graphing the equations, a table of values must be constructed.

$y = 2x + 6$

x	y
−3	0
−2	2
−1	4
0	6
1	8
2	10
3	12

$y = 5x − 3$

x	y
−2	−13
−1	−8
0	−3
1	2
2	7
3	12

Draw both equations on the same set of axes using the data from the table of values. Label the graph clearly.

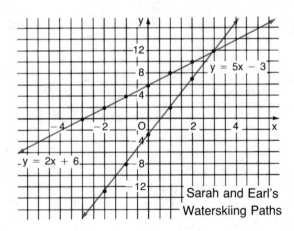

Sarah and Earl's Waterskiing Paths

(b) From the graph, it is evident that their paths will cross at the point given by the coordinates, (3, 12). This point is called the point of intersection. It is a solution to both equations. Check by substituting (3, 12) in the two equations.

EXERCISE 13.5

B 1. (a) Graph the two lines represented by each of the following equations, using the same axes.
   (i) $y = 2x, x \in R$
   (ii) $y = x + 3, x \in R$
(b) Locate the coordinates of the point of intersection.

2. Find the coordinates of the point of intersection by graphing the two lines represented by the equations below.
(a) $y = 3x - 1, x \in R$
(b) $y = x - 7, x \in R$

3. (a) If $x \in R$, graph the lines represented by the following equations.
   (i) $y = x + 3$
   (ii) $y = 3 - 2x$
   (iii) $y = 3$
(b) What do you notice about these three lines?

> Three or more lines which intersect at a common point are said to be concurrent.

4. Show that the lines represented by the following equations are concurrent.
(a) $y = -2x, x \in R$
(b) $y = 2x - 4, x \in R$
(c) $y = -x - 1, x \in R$

5. (a) Graph the four lines represented by the following equations on the same axes.
   (i) $y = 2x - 8$
   (ii) $y = 3$
   (iii) $y = -1$
   (iv) $y = 2x + 3$
(b) What figure is formed by the points of intersection of these lines?

How many words of four letters or more can you form using the letters in the word CARTESIAN?

13.6 PROBLEMS SOLVED WITH GRAPHS

In this section we will use relations and their graphs to solve problems.

EXAMPLE. Ace Truck Rentals offers two plans for renting trucks on a daily basis.

Plan A: $50 plus $0.25/km
Plan B: $0.50/km

(a) Which plan is most economical if you plan to drive 100 km in one day?
(b) At what distance will either plan cost the same?

SOLUTION:
The following are three solutions.

METHOD I

Plan A

Distance (km)	Cost ($)
0	50.00
50	62.50
100	75.00
150	87.50
200	100.00
250	112.50
300	125.00

Plan B

Distance (km)	Cost ($)
0	0
50	25.00
100	50.00
150	75.00
200	100.00
250	125.00
300	150.00

METHOD II

Plan A:

$$C_A = 50 + 0.25\,k \quad \text{where k is kilometres driven}$$

Plan B:

$$C_B = 0.50\,k$$

For 100 km

$$C_A = 50 + 0.25(100) \qquad C_B = 0.50(100)$$
$$= 75 \qquad\qquad\qquad = 50$$

For equal costs
$$C_A = C_B$$
$$50 + 0.25\,k = 0.50\,k$$
$$50 = 0.25k$$
$$k = 200$$

METHOD III

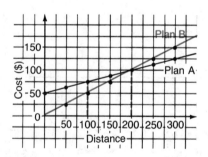

(a) Plan A is more economical by $25 if you drive 100 km.
(b) The plans cost the same at 200 km.

EXERCISE 13.6

B 1. The cost of steel wire is $1.50/m.

(a) Complete the table of values in your notebook.

Length of wire (m)	0	2	5	10	25	30
Cost ($)						

(b) Graph the relation.

(c) Using your graph, calculate the cost of
   (i)   15 m of wire
   (ii) 27.5 m of wire.

(d) Extend your graph to determine the cost of 45 m of wire.

2. In a computer game, the bank was robbed. At 12:30 the robbers left town driving at 80 km/h. At 13:00 the police gave chase at 100 km/h.

(a) Complete the tables.

Time (Robbers)	Kilometres travelled
12:30	0
13:00	40
13:30	
14:00	
14:30	
15:00	
15:30	

Time (Police)	Kilometres travelled
13:00	0
13:30	
14:00	
14:30	
15:00	
15:30	

(b) Graph both sets of information on the same axes.

(c) At what time did the police intercept the robbers? How far had they travelled?

(d) How far apart were the cars at 13:00? At 14:30?

(e) At what time were the cars 20 km apart? 5 km apart?

3.

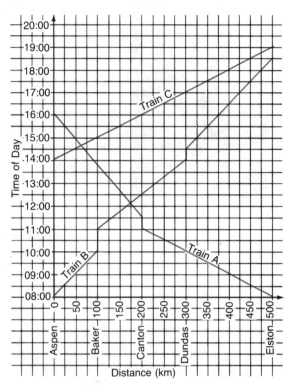

The graph shows the progress of three trains, one travelling from Elston to Aspen and the other two from Aspen to Elston.

(a) At what time does each train start?

(b) When did each train arrive at its destination?

(c) At what time did trains A and B pass each other?

(d) At what time did trains A and C pass each other?

(e) For how long did train A stop at Canton?

(f) How many stopovers did train B make?

(g) What was train B's average speed between Aspen and Baker?

(h) What was train C's average speed between Aspen and Elston?

(i) How far is it from Dundas to Elston?

(j) How far is it from Canton to Aspen?

(k) How long does it take each train to reach its destination?

(l) How far apart are trains A and B at 11:00?

(m) How far apart are trains B and C at 17:00?

(n) How far apart are trains A and B at 09:30?

13.7 SLOPE OF A LINE SEGMENT

In some areas, the steepness of hills on major highways is often given in percentages. The road sign shown indicates that the steepness of the hill is 10%. This means that for every 100 m along the horizontal, the vertical change is 10 m. In mathematics, this ratio is called the slope.

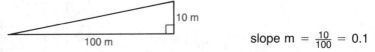

slope m $= \frac{10}{100} = 0.1$

Slope is the measure of the steepness of a line segment or line. In the diagram, EF is steeper than either AB or CD. We find the slope of these lines using the formula

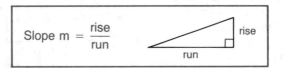

Slope m $= \frac{\text{rise}}{\text{run}}$

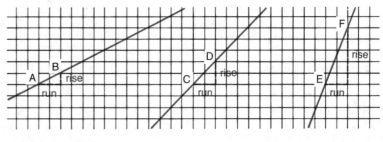

For line AB,	For line CD,	For line EF,
m $= \frac{1}{2}$	m $= \frac{2}{2}$	m $= \frac{5}{2}$
	$= 1$	

EXAMPLE. Calculate the slope of each line in the given diagram.

SOLUTION:
For line AB, the rise is $9 - 3 = 6$, and the run is $4 - 1 = 3$.

$\therefore$ m $= \frac{6}{3} = 2$

For line CD, the rise is $4 - (-1) = 5$, and the run is $10 - 3 = 7$.

$\therefore$ m $= \frac{5}{7}$

The rise is calculated by subtracting the y-coordinates and the run by subtracting the x-coordinates.

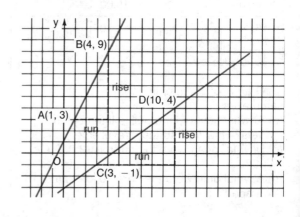

For any two points, (x_1, y_1) and (x_2, y_2) the slope is

$$m = \frac{y_2 - y_1}{x_2 - x_1}$$

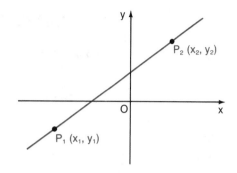

In general, – a line sloping upward to the right has a positive slope
– a line sloping upward to the left has a negative slope
– a line parallel to the y-axis has no slope
– a line parallel to the x-axis has a slope of zero.

EXERCISE 13.7

1. State the slope of each line segment.

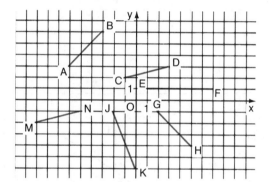

2. Determine the slope of the line passing through each pair of points.

(a) A(5, 6), B(7, 8)
(b) C(3, 4), D(7, 9)
(c) M(9, 3), N(0, 1)
(d) P(0, 0), Q(5, 4)
(e) K(−2, 5), L(0, 8)
(f) A(−2, −3), B(2, 3)
(g) C(3, 4), D(−2, −5)
(h) P(−1, 3), Q(0, −2)
(i) M(−6, 0), N(4, −5)
(j) X(3, −2), Y(7, −2)

3. (a) Draw the line through A(1, 4) and B(−2, 2).
(b) On the same graph, draw the line through P(−1, −1) and Q(2, 1).
(c) What appears to be true about these lines?
(d) Calculate the slope of each line.

Two lines are parallel if they have equal slopes.

Two lines are perpendicular if the product of their slopes is −1.

4. (a) Graph the two lines passing through
(i) A(−2, 3) and B(4, 5)
(ii) P(1, 4) and Q(3, −2)
(b) Calculate the slopes of AB and PQ.
(c) Multiply the two slopes.
(d) Are the lines perpendicular?

5. (a) Find the slope of the diagonals PR and SQ for the rhombus PQRS.
(b) Show that the diagonals of the rhombus PQRS are perpendicular.

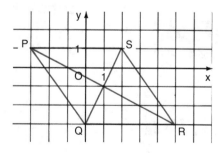

13.8 LENGTH OF A LINE SEGMENT

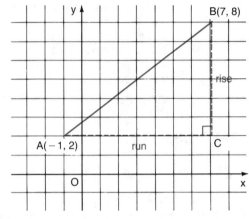

$c^2 = a^2 + b^2$

The Pythagorean Theorem is used to calculate the length of a line segment.

EXAMPLE 1. Calculate the length of the line segment from A(-1, 2) to B(7, 8).

SOLUTION:

The diagram shows the rise and run used to form a right-angled triangle.

The run AC is $7 - (-1) = 8$.
The rise CB is $8 - 2 = 6$.
From the Pythagorean Theorem,

$(AB)^2 = (AC)^2 + (CB)^2$
$(AB)^2 = 8^2 + 6^2$
$\quad\quad = 64 + 36$
$\quad\quad = 100$
$\therefore AB = \sqrt{100}$
$\quad\quad = 10$

Therefore, the line segment AB is 10 units in length.

The length of a line segment from P_1 to P_2 may be expressed as a formula. Since

$$(P_1P_2)^2 = (x_2 - x_1)^2 + (y_2 - y_1)^2$$

$$\ell = \sqrt{(x_2 - x_1)^2 + (y_2 - y_1)^2}$$

EXAMPLE 2. Calculate the length of the line segment joining A(2, -2) to B(4, 2).

SOLUTION:

Let $(x_1, y_1) = (2, -2)$ and $(x_2, y_2) = (4, 2)$.

$$AB = \sqrt{(x_2 - x_1)^2 + (y_2 - y_1)^2}$$
$$AB = \sqrt{(4 - 2)^2 + (2 - (-2))^2}$$
$$\quad = \sqrt{(2)^2 + (4)^2}$$
$$\quad = \sqrt{4 + 16}$$
$$\quad = \sqrt{20}$$
$$\quad = 2\sqrt{5}$$

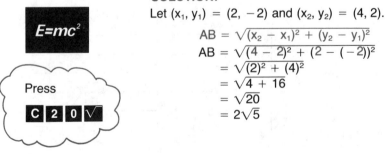

$E=mc^2$

Press

C 2 0 √

EXAMPLE 3. Prove that △ABC is an isosceles triangle.

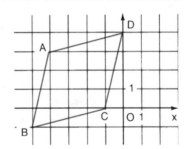

SOLUTION:

$AB = \sqrt{(2 - (-5))^2 + (0 - 4)^2}$
$= \sqrt{(7)^2 + (-4)^2}$
$= \sqrt{49 + 16}$
$= \sqrt{65}$

$BC = \sqrt{(2 - (-1))^2 + (0 - (-3))^2}$
$= \sqrt{(3)^2 + (3)^2}$
$= \sqrt{9 + 9}$
$= \sqrt{18}$
$= 3\sqrt{2}$

$AC = \sqrt{(-1 - (-5))^2 + (-3 - 4)^2}$
$= \sqrt{(4)^2 + (-7)^2}$
$= \sqrt{16 + 49}$
$= \sqrt{65}$

Since AB = AC, △ABC is an isosceles triangle.

EXERCISE 13.8

B 1. Calculate the length of each line segment.
(a) A(0, 5), B(3, 6)
(b) P(2, 4), Q(5, 4)
(c) S(2, 3), T(1, 1)
(d) M(2, 1), N(-3, 2)
(e) A(4, 0), B(0, -3)
(f) X(-5, 1), Y(-1, -1)
(g) M(0, 2), N(5, 7)
(h) E(-3, -1), F(5, 4)

2. The vertices of a quadrilateral are
A(-3, 3), B(5, 3), C(3, -1), and D(-5, -1).
(a) Find the lengths of the sides.
(b) Find the lengths of the diagonals.
(c) Identify figure ABCD.

3. The endpoints of line segment AB are
A(-4, -1) and B(6, 3). Determine whether
M(1, 1) is the midpoint of AB.

4. Show that the triangle formed by joining
the points A(0, 0), B(4, -4), and C(8, 4) is an
isosceles triangle.

5. Show that (0, -2) is the midpoint of the
line segment joining A(-2, 5) to B(2, -9).

6. A rhombus is a quadrilateral with all sides
equal. Show that ABCD is a rhombus.

7. For the △ABC shown,
(a) calculate a, b and c
(b) show that $c^2 = a^2 + b^2$.

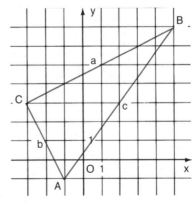

13.9 INTERPOLATING AND EXTRAPOLATING FROM GRAPHS

When obtaining data from experiments, the graph of the results does not always form a smooth curve because of approximation of measurements. In such a case, a curve or line of best fit is drawn through the points.

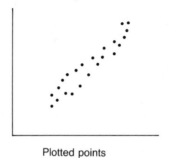

Plotted points

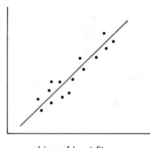

Line of best fit

EXAMPLE. Doug recorded the following information when checking gasoline consumption for his new car.

Litres used	8	10	30	35	15	37	12	16	4.5	6	20
Kilometres Travelled	78	105	325	340	160	395	125	175	40	62	220

(a) Plot the points on a graph and draw the line of best fit.
(b) Estimate the amount of gasoline needed to travel 190 km.
(c) How far can the car travel on 45 L of gasoline?

SOLUTION:

(a)

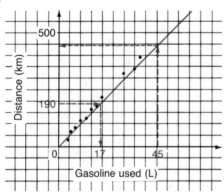

(b) From the graph, 17 L are required to travel 190 km.

> Estimating values from points that lie inside the given range of values is called interpolation.

(c) Extend the graph to include the value for 45 L.
From the graph, the car can travel 440 km on 45 L of gasoline.

> Extending a line to read ordered pairs that occur outside the given range of values is called extrapolation.

EXERCISE 13.9

A 1. The following graph shows the rental charge for construction equipment. The charge consists of a basic float charge plus an hourly rate.

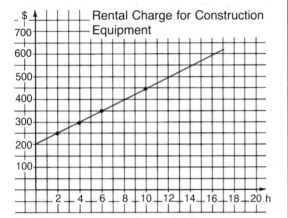

Rental Charge for Construction Equipment

(a) What is the rental cost for the following times?
   (i) 2 h
   (ii) 4 h
   (iii) 6 h
   (iv) 10 h

(b) What is the rental cost for 20 h?
(c) What is the basic float charge?
(d) What is the cost for each additional hour of rental?

B 2. To check the speedometer on her car, Diane drove through a measured kilometre at various speeds. Using the time measured for each trip, she calculated the actual speeds, and recorded the results in the following table.

Speedometer reading (km/h)	20	30	40	50	60
Actual Speed (km/h)	18	25	38.5	45	58

Speedometer reading (km/h)	75	80	90	100	110
Actual Speed (km/h)	70	74	96	92	101

(a) Plot the points and draw the line of best fit.

(b) Estimate the actual speed when the speedometer reads
   (i) 65 km/h
   (ii) 120 km/h

3. The masses and volumes for a variety of gold nuggets were found, with the results shown in the table below.

Volume (cm³)	5	2.5	6.5	2	3.1	4
Mass (g)	99	45	125	40	56	80

Volume (cm³)	7.3	6.3	8.4	8	10.5
Mass (g)	139	119	164	159	200

(a) Construct a graph of these results and draw the line of best fit.
(b) Use extrapolation to determine the mass of 1 cm³ of gold.

C 4. The sides and diagonals of five different squares were measured and the results are recorded in the following table.

Side (cm)	3	5	6	8	10	13
Diagonal (cm)	4.3	6.9	8.6	11.4	14.1	18.2

(a) Construct a graph and draw the line of best fit.
(b) Use your graph to estimate the length of the diagonal of a square whose sides are 11 cm.
(c) What is the length of the sides of a square whose diagonals are 10 cm long?
(d) What is the length of each diagonal of a square whose sides are 15 cm long?
(e) What is the length of each side of a square whose diagonal is 25 cm long?
(f) Calculate the slope of the line of best fit.
(g) Find an equation for the line of best fit.

13.10 NON-LINEAR RELATIONS

Not all the graphs of relations are straight lines. The following is an example.

A ball was tossed from a hot air balloon. The table gives the distance travelled by the ball after it leaves the balloon. The graph of the relation is shown.

Distance (m)	Time (s)
0	0
5	1
20	2
45	3
80	4

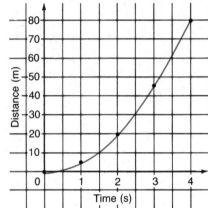

We join the points with a smooth curve. The graph is not a straight line so we have a non-linear relation.
How long will it take the ball to fall 60 m?
How far does the ball fall in 2.5 s?

EXAMPLE. For the relation $y = x^2 + 2$,
(a) list seven ordered pairs in a table of values
(b) graph the relation
(c) use the graph to find the values of x when $y = 4$
(d) use the equation to find the value of y when $x = 2.5$.

SOLUTION:
(a) Choose seven integer values for x and construct a table of values.

(b)

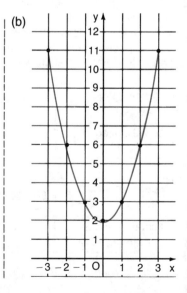

x	y
0	2
1	3
−1	3
2	6
−2	6
3	11
−3	11

(c) From the graph, when y = 4, x $\doteq$ 12 and -1.2.
(d) From the equation

$$y = x^2 + 2$$
$$= (2.5)^2 + 2$$
$$= 8.25$$

$E=mc^2$

EXERCISE 13.10

B 1. (a) Complete the table giving the relationship between the area of a square and the length of each side.

Length of sides (cm)	Area (cm²)
0	
1	
2	
3	
4	

(b) Draw a graph of this relation.
(c) Use the graph to find the length of the sides when the area is 10 cm².

2. The formula for distance travelled is d = st, where d = distance, s = speed, and t = time.
(a) Complete the table for time taken to travel 120 km at various speeds.

Speed (km/h)	Time (h)
20	
30	
40	
60	
80	
120	

(b) Draw a graph of this relation.
(c) Use the graph to determine the time required to travel 120 km at 50 km/h.

3. For the relation y = x² − 1,
(a) list seven ordered pairs in a table of values
(b) draw a graph of the relation
(c) use the graph to find the values of x when y = 2.
(d) use the equation to find the value of y when x = 1.5.

C 4. For the relation x² + y² = 25
(a) complete the table of values
(b) draw a graph of the relation
(c) name the figure.

x	y
0	5
0	−5
	0
	0
4	
4	
−4	
−4	
3	
3	
−3	
−3	

13.11 DIRECT AND PARTIAL VARIATION

The table lists the distance covered by a runner who runs at 12 km/h. The values from the table are plotted on the accompanying graph.

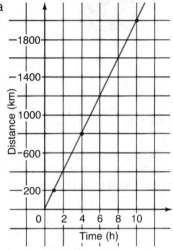

Time (min)	Distance (m)
1	200
4	800
10	2000

The relationship between time and distance covered can be expressed by the formula, d = 200t, where d is the distance in metres and t is the time in minutes.

From the table and the graph, we see that as the time increases, the distance increases. The distance varies directly as the time. This is an example of direct variation. In a direct variation, the ratios of the corresponding values are the same.

$$\frac{200}{1} = \frac{800}{4} = \frac{2000}{10} = 200$$

In this example, d varies directly as t, and we write d ∝ t. For a direct variation, the equation is of the form y = mx.

In some applications, a value can depend on a fixed amount plus a variable amount. Such an application is an example of a partial variation.

EXAMPLE. The cost of printing the school newspaper is $0.05 per copy, plus $10.00 to set up the press.
(a) Prepare a table of values to show the cost of printing the following numbers of copies.
    (i) 10   (ii) 50   (iii) 100   (iv) 1000
(b) Draw a graph to show the variation.

SOLUTION:

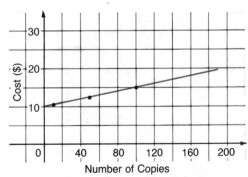

Copies	Cost ($)
10	10.50
50	12.50
100	15.00
1000	60.00

For a partial variation, the equation is of the form y = mx + b.

EXERCISE 13.11

1. Determine whether each of the following tables is an example of a partial variation.

(a)

x	y
2	6
4	12
9	27
15	45

(b)

x	y
5	10
10	15
15	20
20	25

(c)

x	y
1.2	2.4
1.5	3.0
4.2	8.4

(d)

x	y
1.2	3.6
2.2	6.6
2.7	8.1

2. The number of characters that a computer printer will print varies directly as the length of time spent printing. Sarah's printer will print 35 characters in 1 s.

(a) Prepare a table showing the number of characters printed in the following.

2 s, 5 s, 8 s, 10 s

(b) Draw a graph to show the variation from 0 s to 20 s.

(c) How many seconds will it take to print a paragraph with 210 words having an average word length of 5 characters?

3. Taxi fares are $2.90 plus $0.80/km.

(a) Find the fare for each of the following trips.
   (i) 8 km   (ii) 12 km   (iii) 20 km
(b) Draw a graph to show this variation.
(c) How far can you travel for $10.00?

4. In a direct variation, y varies directly as x. When x = 15, y = 45.

(a) Find the value of y when x = 50.
(b) Find the value of y when x = 250.

5. The price of mixed nuts varies directly as the amount purchased. For example, 2.4 kg of nuts cost $16.68.

(a) Prepare a table to show the cost of
   (i) 1 kg   (ii) 2 kg   (iii) 5 kg

(b) Draw a graph to show this variation.
(c) How many kilograms of mixed nuts will you receive for $10.00?

6. Shop time for automobile repairs is worth $42.50/h, based on the time a mechanic works on a car. This is a direct variation.

(a) Prepare a table of values for the following lengths of time.

1, 2, 3, . . . , 8 (hours)

(b) Draw a graph to show this variation.
(c) How long did the mechanic work on an automobile in the shop if the charges are $233.75?

7. The cost of lawn service for commercial buildings is a partial variation. There is a basic service charge plus a charge per hour. The following table shows the cost of lawn service for four commercial properties.

Time (h)	Cost ($)
4	170.00
6	230.00
7.5	275.00

(a) Draw a graph to show this variation.
(b) What is the cost for lawn service taking 3 h of work?
(c) What is the basic service charge?
(d) What is the cost per hour above the basic service charge?

My father was 28 when I was 6. Now he is twice as old as I am. How old am I?

13.12 PROBLEM SOLVING

1. Find the relationship between the sum of the squares of two numbers and the square of their sum.

2. Find the smallest positive integer that meets the following conditions.
(i) When the number is divided by 3, the remainder is 2.
(ii) When the number is divided by 5, the remainder is also 2.
(iii) When the number is divided by 7, the remainder is 1.

3. (a) Determine whether 15% of 50 is the same as 50% of 15.
(b) Generalize this result by considering x% of y, and y% of x.

4. It takes 5 min to travel 1 km at 12 km/h. At 15 km/h, it takes one less minute to travel the same distance.
(a) How much time is saved by increasing the speed from 15 km/h to 30 km/h?
(b) How much time is saved by increasing the speed from 30 km/h to 60 km/h?
(c) At what speed must you travel in order to save 1 min from the time taken to travel the distance at 60 km/h?

5. How can you find the radius of a sphere using only a metre stick?

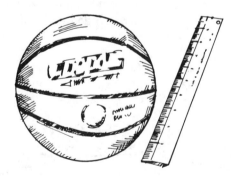

6. A three-ring binder and a pencil cost $10.50. The binder costs $10.00 more than the pencil. What is the cost of two binders and three pencils?

7. About how many words would there be on one page of a newspaper, if there is no advertising or pictures?
(a) Take a guess.
(b) Develop a strategy to estimate the number of words without counting.

8. The square of an integer is n^2. What integer must be added to the square of one integer in order to get the square of the next consecutive integer?

9. How many Friday the thirteenths will next year have?

10. A flower vase usually sells at 25% above the store's cost. During a sale, the vase was sold at a discount of 25%. The sale price was 24.14. What was the cost price of the vase to the store?

11. Numbers that read the same forwards or backwards are called palindromes. Some examples of palindromes are

(a) List all the three-digit palindromes that begin with a 4.
(b) 307 is a three-digit number whose digit sum is 10 (3 + 0 + 7 = 10). List all the three-digit palindromes whose digit sum is 10.

12. The area of the square is 8 × 8 = 64 square units.

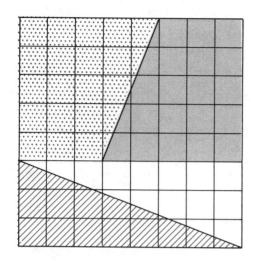

It appears that the pieces of the square have been rearranged to form a rectangle whose area is 13 × 5 = 65 square units.

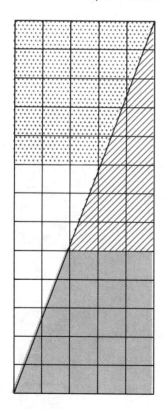

Explain the apparent increase in area.

13. How high would a stack of quarters totalling one million dollars be?

14. What is the common pattern in this set of numbers?

3575	1863	7289
1243	2555	3248

15. The railroad spur is long enough to hold one of the cars A or B, but not the locomotive, L. From the spur, a car may be switched to either direction on the track. How may the position of the cars A and B be switched using the locomotive?

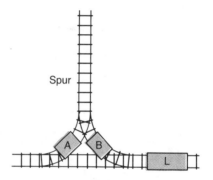

![MIND BENDER]

Determine the pattern. Find the missing number.

15	36	21
5	12	7
27	33	60
9	11	

13.13 REVIEW EXERCISE

1. State the domain and range for each relation.

(a) {(−1, 1), (−2, 4), (−3, 9), (−4, 16)}
(b) {(3, 5), (4, 5), (5, 5), (6, 5)}
(c)

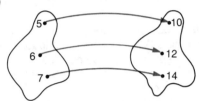

(d)

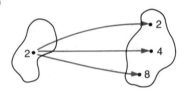

(e)

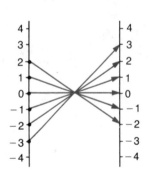

(f)

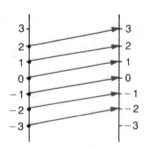

2. For the given relation, state the missing value in each ordered pair.

(a) x → 3x + 1, x ∈ I
(2, ■), (−3, ■), (■, 4), (■, −5), (0, ■)
(b) x → 1 − x, x ∈ I
(5, ■), (−2, ■), (1, ■), (■, 2), (■, −7)

3. State three ordered pairs on each line.

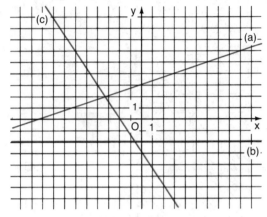

4. For each relation, construct a table of values.

(a) x → 4x − 1, x ∈ {−2, −1, 0, 1, 2}
(b) x → 1 − 2x, x ∈ {−1, 0, 1, 2}
(c) x → x², x ∈ {−4, −2, 0, 2, 4}
(d) x → ⅔x, x ∈ {−6, −3, 0, 3, 6}
(e) x → 0.6x + 1, x ∈ {−10, −5, 0, 5, 10}

5. Complete the table of values in your notebook for each given equation.

(a) y = 2 − x

x	y
2	
1	
0	
−1	
−2	

(b) x + y = 8

x	y
10	
	3
0	
	13
−10	

(c) y − x = 5

x	y
−2	
−1	
0	
	7
	10

(d) x − 2y = 5

x	y
−3	
−1	
0	
1	
3	

6. Construct a table of values and graph the relation described by the equation.
(a) $y = 4x - 1$, $x \in R$, $y \in R$
(b) $y = 1 - 3x$, $x \in R$, $y \in R$
(c) $x = -1$, $y \in R$
(d) $x - y = 5$, $x \in R$, $y \in R$
(e) $y = \frac{2}{3}x + 1$, $x \in R$, $y \in R$
(f) $y = 0.4x - 1$, $x \in R$, $y \in R$
(g) $y = 0.2x - 0.2$, $x \in R$, $y \in R$
(h) $y = -2.5x + 3.1$, $x \in R$, $y \in R$

7. Find the coordinates of the point of intersection of the following two lines by graphing the lines.
(a) $y = 5 - x$, $x \in R$
(b) $y = x - 7$, $x \in R$

8. Determine the slope of the line passing through each pair of points.
(a) A(4, 2), B(8, 6)
(b) P(5, 3), Q(1, 7)
(c) C(0, 3), D(-2, 5)
(d) S(0, 0), T(-1, -4)
(e) A(-2, 5), D(3, 6)
(f) M(4, 0), N(0, 0)
(g) T(-3, -3), X(4, 4)
(h) K(0, 0), L(4, -3)

9. Show that the points P(6, -1), Q(4, 3), and R(0, 11) are collinear.

10. Show that the line segment joining A(-2, 5) to B(1, 8) is parallel to the line segment joining C(6, 8) to D(9, 11).

11. Calculate the length of each line segment.
(a) A(-2, 4), B(5, 4)
(b) M(3, 1), N(2, 2)
(c) P(3, -5), Q(2, 4)
(d) C(-2, -1), D(3, 5)
(e) E(-4, -1), F(2, 0)
(f) H(6, 8), K(-3, -3)

12. Determine whether the triangle whose vertices are A(2, 8), B(1, 1), and C(8, 7) is a right triangle.

13. Determine whether the figure whose vertices are A(-5, 1) B(4, 8), C(5, 3), D(-4, -4) is a parallelogram.

14. Ben and Sue recorded the following measurements for the diameter and circumference of some circular objects.

Diameter (cm)	9.7	6.2	21.2	25.4	32.5
Circumference (cm)	30.5	19.5	66.5	80.0	102

(a) Construct a graph and draw the line of best fit.
(b) Use your graph to estimate the circumference of an automobile hubcap whose diameter is 38 cm.
(c) What is the diameter of a circular light pole whose circumference is 80 cm?
(d) Calculate the slope of the line of best fit.
(e) Find an equation for the line of best fit.

15. For the relation $y = x^2 + 3$,
(a) List five ordered pairs in a table of values.
(b) Draw a graph of the relation.
(c) Use the graph to find two values for x when $y = 5$.
(d) Find the value of y when $x = 0.5$.

16. The amount of high octane fuel that a 747 jet airliner consumes varies directly as the time in the air. The following table shows the amount of fuel used in five flights and the times for the flights.

Time (h)	3.2	1.6	0.75	4.15	2.65
Fuel (t)	6.5	2.7	1.5	8.3	5.2

(a) Draw a graph to show this variation.
(b) How long was the aircraft in the air if it consumed 9 t of fuel?
(c) How much fuel does the aircraft consume per hour?

13.14 CHAPTER 13 TEST

1. Draw an arrow diagram for the following relation.
$$y = x + 2, \quad x \in \{-2, 0, 3, 6, 10\}$$

2. Complete the following table of values for the equation $y = 3 - x$.

x	y
3	
5	
0	
−3	
−6	

3. Construct a table of values and draw the graph of the relation defined by the following.
$$y = 2x - 3, \quad x \in R, y \in R$$

4. Find the point of intersection of the graphs of the lines described by the following equations.
(a) $x + y = 5$
(b) $x - y = 3$

5. Find the slope of the line passing through the points $A(-2, 1)$ and $B(3, 7)$.

6. Find the length of line segment AB having endpoints $A(2, -3)$ and $B(7, 9)$.

7. Marie received the following pay cheques for the indicated hours of work.

Hours of work	13.5	18.5	21.0	9.5
Amount of pay	$87.75	$120.25	$136.50	$61.75

(a) Construct a graph of this relation.
(b) Use the graph to determine Marie's hourly rate of pay.
(c) Use the graph to determine how long, to the nearest half-hour, Marie must work to earn $175.00.

CONGRUENCE TRANSFORMATIONS

CHAPTER

14

Life is itself simple, but the living of life is an infinitely complex experience.
John L. Bilsland

SLIDES, FLIPS, AND TURNS

Three different motions can be seen in the stereo.

The station indicator describes a slide as it moves across the frequency range.

We flip a record over when we want to hear the reverse side.

The volume knob describes a turn as it is adjusted.

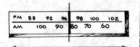 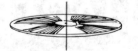

Tile A matches with tile B following a slide to the right. B is called the slide image of A. The slide arrow → indicates the direction and length of the slide. The slide image does not have to touch the original tile after the slide.

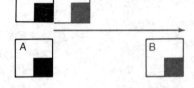

Tile A matches with tile C following a flip about the dotted line. C is called the flip image of A. The dotted line – – – indicates the flip line.

We can also have flips about lines not touching an edge of the original figure, or about lines passing through the figure.

Tile A matches with tile D following a turn about the turn centre ⊙. D is the turn image of A. The turn arrow ⌐ indicates the angle through which the figure is rotated and the dot ⊙ indicates the turn centre. A turn of 180° is called a half-turn.

The turn centre does not have to touch the original figure. It can be in the exterior or interior of the figure.

EXERCISE

1. Which of the figures on the right is a slide image of the original figure? Which is a flip image?

(a)

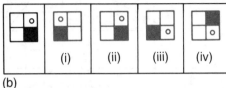

(i) (ii) (iii) (iv)

(b)

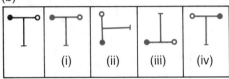

(i) (ii) (iii) (iv)

2. Which of the figures below is a turn image of the original figure? Which is a slide image?

(a)

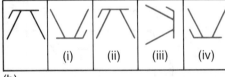

(i) (ii) (iii) (iv)

(b)

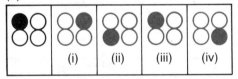

(i) (ii) (iii) (iv)

3. Which of the figures below is a flip image of the original figure? Which is a slide image?

(a)

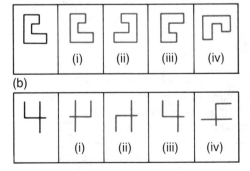

(i) (ii) (iii) (iv)

(b)

(i) (ii) (iii) (iv)

4. Identify the following patterns as slides, flips, or turns.

(a) F ꟻ F ꟻ F ꟻ F ꟻ

(b) 7 7 7 7 7 7 7

(c) Q O Q O Q O

(d) P P P P P P P

(e) T ⊣ ⊥ ⊢ T ⊣ ⊥

(f) B ꓭ ꓭ ꓭ B ꓭ B

5. Identify each figure below as a flip, slide, or turn image of the original figure.

Original	Image			
	(i)	(ii)	(iii)	(iv)
(a)				
(b)				
(c)				
(d)				
(e)				
(f)				
(g)				

14.1 TRANSLATIONS

A translation is the result of a slide. The arrow ST translates the black △ABC to the red image △A'B'C'. We call this matching a mapping of △ABC onto △A'B'C'.

The translation ST moves every point to the right 4 and down 5.

A(2, 11) maps onto A'(6, 6) A → A'
B(1, 7) maps onto B'(5, 2) B → B'
C(5, 9) maps onto C'(9, 4) C → C'
   and △ABC → △A'B'C'

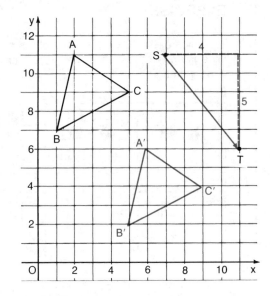

The translation ST can be described mathematically as [4, −5].
The mapping rule is

$$(x, y) \rightarrow (x + 4, y - 5)$$

△RST has sides with lengths

RS = 4
ST = 3
RT = 5

The translation [−6, −4] or the mapping (x, y) → (x − 6, y − 4) gives the image △R'S'T'.
   We see that R'S' = 4
           S'T' = 3
           R'T' = 5
   We also see that ∠R = ∠R'
              ∠S = ∠S'
              ∠T = ∠T'
and △RST ≅ △R'S'T'.

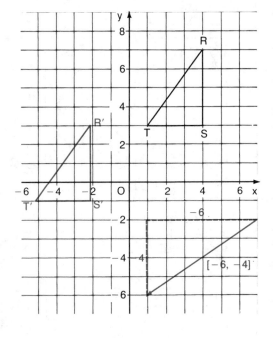

   Notice that R–S–T and R'–S'–T' read in the same direction. In this case it is clockwise (cw). We say that △RST and △R'S'T' have the same sense.

The following are the properties of translations.
(i) The original figure and its image are congruent.
(ii) The original figure and its image have the same sense.

EXERCISE 14.1

A 1. Describe each translation in words.

(a) $(x, y) \rightarrow (x - 3, y + 2)$
(b) $(x, y) \rightarrow (x + 2, y - 7)$
(c) $(x, y) \rightarrow (x, y - 1)$
(d) $(x, y) \rightarrow (x - 2, y - 3)$
(e) $(x, y) \rightarrow (x + 7, y)$
(f) $(x, y) \rightarrow (x - 5, y + 8)$
(g) $[5, -9]$
(h) $[4, 0]$
(i) $[-1, -2]$
(j) $[4, 3]$
(k) $[0, -8]$
(l) $[1, 1]$

2. State each translation arrow as an ordered pair $[x, y]$.

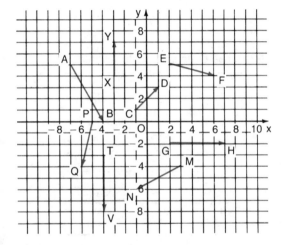

B 3. Write the mapping $(x, y) \rightarrow (\blacksquare, \blacksquare)$, to map the shaded triangle onto each image.

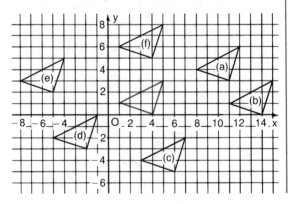

4. Complete the table to show the coordinates of the image of each point under the given translation.

Point (x, y)	Images	
	$(x + 2, y - 3)$	$(x - 3, y + 1)$
$(3, 5)$		
$(-1, 2)$		
$(0, -5)$		
$(-5, -2)$		
$(-3, 0)$		

5. Determine the mapping which will translate each point onto its image.

(a) $(5, 3)$ onto $(2, 1)$
(b) $(-1, 5)$ onto $(3, 2)$
(c) $(0, -1)$ onto $(5, 1)$
(d) $(-5, -1)$ onto $(-3, -3)$
(e) $(4, -1)$ onto $(3, -1)$
(f) $(-8, 0)$ onto $(-10, -2)$

6. Draw each triangle on grid paper and then draw the image for the given translation.

(a) A(2, 1), B(3, 5), C(7, 0)
   $(x, y) \rightarrow (x + 2, y + 4)$
(b) D(-1, 3), E(-4, 5), F(0, 2)
   $(x, y) \rightarrow (x - 4, y - 2)$
(c) R(2, 2), S(5, -1), T(-3, -4)
   $(x, y) \rightarrow (x - 3, y + 5)$
(d) J(-2, -3), K(0, 4), L(-5, 1)
   $(x, y) \rightarrow (x + 6, y - 3)$

7. △ABC has vertices A(1, 1), B(-2, 3) and C(-4, -2).

(a) Determine the coordinates of the vertices of the image △A′B′C′ under the mapping $(x, y) \rightarrow (x + 4, y + 5)$.
(b) Apply the mapping $(x, y) \rightarrow (x - 1, y + 2)$ to the △A′B′C′. Determine the vertices of △A″B″C″.
(c) Determine the translation that maps △ABC onto △A″B″C″.

14.2 REFLECTIONS

A reflection is the result of a flip.
The reflection of △ABC in the line MN is
△A′B′C′. (The equation of line MN is x = 2.)
The reflection line MN is the perpendicular
bisector of the line segments joining
corresponding points of △ABC and △A′B′C′.
If we trace △ABC and flip it, we can match
the tracing of △ABC with the image △A′B′C′
so that

$$AB = A′B′ \quad BC = B′C′ \quad AC = A′C′$$
and $\quad \angle A = \angle A′ \quad \angle B = \angle B′ \quad \angle C = \angle C′$
and $\qquad \triangle ABC \cong \triangle A′B′C′$.

Notice that A–B–C is read in a counter-
clockwise (ccw) direction and A′–B′–C′ is
read in a clockwise (cw) direction. The sense
of the original figure and the image are
reversed.

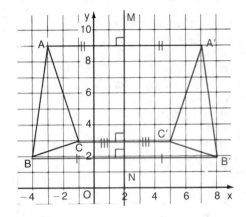

The following are the properties of reflections.
(i) The original figure and its image are congruent.
(ii) The sense of the original figure and the sense of its image are reversed.

EXAMPLE. Find the image of △PQR, with
vertices P(1, 3), Q(−2, 1) and R(4, 0), after a
reflection in the line y = −2.

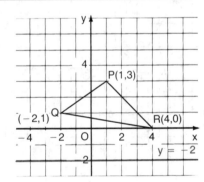

SOLUTION:
Locate the point P′ so that the perpendicular
distance from P to the line y = −2 equals
the perpendicular distance from P′ to the line
y = −2.
The coordinates of P′ are (1, −7).

Locate the points Q′ and R′ in the same way
and join P′–Q′–R′.

$$P(1, 3) \rightarrow P′(1, −7)$$
$$Q(−2, 1) \rightarrow Q′(−2, −5)$$
$$R(4, 0) \rightarrow R′(4, −4)$$

△P′Q′R′ is the image of △PQR after a
reflection in the line y = −2.

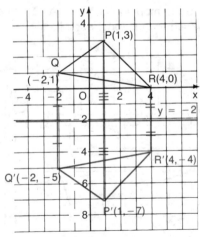

EXERCISE 14.2

A 1. State the coordinates of the image under each reflection.

Point	Reflection	
	In the x-axis	In the y-axis
(3, 5)		
(−2, 1)		
(0, −2)		
(−5, −3)		
(8, 0)		

B 2. Copy each figure on grid paper and draw the image of each figure in the reflection line.

(a) (b)

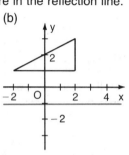

(c) (d)

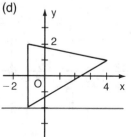

(e) (f)

3. △RST has vertices R(5, 4), S(6, 0), and T(−3, 1). Find the image of △RST after a reflection in

(a) the x-axis
(b) the y-axis.

4. Quadrilateral ABCD has vertices A(6, 1), B(5, 4), C(1, 4), and D(−3, −2). Find the image of quadrilateral ABCD after a reflection in

(a) the line y = 2
(b) the line x = 1.

5. Determine the equation of the reflection line so that

(a) △ABC is the image of △DEF
(b) △KLM is the image of △RST
(c) △RST is the image of △ABC.

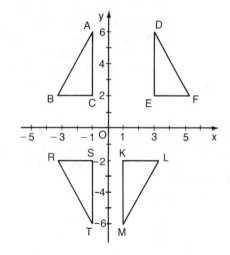

1, 1, 2, 2, 3, 3, 4, 4

An eight-digit number contains two 1s, two 2s, two 3s and two 4s. The 1s are separated by one digit, the 2s by two digits, the 3s by three digits, and the 4s by four digits. What is the number?

14.3 ROTATIONS

A rotation is the result of a turn.
△A′B′C′ is the image of △ABC after a counter-clockwise (ccw) rotation of 90° about the origin.
   We mark the centre of rotation with ⊙ and the direction and amount of rotation with ↰. The amount of rotation is called the angle of rotation.

   If we trace △ABC and rotate it, we can match it with △A′B′C′ so that

   AB = A′B′ BC = B′C′ AC = A′C′
and ∠A = ∠A′ ∠B = ∠B′ ∠C = ∠C′
and   △ABC ≅ △A′B′C′.

   Notice that both A–B–C and A′–B′–C′ are both read in the same direction. Also, the distance between any point on a figure and the centre of rotation does not change in the rotation.

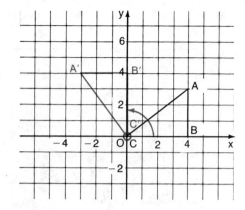

The following are properties of rotations.
(i) The original figure and its image are congruent.
(ii) The original figure and its image have the same sense.

EXAMPLE. △RST has vertices R(0, 4), S(−5, 0) and T(−2, 0). Find the image of △RST after a clockwise (cw) rotation of 180° about the origin.

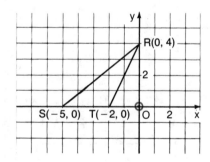

SOLUTION:
R(0, 4) maps onto R′(0, −4)
S(−5, 0) → S′(5, 0)
T(−2, 0) → T′(2, 0)

Join R′–S′–T′.
△R′S′T′ is the image of △RST.

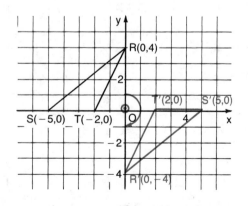

EXERCISE 14.3

A 1. State the image of each point after
(a) a clockwise rotation of 90° about the origin

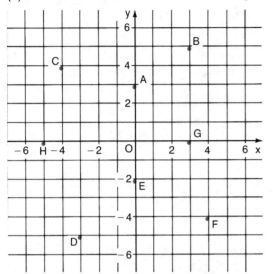

(b) a counter-clockwise rotation of 90° about the origin
(c) a clockwise rotation of 180° about the origin.

B 2. △ABC has vertices A(5, 2), B(0, 3) and C(−3, 0). Find the image of △ABC after a clockwise rotation of 90° about the origin.

3. △DEF has vertices D(−3, 2), E(−5, −1) and F(2, −4). Find the image of △DEF after a counter-clockwise rotation of 90° about the origin.

4. Copy each figure onto grid paper and draw the image after the given rotation.

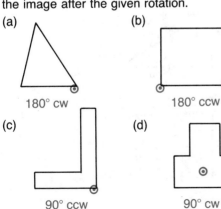

(a)   (b)
180° cw   180° ccw

(c)   (d)
90° ccw   90° cw

5. Complete the table for each rotation about the origin.

Point	90°cw	180°ccw	270°ccw	270°cw
		Image		
(5, 2)				
(−4, 3)				
(−3, −2)				
(3, −1)				
(0, −5)				
(−6, 0)				

6. State the centre of rotation and the amount of rotation for each. The red figure is the image.

(a)   (b)

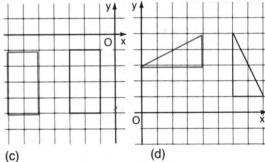

(c)   (d)

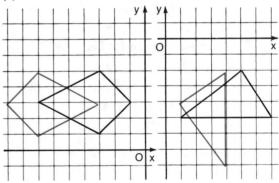

14.4 SPECIAL TRANSFORMATIONS

In this section we investigate the special mappings associated with reflections in the x-axis, the y-axis, and rotations of 180° and 90° about the origin.

A. Reflection in the x-axis

$\triangle ABC \rightarrow \triangle A'B'C'$

$A(5, 4) \rightarrow A'(5, -4)$
$B(1, 2) \rightarrow B'(1, -2)$
$C(6, 1) \rightarrow C'(6, -1)$

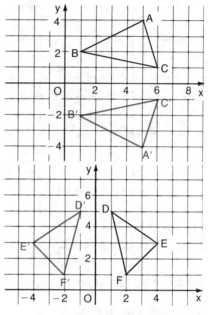

In general, for a reflection in the x-axis,

$(x, y) \rightarrow (x, -y)$

B. Reflection in the y-axis

$\triangle DEF \rightarrow \triangle D'E'F'$

$D(1, 5) \rightarrow D'(-1, 5)$
$E(4, 3) \rightarrow E'(-4, 3)$
$F(2, 1) \rightarrow F'(-2, 1)$

In general, for a reflection in the y-axis,

$(x, y) \rightarrow (-x, y)$

C. Rotation of 180° cw (or 180° ccw)

$\triangle RST \rightarrow \triangle R'S'T'$

$R(5, 4) \rightarrow R'(-5, -4)$
$S(1, 1) \rightarrow S'(-1, -1)$
$T(5, 1) \rightarrow T'(-5, -1)$

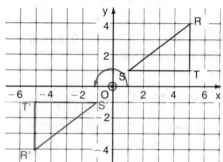

In general, for a rotation of 180° about the origin,

$(x, y) \rightarrow (-x, -y)$

D. Rotation of 90° cw (or 270° ccw)

$\triangle ABC \rightarrow \triangle A'B'C'$

$A(1, 5) \rightarrow A'(5, -1)$
$B(1, 2) \rightarrow B'(2, -1)$
$C(6, 2) \rightarrow C'(2, -6)$

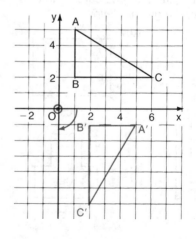

In general, for a rotation of 90° cw (or 270° ccw),

$(x, y) \rightarrow (y, -x)$

E. Rotation of 90° ccw (or 270° cw)

$$\triangle DEF \rightarrow \triangle D'E'F'$$

$$D(2, 6) \rightarrow D'(-6, 2)$$
$$E(2, 1) \rightarrow E'(-1, 2)$$
$$F(6, 1) \rightarrow F'(-1, 6)$$

In general, for a rotation of 90° ccw (or 270° cw),

$$(x, y) \rightarrow (-x, y)$$

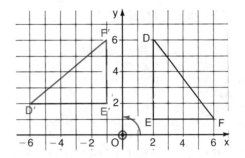

EXERCISE 14.4

B 1. Write the coordinates of the image of each point under each transformation.

(a) A reflection in the x-axis of (2, 3).
(b) A 90° cw rotation about the origin of (−2, 0).
(c) A reflection in the y-axis of (−2, 4).
(d) A 180° ccw rotation about the origin of (−4, 0).
(e) A 90° ccw rotation about the origin of (−1, −2).

2. Write a transformation for each of the following mappings.

(a) $(5, 6) \rightarrow (-5, 6)$
(b) $(2, 3) \rightarrow (-2, -3)$
(c) $(3, 4) \rightarrow (-4, 3)$
(d) $(7, 8) \rightarrow (7, -8)$
(e) $(1, 5) \rightarrow (5, -1)$
(f) $(-4, -5) \rightarrow (5, -4)$
(g) $(3, -4) \rightarrow (3, 4)$
(h) $(2, -1) \rightarrow (-2, 1)$
(i) $(-2, 7) \rightarrow (2, 7)$
(j) $(-5, -6) \rightarrow (-6, 5)$

3. △ABC has vertices A(3, 1), B(6, 2), and C(5, 5). Find the vertices of the image of △ABC for each mapping.

(a) a reflection in the x-axis.
(b) A 90° cw rotation about the origin.
(c) A reflection in the y-axis.
(d) A 180° ccw rotation about the origin.
(e) A 90° ccw rotation about the origin.

4. △DEF has vertices D(4, 3), E(1, 5), and F(0, 0). Find the coordinates of the image of △DEF after the following transformations have been performed in succession.

(a) A reflection in the x-axis.
(b) A 90° cw rotation about the origin.
(c) A reflection in the y-axis.

C 5. △ABC has vertices A(1, 2), B(2, 5), and C(4, 6).

(a) Draw △ABC on grid paper.
(b) Find the coordinates of the image of △ABC after a reflection in the line y = x.
(c) Generalize the mapping in the form $(x, y) \rightarrow (\blacksquare, \blacksquare)$.

6. △RST has vertices R(−1, 7), S(−3, 5), and T(−2, 3).

(a) Draw △RST on grid paper.
(b) Find the coordinates of the image of △RST after a reflection in the line y = −x.
(c) Generalize the mapping in the form $(x, y) \rightarrow (\blacksquare, \blacksquare)$.

14.5 DILATATIONS

A dilatation is often called the size transformation. As in other transformations the image changes position from the original. In this transformation the size of the image figure changes, but the shape does not. Figures with the same shape are similar.

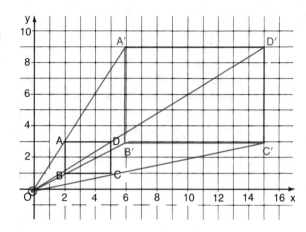

Rectangle ABCD has vertices A(2, 3), B(2, 1) C(5, 1), and D(5, 3). Applying the mapping

$$(x, y) \to (3x, 3y)$$

to the rectangle gives the following.

$$A(2, 3) \to A'(6, 9)$$
$$B(2, 1) \to B'(6, 3)$$
$$C(5, 1) \to C'(15, 3)$$
$$D(5, 3) \to D'(15, 9)$$

Since the ratios of the corresponding sides are equal, the two rectangles are similar. The example illustrates a dilatation that enlarges the original figure by a factor of 3. The centre of the dilatation $\odot$ is the origin and 3 is called the scale factor.

In general,
(i) a dilatation with centre (0, 0) and scale factor k has the mapping rule $(x, y) \to (kx, ky)$
(ii) a dilatation always produces similar figures.

EXAMPLE. △ABC has vertices A(4, 6), B(−6, 2) and C(6, −8). Find the image of △ABC under the mapping $(x, y) \to (\frac{1}{2}x, \frac{1}{2}y)$.

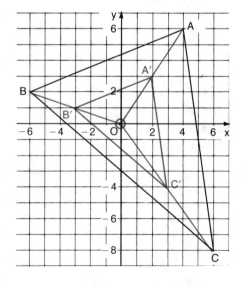

SOLUTION:

For $(x, y) \to (\frac{1}{2}x, \frac{1}{2}y)$,

$$A(4, 6) \to A'(2, 3)$$
$$B(-6, 2) \to B'(-3, 1)$$
$$C(6, -8) \to C'(3, -4)$$

and △ABC → △A'B'C'.

When the scale factor k is >1, the mapping gives an enlargement. When the scale factor is >0 but <1, the mapping gives a reduction.

EXERCISE 14.5

B 1. Complete the table.

Mapping	Original Point	Image	Scale Factor
$(x, y) \rightarrow (6x, 6y)$	$(-2, 5)$	(■, ■)	
$(x, y) \rightarrow (2x, 2y)$	(■, ■)	$(10, 2)$	
$(x, y) \rightarrow$ (■, ■)	$(-1, 0)$	(■, ■)	5
$(x, y) \rightarrow$ (■, ■)	$(-4, ■)$	(■, −3)	$\frac{1}{2}$
$(x, y) \rightarrow (4x, 4y)$	(■, 1)	$(2, ■)$	
$(x, y) \rightarrow$ (■, ■)	$(-2, 4)$	$(-6, 12)$	

2. (a) Draw △ABC where the vertices are A(−2, 2), B(0, 5), and C(3, 3).
(b) Find and draw △A′B′C′ under the dilatation $(x, y) \rightarrow (3x, 3y)$.

3. △RST has vertices R(−5, 2), S(2, 3), and T(−1, −4).
(a) Draw △RST on grid paper.
(b) Find the image of △RST under the mapping $(x, y) \rightarrow (2x, 2y)$.

4. Copy the diagrams on grid paper. Draw the image under the dilatation with the given scale factor.
(a) k = 2

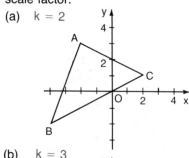

(b) k = 3

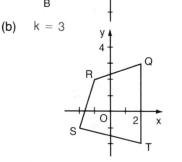

(c) k = 4

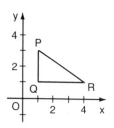

5. (a) Draw △ABC where the vertices are A(1, −1), B(−2, −1), and C(1, 2).
(b) Determine the area of △ABC.
(c) Find and graph △A′B′C′ under the dilatation with scale factor 2.
(d) Determine the area of △A′B′C′.
(e) Find the ratio $\dfrac{\text{Area of } \triangle A'B'C'}{\text{Area of } \triangle ABC}$.

6. (a) Draw any rectangle ABCD on graph paper.
(b) Determine the area of rectangle ABCD.
(c) Find and graph the image of rectangle ABCD under the mapping $(x, y) \rightarrow (4x, 4y)$.
(d) Determine the area of rectangle A′B′C′D′.
(e) Find the ratio of the area of A′B′C′D′ to the area of ABCD.

7. △PQR is mapped onto △P′Q′R′.
(a) State the mapping in the form $(x, y) \rightarrow$ (■, ■).
(b) Determine the area of each triangle.
(c) Find the ratio $\dfrac{\text{Area of } \triangle P'Q'R'}{\text{Area of } \triangle PQR}$.

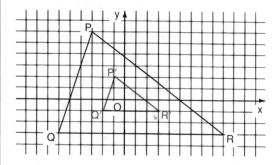

C 8. △PQR has vertices P(3, 5), Q(−2, 6) and R(−4, −2).
(a) Draw △PQR on grid paper.
(b) Draw the image of △PQR under a dilatation with scale factor 2 and centre (1, 1).

14.6 GEOMETRY AND NAVIGATION

Aircraft and ships use a compass for navigating. The pointer attached to the centre of the compass shows the heading or the direction, in which the vehicle is being steered.

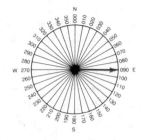

To solve navigation problems, we use arrows called vectors. The direction of the vector is called the heading. The length of the vector represents the speed.

If 1 cm represents a speed of 100 km/h, then the course of an aircraft flying at 600 km/h with a heading of 090° can be represented by the following vector.

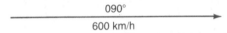

090°
600 km/h

The aircraft above experiences a tailwind of 100 km/h. We can represent the wind by a vector and show the true speed of the aircraft using vector addition.

600 km/h   100 km/h

When the heading and air speed of a plane, and the direction and speed of the wind are known, we can determine the actual direction and speed of the plane. The actual direction of the plane is called the track. The actual speed is called the ground speed.

EXAMPLE 1. An aircraft is flying with a heading of 270° at an air speed of 550 km/h. A south-wind is blowing at a speed of 150 km/h. Determine the track and ground speed of the plane.

SOLUTION:

Step 1   Let 1 cm represent 100 km/h. Draw vector $\overrightarrow{AB}$ to represent the heading and air speed of the plane.

270°
B ←———— A
550 km/h

Step 2   Draw vector $\overrightarrow{BC}$ to represent the direction and speed of the wind.

Step 3   Join AC. The vector $\overrightarrow{AC}$ represents the track and ground speed. By measuring, BAC = 15°, so the track is 285°.
AC = 5.7 cm, so the ground speed is 570 km/h.

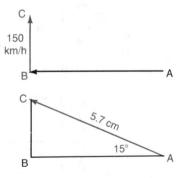

C
150 km/h
B ←———— A

C
5.7 cm
15°
B   A

In Example 1, we saw how the wind altered the direction of the aircraft. In the following examples, we calculate the course that must be taken to overcome the wind.

Suppose you wanted to cross a river from point P on the left side to the right side. The speed and direction of the current is given by the vector c.

If you head directly across intending to reach B, the current carries you to C. In what direction would you aim your craft to reach B?

Using the method of Example 1, we can show that setting a course towards A will bring you to point B.

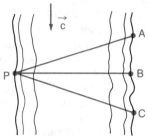

EXAMPLE 2. A pilot wishes to fly the aircraft at 350 km/h in an easterly direction. There is a 50 km/h north wind. What course should the pilot set?

SOLUTION:
Scale: 50 km/h = 1 cm

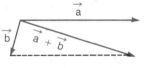

$\overrightarrow{AB}$ is the desired course.
$\overrightarrow{AC}$ represents the wind.
We must find $\overrightarrow{AD}$ so that $\overrightarrow{AB}$ is the resultant of adding $\overrightarrow{AD}$ and $\overrightarrow{AC}$.

A navigator does this by drawing a parallelogram where AC is one side and AB is one diagonal. The other side is the course to set.

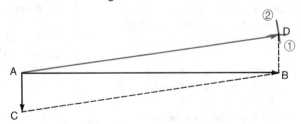

Step 1   Draw this arc with centre B and radius AC.
Step 2   Draw this arc with centre A and radius CB.
Step 3   Label the point of intersection of the arcs D.
Step 4 $\overrightarrow{AD}$ is the required course.
         By measuring
               AD = 7.1 cm so the air speed is 355 km/h.
               ∠DAB = 8° so the track is 82°.

EXAMPLE 3. Prince Albert is North 58° West of Winnipeg. The cruising speed of the aircraft is 360 km/h, and there is a 70 km/h west wind.
(a) What course must be set to fly from Winnipeg to Prince Albert?
(b) What will the ground speed be?

SOLUTION:

Step 1 Draw WE to represent the wind.

Step 2 Draw WA to show the direction to Prince Albert from Winnipeg.

Step 3 With a compass, radius 7.2 cm (360 km/h) and centres W and E, draw arcs ① and ②. Arc ① cuts WA at P.

Step 4 With centre P and radius WE draw arc ③ to cut arc ② at C.

Step 5 WC is the required course. By measuring, ∠NWC = 64° and the course is N64°W.
WP = 6 cm and the ground speed is 300 km/h.

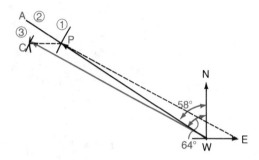

Scale: 50 km/h = 1 cm

EXERCISE 14.6

Answer the following questions using vector diagrams.

B 1. A pilot wishes to fly at 240 km/h toward the west while there is a 30 km/h south wind. Find the course that must be set and the air speed.

2. A boat travels at 20 km/h across a river with a 4 km/h current. Find the direction the boat must take in order to travel directly across the current and also the actual speed of the boat relative to the ground.

3. The air speed of a small aircraft is 250 km/h. The pilot wishes to fly north and there is a west wind of 50 km/h.
(a) What course must the pilot set?
(b) What is the ground speed?

4. A small motorboat has a water speed of 20 km/h in still water. There is a current of 8 km/h.
(a) In what direction should you head the boat to go straight across?
(b) What is the ground speed?

C 5. (a) Find the course required to fly in a direction 30° west of north at 300 km/h while there is a 60 km/h west wind.
(b) What should the air speed be?

6. (a) Find the course required to fly in a south-east direction while the wind blows 50° west of north at 36 km/h. The cruising speed of the aircraft is 240 km/h.
(b) What is the ground speed?

7. A small craft flies at 180 km/h in a direction 50° west of south while there is a 45 km/h south-east wind. Find the ground speed and direction relative to the ground.

8. Find the course that must be set to fly in a direction 30° east of south in a 40 km/h east wind if the aircraft cruises at 300 km/h.

9. Plot the course and calculate the ground speed of an aircraft cruising at 225 km/h in a 50 km/h east wind if you wish to travel north-east.

14.7 CARBON DATING

Archaeologists, law enforcement officers, and private investigators often solve problems using the strategy of working backwards.

Radioactive carbon 14 (C–14) is a form of carbon. All living plants and animals contain the same amount of C–14 per kilogram of mass. When they die, the C–14 changes slowly to nitrogen 14. It takes about 5700 a for half of the C–14 in an object to change to nitrogen 14. We say that C–14 has a half-life of 5700 a.

The table and graph extend the pattern to 34 200 a.

Years after death	Percent of C–14 remaining
0	100
5700	50
11 400	25
17 100	$12\frac{1}{2}$
22 800	$6\frac{1}{4}$
28 500	$3\frac{1}{8}$
34 200	$1\frac{9}{16}$

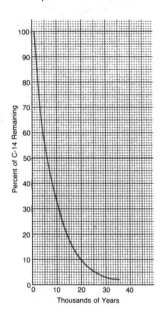

EXERCISE 14.7

1. An archaeologist found bones that contained 10% of the original amount of C–14. Approximately how old were the bones?

2. What percent of C-14 should be left in a fossil that is about 30 000 a old?

3. A scientist estimated that the fossil of a small animal was about 10 000 a old. If this estimate is correct, what percent of C–14 should be remaining?

4. You can use C–14 to find the age of fossils that are less than 50 000 a old. Approximately what percent of C–14 remains after 50 000 a?

14.8 TRAVEL ROUTES ON THE EARTH

Imaginary lines called parallels of
latitude and meridians of longitude have
been "drawn" on the Earth.

The Equator (also an imaginary line)
runs east and west. Other lines drawn
east and west that are parallel to the
Equator are parallels of latitude. The two
poles are 90°. The degrees of latitude
are determined by the angle at the
interior centre of the Earth.

Unlike the parallels of latitude,
meridians of longitude are not parallel to
each other, but meet at the two poles.
The prime meridian is 0°. All other
meridians are measured east and west
from Greenwich, England, and are
measured up to 180°, the international
date-line.

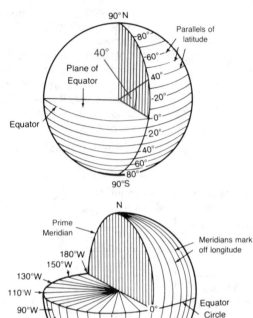

Ottawa and Portland, Oregon both lie on latitude 45° North. Yet, when an airplane
flies from Ottawa to Portland, it will fly a great circle route between the two cities and
not along latitude 45° North. The shortest distance between any two points on a globe
is an arc of a great circle and not a straight line.

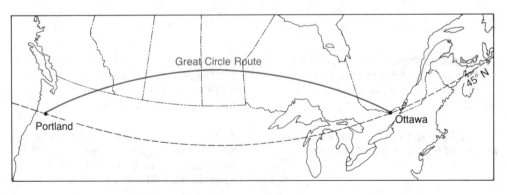

The great circle, which includes Ottawa and Portland, is the imaginary circle passing through the two cities, having its centre at the centre of the Earth.

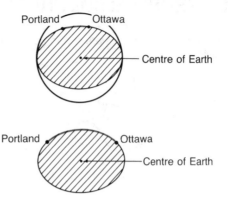

EXERCISE 14.8

1. Verify that the great circle route is the shortest distance between two cities.
(a) Use a piece of string and a globe to measure the distance between two cities on the same parallel of latitude.
(b) Pull the string tight. The string will hug the globe along a great circle. Measure this distance and compare it with the distance found in part (a).

2. Which parallels of latitude and meridians of longitude are great circles?

3. (a) Calculate the circumference of a great circle.
(b) Do all great circles have the same circumference?

4. In plane geometry there is one perpendicular from a point to a line.

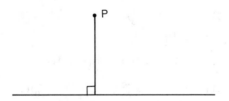

How many perpendiculars can be drawn from the North Pole to the Equator? Use a diagram to illustrate your answer.

5. In plane geometry, the sum of the interior angles of a triangle is 180°. Use a diagram to show that the sum of the angles of a triangle on curved surface of the Earth are greater than 180°.

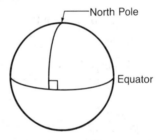

6. On a sphere, as the sum of the interior angles of a triangle gets close to 180°, the area of the triangle gets close to zero. Demonstrate this statement on a diagram.

7. The sum of the angles of a triangle drawn on a sphere varies. What is the largest possible sum that the angles of a triangle on a sphere can have?

14.9 PROBLEM SOLVING

1. Name the wheels that are turning counter-clockwise.

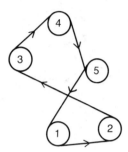

2. What is the number? If you add 9 to it, then multiply by 7, and finally subtract 18, you get 73.

3. Forty trees are evenly spaced around a rectangular field. Fourteen trees form the length. How many form the width?

4. How old will you be in minutes on your next birthday?

5. In how many ways can you make change for fifty cents if at least one coin must be a quarter?

6. What shapes can be made by drawing a line through a square? The line in the diagram gives a pentagon and a right triangle.

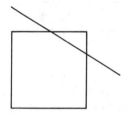

7. Cut the 6 by 4 rectangle into two pieces that will fit together to form a 3 by 8 rectangle.

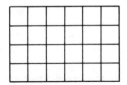

8. The number of cubic centimetres in the volume of a cube is the same number as the number of square units in its surface area. What is the length of an edge of the cube?

9. An ant is at point A. The ant can only walk downward. The ant can reach D in 2 ways. There is only one way the ant can reach point E. In how many ways can the ant reach point F?

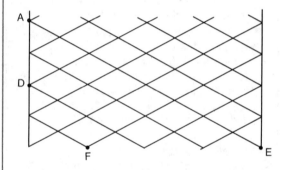

10. Frank has 25 coins to put in three piles. He wants to put an odd number of coins in each pile. In how many different ways can he arrange the coins?

11. Evaluate.

(a) $(1 - \frac{1}{2})$

(b) $(1 - \frac{1}{2})(1 - \frac{1}{3})$

(c) $(1 - \frac{1}{2})(1 - \frac{1}{3})(1 - \frac{1}{4})$

(d) $(1 - \frac{1}{2})(1 - \frac{1}{3})(1 - \frac{1}{4})(1 - \frac{1}{5})$

(e) $(1 - \frac{1}{2})(1 - \frac{1}{3})(1 - \frac{1}{4}) \dots (1 - \frac{1}{99})(1 - \frac{1}{100})$

12. The perimeter of a rectangle is 26 cm. The lengths of the sides are whole numbers. What is the greatest area the rectangle could have?

13. The following are three views of the same object.

Draw a 3-dimensional sketch of the object.

14. Using the digits 1 to 9, find three numbers whose sum is 981 and one number is three times another.

15. Divide and label a sheet of paper as shown below.

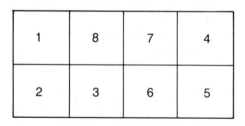

Fold this sheet so the numbers are arranged in numerical order with the number 1 on the top.

16. What is the measure of ∠RST?

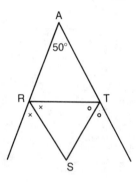

17. When the numbers 24 and 3 are added they give

$$24 + 3 = 27$$

When multiplied, they give the reverse answer.

$$24 \times 3 = 72$$

Find two more pairs of numbers that have this property.

18. How can you cut a circular region into two parts that have the same area but are not congruent?

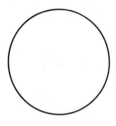

19. Find the area of the square that is inscribed in a circle with a diameter of 12 cm.

Start with the word READ and change one letter at a time to form a new word until you reach BOOK. The best solution has the fewest steps.

R E A D
_ _ _ _
_ _ _ _
_ _ _ _
_ _ _ _
B O O K

14.10 REVIEW EXERCISE

1. State each translation arrow as an ordered pair.

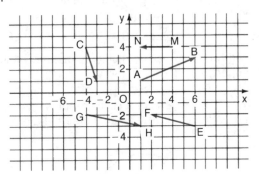

2. Complete the table to show the coordinates of each image point under the given translation.

Point (x, y)	Images	
	(x − 3, y + 2)	(x + 5, y − 7)
(−1, −4)		
(2, −6)		
(0, −5)		
(−3, 0)		
(4, 4)		

3. Draw each triangle on grid paper and then draw the image of the triangle for the given translation.

(a) A(3, 2), B(7, 1), C(4, 5)

        (x, y) → (x − 4, y + 5)

(b) R(−1, −1), S(5, −2), T(0, 6)

        (x, y) → (x + 3, y − 5)

(c) D(−3, −7), E(0, 2), F(1, −5)

        (x, y) → (x − 5, y − 1)

4. Determine the translation which translates each point onto its image.

(a) (2, 1) onto (7, 8)
(b) (−3, −7) onto (3, −1)
(c) (8, −1) onto (−5, 9)
(d) (−4, 6) onto (0, 0)

5. State the coordinates of the image under each reflection.

Point	Images	
	In the x-axis	In the y-axis
(4, 7)		
(−2, −9)		
(5, −6)		
(−7, 9)		

6. △ABC has vertices A(1, 2), B(−4, 2), and C(0, −5). Find the image of △ABC after a reflection in the line x = 2.

7. △DEF has vertices D(−5, −1), E(3, 2), and F(1, −4). Find the image of △DEF after a reflection in the line y = −2.

8. State the image of each point under the following rotations:
(a) 90° ccw about the origin
(b) 180° ccw about the origin
(c) 270° cw about the origin

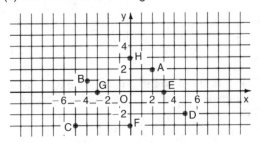

9. Complete the table for each rotation about the origin.

Point	90° cw	180° cw	270° ccw	90° ccw
(2, 4)				
(−3, 7)				
(−5, −1)				
(5, −5)				

10. △ABC has vertices A(2, 0), B(5, 0), and C(4, 6). Find the image of △ABC after a clockwise rotation of 180° about the origin.

11. △RST has vertices R(−4, 5), S(−4, −2), and T(0, −2). Find the image of △RST after a counter-clockwise rotation of 90° about the origin.

12. Write the transformation for each of the following mappings.
(a) (2, 3) → (−2, 3)
(b) (−3, −4) → (−3, 4)
(c) (−1, −2) → (1, 2)
(d) (6, −5) → (5, 6)
(e) (−7, 3) → (3, 7)
(f) (−2, 3) → (2, −3)

13. △ABC has vertices A(1, 1), B(6, 1), and C(1, 5). Find the image of △ABC after the following transformations have been performed in succession.
(a) A reflection in the x-axis.
(b) A reflection in the y-axis.
(c) A 90° cw rotation about the origin.

14. Complete the table.

Mapping	Original Point	Image	Scale Factor
(x, y) → (3x, 3y)	(5, −3)	(■, ■)	
(x, y) → ($\frac{1}{2}$x, $\frac{1}{2}$y)	(−4, −2)	(■, ■)	
(x, y) → (2x, 2y)	(■, ■)	(8, 4)	
(x, y) → (■, ■)	(−2, −3)	(−6, −9)	
(x, y) → (■, ■)	(15, −5)	(5, −1)	

15. △DEF has vertices D(3, 6), E(−2, 1), and F(−1, −4).
(a) Draw the image of △DEF on graph paper.
(b) Find the image of △DEF under the mapping (x, y) → (2x, 2y).

16. △ABC has vertices A(−4, −2), B(6, 6), and C(−6, 8). Find the image of △ABC under the mapping (x, y) → ($\frac{1}{2}$x, $\frac{1}{2}$y).

RUNWAY NUMBERS

Airport runways are numbered according to the angle the runway measures with North on a compass. The compass direction of the runway is always 10 times the runway number. Runway 4 is on a compass bearing of 40°.

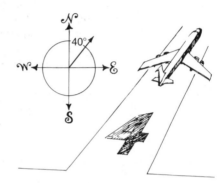

1. What is the compass bearing of runway 16.

2. What is the runway number with a compass bearing of 220°?

3. If the runways in questions 1 and 2 are approached from the opposite direction, what would each runway number be?

Find two numbers x and y such that

$$\frac{x^y}{y^x} = 1, \qquad x \neq y$$

14.11 CHAPTER 14 TEST

1. △RST has vertices R(1, 2), S(−3, 3), and T(0, −3). Find the image of △RST under the translation $(x, y) \rightarrow (x + 3, y - 4)$.

2. △GHK has vertices G(3, 4), H(−1, 6), and K(1, −4).
(a) Find the image of △GHK after a reflection in the x-axis.
(b) Find the image of △GHK after a reflection in the y-axis.

3. △PQR has vertices P(2, 2), Q(7, 2), and R(7, 5). Find the image of △PQR after a clockwise rotation of 90° about the origin.

4. △ABC has vertices A(2, 2), B(−3, 2), and C(−3, −4). Find the image of △ABC after the following transformations have been performed in succession.
(a) A reflection in the x-axis.
(b) A reflection in the y-axis.

5. △DEF has vertices D(−1, −3), E(4, 2), and F(0, −3). Find the image of △DEF under the mapping

$$(x, y) \rightarrow (3x, 3y)$$

14.12 YEAR-END REVIEW

1. Perform the indicated operations.
(a) 24 401 × 53
(b) 365 × 256
(c) 37^2
(d) $\sqrt{625}$
(e) 53 278 ÷ 64 to the nearest tenth

2. If a = 5, b = 3, c = 7, evaluate.
(a) a + b + c
(b) 2a − 3b + 4c
(c) (a + b − c)²
(d) a² + b² − c²
(e) 3a − 5b + 2c
(f) a(b + c)
(g) 2a(3b − c)
(h) −3a(b − c)

3. If x = 2, y = −3, z = −5, evaluate.
(a) x + y + z
(b) 2x − 3y + 4z
(c) 3x − 2y + z
(d) x − 2y − 3z
(e) (x − y + z)²
(f) x² − y² + z²
(g) x(y − z)
(h) 3y(2x + 4z)

4. Simplify.
(a) 6x − 5x
(b) 3x − 7x
(c) 3(x − 2) + 4(2x + 7)
(d) 2x(x + 3) − x(2x − 5)
(e) −3x(x − 1) + 2x(2x + 4)

5. Given E(x) = 3x² + 2x − 5, find
(a) E(0)
(b) E(3)
(c) E(−2)
(d) E(−4)
(e) E(1)
(f) E(−1)

6. Express in scientific notation.
(a) 35 200
(b) 125 000
(c) 0.0375
(d) 0.004 25
(e) 1 450 000
(f) 0.000 875

7. Simplify.
(a) $\frac{1}{2} + \frac{2}{3}$
(b) $\frac{3}{4} + \frac{5}{8}$
(c) $1\frac{1}{2} - \frac{3}{4}$
(d) $3\frac{5}{8} - 1\frac{3}{4}$
(e) $3\frac{3}{5} - 2\frac{1}{2}$
(f) $3\frac{3}{4} + 2\frac{2}{3}$

8. Simplify.
(a) $3\frac{1}{2} \times 1\frac{3}{4}$
(b) $1\frac{1}{2} \div 2\frac{1}{3}$
(c) $3\frac{5}{8} \times 2\frac{1}{4}$
(d) $6\frac{3}{4} \div 3$
(e) $1\frac{1}{2} \div \frac{1}{4}$
(f) $3\frac{3}{8} \div \frac{3}{4}$

9. Express the following ratios in simplest form.
(a) 12 : 18
(b) 12 : 15 : 24

10. Find the unknown value in each of the following proportions.
(a) $\frac{x}{18} = \frac{15}{24}$
(b) $\frac{24}{x} = \frac{30}{10}$

11. If 36 out of 200 people surveyed owned pets, what percentage owned pets?

12. (a) What is 15% of 80?
(b) What is 12.5% of 128?
(c) 45 is 50% of what number?
(d) 63 is 25% of what number?

13. A stereo which regularly sells for $895.00 is on sale at 20% off.
(a) How much is the discount?
(b) What is the sale price of the stereo?

14. Three people invest $42 000, $21 000, and $14 000 in a small business. The business is sold for $500 000, and this money is shared in the same ratio as the original investment. How much would each person receive from the sale?

15. Find the length of the unknown side to the nearest tenth, in each of the following triangles.

(a)
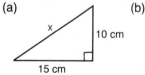

(b)
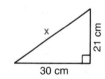

(c)
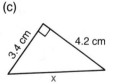

(d)
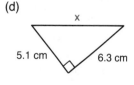

16. Expand and simplify.
(a) 3x(5x − 2) − 2x(x − 1)
(b) 4xy(1 − 3x) − xy(2 − y)

17. Simplify.

(a) $\dfrac{4x^2y^2 - 8xy}{2x}$ (b) $\dfrac{12a^3b - 4ab^3}{4ab}$

18. Factor.

(a) $x^2 - 3x - 18$ (b) $x^2 + 8x + 16$
(c) $t^2 - 100$ (d) $2x^2 + 5x - 3$

19. Solve.

(a) $5t - 3 = 32$
(b) $2 - 3m = 2m - 8$
(c) $2(t - 4) - (t - 1) = 7$
(d) $\dfrac{2m - 1}{3} = 4$

20. Solve and graph, $x \in R$.

(a) $3x - 2 \geqslant 7$
(b) $2(t - 3) - 4 < 3(t + 1)$

21. Susan drove from Chicago to Los Angeles at 80 km/h. She returned at 100 km/h. The total trip took 72 h. How far is it from Chicago to Los Angeles?

22. Calculate the mean, median, and mode of the following sets of data.

(a) 50, 49, 44, 41, 41, 44, 50, 45, 50
(b) 88, 91, 90, 92, 93, 89, 91, 90

23. Calculate the perimeter and area to the nearest tenth.

(a)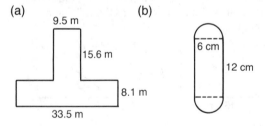

(b)

24. Calculate the surface area and volume to the nearest tenth.

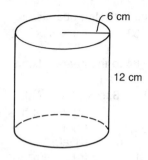

25. Find the missing dimensions.

(a)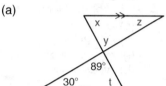

(b)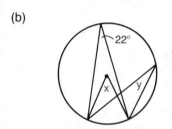

26. Calculate the slope and length of each line segment.

(a) A(1, 1), B(5, 7)
(b) C(−3, 4), D(−5, −9)

27. △ABC has vertices A(1, 1), B(5, 2), and C(3, 7). Determine the coordinates of the vertices of the image △A′B′C′ under

(a) the translation $(x, y) \rightarrow (x - 4, y + 3)$
(b) a reflection in the y-axis
(c) a rotation of 180° about (1, 1).

ANSWERS

AUTHORS' NOTE

The answers to questions requiring rounding or estimating will vary.

REVIEW AND PREVIEW TO CHAPTER 1

SETS

1. {1, 2, 3, 4, 5}
2. {12, 13, 14, 15}
3. {2, 4, 6, 8}
4. {31, 33, 35}
5. {2, 3, 5, 7}
6. {a, e, i, o, u}
7. {21, 28, 35, 42}
8. {Ontario, Erie, Huron, Michigan, Superior}
9. {St. John's, Halifax, Charlottetown, Moncton, Quebec City, Toronto, Winnipeg, Regina, Edmonton, Victoria}
10. {Alabama, Arkansas, Florida, Georgia, Louisiana, Mississippi, North Carolina, South Carolina, Tennessee, Texas, Virginia}

SUBSETS

1. { }, {a}, {b}, {c}, {a, b}, {b, c}, {a, c}, {a, b, c}
2. Yes
3. Yes

INTERSECTION AND UNION

1. (a) {7, 8}
   (b) {5, 6, 7, 8, 9}
   (c) {7, 8}
   (d) {5, 6, 7, 8, 9}
2. (a) {3}
   (b) {3, 4, 5, 6, 7}
   (c) { }
   (d) {1, 2, 3, 4, 5, 6, 7}
   (e) {4, 5}
   (f) {3}
3. (a) {1, 2, 3, 4, 5, 6}
   (b) {0, 1, 2, 3, 4, 5}
   (c) {3, 4, 5, 6, 7, 8}
   (d) {0, 1, 2, 3, 4, 6, 7, 8, ...}
   (e) {4, 5, 6, 7, ...}
   (f) {10, 11, 12, 13, ...}
   (g) {2, 3, 4, 5}
   (h) N
   (i) { }

PROPERTIES OF WHOLE NUMBERS

1. (a) commutative (addition)
   (b) commutative (multiplication)
   (c) associative (multiplication)
   (d) associative (addition)
   (e) additive identity element
   (f) multiplicative identity element
   (g) closure (addition)
   (h) closure (multiplication)
   (i) distributive
2. (a) $2x + 2y$
   (b) $3x + 12$
   (c) $8 + 4t$
   (d) $5m + 40$
   (e) $7x + 63$
   (f) $8n + 88$
   (g) $3x + 3$
   (h) $5y + 15$
   (i) $7t + 21$
   (j) $45 + 9x$
   (k) $10x + 40$
   (l) $2x + 26$
   (m) $3x + 3y + 18$
   (n) $4m + 28 + 4n$
   (o) $5r + 5s + 40$
   (p) $2x - 2y - 6$

EXERCISE 1.1

1. (a) five hundred, twenty-four thousand
   (b) thirteen thousand, five hundred
   (c) six thousand, two hundred fifteen
   (d) twenty-one billion, six hundred twenty-four million, three hundred sixteen thousand, five hundred twenty-eight
   (e) five hundred eight million
2. (a) two hundred thousand
   (b) two hundred thousand
   (c) two million
   (d) twenty thousand
   (e) two billion
3. (a) 13 200 000
   (b) 425 000
   (c) 37 000 000
   (d) 5418
   (e) 1 000 200 000
4. (a) 1387
   (b) 4756
   (c) 200 678
   (d) 11 877
   (e) 72 085
   (f) 75 208
5. (a) 132
   (b) 107
   (c) 1779
   (d) 10 607
   (e) 7253
   (f) 2996
6. (a) 6597
   (b) 12 306
   (c) 264 772
   (d) 179 100
   (e) 47 984 706
   (f) 358 575
7. (a) 152
   (b) 472
   (c) 16
   (d) 456
   (e) 98
   (f) 56

| (g) 125 | (h) 761 | (i) 122 | (j) 48 | (k) 43 | (l) 1004 |

8. (a) 14 229   (b) 36 534   (c) 63   (d) 39 702
(e) 5352   (f) 86   (g) 1 127 578   (h) 43

9. (a) 18 039   (b) 27 642   (c) 8170   (d) 258 750
(e) 1620   (f) 1 192 423   (g) 23

10. (a) 40 141   (b) 182   (c) 525   (d) 4122
(e) 8585   (f) 13 650   (g) 33

11. (a) Marsini, G.; Cloutier, J.; Howe, A.; Skinner, W.
(b) 8572   (c) 119 736

12. 1680 L   13. 50 h   14. 148 000 000 km²

15. (a) France, Spain, Sweden, Finland, Norway
(b) 2 163 000 km²   (c) 222 807 km²

EXERCISE 1.2

1. (a) sixteen and twenty-five hundredths
(b) three hundred twenty-five thousandths
(c) one and six hundred twenty-five thousandths
(d) twenty and ninety-five thousandths
(e) twenty-five ten thousandths
(f) twenty-five hundred thousandths
(g) one hundred twenty-five ten thousandths
(h) twenty-five hundredths
(i) five and six tenths
(j) three and four hundredths

2. (a) 0.01   (b) 0.001   (c) 0.000 01   (d) 0.1   (e) 0.01   (f) 0.000 001

3. (a) 0.4   (b) 0.04   (c) 0.4   (d) 0.004   (e) 0.0004   (f) 40

4. (a) 5.4   (b) 12.125   (c) 105.3   (d) 0.052   (e) 11.013   (f) 4.005

5. (a) $2 \times 1 + 6 \times 0.1 + 2 \times 0.01 + 5 \times 0.001$
(b) $1 \times 10 + 5 \times 1 + 2 \times 0.1 + 3 \times 0.01$
(c) $8 \times 1 + 3 \times 0.1 + 5 \times 0.01$
(d) $8 \times 0.1 + 3 \times 0.01 + 5 \times 0.001$
(e) $2 \times 10 + 4 \times 1 + 3 \times 0.1 + 1 \times 0.0001 + 4 \times 0.000 01$
(f) $6 \times 1 + 2 \times 0.1 + 5 \times 0.001 + 7 \times 0.000 01$
(g) $3 \times 1 + 1 \times 0.1 + 5 \times 0.01$
(h) $1 \times 0.1 + 2 \times 0.01 + 5 \times 0.001$
(i) $1 \times 10 + 2 \times 0.1 + 5 \times 0.01$
(j) $1 \times 100 + 5 \times 0.1$

6. (a) 102.85   (b) 259.581   (c) 64.853 46
(d) 270.492 05   (e) 367.045

7. (a) 140.923   (b) 28.605   (c) 19.85   (d) 2.1758

8. (a) 43.75   (b) 3   (c) 227.5   (d) 10.6625   (e) 0.1625   (f) 8.531 25

9. (a) 6.8   (b) 32.5   (c) 54   (d) 36
(e) 27.4   (f) 3.4   (g) 14.2   (h) 14.3

10. (a) 26.034   (b) 606.031 01   (c) 22.6045   (d) 4.8
(e) 39.3375   (f) 8.4   (g) 6.6875

11. (a) 76.315   (b) 189.02   (c) 13 987.04   (d) 528   (e) 20.675

12. 1941.8 m²   13. 68.5 m   14. 46.94 m   15. $17   16. 1.6 m   17. $1935.65

EXERCISE 1.3

1. (a) 800   (b) 800   (c) 2700   (d) 47 300   (e) 34 900   (f) 26 400
(g) 800   (h) 55 500   (i) 645 600

2. (a) 3.52   (b) 0.24   (c) 25.85   (d) 234.88   (e) 37.54   (f) 0.38
(g) 0.06   (h) 7.02

3. (a) 56.2   (b) 5.9   (c) 4.6   (d) 32.8   (e) 0.5   (f) 4.6
(g) 0.1   (h) 0.0

4. (a) 5.125   (b) 0.526   (c) 1.045   (d) 23.266   (e) 23.264   (f) 5.006
(g) 425.425   (h) 1.125

5. (a) 1418.56   (b) 207 792.4   (c) 1009.34   (d) 24.5952   (e) 21.7   (f) 33.3
(g) 4.25   (h) 0.405

6. (a) 767.28   (b) 1.324 7862   (c) 64.7   (d) 32.478 896   (e) 0.139 7897

7. (a) 150 000   (b) 18 000   (c) 10   (d) 4   (e) 8   (f) 250
(g) 0.5   (h) 2000

8. (a) $20   (b) $180   (c) $1   (d) $2   (e) $300

9. (a) 90   (b) 24   (c) 16   (d) 150

10. (a) $32.8 + 21.7$ (b) 4.25×6.75 (c) $65.72 - 38.6$

EXERCISE 1.4

1. (a) 7   (b) 6   (c) 20   (d) 6   (e) 11   (f) 6
   (g) 3   (h) 2   (i) 35   (j) 28   (k) 6   (l) 1
   (m) 5   (n) 1
2. (a) 53   (b) 45   (c) 25   (d) 25   (e) 193   (f) 126
   (g) 7   (h) 51   (i) 3   (j) 252   (k) 144   (l) 57
   (m) 64   (n) 10.4   (o) 2   (p) 2.1
3. (a) 3   (b) 47   (c) 2   (d) 21   (e) 45   (f) 592
   (g) 738   (h) 39   (i) 76   (j) 16.64   (k) 6.7   (l) 64.96
4. (a) =   (b) =   (c) ≠   (d) ≠   (e) =   (f) ≠

EXERCISE 1.5

1. (a) (i) 43   (ii) 30   (iii) 23   2. (a) (i) 16   (ii) 0   (iii) 8
3. (a) (i) 768   (ii) 6250   (iii) 9375   (iv) 96   (v) 3125
4. (a) (i) 1   (ii) 0.91087047   (iii) 5   (iv) 256   (v) 16
6. (a) 29   (b) 14   (c) 64   (d) 1

EXERCISE 1.6

1. (a) 3   (b) 12   (c) 0   (d) 6.9   (e) 150   (f) 3a
2. (a) 7   (b) 19   (c) 79   (d) 2   (e) 199   (f) 2m − 1
3. (a) 10   (b) 13   (c) 37   (d) 14.5   (e) 607   (f) 7 + 3y
4. (a) 5   (b) 7   (c) 10   (d) 12
   (e) 6   (f) 24   (g) 8   (h) 19
5. (a) 8.5   (b) 70   (c) 7.7   (d) 1.3
   (e) 12   (f) 13.7   (g) 11.6   (h) 6.4
6. E(8) = 68, E(9) = 77, E(10) = 86, E(11) = 95, E(12) = 104
7. E(21) = 698, E(22) = 731, E(23) = 764, E(24) = 797
8. (a) 102   (b) 153   (c) 204   (d) 54.4   (e) 34   (f) 42.5
9. (a) 73   (b) 109   (c) 172   (d) 10.9   (e) 9m − 8   (f) 1
10. (a) 72   (b) 44   (c) 87   (d) 49   (e) 20   (f) 17
   (g) 86   (h) 49   (i) 44   (j) 20   (k) 57   (l) 30
11. (a) 63   (b) 60   (c) 322   (d) 7   (e) 12   (f) 18
   (g) 1   (h) 7   (i) 9   (j) 504

EXERCISE 1.7

1. (a) $3 \times x \times x \times x \times x \times x \times x$ (b) $4 \times y \times y$ (c) $2x \times 2x$
   (d) $t \times t \times t$ (e) $xy \times xy \times xy$ (f) $3 \times rs \times rs$
   (g) $4 \times a \times a \times b \times b$ (h) $(x + y) \times (x + y) \times (x + y)$
2. (a) x^3 (b) y^4 (c) $4x^2y$ (d) $3mn^3$
   (e) $(3x)^3$ (f) $5(x + y)^2$ (g) $(x − y)^2(r + s)^3$
3. (a) 16   (b) 25   (c) 27   (d) 16   (e) 32   (f) 1000
4. (a) 4   (b) 12   (c) 3   (d) 10   (e) 9   (f) 9
5. (a) 4.5   (b) 9   (c) 0.25   (d) 3.375   (e) 6.25   (f) 2.375
6. (a) 1   (b) 4   (c) 9   (d) 9   (e) 3   (f) 8
7. (a) 3   (b) 11   (c) 18   (d) 2   (e) 3.44   (f) $a^2 + 2$
8. (a) 26   (b) 7   (c) 0   (d) 2.375   (e) 20.952   (f) $y^3 − 1$
9. (a) 625   (b) 216   (c) 256   (d) 192
   (e) 224   (f) 144   (g) 2744   (h) 200
10. (a) 13   (b) 25   (c) 24   (d) 9
    (e) 35   (f) 14   (g) 15   (h) 33
11. (a) 5   (b) 2   (c) 4   (d) 3   (e) 2   (f) 1

EXERCISE 1.8

1. (a) 12   (b) 7   (c) 10   (d) 16
   (e) 10   (f) 9   (g) 14   (h) 6
2. (a) 3   (b) 5   (c) 5   (d) 4   (e) 4   (f) 1
3. (a) 6   (b) 8   (c) 9   (d) 8   (e) 10   (f) 15
4. (a) 5   (b) 2   (c) 6   (d) 2   (e) 3   (f) 7
5. (a) 5^9 (b) 2^{11} (c) 7^{10} (d) 5^9 (e) 2^{16} (f) x^{21}
6. (a) x^3 (b) y^{16} (c) m^3 (d) t^9 (e) x^{11} (f) w^{17}
   (g) x^8 (h) y^{21} (i) m^4 (j) x^{18} (k) t (l) m^2

EXERCISE 1.9

1. (a) 24   (b) 14   (c) 13   (d) 12   (e) 20   (f) 23
   (g) 2   (h) 7   (i) 6   (j) 31   (k) 37   (l) 16
   (m) 5   (n) 2   (o) 3   (p) 3
2. (a) 20   (b) 20   (c) 23   (d) 5   (e) 17
   (f) 17   (g) 84   (h) 3   (i) 23   (j) 10
3. (a) 4   (b) 6   (c) 2   (d) 1   (e) 45
   (f) 4   (g) 52   (h) 1035   (i) 202   (j) 12
4. (a) 25   (b) 25   (c) 2   (d) 36   (e) 74
   (f) 124   (g) 12   (h) 72   (i) 1   (j) 1
5. (a) 22.9264   (b) 15   (c) 3.5   (d) 10.55   (e) 1.05
6. (a) 111.216   (b) 1   (c) 4.122 641 509   (d) 41.367
7. (a) 7.48   (b) 17.168   (c) 0.696 528 32
   (d) 1.565   (e) 0.001 481 5529

EXERCISE 1.10

1. (a) binomial   (b) monomial   (c) trinomial   (d) monomial
   (e) binomial   (f) monomial   (g) binomial   (h) trinomial
2. (i) (a) 4   (b) x (ii) (a) 7   (b) x^2y (iii) (a) 1   (b) x
   (iv) (a) 3   (b) x^4y (v) (a) 1   (b) xyz
3. (a) 10x   (b) 9y   (c) 17w   (d) 23x   (e) 5x   (f) 7w
   (g) 5w   (h) 6x   (i) 11s   (j) 15x   (k) 8x   (l) 5w
4. (a) 10x   (b) 13w   (c) 22s   (d) 19t   (e) 21x
   (f) 10w   (g) 2x   (h) 17t   (i) 26s   (j) 4x + 3y
5. (a) 3x   (b) 6w   (c) 11x   (d) 6s   (e) 20t
   (f) 5t   (g) 8x − 3y   (h) 2r   (i) 11x   (j) 10y
6. (a) 9x   (b) 17x   (c) 27w   (d) 12x   (e) 24w   (f) 83x
   (g) 101t   (h) 131x   (i) 175w   (j) 120x   (k) 98w   (l) 124t
7. (a) 18x + 4y   (b) 18t + 20x   (c) 20s + 56y
   (d) $12x^2 + 5x$ (e) 105t + 46   (f) 22x + 12y
   (g) 56x + 22xy   (h) $26x^3 + 14x^2$ (i) 39x + 20
   (j) 4xy + 29x + 15y   (k) $14x^2 + 13x + 6$ (l) $13x^2y + 27xy^2$
   (m) 67r + 17s + 9   (n) $11x^2 + 12x + 32$ (o) $15x^3 + 6x^2 + 102x$
8. (a) 10x; 20   (b) 26x; 52   (c) 37x + 7; 81
   (d) $4x^2 + 4x$; 24   (e) 27x + 6; 60   (f) $4x^2 + 5x$; 26
   (g) $7x^2 + 6x + 7$; 47   (h) $5x^2 + 12x$; 44   (i) $5x^2 + 9x + 4$; 42
9. (a) 5x + 18y; 64   (b) 11x + 10y; 52   (c) 12xy; 72
   (d) $2x^2$; 8   (e) 6x + 15xy; 102   (f) 8y + 7xy; 66
10. (a) 12   (b) 42   (c) 60   (d) 65   (e) 72   (f) 77
11. (a) 15   (b) 16.2   (c) 13.5   (d) 16.25   (e) 25   (f) 23.75
12. (a) 23.4   (b) 15.37   (c) 3.85   (d) 30.25   (e) 30.25   (f) 28.45
13. (a) $(x + y)^2$ (b) $(x + y)^2$ (c) $2x^2 − y^2$ (d) $5x^2 − 2y$ (e) equal

EXERCISE 1.11

1. (a) 28xy   (b) 32wt   (c) 55yx   (d) 42xyw
   (e) 56rst   (f) $45xy^2$ (g) 24xy   (h) 35pqr

2. (a) 15xyz   (b) 12x²wt   (c) 8xyz   (d) 35m²n
3. (a) 8y   (b) 7s   (c) 5   (d) 6r
   (e) 3   (f) 2s   (g) 3y   (h) 5x³
4. (a) 153xyw   (b) 216xyw   (c) 405x²yt   (d) 561rst
   (e) 297xyw   (f) 817x²yw³   (g) 551pqrst   (h) 1075x³y²w⁵
   (i) 18564xyz   (j) 1224p²q²s²
5. (a) 6z   (b) 20   (c) 15y   (d) 123y   (e) 45s
   (f) 21z   (g) 19   (h) 14st   (i) 25t
6. (a) 2y   (b) 6x²   (c) 2y   (d) 3x   (e) xy
   (f) 12   (g) 12   (h) 15w²   (i) 4   (j) 10
7. (a) 24wxy; 576   (b) 0; 0   (c) 4w²xy; 192
   (d) 50wxy; 1200   (e) 12w²x²y; 1728   (f) 24wxy; 576
8. (a) 1367.5   (b) 2168.3   (c) 18.7   (d) 0.2   (e) 33.6
   (f) 7.9   (g) 8.4   (h) 65.1   (i) 601.7   (j) 14.8

EXERCISE 1.12

1. (a) 42 cm   (b) 706 m   2. (a) 128 cm   (b) 572 m
3. (a) 36 cm   (b) 474 m   4. (a) 298 cm   (b) 1046 m
5. (a) 76 cm   (b) 461 m   6. (a) 1984 cm²   (b) 14 847 m²
7. (a) 1521 cm²   (b) 3844 m²   8. (a) 168 cm²   (b) 4061 m²
9. (a) 532 cm²   (b) 3333 m²   10. (a) 92 cm²   (b) 738 m²
11. (a) 96 cm²   (b) 418 m²   12. (a) 30 cm³   (b) 1001 m³
13. (a) 343 cm³   (b) 2197 m³

EXERCISE 1.13

1. (a) 94.2 cm   (b) 879.2 m   2. (a) 314 cm²   (b) 1808.64 m²
3. (a) 4710 cm³   (b) 4019.2 m³   4. (a) 735.25 cm³   (b) 65.42 cm³

EXERCISE 1.14

1. 222 m   2. 270.04 m   3. 2620 cm   4. 680 724 m²
5. 413 449 cm²   6. 64 209.86 cm²   7. 1.729 m³   8. 14 921.28 cm³
9. 7234.56 cm³   10. $523\frac{1}{3}$ cm³   11. (a) 96 m²   (b) 208 m²
12. (a) P = 52 m, A = 102 m²   (b) P = 31.12 m, A = 74.24 m²   (c) P = 51.4 cm, A = 157 cm²
   (d) P = 28.71 m, A = 34.06 m²   (e) P = 42 m, A = 74 m²   (f) P = 57.84 m, A = 132.39 m²

1.16 REVIEW EXERCISE

1. (a) 32 766 250   (b) 221 628   (c) 1 453 660   (d) 256
   (e) 23.395   (f) 580.186   (g) 427.05   (h) 5.789 919 355
2. (a) 32 200   (b) 526 000   (c) 16 400   (d) 0.6
   (e) 12.84   (f) 5.8   (g) 34.84
3. (a) 700   (b) 21   (c) 37.5   (d) 0.4
4. (a) $70   (b) $380   (c) $5   (d) $480   (e) $400
5. (a) 14   (b) 9   (c) 2   (d) 10
   (e) 9   (f) 16   (g) 11   (h) 8
6. (a) 5   (b) 20   (c) 60   (d) 100
7. (a) 7   (b) 14   (c) 5   (d) 60   (e) 25   (f) 4
8. (a) 4   (b) 24   (c) 3   (d) 25
   (e) 15   (f) 20   (g) 100   (h) 125
9. (a) 10x   (b) 11y   (c) 5x   (d) 8x
   (e) 5x   (f) 4y   (g) 8z   (h) 14y
10. (a) 147   (b) 53   (c) 182   (d) 2714   (e) 5   (f) 72
11. (a) 24.75   (b) 11.5   (c) 20.403   (d) 45.79   (e) 17.56
12. (a) 72   (b) 160   (c) 65   (d) 95   (e) 16   (f) 504

13. (a) 59   (b) 29   (c) 132   (d) 21   (e) 12   (f) 1
     (g) $\frac{4}{7}$ (h) 16   (i) 61   (j) 69   (k) 27   (l) 71

14. (a) $83x + 28y$ (b) $58x^2 + 10x$ (c) $16x + 15y + 4$
     (d) $88x^2 + 7x^3$ (e) $41xy + 4yz$ (f) $24r + 19s$

15. (a) 32   (b) 72   (c) 52   (d) 54   (e) 82   (f) 62

16. (a) 594 cm²   (b) 200 cm   (c) 34 104 cm²   (d) 13 774 cm²
     (e) 4896 cm³   (f) 13 cm   (g) 19.125 cm²

17. (a) C = 447.28 cm, A = 18136.64 cm²   (b) C = 263.76 cm, A = 5538.96 cm²
     (c) C = 15.7 m, A = 19.62 m²   (d) C = 11.62 m, A = 10.75 m²

18. 1256 m²   19. 197 100   20. Boris: 7 h; Debbie: 8 h   21. 7.85 cm

1.17 CHAPTER 1 TEST

1. (a) 38 884   (b) 260.791   (c) 7666.9   (d) 32.8
2. (a) 2.658   (b) 34.4   (c) 63 500   3. 48
4. (a) 62   (b) 0.5   (c) 21.1   5. (a) 14   (b) 98   (c) 2
6. (a) 25   (b) 1   7. (a) 10.26   (b) 20
8. (a) 6xyz   (b) $x + 7y + 5xy$ (c) $3x^2 + 8x$ (d) $10x + 5y$
9. 11.34 cm²   10. 4415.625 cm³

REVIEW AND PREVIEW TO CHAPTER 2

PERCENT

1. (a) 0.5   (b) 0.25   (c) 0.75   (d) 0.1   (e) 0.15   (f) 0.2
     (g) 0.21   (h) 0.37   (i) 0.42   (j) 0.81   (k) 0.93   (l) 0.62
     (m) 0.08   (n) 0.05   (o) 0.242   (p) 0.157   (q) 0.604   (r) 0.823
     (s) 0.915   (t) 0.366
2. (a) 24   (b) 144   (c) 55.2   (d) 78   (e) 47.52   (f) 1.6
     (g) 5.39   (h) 2480
3. (a) 297.5   (b) 5742   (c) 386.1   (d) 6.6   (e) 100.8   (f) 130
     (g) 105   (h) 100

PROBLEMS

1. $1125   2. 525 km   3. $66 635   4. $628 125   5. 11 h   6. 125
7. 18 870 000 kg   8. 117 m   9. 2958 kg   10. 13

PERIMETER, AREA, AND VOLUME

1. (a) 30 m   (b) 532 cm   (c) 47 m   (d) 644 m
2. (a) 966 cm²   (b) 225 m²   (c) 45.24 m²   (d) 7623 cm²
3. (a) 198 m³   (b) 729 cm³

EXERCISE 2.1

1. 50 337   2. 01 : 23
1. Possibilities: 15 cm by 7 cm, 10.5 cm by 10 cm, 21 cm by 5 cm, 30 cm by 3.5 cm
4. $4.35   5. 36   6. 24 ways
7. 143.5 cm and 206.5 cm   8. $20.15 and $26.65   9. 81, 82, and 83
10. 450 000 000   11. $940.62   12. 176   13. 120
14. (a) 15:00   (b) 11:00   15. 1134   16. 30 min and 57 s
17. 11 574 d 1 h 46 min 40 s   18. 20
20. January 1, December 31   21. $6500
22. 47, 78, 128   23. 40   24. 7   25. $161.87
26. 1273 km (to the nearest kilometre)   27. 1.5 cm
28. 25.2 m   29. 217   30. $341.60   31. Answers will vary.
32. 237   33. 6   34. 11 250   35. 30 cm
36. one thousand   37. Answers will vary.

EXERCISE 2.2

1. $69.45
2. 14.4°C
3. 0.9 g
4. $842 400
6. 5278 km
7. $647.50
8. 78
9. 8 min 20 s
10. 21.75 m
11. 74
12. Answers will vary.
13. Multiply the price of the new car by $\frac{256}{625}$ to obtain the worth after four years.
14. 1990
15. $935
16. $3648
17. 936 000
18. 110
19. $8.05

EXERCISE 2.3

1. 204
2. (a) 1, 5, 10, 10, 5, 1; 1, 6, 15, 20, 15, 6, 1; 1, 7, 21, 35, 35, 21, 7, 1; 1, 8, 28, 56, 70, 56, 28, 8, 1
   (b) 2048
3. Multiply the smaller of the consecutive numbers by 2 and then add 1.
4. 784

EXERCISE 2.4

1. 631 and 542
2. 7.25
3. 18
4. 32
5. 23, 24, 25, 26, and 27
6. 40 cm by 35 cm
7. 28.5 m and 42.5 m
8. $63\frac{2}{3}°$, $63\frac{2}{3}°$, $52\frac{2}{3}°$

EXERCISE 2.5

3. 56
4. 4
5. 16
6. 3
7. The farmer takes the goat across first. He then comes back and takes the wolf across and brings back the goat. He then takes the cabbage across and comes back for the goat.

EXERCISE 2.6

1. 350 km
2. 16 d
3. 195 cm
4. 21 min
5. 43 min 46.5 s
6. 24
7. $323.37
8. 144
9. $240.01
10. 2 a 140 d
11. 59
12. 708
13. 18.25 m²
14. $2400
15. $8.12
16. 15 km
17. 325

EXERCISE 2.7

1. 24
2. $134
3. 4000
4. 15 : 26
5. $1200
6. $40 000
7. (a) $10 000
(b) $20 736
8. $1000

EXERCISE 2.8

1. −22°C
2. 550.6 m
3. 5
4. 7840 m³
5. 11 h
6. (a) Answers will vary.
(b) Saturday

EXERCISE 2.9

1. Answers will vary.
2. 500 500
3. Answers will vary.
4. 224
5. 0.06 mm
6. 199
7. 45
8. 364
9. Answers will vary.

EXERCISE 2.10

1. 16
2. 0 and 90; 1 and 89; 2 and 88; 3 and 87
3. (a) 240 and 1, 120 and 2, 80 and 3, 60 and 4, 48 and 5, 40 and 6, 30 and 8, 24 and 10, 20 and 12, 16 and 15
   (b) 16 and 15
4. 1, 4, 9, 16, 25, 36, 49   6. $35
8. Sandra: 10 d, Jennifer: 15 d   9. 4 pairs of socks, 3 T-shirts

EXERCISE 2.11

1. 4707 km   2. 689   3. 552   4. 35 h   5. 1152
6. (a) 31, 39, 48   (b) 15, 8, 3   (c) 2, 1, $\frac{1}{2}$
   (d) 21, 34, 55   (e) 13, 16, 15   (f) 14, 16, 18
7. $1\frac{1}{2}$ h

EXERCISE 2.12

1. (a) Regency   (b) $46.67   (c) proximity to river
2. Paul decided to take the train and stay at the Driftwood Hotel (leaving $610 for activities).
3. 10 pro volley balls
   30 pro baseballs
   1 pro basketball, 4 regular
   1 pro football, 5 regular

2.14 REVIEW EXERCISE

1. 9   2. 64, 65, and 66
3. Tom: $67.40, Marcia: $59.50
5. Canada by 613 000 km²   6. $26 077.40   7. 3042   8. 2500
9. 21, 28, 36   10. 13 m by 7 m   11. 3000 cm³   14. 6
15. $27.15   16. $463.75   17. 726.1 km   18. 43 200 min
19. 79   20. Answers will vary.   21. 57   22. 1410
23. 1 + 1 + 1 + 1 + 1 + 1 + 1 + 13 = 20;   1 + 1 + 1 + 1 + 1 + 1 + 1 + 3 + 11 = 20;
    1 + 1 + 1 + 1 + 1 + 1 + 5 + 9 = 20;   1 + 1 + 1 + 1 + 1 + 1 + 1 + 7 + 7 = 20;
    1 + 1 + 1 + 1 + 1 + 3 + 3 + 9 = 20;   1 + 1 + 1 + 1 + 1 + 1 + 3 + 5 + 7 = 20;
    1 + 1 + 1 + 1 + 1 + 5 + 5 + 5 = 20;   1 + 1 + 1 + 1 + 3 + 3 + 3 + 7 = 20;
    1 + 1 + 1 + 1 + 3 + 3 + 5 + 5 = 20;   1 + 1 + 1 + 3 + 3 + 3 + 3 + 5 = 20;
    1 + 1 + 3 + 3 + 3 + 3 + 3 + 3 = 20
24. O = 2, K = 3, G = 9   25. (a) $\frac{1}{12}$ km   (b) $\frac{5}{6}$ km   26. 21, 24, 27

2.15 CHAPTER 2 TEST

1. $306   2. 3 min   3. 15, 9, 2   4. 38 m and 29 m
5. 9   6. 8   7. $84.49   8. $303

REVIEW AND PREVIEW TO CHAPTER 3

WORDS AND NUMBERS

1. (a) 1056 + 927, 1983   (b) 125 × 73, 9125
   (c) 93 − 68, 25   (d) 958 − 563, 395
   (e) 2 × 2385, 4770   (f) 500 − (85 + 132), 283
   (g) 89², 7921   (h) 95 × 95, 9025

(i) $\dfrac{186 + 254}{2}$, 220

(j) $\dfrac{658}{14}$, 47

(k) $18^2 - 2 \times 18$, 288

(l) 6^3, 216

(m) $(25 \times 6) + (981 - 207)$, 924

(n) $\dfrac{56 + 48 + 79 + 46 + 96}{5}$, 65

(o) $1027 - 127$, 900

(p) $56 \times 9 - 207$, 297

(q) $\dfrac{435 + 863}{22}$, 59

(r) $537 - 189$, 348

(s) $102 \times 50 - (43 + 97)$, 4960

(t) 15^2, 225

(u) $\dfrac{56 \times 81}{14}$, 324

(v) $1853 - 475$, 1378

NUMBER LINES

11. $\{x \mid 2 \leqslant x \leqslant 5\}$
13. $\{x \mid 5 \leqslant x \leqslant 12\}$
15. $\{x \mid 0 \leqslant x \leqslant 12, x \neq 4\}$

12. $\{x \mid 1 \leqslant x \leqslant 6\}$
14. $\{x \mid 0 \leqslant x \leqslant 3\}$
16. $\{x \mid 0 \leqslant x \leqslant 6\}$

SUBSTITUTION

1. (a) 10   (b) 1   (c) 70   (d) 0   (e) 24
2. (a) 13   (b) 70   (c) 26   (d) 5
3. (a) 12.5   (b) 2.5   (c) 37.3   (d) 14.5
4. (a) 3.42   (b) 3.2   (c) 5.03   (d) 4.55
5. (a) 1.6   (b) 20.25   (c) 2.25   (d) 3.4   (e) -2.2
6. (a) 149   (b) 145   (c) 1   (d) 1
   (e) 125   (f) 124   (g) 79
7. (a) -0.03 (b) -5.574 (c) -27.438 (d) 1.936   (e) -1.186
8. (b) 4.9 m   (c) 14.7 m   (d) 44.1 m

EXERCISE 3.1

1. (a) -6 (b) -4 (c) -3 (d) $+7$
   (e) $+1560$ (f) $+560$ (g) -5 (h) -20
2. (a) The set of integers greater than negative 3.
   (b) The set of integers less than positive 5.
   (c) The set of integers greater than positive 8.
   (d) The set of integers less than negative 6.
   (e) The set of integers greater than negative 2 and less than positive 5.
   (f) The set of integers greater than negative 1 and less than positive 5.
   (g) The set of integers greater than negative 3 and less than positive 2.
   (h) The set of integers greater than negative 2 and less than positive 3.
   (i) The set of integers greater than negative 7 and less than positive 1.
   (j) The set of integers greater than negative 3, less than positive 5, and not equal to 1.
3. (a) $>$ (b) $>$ (c) $<$ (d) $>$ (e) $>$ (f) $>$
   (g) $<$ (h) $>$ (i) $>$ (j) $<$ (k) $<$ (l) $<$
4. (a) $\{x \mid x \geqslant -2, x \in I\}$ (b) $\{x \mid -3 \leqslant x \leqslant 3, x \in I\}$
   (c) $\{x \mid x \geqslant 0, x \in I\}$ (d) $\{x \mid x \leqslant 0, x \in I\}$
   (e) $\{x \mid x \geqslant -1, x \in I\}$ (f) $\{x \mid x \leqslant -4, x \in I\}$
   (g) $\{x \mid -1 \leqslant x \leqslant 1, x \in I\}$
5. (a) (i) $\{-1, 0, 1, 2, ...\}$ (ii) $\{..., -1, 0, 1, 2, 3, 4\}$
   (iii) $\{..., -7, -6, -5\}$ (iv) $\{..., -3, -2, 0, 1, 2, ...\}$
   (v) $\{-2, -1, 0, 1, ...\}$ (vi) $\{-1, 0, 1, 2\}$
   (vii) $\{0, 1, 2, 3, 4\}$ (viii) $\{..., -3, -2, -1, 3, 4, 5, ...\}$
   (ix) $\{-3, -2, -1, 0\}$ (x) $\{0\}$
6. (a) $\{2, 3\}$ (b) $\{-3, -2, -1, 0, 1, 2\}$ (c) $\{0, 1, 2, 3\}$ (d) $\{\ \}$
7. (a) (i) $\{-2, -1, 0, 1, 2\}$ (ii) $\{..., -2, -1, 0, 3, 4, 5, ...\}$ (iii) $\{-4, -3, -2, -1, 0\}$

EXERCISE 3.2

1. (a) 15   (b) 2   (c) -2 (d) -7 (e) 0   (f) -22
   (g) -12 (h) -10 (i) 17   (j) 9   (k) -22 (l) -17

2. (a) 3   (b) 2   (c) 6   (d) 1   (e) −4
    (f) 0   (g) −10   (h) −17   (i) −3   (j) −10
3. (a) 3   (b) 9   (c) −5   (d) −13   (e) −11   (f) 0
    (g) 0   (h) −1   (i) −21   (j) −14   (k) −15   (l) −16
4. (a) 4   (b) 12   (c) 9   (d) −8   (e) 5
    (f) −5   (g) 1   (h) −10   (i) 17   (j) 3
5. (a) 14   (b) 5   (c) 8   (d) −5   (e) 3   (f) 12
    (g) 0   (h) −18   (i) −3   (j) −1   (k) −5   (l) −4
    (m) 0   (n) −6   (o) −1   (p) 4
7. (a) −5°C   (b) −2°C   (c) −9°C   8. (b) −5°C
9. (a) −5, +1, −2, 0, +6   (b) 0
10. double bogey: +2, bogey: +1, par: 0, birdie: −1, eagle: −2
11. (a) Neither.   (b) 35   12. (a) 8848 m   (b) 5895 m   (c) 6194 m
13. 6194 m   14. \$34 094.00

EXERCISE 3.3

1. (a) −3   (b) 56   (c) −19
    (d) No distinct opposite   (e) 1   (f) 15
    (g) −2   (h) −5   (i) 4
2. (a) 5   (b) 0   (c) −3   (d) −10   (e) 20   (f) 10
    (g) 3   (h) 14   (i) 5   (j) 0   (k) −7   (l) −7
3. (a) 3   (b) 7   (c) 8   (d) 4   (e) −15   (f) −7
    (g) 5   (h) −15   (i) 0   (j) 21   (k) −12   (l) −2
    (m) −14   (n) 3   (o) 9   (p) −12
4. (a) 30   (b) 3   (c) 23   (d) −8   (e) 49   (f) 0
    (g) 57   (h) −7   (i) −29   (j) −21   (k) −26   (l) −40
    (m) −36   (n) −38   (o) −53   (p) 6
5. (a) 3   (b) −100   (c) 32   (d) −14   (e) 0   (f) −19
    (g) −14   (h) −15   (i) −22   (j) 0   (k) −5   (l) −8
    (m) 8   (n) 14
6. Neonex: +24, Nordeen: +12, Normick P: −14, Redstone: −37, Rolland, −6, Superior A: −27

EXERCISE 3.4

1. (a) 15   (b) −12   (c) −36   (d) 8   (e) 0   (f) 28
    (g) 21   (h) −35   (i) −35   (j) 4   (k) 0   (l) −30
    (m) 56   (n) −60   (o) 99   (p) −8   (q) 0   (r) 6
2. (a) 40   (b) −24   (c) 36   (d) −30   (e) −8
    (f) 60   (g) 0   (h) −45   (i) −1   (j) −28
3. (a) 25   (b) 16   (c) −1   (d) 9   (e) −27
    (f) 16   (g) −20   (h) −36   (i) 24   (j) −1
4. (a) (i) −3   (ii) −3   (b) (i) 25   (ii) 25   (c) (i) 48   (ii) 48
5. (a) 20   (b) −28   (c) −33   (d) −20   (e) −25
    (f) −24   (g) −56   (h) 48   (i) 14   (j) 0
6. (a) 17   (b) 20   (c) 72   (d) −24   (e) −8
    (f) 20   (g) 20   (h) 22   (i) 22   (j) −7
    (k) 34   (l) −18   (m) 40   (n) −53
8. (a) −15   (b) 10   (c) 5   (d) 25
    (e) 25   (f) 125   (g) −100   (h) 400
9. (a) −12   (b) 12   (c) −60   (d) 36   (e) 144   (f) 48
    (g) −36   (h) −96   (i) 144   (j) 144   (k) 2304   (l) −288
    (m) −36   (n) 144   (o) 192   (p) −144

EXERCISE 3.5

1. (a) −2   (b) −5   (c) 2   (d) 4   (e) −5
    (f) −8   (g) 3   (h) 7   (i) −1   (j) −9
    (k) 2   (l) 0   (m) 15   (n) −3   (o) −3
2. (a) −5   (b) −1   (c) 5   (d) 9   (e) −28   (f) −17

(g) 4   (h) 9   (i) -5 (j) -20 (k) -49 (l) 23

(m) 0   (n) -1 (o) 1   (p) -3

3. (a) -4 (b) 2   (c) -1 (d) 45   (e) -10 (f) -8

(g) -1 (h) -1 (i) -15 (j) 6   (k) -6 (l) 2

(m) -1 (n) 13   (o) -2 (p) -3 (q) 8   (r) -8

4. 3°C   5. (a) 7°C   (b) -1°C

6. (a) 78°C   (b) 3°C/km (approximate)

7. (a) 2   (b) 8°C   (c) -5°C

EXERCISE 3.6

1. CM Yachts   2. Advocate and Black P A

3. 40¢   4. 0   5. 0

6. (a) $120 loss   (b) $275 gain   (c) $30 loss   (d) Neither gain nor loss.

(e) $40 loss   (f) $169 gain

7. $-$$100   8. $+$$20

EXERCISE 3.7

1. (a) -10 (b) 3   (c) -8 (d) 4   (e) 4   (f) -8

(g) 5   (h) 8

2. (a) -16 (b) -48 (c) -6 (d) -10 (e) 10   (f) 32

(g) -4 (h) 2   (i) 24   (j) -12 (k) -14 (l) -5

3. (a) -5 (b) 3   (c) 15   (d) -2 (e) 8   (f) -8

(g) -25 (h) -9

4. (a) 5   (b) -3 (c) 1   (d) 11   (e) -19 (f) -39

5. (a) 21   (b) -12 (c) 7   (d) -20 (e) 0   (f) -2

(g) -2 (h) 8   (i) 19   (j) -12 (k) -2 (l) -45

6. (a) 10   (b) -3 (c) -14 (d) 36   (e) -27 (f) 1

(g) 64   (h) -8 (i) -25 (j) -6

8. (a) -5 (b) -3 (c) 1   (d) 7   (e) 15   (f) -3

9. (a) 0   (b) -2 (c) 20   (d) 25   (e) -16 (f) 32

(g) 64   (h) -12 (i) -8 (j) -12 (k) 34   (l) 20

10. (a) 4   (b) -6 11. (a) 90   (b) -245 (c) 5050   (d) -1275

12. The dart hits the ground.

13. (b) The dart is falling for those times.

14. (a) L.S. = 1, R.S. = 1   (b) L.S. = 25, R.S. = 25

(c) L.S. = 13, R.S. = 13   (d) L.S. = 13, R.S. = 13

(e) L.S. = -35, R.S. = -35 (f) L.S. = 19, R.S. = 19

(g) L.S. = 169, R.S. = 169   (h) L.S. = 0, R.S. = 0

(i) L.S. = -5, R.S. = -5

EXERCISE 3.8

1. (a) $19x$ (b) $8x^2$ (c) $3y$ (d) $-8xy$ (e) $3x^2$ (f) $-11y$

(g) $-17y$ (h) $12z$ (i) $-12xy$ (j) $9y^3$ (k) $10wx$ (l) $-13x$

2. (a) $5x$ (b) $13x^2$ (c) $2y$ (d) $-7z$ (e) $-3x^2$ (f) $-25x$

(g) $-3x$ (h) $-18xy^2$ (i) 0   (j) $-4x$ (k) $9x$ (l) 0

(m) $4x$ (n) $12z^2$ (o) $-15xy$

3. (a) $10x$ (b) $-3y$ (c) $3z$ (d) $-x$ (e) x^2 (f) $-3w$

(g) $-2y$ (h) $-15xy$ (i) $-23x$ (j) $5w$ (k) $-21p$ (l) $7x^2y$

(m) $-11x$ (n) $-5w$ (o) 0   (p) $-10x$

4. (a) $12x - 5y$ (b) $15xy + 2$ (c) $10x + 19$ (d) $-2y^2$

(e) $-4xyz - 7xy$ (f) $26z - 10y$ (g) $9x^2 + 13$ (h) $-3x + 2y$

(i) $24x - 23z$ (j) $-2 - 6x^2$

5. (a) $6x, -18$ (b) $2x^2 + 3x, 9$ (c) $x, -3$ (d) $x^2 + 2x, 3$

(e) $10x, -30$ (f) $3x^2 + 4x, 15$ (g) $x^3 + 5x, -42$ (h) 0, 0

6. (a) $5xy - 3x, -24$ (b) $3y, 9$ (c) $xyz, 6$

(d) $x^2 + 2xy, -8$ (e) $3x + 2y + 2z, -2$ (f) $-yz - y^2, -6$

7. (a) $P = 12x$ (b) 84   8. (a) $P = 20x$ (b) 100   9. $35x$

10. (a) 5   (b) 15   (c) 25

EXERCISE 3.9

1. (a) $-30xy$ (b) $-6wx$ (c) $-77yz$ (d) $72xyz^2$
   (e) $-2x$ (f) $7xy$ (g) $-7xy$ (h) $-5y$
2. (a) $-24xy$ (b) $48wxyz$ (c) $36xyz$ (d) $-10xyz$
3. (a) $-7y$ (b) $-3x$ (c) $2y$ (d) $-11y$ (e) $8r$ (f) $-4y^3$
4. (a) $-85xy$ (b) $-128wxy$ (c) $165xyz$ (d) $221wxy$
   (e) $243x^2y$ (f) $-675x^3yz^2$ (g) $238rs^2$ (h) $288rst^3$
5. (a) $6y$ (b) $5yz$ (c) $-14y$ (d) $4w$
   (e) $29y$ (f) $-42wy$ (g) $32pq$ (h) $-5y^2$
6. (a) $-4x$ (b) $51x$ (c) 2 (d) 12

EXERCISE 3.10

1. (a) $3x + 6$ (b) $5x - 10$ (c) $8 - 4x$ (d) $-36 + 6x$ (e) $3x + 3y$
   (f) $2x - 6y$ (g) $-3x - 3$ (h) $2x - 6$ (i) $2x + 8$ (j) $12 + 4x$
2. (a) $6x + 18$ (b) $-15y + 35$ (c) $-3x - 3y$ (d) $-6x + 4$
   (e) $-x - 5$ (f) $4x^3 + 20$ (g) $12x + 24y$ (h) $-6x - 18$
   (i) $-3x - 5$ (j) $-8x^2 - 8$ (k) $4x - 3$ (l) $-12x^2 + 20$
3. (a) $8x - 1$ (b) -14 (c) $x - 2$ (d) $-8x - 22$ (e) $-x + 22$
   (f) $-6x + 16$ (g) $9x - 30$ (h) $-5x - 13$ (i) $7x - 21$ (j) $7x - 28$
4. (a) $3x^2 + 6x - 15$ (b) $10x^2 - 25x + 15$ (c) $-12x^2 - 16x + 4$ (d) $-2x^2 + 4x - 8$
   (e) $6x^2 - 6x + 6$ (f) $14x^2 + 35x - 21$ (g) $-2x^2 - 6$
5. (a) $3x + 1$ (b) $2.5x + 2.5$ (c) $4x + 3$ (d) $-2x + 10$ (e) $-7x + 3$
6. (a) $4x - 1, -9$ (b) $11x + 6, -16$ (c) $6x, -12$ (d) $15x^2 + 7, 67$
   (e) $8x + 1, -15$ (f) $17x^3 - 2, -138$ (g) $23x + 3, -43$ (h) $14x + 34, 6$
7. (a) $2x - 22$ (b) $-3y - 20$ (c) $3x - 7y$ (d) $11x - 13$
   (e) $10z^3 + 4z^2$ (f) $15xy - 45xy$ (g) $13xy - 4x - 9y$ (h) $3x - 15$
   (i) $2xy + 14$ (j) $18z - 30$
8. (a) $4x - 2$ (b) $y - 2$ (c) $-3x - 5$
   (d) $14y + 3$ (e) $-7y^2 - 5$ (f) $-3x^4 + 14x^3 - 23x^2$
   (g) $8x + 3$ (h) $4x - 15$ (i) $x - 1$
   (j) $y^2 - 6$
9. (a) $15x^2 - 10x$ (b) $3y - 6y^2$
10. (a) $48x^2$ (b) $10x^2$ (c) $58x^2$ 11. $75y^2$
12. (a) $70y^5$ (b) $108x^2$ (c) $27x^2$
13. (a) $40y^4$ (b) $3y^4$ (c) $37y^4$

EXERCISE 3.11

1. (a) Divisible by 3.   (b) Not divisible by 3.   (c) Divisible by 3.   (d) Not divisible by 3.
2. (a) 1, 0   (b) 5, 3   (c) $-3, -1$ 3. (a) $-10, -17$ (b) $-12, 156$
   2, 3   10, 8 $-2, \ 1$ $-8, -13$ $-9, 90$
   3, 8   15, 13 $-1, \ 3$ $-6, -9$ $-6, 42$
   4, 15   20, 18   0, 5 $-4, -5$ $-3, 12$
      25, 23   1, 7 $-2, -1$ 0, 0
      30, 28   2, 9   0, 3   3, 6
            2, 7   6, 33
            4, 11   9, 72
            6, 15   12, 132
            8, 19
            10, 23

EXERCISE 3.12

1. (a) 15   (b) 8   (c) -6 (d) 36
   (e) -8 (f) -8 (g) 5   (h) 30
2. (a) $5*6.3$ (b) $-12.3/3$ (c) $2.4 \uparrow 2$ (d) $1.7 + 4.9$
   (e) $6.2/12.7$ (f) $2.5 \uparrow 3$ (g) $3.7*2.8$
3. (a) $2.4*(6.5 + 2.9)$ (b) $(7.1 + 2.4)*(3.7 - 6.3)$ (c) $(2.4 - 1.8) \uparrow 2$
   (d) $(-1.6) \uparrow 2 + 7.23$ (e) $(-3.8) \uparrow 2/(2.1*4.3)$ (f) $(6.7*2.4)*3.6$

4. (a) 17 (b) 11 (c) 57 (d) 144 (e) 18 (f) 0.68

5. (a) (2.5 − 3)↑2 (b) 7↑3 − 2 (c) (11.5 − 3)↑2 (d) (3*2)↑2
   (e) 3.6/0.4 (f) 2↑5 (g) (2.1 + 3.9)↑2

6. (a) x + y (b) x*y (c) 3.2*x (d) x↑2 + y↑2
   (e) (x + y)↑2 (f) x*y/z (g) x*(x − y) (h) x*y − x↑2

7. (a) ℓ*w (b) 2*(ℓ + w) (c) 0.5*b*h (d) 3.14*d
   (e) 3.14*r↑2 (f) (a + b)*h/2 (g) s↑3 (h) 4*s
   (i) a + b + c (j) p*r*t

8. (a) 10.81 (b) 49 (c) 27.38 (d) 6.76 (e) 46.74 (f) 15.21
   (g) −2

EXERCISE 3.13

2. (a) 246.49 (b) −3375 (c) 32 (d) 2
   (e) 2 (f) 235.5 (g) 33.25 (h) 130

3. (a) NEW (b) NEW
```
   10 PRINT 5.6*7.8        10 PRINT 64.7 - 21.9
   20 END                  20 END
   RUN                     RUN
```
   (c) NEW (d) NEW
```
   10 PRINT 736.3*0.675    10 PRINT 1.065↑5
   20 END                  20 END
   RUN                     RUN
```

4. (a) NEW (b) NEW
```
   10 PRINT (5.75 + 3.68)/2.5      10 PRINT (6.8*5.9)/(3.57/0.7)
   20 END                          20 END
   RUN                             RUN
```
   (c) NEW (d) NEW
```
   10 PRINT 3.14*6.2↑2     10 PRINT 6.28*4.25/15.275
   20 END                  20 END
   RUN                     RUN
```

5. (a) 62.27
   (b) Since the display is positive, (3.25 + 9.58)^2 must be larger than 3.25^2 + 9.58^2.

6. (a) NEW
```
   10 PRINT (6.75 + 9.64)*(6.75 - 9.64) - (6.75↑2 - 9.64↑2)
   20 END
   RUN
```
   (b) NEW
```
   10 PRINT 5.25↑2 + 4.15↑2 - (5.25 + 4.15)↑2
   20 END
   RUN
```
   (c) NEW
```
   10 PRINT (3.2 - 1.4)*(3.2↑2 + 3.2*1.4 + 1.4↑2) - (3.2↑3 - 1.4↑3)
   20 END
   RUN
```
   (d) NEW
```
   10 PRINT (11.35 - 4.38)↑2 - (11.35↑2 - 4.38↑2)
   20 END
   RUN
```

7. (a) NEW
```
   10 PRINT 3*3.4↑3 - 2*3.4↑2 + 7*3.4 - 2.675
   20 END
   RUN
```
   Display: 115.917
   (b) NEW
```
   10 PRINT 3*6.8↑3 - 2*6.8↑2 + 7*6.8 - 2.675
   20 END
   RUN
```
   Display: 895.741

EXERCISE 3.14

2. (a) 13 (b) 3.75, 37.5 (c) 2.5, 6.25 (d) 3.5, 4.8, 8.3
   (e) 12, 13, −1 (f) 5, 12, 169 (g) 15, 25, 20

3. (a) NEW
       10 X = 7.5
       20 PRINT X + 4
       30 END
       RUN
   (c) NEW
       10 X = 9
       20 PRINT X - 12
       30 END
       RUN
   (e) NEW
       10 X = 2.6
       20 PRINT 5*X↑2
       30 END
       RUN
   (g) NEW
       10 R = 2.5
       20 PRINT 3.14*R↑2
       30 END
       RUN

   (b) NEW
       10 X = 8.2
       20 PRINT X↑3
       30 END
       RUN
   (d) NEW
       10 Y = 1.035
       20 PRINT Y↑6
       30 END
       RUN
   (f) NEW
       10 X = 1.8
       20 PRINT 2*X - 3
       30 END
       RUN

4. (a) NEW
       10 X = 7.5
       20 Y = 2.7
       30 PRINT X + Y
       40 END
       RUN
   (c) NEW
       10 X = 5.75
       20 Y = 4.23
       30 PRINT (X - Y)↑2
       40 END
       RUN

   (e) NEW
       10 X = 3.25
       20 Y = 4.65
       30 Z = 5.55
       40 PRINT X↑2 + Y↑2 + Z↑2
       50 END
       RUN

   (b) NEW
       10 X = 3.5
       20 Y = 2.4
       30 PRINT (X + Y)↑2
       40 END
       RUN
   (d) NEW
       10 X = 7.87
       20 Y = 4.35
       30 Z = 7.12
       40 PRINT X + Y + Z
       50 END
       RUN
   (f) NEW
       10 X = 3.2
       20 Y = 5.7
       30 Z = 9.3
       40 PRINT (X + Y + Z)↑2
       50 END
       RUN

5. (a) NEW
       10 X = 3
       20 PRINT X↑3 + X↑2 + 1
       30 END
       RUN
   (c) NEW
       10 X = 4.5
       20 PRINT 2*X↑2 - 3*X + 7.25
       30 END
       RUN
   (e) NEW
       10 X = 3.3
       20 PRINT (X + 3)↑3
       30 END
       RUN

   (b) NEW
       10 X = 5
       20 PRINT 2*X↑2 + 3*X - 7
       30 END
       RUN
   (d) NEW
       10 X = 3.3
       20 PRINT X↑3 + 3*X↑2 + 3*X + 1
       30 END
       RUN
   (f) NEW
       10 X = 5.8
       20 PRINT (X + 1)↑2 - (X↑2 + 1)
       30 END
       RUN

6. NEW
   10 X = 5.6
   20 Y = 2.3
   30 Z = 1.2
   40 PRINT (X + Y - Z)↑2 - (X↑2 + Y↑2 + Z↑2)
   50 END
   RUN

EXERCISE 3.15

2. (a) (i) 3.5, 17.25   (ii) −5, 30   (iii) 11.2, 130.44   (iv) −12, 149
   (b) (i) 4, 5, 77   (ii) 3.5, 4.2, 53.9   (iii) −7, −9, 274
   (c) (i) 36.95   (ii) 106   (iii) −282
   (d) (i) 4   (ii) 100   (iii) 0.0049

3. (a) NEW
```
10 INPUT X
20 E = 3*X↑2 + 5*X + 3
30 PRINT X, E
40 END
RUN
```

(b) NEW
```
10 INPUT X
20 E = 5*X↑2 - 2*X + 7
30 PRINT X, E
40 END
RUN
```

(c) NEW
```
10 INPUT X
20 INPUT Y
30 E = (X + Y)↑2
40 PRINT X, Y, E
50 END
RUN
```

4. (a) NEW
```
10 INPUT X
20 E = X↑2 - 4*X - 1
30 PRINT X, E
40 END
RUN
```

5. (a) NEW
```
10 INPUT X
20 E = -X↑2 - 2*X + 3
30 PRINT X, E
40 END
RUN
```

EXERCISE 3.16

1. (a) Program will repeat for values of X ranging from 1 to 7 in increments of 1.
   (b) Program will repeat for values of X ranging from −5 to 3 in increments of 2.
   (c) Program will repeat for values of X ranging from −2 to 2 in increments of 0.5.
   (d) Program will repeat for values of X ranging from −2 to 2 in increments of 0.25.

2. NEW
```
10 FOR X = -5 TO 5 STEP 2
20 E = 2*X - 5
30 PRINT X, E
40 NEXT X
50 END
RUN
```

3. (a)

−5,	44
−4,	30
−3,	18
−2,	8
−1,	0
0,	−6
1,	−10
2,	−12
3,	−12
4,	−10
5,	−6

(b) X = −1

4. (a)

−3,	22
−2.5,	15
−2,	9
−1.5,	4
−1,	0
−0.5,	−3
0,	−5
0.5,	−6
1,	−6
1.5,	−5
2,	−3
2.5,	0
3,	4

(b) X = −1 and X = 2.5

5. (a) NEW
```
10 FOR X = 1 TO 12
20 PRINT X
30 NEXT X
40 END
RUN
```

(b) NEW
```
10 FOR X = 1 TO 12
20 PRINT X↑3
30 NEXT X
40 END
RUN
```

(c) NEW
```
10 FOR X = 2 TO 20 STEP 2
20 PRINT X
30 NEXT X
40 END
RUN
```

(d) NEW
```
10 FOR X = 1 TO 19 STEP 2
20 PRINT X
30 NEXT X
40 END
RUN
```

6. (a) NEW
```
10 FOR X = -3 TO 5
20 E = X↑2 - 4*X - 1
30 PRINT X, E
40 NEXT X
50 END
RUN
```

(b) −5 (when X = 2).

7. (a) NEW
```
10 FOR X = -4 TO 3
20 E = X↑2 - 1
30 PRINT X, E
40 NEXT X
50 END
RUN
```

(b) NEW
```
10 FOR X = -5 TO 3
20 E = 2*X↑2 - 5*X - 3
30 PRINT X, E
40 NEXT X
50 END
RUN
```

(c) NEW
```
10 FOR X = -3 TO 3
20 E = (X - 1)↑3
30 PRINT X, E
40 NEXT X
50 END
RUN
```

(d) NEW
```
10 FOR X = -2 TO 3
20 E = 3*X↑3 - 2*X
30 PRINT X, E
40 NEXT X
50 END
RUN
```

8. NEW
```
10 FOR X = -10 TO 10 STEP 10
20 E = 3*X↑2 - 5*X + 7
30 PRINT X, E
40 NEXT X
50 END
RUN
```

9. NEW
```
10 FOR X = -2 TO 3 STEP 0.5
20 E = (2*X - 1)↑2
30 PRINT X, E
40 NEXT X
50 END
RUN
```

10. NEW
```
10 FOR X = -2 TO 4 STEP 0.5
20 E = X*(X - 2)
30 PRINT X, E
40 NEXT X
50 END
RUN
```

11. (a) (i) NEW
```
10 FOR X = 0 TO 1 STEP 0.1
20 Y = X↑2
30 PRINT X, Y
40 NEXT X
50 END
RUN
```
   (b) 0 and 1

12. (b) An addition table from 1 to 12.

(ii) NEW
```
10 FOR X = 0 TO 1 STEP 0.1
20 Y = X↑4
30 PRINT X, Y
40 NEXT X
50 END
RUN
```

(c) 30z = X*Y

EXERCISE 3.19

1. 31
2. 2, 3, and 4
3. (a) 320   (b) (i) 500   (ii) $175.00
4. (a) 8   (b) 276
5. 43
6. 15   7. 6   8. 12, 13
9. 4 and 5 or -5 and -4
10. (b) $150
   (c) $487.50 and $637.50
11. (a) $34 = 6 + 28$
   (b) $73 = 28 + 45$
   (c) $88 = 10 + 78$
12. (a) 13
   (b) 0
   (c) 26
   (d) Vancouver, British Columbia
   (e) Churchill, Manitoba
   (f) 37
   (g) 13
13. length 40 cm, width 20 cm
14. 40 cm by 20 cm
15. 51 cm by 24 cm
16. 35
17. 631 and 542
18. 26 cm by 32 cm
19. -1656 m

3.20 REVIEW EXERCISE

1. (a) 12   (b) -10 (c) -6 (d) -3 (e) -9 (f) 0
   (g) 8x   (h) $5x^2$ (i) $-12xy$ (j) $-x^3$ (k) y   (l) $-5x^3$
2. (a) -2 (b) -17 (c) -5 (d) 3   (e) 2   (f) 14
   (g) 5x   (h) $-20y$ (i) $8y^2$ (j) $-7xy$ (k) $-2w^2$ (l) 7y
3. (a) -18 (b) 30   (c) 64   (d) 0   (e) -14 (f) -56
   (g) -81 (h) -27 (i) -3 (j) 4   (k) -15 (l) -16
   (m) -6 (n) 8   (o) -11 (p) -3
4. (a) 9   (b) 5   (c) -4 (d) 3   (e) 11   (f) 16
   (g) 16   (h) -12 (i) -16 (j) -7 (k) 1   (l) 4
5. (a) -3 (b) -9 (c) 6   (d) -3 (e) 20   (f) 49
   (g) -1 (h) 7   (i) -7 (j) -5 (k) -5 (l) 4
   (m) 2   (n) -15 (o) -2 (p) 4
7. (a) -1 (b) -17 (c) 125   (d) -41 (e) 18   (f) 13
8. (a) 11   (b) 1   (c) 2   (d) 46   (e) 236   (f) -44
10. (a) 3x   (b) $-5y$ (c) $-2w$ (d) $-xy$
   (e) $10x - 8$ (f) 0   (g) $7 + 3x$ (h) $8y - 9x$
   (i) 6xy   (j) $9xy^2 + 8y$ (k) 2x   (l) $8x^2 - 12x + 6$
   (m) 0   (n) $-2y - 10$
11. (a) $-15xy$ (b) $8x^4$ (c) $-15x^5$ (d) $3x^2$
   (e) $-6x^2y$ (f) $-24x^4y^5$ (g) $-30xy^2$ (h) $-21x^7$
   (i) $-30y^5$ (j) $-x^2y^2$ (k) $72w^2$ (l) $5x^2y^4$
12. (a) $-8x^2$ (b) $-3x^2$ (c) 5   (d) $-x^4$
   (e) $-t$ (f) $-3y^4$ (g) $-8z$ (h) -1
   (i) $3x^2$ (j) $-4x^4$ (k) $-4w^2$ (l) $-3x^4z$
13. (a) $10x + 10$ (b) $3x + 38$ (c) $7w - 7$ (d) $8x^2 + 10x$
   (e) $11y - 13$ (f) $-5x^2 + 5x$ (g) -26 (h) $6y - 5x + 11$
   (i) $-9xy + 5$ (j) $8x - 9$ (k) $-7x^2 + 4x$ (l) $x - 17$
   (m) $9y - 13$
14. (a) 27   (b) 1   (c) 45   (d) 8   (e) 12   (f) 81
15. 16
16. 2.5, 1.6, 0.2
17. NEW
```
10 PRINT (4.5↑2 + 3.85)/(2.6*5.7)
20 END
RUN
```

18. (a) NEW
```
10 INPUT X
20 E = 5*X↑2 - 7*X
30 PRINT X, E
40 END
RUN
```
(b) (i) 66   (ii) 0   (iii) 90   (iv) 294

19. NEW
```
10 FOR X = 2 TO 10 STEP 2
20 PRINT X, X↑2
30 NEXT X
40 END
RUN
```

20. NEW
```
10 FOR X = 1 TO 11
20 E = 2*X↑2 - 8*X + 7
30 PRINT X, E
40 NEXT X
50 END
RUN
```

21. NEW
```
10 FOR X = -1 TO 1 STEP 0.5
20 E = 1 - X↑3
30 PRINT X, E
40 NEXT X
50 END
RUN
```

3.21 CHAPTER 3 TEST

2. (a) -27 (b) 28   (c) -40 (d) 4   (e) -6
   (f) -6 (g) -27 (h) 4   (i) 60   (j) -8
   (k) 7   (l) -4 (m) 7   (n) -3 (o) 4
3. (a) -2 (b) -20 (c) 12   (d) 12   (e) 18   (f) 6
4. (a) -3 (b) -7 (c) -13 5. -780
6. (a) $-4x$ (b) $4x^4 + 3x^2 - 3x$ (c) $-4y$ (d) $-8x^2 + 5x + 4$
7. (a) $-10x + 15$ (b) $-15xy$ (c) $6x + 13$ (d) 0.5   8. 6
9. NEW
```
10 FOR X = -5 TO 5
20 E = X*(X - 5)
30 PRINT X, E
40 NEXT X
50 END
RUN
```

REVIEW AND PREVIEW TO CHAPTER 4

COMMON FRACTIONS

1. (a) 4   (b) 6   (c) 2   (d) 1   (e) 6   (f) 10
   (g) 7   (h) 10   (i) 7   (j) 23   (k) 5   (l) 4
2. (a) $<$ (b) $<$ (c) $>$ (d) $<$
   (e) $>$ (f) $<$ (g) $<$ (h) $>$
3. (a) $\frac{3}{5}$ (b) $\frac{3}{7}$ (c) $\frac{7}{10}$ (d) $\frac{5}{18}$ (e) $1\frac{1}{4}$ (f) $\frac{1}{8}$
   (g) $1\frac{2}{3}$ (h) $2\frac{1}{4}$ (i) $\frac{1}{12}$ (j) $1\frac{5}{8}$ (k) $2\frac{1}{2}$ (l) $\frac{3}{4}$
   (m) $2\frac{1}{4}$ (n) $2\frac{3}{8}$ (o) 0   (p) $1\frac{5}{8}$ (q) $2\frac{1}{2}$ (r) $1\frac{7}{8}$
4. (a) $\frac{17}{30}$ (b) $1\frac{5}{12}$ (c) $2\frac{3}{20}$ (d) 1
   (e) $\frac{13}{24}$ (f) $4\frac{7}{15}$ (g) $1\frac{9}{35}$ (h) $2\frac{19}{24}$
5. (a) $\frac{6}{35}$ (b) $\frac{1}{8}$ (c) $\frac{1}{4}$ (d) $\frac{5}{9}$ (e) $\frac{3}{4}$ (f) $\frac{3}{4}$
   (g) 7   (h) $2\frac{3}{16}$ (i) $-\frac{7}{4}$ (j) $\frac{7}{4}$ (k) $4\frac{4}{5}$ (l) 3
6. (a) $3\frac{1}{3}$ (b) $1\frac{1}{5}$ (c) $\frac{1}{3}$ (d) $\frac{5}{9}$ (e) $\frac{1}{2}$ (f) 4
   (g) $\frac{1}{4}$ (h) $\frac{1}{5}$ (i) $\frac{1}{28}$ (j) 4   (k) 6   (l) $\frac{2}{3}$
7. (a) $1\frac{1}{5}$ (b) $\frac{7}{16}$ (c) $4\frac{1}{6}$ (d) 1
   (e) $1\frac{7}{8}$ (f) $\frac{13}{24}$ (g) $1\frac{11}{30}$ (h) $\frac{11}{20}$

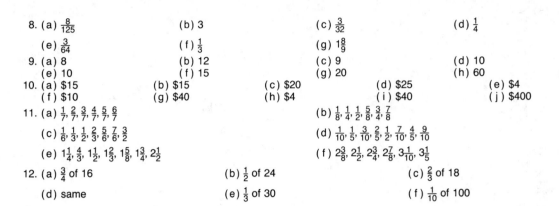

8. (a) $\frac{8}{125}$ (b) 3 (c) $\frac{3}{32}$ (d) $\frac{1}{4}$
   (e) $\frac{3}{64}$ (f) $\frac{1}{3}$ (g) $1\frac{8}{9}$
9. (a) 8 (b) 12 (c) 9 (d) 10
   (e) 10 (f) 15 (g) 20 (h) 60
10. (a) $15 (b) $15 (c) $20 (d) $25 (e) $4
    (f) $10 (g) $40 (h) $4 (i) $40 (j) $400
11. (a) $\frac{1}{7}, \frac{2}{7}, \frac{3}{7}, \frac{4}{7}, \frac{5}{7}, \frac{6}{7}$
    (b) $\frac{1}{8}, \frac{1}{4}, \frac{1}{2}, \frac{5}{8}, \frac{3}{4}, \frac{7}{8}$
    (c) $\frac{1}{6}, \frac{1}{3}, \frac{1}{2}, \frac{2}{3}, \frac{5}{6}, \frac{6}{2}$
    (d) $\frac{1}{10}, \frac{1}{5}, \frac{3}{10}, \frac{2}{5}, \frac{1}{2}, \frac{7}{10}, \frac{4}{5}, \frac{9}{10}$
    (e) $1\frac{1}{4}, \frac{4}{3}, 1\frac{1}{2}, 1\frac{2}{3}, \frac{15}{8}, 1\frac{3}{4}, 2\frac{1}{2}$
    (f) $2\frac{3}{8}, 2\frac{1}{2}, 2\frac{3}{4}, 2\frac{7}{8}, 3\frac{1}{10}, 3\frac{1}{5}$
12. (a) $\frac{3}{4}$ of 16 (b) $\frac{1}{2}$ of 24 (c) $\frac{2}{3}$ of 18
    (d) same (e) $\frac{1}{3}$ of 30 (f) $\frac{1}{10}$ of 100
13. 170 14. $\frac{1}{3}$

EXERCISE 4.1

1. (a) $\frac{-2}{-5}, \frac{4}{10}$ (b) $\frac{1}{-3}, \frac{-3}{9}$ (c) $3\frac{2}{4}, 3\frac{3}{6}$ (d) $\frac{-9}{-13}, \frac{18}{26}$ (e) $\frac{-14}{16}, \frac{21}{-24}$ (f) $-1\frac{2}{10}, \frac{-6}{5}$
   (g) $\frac{-2}{1}, \frac{-4}{2}$ (h) $\frac{-4}{-1}, \frac{8}{2}$ (i) $\frac{6}{7}, \frac{42}{49}$ (j) $\frac{-5}{7}, \frac{5}{-7}$ (k) $\frac{18}{8}, 2\frac{1}{4}$ (l) $\frac{-5}{-11}, \frac{10}{-22}$
3. (a) $2, \frac{17}{10}, 1\frac{1}{5}, \frac{3}{4}, \frac{1}{2}, -\frac{2}{3}, -1, \frac{-7}{4}$ (b) $\frac{3}{4}, \frac{7}{10}, \frac{2}{3}, 0, \frac{-2}{5}, \frac{3}{-4}, -\frac{4}{5}$ (c) $\frac{7}{3}, \frac{11}{9}, \frac{6}{5}, \frac{5}{8}, \frac{-3}{8}, \frac{-13}{15}, \frac{-5}{2}$
   (d) $\frac{3}{4}, \frac{2}{3}, \frac{5}{8}, \frac{2}{5}, \frac{-1}{2}, \frac{-3}{4}$ (e) $\frac{5}{2}, \frac{7}{3}, 1\frac{7}{8}, 1\frac{3}{4}, 1\frac{1}{2}, \frac{9}{7}$ (f) $\frac{-2}{5}, -\frac{3}{7}, -\frac{1}{2}, \frac{-5}{8}, -\frac{2}{3}, -\frac{3}{4}$

EXERCISE 4.2

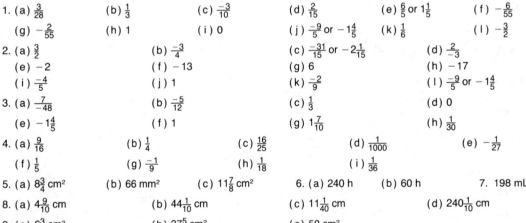

1. (a) $\frac{3}{28}$ (b) $\frac{1}{3}$ (c) $\frac{-3}{10}$ (d) $\frac{2}{15}$ (e) $\frac{6}{5}$ or $1\frac{1}{5}$ (f) $-\frac{6}{55}$
   (g) $-\frac{2}{55}$ (h) 1 (i) 0 (j) $\frac{-9}{5}$ or $-1\frac{4}{5}$ (k) $\frac{1}{6}$ (l) $-\frac{3}{2}$
2. (a) $\frac{3}{2}$ (b) $\frac{-3}{4}$ (c) $\frac{-31}{15}$ or $-2\frac{1}{15}$ (d) $\frac{2}{-3}$
   (e) -2 (f) -13 (g) 6 (h) -17
   (i) $\frac{-4}{5}$ (j) 1 (k) $\frac{-2}{9}$ (l) $\frac{-9}{5}$ or $-1\frac{4}{5}$
3. (a) $\frac{7}{-48}$ (b) $\frac{-5}{12}$ (c) $\frac{1}{3}$ (d) 0
   (e) $-1\frac{4}{5}$ (f) 1 (g) $1\frac{7}{10}$ (h) $\frac{1}{30}$
4. (a) $\frac{9}{16}$ (b) $\frac{1}{4}$ (c) $\frac{16}{25}$ (d) $\frac{1}{1000}$ (e) $-\frac{1}{27}$
   (f) $\frac{1}{5}$ (g) $\frac{-1}{9}$ (h) $\frac{1}{18}$ (i) $\frac{1}{36}$
5. (a) $8\frac{3}{4}$ cm² (b) 66 mm² (c) $11\frac{7}{8}$ cm² 6. (a) 240 h (b) 60 h 7. 198 mL
8. (a) $4\frac{9}{10}$ cm (b) $44\frac{1}{10}$ cm (c) $11\frac{1}{40}$ cm (d) $240\frac{1}{10}$ cm
9. (a) $6\frac{3}{4}$ cm² (b) $37\frac{5}{8}$ cm² (c) 50 cm²

EXERCISE 4.3

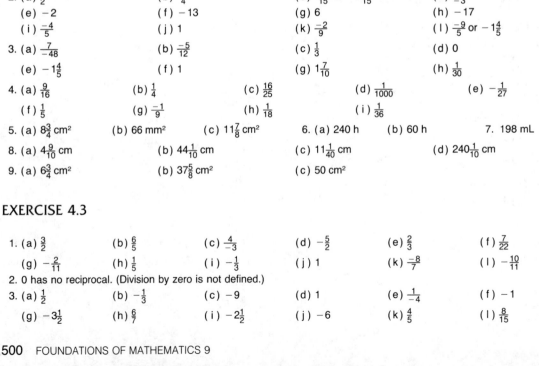

1. (a) $\frac{3}{2}$ (b) $\frac{6}{5}$ (c) $\frac{4}{-3}$ (d) $-\frac{5}{2}$ (e) $\frac{2}{3}$ (f) $\frac{7}{22}$
   (g) $-\frac{2}{11}$ (h) $\frac{1}{5}$ (i) $-\frac{1}{3}$ (j) 1 (k) $\frac{-8}{7}$ (l) $-\frac{10}{11}$
2. 0 has no reciprocal. (Division by zero is not defined.)
3. (a) $\frac{1}{2}$ (b) $-\frac{1}{3}$ (c) -9 (d) 1 (e) $\frac{1}{-4}$ (f) -1
   (g) $-3\frac{1}{2}$ (h) $\frac{6}{7}$ (i) $-2\frac{1}{2}$ (j) -6 (k) $\frac{4}{5}$ (l) $\frac{8}{15}$

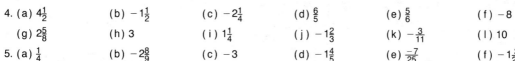

4. (a) $4\frac{1}{2}$ (b) $-1\frac{1}{2}$ (c) $-2\frac{1}{4}$ (d) $\frac{6}{5}$ (e) $\frac{5}{6}$ (f) -8

(g) $2\frac{5}{8}$ (h) 3 (i) $1\frac{1}{4}$ (j) $-1\frac{2}{3}$ (k) $-\frac{3}{11}$ (l) 10

5. (a) $\frac{1}{4}$ (b) $-2\frac{8}{9}$ (c) -3 (d) $-1\frac{4}{5}$ (e) $\frac{-7}{25}$ (f) $-1\frac{3}{25}$

6. 92 km/h 7. (a) $37\frac{1}{2}$ L (b) 8 km 8. 7 9. $1\frac{1}{2}$ cm 10. 9 cm

11. (a) (i) \$5302.50 (ii) \$5215.00 (b) \$240.00
(c) (i) \$262.50 increase (ii) \$2000.00 increase (iii) no change (iv) \$44.38 increase
(d) 400 (e) 30 000 (f) 320

EXERCISE 4.4

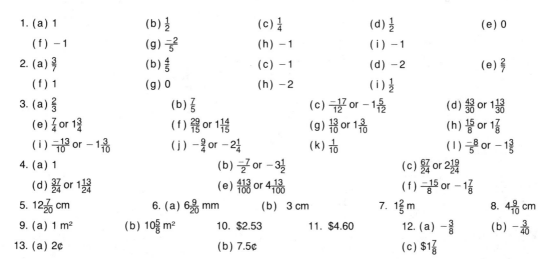

1. (a) 1 (b) $\frac{1}{2}$ (c) $\frac{1}{4}$ (d) $\frac{1}{2}$ (e) 0

(f) -1 (g) $\frac{-2}{5}$ (h) -1 (i) -1

2. (a) $\frac{3}{7}$ (b) $\frac{4}{5}$ (c) -1 (d) -2 (e) $\frac{2}{7}$

(f) 1 (g) 0 (h) -2 (i) $\frac{1}{2}$

3. (a) $\frac{2}{3}$ (b) $\frac{7}{5}$ (c) $\frac{-17}{12}$ or $-1\frac{5}{12}$ (d) $\frac{43}{30}$ or $1\frac{13}{30}$

(e) $\frac{7}{4}$ or $1\frac{3}{4}$ (f) $\frac{29}{15}$ or $1\frac{14}{15}$ (g) $\frac{13}{10}$ or $1\frac{3}{10}$ (h) $\frac{15}{8}$ or $1\frac{7}{8}$

(i) $\frac{-13}{10}$ or $-1\frac{3}{10}$ (j) $-\frac{9}{4}$ or $-2\frac{1}{4}$ (k) $\frac{1}{10}$ (l) $\frac{-8}{5}$ or $-1\frac{3}{5}$

4. (a) 1 (b) $\frac{-7}{2}$ or $-3\frac{1}{2}$ (c) $\frac{67}{24}$ or $2\frac{19}{24}$

(d) $\frac{37}{24}$ or $1\frac{13}{24}$ (e) $\frac{413}{100}$ or $4\frac{13}{100}$ (f) $\frac{-15}{8}$ or $-1\frac{7}{8}$

5. $12\frac{7}{20}$ cm 6. (a) $6\frac{9}{20}$ mm (b) 3 cm 7. $1\frac{2}{5}$ m 8. $4\frac{9}{10}$ cm

9. (a) 1 m² (b) $10\frac{5}{8}$ m² 10. \$2.53 11. \$4.60 12. (a) $-\frac{3}{8}$ (b) $-\frac{3}{40}$

13. (a) 2¢ (b) 7.5¢ (c) $\$1\frac{7}{8}$

(d) Cott Bev and Costain Ltd; Crownx A w and Crownx B w (e) $13\frac{1}{6}$¢

EXERCISE 4.5

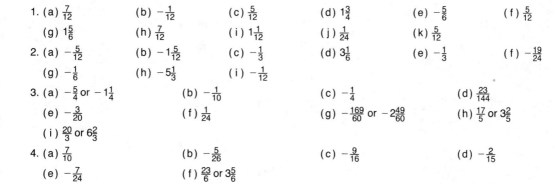

1. (a) $\frac{7}{12}$ (b) $-\frac{1}{12}$ (c) $\frac{5}{12}$ (d) $1\frac{3}{4}$ (e) $-\frac{5}{6}$ (f) $\frac{5}{12}$

(g) $1\frac{5}{6}$ (h) $\frac{7}{12}$ (i) $1\frac{1}{12}$ (j) $\frac{1}{24}$ (k) $\frac{5}{12}$

2. (a) $-\frac{5}{12}$ (b) $-1\frac{5}{12}$ (c) $-\frac{1}{3}$ (d) $3\frac{1}{6}$ (e) $-\frac{1}{3}$ (f) $-\frac{19}{24}$

(g) $-\frac{1}{6}$ (h) $-5\frac{1}{3}$ (i) $-\frac{1}{12}$

3. (a) $-\frac{5}{4}$ or $-1\frac{1}{4}$ (b) $-\frac{1}{10}$ (c) $-\frac{1}{4}$ (d) $\frac{23}{144}$

(e) $-\frac{3}{20}$ (f) $\frac{1}{24}$ (g) $-\frac{169}{60}$ or $-2\frac{49}{60}$ (h) $\frac{17}{5}$ or $3\frac{2}{5}$

(i) $\frac{20}{3}$ or $6\frac{2}{3}$

4. (a) $\frac{7}{10}$ (b) $-\frac{5}{26}$ (c) $-\frac{9}{16}$ (d) $-\frac{2}{15}$

(e) $-\frac{7}{24}$ (f) $\frac{23}{6}$ or $3\frac{5}{6}$

5. (a) -8 (b) $-\frac{73}{40}$ or $-1\frac{33}{40}$ 6. (a) -1 (b) $\frac{15}{16}$

EXERCISE 4.6

1. (a) 0.02 (b) 0.05 (c) -0.6 (d) 0.1875 (e) -0.625

(f) 0.28 (g) 1.1875 (h) -0.425 (i) $-0.343\,75$

2. (a) $0.\overline{3}$, 3, 1
(d) $0.6\overline{1}$, 1, 1
(g) $0.87\overline{0}$, 0, 1
(j) $-0.\overline{428\,571}$, 428 571, 6
3. $-0.107\,142\,\overline{85}$, $-0.\overline{1}$, $-0.0\overline{94}$, $-0.0\overline{9}$, $-0.0\overline{8}$
4. (a) $0\overline{58\,823\,529\,411\,7647}$, 16

(b) $0.\overline{63}$, 63, 2
(e) $-1.\overline{6}$, 6, 1
(h) $-1.1\overline{8}$, 18, 2
(k) $5.\overline{6}$, 6, 1

(c) $-0.0\overline{45}$, 45, 2
(f) $-0.\overline{8}$, 8, 1
(i) $-0.2\overline{3}$, 3, 1
(l) $-0.\overline{384\,615}$, 384 615, 6

(b) $2\overline{17\,391\,304\,347\,826\,086\,9565}$, 22

EXERCISE 4.7

1. (a) $\frac{3}{10}$
(b) $\frac{1}{4}$
(c) $-\frac{3}{5}$
(d) $-\frac{3}{2}$
(e) $\frac{15}{4}$
(f) $\frac{1}{8}$

(g) $-\frac{15}{8}$
(h) $\frac{9}{50}$
(i) $\frac{103}{20}$
(j) $-\frac{1001}{10}$
(k) $\frac{59}{25}$
(l) $\frac{9}{400}$

3. (a) $\frac{1}{3}$
(b) $\frac{4}{9}$
(c) $\frac{13}{99}$
(d) $\frac{4}{11}$
(e) $\frac{5}{9}$
(f) $\frac{4}{15}$

(g) $\frac{7}{45}$
(h) $\frac{97}{330}$
(i) $3\frac{16}{99}$
(j) $\frac{52}{99}$
(k) $1\frac{7}{30}$
(l) $\frac{12}{185}$

4. (a) (i) $\frac{2}{5}$
(ii) $\frac{1}{2}$
(iii) $\frac{4}{5}$
(iv) $\frac{9}{10}$
(v) $\frac{53}{100}$
(vi) $\frac{27}{50}$

(c) (i) $\frac{3}{5}$
(ii) 1

EXERCISE 4.8

1. (a) 65.6
(g) 150
(m) 0.0654
2. (a) 42
(g) 8
3. (a) 95.4030
4. (a) 24 mm²
5. (a) 108 cm²

(b) 4860
(h) 186 000
(n) 0.001 99
(b) 100
(h) 5
(b) 500.625
(b) 144 m²
(b) 0.005 m²

(c) 959
(i) 0.236
(o) 0.000 660
(c) 600
(i) 5
(c) 81.324 32
(c) 56
(c) 0.1 m²

(d) 1.07
(j) 6.01
(p) 19.9
(d) 60
(j) 100
(d) 22.6231
(d) 0.008

(e) 7.92
(k) 880
(e) 1000
(k) 9
(e) 20.840

(f) 12.9
(l) 700
(f) 8
(l) 3
(f) 17.3955

EXERCISE 4.9

1. (a) x^7
(f) x
2. (a) x^9
(f) $\frac{1}{x^5}$
(k) y^6
3. (a) 10^{11}
(g) 10^3
4. (a) 1
(g) $\frac{1}{16}$
5. (a) 1
(g) $\frac{27}{8}$
6. (a) $\frac{1}{x^5}$
(g) $\frac{1}{z^6}$

(b) y^6
(g) $\frac{1}{x^2}$
(b) x^4
(g) $\frac{1}{x^4}$
(l) $\frac{1}{x^2}$
(b) 10^2
(h) $\frac{1}{10^3}$
(b) -8
(h) $\frac{1}{1000}$
(b) $\frac{9}{16}$
(h) 1
(b) y^7
(h) $\frac{1}{x^6}$

(c) 1
(h) 1
(c) $\frac{1}{y^3}$
(h) $\frac{1}{y^5}$
(m) 1
(c) 10^2
(i) $\frac{1}{10^3}$
(c) -1
(i) 1000
(c) $\frac{1}{25}$
(i) 4
(c) w^{13}
(i) $\frac{1}{x^4}$

(d) x^{-7}
(i) $\frac{1}{y^4}$
(d) 1
(i) w^{10}
(d) 10^5
(j) $\frac{1}{10^2}$
(d) $\frac{1}{100}$
(j) $\frac{-1}{8}$
(d) 3
(j) $-\frac{1}{8}$
(d) x^7
(j) $\frac{1}{y^4}$

(e) x^{-8}
(j) $\frac{1}{m^2}$
(e) w^5
(j) x^3
(e) $\frac{1}{10^6}$
(k) 1
(e) $\frac{1}{27}$
(k) $\frac{1}{32}$
(e) 10
(k) -8
(e) y
(k) $\frac{1}{x}$

(f) x
(f) $\frac{1}{10^5}$
(l) 10^6
(f) $\frac{1}{16}$
(l) -1
(f) 4
(l) 1000
(f) $\frac{1}{x^2}$
(l) $\frac{1}{y^7}$

7. (a) $1\frac{1}{3}$ (b) $\frac{7}{10}$ (c) $\frac{1}{48}$ (d) $\frac{5}{6}$

   (e) $\frac{17}{72}$ (f) 9   (g) 9   (h) 5

EXERCISE 4.10

2. (a) 3.71×10^2 (b) 5.6×10^3 (c) 1.82×10^1 (d) 1.73×10^8
   (e) 4.5×10^0 (f) 2.9×10^5 (g) 5.962×10^2 (h) 8×10^0
   (i) 8×10^5 (j) $3.500\ 65 \times 10^3$ (k) 4.87×10^2 (l) 1×10^{12}
3. (a) 5.68×10^3 (b) 1.08×10^4 (c) 3.76×10^5 (d) 5.29×10^4
   (e) 1.79×10^8 (f) 9.98×10^5 (g) 4.90×10^1 (h) 3.77×10^2
4. (b) 6 places to the right.

EXERCISE 4.11

1. (b) (i) 2.95×10^{-2} (ii) 5×10^{-1} (iii) 8.2×10^{-3} (iv) 6.53×10^{-1} (v) 1×10^{-6}
   (vi) 6.32×10^{-1} (vii) 1.02×10^{-2} (viii) 3.5×10^{-4} (ix) $7.9\overline{7}9 \times 10^{-1}$
2. (b) 4 places to the left.
   (c) (i) 0.579   (ii) 7.5   (iii) 0.000 92   (iv) 0.000 000 001 03   (v) 0.0069   (vi) 0.000 01
   (vii) 0.000 000 42   (viii) 0.000 000 06   (ix) 0.0753   (x) 0.000 003 51
3. (a) 1.9×10^{-3} (b) 3.4×10^{-1} (c) 4.4×10^{-5}
   (d) 6.0×10^{-1} (e) 8.4×10^{-4} (f) 2.6×10^{-2}

EXERCISE 4.12

1. (a) 3.30×10^6 (b) 1.40×10^{-4} (c) 9.57×10^{-1} (d) 3.97×10^{-2} (e) 1.00×10^7
   (f) 5.91×10^{-1} (g) 4.92×10^{-5} (h) 2.85×10^4 (i) 7.08×10^7 (j) 5.06×10^{-1}
2. (a) 6×10^3 (b) 2×10^4 (c) 8×10^{-1} (d) 3×10^{19} (e) 1×10^9
   (f) 7×10^{-1} (g) 3×10^6 (h) 5×10^2 (i) 3×10^9 (j) 2×10^{-5}
   (k) 1×10^8 (l) 3×10^4 (m) 2×10^{-2} (n) 3×10^5 (o) 1
   (p) 4×10^{-5}

EXERCISE 4.13

1. (a) 2.1   (b) -3.75 (c) -0.3 (d) 7.5
2. (a) -1.5 (b) -3.5 (c) -5.5 (d) 1.5
3. (a) 6.5   (b) 9.6   (c) -0.6 (d) 4.5   (e) 10.3   (f) -17.3
   (g) 8.4   (h) 13.4   (i) 1.69   (j) 30.72   (k) 11.93   (l) 9.791
   (m) 20.25   (n) 8.6   (o) 9.54   (p) -4.16
4. (a) 78.5 m²   (b) 7.1 mm²   5. (a) 19 cm³   (b) 0.2 cm³
6. (a) 340 cm²   (b) 4 mm²   7. (a) 2.1 m²   (b) 2.2 cm²   8. (a) 70 m   (b) 140 km

EXERCISE 4.15

2. 31 a
3. Alaska, Washington, Idaho, Montana, North Dakota, Minnesota, New York, Vermont, New Hampshire, Maine
4. (a) Neither   (b) Neither profit nor loss.
5. 29   6. 4 and 5   7. (a) $7.50   (b) $6.25
8. $43.18   9. 28 a
10. 1st pile: 27 pennies
     2nd pile: 25 pennies
     3rd pile: 18 pennies
     4th pile: 16 pennies
     5th pile: 14 pennies
11. $856.07   12. 12 and 14   13. 56   14. $140.00
15. (a) 39, 47   (b) 65, 82   (c) 10, 5   16. one   18. $9216.00   19. 84×27

4.16 REVIEW EXERCISE

1. $Q = \{\frac{a}{b} \mid a, b \in I, b \neq 0\}$

2. (a) $\frac{5}{-6}$ (b) $\frac{-1}{2}$ (c) -2 (d) $\frac{7}{8}$ (e) 0

  (f) -1 (g) $\frac{1}{-2}$ (h) $\frac{1}{3}$ (i) $\frac{-1}{7}$

3. (a) $\frac{3}{2}$ (b) $\frac{1}{5}$ (c) 2   (d) $\frac{3}{-5}$ (e) $\frac{-1}{6}$

  (f) $-\frac{10}{3}$ (g) $-\frac{2}{3}$ (h) $\frac{4}{11}$ (i) $\frac{13}{-11}$

4. (a) 1.36×10^4 (b) 3.562×10^6 (c) 5.6×10^{-1} (d) 3.75×10^1 (e) 8.56×10^{-4}
  (f) 2×10^{-5} (g) 1×10^{-2} (h) 2.1×10^{-7} (i) 7.5817×10^2

5. (a) $-\frac{1}{4}$ (b) $\frac{1}{6}$ (c) $\frac{5}{6}$ (d) $-\frac{16}{5}$ (e) $-\frac{4}{5}$ (f) $\frac{3}{2}$

  (g) $-\frac{5}{3}$ or $-1\frac{2}{3}$ (h) 2   (i) $\frac{3}{8}$ (j) $1\frac{7}{10}$ (k) -10 (l) -19

6. (a) $\frac{-7}{10}$ (b) $\frac{-3}{2}$ or $-1\frac{1}{2}$ (c) $-\frac{3}{2}$ or $-1\frac{1}{2}$ (d) $\frac{12}{5}$ or $2\frac{2}{5}$

  (e) 3   (f) $-\frac{9}{2}$ or $-4\frac{1}{2}$ (g) -4 (h) $\frac{2}{-9}$

7. (a) $\frac{-1}{12}$ (b) $\frac{-7}{8}$ (c) 1   (d) $\frac{-7}{20}$

  (e) $\frac{13}{12}$ or $1\frac{1}{12}$ (f) $\frac{-11}{12}$ (g) $\frac{43}{24}$ or $1\frac{19}{24}$ (h) 0

  (i) $\frac{1}{3}$ (j) $\frac{-7}{2}$ or $-3\frac{1}{2}$ (k) $\frac{1}{12}$ (l) $-\frac{25}{4}$ or $-6\frac{1}{4}$

8. (a) $\frac{-11}{6}$ or $-1\frac{5}{6}$ (b) 10   (c) $\frac{7}{10}$ (d) $\frac{1}{24}$ (e) $\frac{13}{10}$ or $1\frac{3}{10}$

  (f) $\frac{-7}{2}$ or $-4\frac{2}{31}$ (g) $\frac{3}{8}$ (h) $-\frac{1}{16}$ (i) -4 (j) $\frac{64}{81}$

9. (a) -3.84 (b) -7 (c) -12.6 (d) -5.76 (e) 3.56
  (f) 6.76   (g) -1.24 (h) $-5.1\overline{3}$ (i) 0.62

10. (a) $\frac{1}{x^2}$ (b) x (c) x^7 (d) y^9 (e) $\frac{1}{x^5}$ (f) $\frac{1}{y^7}$

  (g) x^8 (h) $\frac{1}{y^5}$ (i) x^{11} (j) x^2 (k) $\frac{1}{y^5}$ (l) x^6

11. (a) 1   (b) $\frac{1}{32}$ (c) $-\frac{1}{27}$ (d) $\frac{1}{9}$ (e) $\frac{1}{16}$ (f) 1

  (g) $\frac{3}{2}$ (h) 4   (i) $\frac{4}{3}$ (j) 12   (k) 4   (l) 5

12. (a) 41.3   (b) 7.38   (c) 173   (d) 0.392   (e) 2.06
  (f) 5 730 000   (g) 1.80   (h) 0.002 19   (i) 0.280

13. (a) 6.95×10^{21} kg   (b) 2.7×10^8 (c) 1×10^{-9} (d) 5×10^{-5} cm
  (e) 5.2×10^3 mL   (f) 2.8×10^{-8} cm   (g) 8×10^9 a   (h) 1.5×10^8 km
  (i) 1.67×10^{-24} g   (j) 1×10^{-6} (k) 4×10^4 km

14. 503 cm²

4.17 CHAPTER 4 TEST

1. $-\frac{40}{45}$, $-\frac{39}{45}$, $-\frac{36}{45}$ or $-\frac{8}{9}$, $-\frac{13}{15}$, $-\frac{4}{5}$

2. (a) $-\frac{7}{2}$ or $-3\frac{1}{2}$ (b) $\frac{7}{10}$ (c) $\frac{7}{3}$ or $2\frac{1}{3}$ (d) $\frac{1}{10}$

3. (a) (i) 0.051   (ii) $0.\overline{740}$ (iii) $-0.156\ 25$
  (b) (i) period 0, length 1   (ii) period 740, length 3   (iii) period 0, length 1

4. (a) $-\frac{11}{16}$ (b) $\frac{16}{33}$ (c) $\frac{11}{450}$ 5. 40

6. (a) 4.82×10^{14} (b) 7.9×10^{-8} 7. 40 cm²

4.18 CUMULATIVE REVIEW FOR CHAPTERS 1 TO 4

1. (a) 2 457 664   (b) 813   (c) 350 444   (d) 32 577
  (e) 1415.015   (f) 66.45   (g) 36.1   (h) 19.6
2. (a) 4700   (b) 45 000   (c) 750 000   (d) 0.7   (e) 1.8   (f) 3.12

3. (a) 47.75　　　　　　　(b) 0.8　　　　　　　(c) 20.9　　　　　　　(d) 4.28

4. (a) 32　　　(b) 101　　　(c) 70　　　(d) 396　　　(e) $20\frac{1}{3}$　　　(f) 60

5. (a) $51x + 6y$　　　(b) $3x^2 + 3xy$　　　(c) $15r^2 + 2s^2$　　　(d) $7t^2 - 5s^2$

6. (a) 146.6 m　　　(b) 16.77 cm^2　　　(c) 731.5 m^3

7. (a) 48　　　(b) 100　　　(c) 82　　　8. $25.01

9. 56, 57, 58, 59　　　10. 6　　　11. $242.22　　　12. 08 : 15

13. 11 min　　　14. 02:00 on January 4　　　15. 15th week

16. (a) -11　　　(b) -16　　　(c) 6　　　(d) $-x^2$　　　(e) $-12xy$　　　(f) 5 m^2

17. (a) -14　　　(b) 1　　　(c) 26　　　(d) a　　　(e) 12 a　　　(f) $-2t^2$

18. (a) 42　　　(b) -6　　　(c) -54　　　(d) -4　　　(e) -8　　　(f) 2

　　(g) 4　　　(h) 14　　　(i) 8　　　(j) -11　　　(k) 13　　　(l) 1

19. (a) $2x$　　　(b) $-y + 5$　　　(c) $18x^2 + 4xy$　　　(d) $27xy$　　　(e) 4 m^2

20. (a) $5x - 4$　　　(b) $9t + 2$　　　(c) $-2x + 18$　　　(d) $-4x - 19$　　　(e) $19x^2 - 9$

21. (a) 17　　　(b) 34　　　(c) 1　　　(d) 2　　　(e) 9　　　(f) 66

22. NEW
```
10 INPUT X
20 E = 2*X↑2 + 3*X - 4
30 PRINT X, E
40 END
RUN
```

23. (a) 9.7×10^4　　　(b) 3×10^6　　　(c) 1.2×10^{-1}

　　(d) 7.1×10^{-5}　　　(e) 4×10^{-3}　　　(f) 7.9×10^5

24. (a) $\frac{-2}{15}$　　　(b) $-\frac{1}{3}$　　　(c) 8　　　(d) $-\frac{3}{4}$

　　(e) $\frac{25}{12}$ or $2\frac{1}{12}$　　　(f) $-\frac{12}{5}$ or $-2\frac{2}{5}$　　　(g) $-\frac{3}{16}$　　　(h) $-\frac{14}{5}$ or $-2\frac{4}{5}$

25. (a) $-\frac{1}{4}$　　　(b) -1　　　(c) $-\frac{3}{20}$　　　(d) $\frac{25}{8}$ or $3\frac{1}{8}$　　　(e) $\frac{47}{6}$ or $7\frac{5}{6}$　　　(f) $-\frac{1}{6}$

26. (a) x^{13}　　　(b) x^6　　　(c) x^6　　　(d) x^7

27. (a) $\frac{1}{8}$　　　(b) 1　　　(c) 3　　　(d) 4　　　(e) 4　　　(f) $\frac{4}{3}$ or $1\frac{1}{3}$

28. (a) 5000　　　(b) 29　　　(c) 436 000　　　(d) 7.3

　　(e) 623 000 000　　　(f) 10 500　　　(g) 42 000 000　　　(h) 5350

　　(i) 1 960 000 000 000　　　(j) 6 018 000

29. (a) 12　　　(b) 36　　　(c) 36　　　(d) 17　　　(e) 1

30. $-4, 12$
　　$-3, 6$
　　$-2, 2$
　　$-1, 0$
　　$0, 0$
　　$1, 2$
　　$2, 6$
　　$3, 12$
　　$4, 20$

REVIEW AND PREVIEW TO CHAPTER 5

DECIMALS AND FRACTIONS

1. (a) 6.4　　　(b) 15.6　　　(c) 1.9　　　(d) 7　　　(e) 3　　　(f) 12.9
　　(g) 4.5　　　(h) 0.5　　　(i) 1.4　　　(j) 4.5　　　(k) 45.5　　　(l) 8.4
　　(m) 0.07　　　(n) 2.2　　　(o) 0.9　　　(p) 0.08　　　(q) 0.27　　　(r) 0.002

2. (a) 45.6　　　(b) 1874.4　　　(c) 62.736　　　(d) 1.3923
　　(e) 187.55　　　(f) 4555.32　　　(g) 24.071 43　　　(h) 1.764 52

3. (a) 3.1　　　(b) 0.42　　　(c) 0.19　　　(d) 0.032　　　(e) 0.03　　　(f) 0.018
　　(g) 0.06　　　(h) 0.07　　　(i) 0.038　　　(j) 0.03　　　(k) 0.25　　　(l) 0.4
　　(m) 0.0001　　　(n) 1.01　　　(o) 0.71　　　(p) 0.07

4. (a) 1.2　　　(b) 6.3　　　(c) 0.56　　　(d) 0.06　　　(e) 0.03　　　(f) 0.3
　　(g) 0.02　　　(h) 1.9　　　(i) 0.032　　　(j) 0.03　　　(k) 0.0001　　　(l) 0.001

5. (a) 18.5　　　(b) 12.7　　　(c) 0.0317　　　(d) 31.6　　　(e) 37.04　　　(f) 0.231
　　(g) 0.51　　　(h) 0.112　　　(i) 0.63　　　(j) 0.006 86　　　(k) 0.001 25　　　(l) 0.008

6. (a) 217.887 12　　　(b) 4.818 44　　　(c) 15.7696　　　(d) 6.175 216
　　(e) 360　　　(f) 3.9　　　(g) 1.2852　　　(h) 24.22

7. (a) 0.125　　　(b) 0.25　　　(c) 0.375　　　(d) 0.5　　　(e) 0.625　　　(f) 0.75

8. (a) $\frac{1}{4}$ (b) $\frac{2}{5}$ (c) $\frac{7}{20}$ (d) $\frac{3}{4}$ (e) $\frac{7}{8}$

    (f) $\frac{3}{5}$ (g) $\frac{3}{8}$ (h) $\frac{1}{5}$ (i) $\frac{2}{25}$

9. (a) 0.333   (b) 0.667   (c) 0.429   (d) 0.875   (e) 0.182   (f) 0.455

10. (a) $\frac{3}{11}$ (b) $\frac{8}{9}$ (c) $\frac{4}{11}$ (d) $\frac{5}{9}$ (e) $\frac{2}{9}$

     (f) $\frac{19}{45}$ (g) $\frac{12}{37}$ (h) $\frac{139}{330}$ (i) $\frac{34}{111}$

11. (a) $\frac{1}{2}, \frac{5}{9}, \frac{3}{5}, \frac{5}{8}, \frac{3}{4}$ (b) $\frac{1}{3}, \frac{5}{12}, \frac{8}{19}, \frac{4}{9}, \frac{5}{11}, \frac{7}{12}$ (c) $\frac{2}{5}, \frac{10}{17}, \frac{5}{7}, \frac{3}{4}, \frac{5}{6}$ (d) $\frac{3}{4}, \frac{10}{13}, \frac{5}{6}, \frac{6}{7}, \frac{11}{12}$

     (e) $\frac{20}{24}, \frac{18}{20}, \frac{12}{13}, \frac{15}{16}, \frac{17}{18}$

12. (a) $\frac{4}{5}$ (b) $\frac{2}{3}$ (c) $\frac{1}{2}$ (d) $\frac{7}{6}$ $(1\frac{1}{6})$ (e) $\frac{7}{10}$

     (f) $\frac{19}{15}$ or $1\frac{4}{15}$ (g) $\frac{31}{30}$ or $1\frac{1}{30}$ (h) $\frac{53}{30}$ or $1\frac{23}{30}$ (i) $\frac{163}{60}$ or $2\frac{43}{60}$

13. (a) $5\frac{11}{24}$ (b) $8\frac{1}{4}$ (c) $5\frac{5}{6}$ (d) $7\frac{7}{12}$

     (e) $3\frac{1}{4}$ (f) $4\frac{3}{8}$ (g) $3\frac{1}{4}$ (h) $8\frac{1}{4}$

14. (a) $3\frac{1}{2}$ (b) $3\frac{3}{4}$ (c) $5\frac{3}{4}$ (d) $4\frac{2}{3}$

     (e) $6\frac{3}{4}$ (f) $2\frac{3}{4}$ (g) $3\frac{5}{6}$ (h) $4\frac{11}{12}$

15. (a) $\frac{1}{6}$ (b) $\frac{15}{32}$ (c) $\frac{3}{20}$ (d) $\frac{1}{2}$

     (e) $\frac{2}{7}$ (f) $\frac{6}{25}$ (g) $\frac{3}{8}$ (h) $\frac{4}{15}$

16. (a) 216   (b) 128.75   (c) 454   (d) 1875   (e) 649   (f) 3900

17. (a) $\frac{4}{3}$ or $1\frac{1}{3}$ (b) $\frac{3}{4}$ (c) 2   (d) $\frac{1}{2}$

     (e) 3   (f) $\frac{1}{3}$ (g) $12\frac{1}{2}$ (h) 2

18. (a) $\frac{7}{8}$ (b) $4\frac{5}{8}$ (c) 11   (d) $10\frac{1}{2}$ (e) 3

19. (a) $\frac{1}{2}$ of 670   (b) $\frac{3}{4}$ of 200

EXERCISE 5.1

1. (a) 2 : 1   (b) 1 : 3   (c) 2 : 3   (d) 6 : 1   (e) 3 : 2   (f) 2 : 5
   (g) 5 : 2   (h) 3 : 1   (i) 3 : 5   (j) 9 : 10   (k) 2 : 11   (l) 1 : 3
2. (a) 2 : 10   (b) 6 : 4   (c) 14 : 2   (d) 3 : 4   (e) 4 : 9   (f) 2 : 5
   (g) 21 : 15   (h) 12 : 9   (i) 10 : 100
3. (a) 3 : 7   (b) 250 : 13   (c) 3 : 2   (d) 4 : 3
   (e) 3 : 10   (f) 12 : 5   (g) 1 : 20   (h) 9 : 4
4. (a) 96 m/s   (b) \$12.50/h   (c) 30 kg/\$ (d) 26 cm/m
   (e) $85\frac{1}{3}$ w.p.m.   (f) $383\frac{1}{9}$ km/h
5. (a) 5 : 32   (b) 3 : 5   (c) 15 : 16   (d) 1 : 2   (e) 19 : 5   (f) 2 : 15
6. 5 : 1

EXERCISE 5.2

1. (a) 4 : 3 : 5   (b) 4 : 4 : 4   (c) 10 : 3 : 3   (d) 8 : 6 : 3
2. (a) 15 : 5 : 12   (b) 3 : 2 : 12   (c) 5 : 12 : 15
3. (a) 36 : 28 : 60   (b) 9 : 7 : 15

EXERCISE 5.3

1. (a) not equivalent   (b) not equivalent   (c) not equivalent   (d) equivalent
   (e) equivalent   (f) equivalent   (g) not equivalent   (h) not equivalent
2. (a) 4 : 1   (b) 5 : 1   (c) 1 to 4   (d) 9 to 1   (e) $\frac{1}{2}$ (f) $\frac{5}{2}$

   (g) 19 : 36   (h) 16 : 3   (i) 3 : 2 : 5   (j) 8 : 15 : 24   (k) $\frac{4}{5}$ (l) $\frac{5}{8}$

3. (a) 6   (b) 16   (c) 7   (d) 22.4   (e) 2.5
 (f) 5   (g) 45   (h) 20   (i) 2.5   (j) 72
4. (a) $x = 2\frac{1}{3}$ (b) $x = 9.8$ (c) $x = 12, y = 16$ (d) $x = 12, y = 20$
 (e) $x = 10, y = 30$ (f) $x = 30, y = 22$ (g) $x = 6, y = 9$
5. 29.75 cm   6. 38 400 people   7. (a) 35 jobs   (b) 286 bids   (c) 52 bids
8. 5 : 5   9. 9 : 16   10. (a) 24 jackets   (b) $3680

EXERCISE 5.4

1. Elaine receives $900, Kasmir $600   2. 0.6 m   3. 63
4. $225 000, $168 750, $56 250   5. 72 small, 180 medium, 144 large   6. 195 tenders
7. (a) 50 : 24 : 25   (b) $75 758, $36 364 and $37 879
8. 148 kg copper (to the nearest kilogram)   9. $21.60
10. 25 laps   11. 11 km (to the nearest kilometre)
12. two sides of 33 cm, one side of 55 cm
13. plumber $2495.25, mechanic $1386.25, accountant $1663.50
14. 21 nickels, 56 dimes, 28 quarters

EXERCISE 5.5

1. (a) $3.99/L   (b) $1.53/L   (c) $7.92/kg
2. (a) 500 mL for $0.85   (b) same value   (c) 20 kg for $25.00

EXERCISE 5.6

1. 4 h   2. $1\frac{1}{2}$ d
3. 1 d 5 h 43 min (to the nearest minute) or $1\frac{5}{7}$ working days   4. 51 min (to the nearest minute) or $\frac{6}{7}$ h
5. 2 h 43 min 38 s (to the nearest second) or $2\frac{8}{11}$ h   6. 30 min

EXERCISE 5.7

1. $305.15   2. 82.5 km
3. (a) 13 t   (b) 4.5 h   4. (a) $233.80   (b) 41 h
5. (a) $76.78   (b) 39 m   6. (a) $64.02   (b) 151 shares
7. (a) 442.5 d   (b) 111 times   8. (a) 6000 km   (b) 7.25 h
9. (a) 12.5 h   (b) 3625 m²   10. (a) $1028.34   (b) 12
11. (a) 4 h 42 min 21 s (to nearest second) $4\frac{12}{17}$ h   (b) 51 cm
12. 3600 kJ   13. (a) 12 kJ   (b) 153 kJ   14. (a) 16.6 kJ   (b) 90.6 g
15. (a) 4 315 000 km (to the nearest thousand kilometres)   (b) 8 min 41.4 s (to the nearest tenth of a second)
16. (a) 342 billion litres   (b) 5.25 d

EXERCISE 5.8

2. (a) 15%   (b) 60%   (c) 9%   (d) 98%   (e) 150%
 (f) 62.5%   (g) 12.5%   (h) 6.25%   (i) 93.75%   (j) 40%
3. (a) 0.35   (b) 0.1   (c) 0.03   (d) 0.055
 (e) 0.01   (f) 1.25   (g) 0.0675   (h) 0.001
4. (a) 25%   (b) 75%   5. 0.77% (to two decimal places)
6. 3.6% (to the nearest tenth of a percent)   7. 23.0% (to the nearest tenth of a percent)

EXERCISE 5.9

1. (a) 2.5   (b) 6   (c) 30   (d) 9
   (e) 53   (f) 8   (g) 18   (h) 36
2. (a) 10%   (b) 20%   (c) 5%   (d) 100%
   (e) 20%   (f) $6\frac{2}{3}$%   (g) 25%   (h) $33\frac{1}{3}$%
3. (a) $25   (b) $13.65   (c) $9.14   (d) $1.50
   (e) $26.70   (f) $2125.00   (g) $2275.00   (h) $5312.50
4. (a) 48%   (b) 40%   5. 40 students
6. (a) Royals, $41\frac{2}{3}$%; Pirates $39\frac{1}{16}$%   (b) Royals
7. (a) 25%   (b) 125%   8. $2 880 000   9. 3.375 million dollars
10. 35% (to the nearest percent)

EXERCISE 5.10

1. (a) $1.75   (b) $6.30   (c) $1715   (d) $2.76
   (e) $5.60   (f) $1736   (g) $34.65   (h) $3.96
2. (a) $22.44   (b) $1.57   (c) $24.01
3. (a) $1199.70   (b) $26.94   (c) $0.89
4. (a) $240.75   (b) $85.55   (c) $7.22   5. $39.95
6. $17 500   7. (a) $188.68   (b) $186.92   (c) $185.19

EXERCISE 5.11

1. (a) (i) $2.24   (ii) $108.75   (iii) $19.42   (iv) $4.49
   (b) (i) $12.71   (ii) $616.25   (iii) $110.08   (iv) $25.46
2. (a) $4.90   (b) $3.92   (c) $6.37
3. 24%   4. 12.8% (to the nearest tenth of a percent)
5. (a) 16.4% (to the nearest tenth of a percent)   (b) 33.1% (to the nearest tenth of a percent)
   (c) 49.9% (to the nearest tenth of a percent)

EXERCISE 5.12

1. (a) 0.07   (b) 0.05   (c) 0.08   (d) 0.12   (e) 0.1
   (f) 0.22   (g) 0.005   (h) 0.14   (i) 0.06
2. (a) $\frac{1}{2}$ (b) $\frac{6}{73}$ (c) $\frac{1}{12}$ (d) $\frac{20}{73}$
   (e) $\frac{24}{365}$ (f) $1\frac{7}{73}$ (g) $\frac{3}{4}$ (h) $\frac{60}{73}$
3. (a) $1050   (b) $2400   (c) $420   (d) $5600   (e) $171.50   (f) $3000
4. (a) $4.44   (b) $80   (c) $61.64   (d) $177.53   (e) $23.01
5. $2571.43   6. $5625   7. $6900

EXERCISE 5.13

1. (a) $2450.09   (b) $6802.44   (c) $9231.74   (d) $6122.20
2. (a) $4720.56   (b) $4761.71   (c) $8806.20   (d) $12 078.82
3. $1295.03   4. $471.71   5. (ii)   6. $1524.25   7. $601.27

EXERCISE 5.14

1. 56.25%   2. 21%   3. (a) 30 cm by 30 cm   (b) 43.75%
4. 200%   5. (a) 20 cm by 30 cm   (b) 75%

EXERCISE 5.19

1. Starting from the top and moving clockwise: 31, 33, 37, 39, 32, 34, 35, 36, 38
2. 157, 159, 179, 359, 517, 519, 539, 719
3. (a) 8   (b) 0   (c) 24   (d) 6   4. 5039   5. 287.5 m
6. (a) 52 more Tuesdays   (b) Thursday
7. The radio station broadcasts on a frequency of 980 kHz
8. 6 ten-dollar bills, and 4 one-dollar bills or 2 twenty-dollar bills, 4 five-dollar bills, and 4 one-dollar bills
9. $6.87   10. 72 steps   11. 9
13. (a) 88 and 89   (b) Yes, at pages 79 and 80.
14. 3, 5; 11, 13; 17, 19; 29, 31; 41, 43; 59, 61; 71, 73
15. Wheels numbered 1, 2, 3, and 4 are turning clockwise.
17. (a) $53\frac{1}{3}$ L   (b) 262.5 km
18. Pour four half-full glasses into two empty glasses to make nine full glasses, three half-full glasses, and nine empty glasses. All are divisible by 3.
20. Draw one marble from the box labelled "Red and Black," depending on its colour, you will know how to adjust the other labels.

5.20 REVIEW EXERCISE

1. (a) 4 : 7   (b) 5 : 3   (c) 2 : 5   (d) 1 : 4
   (e) 9 : 1   (f) 9 : 5   (g) 4 : 1
2. (a) 6 m/s   (b) 40 kg/$ (c) 80 km/h   (d) 49 m/min
   (e) $50/h   (f) 0.79 L/$ (g) $1.26/L
3. (a) 15 : 5 : 3   (b) 75 : 25 : 15   (c) $1.15
4. (a) $2\frac{1}{2}$ (b) $2\frac{2}{15}$ (c) $3\frac{1}{2}$ (d) $3\frac{4}{5}$
5. $\ell = 36$ cm, h = 12 cm   6. (a) 252 people   (b) 36 people   7. 32 cm by 20 cm
8. (a) 1 : 1   (b) 3 : 5 : 5   (c) 75 bananas, 125 oranges
9. $60 810.81, $87 837.84, $101 351.35
10. (a) $2.63/L   (b) $0.025/g   (c) $0.011/g
11. (a) 1.5 kg for $9.95   (b) $13.85/h   12. 66 min 40 s
13. (a) $2.40   (b) $6.28   (c) $3.50   (d) $6.59
   (e) $319.93   (f) $8   (g) $24.38
14. (a) 156.25%   (b) 20%   (c) 125%   (d) 20%   (e) 62.5%   (f) 156.25%
15. (a) 350   (b) 433.3   (c) 128   (d) 361.1   (e) 44.8   (f) 131.8
16. 35.8% (to the nearest tenth of a percent)   17. 7.8%
18. (a) $0.69   (b) $17.19   19. 5.6%   20. $2 896 175
21. $57.17   22. $42.75   23. $19.42   24. $13.28   25. $66   26. $0.77
27. (a) 25 cm by 20 cm   (b) 56.25%

5.21 CHAPTER 5 TEST

1. 15 : 8   2. 16 : 4 : 7   3. (a) 4.8   (b) 20   4. 25 : 64
5. (a) 3 : 4 : 5   (b) $3000, $4000, $5000   6. 12.5 min
7. (a) $3.75   (b) 37.5%   (c) 500   8. $42.75   9. $22.75   10. $67.81

REVIEW AND PREVIEW TO CHAPTER 6

EXPONENT LAWS

1. (a) 3^9 (b) 5^{22} (c) 2^5 (d) 1
   (e) 3^8 (f) 1   (g) 4^6 (h) 3^2
2. (a) $\frac{1}{4}$ (b) $\frac{1}{4}$ (c) $\frac{1}{3^{10}}$ (d) $\frac{1}{64}$ (e) 1   (f) $\frac{1}{4}$
3. (a) 1   (b) 10^6 (c) $\frac{1}{10^6}$ (d) 1   (e) 10^4 (f) 10^2

4. (a) 2   (b) $\frac{27}{8}$ (c) $\frac{1}{64}$ (d) 1

   (e) $\frac{1}{32}$ (f) 72   (g) 17   (h) $\frac{1}{9}$

5. (a) x^{14} (b) y^7 (c) m^7 (d) x^4 (e) 1

   (f) t   (g) $\dfrac{1}{x^6}$ (h) $\dfrac{1}{y^{20}}$ (i) 1 $(m \neq 0)$ (j) n^{14}

6. $2^{-3} + 3^{-2}$ is larger.

POWERS OF TEN

1. (a) 23 000   (b) 0.78   (c) 570   (d) 12.3   (e) 560 000   (f) 7.3
   (g) 0.3   (h) 0.56   (i) 2000   (j) 43 900   (k) 6   (l) 2.5
2. (a) 0.34   (b) 0.000 67   (c) 19   (d) 0.0006
   (e) 4 000 000   (f) 36 000   (g) 0.0999   (h) 230 000
   (i) 0.8   (j) 9.9   (k) 0.0008   (l) 2.5

MENTAL MATH

1. (a) 111   (b) 335   (c) 20   (d) 808   (e) 112   (f) 1300
   (g) 30   (h) 1110   (i) 9   (j) 555   (k) 212   (l) 5005
2. (a) 425   (b) 800   (c) 321   (d) 129   (e) 668   (f) 767
   (g) 101   (h) 969   (i) 729   (j) 808   (k) 1100   (l) 43 200
3. (a) 797   (b) 256   (c) 130   (d) 369   (e) 876   (f) 9801
   (g) 40   (h) 8800   (i) 656   (j) 644   (k) $333\frac{2}{3}$ (l) 484
4. (a) -4 (b) 64   (c) 27   (d) 5   (e) 9   (f) 62
   (g) 134   (h) 645   (i) 43   (j) 1515   (k) 803   (l) 221
   (m) 90

EQUATIONS

1. (a) x = 3   (b) t = 8   (c) w = 3   (d) y = 7   (e) x = 3   (f) s = 13
2. (a) 6   (b) -2 (c) 2   (d) 4   (e) 4   (f) 13

NUMBER LINES

2. (a) $x < 4, x \in w$ (b) $x > 2, x \in w$ (c) $x \leq 3, x \in w$ (d) $x > -3, x \in I$
   (e) $x < 4, x \in I$ (f) $x \geq -3, x \in I$

EXERCISE 6.1

2. (a) 43   (b) 1806   (c) 1892   (d) 2025
3. (a) 1, 3, 5, 7, 9, 11, 13, 15, 17, 19, 21, 23, 25, 27
   (b) 91 and 105
4. 153 and 171
5. (a) $21 = 4^2 + 2^2 + 1^2$ (b) $36 = 6^2$
   (c) $126 = 11^2 + 2^2 + 1^2$ (d) $143 = 9^2 + 7^2 + 3^2 + 2^2$
   (e) $280 = 14^2 + 8^2 + 4^2 + 2^2$ (f) $351 = 18^2 + 5^2 + 1^2 + 1^2$
   (g) $5053 = 71^2 + 2^2 + 2^2 + 2^2$ (h) $1000 = 30^2 + 8^2 + 6^2$

EXERCISE 6.2

1. (a) 8   (b) 6   (c) 10   (d) 1   (e) 16   (f) 144
   (g) 0   (h) 121   (i) $\frac{4}{5}$ (j) $\frac{1}{2}$ (k) $\frac{4}{9}$ (l) $\frac{1}{9}$
2. (a) 3   (b) 17   (c) 14   (d) 50   (e) 81   (f) 9
   (g) 24   (h) 5   (i) 31   (j) 14   (k) 42   (l) $\frac{2}{3}$
   (m) $\frac{5}{6}$ (n) 5   (o) $\frac{2}{3}$
3. (a) 20   (b) 25   (c) 17   (d) 2   (e) 100   (f) 100
   (g) $\frac{1}{2}$ (h) 3   (i) $\frac{5}{4}$ (j) 4   (k) 5   (l) 20

4. (a) 4.5   (b) 22.4   (c) 2.1   (d) 5.6   (e) 2.7   (f) 1.9
   (g) 5.7   (h) 0.6   (i) 26.5   (j) 26.5   (k) 0.8   (l) 4.3
5. (a) 14.1 cm   (b) 22.4 m   (c) 27.7 cm
6. (a) 1.7   (b) 2.8   (c) 15.7   (d) 17.0   (e) −1.7   (f) 8.5
   (g) 1.4   (h) 8.4   (i) 18.0   (j) 16.5   (k) 2.2   (l) 1.7
   (m) 3.3

EXERCISE 6.3

1. (a) 12   (b) 16   (c) 18   (d) 25
2. (a) 21   (b) 23   (c) 26   (d) 29   (e) 31   (f) 32
1. (a) 3.9   (b) 8.2   (c) 13.8   (d) 15.8
2. (a) 18.4   (b) 21.9   (c) 25.3   (d) 28.3   (e) 37.4   (f) 42.4

EXERCISE 6.4

1. (a) 8.8 s (to nearest tenth of a second)
   (b) 1.8 s longer (to nearest tenth of a second)
2. 1.6 (to nearest tenth)
3. (a) 14.0 s   (b) 22.2 s
4. (a) 54 m²   (b) 336 cm²
5. (a) 6 400 000 m (to nearest million metres)
   (b) 3079 m/s ($\doteqdot$ 11 084 km/h)

EXERCISE 6.5

1. (a) $y^2 + z^2 = x^2$ (b) $x^2 + y^2 = w^2$
   (c) $5^2 + 8^2 = y^2$ (d) $x^2 + x^2 = y^2$ or $2x^2 = y^2$
   (e) $x^2 + 9^2 = 12^2$ (f) $s^2 + w^2 = t^2$
   (g) $q^2 + r^2 = p^2$ (h) $4^2 + 5^2 = x^2$
2. (a) $x = 10$ (b) $y = 20$ (c) $p = 5$ (d) $x = 7$
3. (a) $x = 10.6$ m   (b) $y = 14.3$ cm   (c) $t = 20.2$ m
   (d) $x = 22.0$ m   (e) $r = 21.2$ m   (f) $m = 24.1$ m

EXERCISE 6.6

1. 31.9 m   2. 27.5 m
3. 6.9 m (to nearest tenth of a metre)   4. 34.4 cm (to nearest tenth of a centimetre)
5. 24.3 m

EXERCISE 6.7

1. (i) (a) 1.5   (b) $\sqrt{2}$
   (ii) (a) 0.55   (b) 0.515 115 111 511 115 ...
   (iii) (a) 0.634   (b) 0.634 334 333 4 ...
   (iv) (a) 0.23   (b) 0.232 232 223 ...
2. (a) 1   (b) 3   (c) 4

EXERCISE 6.8

1. 30 d (approximately)   2. Taurus, Libra   3. (a) Sagittarius   (b) Gemini
4. In Scorpio

EXERCISE 6.9

1. (a) $\frac{1}{2}$ (b) $\frac{2}{3}$ (c) $\frac{3}{4}$ (d) $\frac{4}{5}$ (e) $\frac{98}{99}$
2. 25 and 36   3. 40 and 8   4. (a) 54 × 632   (b) 24 × 356
5. (a) approximately 275 m   (b) 135 balls   6. 7   7. 21
8. 48 cubes
9. Wheels numbered 1, 3, 4, and 5 are turning counter-clockwise.
10. (a) 31°C   (b) (i) 0°C   (ii) +7°C   (iii) +9°C   (iv) +29°C
     (c) −5°C   (d) 5°C   (e) (i) 16°C below average   (ii) 15°C above average
11. 1st pile: 27 dimes; 2nd pile: 25 dimes; 3rd pile: 18 dimes; 4th pile: 16 dimes; 5th pile: 14 dimes
13. 49°S, 108°E   14. 10 times   15. Approximately 73 beats per minute.
16. 1.6 km   17. 20, 35, 56   18. $8.02
19. 28 + 30 + 32 = 90; 44 + 46 = 90; 10 + 12 + 14 + 16 + 18 + 20 = 90;
     2 + 4 + 6 + 8 + 10 + 12 + 14 + 16 + 18 = 90

6.10 REVIEW EXERCISE

1. (a) 9   (b) 100   (c) 0   (d) 1   (e) 13   (f) 20
     (g) $\frac{3}{4}$ (h) $\frac{1}{4}$ (i) 625
2. (a) 5   (b) 27   (c) 35   (d) 8   (e) 9   (f) $\frac{12}{7}$
     (g) $\frac{1}{3}$ (h) 4   (i) $\frac{3}{2}$ (j) 4   (k) 11   (l) $\frac{4}{3}$
3. (a) 8.7   (b) 14.2   (c) 4.5   (d) 21.2   (e) 7.6   (f) 11.8
     (g) 28.8   (h) 83.1
4. (a) 6.3 cm   (b) 7.5 m   (c) 5.8 m   (d) 12.2 m
5. 3.7 cm   6. 11.2 cm   7. 13.7 m   8. 2.2 m   9. 24.4 km
10. (a) 324 m/s (nearest one)   (b) 340 m/s   (c) 352 m/s (nearest one)
11. 17 cm

6.11 CHAPTER 6 TEST

1. (a) 4   (b) 18   (c) 18   (d) 3
2. (a) 7.9   (b) 4.7   (c) 0.7   (d) 12.4
3. 43.2 km   4. (a) 12.8 m   (b) 19.0 cm   5. 13.6 m

REVIEW AND PREVIEW TO CHAPTER 7

SIMPLIFYING ALGEBRAIC EXPRESSIONS

1. (a) $-3x + 7$ (b) $9x^2 + 3x - 6$ (c) $4y + 1$ (d) $-9t - 6$
2. (a) $-8xy - 3x$ (b) $6x^2 - 4x + 14$ (c) $5xy - x - y$ (d) $15x^2 - 3x$
3. (a) $6x - 3xy + 7$ (b) $22y - 33$ (c) $-5y^2 - 11y$ (d) $-9y + 5$
4. (a) $-17y^2 - 4y - 7$ (b) $x^3 - 16x^2 + 22$
     (c) $16xy - 17yz - 7xz$ (d) $5y^2 - 6y + 1$
5. (a) $9xy - 2y^2$ (b) $-t - 2s + 9$ (c) $15x^2 - 9x$ (d) $6x - 13y + 1$
6. (a) $2x - 14$ (b) $8x^2 - 12x + 4$ (c) $4x^2 - 12x + 8$ (d) $42x - 14y + 21$
7. (a) $-12x + 18y - 3$ (b) $-24 + 16x - 32y$ (c) $8x - 8y - 48$ (d) $-x - 13y$
8. (a) $22x - 66y - 11$ (b) $3x^2 - 16x + 1$ (c) $5x - 4$ (d) $8x - 19$
9. (a) $15x + 24y$ (b) $-8s - 6t$ (c) $17xy + 14z + 6$ (d) $15x - 13y$
10. (a) $17x - 14z - 22$ (b) $16x - 20y + 12$ (c) $6s + 18t - 7$ (d) $16x - 28y - 2b$

AREA

1. 15.6 m²   2. 5346 cm²   3. 143 m²   4. 24 m²
5. 327.61 m²   6. 1849 mm²   7. 254.34 m²   8. 14.13 m²
9. 332.91 m²   10. 78.76 m²

VOLUME

1. 180 m³   2. 169.56 cm³   3. 120 m³   4. 252 m³

EXERCISE 7.1

1. (a) monomial   (b) binomial   (c) trinomial   (d) monomial
   (e) monomial   (f) trinomial   (g) monomial   (h) binomial
2. (a) 1   (b) 2   (c) 0   (d) 7
   (e) 4   (f) 6   (g) 3   (h) 11
3. (a) 6   (b) 3   (c) 1   (d) 5   (e) 4
   (f) 11   (g) 1   (h) 15   (i) 5   (j) 5
4. The binomial $2\pi r^2 + 2\pi rh$ represents the surface area of a cylinder of radius r and height h.
   The trinomial $2\ell w + 2\ell h + 2wh$ represents the surface area of a box with dimensions ℓ by w by h.
5. (a) $x^5 - x^3 + x^2 + 1$ (b) $5x^2 - 4x + 3$
   (c) $4x^2 - 3ax + 6a^2$ (d) $x^4 + p^4x^3 + 24px^2 - 11p^2x$
   (e) $-4x^6 + 4m^2x^3 - 5m^3x^2 - 3mx$
6. (a) $1 + x - x^2 - x^3 + x^5$ (b) $4 - x + x^3 + 2x^4$
   (c) $5 - 4xy^2 + 3x^2y + 3x^3$ (d) $-2xy - 5x^2y^4 + 3x^3y^4 + 7x^4$
   (e) $1.7 - 0.3x - 1.5x^2 + 0.4x^3$ (f) $y + x$
7. (a) 700 cm³   (b) 87.6 cm³   8. 4212 cm³

EXERCISE 7.2

1. (a) $5x + 1$ (b) $3x^2 - 12x + 5$ (c) $-4y - 3$ (d) $4x^2 + 3x$
2. (a) $4x + 7$ (b) $5x^2 + 5x - 8$ (c) $5x - 7y + 3$ (d) $3x^2 + 2x - 2$
3. (a) $x^3 + x + 9$ (b) $x^2 - 5x + 2$
   (c) $y^3 + 6y^2 - 3y + 2$ (d) $z^2 - 11z + 13$
   (e) $x^2 + 2xy + y^2$ (f) $3y^3 - 2y^2 + 15$
   (g) $m + n - y - z$ (h) $9x^3 - 2x^2 + 4x + 4$
4. (a) $4x^2 - 8x + 3$ (b) $3y^2 - 2y - 11$ (c) $3m^2 - 9m + 6$
   (d) $-6t + 12$ (e) $11s^2 + 8s + 12$ (f) $2d^2 - 10d + 3$
5. (a) $4x^2 + xy + 2y^2$ (b) $14t^2 - 4st$ (c) $15y^2 - 4y + t$
   (d) $10a^2b + 6ab^2 - 3a^2b^2$ (e) $-2x^2 - 2x + 6$ (f) $4s^2t - 4st + 6st^2$
6. (a) $4x^2 + 3x + 11$ (b) $5t^2 + 2t - 11$ (c) $3x^2 - 3xy$ (d) $3m^2 + 11n^2$
7. (a) $3x^2 + 12x + 10$ (b) $5x^2 + xy + 5y^2$ (c) $11t^2 + 6t + 9$
8. (a) $x^2 + \frac{2}{3}x + 1$ (b) $2t^2 + \frac{7}{3}t + 2$ (c) $\frac{3}{4}m^2 - m + \frac{1}{2}$
   (d) $0.8t^2 - 0.4t + 1.9$ (e) $2.8y^2 + 1.3y + 11.6$ (f) $4x^2 - 0.7x - 13$

EXERCISE 7.3

1. (a) $-x - y - 3$ (b) $3x + 4$ (c) $x - 1$ (d) $-2y$
   (e) $2x^2 - 5x - 2$ (f) $13x^3 - 3x^2 - 13y^3 + 3y^2$
   (g) $7y^2 - 2xy - 8x^2$
2. (a) $-x^2 - 12x + 7$ (b) $-15x^2 + 16$ (c) $5 - 7x + x^2$
   (d) $-4x^2 + 3x - 15$ (e) $-12x^2 + 16x - 18$ (f) $2x^2 + 25x - 10$
3. (a) $2t^2 - 3t + 8$ (b) $5y^2 + 5y - 9$ (c) $4x^2 - 2x - 3$
   (d) $3m^3 - m^2 - m + 2$ (e) $-x^2 + 3x - 5$ (f) $2t^3 + t^2 + 5$
4. (a) $3x^2 + 5x + 8$ (b) $5m^2 - m$ (c) $-8t^2 - 9t - 6$
   (d) $-x^2 + 4xy$ (e) $-4m^2 + mn - 3n^2$
5. (a) $-2x^2 - 2x + 12$ (b) $-4t^2 + 7t + 8$ (c) $6m^3 - 7m^2 + m + 5$
   (d) $-r^2 + 10r - 1$ (e) $2p^2 - 6pq + 3q^2$
6. (a) $4x^2 - 5x - 2$ (b) $t^2 - 2st + 2s^2$ (c) $13m^2 - 3m + 4$
   (d) $6x^2 + xy - 2y^2$ (e) $3a^2b + 3ab - 2ab^2$ (f) $4c^2 - 3cd + 8d^2$
7. $-9x - 4$ 8. (a) $3x - 16y$ (b) $2x^2 - 4x + 22$
9. (a) $-2x^2 + 7$ (b) $-0.7y^2 - 1.3y + 1.1$ (c) $\frac{1}{3}x^2 - \frac{1}{2}x - \frac{1}{4}$
   (d) $-0.2t^2 - 4.2t + 0.7$ (e) $\frac{5}{8}x^3 + \frac{5}{4}x^2 - \frac{15}{2}$

EXERCISE 7.4

1. (a) 2^6 (b) 3^5 (c) t^6 (d) $(-3)^4$
3. (a) x^9 (b) w^{10} (c) t^7 (d) s^{13} (e) m^{13} (f) t^{14}
   (g) 2^{10} (h) 3^{12} (i) x^4w^5 (j) 5^8 (k) r^{30} (l) x^8
   (m) 4^5 (n) x^6y^7 (o) 2^{15} (p) 3^22^3
4. (a) $2x^5$ (b) $-18w^6$ (c) $45m^{12}$ (d) $48x^{17}$ (e) $60x^6$ (f) $-42w^{12}$
   (g) $140t^5$ (h) $-64s^7$ (i) $162x^{11}$ (j) $-90t^6$
5. (a) $12x^3y^5$ (b) $35s^5t^5$ (c) $160x^8y$ (d) $-70w^7xy$
   (e) $130w^{10}x^7y$ (f) $57m^8n^5$ (g) $45w^{11}x^4y$ (h) $42s^8t^{12}$
   (i) $180x^6y^9$ (j) $7x^{11}y^{11}$ (k) $54m^{11}n^3$ (l) $84x^5y^4$
   (m) $168x^4y^4$ (n) $-210w^2x^6$ (o) $168r^3s^6$ (p) $-84a^6b^4$
6. (a) $12a^3b$ (b) $4a^6$ (c) $52m^4n^2$ (d) $40x^2y^3$
7. (a) $3x^6y^8$ (b) $\frac{1}{2}x^4y^5$ (c) $-\frac{3}{5}a^4b^{10}$ (d) $-3s^3t^4$
   (e) $8a^3b^3c$ (f) $-3p^3q^8$
8. (a) x^9 (b) m^{a+4} (c) y^{2x-1} (d) x^{3a-1}

EXERCISE 7.5

1. (a) x^6 (b) x^6 (c) y^{10} (d) z^9 (e) x^{15} (f) y^{20}
   (g) z^3 (h) x^{24} (i) 3^4 (j) 2^4 (k) 2^6 (l) 3^9
2. (a) x^4y^4 (b) p^6q^6 (c) a^7b^7 (d) $8x^3$
   (e) $9a^2b^2c^2$ (f) $625m^4n^4$ (g) $64r^3s^3t^3$ (h) $4x^2y^2$
3. (a) $x^{12}y^8$ (b) m^6n^{18} (c) $r^5s^{10}t^{15}$ (d) $a^4b^2c^8$
   (e) $m^{18}n^{12}p^{18}$ (f) $d^3e^3f^9$
4. (a) $8a^6b^6$ (b) $25x^6y^8$ (c) $7776m^5n^{10}$ (d) $81r^8s^{12}t^{16}$
   (e) $4x^6y^8$ (f) $-343a^9b^{12}c^3$ (g) $256m^{24}n^8p^{12}$ (h) $-125a^9b^6c^{18}$
   (i) $-r^{15}s^{20}t^{10}$ (j) $81d^4e^6f^2$ (k) $-x^3y^3z^9$ (l) $-32a^{20}b^{25}c^{30}$
5. (a) $500x^{10}y^9$ (b) $1728a^{12}b^9c^6$ (c) $16d^{16}e^{22}$
   (d) $36x^{14}y^6$ (e) $1024x^{11}y^7$ (f) $-32x^{32}y^{21}$
6. (a) $36x^{16}y^{14}$ (b) $162x^6y^8$ (c) $-80a^8b^{15}$
7. (a) $0.16x^6y^2$ (b) $\frac{1}{8}x^{12}y^9$ (c) $\frac{16}{81}m^{16}n^4$
   (d) $0.008r^9s^6t^3$ (e) $250x^{16}y^{17}$ (f) $-2x^{24}y^{19}$

EXERCISE 7.6

1. (a) $3x + 6$ (b) $-2t + 6$ (c) $-2x + 2y$ (d) $12b - 21$ (e) $x^2 - 2x$
   (f) $-3x^2 + 5x$ (g) $-6x^2 + 15x$ (h) $6x^3 - 4x^2$ (i) $x^2y + xy^2$ (j) $-x^2y + xy^2$
2. (a) $5x - 4$ (b) $2x - 6$ (c) $t - 5$ (d) $-s - 4$ (e) $17x - 16$
   (f) $8x - 2$ (g) $-y + 1$ (h) $3x - 2$ (i) $5x - 7$ (j) $-11x + 8$
3. (a) $10x - 25$ (b) $6t - 5$
   (c) $5y - 16$ (d) $3a^2 + 7a + 2ax + 2x$
   (e) $-3x^2 - 8x$ (f) $5x + y - z$
   (g) $8x^2 - 11x + 4$ (h) $n - 28$
   (i) $-8w - 15$ (j) $12x^2 + 2x$
4. (a) $7x^2 - 16xy - 5y^2$ (b) $3x^2 + 4x + 5xy - 5y - 2y^2$
   (c) $9x^2 - 6x + 5y - 5y^2$ (d) $-5xy^2$
   (e) $-3x^3y$ (f) $-xy$
   (g) $2x^3y + 5x^2y^2$ (h) $7x^2y^2 - 11xy^3$
5. (a) $4x - 6y$ (b) $-0.5x + 1.5y$ (c) $0.34x - 0.03y$
   (d) $4x - 3y$ (e) $0.2x^2 - 0.4xy + 0.3y^2$
6. (a) $-7y$ (b) $x^2 + 2xy$ (c) $3x^2 - 3xy + 2y^2$
   (d) $8x + 13y$ (e) $3x + 14y$
7. (a) $6x^3 - 21x^2$ (b) $15y^4 - 12.5y^3$ 8. $6x^3 + 15x^2$
9. (a) $4x - 36$ (b) $-19x^2 + 24x$ (c) $-2x^2 - 44x$ (d) $10x^2 - 3x$ (e) $7x^2 - x$

EXERCISE 7.7

1. (a) $2x^4$ (b) $3t$ (c) $-5m^4$ (d) $-4s^5$ (e) $2x^2$ (f) $7a^2b^3$
   (g) $-9xy^4$ (h) $-3m^2$ (i) $4de^4$ (j) $-8bc$

2. (a) $5xy^4$ (b) $-12a^2b^3$ (c) $-4m^2n^7$ (d) $5x^4y^9$ (e) $-a^2bc$ (f) $4xy$

3. (a) $\dfrac{2b}{a^2}$ (b) $\dfrac{3x}{y}$ (c) $\dfrac{-3}{m^3}$ (d) $\dfrac{-2x}{yz^2}$

(e) $\dfrac{4}{3}$ (f) $\dfrac{-3x^2}{2y^2}$ (g) $\dfrac{-5r}{6st^2}$ (h) $\dfrac{-2}{3m^4n^3}$

4. (a) $2x^2y^4$ (b) $4a^2b^2$ (c) $\dfrac{-4}{mn^5}$ (d) $3xy$ (e) $\dfrac{4}{3}xy$

(f) $\dfrac{-11a^5}{b^4}$ (g) $\dfrac{-m^{10}}{6n^7}$ (h) $\dfrac{s^2t}{4}$ (i) $\dfrac{3z^2}{4x^4}$ (j) $\dfrac{2z^2}{3xy}$

5. (a) $3x^2y^7$ (b) $6a^2b$ 6. (a) 8 (b) -16 (c) -12 (d) -28

7. $8x^3y^3 + 18x^2y^4$

EXERCISE 7.8

1. (a) $4x$ (b) $4y$ (c) xy (d) 2
   (e) $-6u$ (f) $2x$ (g) $-4x$ (h) $-2y$
2. (a) $x + y$ (b) $xy + x$ (c) $y^2 - 1$ (d) $x + 2$
   (e) $x + 2y$ (f) $2x - 1, y \neq 0$ (g) $1 - 2x, x \neq 0$ (h) $x - 2y, x, y \neq 0$
3. (a) $x - 2, x \neq 0$ (b) $2x^2 - 3x + 1, x \neq 0$
   (c) $-8yz - 2y + 4z, x \neq 0$ (d) $2x^2 + x - 3, x \neq 0$
   (e) $x^3 - 4x + 3, x \neq 0$ (f) $-3y + a$
4. (a) $2x - 3$ (b) $4x^2$ (c) $x^2 - 2x + 3$
5. (a) $4x^2y - 3xy$ (b) $-4m^2n + 2n^2 + 6mn$ (c) $3a^3b + 4a - 2b$

   (d) $6x^2y^2 + 2xy + 1$ (e) $z - 2xz + 3yz^3$ (f) $\dfrac{3a}{c} - \dfrac{2b}{c} + 4$

   (g) $-x^4 + x^3 - x^2 + x + 1$

6. (a) $1 + \dfrac{3}{x}$ (b) $-2m + 1 + \dfrac{3}{m}$ (c) $2n - \dfrac{4n^2}{m} - \dfrac{6n^3}{m^2}$

7. (a) $2a - b$ (b) $3x + 2$

EXERCISE 7.9

1. (a) $2 \times 2 \times x \times x \times x \times y$ (b) $-1 \times 2 \times 2 \times 2 \times 3 \times a \times a \times a \times a \times b \times b$
   (c) $2 \times 2 \times 3 \times 3 \times x \times x \times x \times y \times y \times y \times y \times z$ (d) $-1 \times 2 \times 3 \times 3 \times a \times a \times a \times a \times b \times b \times c$
   (e) $-1 \times 2 \times 2 \times 2 \times 2 \times 2 \times x \times x \times x \times x \times x \times y \times y \times z \times z$
   (f) $2 \times 2 \times 2 \times 2 \times a \times a \times b \times c$
2. (a) 3 (b) 4 (c) 10 (d) 8 (e) 30 (f) 7
3. (a) 2 (b) 4 (c) 6 (d) 12 (e) 2 (f) 4
4. (a) $4x$ (b) $2ab$ (c) $3x^2y$ (d) $7a^2b$ (e) $2a^2x$ (f) 2
5. (a) $6a$ (b) $2x$ (c) $5xy$ (d) $7ab$ (e) $4mn$ (f) $4rs$
   (g) 3
6. (a) ab (b) $2xy^2$ (c) m^2n^{n-1} (d) 4 (e) $-3ab$ (f) $4x^2z$
   (g) $-3p$ (h) $-3ab^2c^3$ (i) $-q$ (j) $-5y$ (k) $8x$ (l) $-7x$

EXERCISE 7.10

1. (a) $3x + 15$ (b) $2y - 14$ (c) $3x^2 - 3x$
   (d) $5x - 10x^2$ (e) $3x - 6x^2 + 3x^3$ (f) $-8y + 6y^2$
2. (a) 3 (b) 5 (c) $2z$ (d) $7x$ (e) $4y$
   (f) $3x$ (g) $3x$ (h) b (i) xy (j) $11t$
3. (a) $x^2 + 4$ (b) $y + 3$ (c) $x^2 - 5$ (d) $4x + y$ (e) $x + z$
   (f) $x + y$ (g) $x + 3$ (h) $3x - 1$ (i) $4x - 1$ (j) $2xy - 3$
4. (a) $6x^2 - 21x$ (b) $4x^3 - 4x^2y$ (c) $14x^2 - 6xy$
   (d) $5xy^2 + 5x^3y$ (e) $3x^2 - 3x^2y$ (f) $14s^2 - 21st$
   (g) $7x^2y^2 + 7x^2y$ (h) $2xy^2z + 4xy^2$ (i) $3x^2 + 3xy - 3x^2y$
   (j) $10y^3 - 15y^2 + 25y$
5. (a) $5(x - 2)$ (b) $2x(3x + 4)$ (c) $6y(x + 3)$
   (d) $7y(y + 3)$ (e) $5z^2(z + 2)$ (f) $3x^3(x - 2)$

(g) $4xy(2z - 3w)$ (h) $7yz(x^2 + 2z^2)$ (i) $y^2(35 - 18y)$
(k) $12xyc(2y + xc)$
6. (a) $x(3x + 2y + 1)$ (b) $x(6y + 5z + 3)$ (c) $2x(2y + z + 3a)$
   (e) $3xy(1 - 2x + 4y)$ (f) $3(4xy - 3x^2 + 2z^2)$ (h) $5xy(3x + 1 - 4y)$
   (i) $5xt(xt - 2t + 3x)$
7. (a) $(a + b)(x + y)$ (b) $(x - 2)(x + 3)$
   (c) $(5 - x)(2x - 3)$ (d) $(3x + 2y)(x + y)$
   (e) $(3x - 2)(2x + 1)$ (f) $(x - 2y)(3x + 9y)$ or $3(x - 2y)(x + 3y)$
8. (a) $(x + 3)(y + 6)$ (b) $(2x + 1)(y - 3)$ (c) $(x - 1)(y + 1)$ (d) $(x - 7)(y - 2)$
   (e) $(10x + 9)(y + 2)$ (f) $(x + 2)(y + 2)$ (g) $(x + 3)(y - 2)$ (h) $(x - 2)(y + 4)$

EXERCISE 7.11

1. (a) $x^2 + 7x + 10$ (b) $x^2 + 7x + 12$ (c) $x^2 + 3x + 2$
   (d) $x^2 - 5x + 6$ (e) $x^2 - 6x + 8$ (f) $x^2 - 8x + 15$
2. (a) $x^2 + 3x - 4$ (b) $t^2 + 2t - 15$ (c) $x^2 + 4x - 12$ (d) $x^2 - 2x - 15$
   (e) $p^2 - 3p - 4$ (f) $x^2 - x - 20$ (g) $q^2 - 4q - 21$ (h) $x^2 + 3x - 10$
   (i) $r^2 + r - 12$ (j) $t^2 - 18t + 77$
3. (a) $x^2 + 9x + 14$ (b) $x^2 + 5x - 14$ (c) $x^2 - 5x - 14$ (d) $x^2 - 3x - 18$
   (e) $x^2 - 25$ (f) $x^2 + 13x + 42$ (g) $x^2 - x - 12$ (h) $x^2 + x - 20$
   (i) $x^2 - x - 6$ (j) $x^2 + 18x + 80$
4. (a) $x^2 - 6x - 16$ (b) $x^2 - x - 20$ (c) $x^2 - 6x + 8$
   (d) $x^2 - 2x - 15$ (e) $x^2 + 4x - 21$ (f) $x^2 + 4x - 21$
5. (a) $6x^2 + 11x + 3$ (b) $15y^2 + 11y + 2$ (c) $6x^2 - 11x - 35$ (d) $6z^2 - 29z + 28$
   (e) $6y^2 - y - 40$ (f) $3x^2 + 31x - 22$ (g) $6x^2 + 11x - 35$ (h) $25z^2 - 4$
   (i) $6x^2 + 11x - 35$ (j) $6 - 11y - 35y^2$ (k) $8z^2 - 26z + 15$ (l) $6x^2 - 31x - 11$
   (m) $5x^2 + 22x - 15$ (n) $6x^2 - x - 40$
6. (a) $x^2 + 3x - 4$ (b) $2x^2 + 7x + 5$ (c) $15x^2 - 11x - 14$
7. (a) $30x^2 - 21x - 36$ (b) $36x^2 - 4$ (c) $-24 + 2x + 2x^2$ (d) $60 - 55x + 10x^2$
8. (a) $x^2 - 2x - 15$ (b) $6x^2 + 13x + 6$ (c) $-3x^2 + 3x + 60$
   (d) $27x^2 - 3$ (e) $10x^2 + 5x - 75$ (f) $4x^2 - 1$
9. (a) $28.26x^2 - 37.68x + 12.56$ (b) $10x^2 + 11x + 1$ (c) $50.24 - 12.56x$

EXERCISE 7.12

1. (a) 5, 6; 3, 4; 3, 5; 1, 12; 7, 11; $-2, -5$; $-3, -5$; $-5, -5$; $-3, -4$; $-1, -6$
   (b) $-4, 3$; $-3, 4$; $-8, 5$; $-3, 5$; 10, 15; 10, 25; $-1, 5$; $-7, 6$; $-12, 5$; $-6, 8$
2. (a) $(x + 3)(x + 5)$ (b) $(x + 5)(x - 3)$ (c) $(x - 3)(x - 2)$
   (d) $(x - 7)(x + 8)$ (e) $(x + 5)(x + 5)$ (f) $(x - 3)(x - 3)$
3. (a) $x + 5$ (b) $x + 2$ (c) $x + 4$ (d) $x + 1$ (e) $x + 9$ (f) $x - 5$
   (g) $x - 3$ (h) $x - 1$ (i) $x + 4$ (j) $x + 5$ (k) $x - 3$ (l) $x - 2$
4. (a) $(a + 3)(a + 4)$ (b) $(t + 1)(t + 4)$ (c) $(b - 2)(b - 3)$ (d) $(x - 1)(x - 3)$
   (e) $(x + 1)(x + 2)$ (f) $(x - 1)(x - 7)$ (g) $(x + 1)(x + 8)$ (h) $(a - 2)(a - 4)$
   (i) $(a - 1)(a - 9)$ (j) $(y - 2)(y - 10)$ (k) $(x - 1)(x - 5)$
5. (a) $(m - 1)(m + 3)$ (b) $(t - 3)(t + 1)$ (c) $(x - 2)(x + 1)$ (d) $(x - 1)(x + 2)$
   (f) $(a - 4)(a + 3)$ (g) $(x + 4)(x - 3)$ (h) $(x - 5)(x + 4)$ (i) $(x - 6)(x + 7)$
   (k) $(y - 3)(y + 5)$ (l) $(x - 8)(x + 11)$
6. (a) $(y - 5)(y + 6)$ (b) $(t - 7)(t + 1)$ (c) $(b + 2)(b + 3)$ (d) $(x - 1)(x + 6)$
   (e) $(x - 3)(x + 10)$ (f) $(x - 8)(x + 1)$ (h) $(y - 7)(y + 3)$ (i) $(a - 5)(a + 8)$
   (j) $(y - 11)(y - 11)$ (k) $(a + 10)(a + 15)$ (l) $(x - 12)(x + 7)$
7. (a) $3(y - 3)(y - 4)$ (b) $5(x - 1)(x - 6)$ (c) $5(x + 1)(x + 2)$ (d) $6(x - 3)(x + 5)$
   (e) $y(y - 3)(y + 4)$ (f) $5(x - 5)(x + 4)$ (g) $a(x - 3)(x - 25)$ (h) $5a(x + 3)(x + 5)$
   (i) $2x^2(x + 2)(x + 6)$ (j) $3x(x - 1)(x + 6)$ (k) $3(x + 4)(x + 6)$ (l) $3b(x + 2)(x + 2)$
8. (a) 4   (b) -5 (c) -10 (d) -9
9. (a) $(2x + 1)(2x + 3)$ (b) $(3y - 1)(3y - 4)$ (c) $(2x - 3)(2x - 4)$
   (d) $(a + b - 2)(a + b - 3)$

EXERCISE 7.13

1. (a) 6, 7; $-6, 7$; $-7, 6$; 3, 11; $-12, 10$ (b) $-8, -9$; $-6, 11$; $-11, 4$; $-4, 9$; 5, 12

2. (a) $(5x + 2)(3x + 4)$ (b) $(3x - 7)(2x + 3)$ (c) $(4x + 3)(2x - 5)$ (d) $(3x - 2)(x + 4)$
   (e) $(6x + 5)(2x + 3)$ (f) $(3a - 2b)(x + y)$ (g) $(5x + 2)(3x + 4)$ (h) $(2x - 5)(x - 3)$
3. (a) $(9x + 10)(x + 1)$ (b) $(5x + 3)(2x + 1)$ (c) $(2x - 3)(x - 4)$ (d) $(2x - 5)(3x - 2)$
   (e) $(5x + 2)(3x + 4)$ (f) $(2x - 5)(3x - 1)$ (g) $(4x + 3)(3x + 2)$ (h) $(5x - 4)(3x - 4)$
   (i) $(2x + 5)(3x + 2)$ (j) $(4x - 5)(4x + 1)$
4. (a) $(2x + 5)(3x - 2)$ (b) $(2x - 3)(4x + 1)$ (c) $(4x + 7)(2x - 3)$ (d) $(5x + 3)(4x - 3)$
   (e) $(5x - 2)(3x + 4)$ (f) $(3x - 2)(3x - 2)$ (g) $(6x - 5)(2x + 1)$ (h) $(2x - 5)(2x + 3)$
   (i) $(5x + 6)(4x - 3)$ (j) $(5x + 4)(4x - 1)$
5. (a) $(2x - 5)(x + 3)$ (b) $(7x + 2)(x + 7)$ (c) $(x - 5)(2x - 9)$ (d) $(2x + 5)(5x - 2)$
   (e) $(x - 4)(3x + 7)$ (h) $(2x + 5)(5x - 3)$ (i) $(2x + 1)(3x - 11)$ (j) $(2x + 3)(8x - 5)$
6. (a) $(2x - 1)(3x - 4)$ (b) $(3x + 4)(7x + 8)$ (c) $(2x + 5)(7x + 3)$ (d) $(4x - 3)(5x + 8)$
   (e) $(3x + 2)(5x - 9)$ (f) $(2x - 3)(5x + 2)$ (g) $(x - 4)(3x + 2)$ (h) $(2x - 3)(9x + 4)$
   (i) $(3x + 2)(12x - 5)$ (j) $(5x + 2)(5x + 3)$
7. (a) $(x + 9)(2x + 5)$ (b) $(2x + 5)(7x - 2)$ (c) $(3x - 5)(6x + 7)$ (d) $(2x - 9)(4x - 5)$
   (e) $(2x - 3)(7x + 3)$ (f) $(x - 8)(3x - 7)$ (g) $(x + 8)(3x + 5)$ (h) $(x - 12)(2x - 5)$
8. (a) $2(x + 3)(2x - 5)$ (b) $4(x + 3)(3x - 2)$ (c) $2(x - 5)(7x - 2)$
   (d) $3(2x - 1)(2x + 3)$ (e) $5(x - 2)(2x - 1)$ (f) $7(x + 1)(x + 2)$
   (g) $6(2x + 5)(3x - 2)$ (h) $8(x + 5)(5x - 2)$ (i) $3(x + 3)(2x - 5)$
   (j) $(3x - 2)(21x + 3)$ (l) $4(2x - 9)(3x + 5)$

EXERCISE 7.14

1. (a) $x^2 - 4$ (b) $y^2 - 1$ (c) $r^2 - 25$ (d) $s^2 - 36$ (e) $v^2 - 100$ (f) $w^2 - 144$
   (g) $25x^2 - 1$ (h) $9x^2 - 1$ (i) $1 - x^2$ (j) $t^2 - 36$ (k) $z^2 - 9$ (l) $1 - 16x^2$
   (m) $16 - t^2$ (n) $1 - 4x^2$ (o) $9 - x^2$ (p) $25 - m^2$
2. (a) $4x^2 - 9$ (b) $9x^2 - 49$ (c) $25y^2 - 36$ (d) $25x^2 - 9y^2$
   (e) $4t^2 - 49$ (f) $9r^2 - 4s^2$ (g) $121x^2 - 25y^2$ (h) $25p^2 - 144q^2$
   (i) $16s^2 - 169t^2$ (j) $49x^2 - 64v^2$ (k) $100x^2 - 225y^2$ (l) $81x^2 - 121y^2$
   (m) $x^2y^2 - 4$
3. (a) $x^4 - 1$ (b) $x^4 - 9$ (c) $2x^2 - 2$ (d) $5x^2 - 20$
   (e) $27 - 3y^2$ (f) $x^3 - xy^2$ (g) $x^4 - 81$ (h) $20s^3 - 125s$
   (i) $x^4 - 400$ (j) $75z - 12z^3$ (k) $x^4 - 16$ (l) $27x^4 - 3x^2$

EXERCISE 7.15

1. (a) $x - 4$ (b) $2x - 1$ (c) $x + 6$ (d) $3y - 2$
   (e) $x - 5$ (f) $5 - x$ (g) $x + y$ (h) $s - t$
2. (a) $(x + 9)(x - 9)$ (b) $(9 + y)(9 - y)$ (c) $(x + 10)(x - 10)$ (d) $(x + 11)(x - 11)$
   (e) $(y + 12)(y - 12)$ (f) $(x + 2y)(x - 2y)$ (g) $(10x + 1)(10x - 1)$ (h) $(1 + 11y)(1 - 11y)$
3. (a) $(3x + 5)(3x - 5)$ (b) $(2y + 7)(2y - 7)$ (c) $(5x + 6)(5x - 6)$
   (d) $(10x + 9)(10x - 9)$ (f) $(3x + 4)(3x - 4)$ (h) $(11x + 10)(11x - 10)$
4. (a) $(xy + 1)(xy - 1)$ (b) $(3 + xy)(3 - xy)$ (c) $(5 + 4xy)(5 - 4xy)$
   (d) $(6xy + 1)(6xy - 1)$ (f) $(10s + tx)(10s - tx)$ (g) $(4x + 5ty)(4x - 5ty)$
5. (a) $4(x + 4)(x - 4)$ (b) $3(x + 1)(x - 1)$ (c) $(x^2 + 4)(x + 2)(x - 2)$
   (d) $(x^2 + 9)(x + 3)(x - 3)$ (e) $(9x^2 + 5y^2)(9x^2 - 5y^2)$ (f) $x(x - 6)$
   (g) $4xy$ (h) $(x + y + z)(x + y - z)$ (i) $3(2x - 3)$
6. (a) $(60 + 40)(60 - 40); 2000$ (b) $(125 + 25)(125 - 25); 15\,000$
   (c) $(112 + 111)(112 - 111); 223$ (d) $(252 + 248)(252 - 248); 2000$
   (e) $(70 + 30)(70 - 30); 4000$ (f) $(55 + 45)(55 - 45); 1000$
   (g) $(93 + 7)(93 - 7); 8600$ (h) $(68 + 32)(68 - 32); 3600$

EXERCISE 7.16

1. (a) $x^2 + 2x + 1$ (b) $x^2 + 6x + 9$ (c) $x^2 + 10x + 25$
   (d) $y^2 - 4y + 4$ (e) $y^2 - 8y + 16$ (f) $y^2 - 10y + 25$
   (g) $x^2 + 2xy + y^2$ (h) $x^2 - 2xy + y^2$ (i) $1 + 4y + 4y^2$
   (j) $25 - 10s + s^2$ (k) $9 + 6t + t^2$ (l) $49 + 14z + z^2$
   (m) $a^2 + 2ax + x^2$ (n) $x^2 - 18x + 81$ (o) $r^2 + 10r + 25$
   (p) $9 - 6y + y^2$ (q) $4x^2 - 4x + 1$ (r) $9z^2 + 6z + 1$
   (s) $1 - 6x + 9x^2$ (t) $1 + 10y + 25y^2$ (u) $v^2 - 12v + 36$

2. (a) $4x^2 + 12x + 9$ (b) $25x^2 - 20x + 4$ (c) $50x^2 + 60x + 18$
   (d) $4y^2 - 20y + 25$ (e) $16 - 8y + y^2$ (f) $12 - 60y + 75y^2$
   (g) $9z^2 + 42z + 49$ (h) $4z^2 - 20z + 25$ (i) $100 - 40z + 16z^2$
   (j) $9t^2 + 48t + 64$ (k) $49 + 56s + 16s^2$ (l) $-8r^2 + 72r - 162$
3. (a) $x^2y^2 + 2xy + 1$ (b) $s^2t^2 - 6st + 9$ (c) $5p^2q^2 + 20pq + 20$
   (d) $9x^2y^2 + 6xy + 1$ (e) $y^2z^2 + 14yz + 49$ (f) $75y^2 - 30xyz + 3x^2z^2$
   (g) $4x^2y^2 - 12xy + 9$ (h) $25x^2z^2 + 80xz + 64$ (i) $36x^2y^2 + 96xy + 64$
   (j) $25x^2 + 70xyz + 49y^2z^2$ (k) $4x^2y^2 - 36xy + 81$ (l) $-25r^2s^2 - 20rst - 4t^2$
4. (a) $(x + 9)^2$ (b) $(x - 7)^2$ (c) $(3t + 2)^2$
   (d) $(5m - 7)^2$ (e) $(10t - 1)^2$ (f) $(8m + 7)^2$

EXERCISE 7.17

1. (a) $2x^2 + x - 3$ (b) $x^2 + 5x - 14$ (c) $6x^2 + x - 35$ (d) $12x^2 + 29x + 15$
2. (a) $x^3 - 7x^2 + 12x - 4$ (b) $3x^3 + 5x^2 - 27x + 4$
   (c) $6x^3 - 7x^2 - 11x + 10$ (d) $2x^3 - 5x^2 - 19x + 15$
   (e) $x^4 - 4x^3 - 4x^2 + 13x - 6$ (f) $x^4 + 2x^3 + 17x - 10$
   (g) $6x^4 - 19x^3 + 4x^2 + 19x - 10$ (h) $6x^4 - 16x^3 - 13x^2 + 40x - 5$
3. (a) $x^3 + 4x^2 + 4x + 1$ (b) $2x^3 - 9x^2 + 13x - 6$
   (c) $3x^3 + 7x^2 + x + 21$ (d) $2y^3 + y^2 - 12y + 9$
   (e) $3y^3 - 14y^2 + 18y - 9$ (f) $6x^3 + 9x^2 + 10x + 15$
4. (a) $6s^3 - 19s^2 + 19s - 6$ (b) $10t^3 - 21t^2 + 5t + 6$
   (c) $5x^3 + 17x^2 - 12x$ (d) $8 - 18t + 11t^2 - 3t^3$
   (e) $2v^3 - 13v^2 + 31v - 35$ (f) $6r^3 - r^2 - r + 21$
   (g) $6x^3 + 3x^2 - 2x - 1$
5. (a) $6x^3 + 5x^2 - 17x + 20$ (b) $2 - 7x + 8x^2 - 3x^3$
6. (a) $5x - y$ (b) $5y - 16$ (c) $3x^2 - 5x$ (d) $3x^2 + x + 12$
   (e) $2x^2 + 11x + 6$ (f) $2y^2 + 5y - 1$
7. (a) $2x^2 + 10x + 44$ (b) $-x^2 + 32x - 12$ (c) $-y^2 - 3y + 8$ (d) $2x^2 + 13x + 51$
8. (a) $-x^2 + 28x + 23$ (b) $-8x^2 + 18x - 23$ (c) $-30x + 55$ (d) $8x^2 - 25x - 73$
9. (a) $3x^2 - 20x + 46$ (b) $x^2 - 10x + 19$ (c) $x^2 - 3$ (d) $-7x + 13$
   (e) $18x^2 - 76x + 13$ (f) $144x + 72$
10. (a) $x^3 + 3x^2 + 3x + 1$ (b) $x^3 + 6x^2 + 12x + 8$ (c) $x^3 + 9x^2 + 27x + 27$
    (d) $3x^3 - 6x^2 - 39x + 18$ (e) $-4x^3 + 4x^2 + 20x - 24$
11. (a) $5x^2 - 5y^2$ (b) $3x^2 + 50x - 5$ (c) $5x^2 - 36x + 7$
    (d) $5x^2 - 26x + 179$ (e) $-3x^2 + 2xy + 8y^2$ (f) $5x^2 + 8xy + 14y^2$
    (g) $-21x^2 + 21$ (h) $x^2 - 38x + 41$ (i) $-6x - 27$
    (j) $-6x^2 - 48x + 25$
12. (a) $x^3 - 9x^2 + 24x - 9$ (b) $2y^3 + 13y^2 + 25y - 10$

EXERCISE 7.18

1. approximately 11.6 d   2. 961   3. 28%   4. 38, 39, and 40
5. $x^2 - y^2$
6. Caroline's transportation budget will be exhausted after the 24th week. She will need $266.67 to complete the year.
8. 8   9. 83   10. (a) 10   (b) 6   11. 602 070   12. $30.89
13. 506.5 m^3 15. (a) 380 games   (b) $n(n - 1)$ games
16. Sam walked 16 km, Cory walked 27 km.
17. 120 posts   18. 15   19. $1.76   20. 16 m and 24 m
21. 61 m^2 22. 40 squares   23. 1 and 4

7.19 REVIEW EXERCISE

1. (a) 5   (b) 3   (c) 7
2. (a) $6x^2 + x - 12$ (b) $8y^2 - y - 15$ (c) $2m^2 - 4m - 7$ (d) $-4t^2 - t + 14$
3. (a) $x^2 + 8x + 16$ (b) $-4t^2 - 12t - 15$ (c) $3m^2 - 7m - 5$ (d) $10y^2 - y - 6$
4. (a) $20x^5y^5$ (b) $-6m^5nt$ (c) $99r^5s^3t^4$ (d) $48x^7y$
5. (a) $35x^4y$ (b) $25x^4y^2$

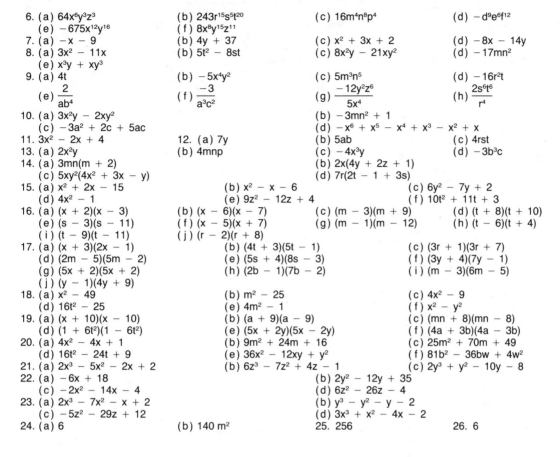

6. (a) $64x^6y^3z^3$ (b) $243r^{15}s^5t^{20}$ (c) $16m^4n^8p^4$ (d) $-d^9e^6f^{12}$
   (e) $-675x^{12}y^{16}$ (f) $8x^8y^{15}z^{11}$
7. (a) $-x - 9$ (b) $4y + 37$ (c) $x^2 + 3x + 2$ (d) $-8x - 14y$
8. (a) $3x^2 - 11x$ (b) $5t^2 - 8st$ (c) $8x^2y - 21xy^2$ (d) $-17mn^2$
   (e) $x^3y + xy^3$
9. (a) $4t$ (b) $-5x^4y^2$ (c) $5m^3n^5$ (d) $-16r^2t$
   (e) $\dfrac{2}{ab^4}$ (f) $\dfrac{-3}{a^3c^2}$ (g) $\dfrac{-12y^2z^6}{5x^4}$ (h) $\dfrac{2s^6t^6}{r^4}$
10. (a) $3x^2y - 2xy^2$ (b) $-3mn^2 + 1$
    (c) $-3a^2 + 2c + 5ac$ (d) $-x^6 + x^5 - x^4 + x^3 - x^2 + x$
11. $3x^2 - 2x + 4$ 12. (a) $7y$ (b) $5ab$ (c) $4rst$
13. (a) $2x^2y$ (b) $4mnp$ (c) $-4x^3y$ (d) $-3b^3c$
14. (a) $3mn(m + 2)$ (b) $2x(4y + 2z + 1)$
    (c) $5xy^2(4x^2 + 3x - y)$ (d) $7r(2t - 1 + 3s)$
15. (a) $x^2 + 2x - 15$ (b) $x^2 - x - 6$ (c) $6y^2 - 7y + 2$
    (d) $4x^2 - 1$ (e) $9z^2 - 12z + 4$ (f) $10t^2 + 11t + 3$
16. (a) $(x + 2)(x - 3)$ (b) $(x - 6)(x - 7)$ (c) $(m - 3)(m + 9)$ (d) $(t + 8)(t + 10)$
    (e) $(s - 3)(s - 11)$ (f) $(x - 5)(x + 7)$ (g) $(m - 1)(m - 12)$ (h) $(t - 6)(t + 4)$
    (i) $(t - 9)(t - 11)$ (j) $(r - 2)(r + 8)$
17. (a) $(x + 3)(2x - 1)$ (b) $(4t + 3)(5t - 1)$ (c) $(3r + 1)(3r + 7)$
    (d) $(2m - 5)(5m - 2)$ (e) $(5s + 4)(8s - 3)$ (f) $(3y + 4)(7y - 1)$
    (g) $(5x + 2)(5x + 2)$ (h) $(2b - 1)(7b - 2)$ (i) $(m - 3)(6m - 5)$
    (j) $(y - 1)(4y + 9)$
18. (a) $x^2 - 49$ (b) $m^2 - 25$ (c) $4x^2 - 9$
    (d) $16t^2 - 25$ (e) $4m^2 - 1$ (f) $x^2 - y^2$
19. (a) $(x + 10)(x - 10)$ (b) $(a + 9)(a - 9)$ (c) $(mn + 8)(mn - 8)$
    (d) $(1 + 6t^2)(1 - 6t^2)$ (e) $(5x + 2y)(5x - 2y)$ (f) $(4a + 3b)(4a - 3b)$
20. (a) $4x^2 - 4x + 1$ (b) $9m^2 + 24m + 16$ (c) $25m^2 + 70m + 49$
    (d) $16t^2 - 24t + 9$ (e) $36x^2 - 12xy + y^2$ (f) $81b^2 - 36bw + 4w^2$
21. (a) $2x^3 - 5x^2 - 2x + 2$ (b) $6z^3 - 7z^2 + 4z - 1$ (c) $2y^3 + y^2 - 10y - 8$
22. (a) $-6x + 18$ (b) $2y^2 - 12y + 35$
    (c) $-2x^2 - 14x - 4$ (d) $6z^2 - 26z - 4$
23. (a) $2x^3 - 7x^2 - x + 2$ (b) $y^3 - y^2 - y - 2$
    (c) $-5z^2 - 29z + 12$ (d) $3x^3 + x^2 - 4x - 2$
24. (a) 6 (b) 140 m^2 25. 256 26. 6

7.20 CHAPTER 7 TEST

1. (a) $9x^2 - 2x - 11$ (b) $7t^2 - t + 4$ (c) $-20x^3y^9$ (d) $6x^2$
2. (a) -11 (b) $x^2y + 4xy^2$ 3. $2x^2y - 3xy^2 + 2xy$
4. (a) $2y(x - 3z + 4)$ (b) $5mn^2(4m^2 - mn + 2)$
5. (a) $6x^2 + 13x - 5$ (b) $25t^2 - 10t + 1$
6. (a) $(x - 4)(x + 5)$ (b) $(3x + 4)(3x - 4)$ (c) $(t + 5)(2t - 1)$ (d) $(2m - 3)(3m - 7)$
7. (a) $2x^3 + x^2 - 7x - 2$ (b) $-16x^2 - 39x + 13$

REVIEW AND PREVIEW TO CHAPTER 8

ALGEBRA, EQUATIONS, AND INEQUALITIES

1. (a) $45x$ (b) $60x$ (c) $43y$
   (d) $42xy$ (e) $-19x^2$ (f) $39t$
   (g) $25x + 97y$ (h) $86x^2 - 34x$ (i) $8x^2 + 32x + 3$
   (j) $101 - 53s + 48t$ (k) $107 - 59x + 81y$ (l) $58 - 107z + 62x^2$
   (m) $43xy - 74x^2$ (n) $41x^3 - 53x^2 - 9x + 114$ (o) $-2xy + 101x - 49y$
   (p) $158x - 112y + 2$ (q) $238x + 381y$ (r) $-52.8x - 24.1y$
   (s) $-32.3x^2 + 47.3y$
2. (a) $130.3t - 95.2s$ (b) $-376.3 - 91.3t$ (c) $-12x^3 + 46.6x$
   (d) $9.48x + 0.87y$ (e) $-41.6 + 136x$ (f) $-2.45x$
   (g) $-42.3x^2 + 115.9x$ (h) $6.37x^3 + 6.84x^2 + 1.16x$ (i) $6.43y^2 - 2.19y$
   (j) $1.07x^2 + 6.39x$ (k) $2x$

3. (a) 5x + 20
   (d) −72t + 63s − 459
   (g) −52y + 403x + 143
   (j) 3.2x³ − 2.8x² + 5.2x
   (b) 39x − 91
   (e) −52x² + 204x + 44
   (h) 260x² − 572x + 832
   (k) −55.2x − 119.6y + 46
   (c) −3x² + 9x + 14
   (f) 57x³ − 76x² − 152x + 114
   (i) −170 + 238x² − 1122x
   (l) 7.42t − 7.28s + 13.3
4. (a) 4   (b) 7   (c) 2   (d) −32   (e) 1
   (f) 11   (g) 25   (h) −86   (i) −27   (j) 27
5. (a) 9   (b) −45   (c) −19   (d) 17   (e) 12
   (f) 181   (g) 58   (h) 7   (i) −106   (j) −8
6. (a) 640   (b) 30   (c) 2160   (d) 4050
   (e) 529.20   (f) 11.25   (g) 80   (h) 112.50
7. (a) x = 7   (b) x = 8   (c) x = 12   (d) x = 22   (e) x = 10   (f) x = 8
   (g) x = 7   (h) x = −4   (i) x = −8   (j) x = −7   (k) x = −2   (l) x = 3
   (m) x = 5   (n) x = −5   (o) x = 7   (p) x = 16
8. (a) x = 21   (b) x = 7   (c) x = 5   (d) x = 3   (e) x = 10   (f) x = 25
   (g) x = 3   (h) x = 7   (i) x = 4.8   (j) x = 14   (k) x = 9   (l) x = −3
   (m) x = −6   (n) x = −15   (o) x = 7   (p) x = −3

FLOW CHARTS

1. (a) −5,   24
       −4,   15
       −3,   8
       −2,   3
       −1,   0
        0, −1
        1,   0
        2,   3
        3,   8
        4,   15

   (b) 5, 8
       6, 11
       7, 14
       8, 17
       9, 20

EXERCISE 8.1

1. (a) S = {2}   (b) S = ϕ   (c) S = {2}   (d) S = ϕ
   (e) S = {2,3,4}   (f) S = {1,2,4}   (g) S = {3,4}   (h) S = {1,2,3,4}
   (i) S = {2,3,4}   (j) S = {1,2}
2. (a) consistent   (b) inconsistent   (c) consistent
   (d) inconsistent   (e) consistent   (f) inconsistent
3. (a) S = {2}   (b) S = {3}   (c) S = {3,4}
   (d) S = {1,2,3}   (e) S = {1,3,4}   (f) S = {4}
4. (a) S = {5}   (b) S = {3}   (c) S = {4}
   (d) S = {6}   (e) S = {2,3,4,5,6,7,8}   (f) S = ϕ
   (g) S = {2}   (h) S = {1,2,4,5,6,7,8}   (i) S = {2}
   (j) S = ϕ   (k) S = {3}   (l) S = ϕ
   (m) S = {3}   (n) S = {8}   (o) S = ϕ
   (p) S = {6,7,8}
5. (a) S = {2}   (b) S = {4}   (c) S = {...,−2,−1,0,1,3,4,5,...}

   (d) S = {6,7,8,...}   (e) S = {11}   (f) S = {...,−2,−1,0,1,2,4,5,6,...}

   (g) S = {5}   (h) S = {4,5,6,...}

EXERCISE 8.2

1. (a) 4(x + 7)   (b) 5x − 3   (c) $\frac{x}{3}$ + 6   (d) 5(x − 3)   (e) (x + 4)²   (f) $\frac{x - 12}{4}$
2. (a) subtract 3, divide by 5   (b) divide by 3, add 2
   (c) add 3, divide by 5   (d) divide by 4, subtract 3
   (e) subtract 5, divide by −2   (f) subtract 1, multiply by −2
3. (a) 60   (b) 31   (c) 5   (d) 4.8   (e) −320   (f) 16.39
4. (a) x = 6   (b) x = 13   (c) x = −5   (d) x = 8   (e) x = −8   (f) x = 16
   (g) x = 4   (h) x = 1.2   (i) x = 1.5
5. (a) x = 2   (b) x = 39   (c) x = 0   (d) x = 50   (e) x = 6   (f) x = −2

EXERCISE 8.3

1. (a) $x = 2$ (b) $x = 6$ (c) $x = 15$ (d) $y = 20$ (e) $t = 2$ (f) $x = 7$
   (g) $y = 13$ (h) $z = -10$ (i) $x = 16$ (j) $x = 20$ (k) $x = 1$ (l) $y = -10$
   (m) $x = -7$ (n) $t = -5$ (o) $x = -4$ (p) $t = 5$ (q) $x = -73$ (r) $t = -30$
   (s) $x = 2$ (t) $m = -9$
2. (a) $x = 12$ (b) $x = 60$ (c) $x = -47$ (d) $x = 15$ (e) $x = -23$ (f) $t = 52$
   (g) $y = -29$ (h) $x = -15$ (i) $t = -42$ (j) $x = 5$ (k) $x = -88$ (l) $s = 81$
3. (a) $x = 7$ (b) $t = -45$ (c) $t = -23$ (d) $x = -40$ (e) $t = 18$ (f) $y = -44$
   (g) $y = 53$ (h) $z = 66$ (i) $x = 52$ (j) $x = -55$
4. (a) $x = 22$ (b) $x = -1$ (c) $x = -32$ (d) $x = 19$ (e) $x = 26$ (f) $x = 7$
   (g) $x = 34$ (h) $x = -23$ (i) $x = -46$ (j) $x = 167$ (k) $y = 92$ (l) $t = -11$
5. (a) $x = 3.1$ (b) $x = 2.51$ (c) $t = 20.7$ (d) $y = -1.89$ (e) $x = -1.53$ (f) $s = -3.45$
   (g) $x = 14.7$ (h) $x = -2.9$ (i) $x = -41.8$ (j) $x = -5.37$ (k) $y = -19.3$ (l) $x = 4.028$

EXERCISE 8.4

1. (a) $x = 5$ (b) $x = 5$ (c) $x = 7$ (d) $x = 6$ (e) $y = -7$ (f) $t = 3$
   (g) $s = -8$ (h) $z = -5$ (i) $x = 2$ (j) $y = 8$ (k) $x = 0$ (l) $t = 1$
   (m) $x = 12$ (n) $y = -9$ (o) $x = 4$ (p) $t = 3$ (q) $s = -9$ (r) $y = 4$
   (s) $x = 3$ (t) $x = -2$
2. (a) $x = 9$ (b) $x = 36$ (c) $x = 22$ (d) $t = 48$ (e) $t = -37$ (f) $x = 67$
   (g) $t = -11$ (h) $x = 245$ (i) $t = -33$ (j) $x = -104$ (k) $y = -21$ (l) $x = 86$
3. (a) $x = 28$ (b) $x = 21$ (c) $x = 36$ (d) $x = 13$ (e) $x = \frac{1}{2}$ (f) $y = \frac{1}{3}$

   (g) $t = -5$ (h) $x = -13$ (i) $y = \frac{1}{5}$ (j) $x = 2$ (k) $x = -3$ (l) $s = -4$
4. (a) $x = 2$ (b) $x = -1$ (c) $y = 9$ (d) $t = -38$ (e) $x = -3$ (f) $x = -2$

   (g) $x = 2$ (h) $x = 0$ (i) $x = 3$ (j) $x = -\frac{1}{2}$ (k) $x = -15$ (l) $x = \frac{1}{3}$
5. (a) $x = 2.6$ (b) $x = 1.47$ (c) $x = 0.9$ (d) $x = -2$ (e) $x = 0.3$ (f) $x = -1$
   (g) $x = 8$ (h) $x = 9$ (i) $x = 0.6$

EXERCISE 8.5

1. (a) $x = 14$ (b) $x = 15$ (c) $t = 42$ (d) $x = 16$ (e) $y = 33$ (f) $x = -20$
   (g) $x = -14$ (h) $s = 0$
2. (a) No (b) Yes (c) Yes (d) Yes (e) No (f) No
3. (a) $x = 30$ (b) $x = -20$ (c) $x = -42$ (d) $s = -42$ (e) $x = -12$ (f) $x = -35$
   (g) $x = 24$ (h) $x = -30$ (i) $x = -1$
4. (a) $x = 27$ (b) $x = 13$ (c) $x = 2$ (d) $x = 8$ (e) $x = 2$ (f) $x = -27$
5. (a) $x = -\frac{7}{3}$ (b) $x = 4$ (c) $x = 26$ (d) $x = -\frac{14}{11}$ (e) $x = -\frac{25}{2}$ (f) $x = 2$

EXERCISE 8.6

1. (a) $x = 2$ (b) $x = 5$ (c) $x = 2$ (d) $y = -8$ (e) $y = -11$ (f) $y = 5$
   (g) $m = -1$ (h) $x = -4$ (i) $y = 2$ (j) $x = 2$
2. (a) $x = -2$ (b) $y = 1$ (c) $x = -2$ (d) $x = -1$ (e) $y = -6$ (f) $x = -1$
   (g) $x = 5.2$ (h) $x = 3.9$ (i) $x = 4.5$ (j) $x = 4.7$ (k) $x = 0.45$ (l) $x = 2.8$
   (m) $x = 6.1$ (n) $x = 6.5$ (o) $x = 4.7$ (p) $x = 5.5$

EXERCISE 8.7

1. (a) $x = \dfrac{c + b}{a}$ (b) $x = ab - a$ (c) $x = \dfrac{-2ab}{a - b}$ (d) $x = \dfrac{a + b}{a - b}$ (e) $x = 1$ (f) $x = 2$

   (g) $x = \dfrac{2ac}{b - a}$ (h) $x = a + b$ (i) $x = 0$ (j) $x = -1$

2. (a) $R = \dfrac{E}{I}$ (b) $r = \dfrac{I}{Pt}$ (c) $d = \dfrac{C}{\pi}$

3. (a) $r = \dfrac{c}{2\pi}$ (b) $x = \dfrac{y - b}{m}$ (c) $x = \dfrac{y}{m} + a$ (d) $h = \dfrac{2A}{b}$

  (e) $h = \dfrac{2A}{a + b}$ (f) $a = \dfrac{2(v - ut)}{t^2}$ (g) $\ell = A - P$ (h) $S = \dfrac{D}{T}$

  (i) $\ell = \dfrac{P}{2} - w$ (j) $a = x - \dfrac{y}{m}$ (k) $a = \dfrac{2s}{n} - \ell$ (l) $n = \dfrac{t - a}{d} + 1$

EXERCISE 8.8

1. (a) 455 km (b) 6.5 h (c) 734 km/h (d) $94\frac{2}{7}$ h (e) 143 a (f) $R = \dfrac{D}{T}$

2. (a) 550 km/h (b) 563 km/h (c) 45 km/h
   (d) 45 km/h (e) 3.3 h (f) 8 h
   (g) $a = g - w$ (tailwind), $a = g + w$ (headwind)

3. (a) 10 250 kJ (b) 16 500 kJ (c) $t = \dfrac{15\ 250 - E_f}{125}$

4. (a) \$347.70 (b) \$509.55 (c) 468 km (d) 3 d (e) $k = \dfrac{C - 19.95d}{0.24}$

5. (a) 77 kg (to nearest kilogram) (b) approximately 172 cm (c) $h = \dfrac{7m}{6} + 90$

6. (a) 54.3 m (b) 442.2 m (c) 8 s (d) $t^2 = \dfrac{d}{4.9}$

7. (a) 348.5 m/s (b) 332.5 m/s

8. (a) 1.63 (b) 2.76 (c) 63 (d) $i = \dfrac{9r}{ERA}$

EXERCISE 8.9

1. $c = \dfrac{n}{2} + 10$ 2. (c) $2s^2 = d^2$

EXERCISE 8.10

1. (a) $\{x \mid x > 4, x \in R\}$ (b) $\{x \mid x < 5, x \in R\}$ (c) $\{x \mid x > -4, x \in R\}$
   (d) $\{x \mid x < -2, x \in R\}$ (e) $\{x \mid x \geqslant -5, x \in R\}$ (f) $\{x \mid x \leqslant -6, x \in R\}$
   (g) $\{x \mid x < -7, x \in R\}$ (h) $\{x \mid x \geqslant -11, x \in R\}$ (i) $\{x \mid x < -11, x \in R\}$
   (j) $\{x \mid x \geqslant 1, x \in R\}$ (k) $\{x \mid x \leqslant -4, x \in R\}$ (l) $\{x \mid x > 1, x \in R\}$
   (m) $\{x \mid x \leqslant 3, x \in R\}$ (n) $\{x \mid x > -17, x \in R\}$ (o) $\{x \mid x < 1, x \in R\}$
   (p) $\{x \mid x \leqslant -3, x \in R\}$
2. (a) $x < 7$ (b) $x \geqslant -11$ (c) $t \leqslant 1$ (d) $s > -18$ (e) $y \leqslant -11$ (f) $w > -20$
3. (a) $x > 11$ (b) $y \leqslant -16$ (c) $x > -13$ (d) $x \geqslant -5$ (e) $x < -9$ (f) $x \leqslant 18$
   (g) $w < 3$ (h) $w \geqslant 66$ (i) $w < 113$
4. (a) $x > -1.1$ (b) $y \leqslant -20.5$ (c) $x \leqslant -2.2$ (d) $x \geqslant 1.9$

EXERCISE 8.11

1. (a) $\{x \mid x > 3, x \in R\}$ (b) $\{y \mid y < 4, y \in R\}$ (c) $\{t \mid t \leqslant 5, t \in R\}$
   (d) $\{z \mid z \geqslant 2, z \in R\}$ (e) $\{x \mid x \leqslant -3, x \in R\}$ (f) $\{x \mid x < 4, x \in R\}$
   (g) $\{y \mid y > -10, y \in R\}$ (h) $\{t \mid t \geqslant -2, t \in R\}$ (i) $\{z \mid z < -3, z \in R\}$
   (j) $\{x \mid x \geqslant 6, x \in R\}$ (k) $\{x \mid x > -2, x \in R\}$ (l) $\{t \mid t > -1, t \in R\}$
2. (a) $x \leqslant 2$ (b) $y > 3$ (c) $z < 3$ (d) $x > -4$
   (e) $x < 2$ (f) $x \leqslant 13$ (g) $x \geqslant -6$ (h) $x \geqslant 4$
   (i) $y < -6$ (j) $x > 6$ (k) $t \leqslant 0$ (l) $x < 79$

3. (a) $t \geq -14$ (b) $x > \frac{3}{2}$ (c) $x \leq 9$ (d) $x > -3$ (e) $x < 33$ (f) $z > \frac{5}{3}$
   (g) $y \in R$ (h) $x < 20$ (i) $x \leq 1$ (j) $S = \phi$

EXERCISE 8.12

1. (a) $\{x \mid x > 16, x \in R\}$ (b) $\{x \mid x < 15, x \in R\}$ (c) $\{t \mid t \leq -4, t \in R\}$
   (d) $\{z \mid z \geq -10, z \in R\}$ (e) $\{x \mid x > -3, x \in R\}$ (f) $\{t \mid t \leq 5, t \in R\}$
   (g) $\{z \mid z \leq 0, z \in R\}$ (h) $\{x \mid x < 12, x \in R\}$ (i) $\{x \mid x \leq 12, x \in R\}$
   (j) $\{x \mid x < -18, x \in R\}$ (k) $\{t \mid t \geq 3, t \in R\}$ (l) $\{x \mid x < -15, x \in R\}$

2. (a) $x < -3$ (b) $x \leq 16$ (c) $x < 4$ (d) $x < \frac{3}{2}$ (e) $x > -\frac{3}{2}$ (f) $x \leq 18$
   (g) $x > \frac{5}{2}$ (h) $x \geq -16$ (i) $x > \frac{4}{7}$ (j) $x \leq \frac{1}{4}$ (k) $x \geq \frac{2}{3}$ (l) $x > 1$

3. (a) $x > -10$ (b) $x \geq -7$ (c) $x \geq 2$ (d) $x > -\frac{3}{2}$ (e) $x \geq 3$ (f) $x > 47$
   (g) $x \leq -1$

EXERCISE 8.13

1. (a) $x \geq \frac{4}{3}$ (b) $x < \frac{5}{2}$ (c) $x \geq 18$ (d) $x > -8$ (e) $x \geq 2$ (f) $x > -2$
   (g) $x > -9$ (h) $x \geq -14$ (i) $x \leq -19$ (j) $x \leq -3$ (k) $x > 13$

EXERCISE 8.14

1. 4 times older   2. Wheels numbered 1 and 2.   3. Answers will vary.
4. \$4.75   5. \$5.50   6. 6, 4, 6, 4
7. Answers will vary.
8. (a) 2   (b) 6   (c) 10   (d) 36
9. 8 times   10. 10   11. 51, 52, 53, 54, 55
12. 8
13. (a) 15, 18, 21   (b) $-2, -8, -15$ (c) 31, 63, 127
   (d) 26, 37, 50   (e) 3, 3, 3
14. Answers will vary.   15. 17 nickels, 14 dimes   16. 23 nickels, 11 dimes
17. \$3.50   19. During the seventh year the car will have doubled in value.
20. 72, 73 , 74   21. (a) 18   (b) 29

8.15 REVIEW EXERCISE

1. (a) inconsistent   (b) consistent   (c) consistent
   (d) inconsistent   (e) inconsistent   (f) consistent
2. (a) $S = \{3\}$ (b) $S = \{6\}$ (c) $S = \{2\}$ (d) $S = \{-9\}$
   (e) $S = \{3\}$ (f) $S = \{-6\}$ (g) $S = \{13\}$ (h) $S = \{0\}$
   (i) $S = \{8\}$ (j) $S = \{0\}$ (k) $S = \{-5\}$ (l) $S = \{7\}$
   (m) $S = \{-5\}$ (n) $S = \{-6\}$ (o) $S = \{10\}$ (p) $S = \{-10\}$
   (q) $S = \{10\}$ (r) $S = \{-12\}$ (s) $S = \{14\}$ (t) $S = \{0\}$
3. (a) $\{x \mid x > 3, x \in R\}$ (b) $\{t \mid t < 8, t \in R\}$ (c) $\{y \mid y \leq -6, y \in R\}$
   (d) $\{x \mid x \geq 4, x \in R\}$ (e) $\{x \mid x > -1, x \in R\}$ (f) $\{x \mid x > -3, x \in R\}$
   (g) $\{x \mid x \leq 7, x \in R\}$ (h) $\{x \mid x < -18, x \in R\}$ (i) $\{x \mid x \leq -15, x \in R\}$
   (j) $\{x \mid x > -15, x \in R\}$ (k) $\{x \mid x > -1, x \in R\}$ (l) $\{t \mid t \leq 12, t \in R\}$
   (m) $\{x \mid x < 7, x \in R\}$ (n) $\{x \mid x > 17, x \in R\}$ (o) $\{y \mid y \leq 0, y \in R\}$
   (p) $\{x \mid x < 0, x \in R\}$ (q) $\{x \mid x \geq -2, x \in R\}$ (r) $\{x \mid x < 10, x \in R\}$
   (s) $\{x \mid x < 0, x \in R\}$ (t) $\{x \mid x \leq -3, x \in R\}$
4. (a) $x = 33$ (b) $x = 16$ (c) $x = 23$ (d) $t = 30$ (e) $x = 144$ (f) $x = 104$
   (g) $x = 72$ (h) $x = -15$ (i) $x = 27$ (j) $t = -37$ (k) $w = 7$ (l) $x = -12$
   (m) $w = 10$ (n) $t = -3$ (o) $m = 64$
5. (a) $t = 9$ (b) $x = 8$ (c) $x = -6$ (d) $x = -3$ (e) $w = -1$ (f) $S = \phi$
   (g) $x = 10$ (h) $x = 7$ (i) $x = 39$ (j) $x = -17$ (k) $x = 12$ (l) $x = 4$
6. 5.4 h   7. (a) (i) 110 L   (ii) 300 L   (b) 56 min

8. (a) (i) 825 L   (ii) 165 L   (b) 60 min
9. (a) 3.76 L   (b) 2.98 L   (c) 0.03 L
10. (a) $x \geq 2$ (b) $t > -4$ (c) $x \leq -2$ (d) $x < 9$ (e) $t \geq 3$ (f) $t > 2$
    (g) $t < -10$ (h) $w < -7$ (i) $s \leq -2$
11. (a) $x > -10$ (b) $x \geq -7$ (c) $x \geq -5$ (d) $x \leq 8$ (e) $x > 4$ (f) $x > 3$
12. (a) $x = 2.8$ (b) $t = 1$ (c) $w = 2$ (d) $x = -0.8$ (e) $x = 16$ (f) $x = -1.8$
13. (a) $w = \dfrac{P}{2} - \ell$ (b) $b = \dfrac{2A}{h} - a$ (c) $d = \dfrac{t - a}{n - 1}$ (d) $\ell = \dfrac{2S}{n} - a$
14. (a) $x < 22$ (b) $x \leq 28$ (c) $x \geq 10$ (d) $x > 7$

8.16 CHAPTER 8 TEST

1. subtract 3, divide by -2
2. (a) $x = 4$ (b) $x = -13$ (c) $x = 12$
3. (a) $x \geq -1$ (b) $x > 1$ (c) $x \leq 4$
4. (a) $x = 2$ (b) $x = -4$ (c) $x \geq 2$ (d) $x = -\dfrac{7}{2} = -3.5$
5. (a) $x = \dfrac{b}{a + b}$ (b) $h = \dfrac{2A}{a + b}$
6. (a) 1970   (b) $c = 1.5n + 45$ (c) \$2445

8.17 CUMULATIVE REVIEW FOR CHAPTERS 5 TO 8

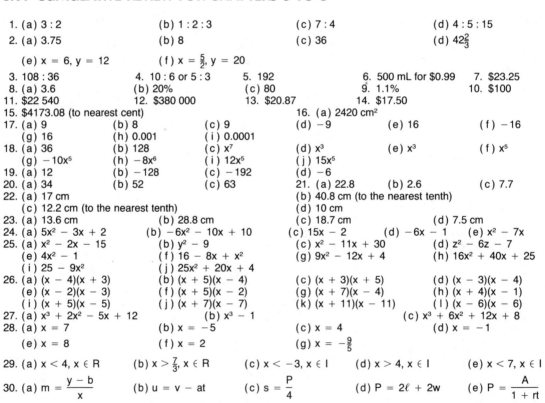

1. (a) $3 : 2$ (b) $1 : 2 : 3$ (c) $7 : 4$ (d) $4 : 5 : 15$
2. (a) 3.75   (b) 8   (c) 36   (d) $42\frac{2}{3}$
    (e) $x = 6, y = 12$ (f) $x = \frac{5}{2}, y = 20$
3. $108 : 36$ 4. $10 : 6$ or $5 : 3$ 5. 192   6. 500 mL for \$0.99   7. \$23.25
8. (a) 3.6   (b) 20%   (c) 80   9. 1.1%   10. \$100
11. \$22 540   12. \$380 000   13. \$20.87   14. \$17.50
15. \$4173.08 (to nearest cent)   16. (a) 2420 cm²
17. (a) 9   (b) 8   (c) 9   (d) -9 (e) 16   (f) -16
    (g) 16   (h) 0.001   (i) 0.0001
18. (a) 36   (b) 128   (c) x^7 (d) x^3 (e) x^3 (f) x^5
    (g) $-10x^5$ (h) $-8x^6$ (i) $12x^5$ (j) $15x^5$
19. (a) 12   (b) -128 (c) -192 (d) -6
20. (a) 34   (b) 52   (c) 63   21. (a) 22.8   (b) 2.6   (c) 7.7
22. (a) 17 cm   (b) 40.8 cm (to the nearest tenth)
    (c) 12.2 cm (to the nearest tenth)   (d) 10 cm
23. (a) 13.6 cm   (b) 28.8 cm   (c) 18.7 cm   (d) 7.5 cm
24. (a) $5x^2 - 3x + 2$ (b) $-6x^2 - 10x + 10$ (c) $15x - 2$ (d) $-6x - 1$ (e) $x^2 - 7x$
25. (a) $x^2 - 2x - 15$ (b) $y^2 - 9$ (c) $x^2 - 11x + 30$ (d) $z^2 - 6z - 7$
    (e) $4x^2 - 1$ (f) $16 - 8x + x^2$ (g) $9x^2 - 12x + 4$ (h) $16x^2 + 40x + 25$
    (i) $25 - 9x^2$ (j) $25x^2 + 20x + 4$
26. (a) $(x - 4)(x + 3)$ (b) $(x + 5)(x - 4)$ (c) $(x + 3)(x + 5)$ (d) $(x - 3)(x - 4)$
    (e) $(x - 2)(x - 3)$ (f) $(x + 5)(x - 2)$ (g) $(x + 7)(x - 4)$ (h) $(x + 4)(x - 1)$
    (i) $(x + 5)(x - 5)$ (j) $(x + 7)(x - 7)$ (k) $(x + 11)(x - 11)$ (l) $(x - 6)(x - 6)$
27. (a) $x^3 + 2x^2 - 5x + 12$ (b) $x^3 - 1$ (c) $x^3 + 6x^2 + 12x + 8$
28. (a) $x = 7$ (b) $x = -5$ (c) $x = 4$ (d) $x = -1$
    (e) $x = 8$ (f) $x = 2$ (g) $x = -\frac{9}{5}$
29. (a) $x < 4, x \in R$ (b) $x > \frac{7}{3}, x \in R$ (c) $x < -3, x \in I$ (d) $x > 4, x \in I$ (e) $x < 7, x \in I$
30. (a) $m = \dfrac{y - b}{x}$ (b) $u = v - at$ (c) $s = \dfrac{P}{4}$ (d) $P = 2\ell + 2w$ (e) $P = \dfrac{A}{1 + rt}$

REVIEW AND PREVIEW TO CHAPTER 9
EQUATIONS AND INEQUALITIES

1. (a) $x = 12$ (b) $x = 17$ (c) $m = 8$ (d) $y = 2$ (e) $n = 0$ (f) $z = 15$

(g) x = 5   (h) y = 4   (i) m = 2   (j) x = −6   (k) x = 2   (l) y = 2
2. (a) x = 2.1   (b) y = 1.6   (c) x = 9   (d) x = 14.1   (e) x = 1.6
   (f) x = 4.8   (g) x = 1   (h) x = 0.5   (i) x = 1
3. (a) x < 5   (b) x < 4   (c) y ⩽ 6   (d) n ⩾ 6   (e) x ⩾ 1
   (f) x > 2   (g) x > −2   (h) x < 2   (i) x ⩽ −1   (j) x ⩾ 4
   (k) x > $\frac{3}{2}$ (l) x < $-\frac{20}{3}$ (m) x ⩾ $-\frac{9}{2}$ (n) x ⩾ $-\frac{4}{3}$
4. (a) y = 3   (b) x = 1   (c) m = 3   (d) y = −9
   (e) x = 0   (f) x = 3   (g) y = −1   (h) x = 4
5. (a) (i) 325 000   (ii) 166 000   (iii) 24 000   (iv) 3 206 000
   (b) (i) 25.6   (ii) 0.6   (iii) 5.7   (iv) 12.5
   (c) (i) 465 924   (ii) 46   (iii) 325   (iv) 4
6. (a) 500 500   (b) 1 283 601

FRACTIONS

1. (a) $4\frac{1}{6}$ (b) $\frac{5}{8}$ (c) $6\frac{1}{4}$ (d) $1\frac{1}{4}$
   (e) $1\frac{11}{12}$ (f) $2\frac{1}{12}$ (g) $5\frac{1}{8}$
2. (a) $\frac{1}{2}$ (b) 4   (c) $1\frac{2}{13}$ (d) $1\frac{23}{40}$
   (e) $4\frac{1}{16}$ (f) $6\frac{1}{4}$ (g) $5\frac{11}{16}$
3. (a) 0.625   (b) 0.636   (c) 0.8   (d) 0.889
   (e) 0.583   (f) 0.417   (g) 0.833   (h) 0.167
4. (a) $\frac{3}{4}$ (b) $\frac{7}{20}$ (c) $\frac{12}{25}$ (d) $\frac{9}{100}$
   (e) $\frac{5}{9}$ (f) $\frac{4}{11}$ (g) $\frac{8}{11}$ (h) $\frac{2}{33}$
   (i) $\frac{235}{999}$ (j) $\frac{14}{33}$ (k) $\frac{1}{2}$ (l) $\frac{3}{10}$

PERIMETER

1. (a) 9.3 cm   (b) 17.2 m   (c) 17 m   (d) 12 m   (e) 36 m   (f) 32.2 m
   (g) 23.4 m   (h) 29.4 m   (i) 14 m   (j) 28 cm

EXERCISE 9.1

1. (a) x + 7   (b) 2n   (c) y + 8   (d) 5n   (e) x + 6   (f) 4n
   (g) x − 3   (h) n − 2   (i) 9n   (j) n − 11   (k) $\frac{x}{6}$ (l) n + 15
   (m) a + 3   (n) a − 2   (o) 25n   (p) 10y   (q) 7x   (r) x − 8
   (s) 8 − x
2. (a) 5n + 3   (b) 2s − 13   (c) 3h + 2   (d) 6n − 4
   (e) a + 2a   (f) 6p − 5   (g) x + (x + 1)   (h) x(x + 1)
   (i) $\frac{d}{2}$ + 7   (j) 2(a + 3)   (k) 5(a − 2)
4. (a) 6n, n   (b) a, 3a   (c) s, 9s   (d) w, 5w   (e) p, 10p   (f) s, 8s
   (g) h, 20h   (h) v, $\frac{v}{2}$ (i) b, $\frac{b}{3}$
6. (a) a, a + 3   (b) a, a − 6   (c) w, w + 15   (d) c, c + 13
   (e) N, N − 1335   (f) b, b + 20   (g) h, h − 53

EXERCISE 9.2

1. (a) d = 3440 h
   (b) (i) 172 m   (ii) 34 400 m   (iii) 6295.2 m   (iv) 3 663 600 m
2. (a) LP = 1.25CP
   (b) (i) $10 950   (ii) $12 287.50   (iii) $13 412.50   (iv) $24 250
3. (a) d = 40 200t
   (b) (i) 281 400 km   (ii) 3 216 000 km   (iii) 7 095 300 km   (iv) 38 039 250 km

4. (a) S = 8.75h
   (b) (i) $87.50　　(ii) $262.50　　(iii) $328.13　　(iv) $450.63
5. (a) LL = 11t
   (b) (i) 2.2 m　　(ii) 11 m　　(iii) 110 m　　(iv) 275 m
6. (a) d = 330t
   (b) (i) 660 m　　(ii) 2310 m　　(iii) 4455 m
7. (a) E = 0.05S + 250
   (b) (i) $6486.15　　(ii) $3345　　(iii) $4666.50
8. (a) E = 15 600, if S ≤ 300 000
      E = 15 600 + 0.06(S − 300 000), if S > 300 000
   (b) (i) $48 600　　(ii) $29 100　　(iii) $15 600　　(iv) $42 416.40
9. (a) $n = \dfrac{t}{4}$　　(b) (i) 360　　(ii) 2520　　(iii) 10 800　　(iv) 131 400
10. (a) $n = \dfrac{t}{18}$　　(b) (i) 4800　　(ii) 33 600　　(iii) 144 000　　(iv) 1 752 000

EXERCISE 9.3

1. (a) 5n = 15　　(b) 2a = 30　　(c) n + 7 = 13　　(d) n − 2 = 11
   (e) n − 6 = 14　　(f) a − 2 = 10　　(g) a + 5 = 21
2. (a) 2[x + (x + 5)] = 24　　(b) 2[x + (x + 2)] = 24　　(c) 2[x + 3x] = 24
3. (a) 5n + 8 = 63　　(b) 3n + 15 = 75
   (c) 11p = 6.93　　(d) P − S = 3, S + P = 33
   (e) 6n − 3 = 93　　(f) P − B = 10, P + B = 36
   (g) B − Y = 3, B + Y = 13　　(h) K = 2M, K + M = 78
   (i) LE − LO = 77, LO + LE = 698　　(j) D − T = 5, D + T = 19
   (k) SL − RG = 24, SL + RG = 6090　　(l) $AO = \dfrac{PO}{2}$, AO + PO = 250 000 000
   (m) BR + LG = 107, BR − LG = 13　　(n) S = 110E, S + E = 1 405 000

EXERCISE 9.4

1. 16.4　　2. 20　　3. 15　　4. −8　　5. 13 and 39
6. 19 and 41　　7. 15 and 30　　8. 34 m by 30 m
9. 81, 82, 83　　10. 121, 122, 123, 124　　11. −25, −24, −23, −22, −21
12. 12 and 24　　13. 5 and 13　　14. 1724 km　　15. 6 and 18
16. 240 m and 60 m　　17. Dave: $330, Bill: $165, Fred: $55
18. Suez Canal: 161.9 km, Panama Canal: 81.6 km　　19. 29 m by 8 m
20. 82, 84, 86　　21. 91, 93, 95, 97
22. Sam: 12a, Bill: 8a, Mary: 24a　　23. 24a
24. base 17 cm, sides 31 cm　　25. 48a

EXERCISE 9.5

2. (a) x, 35 − x　　(b) x, 87 − x　　(c) x, 200 − x　　(d) x, 34 − x
   (e) x, 16 − x　　(f) x, 115 − x　　(g) x, 257 − x　　(h) x, 63 − x
3. 31 and 42　　4. 61 and 24　　5. 9
7. 52 and 73　　8. 19　　9. 15　　6. 7
10. 10 two-dollar bills and 20 five-dollar bills
11. 12 km　　12. 60 and 20

EXERCISE 9.6

1. $1\frac{1}{3}$ h　　2. $2\frac{2}{5}$ h　　3. $4\frac{4}{9}$ h　　4. $3\frac{3}{7}$ h　　5. 10 min　　6. $13\frac{1}{3}$ min
7. $17\frac{1}{7}$ min　　8. (i)　　9. $3\frac{3}{7}$ h　　10. 4 h　　11. $2\frac{2}{3}$ h

EXERCISE 9.7

1. (a) 240 km   (b) 12 h   (c) 100 km/h   (d) 420 km   (e) 3.5 h
4. 222.25 km/h   5. 293.3 km/h   6. 171.4 km/h   7. 5600 km   8. 1.5 h
9. 1.5 h   10. 1.5 h   11. 720 km   12. 1.75 h   13. 3.5 h   14. 450 km
15. 87.5 km

9.8 REVIEW EXERCISE

1. (a) 7n   (b) n + 9   (c) a − 3   (d) n − 4
 (e) a + 6   (f) 5y   (g) 7n − 4   (h) 3n − 5
 (i) x + (x + 1) + (x + 2)
2. (a) n + 10 = 63   (b) a − 5 = 13   (c) n − 7 = 6
 (d) 6n + 4 = 40   (e) 2n − 3 = 7
3. 43   4. 21   5. 13   6. 56 m by 49 m
7. 6   8. 463   9. 53.25 km   10. 96, 97, 98
11. 714   12. 4191   13. 68 and 49   14. 68   15. 9 dimes
16. 5   17. 40 min   18. $37\frac{1}{3}$ min
29. 2 h   20. 2700 km   21. 1.2 h   22. $1\frac{11}{13}$ h   23. 80 km
24. 15 km/h and 30 km/h

9.9 CHAPTER 9 TEST

1. (a) 25 − x   (b) x − 3   (c) $\frac{x}{3}$

 (d) $\frac{x + 2}{5}$ (e) x, x + 1, x + 2   (f) x, x + 2, x + 4
2. (a) SP = 1.32 CP   (b) $489.94
3. (a) 2x + (x − 3) = 12   (b) (Jason + 5 + 3) + (Jason + 3) = 34   (c) $\frac{x}{75} + \frac{x}{100} = 7$
4. 35, 37, 39   5. $3\frac{3}{7}$ h   6. $10\frac{2}{9}$ h

REVIEW AND PREVIEW TO CHAPTER 10

PERCENT

1. (a) 0.25   (b) 0.1   (c) 0.4   (d) 0.45   (e) 0.65
 (f) 1.0   (g) 0.63   (h) 0.05   (i) 0.01   (j) 0.255
 (k) 0.076   (l) 0.125   (m) 0.124   (n) 1.09   (o) 2.3
 (p) 0.0775   (q) 1.53   (r) 0.099   (s) $0.0\overline{3}$ (t) $0.\overline{6}$
2. (a) 75%   (b) 50%   (c) 70%   (d) 15%   (e) 14%   (f) 25%
 (g) 10%   (h) 67%   (i) 8%   (j) 81%   (k) 320%   (l) 150%
3. (a) 30   (b) 42   (c) 135   (d) 147   (e) 28.35   (f) 5.2
 (g) 42.5   (h) 275   (i) 18.6   (j) 121.6   (k) 0.4   (l) 0.2
4. $33\frac{1}{3}$%   5. 20%   6. 10%   7. $16\frac{2}{3}$%   8. $14\frac{2}{7}$%   9. 200%
10. $371\frac{3}{7}$%   11. 180   12. 120   13. 300   14. 48 students
15. $69.55   16. $252   18. $472
20. (a) 10 714   (b) 17 143   (c) 42 857
22. 26 000 vehicles

EXERCISE 10.1

1. (a) encyclopedia   (b) testing   (c) telephone survey
 (d) telephone surveys (phone-in)   (e) encyclopedia   (f) encyclopedia

(g) questionnaires   (h) questionnaires   (i) testing
(j) questionnaires   (k) measurement   (l) questionnaires
2. (a) testing the flares destroys the product
   (b) agricultural, pharmaceutical
   (c) automotive, telecommunications, security (alarms, locks, ...)

EXERCISE 10.2

1. 69 000 watch CHRT, 90 000 watch CJLP, 60 000 watch CBC, 48 000 watch WXNT, 33 000 watch WRQT
2. (b) 90 000 prefer Italian, 200 000 prefer Canadian, 140 000 prefer French, 70 000 prefer Chinese
3. (a) The majority of trips taken are fewer than 10 km from home, which accounts for the higher accident rate within 10 km of home.
   (b) The people surveyed may not be representative of the population.
   (c) If there are more than two parties 40% may be a majority.

EXERCISE 10.3

1. bingo, lotteries, raffles, playing cards, and tournaments
2. The tickets should be well mixed and the same size.
3. Put 100 equally sized slips of paper in a container, 10 with the letter F, 20 with the letter D, 30 with the letter C, and 40 with the letter P. Agree (by random selection if necessary) on a person to draw a ticket from the container. Thus, the initial drawn decides who shall get the boat for July 1.
4. Assign each of the people a number from 00 to 59. Begin at the top of the table and record the digits in groups of two horizontally, disregarding any group of two beginning with the digits 6, 7, 8, or 9. This method gives 21, 58, 04, 07, 41, 38, 20, and 18 as the first 8 numbers.
6. Begin at the top of the table and record the digits in groups of one horizontally. Interpret even digits (0, 2, 4, 6, 8) as heads and odd digits (1, 3, 5, 7, 9) as tails.
7. Begin at the top of the table and record the digits in groups of one horizontally, disregarding the digits 0, 7, 8, and 9. Interpret the digits obtained as face values of a die.

EXERCISE 10.4

1. (a) Uranus: 11 h, Earth: 24 h, Jupiter: 9.5 h, Mars: 24 h, Neptune: 16 h, Saturn: 10 h
   (b) Earth and Mars; Uranus, Jupiter, and Saturn   (c) 11
2. (a) 110 on Monday, 120 on Tuesday, 130 on Wednesday, 150 on Thursday, 140 on Friday, 160 on Saturday
   (b) Thursday, Friday, and Saturday

3. (a) 07:00   (b) 70 km   (c) 70 km/h   (d) $2\frac{1}{2}$ h   (e) 17.5 km
   (f) 12:00   (g) 82 km/h   (h) 2 h   (i) 350 km   (j) 102.5 L

EXERCISE 10.5

2. (b) Swimming: 18.75%, Boating: 6.25%, Camping: 7.5%, Snow-skiing: 11.25%, Water-skiing: 5%, Sailing: 5%, Horseback riding: 3.75%, Bicycling: 20%, Ice Skating: 22.5%

EXERCISE 10.7

1. (a) $3000 on tuition, $2400 on food, $2880 on room, $1200 on travel, $600 on books, $1920 other
   (b) clothing, entertainment
2. (a) $1 800 000   (b) $720 000   (c) $720 000
   (d) $450 000   (e) $450 000   (f) $360 000
3. (a) (i) 40 kg   (ii) 16 kg   (iii) 14.4 kg   (iv) 9.6 kg
5. Food Stores: 28.6 billion, Automotive Dealers: 24.7 billion, General Merchandise: 20.8 billion, Gasoline Service Stations: 9.1 billion, Drug and Liquor: 6.5 billion, Building and Hardware: 6.5 billion, Furniture: 5.2 billion, Apparel: 6.5 billion, Other: 22.1 billion
6. (a) $1.60   (b) $2.60   (c) $4.00
7. Home and Other Mortgages: 136.5 billion, Instalment and Credit: 52.5 billion, Loans: 12.6 billion, Other: 8.4 billion

9. Music: 4536 min, Commercials: 2016 min, News: 1512 min, Sports: 1008 min, D.J. Talk: 1008 min

EXERCISE 10.8

1. (a) Concorde jet: 150 people, Mayflower: 130 people, Gondola: 5 people, Double-decker bus: 70 people
   (b) 26   (c) 19

EXERCISE 10.9

1. (a) 9   (b) no mode   (c) 24   (d) 9 and 18   (e) 41   (f) no mode
2. (a) 10.5, 9.5, no mode   (b) 18, 13, no mode   (c) 5, 5, 4 and 6   (d) 48, 41, no mode
   (e) 36, 34, 23   (f) 128.2, 127.5, 103 and 153   (g) 8, 8.2, no mode
3. 81.25
4. Yes, since there are 5 weeks the median weekly salary is Paul's salary for the third week.
5. (a) 16   (b) 16   6. 204

EXERCISE 10.10

1. (a) mode   (b) median   (c) median   (d) mean   (e) mean
   (f) mode   (g) median   (h) mean   (i) median
2. mode   3. No, unless both towns have the same number of people.   4. 7
5. (a) 12, 11.2, 10.9   (b) median   6. (a) 3.5, 3, 2   (b) median   7. 4
8. mean: 54.4 w.p.m.; 4 had speeds greater than the mean   9. (a) $10.74   (b) $10
10. Yes, 5 additional employees are needed.
11. While half the tires last fewer than 24 000 km, some last considerably longer producing a mean lifetime
   of 34 000 km.

EXERCISE 10.11

1. (a) {red, black}   (b) {clubs, diamonds, hearts, spades}
   (c) {(H, 1), (H, 2), (H, 3), (H, 4), (H, 5), (H, 6), (T, 1), (T, 2), (T, 3), (T, 4), (T, 5), (T, 6)}
2. (a) {R, B, G, Y}   (b) {(R, B), (R, G), (R, Y), (B, G), (B, Y), (G, Y)}
   (c) {(R, B, G), (R, B, Y), (R, G, Y), (B, G, Y)}   (d) {(R, B, G, Y)}

EXERCISE 10.12

1. (a) $\frac{1}{13}$ (b) $\frac{3}{13}$ (c) $\frac{1}{4}$ (d) $\frac{3}{26}$ (e) $\frac{3}{52}$
2. (a) $\frac{1}{4}$ (b) $\frac{1}{13}$ (c) $\frac{3}{13}$ (d) $\frac{1}{52}$
3. (a) $\frac{1}{18}$ (b) $\frac{1}{18}$ (c) $\frac{5}{36}$ (d) $\frac{5}{36}$ (e) $\frac{1}{6}$ (f) $\frac{1}{9}$
   (g) 0   (h) 0
4. (a) $\frac{3}{7}$ (b) $\frac{1}{14}$ (c) $\frac{3}{14}$
5. (a) $\frac{3}{10}$ (b) $\frac{1}{10}$ (c) $\frac{3}{5}$ (d) 1   (e) 0
6. (a) $\frac{20}{37}$ (b) $\frac{17}{37}$ (c) $\frac{3}{37}$ (d) $\frac{9}{37}$ (e) $\frac{16}{37}$ (f) 0
7. (a) $\frac{1}{4}$ (b) $\frac{1}{8}$ (c) $\frac{1}{16}$ (d) 0   8. 0, 1

EXERCISE 10.13

1. 0.4   2. (a) 0.22   (b) 0.2   4. (a) 0.025   (b) 250
5. (a) 0.99   (b) 24 750   6. (a) $\frac{21}{46}, \frac{25}{46}$ (b) $\frac{11}{46}$ (c) $\frac{6}{11}$

7. (a) Robinson: 0.366, Kaline: 0.399, Mantle: 0.290, Ruth: 0.261, Gehrig: 0.281, Williams: 0.344, Jackson: 0.281, Carew: 0.284

(b) 0.313

EXERCISE 10.14

1. 2   2. 10   3. $50 390.62   4. 60°

5. 235.5 (using $\pi = 3.14$)   6. 210   7. 88

9. The distance from Roosevelt Field to Le Bourget is 5790 km. Therefore, the average speed is about 173 km/h.

10. First weigh any six coins — three on each pan. If they balance, then the counterfeit coin is one of the remaining two coins and may be found by weighing these two against each other. If they do not balance, then the counterfeit coin is contained in the group of three that weighs less, and if we now weigh any two of these coins we will find the counterfeit coin. (If these two balance, then the counterfeit coin is the third. If they do not balance the counterfeit coin is evident.)

11. Engineer: Lee, Computer Operator: Roberts, Conductor: Jones

12. 26   13. $\frac{7}{4}$ 14. 35   15. 6

10.15 REVIEW EXERCISE

3. (a) (i) 64   (ii) 62   (iii) 65   (iv) 70   (b) 261 students

4. (a) 8, 7, 6   (b) 12.3, 10.5, 5 and 14   (c) 30.6, 31.5, no mode

5. (a) 2.6, 2, 1 and 2   (b) mean

6. (a) $\frac{1}{4}$ (b) $\frac{1}{13}$ (c) $\frac{1}{26}$ 7. 0.89

8. (a) 0.935   (b) 0.062   (c) 0.035   (d) 91%   (e) 3.74%   (f) 6.2%

9. (a) 6   (b) $\frac{1}{3}$

10.16 CHAPTER 10 TEST

3. (a) 10, 9.5, 9   (b) 145, 144, no mode   4. (a) $\frac{1}{2}$ (b) $\frac{3}{10}$ (c) $\frac{7}{10}$

5. (a) $\frac{1}{8}$ (b) $\frac{3}{8}$

REVIEW AND PREVIEW TO CHAPTER 11

METRIC UNITS

1. (a) 4400 m   (b) 70 m   (c) 600 m   (d) 3.5 m

2. (a) 130 cm   (b) 45 cm   (c) 77 cm   (d) 0.025 cm

3. (a) 7.5 ha   (b) 1000 ha   (c) 50 ha   (d) 500 ha

4. (a) 1 200 000 m²   (b) 30 000 m²   (c) 700 000 m²   (d) 2000 m²

5. (a) 8000 cm²   (b) 3 cm²   (c) 15 cm²   (d) 2500 cm²

6. (a) 3.5 L   (b) 0.0006 L   (c) 5200 L   (d) 250 L

7. (a) 8400 kg   (b) 8 kg   (c) 500 kg   (d) 0.075 kg

8. (a) 8.76×10^{12} km   (b) 8.76×10^{15} m

9. 9.976×10^{11} 10. 100 pin-heads   11. 8 241 400 ha

12. 7×10^{20} L   13. 22 times heavier

PROBLEM SOLVING: SEARCH FOR A PATTERN

1. (a) 24 (multiply vertically opposite values by 2)   (b) $8^2 - 50 = 14$, $5^2 - 26 = -1$

(c)
20
26

(d) 4 (add inner values, subtract outer values)

2. (a) 10, 3   (b) 25, 30   (c) 17   (d) 65   (e) 94

EXERCISE 11.1

1. (a) 47.4 cm   (b) 219.24 m   (c) 587.2 km
   (d) 402 cm   (e) 1389.6 m   (f) 5.12 cm
2. (a) 65.6 m   (b) 485.5 m   (c) 152.5 cm   (d) 1245.1 km
3. (a) x = 205.1 m   (b) y = 0.77 cm
4. 67.6 cm   5. (a) 1710.8 m   (b) $15 380.09   (c) $19 952.84
6. 109.8 m

EXERCISE 11.2

1. (a) 565.2 m   (b) 209.1 cm   (c) 1.3 cm   (d) 113.0 m
2. 114 cm   3. 189 m   4. (a) 54.84 m   (b) 26.71 cm
5. (a) 25.12 m   (b) 25.12 m
   (c) The circumference of the larger circle equals the circumference of the 3 smaller circles.
6. (a) 40 000 km   (b) 28   (c) 11 765

EXERCISE 11.3

1. (a) 315 m^2 (b) 63.7 cm^2 (c) 205.8 m^2 (d) 8384 m^2
2. (a) 2601 m^2 (b) 676 cm^2 (c) 94.09 m^2 (d) 129.96 cm^2
3. (a) 507 cm^2 (b) 925 cm^2 (c) 80 m^2 (d) 720 cm^2
4. (a) 192 cm^2 (b) 8305 cm^2
6. $2683.20   7. 230 m   8. 95.4 m

EXERCISE 11.4

1. (a) 84 cm^2 (b) 198 cm^2 (c) 144 m^2 (d) 33.8 m^2
   (e) 405 m^2 (f) 114.5 m^2 (g) 69.36 cm^2 (h) 250.32 m^2
   (i) 43.43 m^2 (j) 3 m^2 (k) 45 m^2 (l) 3065.665 m^2
2. (a) 16.12 m^2 (b) 112.16 cm^2 (c) 651.755 m^2 (d) 82.8 m

EXERCISE 11.5

1. (a) 379.9 m^2 (b) 475.1 cm^2 (c) 260.0 m^2 (d) 96 162.5 m^2
2. (a) 26.4 m^2 (b) 2461.8 cm^2 (c) 481.6 m^2 (d) 147.0 cm^2
3. (a) 18.9 m^2 (b) 5504 m^2 4. 9426 m^2 5. (a) 89.25 m^2 (b) 36.56
6. 251.2 m^2 (using π = 3.14)   7. 4 − π in both cases.

EXERCISE 11.8

1. (a) 52 m^2 (b) 346 m^2 (c) 43.6 cm^2 (d) 270 000 mm^2
2. (a) 584.016 m^2 (b) 432.6 m^2 (c) 252 cm^2 3. $491.55

EXERCISE 11.9

1. (a) 1155.5 cm^2 (b) 306.2 m^2 (c) 720.9 cm^2
   (d) 942 cm^2 (e) 400.9 m^2 (f) 1149.5 cm^2
2. (a) 160 m^2 (b) 499.8 m^2 3. 3140 m^2 4. 7 m^2

EXERCISE 11.10

1. (a) 198 m³   (b) 111.52 cm³   (c) 3 036 000 m³
2. (a) 850 m³   (b) 60 000 cm³   (c) 3300.224 m³   (d) 2808 m³
3. (a) 115 m³   (b) 115 000 L   (c) 6 h 23 min 20 s

EXERCISE 11.11

2. (a) 3052.1 m³   (b) 360.0 m³   (c) 1299.8 cm³
    (d) 15 274 734.1 m³   (e) 464.6 cm³   (f) 51 776.8 m³
3. (a) 55.488 m³   (b) 323.532 cm³   (c) 270 cm³   (d) $1564\frac{1}{3}$ m³
4. 49 850.64 cm³   5. 91

EXERCISE 11.12

1. (a) 314 m³, 282.6 m²   (b) 2411.5 cm³, 1205.8 cm²   (c) 2512.0 cm³, 1130.4 cm²
    (d) 75.4 cm³, 108.7 cm²   (e) 3014.4 cm³, 1331.0 cm²   (f) 1055.0 cm³, 975.6 cm²
2. 12 560 cm³   3. 159.9 cm³

EXERCISE 11.13

1. (a) 1256 m², 4186.7 m³   (b) 422.5 m², 816.9 m³
    (c) 20 096 m², 267 946.7 m³   (d) 84.9 cm², 73.6 cm³
    (e) 3629.8 m², 20 569.1 m³   (f) 51 445.8 cm², 1 097 509.5 cm³
2. S.A. = 2386.4 cm², V = 9838.7 cm³
3. (a) S.A. of cube is 2400 cm²   (b) S.A. of sphere is 1256 cm²   (c) 157 : 300

EXERCISE 11.14

1. 1400 m   2. 0.35 m³   3. 24.56 m   4. (a) 4534.2 m²   (b) 28 716.3 m³
5. P = 60 m, A = 111 m²   6. 278 m   7. 5 m³
8. 6.868 75 m³   9. 9914 cm³   10. 26.8 m²   11. 526.24 m²   12. 10

EXERCISE 11.15

2. (a) Toronto   (b) Los Angeles   (c) Uranium City
    (d) Fredericton   (e) Churchill   (f) Vancouver
    (g) Moncton   (h) Montreal   (i) Hamilton
    (j) Halifax   (k) Winnipeg   (l) Calgary
3. 7 and 21
4. (a) Her brother assumed an equal length of time for both trips.
    (b) 48 km/h
5. (b)   6. 60 cm long, 30 cm wide
7. 48   8. Yes   9. $25.05   10. 15
11. One pizza with a diameter of 40 cm.
14. $420.60   15. 3000
16. The sequence decreases alternately by 2 and 3. Next number: 8.

11.16 REVIEW EXERCISE

1. (a) 97.8 m   (b) 263.76 m   (c) 148.8 cm   (d) 74.84 cm
2. (a) 1575 cm²   (b) 1728 m²   (c) 78.44 cm²   (d) 5696 m²
3. (a) 5805.86 cm²   (b) 104.52 m²   4. (a) 432 cm²   (b) 1970.4 m²
5. (a) 1055.0 cm²   (b) 238.6 m²   6. (a) 6137.208 m³   (b) 38 016 cm³

7. $1877\frac{1}{3}$ cm³

8. 16 729.9 m³

9. (a) V $= 1674\frac{2}{3}$ m³, S.A. $= 906.5$ m²

(b) V $= 113\ 040$ m³, S.A. $= 11\ 304$ m²

10. (a) 28.5 m²

(b) 7 m²

(c) 4

11. (a) 1 046 863 440 000 km³ (Earth), 20 569 093 330 km³ (moon)

(b) 51

11.17 CHAPTER 11 TEST

1. (a) 105 cm
(b) 62.8 cm

2. (a) 6300 m²
(b) 379.94 m²
(c) 299.7 m²

3. (a) S.A. $= 4408$ cm², V $= 19\ 448$ cm³

(b) S.A. $= 11\ 329.12$ m², V $= 91\ 185.6$ m³

(c) S.A. $= 20\ 096$ cm², V $= 267\ 946\frac{2}{3}$ cm³

(d) S.A. $= 3520.3$ m², V $= 12\ 560$ m³

REVIEW AND PREVIEW TO CHAPTER 12

MEASURING, DRAWING, AND CLASSIFYING ANGLES

1. (a) 30°
(b) 70°
(c) 70°
(d) 50°
(e) 60°
(f) 85°

(g) 145°
(h) 110°
(i) 165°

2. (a) 20°
(b) 15°
(c) 45°
(d) 48°
(e) 85°
(f) 78°

(g) 165°
(h) 103°
(i) 118°

4. (a) 49°
(b) 35°
(c) 6°
(d) 83°

5. (a) 124°
(b) 74°
(c) 167°
(d) 86°
(e) 90°
(f) 1°

6. (a) acute
(b) obtuse
(c) straight
(d) reflex

(e) right
(f) right
(g) acute
(h) obtuse

7. (a) x $= 104°$, y $= 76°$, z $= 104°$
(b) x $= 147°$

CLASSIFYING TRIANGLES

1. (a) isosceles
(b) isosceles
(c) right
(d) obtuse

2. (a) equilateral
(b) scalene
(c) isosceles
(d) isosceles

EXERCISE 12.1

1. (a) x $= 64°$
(b) y $= 151°$
(c) x $= 70°$, y $= 70°$
(d) t $= 106°$

2. (a) x $= 90°$, y $= 59°$, z $= 149°$, t $= 121°$
(b) x $= 52°$, y $= 67°$, w $= 119°$

(c) x $= 57°$, y $= 57°$, z $= 123°$, t $= 37°$
(d) x $= 55°$, y $= 85°$, z $= 95°$

(e) x $= 18°$, y $= 81°$, m $= 53.5°$, n $= 53.5°$

4. (a) 90°
(b) 108°
(c) 120°

EXERCISE 12.2

1. (a) (i) SAS
(ii) HS
(iii) ASA
(iv) SSS

(b) (i) $\angle B = \angle E$, $\angle C = \angle F$, BC $=$ EF
(ii) $\angle A = \angle R$, $\angle C = \angle N$, AB $=$ RM

(iii) $\angle R = \angle P$, SR $=$ QP, RT $=$ PW
(iv) $\angle A = \angle G$, $\angle B = \angle H$, $\angle C = \angle K$

2. (a) ASA, x $= 2.5$, y $= 2.0$
(b) SSS, x $= 40°$, y $= 65°$, z $= 75°$

3. (a) AB $=$ DE, $\angle ABC = \angle DEF$, BC $=$ EF, $\triangle ABC \cong \triangle DEF$ (SAS)

(b) $\angle ADB = \angle ADC$, AB $=$ AC, AD $=$ AD, $\triangle ABC \cong \triangle ADC$ (HS)

4. (a) (i) ASA
(ii) ASA
(iii) ASA
(iv) HS
(v) SSS
(vi) HS

(b) (i) SR $=$ SQ, RT $=$ QT, $\angle SRT = \angle SQT$

(ii) AB $=$ DE, CD $=$ CB, $\angle ABC = \angle EDC$

(iii) $\angle BAD = \angle DCB$, AB $=$ CD, AD $=$ CB

(iv) SM $=$ TM, $\angle MSR = \angle MTR$, $\angle SRM = \angle TRM$

(v) $\angle XYW = \angle ZYW$, $\angle XWY = \angle ZWY$, $\angle WXY = \angle WZY$

(vi) BC $=$ DC, $\angle BAC = \angle DAC$, $\angle BCA = \angle DCA$

EXERCISE 12.6

3. (a) a = 110°, b = 70°, c = 110°, d = 70°, e = 110°, f = 70°, g = 110°
   (b) m = 110°, r = 70°, s = 110°, t = 70°, x = 70°, y = 110°, z = 70°
   (c) a = 120°, b = 60°, c = 120°, d = 120°, e = 60°
   (d) x = 75°, y = 105°, z = 75°
4. (a) x = 95°, y = 35°, z = 50°   (b) x = 90°, y = 90°, z = 90°
   (c) x = 23°, y = 32°   (d) x = 45°, y = 80°, z = 55°
   (e) x = 31°, y = 108°, z = 77°   (f) x = 70°, y = 80°, z = 30°
   (g) x = 70°, y = 50°, z = 70°   (h) x = 50°, y = 70°, z = 60°, w = 70°

EXERCISE 12.9

1. (a) OA   (b) CD   (c) CE   (d) CFE   (e) AOD   (f) CAD
4. Connect the hospitals with two straight lines and construct the right bisectors of these lines. The point of intersection of these lines is where to locate the Emergency Station.
5. Construct two non-parallel chords and the right bisectors of these chords. The point of intersection of the bisectors locates the centre of the fort from which the radius may be determined.

EXERCISE 12.10

4. (a) x = 35°   (b) x = 40°   (c) y = 90°   (d) x = 300°
   (e) t = 55°   (f) m = 30°   (g) y = 25°   (h) m = 41°, n = 32°
5. (a) x = 20°, y = 40°   (b) x = 90°, y = 90°, z = 50°
   (c) x = 25°, y = 25°, z = 25°   (d) x = 50°, y = 50°
   (e) x = 62°, y = 47°, t = 37°, m = 71°   (f) x = 61°, y = 52°, m = 113°

EXERCISE 12.11

3. (a) x = 106°, y = 88°
   (b) x = 110°, y = 70°
   (c) x = 95°, y = 85°, z = 45°
   (d) a = 88°, b = 92°, c = 89°, d = 91°
   (e) a = 96°, b = 92°, c = 84°, d = 88°, e = 92°, f = 96°
4. (a) x = 37°, y = 26°, z = 26°
   (b) x = 21°, y = 21°, r = 68°, t = 138°, m = 47°
   (c) x = 29°, y = 31°, s = 38°, t = 38°, m = 111°

EXERCISE 12.12

1. e = 8, d = 12   2. x = 4, z = 3   3. p = 6, q = 9   4. $x = 6\frac{2}{3}$, $y = 15\frac{5}{9}$
5. d = 2, e = $2\frac{1}{2}$, x = 60°   6. a = $6\frac{2}{5}$, b = $8\frac{4}{5}$ 7. a = 3, d = 5   8. e = 3, f = 4
9. 12.4 m   10. 62.7 m   11. 164.2 m   12. 42.9 m

EXERCISE 12.13

1. (a) the turtle turns 30° clockwise   (b) the turtle turns 45° counter-clockwise
   (c) the turtle turns 270° clockwise   (d) the turtle moves 100 units forward
   (e) the turtle moves 25 units backward   (f) the turtle turns 100° counter-clockwise
2. (a) equilateral triangle of side 100 units   (b) rectangle with dimensions 100 units by 50 units
3. (a) equilateral triangle of side 100 units   (b) regular polygon with 60 (equal) sides of 2 units
   (c) regular polygon with 90 (equal) sides of 1 unit   (d) regular polygon with 120 (equal) sides of 1 unit
   (e) regular polygon with 180 (equal) sides of 1 unit   (f) regular polygon with 360 (equal) sides of 1 unit
4. a 32 point star

EXERCISE 12.14

1. (a) 16   (b) 25   (c) 36   (d) 49   (e) 31 741 956   (f) n^2
2. 1 cm^2 3. $\angle 1 + \angle 2 + \angle 3 = 360°$
4. 14 possibilities (provided the bags are not distinguishable)
5. 65   6. (a) 174   (b) 173   (c) 177 .
7. $1.69 (3 quarters, 9 dimes, and 4 pennies)   8. February and March
9. (a) 64 m   (b) $814.91   (c) 32 posts   (d) $496   (e) $1740.91
10. $64 = 9 + 15 + 4 + 36$
11. 343   12. 24 cm   14. 126.1 km

12.15 REVIEW EXERCISE

5. (a) $x = 65°$, $y = 69°$, $z = 46°$ (b) $x = 55°$, $y = 55°$, $z = 25°$
   (c) $x = 50°$, $y = 40°$, $z = 50°$ (d) $x = 61°$, $y = 71°$, $z = 48°$
   (e) $x = 57°$, $y = 123°$, $z = 57°$ (f) $x = 99°$, $y = 81°$, $z = 99°$
   (g) $x = 47°$, $y = 48°$, $z = 48°$ (h) $x = 50°$, $y = 20°$
   (i) $x = 35°$, $y = 98°$, $z = 82°$ (j) $x = 70°$, $y = 25°$, $z = 25°$
   (k) $x = 33°$, $y = 82°$, $z = 98°$ (l) $x = 99°$, $y = 81°$, $z = 111°$
6. (a) $x = 4$, $y = 4$ (b) $x = 42°$, $y = 276°$, $z = 42°$
   (c) $x = 90°$, $y = 50°$, $z = 40°$ (d) $x = 45°$, $y = 90°$, $z = 45°$
   (e) $x = 60°$, $y = 120°$, $z = 240°$ (f) $x = 52°$, $y = 52°$, $z = 52°$
   (g) $x = 32.5°$, $y = 100°$, $z = 17.5°$ (h) $x = 65°$, $y = 65°$, $z = 65°$
   (i) $x = 45°$, $y = 45°$ (j) $x = 45°$
7. (a) $a = 2$, $x = 43°$ (b) $x = 25°$, $d = 9\frac{3}{5}$ (c) $b = 11.6$

8. (c) $\dfrac{AE}{AC} = \dfrac{AD}{AB} = \dfrac{DE}{BC} = \dfrac{1}{2}$

12.16 CHAPTER 12 TEST

1. (a) $x = 159°$, $y = 92°$, $w = 53°$ (b) $x = 30°$
   (c) $x = 115°$ (d) $x = 108°$, $y = 108°$, $z = 108°$, $w = 72°$
2. (a) (i) SSS   (ii) $\angle ABC = \angle ADC$, $\angle BAC = \angle DAC$, $\angle BCA = \angle DCA$
   (b) (i) SAS   (ii) $PQ = TS$, $\angle P = \angle T$, $\angle Q = \angle S$
3. $x = 9.6$, $y = 8.75$

12.17 CUMULATIVE REVIEW FOR CHAPTERS 9 TO 12

1. 110, 111, 112, 113   2. 88 m by 45 m   3. 21 dimes
4. (a) $1400   (b) $60   5. $9.30 Canadian
6. 1200 km   7. 4 h   8. (b) 22 400 people
9. If the population being sampled is spread out over a very large area, for instance, the whole country, then long distance charges would make a telephone survey too costly. The cost of mailing a questionnaire is constant throughout all regions of a country.
11. (a) 26, 27, 27   (b) 171, 174, no mode
12. (a) $\frac{1}{12}$ (b) $\frac{1}{4}$
13. (a) 52 m   (b) 75.4 cm
14. (a) 314 m^2 (to nearest one)   (b) 134.4 cm^2
   (c) 96.2 m^2 (to nearest tenth)   (d) 57 m^2
15. (a) 527.5 cm^2 (b) 392.8 m^2
16. (a) 803.8 cm^3 (b) 523 333.3 cm^3
17. (a) $r = 81°$, $s = 57°$, $t = 42°$ (b) $x = 79°$, $y = 61°$, $z = 40°$
   (c) $x = 42°$ (d) $x = 101°$, $y = 41°$, $z = 38°$
18. (a) $a = 6\frac{6}{7}$, $b = 8\frac{4}{7}$ (b) $r = 10\frac{10}{17}$, $s = 11\frac{3}{17}$

REVIEW AND PREVIEW TO CHAPTER 13

SET NOTATION

1. (b) {0, 1, 2, 3, 4}   (c) {−1, 0, 1, 2, 3, ...}   (d) {..., −3, −2, −1}   (e) {..., −2, −1, 0, 1, 2, 3, 4}
   (f) {3, 4, 5, 6}   (g) {1, 2, 3, 4, 5, 6, 7, 8}   (h) {−1, 0, 1, 2}   (i) {−4, −3, −2, −1}

THE PYTHAGOREAN THEOREM

1. (a) 9.2 cm   (b) 8.1 m   (c) 13.9 cm   (d) 31.9 m

EXERCISE 13.1

1. (b) {(3, 1), (4, 2), (5, 3), (6, 4), (7, 5)}
   (c) The number of triangles is 2 less than the number of sides.
   (d) $t = n − 2$ (e) $t = 12$
2. (b) (i) {(1, 4), (2, 8), (3, 12), (4, 16)} (ii) {(1, 1), (2, 4), (3, 9), (4, 16)}
   (c) $P = 4n$ (d) 84
   (e) $A = n^2$ (f) 361
3. (a) $E = 9.75h$ (b) $224.25   (e) 80 h
4. (a) $y = −x + 10$ (b) $y = x − 2$ (c) $y = x^2$ (d) $y = x − 1$

EXERCISE 13.2

1. (a) {−2, −1, 0, 1}   (b) {0, 1, 2, 3}   (c) {−2}   (d) {0, 1, 2, 3}
   (e) {−1, 0, 1}
2. (a) {3, 5, 7, 9}   (b) {2, 4, 6, 8}   (c) {1}   (d) {1, 4}
   (e) {−2, −1, 1, 2}
3. (a) 6   (b) −3   (c) 4   (d) 0   (e) −15   (f) 15
   (g) −6   (h) −21
4. (a) 7   (b) 1   (c) −1   (d) 3   (e) −7   (f) −3
   (g) 4   (h) −1
5. (b) (i) {(0, −2), (1, 1), (2, 4), (3, 7)}
        (ii) {(−2, 3), (−1, 2), (0, 1), (1, 0), (2, −1)}
        (iii) {(−1, 2), (0, 0), (1, 2), (2, 8), (3, 18)}
        (iv) {(0, 0), (2, $\frac{3}{2}$), (4, 3), (6, $\frac{9}{2}$), (8, 6)}
        (v) {(0, 0), (5, 1), (10, 2), (15, 3)}
6. (a) $x − 5$ (b) $2x$ (c) $\frac{1}{3}x$ (d) $5x + 3$ (e) $\frac{1}{2}x − 1$
7. (a) $3x$, {1, 2, 3, 4}   (b) $x − 2$, {2, 3, 4, 5}   (c) x^2, {1, 2, 3, 4}
   (d) $\frac{x}{2}$, {−2, −4, −6, −8}   (e) $x + 1$, {−1, 0, 1, 2}   (f) x^2, {−3, −2, 2, 3}
8. (b) {−7, −2, 3, 8, 13}   9. (b) {1, 2, 3, 4, 5}

EXERCISE 13.3

1. (a) A(1, 4), B(0, 2), C(6, 1), D(4, 0), E(1, −1), F(6, −2), G(0, −6), H(−1, −4), I(−1, −1), J(−2, 0), K(−6, −3),
   L(−6, 1), M(−3, 2), N(−1, 7), O(−4, 5), P(0, 6).
   (b) L, M   (c) P, B, G, Q   (d) A, E
2. (a) (−1, −2), (0, −2), (1, −2)   (b) (0, 2), (1, 1), (2, 0)   (c) (−1, −1), (0, 2), (1, 5)
3. (a) AB: 10, CD: 5, EF: 2, GH: 3   (b) AB: (−1, 4), CD: (−7, −1.5), EF: (0, 1), GH: (5, −1.5)
4. RIGHT ON!
5. (b) (0, $\frac{3}{2}$), (3, 3), (−9, −3)
6. (a) triangle   (b) right angle triangle   (c) rectangle
   (d) parallelogram   (e) hexagon
7. (b) (1, −2)   8. (b) (6, 3) or (−6, −1)
9. (c) (5, 0), (0, −5), (3, 4), (−3, −4)   10. MATH IS FUN?

EXERCISE 13.4

1. (a) 10   (b) 2   (c) -2 (d) 3   (e) 2   (f) $\frac{1}{2}$
2. (a) $y = 5x$ (b) $y = 3x$ (c) $y = \frac{1}{2}x$
3. (a) $y = x + 1$ (b) $y = 2x$ (c) $y = -x$ (d) $y = x - 3$

EXERCISE 13.5

1. (b) (3, 6)
2. $(-3, -10)$
3. (b) They are concurrent at (0, 3).
4. They are concurrent at $(1, -2)$.
5. (b) a parallelogram

EXERCISE 13.6

1. (c) (i) \$22.50   (ii) \$41.25   (d) \$67.50
2. (c) 15:00, 200 km
   (d) 40 km (apart at 13:00), 10 km (apart at 14:30)
   (e) 14:00 (20 km apart), 14:45 (5 km apart)
3. (a) Train A 08:00, Train B 08:00, Train C 14:00
   (b) Train A 16:00, Train B 18:30, Train C 19:00
   (c) 12:10   (d) 14:40   (e) 30 min
   (f) 2   (g) 50 km/h   (h) 100 km/h
   (i) 200 km   (j) 200 km
   (k) Train A 8 h, Train B $10\frac{1}{2}$ h, Train C 5 h
   (l) 100 km   (m) 125 km   (n) 275 km

EXERCISE 13.7

1. AB: 1, CD: $\frac{1}{4}$, EF: 0, GH: -1, JK: $-\frac{5}{2}$, MN: $\frac{1}{4}$
2. (a) 1   (b) $\frac{5}{4}$ (c) $\frac{2}{9}$ (d) $\frac{4}{5}$ (e) $\frac{3}{2}$ (f) $\frac{3}{2}$
   (g) $\frac{9}{5}$ (h) -5 (i) $-\frac{1}{2}$ (j) 0
3. (c) They are parallel.   (d) Each line has slope $\frac{2}{3}$.
4. (b) AB has slope $\frac{1}{3}$, PQ has slope -3.   (c) The product is -1.
   (d) Yes
5. (a) PR has slope $-\frac{1}{2}$, QS has slope 2.
   (b) The product of the slopes of the diagonals is -1 and so the diagonals are perpendicular.

EXERCISE 13.8

1. (a) $\sqrt{10}$ (b) 3   (c) $\sqrt{5}$ (d) $\sqrt{26}$ (e) 5   (f) $2\sqrt{5}$
   (g) $5\sqrt{2}$ (h) $\sqrt{89}$
2. (a) Two sides of length $2\sqrt{5}$ and two of length 8.
   (b) $2\sqrt{13}$ and $2\sqrt{29}$ (c) parallelogram
3. Yes, it is the midpoint.
7. (a) $a = 4\sqrt{5}$, $b = 2\sqrt{5}$, $c = 10$

EXERCISE 13.9

1. (a) (i) \$250   (ii) \$300   (iii) \$350   (iv) \$450

(b) $700   (c) $200   (d) $25

2. (b) (i) 62 km/h   (ii) 115 km/h   3. (b) 20 g

4. (b) 15.5 cm   (c) 7.1 cm   (d) 21.1 cm

(e) 17.8 cm   (f) 1.4   (g) d = 1.4s

EXERCISE 13.10

1. (c) approximately 3.2 cm   2. (c) 2.4 h   3. (c) approximately 1.7   (d) 1.25

4. (c) circle

EXERCISE 13.11

1. (a) No   (b) Yes   (c) No   (d) No

2. (c) 30 s   3. (a) (i) $9.30   (ii) $12.50   (iii) $18.90   (c) approximately 9 km

4. (a) 150   (b) 750

5. (a) (i) $6.95   (ii) $13.90   (iii) $34.75   (c) approximately 1.4 kg

6. (c) $5\frac{1}{2}$ h

7. (b) $140.00   (c) $50.00   (d) $30.00

EXERCISE 13.12

1. $(x + y)^2 = x^2 + y^2 + 2xy$ 2. 92

3. (a) Yes   (b) x% of y is the same as y% of x.

4. (a) 3 min   (b) 4 min   (c) No speed is fast enough.

6. $21.25

8. If the one integer is n, then we must add 2n + 1 to the square of n to obtain $(n + 1)^2$ — the square of the next consecutive integer.

10. $25.75

11. (a) 404, 414, 424, 434, 444, 454, 464, 474, 484, 494

(b) 181, 262, 343, 424, 505

13. Approximately 6 km.

14. In each of the numbers, the first two digits form a number that is the product of the second two digits.

EXERCISE 13.13

1. (a) D = {−1, −2. −3, −4}, R = {1, 4, 9, 16}   (b) D = {3, 4, 5, 6}, R = {5}

(c) D = {5, 6, 7}, R = {10, 12, 14}   (d) D = {2}, R = {2, 4, 8}

(e) D = {−3, −2, −1, 0, 1, 2}, R = {−2, −1, 0, 1, 2, 3}

(f) D = {−3, −2, −1, 0, 1, 2}, R = {−2, −1, 0, 1, 2, 3}

2. (a) 7, −8, 1, −2, 1   (b) −4, 3, 0, −1, 8

3. (a) (0, 3), (3, 4), (−9, 0)   (b) (−1, −2), (0, −2), (1, −2)   (c) (−2, 0), (0, −3), (−4, 3)

7. (6, −1)

8. (a) 1   (b) −1   (c) −1   (d) 4   (e) $\frac{1}{5}$ (f) 0

(g) 1   (h) $-\frac{3}{4}$

9. They all lie on the line y = −2x + 11.

10. Both segments have slope 1.

11. (a) 7   (b) $\sqrt{2}$ (c) $\sqrt{82}$ (d) $\sqrt{61}$ (e) $\sqrt{37}$ (f) $\sqrt{202}$

12. No   13. Yes

14. (b) 119.3 cm   (c) 25.5 cm   (d) 3.14   (e) C = 3.14d

15. (a) (0, 3), (1, 4), (−1, 4), (2, 7), (−2, 7)

(c) 1.4 and −1.4   (d) 3.25

16. (a) 4.5 h   (c) 2 t

4. (4, 1)   5. $\frac{6}{5}$ 6. 13   7. (b) $6.50   (c) 27 h

REVIEW AND PREVIEW TO CHAPTER 14

SLIDES, FLIPS, AND TURNS

1. (a) (i) flip image   (ii) slide image   (iii) neither   (iv) flip image
   (b) (i) slide image   (ii) neither   (iii) flip image   (iv) flip image
2. (a) (i) turn image   (ii) slide image   (iii) turn image   (iv) neither
   (b) (i) turn image   (ii) turn image   (iii) slide image   (iv) turn image
3. (a) (i) slide image   (ii) flip image   (iii) flip image   (iv) neither
   (b) (i) flip image   (ii) flip image   (iii) slide image   (iv) neither
4. (a) flips   (b) slides   (c) turns or flips
   (d) slides   (e) turns   (f) flips
5. (a) (i) flip image   (ii) turn image   (iii) slide image   (iv) turn image
   (b) (i) flip image   (ii) turn image   (iii) flip image   (iv) slide image
   (c) (i) turn image   (ii) flip image   (iii) turn image   (iv) slide image
   (d) (i) flip image   (ii) slide image   (iii) turn image   (iv) turn image
   (e) (i) turn image   (ii) flip image   (iii) flip image   (iv) flip image
   (f) (i) slide image   (ii) flip image   (iii) turn image   (iv) slide image
   (g) (i) slide image   (ii) flip image   (iii) flip image   (iv) turn image

EXERCISE 14.1

1. (a) The translation moves every point to the left 3 and up 2.
   (b) The translation moves every point to the right 2 and down 7.
   (c) The translation moves every point down 1.
   (d) The translation moves every point to the left 2 and down 3.
   (e) The translation moves every point to the right 7.
   (f) The translation moves every point to the left 5 and up 8.
   (g) The translation moves every point to the right 5 and down 9.
   (h) The translation moves every point to the right 4.
   (i) The translation moves every point to the left 1 and down 2.
   (j) The translation moves every point to the right 4 and up 3.
   (k) The translation moves every point down 8.
   (l) The translation moves every point to the right 1 and up 1.
2. AB = [3, −5], CD = [2, 2], EF = [4, −1], GH = [5, 0], MN = [−4, −2], PQ = [−1, −4], TV = [0, −5], XY = [0, 3]
3. (a) (x + 7, y + 3)   (b) (x + 10, y)   (c) (x + 2, y − 5)
   (d) (x − 6, y − 3)   (e) (x − 9, y + 2)   (f) (x, y + 5)
5. (a) (x, y) → (x − 3, y − 2)   (b) (x, y) → (x + 4, y − 3)   (c) (x, y) → (x + 5, y + 2)
   (d) (x, y) → (x + 2, y − 2)   (e) (x, y) → (x − 1, y)   (f) (x, y) → (x − 2, y − 2)
7. (a) A′(5, 6), B′(2, 8), C′(0, 3)   (b) A″(4, 8), B″(1, 10), C″(−1, 5)   (c) (x, y) → (x + 3, y + 7)

EXERCISE 14.2

3. (a) R′(5, −4), S′(6, 0), T′(−3, −1)   (b) R′(−5, 4), S′(−6, 0), T′(3, 1)
4. (a) A′(6, 3), B′(5, 0), C′(1, 0), D′(−3, 6)   (b) A′(−4, 1), B′(−3, 4), C′(1, 4), D′(5, −2)
5. (a) x = 1   (b) x = 0   (c) y = 0

EXERCISE 14.3

1. (a) A′(3, 0), B′(5, −3), C′(4, 4), D′(−5, 3), E′(−2, 0), F′(−4, −4), G′(0, −3), H′(0, 5)
   (b) A′(−3, 0), B′(−5, 3), C′(−4, −4), D′(5, −3), E′(2, 0), F′(4, 4), G′(0, 3), H′(0, −5)
   (c) A′(0, −3), B′(−3, −5), C′(4, −4), D′(3, 5), E′(0, 2), F′(−4, 4), G′(−3, 0), H′(5, 0)

2. A′(2, −5), B′(3, 0), C′(0, 3)
6. (a) (−4, −3), 180°
   (c) (−5, 3), 180°

3. D′(−2, −3), E′(1, −5), F′(4, 2)
(b) (4, 1), 90° counter-clockwise
(d) (4, −5), 90° counter-clockwise

EXERCISE 14.4

1. (a) (2, −3) (b) (0, 2) (c) (2, 4) (d) (4, 0) (e) (2, −1)
2. (a) (x, y) → (−x, y) (b) (x, y) → (−x, −y) (c) (x, y) → (−y, x) (d) (x, y) → (x, −y)
   (e) (x, y) → (y, −x) (f) (x, y) → (−y, x) (g) (x, y) → (x, −y) (h) (x, y) → (−x, −y)
   (i) (x, y) → (−x, y) (j) (x, y) → (y, −x)
3. (a) A′(3, −1), B′(6, −2), C′(5, −5) (b) A′(1, −3), B′(2, −6), C′(5, −5)
   (c) A′(−3, 1), B′(−6, 2), C′(−5, 5) (d) A′(−3, −1), B′(−6, −2), C′(−5, −5)
   (e) A′(−1, 3), B′(−2, 6), C′(−5, 5)
4. D′(3, −4), E′(5, −1), F′(0, 0)
5. (b) A′(2, 1), B′(5, 2), C′(6, 4) (c) (x, y) → (y, x)
6. (b) R′(−7, 1), S′(−5, 3), T′(−3, 2) (c) (x, y) → (−y, −x)

EXERCISE 14.5

2. (b) A′(−6, 6), B′(0, 15), C′(9, 9)
5. (b) $\frac{9}{2}$
   (d) 18
6. Answers will vary.
7. (a) (x, y) → ($\frac{1}{3}$x, $\frac{1}{3}$y)
   (b) Area of △PQR: 67.5
      Area of △P′Q′R′: 7.5

3. (b) R′(−10, 4), S′(4, 6), T′(−2, −8)
(c) A′(2, −2), B′(−4, −2), C′(2, 4)
(e) 4

(c) $\frac{1}{9}$

EXERCISE 14.6

1. air speed: 242 km/h, course: W7°S
2. actual speed: 19.6 km/h
   direction: upstream, 11.5° with a perpendicular to the river
3. (a) N11.5°W (b) 245 km/h
4. (a) upstream, 24° with a perpendicular to the river (b) 18 km/h
5. (a) N39°W (b) 335 km/h 6. (a) E44°S (b) 202 km/h
7. Direction (relative to the ground) S68°W
   Speed (relative to the ground) 190 km/h
8. course: S37°E
9. course: N54°E
   ground speed: 187 km/h

EXERCISE 14.9

1. 1, 2, and 5 2. 4 3. 8 4. Answers will vary.
5. 13
6. rectangles, trapezoids, and isosceles right triangles (in addition to those supplied in the problem)
8. 6 cm 9. 27 10. 16
11. (a) $\frac{1}{2}$ (b) $\frac{1}{3}$ (c) $\frac{1}{4}$ (d) $\frac{1}{5}$ (e) $\frac{1}{100}$
12. 42 cm² 14. 129, 387, and 465 16. 65°
17. 9 and 9, 2 and 47 19. 72 cm²

14.10 REVIEW EXERCISE

1. AB = [5, 2], CD = [1, −3], EF = [−4, 1], GH = [5, −1], NM = [−3, 0]
4. (a) (x, y) → (x + 5, y + 7) (b) (x, y) → (x + 6, y + 6)

(c) $(x, y) \rightarrow (x - 13, y + 10)$ (d) $(x, y) \rightarrow (x + 4, y - 6)$

6. The image has vertices: A'(3, 2), B'(8, 2), C'(4, −5)
7. The image has vertices: D'(−5, −3), E'(3, −6), F'(1, 0)
8. (a) A'(−2, 2), B'(−1, −4), C'(3, −5), D'(2, 5), E'(0, 3), F'(3, 0), G'(0, −3), H'(−3, 0)
   (b) A'(−2, −2), B'(4, −1), C'(5, 3), D'(−5, 2), E'(−3, 0), F'(0, 3), G'(3, 0), H'(0, −3)
   (c) A'(−2, 2), B'(−1, −4), C'(3, −5), D'(2, 5), E'(0, 3), F'(3, 0), G'(0, −3), H'(−3, 0)
10. The image has vertices: A'(−2, 0), B'(−5, 0), C'(−4, −6)
11. The image has vertices: R'(−5, −4), S'(2, −4), T'(2, 0)
12. (a) $(x, y) \rightarrow (-x, y)$ (b) $(x, y) \rightarrow (x, -y)$
    (c) $(x, y) \rightarrow (-x, -y)$ (d) $(x, y) \rightarrow (-y, x)$
    (e) $(x, y) \rightarrow (y, -x)$ (f) $(x, y) \rightarrow (-x, -y)$
13. The image has vertices: A'(−1, 1), B'(−1, 6), C'(−5, 1)
15. (b) The image has vertices: D'(6, 12), E'(−4, 2), F'(−2, −8)
16. The image has vertices: A'(−2, −1), B'(3, 3), C'(−3, 4)

14.11 CHAPTER 14 TEST

1. The image has vertices: R'(4, −2), S'(0, −1), T'(3, −7)
2. (a) The image has vertices: G'(3, −4), H'(−1, −6), K'(1, 4)
   (b) The image has vertices: G'(−3, 4), H'(1, 6), K'(−1, −4)
3. The image has vertices: P'(2, −2), Q'(2, −7), R'(5, −7)
4. The image has vertices: A'(−2, −2), B'(3, −2), C'(3, 4)
5. The image has vertices: D'(−3, −9), E'(12, 6), F'(0, −9)

14.12 YEAR–END REVIEW

1. (a) 1 293 253   (b) 93 440   (c) 1369   (d) 25   (e) 832.5
2. (a) 15   (b) 29   (c) 1   (d) −15
   (e) 14   (f) 50   (g) 20   (h) 60
3. (a) −6   (b) −7   (c) 7   (d) 23
   (e) 0   (f) 20   (g) 4   (h) 144
4. (a) x   (b) −4x   (c) 11x + 22   (d) 11x   (e) $x^2 + 11x$
5. (a) −5   (b) 28   (c) 3   (d) 35   (e) 0   (f) −4
6. (a) 3.52×10^4 (b) 1.25×10^5 (c) 3.75×10^{-2}
   (d) 4.25×10^{-3} (e) 1.45×10^6 (f) 8.75×10^{-4}
7. (a) $1\frac{1}{6}$ (b) $1\frac{3}{8}$ (c) $\frac{3}{4}$ (d) $1\frac{7}{8}$ (e) $1\frac{1}{10}$ (f) $6\frac{5}{12}$
8. (a) $6\frac{1}{8}$ (b) $\frac{9}{14}$ (c) $8\frac{5}{32}$ (d) $2\frac{1}{4}$ (e) 6   (f) $4\frac{1}{2}$
9. (a) 2 : 3   (b) 4 : 5 : 8   10. (a) 11.25   (b) 8   11. 18%
12. (a) 12   (b) 16   (c) 90   (d) 252
13. (a) $179   (b) $716
14. $272 727.27, $136 363.64, $90 909.09
15. (a) 18.0 cm   (b) 36.6 cm   (c) 5.4 cm   (d) 8.1 cm
16. (a) $13x^2 - 4x$ (b) $2xy - 12x^2y + xy^2$
17. (a) $2xy^2 - 4y$ (b) $3a^2 - b^2$
18. (a) (x − 6)(x + 3)   (b) (x + 4)(x + 4)   (c) (t − 10)(t + 10)   (d) (2x − 1)(x + 3)
19. (a) t = 7   (b) m = 2   (c) t = 14   (d) m = 6.5
20. (a) x ⩾ 3   (b) t > −13
21. 3200 km
22. (a) 46, 45, 50   (b) 90.5, 90.5, 90, and 91
23. (a) 114.4 m, 419.6 m²   (b) 42.8 cm, 100.3 cm²
24. 678.2 cm², 1356.5 cm³
25. (a) t = 61°, y = 89°, x = 61°, z = 30°   (b) x = 44°, y = 22°
26. (a) $\frac{3}{2}$, 7.2 units   (b) $\frac{13}{2}$, 13.2 units
27. (a) A'(−3, 4), B'(1, 5), C'(−1, 10)   (b) A'(−1, 1), B'(−5, 2), C'(−3, 7)
    (c) A'(1, 1), B'(−3, 0), C'(−1, −5)

GLOSSARY

acute angle   An angle whose measure is between 0° and 90°.

acute triangle   A triangle with all angles acute.

additive inverse   The additive inverse of a real number, a, is $(-a)$ such that
$$a + (-a) = -a + a$$
$$= 0$$

adjacent angles   Two angles with a common vertex, a common side, and no interior points in common.

alternate angles   Two angles between two lines on opposite sides of a transversal.

altitude of a triangle   A line from a vertex, perpendicular to the opposite side.

angle   A figure formed by two rays with a common endpoint called the vertex.

angle bisector   A ray that divides an angle into two angles having the same measure.

area   The number of unit squares contained in a region.

average   The average of n numbers is the sum of the numbers divided by n.

axiom   A statement that is assumed to be true; also called a postulate.

axis   A number line used for reference in locating points on a coordinate plane.

axis of symmetry   A line that is invariant under a reflection.

bar graph   A graph using bars to represent data.

base of a trapezoid   One of the parallel sides of a trapezoid.

BASIC   Beginners All-purpose Symbolic Instruction Code is a computer language.

binomial   A polynomial consisting of two terms.

broken line graph   A graph using line segments to represent data.

central angle of a circle   An angle subtended by an arc of a circle with the vertex at the centre.

centroid   The point of intersection of the three medians of a triangle.

chord of a circle   A line segment having its endpoints on the circumference.

circle   The set of all points in the plane that are equidistant from a fixed point called the centre.

circle graph   A graph using sectors of a circle to represent data.

circumcentre   The centre of the circle, which passes through the three vertices of a triangle.

circumference   The perimeter of a circle.

circumscribed circle   A circle is circumscribed about a polygon if all the vertices of the polygon lie on the circle.

collinear points   Points that lie in the same straight line.

complementary angles   Two angles whose sum is 90°.

concentric circles   Circles having the same centre.

conditional statement   A statement that can be written in an "if ... then" form.

congruent angles   Angles with the same measure.

congruent figures   Two figures are congruent if they are equal in all respects; there exists an isometry that maps one figure onto the other.

consecutive even (odd) numbers   Numbers obtained by counting by twos from any even (odd) number.

consecutive numbers   Numbers obtained by counting by ones from any given number.

construction   The process of drawing a geometric figure using only ruler and compass.

coordinate   A real number paired with a point on a number line.

coordinate plane   A one-to-one pairing of all ordered pairs of real numbers with all points of a plane. Also called the Cartesian coordinate plane.

corollary   A theorem that follows directly from the proof of another theorem.

degree   A unit of angle measure equal to $\frac{1}{360}$ of a rotation.

degree of a monomial   The sum of the exponents of the variables.

degree of a polynomial   The largest sum of the exponents of all the variables in any one term of the polynomial.

diagonal   A line segment with endpoints on two non-adjacent vertices of a polygon.

diameter of a circle   A chord that contains the centre of the circle. The largest chord.

dilatation A transformation that maps each point of a figure to an image point so that for a centre C and a point P, CP' = k(CP) where k is the scale factor.

direct variation A function defined by a function of the form y = kx.

distance from a point to a line The length of the perpendicular segment drawn from the point to the line.

domain of a variable The set of numbers that can serve as replacements for a variable.

END command A BASIC program command which halts the execution of a program.

equation An open sentence formed by two expressions separated by an equal sign.

equidistant At the same distance.

equilateral triangle A triangle with all sides equal.

event Any possible outcome for an experiment in probability.

exponent The number of times the base occurs in a power.

expressing in simplest form Dividing the numerator and denominator of a fraction by the highest common factor.

exterior angle of a polygon An angle formed by extending one side of a polygon and the other side of the same vertex.

factor Number that is multiplied by another number to give a product.

factorial notation Notation used to indicate the product of consecutive integers beginning with 1.

$$n! = 1 \times 2 \times 3 \times ... \times (n - 1) \times n$$

factoring Finding the factors of a number or expression over a given set.

FOR – NEXT statement A statement used in BASIC to loop through a series of statements several times.

formula An equation that states the relationship among quantities that can be represented by variables.

frequency of an event The number of times an event has taken place.

glide reflection The composition of a translation and a line reflection.

greatest common factor The greatest integer that is a factor of two or more integers.

greatest monomial factor The factor of two or more monomials that has the greatest coefficient and the greatest degree.

histogram A bar graph used to summarize and display a large set of data.

hypotenuse The side opposite the right angle in a right triangle.

identity An equation whose sides are equivalent expressions. The equation is true for every value of the variable.

identity elements The identity element for addition is 0 since a + 0 = a. The identity element for multiplication is 1 since a × 1 = a.

image The image of A is A' following a transformation.

included angle The angle whose rays contain the sides of a triangle.

indirect reasoning Assuming the opposite of what is to be proved and showing that this leads to a contradiction.

inequality Two expressions separated by an inequality symbol.

inscribed angle An angle subtended by an arc of a circle with its vertex on the circumference.

inscribed polygon A polygon with its vertices on the circle.

integer A member of the set $\{..., -3, -2, -1, 0, 1, 2, 3, ...\}$.

intersection The elements that two sets have in common.

irrational number A real number that cannot be expressed in the form $\frac{a}{b}$, where a, b $\in$ I, and b $\neq$ 0.

isometry A transformation that preserves lengths and angles.

isosceles triangle A triangle with two sides equal.

lateral area The sum of the areas of the faces of a polyhedron other than the base.

least common multiple The monomial with the smallest positive coefficient and smallest degree that is a multiple of several monomials.

LET statement Assigns a value or an expression to a variable in a BASIC computer program.

line segment Two points on a line and the points between them.

line symmetry   A figure has line symmetry if there is a line such that the figure coincides with its reflection image over the line.

linear equation   An equation in which each term is either a constant or has degree 1.

linear function   A function of the form $f(x) = mx + b$.

locus   A set of points that satisfy a given condition.

mapping   A mapping illustrates how each element in the domain of a function is paired with each element in the range. A correspondence of points between an object and its image.

mass   The amount of matter in an object. The base unit for measuring mass is the kilogram.

mean   The sum of the values divided by the number of values.

median   When a set of numbers is arranged in order from smallest to largest, or largest to smallest, the median is the middle number.

midpoint   The point that divides a line segment into two equal parts.

mixed number   A number that is part whole number and part fraction.

mode   The number that occurs most often in a set of numbers.

monomial   A number, a variable, or a product of numbers and variables.

mutually exclusive events   Events that cannot both occur at the same time.

natural numbers   The set of numbers {1, 2, 3, 4, 5, 6, ...}.

net   A pattern for constructing a polyhedron.

NEW   A BASIC command which clears the previous program from computer memory.

nonagon   A polygon with nine sides.

number line   A pictorial representation of a set of numbers.

numeral   A symbol that represents a number.

obtuse angle   An angle whose measure is greater than 90° but less than 180°.

obtuse triangle   A triangle with one obtuse angle.

octagon   A polygon with eight sides.

octahedron   A polyhedron with eight faces.

order of operations   The rules to be followed when simplifying expressions. These rules are sometimes referred to as BODMAS or BEDMAS.

ordered pair   A pair of numbers used to name a point on a graph.

origin   The intersection of the horizontal and vertical axes on a graph. It is described by the ordered pair (0, 0).

orthocentre   The point where the altitudes of a triangle intersect.

outcome   The result of an experiment or a trial.

palindrome   A number such as 232 that reads the same forwards and backwards.

parallel lines   Two lines in the same plane that never meet.

parallelogram   A quadrilateral with opposite sides parallel.

parameter   An arbitrary constant.

partial variation   A relation between two variables that involves a fixed amount plus a variable amount such as $C = nd + 15$.

pentagon   A polygon with five sides.

percent   A fraction (or ratio) in which the denominator is 100.

perimeter   The distance around a polygon.

perpendicular bisector   The line that cuts a line segment into two equal parts at right angles.

perpendicular lines   Lines that intersect at right angles.

Pi (π)   The quotient that results when the circumference of a circle is divided by the diameter.

pictograph   A graph using pictures to represent data.

polygon   A closed figure formed by line segments.

polyhedron   A three-dimensional object having polygons as faces.

polynomial   A monomial or the sum of monomials.

population   The entire set of items from which data are taken.

postulate   A statement that is accepted without proof.

power   A product obtained by using a base as a factor one or more times.

prime number   A number with exactly two factors — itself and 1.

principal square root   The positive square root.

prism   A polyhedron with two parallel and congruent bases in the shape of polygons.

probability   The probability of an event occurring is the ratio of the number of favourable outcomes to the number of possible outcomes.

proportion   An equation that states that two ratios are equal.

pyramid   A polyhedron with three or more triangular faces and the base in the shape of a polygon.

Pythagorean theorem   The area of the square drawn on the hypotenuse of a right-angled triangle is equal to the sum of the areas of the squares drawn on the other two sides.

quadrant   One of the four regions formed by the intersection of the x-axis and y-axis.

quadrilateral   A polygon with four sides.

quotient   The result of a division.

radical sign   The symbol $\sqrt{}$.

radius   The length of the line segment that joins the centre and a point on the circumference of a circle.

random sample   A sample in which each member of the population has the same chance of being selected.

range   The set of all second coordinates of the ordered pairs of a relation. The set of all values of a function f(x).

rate   A ratio of two measurements having different units.

ratio   A comparison of two numbers.

rational number   A number that can be expressed as the ratio of two integers.

ray   Part of a line extending in one direction without end.

real numbers   The set of all the rational and irrational numbers.

reciprocals   Two numbers that have a product of 1.

rectangle   A parallelogram with four right angles.

rectangular hyperbola   A hyperbola whose equation is xy = k.

reflection   A transformation that maps an object into an image by a reflection in a line.

reflex angle   An angle whose measure is greater than 180° and less than 360°.

regular polygon   A polygon in which all sides and angles are equal.

relation   A set of ordered pairs.

repeating decimal   A decimal in which one or more digits repeat without end.

rhombus   A parallelogram in which all sides are equal.

right angle   An angle whose measure is 90°.

right cone   A cone in which the axis is perpendicular to the base.

right cylinder   A cylinder in which the sides are perpendicular to the bases.

right prism   A prism in which the lateral edges are perpendicular to the bases.

right triangle   A triangle with one right angle.

root of an equation   A solution of the equation.

rotation   A transformation that maps an object onto its image by a rotation about a point.

rotational symmetry   A figure has rotational symmetry if it maps onto itself after a turn.

rounding   The process of replacing a number by an approximate number.

scale drawing   A drawing in which distances are reductions or enlargements of actual distances.

scale factor   The multiplication factor used in dilatations (enlargements and reductions).

scalene triangle   A triangle with no two sides equal.

scientific notation   Numbers written with one digit (not zero) to the left of the decimal place and a power of ten.
$$2700 = 2.7 \times 10^3$$

sector angle   An angle with vertex at the centre of a circle and subtended by an arc of the circle.

sector of a circle   A region bounded by two radii and an arc.

segment of a circle   A region bounded by a chord and an arc.

set   A collection of objects.

shell   A three-dimensional object whose interior is empty.

similar figures   Figures having corresponding angles equal and corresponding sides proportional.

skeleton   A representation of the edges of a polyhedron.

slope of a line   For a non-vertical line containing two distinct points (x_1, y_1) and (x_2, y_2), the slope is
$$m = \frac{y_2 - y_1}{x_2 - x_1}$$

solid   A three-dimensional object whose interior is completely filled.

solution   A replacement for a variable that results in a true sentence.

sphere   The set of all points in space that are a given distance from a given point.

square   A quadrilateral with four congruent sides and four right angles.

square root   The square root of a number is the number that multiplies itself to give the number.

standard form of a linear equation   A linear equation written in the form
$Ax + By + C = 0$.

statistics   The science of collecting and analysing numerical information.

stem and leaf plot   A graph using digits of numbers to display data.

straight angle   An angle whose measure is 180°.

supplementary angles   Two angles whose sum is 180°.

surface area   The sum of all the areas of all faces of a polyhedron.

term of a polynomial   The product of one or more numerical factors and variable factors.

terminating decimal   A decimal whose digits terminate.

tessellation   A repeated pattern of geometric figures that will completely cover a surface.

tetrahedron   A polyhedron with four triangular faces.

theorem   A mathematical statement that can be proved.

transformation   A mapping that maps the points of a plane onto the points of the same plane.

translation   A transformation that maps an object onto its image so that each point in the object is moved the same distance and direction.

transversal   A line that intersects two lines in the same plane in two distinct points.

trapezoid   A quadrilateral with one pair of parallel sides.

tree diagram   A diagram illustrating the possible outcomes of consecutive events.

triangle   A polygon with three sides.

trinomial   A polynomial with three terms.

union of sets   The set of all elements that belong to at least one of the sets.

value of a function   For every given element of the domain of a function there is a corresponding element in the range, called the value of the function.

variable   A letter or symbol used to represent a number.

vertex of a parabola   The point of intersection of a parabola and its line of symmetry.

vertex of a polygon   The point where two adjacent sides meet in a polygon.

vertex of an angle   The common endpoint of two rays.

volume   The number of cubic units contained in a solid.

whole numbers   Numbers in the set
$\{0, 1, 2, 3, 4, 5, ...\}$.

x-axis   The horizontal line used as a scale for the independent variable in the Cartesian coordinate system.

x-intercept   The x-coordinate of the point where a curve crosses the x-axis.

y-axis   The vertical line used as a scale for the dependent variable in the Cartesian coordinate system.

y-intercept   The y-coordinate of the point where a curve crosses the y-axis.

zero-product property   If $ab = 0$, then $a = 0$ or $b = 0$.

INDEX

pattern, searching for   48
rate of work problems   310
ratios, with   168
tables, by constructing   60
working backwards   54
Product of polynomials   250
Product of powers   226
Product of two binomials   240
Proportion and percent   176
Proportions   166
Protractor   388
Pyramid
 surface area of   372
 volume of   376
Pythagoras   198
Pythagorean Theorem   204, 426
 applications of   206
Pythagorean triple   253

Quadrilateral
 area of   29
 cyclic   410
 exterior angle   410
 perimeter of   29
Quotient of powers   232

Radius   279, 360, 406
Random number tables   326
Random sample   322
Random sampling   326
Range   430
Rate   163
 applications of   170
 percent   174
 Rule of Three   172
Rate of travel   312
Rate of work solving
   problems   310
Ratio   162
 applications of   168
 proportion, and   166
 three-term   165
Rational numbers   208
 addition of   129
 algebraic expressions, and   148
 division of   126
 equivalent forms, and   122
 fractional form   122
 multiplication of   124
 order of operations   132
 subtraction of   129
Real numbers   208
Reciprocals   126
Rectangle
 area of   29, 362
 perimeter of   28
Reflection geometry   405
Reflections   462, 466
Reflex angle   389
Relations
 domain   430
 linear   435
 mapping of   430
 non-linear   448
 ordered pairs, and   428

range   430
 representation of   430
Right angle   389
Right bisector   398, 405
Right cylinder   372
Right prism   370
Right pyramid   372
Rotations   464, 466
Rounding
 estimating, and   138
 key digit   138
 numbers, of   8
 rules   138
 significant digits   138
Rule of Three   172

Sales tax   178
Sample size   322
Samples, predictions from   324
Scale drawings   185
Scalene triangle   391
Scientific notation   145
 estimating using   147
 large numbers   145
 significant digits   147
 small numbers   146
Sector   406
Segment   406
Semi-circle   406
Series   91
Set
 definition   2
 domain   430
 empty   261
 intersection   2
 mapping   430
 member of   426
 notation   426
 ordered pairs and relation   429
 range   430
 subset   3
 union   3
Sign rules   95
Significant digits   138
Similar triangles   412
Simple interest   180
Slide image   458. See also
   Translation
Slope   442
Small numbers   146
Speed   312, 470
Sphere
 surface area of   379
 volume of   30, 379
Square
 area of   29, 362
 perfect   196
 perimeter of   28, 358
Square root   198
 applications of   202
 graph, from a   215
 Newton's method, finding
   by   201
 principal   198
 radical sign   198

subtraction, finding by   201
Statistics   322
 average   338
 central tendency, measure
   of   338
 mean   338
 median   338
 mode   338
 population   322
 predictions using samples   324
 probability and   342
 random number tables   326
 random sample   322
 random sampling   326
 sample size   322
 statistical inference   322
Straight angle   389
Substitution   75
Subtraction
 equations, solving using   264
 inequalities, solving using   280
 integers, of   82
 monomials, of   92
 polynomials, of   224
 rational numbers, of   129
 rule for equations   264
Subtraction property of order   280
Supplementary angles   389
Surface area. See Area
Symbols
 division   10
 grouping   10
 variable   14

Theorem, Pythagorean   204, 426
Time and motion   312
Transformations. See also
   Mapping
 dilatations   468
 reflections   462
 rotations   464
 size   468
 special   466
 translations   460
Translation   460
Transversal and parallel
   lines   402
Trapezoid, area of   29, 365
Triangle
 altitude   400
 area of   29, 364
 circumcircle of   398
 congruence   394
 equilateral   358, 391
 formula for area of   371
 isosceles   391
 orthocentre of   400
 perimeter of   28, 358
 right   204
 scalene   391
 similar   412
 sum of interior angles   392
Triangular numbers   196
Trinomial   220
 factoring of   242, 244

PHOTOGRAPH CREDITS

p. 5: Courtesy of NASA. p. 35: Air Canada 747. p. 43: A B.C. ferry, one of 38 vessels in the B.C. Ferries' fleet, sailing through Active Pass en route to Tsawwassen Terminal. p. 44: Photograph courtesy of the Canadian 5 Pin Bowlers' Association. p. 47: (left) Photo courtesy of the B.C. Government; (right) Photo courtesy of PJ's Pet Centres. p. 53: (right) Courtesy from General Motors of Canada. p. 55: (top) Photography of component stereo system courtesy of Matsushita Electric of Canada Limited; (centre) Photo courtesy of Sea Ray Boats. p. 57: Courtesy of Jamieson Crozier. p. 59: Reprinted with the permission of Fitness and Amateur Sport Canada. p. 60: Photo courtesy of Century Fence Ltd. p. 61: (left) Promotion Australia; (right) The Royal Life Saving Society of Canada. p. 63: Photography by Graig Abel. p. 64: Government of B.C. p. 71: Photo: Toronto Transit Commission. p. 103: Courtesy of AT&T. p. 162: White Rose Crafts & Nursery Sales Limited. p. 167: CHCH TV — Hamilton. p. 170: Tide is a trademark of Procter & Gamble Inc. p. 186: The *Cats* Company of Canada. p. 202: Photo courtesy: Travel Manitoba. p. 277: Courtesy of NASA. p. 288: Courtesy of Variety Village Sport Training & Fitness Centre. p. 301: Metropolitan Toronto Police Museum. p. 315: Air Canada 747. p. 317: The Bettmann Archive. p. 323: Photo courtesy of Dalhousie University. p. 327: Photo courtesy of Sea Ray Boats. p. 350: National Baseball Library. p. 380: Courtesy of U.S. Department of Defense. p. 381: Ontario Ministry of Industry & Tourism. p. 418: Photo courtesy of the Canadian 5 Pin Bowlers' Association. p. 452: Photograph courtesy of Heidelberg Canada.

HILL PARK SECONDARY SCHOOL

25 HIGH STREET
HAMILTON, ONTARIO
L8T 3Z4